W9-CFL-044

The Sessile Barnacles, Cirripedia, Contained In The Collections Of The U. S. National Museum: Including A Monograph Of The American Species

Henry Augustus Pilsbry

In the interest of creating a more extensive selection of rare historical book reprints, we have chosen to reproduce this title even though it may possibly have occasional imperfections such as missing and blurred pages, missing text, poor pictures, markings, dark backgrounds and other reproduction issues beyond our control. Because this work is culturally important, we have made it available as a part of our commitment to protecting, preserving and promoting the world's literature. Thank you for your understanding.

SMITHSONIAN INSTITUTION
UNITED STATES NATIONAL MUSEUM
Bulletin 93

THE SESSILE BARNACLES (CIRRIPEDIA) CONTAINED IN THE COLLECTIONS OF THE U. S. NATIONAL MUSEUM; INCLUDING A MONOGRAPH OF THE AMERICAN SPECIES

BY

HENRY A. PILSBRY

*Special Curator of the Department of Mollusca, Academy
of Natural Sciences of Philadelphia*

NEW YORK
PUBLIC
LIBRARY

WASHINGTON
GOVERNMENT PRINTING OFFICE
1916

DUPLICATE
TO BE KEPT
. . . T

745677

BULLETIN OF THE UNITED STATES NATIONAL MUSEUM.

Issued July 31, 1916.

II

NEW YORK
PUBLIC
LIBRARY

ADVERTISEMENT.

The scientific publications of the United States National Museum consist of two series, the *Proceedings* and the *Bulletins*.

The *Proceedings*, the first volume of which was issued in 1878, are intended primarily as a medium for the publication of original, and usually brief, papers based on the collections of the National Museum, presenting newly-acquired facts in zoology, geology, and anthropology, including descriptions of new forms of animals, and revisions of limited groups. One or two volumes are issued annually and distributed to libraries and scientific organizations. A limited number of copies of each paper, in pamphlet form, is distributed to specialists and others interested in the different subjects as soon as printed. The date of publication is printed on each paper, and these dates are also recorded in the tables of contents of the volumes.

The *Bulletins*, the first of which was issued in 1875, consist of a series of separate publications comprising chiefly monographs of large zoological groups and other general systematic treatises (occasionally in several volumes), faunal works, reports of expeditions, and catalogues of type-specimens, special collections, etc. The majority of the volumes are octavos, but a quarto size has been adopted in a few instances in which large plates were regarded as indispensable.

Since 1902 a series of octavo volumes containing papers relating to the botanical collections of the Museum, and known as the *Contributions from the National Herbarium*, has been published as bulletins.

The present work forms No. 93 of the *Bulletin* series.

RICHARD RATHBUN,
Assistant Secretary, Smithsonian Institution,
In charge of the United States National Museum.

WASHINGTON, D. C., June 8, 1916.

PREFACE.

The sessile barnacles are one of the dominant groups of littoral animals. In vast profusion of individuals they inhabit the zone between high-water mark and the hundred-fathom line. Their free nauplii form an appreciable part of the food available for bivalve mollusks and other animals subsisting on the plankton. The adult barnacles, together with mollusks, are part of the food of bottom-feeding fishes. In Japan barnacles are extensively utilized for fertilizer, as fish and Limulus are with us. On the other side of the account, it may be mentioned that barnacles are most widely known as the chief organisms fouling ships' bottoms.

Although barnacles offer a wide field for systematic and ecological study, they have been neglected by American naturalists. In the early days of zoology they were classed with the mollusks, and were collected by conchologists. After the group was transferred to the Crustacea, conchologists lost interest, and but few students of Crustacea took it up. Fortunately the Cirripedes found a historian in Charles Darwin. His Monograph on the Subclass Cirripedia is one of the most brilliant morphologo-systematic studies to be found in the whole field of systematic zoological literature. In recent years the works of P. P. C. Hoek and A. Gruvel, inspired by the high ideals of Darwin, have stimulated renewed research, and a substantial advance in our knowledge of barnacles must result from the work of zoologists and paleontologists who have taken up the group in England, Germany, Italy, India, and New Zealand.

In America there is opportunity for systematic and faunistic work on the southern and Pacific coasts especially, while the entire seaboard abounds in cirripede material for the investigator of the problems of ecology and evolution.

H. A. PILSBRY.

PHILADELPHIA, *May 1, 1916.*

v

CONTENTS.

Descriptions of genera and species—Continued.
Suborder Balanomorpha—Continued.
Family Balanidae—Continued.
Subfamily Balaninae—Continued.

Descriptions of genera and species—Continued.
Suborder Balanomorpha—Continued.
Family Balanidae—Continued.
Subfamily Balaninae—Continued.

THE SESSILE BARNACLES (CIRRIPEDIA) CONTAINED IN THE COLLECTIONS OF THE U. S. NATIONAL MUSEUM; INCLUDING A MONOGRAPH OF THE AMERICAN SPECIES.

By Henry A. Pilsbry,

Special Curator of the Department of Mollusca, Academy of Natural Sciences of Philadelphia.

INTRODUCTION.

This work is a continuation of the author's report on the Cirripedia contained in the United States National Museum, of which the portion relating to pedunculate forms was published in 1907. It was at first intended to record the species of sessile Cirripedia in the Museum, with their localities, and to describe and figure new forms. As the collection was worked over, its wealth in American barnacles became apparent. It contains nearly every known species of the Western Hemisphere, many of them in hundreds, even thousands, of individuals, often showing aspects of variation special to American waters. This has led to an alteration in the scope of the work, which may be described as a monograph on American sessile barnacles, with the records of foreign species contained in the Museum interpolated in systematic order. In cases where extended investigation of Old World barnacles has been essential to a right appreciation of our own, the results have been included herein. It is believed that these interpolations will not seriously detract from the use of the work for the determination of American species, while it is an advantage to have all the information relating to a given species or genus in one place.

The deep-water barnacles of our coast are nearly all new to science, but a majority of the American littoral species have been described in Darwin's monograph.[1] His grasp of detail was so comprehensive and his language so lucid that one can not expect to improve upon them. In the field he covered one can not do better than to imitate. Yet it has been possible to extend the work in certain directions. By the use of higher powers than were commonly used upon such objects 60 years ago, important features, unknown to Darwin, are found in the cirri. Various reforms in classification have been under-

---

[1] A Monograph on the Subclass Cirripedia, the Balanidæ, the Verrucidæ. London, 1854.

taken. Moreover, the vast collections from American waters extend our knowledge of the distribution of species, both geographic and bathymetric.

The study of large series of the widely distributed or so-called cosmopolitan species of barnacles shows that, with the exception of pelagic and deep-sea forms, they may be divided into subspecies which conform in distribution to the faunal provinces usually recognized by workers in marine zoology, and determined by conditions of temperature, currents, land barriers, and depth. The definition of these subspecies or local races has hitherto received but little attention in this group.

The walls of Balani have been inadequately illustrated in former works. With the more intensive study of racial characters now undertaken in all branches of zoology, the external characters of barnacles become of importance. The extraordinary plasticity of the Balanid organization makes discrimination between racial characters and those controlled by environmental conditions a matter of extreme difficulty. Ecological and biometrical studies of some of the abundant species are much needed in this connection. Numerous figures are given herein to serve as standards of comparison for those who may take up such local work.

By the copious illustration of American forms, by large-scale drawings and photographs, their identification should be easier. Until one has studied barnacles deeply enough to have standards of comparison, even the inimitable descriptions of Darwin are difficult to follow, especially if one is dealing with forms differing somewhat from those described. The appeal to the eye will often relieve the student from uncertainty. "Identifying by the pictures" may be a primitive and superficial method, yet such short cuts are permissible in case one merely needs the name of an animal which has been taken as the subject of embryological, ecological, or other non-systematic studies. The student must be warned, however, that many species have parallel mutations, vary in the same way under similar conditions, so that external form by itself is rarely a reliable criterion. The opercular valves, the details of structure of the plates of the wall, and the structure of the feet are the important characters.

For the main facts of cirripede structure the student will naturally consult one of the standard treatises on zoology, such as that of Lankester. Matter relating to the group in general has therefore been restricted in this work to a brief explanation of the terms used in systematic descriptions, in large part adapted from Darwin's monograph.

The work is based upon the specimens contained in the United States National Museum, but to complete the account of American forms, some illustrations and descriptions have been drawn from material in the collection of the Academy of Natural Sciences of Philadelphia. By the courtesy of Mr. Samuel Henshaw, I have been able to study a series of Antillean deep-water forms, collected by the United States Coast Survey steamer *Blake*, and contained in the Museum of Comparative Zoology. This material has added considerable to the account of American Verrucidæ.

Mr. John B. Henderson has furnished various deep-water species dredged by his yacht *Eolis*.

Several illustrations from the Bulletin of the Bureau of Fisheries were lent by the Hon. George M. Bowers, late commissioner.

Dr. W. H. Dall generously placed in my hands his fine examples of *Tamiosoma*.

Mr. Thomas H. Withers, of the British Museum, supplied photographs of the type of *Lepas balanus* Linnæus. Mr. C. Forster Cooper kindly lent the type of *Balanus æneas* from the University Museum of Zoology, Cambridge.

Miss Mary J. Rathbun, Dr. Paul Bartsch, Dr. Thomas Barbour, and others mentioned in the text have furthered the work in various ways. For all of these favors I wish to offer sincere thanks.

Finally, I would express my appreciation of the faithful work of Miss Helen Winchester, who made the drawings and retouched the photographs of the work.

TERMINOLOGY OF THE PLATES OF SESSILE BARNACLES.

The armor of sessile barnacles is essentially similar to that of the capitulum of pedunculate forms in being composed of calcareous plates connected by chitinous intervals. Only the plates (scuta and terga) bounding the cavity for the mouth, feet, etc., are movable, the rest being so interlocked that they form a rigid *wall*, the plates of which are termed *compartments*. The chitinous band surrounding the scuta and terga (or opercular valves) and connecting them with the wall is called the *opercular membrane*. This membrane is moulted like the exoskeleton of the limbs, and unlike other external hard parts, which are permanent.[1]

The terminology of the plates is shown in figures 1 to 5. The scuta, terga, carina, and rostrum are clearly homologous with those of pedunculate barnacles. The lateral compartments are homologous with part of the latera of the genus *Mitella;* probably they are homologous with the three pairs of latera which are retained in the genus *Calantica*.

The exposed median triangle of each compartment is the *paries* (*pl.* parietes). The edges of the compartments overlapping adjacent compartments are called *radii* when they are differentiated from the parietes by an alteration in the direction of the lines of growth. The underlapping edges are called *alæ*. The membrane or calcareous plate upon which the barnacle stands is termed the *basis*.

---

[1].It should be noted that in some genera, such as *Tubicinella*, the upper layers of the wall, and in various *Coronulinæ* the upper layers of the opercular valves are deciduous.

Structure of the individual compartments.—If the basal margin of a compartment, for instance of *Balanus tintinnabulum*, be examined, it appears sufficiently complicated, being composed of an outer and inner lamina, separated by longitudinal septa, which are denticulated at their bases; and the tubes formed by these longitudinal septa are crossed by transverse septa. On the other hand, in some cases, as in the genera *Chthamalus* and *Elminius*, each compartment consists of a simple shelly layer. These two extreme states graduate into each other (in different genera); we have, firstly, on the internal surface, quite irregular points and ridges; these become regular (in some other genera), causing the internal surface to be longitudinally ribbed; then these ribs themselves become finely furrowed on their sides and at their lower ends, producing sharp, minute ridges, the ends of which I have called the denticuli; and lastly, some of the denticuli on the adjoining longitudinal septa become united into a solid layer, forming the internal lamina of the wall. (Darwin, p. 43.)

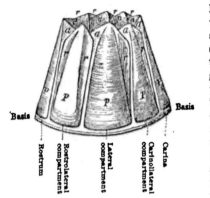

Fig. 1.—Wall of a Balanomorph barnacle. *a, a*, Alæ. *p, p*, Parietes. *r, r*, Radii. Part of the sheath is visible in the orifice. In Balanus and many other genera the rostrum and rostrolateral compartments are concrescent, not separate as shown here (diagrammatic; after Darwin).

Growth of the compartments takes place at the basal margin and usually at the sutures also, where the increment is at right angles to that of the parietes, and forms the radii. In species which do not increase the diameter of the cone and orifice by the interposition of radii, the orifice is enlarged as the animal grows by wearing away of the summit of the cone.

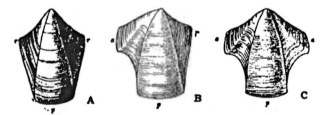

Fig. 2.—*a*, Compartment with two radii, serving either as a rostrolateral or as a rostrum concrescent with the rostrolaterals, as in Balanus. *b*, Lateral or carinolateral compartment. *c*, Carina or rostrum. Letters as in Fig. 1 (after Darwin).

The upper ends of the pores or tubes in the parietes are more or less extensively filled up with calcareous material, occasionally differing in color from that of the rest of the wall. In the genus *Tetraclita*, *inter alia*, the outer lamina of the wall is ordinarily disintegrated and fugacious in adults, leaving a columnar or tessellated surface, formed of the harder filling of the parietal tubes.

The lateral edges of the radii are often provided with fine transverse ridges or septa, usually having denticulate edges. These fit into recipient grooves of similar shape on the opposed sutural edges outside of the alæ. In a few forms the radii are permeated with pores which open in the intervals between the septa, and have a direction at right angles with the pores of the parietes. (See plate 10, fig. 2, where the denticulate septa and the ends of the parietal pores are shown.)

The basis, when calcareous, may be either solid or provided with radiating pores, or it may have radiating ridges on the upper surface.

Homologies of the plates of the wall.— In the absence of paleontologic evidence, we may assume that all acorn barnacles descended from a primitive stock having eight mural compartments. The most generalized genus now existing, *Catophragmus*,

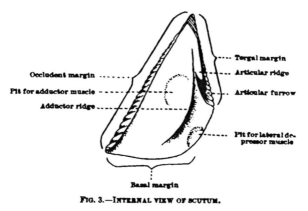

FIG. 3.—INTERNAL VIEW OF SCUTUM.

has eight main compartments, with numerous smaller ones outside, the latter representing the upper scales of the peduncle of pedunculate ancestral forms.

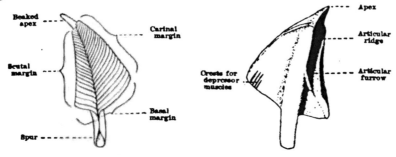

FIG. 4.—EXTERNAL AND INTERNAL VIEWS OF TERGUM.

Darwin and others have compared this structure with that of the pedunculate genus, *Pollicipes* (*Mitella*). A nearer likeness, perhaps, exists with *Scyllælepas*, in which there has been further specialization of the plates. *Brachylepas*, though superficially like *Catophragmus*, is evidently not in the line of descent of the *Balanomorpha*. On account of the different system of imbrication of the plates, it does not seem likely that the *Balanomorpha* descended from Mesozoic *Scyllælepas*, but rather that both had a common ancestor.

In most recent barnacles the number of compartments has been reduced, and it becomes important to determine the homologies of those remaining. This is partly to be done by attention to the articulating edges of the compartments.

The carina and rostrum are nearly alike in primitive forms, both being bilaterally symmetrical, and having *alæ on both sides*, therefore overlapped by the adjacent compartments. There is no certain means of distinguishing them apart when detached, but the carina is usually more narrowly curved or bent than the rostrum of the same species.

The carinolateral and lateral compartments are asymmetrical, having *alæ on their rostral edges*, and radii, or *an overlapping border, on the carinal edges*. There is no significant difference between these two compartments when detached, though the lateral is wider in most genera.

The rostrolateral compartments have no alæ, both sides overlapping the adjacent compartments, thus differing essentially from all of the other plates of the wall.

Departures from the structure just described are due to concrescence of compartments. Reasoning from the conditions in species still in transition stages, we may infer that reduction in the number of compartments has taken place by two modes:

1. Reduction by elimination. In *Acasta* and *Conopea* the carinolateral compartment is usually very narrow. In *Acasta sporillus* it has been almost crowded out, and does not reach to the basis. In *Conopea cornuta* it has entirely disappeared. In some other genera this compartment appears to be wanting.[1]

2. Reduction by concrescence. In *Chelonibia* the rostrolateral compartments and rostrum are calcified together, but traces of the sutures are usually discernable. In *Pachylasma crinoidophilum* the same compartments are united by fine linear sutures, but can be separated; in *P. darwinianum* they are calcified together externally, but the sutures are visible inside; finally in *P. giganteum* these compartments are united by sutures in the earliest sessile stage, but afterwards they become completely concrescent, so that no trace whatever of the tripartite nature of the compartment is visible. The result of this concrescence is that the composite rostrum (rostrum plus rostral latera) has radii or overlapping borders on both sides, these being the original overlapping borders of the rostral latera. Having this transition series, among others before us, it seems highly probable

---

[1] In such genera as *Tetraclita* and *Chthamalus*, in which the carinolateral compartments are absent, they may be fused with the lateral compartments or with the carina; but seeing that they are normally developed later than the other valves, it appears to be the simplest theory to assume, until the contrary be proved, that they are aborted. Finally, the somewhat unexpected conclusion that the shell (not including the operculum) of sessile cirripedes normally consists of eight valves—four belonging to an upper whorl and four to a lower whorl, all forced into a single ring, and often more or less fused together, though not strictly proved, is rendered highly probable. (Darwin.)

that *in all cases where the rostrum has radii, or overlaps the adjacent compartments, it is a composite plate,* formed by the concrescence of both rostral latera with the true rostrum. This is the case with all recent Balanidæ and part of the Chthamalidæ. It is inexact to term the compartment formed by fusion of rostrum with the rostral latera a "rostrum," in *Balanus,* for example, as it is not equivalent to the rostrum in the less modified Chthamalidæ, the Verrucidæ, or 'the pedunculate cirripedes. So long, however, as the true constitution of the plate is understood, the inconsistent terminology is perhaps of no great moment.

The chief modifications in the arrangement of the compartments due to concrescence or to elimination are represented diagrammatically in figure 5. Having examined a very great majority of the known species of sessile cirripedes, I find that the evidence supports Darwin's

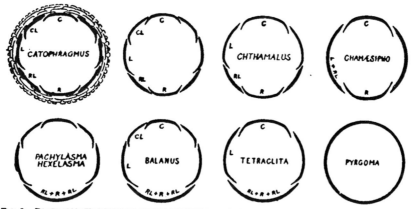

Fig. 5.—DIAGRAMS SHOWING THE MODES OF IMBRICATION AND THE HOMOLOGIES OF COMPARTMENTS IN CHTHAMALIDÆ AND BALANIDÆ. *c,* CARINA. *cl,* CARINOLATERAL COMPARTMENT. *l,* LATERAL. *r,* ROSTRUM. *rl,* ROSTROLATERAL. THE SECOND DIAGRAM REPRESENTS OCTOMERIS.

views of the homologies of the compartments, so far as he definitely expressed himself, and is opposed to the interpretations of Gruvel.[1]

The question of homologies of the wall plates is by no means academic. Our conceptions of the classification and phylogeny of the group depend upon our understanding of these homologies.

The cirri are always well developed in sessile barnacles, and there is much less diversity in the arrangement of the spines than in the *Lepadomorpha.* The first two or three pairs of cirri bear dense, brushlike tufts of spines; the later cirri bear spines in pairs, two to eight or ten pairs on each segment. The number of pairs of spines is a useful specific character, though subject to some variation in polymorphic species. In descriptions the count is made in the median third of the cirrus, where the maximum number is found.

---

[1] Gruvel, Monographie des Cirrhipèdes, p. 194, fig. 213, where Professor Gruvel's views of the homologies of the compartments are given.

There are sometimes bunches of short spines on the anterior face between the spines of the pairs. In the species figured (fig. 6) the posterior ramus of the first cirrus and both rami of the second are formed of what Darwin termed "protuberant segments."

In many species of *Balanus* there are minute "spinules" variously arranged on the outer faces of the segments of some of the cirri, particularly the third and fourth, as shown in figure 8 and many others. Sometimes the spinules are enlarged on the anterior margin of the cirrus, forming "teeth," as in *Acasta* (fig. 80) and some Balani.

In the evolution of barnacles the cirri have been successively modified from before backward. In the least modified forms the second cirrus, or only its anterior ramus, has assumed the form and chæto-taxy of the first cirrus. In more advanced forms the second and third cirri are so modified. In a few, the fourth cirrus also shows

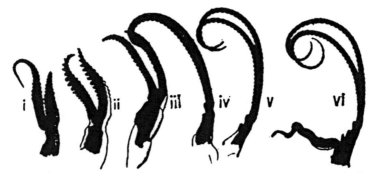

FIG. 6.—CIRRI OF THE RIGHT SIDE OF BALANUS ROSTRATUS ALASKENSIS, FROM KODIAK, ×3. CAT. No. 3415. THE PENIS IS SEEN AT THE BASE OF THE SIXTH CIRRUS. THE SPINES ARE NOT SHOWN IN THIS PHOTOGRAPHIC FIGURE.

some modification. The modification of the cirri is therefore one of the indices to the evolutionary rank of a species.

On account of the fact that a barnacle grows at the base and sutures, and not at the orifice, it receives the impression of the supporting surface, and often reproduces its sculptural features. A specimen growing on a scallop shell may bear, vicariously, the ribs of the shell, as in plate 33, figure 2a. Exactly the same effect, from the same cause, is sometimes seen in sedentary, limpetlike mollusks. This vicarious sculpture may be superimposed upon that proper to the barnacle, or the conflict of the two patterns may result in neither being distinctly expressed. Very often the sculpture of the supporting surface seems to have no effect whatever on that of the barnacle, even when the latter has a smooth surface.

The shapes of barnacles are often controlled by the size and shape of the supporting object, but they show little if any choice between such solid objects as occur in their vicinity. Many, but apparently not all, of the littoral species attach to ship bottoms; a few forms are known from no other source. Such specimens are often found in museums, labeled merely with the locality where they were taken off of the ship, or picked up where they had dropped or been cleaned off. Such specimens may often be known by the paint or rust adhering to the base, or they may show the grain of the planks. On such smooth surfaces a barnacle is likely to develop a beautifully symmetrical cone, whereas others of the same race, growing on an uneven natural surface, are likely to be irregular, unsymmetrical, or cylindrical.

Most of the species which develop a conic wall when growing alone become lengthened and cylindric when crowded. The transitions of form are frequently seen in the same group, as in plate 44, figure 2. Very much lengthened forms often result where barnacles grow solitary on small objects, as in figures 5–5b of plate 40.

Like many originally bilateral animals which have become fixed, the sessile cirripedes approximate more or less to a superficial radial symmetry. This is especially marked in the whale and turtle barnacles, in which the incidence of external forces is practically equal on all sides.

MATERIAL EXAMINED.

In the census of species and subspecies of known recent sessile cirripedes, given in the first column of the following table, several forms of doubtful specific or subspecific status are admitted. The other columns contain species and subspecies contained in the National Museum.

Genera.	Total of recent forms.		Contained in the U. S. Nat. Mus.		Types contained in U. S. Nat. Mus.	
	Species.	Sub-species or "varieties."	Species.	Sub-species.	Species.	Sub-species.
Balanus	75	46	50	28	13	19
Acasta	16	......	6	......	3	......
Tetraclita	7	7	6	7	......	4
Elminius	7	......	2	......	......	......
Creusia	1	2	1	......	......	......
Pyrgoma	11	......	2	......	......	......
Pyrgopsis	1	......	......	......	......	......
Chelonibia	4	2	3	2	......	1
Coronulinæ (8 genera)	14	1	9	1	1	......
Chthamalus	18	4	16	3	7	3
Chamæsipho	2	......	......	......	......	......
Pachylasma	5	......	4	......	3	......
Hexelasma	6	......	2	......	2	......
Bathybalanus	1	......	......	......	......	......
Octomeris	2	......	1	......	......	......
Catophragmus	3	......	2	......	1	......
Verruca	50	5	18	2	17	2
	223	67	122	43	47	29

In addition to material tabulated above, I have had available for study several species contained in the collection of the Academy of Natural Sciences of Philadelphia, including the types of five species and four subspecies, and from the Museum of Comparative Zoology the types of two subspecies. So far as I know, this includes all but one of the types of recent sessile cirripedes contained in or described from American museums.[1]

The British Museum, containing the types of Darwin's monograph and of Hoek's *Challenger* report, etc., possesses more types of sessile cirripedes than any other museum, at least 34 per cent of the total number of accepted species. The United States National Museum stands next, having types of about 21 per cent of the valid species and about 43 per cent of the subspecies. Other museums contain comparatively few types. Many types of the older (pre-Darwinian) species are lost, or at least the present location of the type-specimens is not known. The calculations above do not include types of forms generally admitted to be synonyms.

DISTRIBUTION OF AMERICAN BALANOMORPH BARNACLES.

The distribution of Verrucidæ has been considered separately (p. 18). In the following list the species are arranged systematically, the geographic ranges of Atlantic species being printed in roman, of Pacific species in italic type.

Species.	American distribution.	Occurrence elsewhere.
Balanus tintinnabulum antillensis.	Cuba to Brazil	
t. californicus	*Santa Barbara to San Diego, Cal.*	
t. peninsularis	*Cape St. Lucas, Lower California*	
t. coccopoma	*Mazatlan to Panama*	
t. galapaganus	*Galapagos Islands*	
t. concinnus	*Peru to Strait of Magellan*	
psittacus	*Peru to Strait of Magellan*	
eburneus	Massachusetts Bay to Caribbean Sea	
improvisus	Nova Scotia to Patagonia; ? *West Colombia.*	Europe; Red Sea.
amphitrite niveus	Vineyard Sound to southern Brazil	?
a. inexpectatus	*Gulf of California*	
peruvianus	*Peru*	
concavus pacificus	*California to Peru*	
regalis	*West coast of Lower California*	
poecilus	*West coast of South America*	
trigonus	West Indies to southern Brazil; *southern California to Peru.*	West and South Africa; Japan to Australia.
spongicola	Venezuela to Brazil	English Channel to South Africa; Seychelles.
calidus	West Florida to Yucatan and St. Vincent.	
lævis	Rio Negro to Cape Horn, *north to Peru*	
aquila	*Monterey to San Diego, Cal*	
nubilis	*Southern Alaska to Santa Cruz, Cal.*	
flos	*California*	
rostratus alaskensis	*Alaska*	
r. apertus	*Bering Sea*	
r. dalli	*Bering Sea*	
r. heteropus	*Puget Sound*	
balanus	Arctic Ocean to Long Island; *Bering Sea*	Northern Europe.
b. pugetensis	*Puget Sound*	
crenatus	Arctic Ocean to Long Island; *Bering Sea to Santa Barbara, Cal.*	Europe, Mediterranean; northern Japan.
c. curvisculum	*Alaska*	
c. delicatus	*California*	
glandula	*Aleutian Islands to San Diego*	

[1] The type of *Euraphia kembelli* Conrad appears to be lost.

Species.	American distribution.	Occurrence elsewhere.
Balanus balanoides	Arctic Ocean to Delaware Bay; *Alaska south to Sitka.*	Northern Europe.
b. calcaratus	Alaska.	
cariosus	Bering Sea to Oregon.	Northern Japan.
hesperius	Alaska.	Saghalin Island.
h. lævidomus	Aleutian Islands to Monterey.	
hockianus	Bering Sea.	
hameri	Nova Scotia to off Chesapeake Bay (in deep water southward).	Northern Europe.
evermanni	Bering Sea to southern Alaska.	
flosculus	Peru and Chile.	Kuril Islands.
f. sordidus	Tierra del Fuego.	
declivis	Bermuda; Antilles.	
orcutti	Lower California.	
galeatus	South Carolina to West Indies; *southern California.*	
Acasta cyathus	Florida to Colon.	Madeira; ? Gulf of Manaar.
Tetraclita squamosa stalactifera	Florida to southern Brazil; *Gulf of California to Nicaragua.*	
s. panamensis	Panama to Peru.	
s. milleporosa	Galapagos Islands.	
s. rubescens	Farallones to southern California.	
radiata	West Indies.	? New South Wales; Sumatra.
Elminius kingii	Tierra del Fuego; Falkland Islands.	
Chelonibia testudinaria	Rhode Island to Brazil; *Lower California to Galapagos.*	World-wide in Tropic and warm Temperate Zones.
manati lobatibasis	Florida.	*C. manati* West African.
caretta	Delaware Bay to Cape Fino, Brazil.	Nearly world-wide in warm seas.
patula	Florida and West Indies.	Do.
Coronula diadema	Greenland to West Indies; *Bering Sea to Lower California.*	World-wide.
reginæ	Newfoundland; *Aleutian Islands to Oregon.*	North Atlantic and Pacific.
complanata	Chile.	Southern Hemisphere generally.
Cryptolepas rachianecti	Bering Sea to Lower California.	Hawaiian Islands?
Xenobalanus globicipitis	New England.	North Atlantic.
Platylepas hexastylos	Delaware Bay to West Indies.	Mediterranean; Tropics.
h. ichthyophila	Florida, western.	
decorata	Galapagos Islands.	
Cylindrolepas darwiniana	West Indies.	
Stomatolepas præpustator	Dry Tortugas.	? Mediterranean.
Chthamalus fragilis	Woods Hole to West Indies.	
stellatus angustitergum	Florida; Bahamas.	*C. stellatus*, Europe; West Africa.
s. bisinuatus	Southern Brazil.	
dalli	Unalaska.	
fissus	Southern California.	
anisopoma	Gulf of California.	
panamensis	Panama.	
imperatriz	Panama.	
cirratus	Peru; Chile.	
scabrosus	Peru to Tierra del Fuego; Falkland Islands.	
Hexelasma americanum	Off South Carolina.	
Octophragmus imbricatus	Bermuda; Antigua.	

NOTES ON FOSSIL BARNACLES.

The limits of this work do not allow of any discussion of the American tertiary barnacles, except in the case of *Balanus concavus*, which also occurs as a recent species. On account of the importance of the subject, some notes are given on supposed Palæozoic Balanidæ.

Protobalanus hamiltonensis Whitfield [1] from the Marcellus shale, Hamilton group of the Devonian of New York, is described as having 12 wall plates and perhaps 7 opercular valves. It has a certain superficial resemblance to *Balanus*, but is morphologically inconsistent with the Balanomorph barnacles. I doubt very much whether *Protobalanus* is a cirripede, but if so it must represent a group unrelated to any known Mesozoic or later form.

[1] Bull. Amer. Mus. Nat. Hist., vol. 2, 1889, p. 67, pl. 13, fig. 22.

In *Palæocreusia devonica* J. M. Clarke, from the Corniferous limestone of New York,[1] the form is practically that of *Pyrgoma*. It is embedded in a *Favosites* colony, which has also overgrown the upper surface. No compartments are visible and no opercular valves found. While the fossil presents no characters differentiating it from the modern *Pyrgoma*, yet it is also utterly without features definitely placing it in the *Cirripedia*. The question is not whether *Palæocreusia* is a close relative of *Creusia*—this is practically excluded by the fact that *Creusia* and *Pyrgoma* are highly specialized forms of the most recent family of barnacles—but whether it is a cirripede at all.

CLASSIFICATION.

The modern classification of cirripedes began with Leach, who, in 1825, proposed the following arrangement. I add the contents of the families in brackets:

Class CIRRIPEDES.
  Order 1. Campylosomata.
    Family Clytiadæ [*Conchoderma*].
      Pollicipedidæ [*Lepas, Scalpellum, Pollicipes*, etc.]
      Ibladæ [*Ibla*].
  Order 2. Acamptosomata.
    Family Coronuladæ [Tubicinella, Coronula, Chelonibia].
      Balanidæ [*Pyrgoma, Acasta, Balanus, Tetraclita, Eliminus*, etc.].
      Clistadæ [*Verruca*].

Darwin revised this classification in 1852–1854. His chief additions to the system of sessile barnacles were the demonstration of important differences in the morphology of the turtle barnacles (*Chelonibia*) and the whale barnacles, and the separation of the Chthamalinæ from the Balaninæ. In addition to this, he established the genera upon sound morphological characters, demonstrated their affinities with wonderful insight, and defined the species, which had before been in the greatest confusion. Darwin's monograph has been the basis of all subsequent systematic work, and is still the chief work of reference.

The family and generic classification of this work is substantially that of Darwin. The principal departures are that the turtle barnacles are removed from the Balaninæ to form a separate subfamily; the arrangement of the Coronulinæ is altered, considerable changes have been made in the subgeneric arrangement of the Balani, and the grade of supergeneric groups has been raised. I consider Darwin's subfamilies as families, and his primary divisions of subfamilies may then be ranked as subfamilies. Such an alteration of taxonomic values has been general throughout zoology during the last half century. It should in no way obscure the fact that the system of the *Cirripedia Thoracica* is still essentially Darwinian.

---

[1] Palæontology of New York, vol. 7, 1888, p. 210, pl. 36, figs. 24–20.

The new classification of sessile barnacles proposed by Professor Gruvel,[1] cast aside Darwin's principles. The families were based upon the number of compartments in the wall—eight, six, or four. This system seems to me to be retrogressive at every point. His family Octomeridæ is a natural group, though *Pachylasma* forms a complete transition to his Hexameridæ, and *Chelonibia* should logically have been included. His Hexameridæ contains genera with six compartments, but *they are not the same six* in the different genera, as may be seen by a comparison of *Balanus* and *Chthamalus*, the walls being constituted as follows, counting from the carina.

Balanus.	*Chthamalus.*
1. Carina.	1. Carina, carinolatera wanting.
2, 3. Carinolatera.	2, 3. Latera.
4, 5. Latera.	4, 5. Rostrolatera.
6. Rostrolatera+rostrum.[2]	6. Rostrum.

The numerical agreement upon which Professor Gruvel's family is based is, therefore, due to the incident that members of two collateral phyletic series have independently reached the hexamerous stage. In *Balanus* it has been reached by complete concrescence of the rostrum with the rostrolatera, while in *Chthamalus* the rostrolatera remain as large, independent compartments, but the elimination of carinolatera brings the number of mural plates down to six. Meantime, the characters of the labrum, mandibles, and cirri show that the relationship between the genera is not close, wholly confirming the conclusion drawn from the homologies of the wall plates.

The family Tetrameridæ Gruvel is heterogeneous by including *Chamæsipho*. This genus has a simple rostrum with alæ, as in *Chthamalus*, while the other genera have the rostrum composite, as in *Balanus*, with which they also agree in the structure of the labrum and cirri.

The usual classification of sessile barnacles as a suborder Operculata, with the tribes Symmetrica and Asymmetrica, is unsatisfactory for the reason that the two divisions or tribes are not directly related. The Asymmetrica (Verrucidæ) and the Symmetrica (Balanidæ, Chthamalidæ) are two entirely independent derivatives from the pedunculate group. We have, then, the following Suborders of the Order *Thoracica:*

Suborder TURRILEPADOMORPHA.

The elongated body is not differentiated into capitulum and peduncle and is covered with longitudinal series of large, similar, imbricating plates. Palæozoic.

Families: LEPIDOCOLEIDÆ, TURRILEPADIDÆ.

---

[1] Monographie des Cirrhipèdes ou Thecostraces, 1905, pp. 8, 9, Paris.

[2] The rostrum in *Balanus* is morphologically the rostrum concrescent with the rostrolateral compartments, but it is not so in *Chthamalus*. Professor Gruvel's diagrams, *Monographie*, p. 104, are inaccurate as to the homologies of the compartments.

Suborder LEPADOMORPHA.

Usually elongate and differentiated into capitulum and peduncle, the former protected by larger plates of specialized shapes, or sometimes all plates are wanting. Mesozoic to Recent.

Families: LORICULIDÆ (*Loricula, Archæolepas*), BRACHYLEPADIDÆ (if distinct from SCALPELLIDÆ), SCALPELLIDÆ, LEPADIDÆ.

Suborder VERRUCOMORPHA.

Depressed, sessile, protected by an asymmetrical wall of four dissimilar plates immovably articulated together—carina, rostrum, a tergum, and a scutum; some lateral wall-plates are sometimes present on one side. The other tergum and scutum form a movable lid closing the orifice. Mesozoic to Recent.

Family: VERRUCIDÆ.

Suborder BALANOMORPHA.

Sessile, the wall bilaterally symmetrical, composed of carina, rostrum, and one to three pairs of lateral compartments; opercular valves paired, furnished with depressor muscles, or rarely wanting. Mesozoic to Recent.

Families: CHTHAMALIDÆ, BALANIDÆ.

The first two suborders have hitherto been grouped together as *Cirripedia Pedunculata;* the last two as *Cirripedia Operculata* or *Sessilia,* with the divisions *Asymmetrica* and *Symmetrica.* The *Pedunculata* and *Operculata* of recent authors are exactly equivalent to the groups Campylosomata and Acamptosomata of Leach.[1]

DESCRIPTIONS OF GENERA AND SPECIES.

Suborder VERRUCOMORPHA.

Family VERRUCIDÆ Darwin.

1825. *Clisiadæ* LEACH, Zoological Journal, vol. 2, p. 210.
1854. *Verrucidæ* DARWIN, Monograph on the subclass Cirripedia, etc., Balanidæ, Verrucidæ, etc., p. 495.
1914. *Verrucidæ* WITHERS, Proc. Zool. Soc. London, p. 946.

"Sessile, asymmetrical, boxlike barnacles, in which a scutum, tergum, rostrum, and carina, with or without a rostral and a carinal latus in addition, are immovably united to form the wall; the remaining scutum and tergum are movable, and form the lidlike top" (Withers). Basis membranous; caudal appendages present. Labrum with a concave edge.

Although the Verrucidæ are grouped as sessile barnacles, they have no near relationship with the Balanidæ. The family comprises two genera: *Verruca* Sowerby (see below) and *Proverruca* Withers, a Lower Devonian genus, "in which a rostral and a carinal latus are present on the rostrocarinal side, and in which none of the valves has developed interlocking ribs."[2]

New light has been thrown on the phylogeny of Verrucidæ by the recent discovery of the Lower Devonian genus *Proverruca* and the

---

[1] Zoological Journal, vol. 2, 1825, pp. 208, 209.   [2] Proc. Zool. Soc. London, 1914, p. 946.

admirable exposition of its structure and significance by Mr. T. H. Withers. Taking such a form as *Scillælepas*—

If we imagine the almost equal development of the rostrum and carina and the suppression on one side of the lateral valves, the scutum and tergum would be allowed to form that side of the wall, and the opposing scutum and tergum would have to lean over at a greater angle to meet them. We should then have only to suppress the subcarina, the median latus, and the peduncle to get a form such as *Proverruca*. This was evidently the history of the form, and although *Scillælepas* may not have been the actual ancestor, it must have been a form somewhat similar. (Withers.)

Further reduction of the wall by loss of the lateral plates, together with the more efficient articulation of the remaining wall compartments, are all that is required to transform *Proverruca* into *Verruca*.

Genus VERRUCA Schumacher.

1817. *Verruca* Schumacher, Essai d'un nouveau système des habitations des Vers Testacés, pp. 35, 91. Monotype, *Verruca strömii=Lepas strömia* Müller.

1817. *Clysia* Savigny, Leach, Journal de Physique, de Chimie, d'Histoire naturelle et des Arts, vol. 85, July 1817, p. 69. Monotype, *C. striata=Balanus striatus* Penn.

1817. *Ochthosia* Ranzani, Opuscoli Scientifici, vol. 1, p. 275; 2, 1818, p. 66. Monotype, *O. stroemia*.

1824. *Clisia* Leach, Encyclopedia Britannica Suppl., vol. 3 (according to Darwin).

1825. *Clisia* Leach, Zoological Journal, vol. 2, p. 210.

1827. *Clitia* Leach, Sowerby, Genera of Shells. Type, *Lepas verruca* Gmelin.

1854. *Verruca* Darwin, Monograph, p. 496.

Verrucidæ without lateral plates additional to the four composing the wall. Type, *V. stroemia*.

The genus is readily distinguished from all other sessile barnacles by the wall composed of four dissimilar plates, the movable top, like the lid of a chest, composed of two plates hinged to the wall along one side.

Terminology of plates.—The scutum in *Verruca* is always smaller than the tergum. The inner face is more or less concave, with raised occludent and tergal borders, an impression or pit for the adductor muscle, and very rarely an adductor ridge. Externally the tergal side or area slopes at an angle with the rest of the valve. The upper border of this slope forms an *apical ridge*, often not visible in a top view. Below this rib there is invariably an *articular furrow*. This is followed by the *articular ribs*, variable in number and position. The last one, terminating at the basotergal angle, is the most constant of all.[1] I have termed it the crescent rib, since it defines the semilunar tergal area of the scutum.

The tergum is trapezoidal, and usually flat or lightly concave within. The exterior is divided into two areas by the last articular

---

[1] This rib, terminating at the baso-tergal angle, was not counted as an articular rib by Darwin, but Hoek and others, I think properly, regard it as articular.

rib, also termed the *diagonal rib*. The upper articular rib terminates in the articular furrow of the scutum; rarely there is a weak rib above it, forming part of the occludent border of the plate.

The fixed scutum and tergum have structures analogous to the lateral plates of Balanidæ. There are median raised triangular areas or parietes, and sunken or diversely sculptured sutural areas like the Balanid radii. These structures are well shown in plate 7, figure 2a. The radius and ala along the scutotergal suture of the fixed plates have been homologized by Darwin with the articular ribs of the movable plates, the parietes being then homologous with the lower articular ribs.

The fixed scutum may be quite plain inside, or there may be a pit for the insertion of the scutal adductor muscle. The lower edge of this pit is sometimes raised, forming an *adductor ridge*. When this ridge projects as a semicircular or spatulate process, I have termed it a *myophore*. (See pl. 1, fig. 3.)

The wall plates are indicated by letters on plate 7, as C, carina; R, rostrum; F. Sc., fixed scutum; F. T., fixed tergum; M. Sc., movable scutum; M. T., movable tergum.

V. strömia sometimes excavates its basal support when this is calcareous, according to Darwin. I have seen no evidence of such action in any American species. The surface sculpture of shells or coral, whether living or dead, seems perfectly sharp and uninjured under the Verrucæ I have investigated.

Verrucæ are modified in shape by the form of the support and sometimes by crowding, but the wall plates do not reproduce the irregularities of the supporting surface, as in *Balanus*, or, at all events, only to a very small degree. On echinoid spines *Verruca* almost always sits with the carinorostral axis parallel to the spine. On corals the position is more variable.

Mouth parts.—I have not found much difference between the mandibles and maxillæ of the various Verrucæ examined. The lower point of the mandible is always multispinose, and the edge of the maxilla very irregular. In these characters *Verruca* resembles the Lepadidæ.

Cirri.—In all but two of the species examined the anterior ramus of cirri i and ii is from two-thirds to as long as the posterior, the rami of other cirri being subequal. The cirri show great specialization in *V. strömia* and *V. alba*. In *V. strömia* the rami of cirrus i are nearly equal, but in ii and iii the anterior ramus is extremely short, less than half as long at the posterior. *V. alba* has the anterior rami of cirri i and ii very short, one-third the length of the posterior, that of cirrus iii being three-fourths the length. In this species the cirri are unusually slender.

In all species examined the rami of cirri iv, v, and vi are nearly alike in length and armature. The segments in nearly every specimen examined have three pairs of spines on the anterior side, the lower pair being very small, and usually there are two unequal spines at the posterior distal angle of each segment. The chætotaxy is so similar that it is hardly necessary to figure cirri of the several species.

FIG. 7.—VERRUCA ALBA, MAXILLA (a) AND MANDIBLE (b) OF SPECIMEN FIGURED IN PL. 2, FIGS. 1–1B.

The relative length and number of segments of the cirri are given in the following table, in all cases from individuals believed to be adult. It is, of course, understood that young barnacles have cirri of fewer segments than old ones.

Species.	Cirrus i.		Cirrus ii.		Cirrus iii.
	Relative length of anterior to posterior rami.	Number of segments of both rami.	Relative length of anterior to posterior rami.	Number of segments of both rami.	Relative length of anterior to posterior rami.
V. strömia	Slightly unequal.	7, 9	<One-half	7, 16	<One-half.
V. alba	One-third	10, 21	One-third	9, 21; 8, 18	Three-fourths.
V. nexa	Subequal	11, 12	Two-thirds	10, 15	Subequal.
V. floridana	Three-fifths	11, 14	Three-fourths		Subequal.
V. calotheca	Two-thirds	10, 12	Slightly unequal		Slightly unequal.
V. c. flavidula	Three-fourths.	9, 14	Three-fourths	11, 15	Subequal.
V. c. heteropoma	...do	12, 13	.....do	11, 14	Subequal.
V. entobapta	Two-thirds	8, 12	Subequal	15, 16	
V. zenthia	Subequal	12, 12	Three-fourths	10, 15	Subequal.
V. euglypta	Subequal	17, 17	Three-fifths	9, 18	Subequal.
V. darwini	Subequal	8, 8	Two-thirds		Subequal.
V. rathbuniana	Slightly unequal.	10, 11	Four-fifths	6, 11	Subequal.
V. kocki	Subequal	10, 12	Slightly unequal	15, 15	Subequal.
V. bicornuta	Subequal	10, 11	Three-fourths	7, 13	Subequal.
V. halotheca	Equal	12, 14	Three-fifths	9, 22	Subequal.

Terminal or caudal appendages.—These are very long in *V. strömia*, *V. spengleri*, *V. lævigata*, and *V. nexa*, described by Darwin, and in *V. alba* and *V. floridana*, being over half the length of cirrus vi, and more than double the length of its protopod. They are shorter though still rather long in *V. entobapta* and *V. calotheca flavidula*. The other species examined by me have short caudal appendages, not much exceeding the length of the protopod of cirrus vi, or even shorter. The actual and relative length follows:

Species.	Caudal appendages.		Protopodite of cirrus v (length in mm.).	Cirrus vi (length in mm.).
	Length in mm.	Number of segments.		
V. alba	2.8	22	0.8 to 1	3.8 to 4.6
V. alba	2.5	28	1	3.8
V. floridana	3.2	23	1	5.5
V. entobapta	2.4	18	1.3	
V. c. flavidula	2.3	14	1.2	5+
V. calotheca	1.8	14	1.5	
V. c. heteropoma	1.6	14	1	5
V. xanthia	1	12		
V. darwini	1.9	11	1.5	
V. hoeki	0.6	8	0.6	3
V. bicornuta	2.6	10	2.4	
V. euglypta	2	10	2.5	
V. halotheca	2	10	2.6	

Distribution of Verruca.—Under this head it may be said that while the genus is of almost world-wide occurrence, there are some extensive areas where no species have yet been found. In the Pacific no *Verruca* is known to exist on the west coast of America from Peru to the Arctic Ocean. Southward along the Asiatic coasts we encounter the genus first in the Philippine Archipelago. *The whole North Pacific is therefore without species.* One, the largest of the genus, is found, however, in the Hawaiian Archipelago. The coasts of tropical and South Africa have as yet afforded no Verrucidæ, and none are known from Australian seas; yet these coasts have not been very closely explored in deep water, near and off the borders of the continental shelf, where these animals have elsewhere been found most frequently.

In the north one species, *V. strömia*, has been reported from Iceland, and in the Antarctic Ocean *V. mitra* was taken by the *Belgica* in 70° south latitude. Only three species, *V. strömia* and *V. spengleri* of Europe, and *V. lævigata* of western South America, live in shallow water. All of the others are truly deep-sea creatures.

Dr. P. P. C. Hoek, in his account of the *Belgica* cirripedia (1907) has given a list of 25 recent species, grouped by geographic provinces. Adding to this list the new species described from the Indian Ocean by Professor Gruvel, and the American species described by myself, we have the following result;

Species.

Eastern North Atlantic and Mediterranean... [1]18

Western North Atlantic and Gulf of Mexico................................... 11

South Atlantic and Antarctic.. 4

West coast of South America.. 1

Hawaiian Islands.. 1

Southwestern Pacific (near Kermadec and Gambier Islands)..................... 2

East Indies (Malay Archipelago and Philippines to the Andamans)............. 13

     Total.. 50

It will be seen by the above table that (except in the North Pacific) Verrucæ are most abundant where the sea bottom has been most assiduously explored, that is, in the North Atlantic. The comparative scarcity of species in other seas may very likely turn out to be due to the imperfection of our knowledge.

While most deep-water Verrucæ are now known from a single station, the geographic distribution of species will, I think, eventually prove to be somewhat extended, where conditions favor; this opinion being based upon the data relating to V. alba, the varying forms under V. calotheca, etc. The limits of their range seem to be determined by temperature, which of course is more or less closely correlated with depth. Thus, V. alba, in its several varieties, has an extension from Barbados to Hatteras, yet always in bottom temperatures of from 71°.3 to 75° F., and depths of 45 to 68 fathoms. V. calotheca, with the two forms I have segregated as races, has an even greater geographic extension, with a known range in temperature of only from 45°.6 to 48°.3 F. Whether the restriction to a narrow range of temperatures which seems indicated by the small number of observations available be due to the direct effect of temperature on the barnacle,[2] or to indirect action through the food supply or other factors, is uncertain. That they are so restricted accounts for the emphatic specific diversity I have found to exist between the warm-water Verrucæ of our continental shelf and the species obtained by European expeditions in the eastern Atlantic.

In the group of V. darwini, bicornuta, and rathbuniana, which live in 1,550 to 1,769 fathoms, bottom temperature 37° to 38°.5 F., we find very closely related species on the two sides of the North Atlantic and as far south as the Antarctic Ocean. It seems likely that this group of forms, living in the depths in temperatures approaching

[1] Seven of the eighteen eastern Atlantic species were briefly diagnosed by Aurivillius, without figures. Until a more complete account of these forms is given they can not be critically compared with really known forms. Doctor Hoek significantly remarks that " Aurivillius and Gruvel have described 10 different species of Verruca as occurring near the Azores; between some of these the differences seem to be very small." It seems curious that the Verrucæ obtained near the Azores by the Travailleur and Talisman (described by Gruvel) should all be different from those dredged in the same waters by the Princesse Alice (described by Aurivillius).

[2] Littoral and pelagic barnacles outside of the Tropics tolerate very considerable variations in temperature.

freezing point (3° to 4° C.), may have a general distribution over the floor of the Atlantic, where the uniformity of conditions in the dark, cold, deeps opposed no barriers to their distribution. These abyssal, cold-water species have a characteristic erect shape not found in any *Verruca* from shallow or warm water.

A certain correlation therefore exists between the shape of the barnacle and its habitat. The shallow-water species, *V. strömia, V. spengleri,* and *V. lævigata,* are all much depressed, having broadly spreading walls, while all of the high species with erect movable plates live in very deep or very cold water. There are also in intermediate depths and temperatures numerous boxlike forms with steep walls and flattened top.

I have given somewhat detailed accounts of several species, such as *V. alba,* since very little is known of the range of variation in *Verruca,* nearly all the species except *V. strömia* and *V. lævigata* being known from one or very few individuals, from a single station. The series of numerous examples from several stations before me for the first time allows some estimate of the kind and degree of variation among individuals and colonies of the deep-water forms. It appears that, as Darwin has noticed in *Balanus,* the individuals of a colony usually resemble one another rather closely. Different colonies of one species may sometimes show rather marked differences, even in the same district, while in others, widely separated, the specimens may be practically identical. It should be noted that the widely separated colonies recorded herein in which the individuals are very similar, occur along the course of the Gulf Stream, such as the colonies of typical *V. alba* in Florida Strait and off Hatteras. The wandering nauplii are doubtless borne northward in a constant stream upon this mighty current.

KEY TO VERRUCÆ OF THE WESTERN ATLANTIC AND CARIBBEAN ZOOLOGICAL PROVINCES.

a^1. Movable plates sloping steeply or nearly erect; parietes of fixed scutum and tergum separated by a large radio-alar area; basal edges of wall not inflexed.

b^1. Apical cavities of fixed tergum and rostrum partitioned off; a partition-like myophore in fixed scutum.............................. *V. euglypta,* p. 39.

b^2. Cavity simple, without partitions, myophore, or distinct adductor pit; fixed tergum with narrow paries.

c^1. Movable scutum and tergum each with one articular rib; no distinct rostro-carinal articular teeth or ribs; size small.................... *V. hoeki,* p. 41.

c^2. Movable scutum with one or two, tergum with one distinct and two very weak articular ribs; rostrocarinal suture serrate; greatest diameter and height about equal.

d^1. Rostrum with 4, carina 5 subequal articular ribs........ *V. bicornuta,* p. 43.

d^2. Rostrum and carina each with 2 distinct and one imperfect rib.

V. rathbuniana, p. 41.

c^3. Similar to c^2, but height decidedly less than greatest diameter.

V. darwini, p. 45.

a^2. Movable plates not steeply sloping, the top more or less flattened; suture or area between parietes of fixed scutum and tergum linear or narrow.

b^1. Base of walls inflexed to form a broad ledge; a depending myophore in the fixed scutum; sculpture weak; apex of rostrum marginal.

V. coraliophila, p. 21.

b^2. Base of walls simple or rarely inflexed; sculpture strong.

c^1. Apex of rostrum not marginal; base of the walls inflexed in the adult stage.

V. nexa, p. 29.

c^2. Apex of rostrum marginal or nearly so; base of the walls not inflexed, but sometimes thickened.

d^1. Rostrum and carina having short ribs above their upper articulating ribs, and curving to the bases of the movable plates; scutum *convex* having 3, tergum 4 articular ribs.............. *V. alba* and subspecies, pp. 25, 28.

d^2. Rostrum having short ribs curving to base of movable scutum, and above the upper articulating rib; carina without such ribs.

e^1. Movable plates each with 4 articular ribs.

f^1. Interlocking teeth and ribs of carina and rostrum subequal.

V. calotheca flavidula, p. 34.

f^2. Upper teeth and ribs of carina and rostrum larger.. *V. calotheca*, p. 33.

e^2. Movable plates each with 3 articular ribs.

f^1. Yellowish; walls subvertical, rather thin-edged; adductor pit shallow, without ridge or myophore................... *V. c. heteropoma*, p. 35.

f^2. Yellow; walls subvertical, blunt-edged; fixed scutum having a pit and adductor ridge, fixed tergum not calloused within.

V. xanthia, p. 36.

f^3. White; walls spreading, thin and sharp-edged; fixed scutum having a high adductor ridge or myophore; fixed tergum calloused within.

V. floridana, p. 31.

d^3. No short ribs above the upper articulating ribs of rostrum and carina, which have marginal apices; basal edge of walls obtuse; movable plates having each 4 articular ribs................................. *V. entobapta*, p. 38.

Section A: METAVERRUCA.

The basal borders of the wall plates are inflexed, forming a wide basal ledge; the fixed scutum bears a depending tongue-shaped adductor ridge or myophore; the apex of the rostrum is marginal; top flattened; sculpture weak.

Type.—V. coraliophila.

VERRUCA CORALIOPHILA, new species.

Plate 1, figs. 1-5.

Type.—Cat. No. 43469, U.S.N.M.

Type-locality.—*Albatross* station 2662-3, 2669, 2671-2, between the Bahamas and Cape Fear.[1]

The barnacle is cream-white, seated upon a branch of white coral. The carinorostral wall slopes somewhat, the scuto tergal wall usually being vertical. The movable scutum and tergum lie parallel to or at a small angle with the plane of the base, each having three articular ribs. The plates of the wall are only weakly sculptured, usually almost

---

[1] For footnote see p. 22.

smooth; their basal borders are broadly inflexed (fig. 2). Both movable valves have three very low, flat ribs.

The movable scutum has the usual crescentic rib, a broad, flat, strongly projecting median articular rib, another very narrow one above it, the rest of the plate having well-spaced, narrow, transverse grooves. Inside there is a deep, oblique articular furrow near the apex, receiving the upper articular ridge of the tergum. This is bounded inside by a short, high ridge back of which is the rather deep pit of the scutal adductor muscle. Nearer the basal edge there are several low callous lumps, variable in form and position (fig. 5.)

The movable tergum has a deep recess in the middle of the scutal border, at the termination of a median articular rib; above this there is a flat, wide upper articular rib, and below it a narrow diagonal rib. The rest of the plate is transversely grooved. The internal face (fig. 5) is nearly flat.

The fixed scutum has only faint sculpture of growth lines outside, or sometimes the triangular area next the occludent edge is vertically grooved. The beak is not produced, but lies in close proximity to that of the movable scutum. From the inside wall a prominent semicircular adductor ridge or myophore depends, concave on its upper face (fig. 3.) Externally, there is a very small radius in the tergal suture; below a small ala on the fixed tergum.

The fixed tergum is about as large as the fixed scutum and similarly sculptured.

The carina and rostrum articulate by a suture weakly zigzag below, but the carina has one large tooth above, between two smaller

---

[1] Some material preserved dry was labeled as from *Albatross* stations 2662-3, 2669, 2671-2. Among other organisms it contained fragments of coral and more or less perfect examples of the following Cirripedia:

Scalpellum longicarinatum Pilsbry.

Calantica superba (Pilsbry).

Verruca coralliophila Pilsbry.

Hexelasma americanum Pilsbry.

These stations are situated as follows:

U. S. F. C. Station.	Position.		Depth in fathoms.	Bottom temperature.
	Latitude north.	Longitude west.		
	° ′ ″	° ′ ″		
2662	29 24 30	79 43 00	434	43.7
2663	29 39 00	79 49 00	421	42.7
2669	31 09 00	79 33 30	352	43.7
2671	31 20 00	72 22 00	280	....
2672	31 31 00	79 05 00	277	54.3

Coral was reported from stations 2669 and 2671. Material preserved wet from station 2669 contained the types of *Calantica superba*; the type of *Hexelasma americanum* is from station 2663; and that of *Scalpellum longicarinatum* is from station 2668. It is therefore impossible to draw any inference as to the particular station or stations which supplied the barnacles of this mixed lot, but this is not of great importance since all of the stations in question are in the same district, and except the last two they do not differ much in depth or temperature.

ones on the rostrum. The straight hinge margin is simple, and the beaks are not produced.

Two specimens measure: Carinorostral length of base 8.5, length between apices 6.3 mm.; diameter of base 7.3 mm.; height of fixed tergum 5.5 mm. C.-R. length of base 14 mm.; between apices 11.2 mm.; diameter of base 8, height of fixed tergum 8 mm.

Internal organs not examined. The specimens were preserved dry.

This species is strongly individualized by its inornate exterior, the apices of the plates not projecting, by the very broadly inflexed basal margins of the wall and by the peculiar, depending adductor ridge or myophore of the fixed scutum.

Four complete individuals and three more or less imperfect ones were preserved, all being dry. Two are seated on the strong, solid branches of a white coral, the others detached. In four of them the carinorostral length scarcely exceeds the other diameter of the base, the others being longer than wide. There is also considerable variation in the degree of development of the external sculpture of the walls as shown in the figures, the longer, more strongly sculptured individuals having the parietes of the fixed scutum and tergum distinctly raised, while in the shorter, smoother form the areas of these plates are nearly even. The myophore and inflexed basal walls are similar in all of the examples.

Figures 1, 2, 4 are drawn to one scale and represent adult barnacles. Figures 2 and 4 are examples which lack the movable plates. Figure 3 represents the interior of the fixed tergum and scutum; figure 5 the interior of the movable tergum and scutum.

Section B: VERRUCA.

Top flattened, the plane of the movable plates not far from parallel with that of the base; radio-alar area between parietes of fixed scutum and tergum small or linear.

Type.— *V. strömia.*

GROUP OF V. STRÖMIA.

Much depressed; basal edges of the spreading wall-plates thin and sharp; adductor ridge or myophore well developed; apex of the rostrum marginal. Rami of first pair of cirri subequal, those of the second and third pairs very unequal, the third pairs being like the second, and unlike the fourth to sixth. Terminal appendages very long. Shallow-water forms.

This group of shallow-water forms is strongly individualized, not only by the depressed form, but especially by the cirri, which are more specialized than in other Verrucae. The group comprises *V. stromia, V. spengleri,* and *V. lævigata.* The second of these species is not contained in the Museum.

Conia monstruosa O. G. Costa,[1] is evidently a *Verruca* of the Italian Tertiary, which has not been noticed by any subsequent author, to my knowledge.

VERRUCA STRÖMIA (O. F. Müller).

1776. *Lepas strömia* O. F. MÜLLER, Zoologiæ Danicæ Prodromus, p. 251.
1789. *Lepas strömia* MÜLLER, Zoologica Danica, vol. 3, p. 21, pl. 94, figs. 1, 2, 3, 4.
1790. *Lepas verruca* SPENGLER, Skrivter af Naturhistorie-Selskabet, vol. 1, p. 194.
1854. *Verruca strömia* Müller, DARWIN, Monograph, etc., p. 518, pl. 21, figs. 1a–f (*q. v.* for synonyms and older references).
1897. *Verruca strömia* Müller, WELTNER, Verzeichnis der bisher beschriebenen recenten Cirripedienarten, Archiv f. Naturg., vol. 1, p. 274.
1900. *Verruca stroemia* Müller, WELTNER, Fauna Arctica, vol. 1, pp. 298, 303–4 (entrance to White Sea).

Type-locality.—North Sea.

Distribution.—Shores of northern Europe north to Iceland and Greenland, south to England and Helgoland; low tide to 90 fathoms. Pliocene and Pleistocene of Great Britain; ?Red Sea.

Specimens in the United States National Museum are from Scarborough, on *Pecten*, Exmouth, south Devon, on sandstone, with *Balanus spongicola*, and the Irish Channel, on *Chrysodomus antiquus* and *Balanus hameri*, all from the Jeffreys collection. There are also numerous examples without definite locality, and one lot from the British Crag, Jeffreys collection. I have looked over a good many shells and barnacles from Greenland without finding *Verruca*.

This common European species is light brown, much depressed, with the walls broadly spreading; rostrum is much the largest plate. Movable scutum and tergum are very small, especially the scutum, both having three articular ribs. The sculpture of fine, crowded growth lines, is quite unlike any deep-water species. Carina, rostrum, and fixed scutum interlock by many subequal ribs, but the suture between fixed scutum and tergum is straight and linear. Inside there is a very large adductor ridge or myophore, in form of a flat, downwardly sloping plate in the fixed scutum. In the fixed tergum there is a similar plate. Sometimes these plates stand almost vertically, partitioning off the cavities of fixed scutum and tergum. Often the apex of the rostrum also is excavated. The contour is rounded when the barnacle stands alone, but they are often crowded, like Balani, producing curious irregularities of shape. Well-grown English examples measure about 8 or 9 mm. in greatest diameter and 2 to 3 mm. high.

According to Darwin the rami of cirrus i are slightly unequal. In cirrus ii the posterior ramus is more than twice as long as the anterior. Cirrus iii is like ii. Terminal appendages are two-thirds to four-

---

[1] Di alcuni Balanidi appartenenti al Regno di Napoli, in Atti Accad. Sci. Napoli, vol. 5, pt. 2, 1843, p. 117, pl. 1, figs. 4, 5, 6, republished as *Creusia monstruosa* Costa, Fauna del Regni Napoli, Cirropedi p. 23.

fifths the length of cirrus vi. A specimen from England examined agrees with these proportions.

This species, the type of the genus, is one of the more highly evolved forms, both in internal structure and the form and articulations of the wall-plates. The fine, crowded growth lines are also a peculiar feature. With *V. lævigata* and *V. spengleri*, it should probably be considered to form a section of the genus apart from the deep-sea species.

VERRUCA LÆVIGATA (Sowerby.)

Plate 8, fig. 2.

1827. *Clitia lævigata* SOWERBY, Genera of Recent and Fossil Shells. Plate of *Clitia*, figs. 1, 3.

1854. *Verruca lævigata* Sowerby, DARWIN, Monograph, etc., p. 520, pl. 21, figs. 3a, 3b.

1897. *Verruca lævigata* Sowerby, WELTNER, Verzeichnis, Archiv für Naturgeschichte, Jahrg. 1897, vol. 1, p. 274.

1903. *Verruca lævigata* Sowerby, GRUVEL, Nouv. Arch. du Muséum (4), vol. 5, p. 99, pl. 1, fig. 10.

Type.—Present location unknown; from "coast of South America, adhering to *Mytilus magellanicus.*"

Distribution.—Tierra del Fuego to Peru (Darwin).

Numerous individuals, Cat. Nos. 43480, 43481, are on a pair of very large specimens of *Balanus psittacus* (Molina), from Talcahuano Bay, Chile, Cat. No. 43482, R. E. C. Stearns coll. One of these is illustrated. *V. lævigata* and *V. strömia* are the only littoral species of the genus known, and the former is the only species known from South America, or, indeed, from any part of the eastern rim of the Pacific. Since its only near relatives live in the north Atlantic, its ancestors probably spread westward in pre-Miocene times before the elevation of the Isthmus of Panama. The individual figured measures 6 mm. in carinorostral diameter.

GROUP OF V. ALBA.

Boxlike, strongly sculptured forms, externally like the Group of *V. calotheca,* but differing in the cirri, which are very slender; cirri i and ii having very unequal rami, the anterior branch about one-third as long as the posterior; cirrus iii with somewhat unequal rami, iv to vi similar with subequal rami; terminal appendages very long.

VERRUCA ALBA Pilsbry.

Plate 2, figs. 1–1b, 2.

1907. *Verruca nexa alba* PILSBRY, U. S. Nat. Mus., Bull. 60, p. 107, pl. 11, figs. 7, 8.

Type.—Cat. No. 9474, U. S. N. M.

Type-locality.—*Albatross* station 2317, Straits of Florida, north latitude 24° 25′ 45″; west longitude 81° 46′ 45″, in 45 fathoms, bottom temperature 75° F., seated on a sea-urchin spine. Other

localities are: *Albatross* station 2268, off Hatteras, north latitude
35° 10' 40''; west longitude 75° 06' 10'', in 68 fathoms, bottom temperature 71°.3 F., and station 2269, in the same locality, 48 fathoms,
bottom temperature 77° F.   On the Pourtalès Plateau, 10 miles
south of Key West, yacht *Eolis*, J. B. Henderson, jr., 1911, all on
spines of *Dorocidaris*.   Off Florida, in 195 fathoms, *Blake* Expedition, in the Museum of Comparative Zoology.

V. alba has a very considerable geographic range—greater than any
other American species so far as we know, but it seems to be restricted
to moderate depths, and it will be noted that the northern stations
have about the same high bottom temperature as the southern, and
all lie in the course of the Gulf Stream.

The barnacle is white, flat topped, with steep or subvertical walls.
The movable scutum is *strongly convex* between the apex and basal
margin, the apex being depressed and somewhat twisted.   It has
three articular ridges and two (or sometimes three) longitudinal ridges
on the occludent area.   The movable tergum has four articular
ridges, the second one very small in the type-specimen (but nearly as
large as the others in another).   The fixed scutum and tergum have
conspicuous, stout, recurved beaks.   The carina and rostrum interlock by one long and some small teeth in each; and above the upper
articulating rib *both carina and rostrum have several short riblets
curving toward and terminating on the scutotergal hinge line.*   There
is a shallow adductor pit in the fixed scutum bounded below by a
curved adductor ridge.   The fixed tergum is calloused inside.   *The
basal edges of the wall are very obtuse,* rather thick.

Length 4, breadth 2.7, height 1.7 mm.

The cirri are very slender.   The first has rami of 11 and 21 segments, the anterior ramus not much exceeding one-third the length
of the posterior.   Cirrus ii similar, of 9 and 19 segments, the anterior
ramus a third as long as the posterior.   The rami of cirrus iii are more
nearly equal, the anterior three-fourths the posterior.   Cirrus vi
about 3.3 mm. long.   The terminal appendage is 2.8 mm. long, with
27 segments, being nearly four times as long as the protopod of
cirrus vi.

The above details from the original specimens, together with the
figures given in my former account, show that *V. alba* is widely
distinct from *V. nexa* Darwin, of which I formerly thought it might
be a variety.

The specimens are apparently adult, judging from the long beaks
of the fixed scutum and tergum, and the thickness of the wall plates.
The specimens from off Hatteras, one from each of the stations mentioned above, are typical in form and sculpture and of about the
typical size, one measuring: carinorostral length 3.9, breadth 2.8,
alt. 1.9 mm.   Specimens from other places differ in some respects.

(1) The *Blake* took four specimens in 195 fathoms off Florida, on a spine of *Dorocidaris abyssicola* A. Agassiz. The base of one of these is drawn in plate 2, figure 2. They are much larger and especially longer than the typical form of *V. alba*. The rostrum extends entirely around the rostral end and its wall slopes outward toward the base. The basal edge is very obtuse, flat, but not inflexed. The rostrum and carina each have 5 articulating teeth and ribs in the largest, but in smaller ones there are four. The right scutum and tergum are movable. In one example a minute rib has split off from the second articular rib of the tergum, a corresponding one appearing also in the scutum. The largest specimen measures: greatest carinorostral length 7 mm., length between apices 5 mm., height 2.5 mm.

The terminal appendages are 2.5 mm. long, of 28 segments (pl. 9, fig. 2). The penis is nearly 3 mm. long, being nearly three times the length of the protopod, and about three-fourths that of cirrus vi.

The cirri and mouth-parts are substantially as described for typical *V. alba*.

(2) The lot taken by Mr. Henderson in the *Eolis*, on the Pourtalès Plateau near Key West (pl. 2, figs. 1–1b), contains numerous examples of all ages, all of them sitting upon *Dorocidaris* spines, and all agreeing in having thinner walls than other colonies seen. The shape is long, as in the *Blake* specimens, the rostrum being produced around the end and outward farther than in the typical *V. alba*. The basal edges are thin in about a dozen individuals of various sizes removed from the spines.

The movable scutum is arched or convex, being depressed and somewhat twisted toward the acute apex. Articular ribs three, counting that terminating at the basotergal angle, the rest of the surface transversely grooved and longitudinally bicostate. Internally it is excavated toward the apex.

The movable tergum has four articular ribs, the second one slightly smaller or very small. The rest of the plate is transversely grooved, often with some short longitudinal ribs.

The fixed scutum and tergum have recurved, produced apices, rather near together. Parietal surfaces irregularly roughened, similar to those of the rostrum and carina. There is a hollow for the adductor muscle, with a narrow adductor ridge below, in the fixed scutum. The rostrum and carina interlock in a zigzag suture produced by about four teeth in each plate, the upper two teeth large in each. The beaks of the plates bend over toward the movable plates, especially that of the rostrum. The scutotergal borders of both rostrum and carina have short, arcuate riblets terminating on the scutal and tergal borders. A large individual measures: Carinorostral length of base 5 mm., between apices 3.8 mm., breadth of base 2.2 mm., greatest height 2.8 mm.

The cirri in the individual figured and another of the same lot are
extremely slender and long, as in typical *V. alba*. Cirrus i of 10 and
21 joints, the shorter ramus about one-third as long as the longer.
Cirrus ii is similar, with 8 and 18, or 9 and 21, joints. In cirrus iii
the shorter ramus is over three-fourths as long as the longer, thus
approaching the condition of the posterior cirri. Terminal appendage
has 22 long joints, is about three times the length of the protopod,
and from over one-half to nearly two-thirds as long as cirrus vi.
The penis is nearly twice as long as the protopod, being 1.2 to 1.7
mm. long. The mandible (fig. 7*b*) has three teeth, and seven or
eight points on the lower angle, the upper tooth being very large
and widely separated from the second. The maxilla (fig. 7*a*) has,
below the upper great spines, a deep recess in which a group of short
spines stands. The projecting lower edge has large and small spines
mingled.

VERRUCA ALBA CARIBBEA, new subspecies.

Plate 2, fig. 4.

Type.—Museum of Comparative Zoology.

Type-locality.—Off Grenada, West Indies, in 92 fathoms, on a spine
of *Dorocidaris affinis* (Philippi), *Blake* expedition. Also off Guadalupe in 150 fathoms, on spine of *D. affinis*, *Blake* expedition.

Twenty-three individuals on one spine of *Dorocidaris* are, with the
exception of a few young specimens, of nearly uniform size. In
sixteen of the lot the right scutum and tergum are movable. Sometimes the first articular ridge of the scutum is very weak and there is
variation in the articulation of the carina and rostrum. As a rule
each has three ribs and teeth. In a few examples the second rib and
tooth of the carina are much broader than in others. The upper rib
of the carina is always quite narrow, and the short ribs terminating
on the tergal margin are either *extremely small*, never more than two
in number, or, in a majority of the specimens, they are *absent or barely
perceptible*. The basal edge of the wall is as obtuse as in the type
form in some examples, thinner in others.

Greatest carinorostral length 4.1, height of fixed tergum 2 mm.

Cirri are as in typical *V. alba*. The teeth of the mandible are
more slender.

Three individuals from off Guadalupe in 150 fathoms, *Blake* collection, are similar, but larger, the largest 4.8 mm. long.

VERRUCA ALBA BARBADENSIS, new subspecies.

Plate 2, figs. 3, 3*a*.

Type.—Museum of Comparative Zoology.

Type-locality.—Off Barbados in 106 fathoms, on the spine of *Dorocidaris bartletti* A. Agassiz, *Blake* expedition.

The shape is more depressed than *V. alba*. The tergal area of the
movable scutum is narrower, its ribs three or four in number are

very narrow; the outer face is less convex, and the plate is not twisted toward the apex. The movable tergum is lengthened in the direction of the diagonal rib, and its articular ribs are unevenly spaced. The recurved beaks of the fixed scutum and tergum are very long. Rostrum and carina interlock by two very large and one small tooth in the rostrum, one very large and two or three small teeth in the carina. There are some very minute, granose ribs above the upper articulating rib of the rostrum, none above that of the carina. The rostrum is the largest and highest plate. It extends around the end of the barnacle, as in *V. alba*. Basal margin of the wall is obtuse. Greatest carinorostral length 3.9 mm.; height of fixed tergum 1 mm.

Three individuals on one spine agree in size and the other features mentioned above, except that one has the fixed tergum lower.

While this and the preceding forms are described as subspecies of *V. alba* of the Gulf Stream, it is not to be supposed that they are derivatives of the Floridian form. The direction of the oceanic currents leads us to conclude that the Caribbean forms represent a southern stock which was also carried northward, where the form described as typical *V. alba* arose.

GROUP OF V. NEXA.

Basal borders of the subvertical wall-plates either inflexed or simple. Fixed scutum without a distinct myophore, though there is an adductor pit. *The apex of the rostrum is removed from the upper edge of the plate.* Sculpture strong.

A group of small, elaborately sculptured forms, distinguished as follows:

a^1. Basal borders of the wall inflexed in the adult stage, West Indies.. *V. nexa* Darwin.
a^2. Basal borders of the wall not inflexed.
b^1. Movable scutum and tergum each with 4 articular ribs, Andaman Islands..*V. koehleri* Gruvel.
b^2. Movable scutum and tergum each with 3 articular ribs, Philippines.
V. intexta Pilsbry.

VERRUCA NEXA Darwin.

Plate 3, figs. 1, 1a, 1b, 1c.

1854. *Verruca nexa* DARWIN, Monograph of the Cirripedia, Balanidæ and Verrucidæ, p. 522, pl. 21, figs. 5.

Type.—British Museum.
Type-locality.—West Indies, on a gorgonian.
Distribution.—*Albatross* station 2324, off Havana, Cuba, in 33 fathoms.

The barnacle [1] is oblong, boxlike, with subvertical side walls and flattened top, the movable plates parallel to the plane of the base.[2]

---

[1] The specimens have now faded nearly to white, but were reddish when I first saw them in 1906.
[2] Professor Gruvel has placed *V. nexa* in the group having the plane of the movable plates ; erpendicular to the base, and in his monograph speaks of it (p. 179) as *non déprimeé;*" also "scutum fixe sans aucune dépression pour l'adducteur." These terms certainly are not applicable to *V. nexa*. I do not know what species was in view.

Wall-plates broadly inflexed at the base.   Apices of the fixed scutum and tergum produced and recurved.

Movable scutum having three strong articular ribs and two other ribs reaching the rostral margin.   Inside it is somewhat excavated near the apex.

Movable tergum having three broad articular ribs, the rest of the plate transversely grooved.

The fixed scutum is radially ribbed, the ribs on the rostral side interlocking with those of the rostrum.   The sutural margin on the tergal side has four short ribs.   Inside there is a low, transverse, adductor ridge, a rounded hollow above it.

Fixed tergum ribbed, contracted above the middle, with short sutural ribs on both sides.

Carina small, with vertically ribbed paries and about seven ribs which interlock with those of the rostrum, the intervals crenulate.

Rostrum somewhat patelliform, the *apex being removed from the margin*.   Carinal and scutal margins are profusely ribbed radially, paries irregularly ribbed vertically.

Carinorostral length, 4.7 mm.; height of fixed tergum, 2.1 mm. The largest specimen of the type lot is said by Darwin to measure 0.2 inch (5 mm.) in greatest diameter.

According to Darwin the rami of cirrus i are subequal, of 11 and 12 segments.   In cirrus ii the shorter ramus is two-thirds as long as the longer, segments 10 and 15.   In cirrus iii the rami are very nearly equal.   The caudal appendages are very long, as in *V. strömia.*

In young individuals the internal ledge of the base is wanting.   In one example there are three longitudinal ribs on the movable scutum in addition to the three articular ribs; the apex of the rostrum is much nearer the upper edge than in the specimen figured, though still removed from it.   The short articular ribs in the suture of fixed scutum and tergum are wanting; the articular ribs of rostrum and carina are fewer, four in each, and more widely spaced; their intervals smooth.   The range of variation in the species is therefore considerable.

By having the apex of the rostrum well removed from the upper margin of the plate, this species differs from all other Atlantic species, and resembles *V. intexta* Pilsbry and *V. koehleri* Gruvel.

GROUP OF V. CALOTHECA.

Boxlike forms with strong sculpture, vertical or moderately sloping walls, their basal edges not inflexed; fixed scutum having an adductor pit and often an adductor ridge or myophore; apex of the rostrum nearly or quite marginal.   Rami of cirri i and ii subequal, or the anterior decidedly over half as long as the posterior; rami of cirri iii to vi nearly equal.   Terminal appendages short or moderately long.

VERRUCA FLORIDANA, new species.

Plate 4, figs. 1 to 1c, 2, 3.

Type.—Cat. No. 1901, A. N. S. P. Cotype, Cat. No. 48095, U. S. N. M.
Type-locality.—South of Key West, Florida, in 90 fathoms, on dead shells of *Voluta dohrni*, living *Pleurotoma albida*, and on *Dorocidaris* spines. *Eolis* expedition, 1911.

The barnacle is white, about as wide as long, varying from square to approximately circular in outline; the opercular plates are quite flat, and usually slope at a low angle with the plane of the base. The plates of the wall are rather thin, and are beveled to an edge at the base, with no trace of inflection.

The movable scutum has three articular ridges, the third or crescentic ridge extending to the basitergal angle. They are parted by two wide, shallow furrows. The rest of the surface has rather widely spaced impressed lines parallel to the rostral border, and cut by one (in the type) or sometimes by two or three curved radial furrows, which do not extend to the apex of the plate (and therefore are not present in young individuals). When detached, this plate is seen to have two low, wide teeth on the tergal border, between the apex and the rostro-tergal angle. Internally the plate is quite smooth, gently concave in the median part.

The movable tergum is nearly square, the carinal border, however, being somewhat longer than the occludent border. It has three strong, well-raised articular ribs, the rest of the plate being sculptured with sunken lines parallel to the carinal margin of the plate and rather widely spaced. The interior face is smooth.

The carina has three wide, low radial ribs from apex to rostral suture, where they terminate in teeth interlocking with those of the rostrum, producing a strongly zigzag suture. Parallel with the upper rib there is an inconspicuous, very narrow riblet along the tergal border.

The rostrum has two principal ribs articulating with those of the carina. There is also a ledge along the scutal border sculptured with several small, curved radial riblets, terminating on the scutal border.

The fixed scutum has a small, recurved apex. The surface is divided into (1) a large triangle bounded by lines connecting the apex and basal extremities, which would be termed the paries in a Balanid, and which has only irregular sculpture consequent upon its base of support; (2) a somewhat smaller triangle above the former one, with its base against the rostrum, sculptured with vertical, spaced lines, and sometimes some radial riblets near the rostrum; (3) a small, densely lineolate area between the apex and the movable scutum; and (4) a very small, vertically lineolate, radiiform triangle toward the fixed tergum. Inside there is a rather small adductor myophore, concave on its upper face, and situated rather high on the plate.

The fixed tergum is a subquadrate plate with the four angles produced. Its surface is divided into four triangles by lines from the corners to the acute, recurved, but scarcely projecting apex. (1) The largest triangle has the basal margin as its base, and is without special sculpture; (2) a small, radially ribbed and concentrically striate aliform triangle toward the fixed scutum; (3) a lineolate triangle between the apices of the two terga; and (4) a long triangle extending between the carina and the movable tergum. The interior of this plate is rather heavily calloused in the middle, but less than in *V. strömia.*

Greatest carinorostral length 7.5 mm.; length between apices 6 mm.; greatest breadth, at right angles to preceding, 7 mm.; height from base to summit of the movable scutum 4 mm.

Other individuals measure: 5, 3.7, 4.8, 2 mm., and 7, 5.6, 6.8, 3 mm.

This species is related to *V. alba* Pilsbry, but it differs by the sculpture of the movable plates by the internal structure of the fixed scutum, and by lacking short, arcuate ribs above the upper articulating rib of the carina. *V. alba* is smaller, so far as known, and since all the individuals seen sit upon narrow echinid spines, the contour is different.

The general shape of the plates of the wall varies among the specimens, being dependent upon the irregularities of the supporting surface. Most of them have spreading walls, as in that selected as type (figs. 1–1c), but in some examples, hampered by a restricted base of support, the walls become steep, the tergo-scutal wall vertical or overhanging. Such an individual is drawn in figure 3. It grew upon a rather small *Dorocidaris* spine, the rostrocarinal axis of the barnacle transverse to the spine, and the base in consequence deeply concave. The greatest rostrocarinal length of this individual is 5 mm.

This species has been somewhat fully figured in order to show the amount and kind of variation to be found among individuals of one colony, brought up in one haul of the dredge. The lot, consisting of 15 individuals, was taken by Mr. John B. Henderson, jr., during the 1911 cruise of the yacht *Eolis.*

Cirrus i has rami of 14 and 11 segments, the shorter ramus three-fifths the length of longer. In cirrus ii the shorter ramus is over two-thirds the length of the longer, the other cirri having subequal rami. The terminal appendage has 23 joints, is more than three times the length of the protopod, decidedly over half the length of cirrus vi.

The penis is very stout, about twice as long as the protopod, sparsely hairy near the end, as usual.

VERRUCA CALOTHECA Pilsbry.

Plate 4, figs. 4, 4a, 4b.

1907. *Verruca calotheca* PILSBRY, U. S. Nat. Mus. Bull., 60, p. 110, pl. 11, figs. 1–3.

Type.—Cat. No. 32907, U.S.N.M.

Type-locality.—*Albatross* Station 2415, north latitude 30° 44'; west longitude 79° 26', off Georgia, 440 fathoms, bottom temperature 45.6 F., on *Calantica superba.*

The type-specimen, the only one known of the typical form, is figured here (pl. 4, figs. 4–4b) to show certain features not noticed in the original account. The suture between fixed scutum and fixed tergum is of the usual structure—a slit, widening upward, occupied by a very narrow radiiform extension of the fixed scutum and above it an obliquely grooved aliform triangle for the fixed tergum.

The movable scutum has four articular ribs (in addition to the usual apical rib, which is very slender and short, articulating above the first tergal rib). The lower or fourth rib terminates at the basitergal angle. Inside there is a deep articular furrow. The interior is deeply concave, with a distinct, rounded adductor pit; near the basal margin there are two grooves (fig. 4a). The scutotergal suture is markedly sinuous.

The movable tergum has four articular ribs and a weak ledge along the occludent margin. Inside there are two basal grooves, as in the scutum (fig. 4b).

The rostrum has, above the upper articular rib, an area upon which there are two slender ribs curving toward the movable plates. This ribbed scutal area is shown in figure 1 of my former paper, but not mentioned in the description.

Internally (pl. 4, fig. 4) the wall-plates are beveled to a sharp, simple edge. There is a very shallow pit or depression for the adductor muscle in the fixed scutum, which is calloused below it. The sutural edges of fixed scutum and tergum are decidedly thickened. In the scutum this thickening is in the lower part of the wall, but in the tergum it is chiefly farther inward, spreading in a rather thick pad in the upper part.

Cirrus i has rami of 10 and 12 joints, the shorter ramus two-thirds the length of the longer. Cirrus ii has the endopod slightly shorter, more hairy, as usual. Cirrus iii is similar, the outer ramus having three pairs of spines on each joint.

The terminal appendages have 14 joints, and are very little longer than the protopod of cirrus vi.

Penis is about two-thirds as long as protopod, and has very few hairs.

Verruca alba Pilsbry is related to *V. calotheca*, but differs by having a distinct pit within the fixed scutum, high on the wall near the tergal border. The sutural edges of fixed scutum and tergum are not so thickened. The rostrum and carina both have short, curved ribs above the upper articulating ribs, and terminating on the borders of the movable scutum and tergum, while in *V. calotheca* these are wanting on the carina. The oblong contour of the base in *V. alba* is probably due to its seat on narrow spines. *V. calotheca*, seated on the flat plate of a barnacle, has a normal, broad base.

VERRUCA CALOTHECA FLAVIDULA, new subspecies.

Plate 5, figs. 2, 2a.

Type.—Cat. No. 32926, U.S.N.M.

Type-locality.—*Albatross* Station 2415, off northern Florida, north latitude 30° 44′; west longitude 79° 26′, in 440 fathoms, bottom temperature 45°.6 F. (or at Station 2416 in 270 fathoms, bottom temperature 53°.8 F.—material from these two hauls, made in one day, was put together). Also Station 2666, near the preceding, north latitude 30° 47′ 30′′; west longitude 79° 49′, in 270 fathoms, bottom temperature 48°.3 F., on the coral *Anisopsammia profunda* Pourtalès, with *Verruca xanthia*.

The barnacle is very pale yellow or faintly brown outside, distinctly yellow within. The base is subcircular. The walls have simple, thin basal edges; interior without myophore or pit in the fixed scutum. Movable plates slope very steeply, about parallel to the plane of the adjacent carinorostral wall (or in some specimens approaching a horizontal position). Apices of the wall-plates project.

The movable scutum resemble that of *V. calotheca*, except that the occludent area has two longitudinal furrows, parting three ribs which attain the hinge margin. Interior deeply concave. Tergo-scutal suture nearly straight, as seen from within, except near the apex, where a small tooth of the tergum enters the scutum.

Tergum as in *V. calotheca*.

Rostrum has a scutal area sculptured with several narrow, granose ribs curving toward and terminating on the scutal border.

Carina with the upper articular rib indistinctly double, but there is no area of short, arcuate ribs above it.

Carinorostral length between apices 8 mm.; height of fixed tergum 5.2 mm.

Cirri i and ii have rapidly tapering rami, the shorter ramus about three-fourths the length of the longer. Cirrus iii is much more slender, with nearly equal rami, the inner one very profusely bristly. Terminal appendage has 14 joints, is three times the length of protopod, but less than half as long as cirrus vi. It resembles that of *V. floridana*, and is much longer than in *V. calotheca*.

This form varies in the pose of the movable plates, which vary from a subvertical to a subhorizontal position in different examples. The sculpture of the movable scutum is somewhat more elaborate than in the type of *V. calotheca*, having three (or, in one individual, four) longitudinal ribs on the occludent area. The color differs, especially inside. The movable plates slope more steeply. The interlocking teeth of the carina and rostrum are more regular and the ribs running to them are stronger. In *V. calotheca* the upper ribs and teeth are decidedly larger than the lower ones. There are also slight differences in the scutotergal sutures, both in the movable and fixed plates. Three specimens were taken at the type-locality; one at Station 2666. All were seated upon coral branches.

VERRUCA CALOTHECA HETEROPOMA, new subspecies.

Plate 5, figs. 1, 1a.

Type.—Cat. No. 32932, U.S.N.M.

Type-locality.—*Albatross* station 2753, near St. Vincent, West Indies, north latitude 13° 34'; west longitude 61° 03', in 281 fathoms, bottom temperature 48° F., on slender, branching coral, and on an echinoid spine. Also *Blake* collection, off St. Vincent, in 88 fathoms, on spines of *Cidaris affinis* Philippi. (Museum of Comparative Zoology.)

This barnacle, known by eight individuals from the type station, and two from an adjacent *Blake* station, resembles *V. calotheca* internally and in most details of external form. It differs by the sculpture of the movable plates. The movable scutum has two broad articular ribs (in *V. calotheca* and *V. c. flavidula* there are four articular ribs), and a much narrower, though more prominent, third crescentic rib terminating at the basitergal angle. There is also a minute rib under the apex, forming the upper border of the tergal edge, as usual.

The movable tergum has three articular ribs, including the diagonal rib (whereas in *V. calotheca* and *V. c. flavidula* there are four). The apex of the rostrum projects. Carinorostral sutural region about as in *V. calotheca*.

Carinorostral length between apices 5.5 mm.; greatest diameter at right angles to the length 5 mm.; height of fixed tergum 2.6 mm.

The rami of cirri i and ii are unequal, the anterior being about three-fourths the length of the posterior ramus. The terminal appendage of 14 segments is about one and one-half times the length of the protopod, and one-third that of cirrus vi. The penis is 2.4 mm. long, about half as long as cirrus vi.

In one individual the median articular rib of the tergum is bifid, and a minute rib split off from the second rib of the scutum articulates in the notch. The apex of the rostrum also is produced somewhat longer than in the others, approaching the form of *V. c. flavidula*. It is this specimen which causes me to consider *heteropoma* a race of *V. calotheca*, notwithstanding the considerable differences between typical specimens.

The locality of this race is distant from that of *V. calotheca*, but the bottom temperatures do not differ much.

VERRUCA XANTHIA, new species.

Plate 6, figs. 1, 1a, 1b.

Type.—Cat. No. 32931, U.S.N.M.

Type-locality.—*Albatross* Station 2666, off Fernandina, Florida, north latitude 30° 47′ 30″; west longitude 79° 49′, in 270 fathoms, bottom temperature 48.3° F. Seated on a coral (*Anisopsammia profunda* Pourtalès) with *Verruca calotheca flavidula.*

The barnacle is pale yellow, about as wide as long, depressed, the movable plates nearly parallel to the plane of the base. Basal edges of the wall rather obtuse, simple. Myophore in the fixed scutum well developed; its upper face concave.

The movable scutum has three articular ribs, two broad and flattened, and a much narrower third or crescentic rib running to the basitergal angle. Inside it is hollowed out under the apical part. The suture between scutum and tergum, as seen from below, has two teeth projecting from the tergum, one near the apex, the other midway.

The movable tergum has three articular ribs.

The fixed scutum is almost smooth externally and has a small radiiform slip on the tergal side.

The fixed tergum has a large, smooth paries in shape of an equilateral triangle, with obliquely grooved aliform triangles on the scutal and carinal sides.

The carina has five ribs articulating at their ends with those of the rostrum, the upper rib much longer than the others.

The rostrum has five articular ribs and a group of short arcuate ribs above, terminating on the scutal border. The apex is erect and marginal. Both carina and rostrum have a low callous submargin within.

Carinorostral length between apices 5 mm.; greatest diameter at right angles to length 5 mm.; height of fixed tergum 3 mm.

Cirrus i has slightly unequal rami tapering and attenuated distally, of 12 joints each. Cirrus ii has rami of 10 and 15 joints, the shorter one three-fourths the length of the longer, both rather profusely spinose. Cirrus iii has subequal, rather profusely spinose rami. Terminal appendage of 12 (?) joints, very minute, 1 mm. long. Penis minute, 0.8 mm. long.

V. xanthia differs from *V. floridana* by the color, the obtuse basal edges of the wall, which is vertical on the ends and overhangs on the tergoscutal side. It has some resemblance to *V. entobapta*, but differs from that by having some short, arcuate riblets on the scutal edge of the rostrum above the first rib which articulates with the carina. The number of articular ribs of the movable plates and the color also differ in the two species.

One specimen somewhat smaller than the type was found in the dry material from *Albatross* stations 2662, 2663, 2669, 2671, 2672, all in the neighborhood of the type-locality. It agrees with the type in the projecting adductor ridge or myophore in the fixed scutum, etc.

The type-specimen has a circular depression on the movable scutum, probably made by a rapacious gastropod, being similar to the unfinished borings often seen on bivalve mollusks. I have seen holes of this kind in several Verrucas.

A variety or race of this species, which may be called *Verruca xanthia insculpta* (pl. 6, fig. 2), is represented by one individual, Cat. No. 32925, U.S.N.M., taken at *Albatross* station 2415 or 2416 (the material from these two stations was not separated), both being very close to the type-locality of *V. xanthia*. It has more pronounced sculpture than the type; the movable scutum being radially ribbed throughout, five ribs extending to its basal margin. The fixed scutum and tergum have strong, well-spaced growth-lines parallel to the basal margin. The fixed scutum has a deep adductor pit within, situated in the upper half of the plate, but the lower margin of the pit does not project as a myophore. The fixed scutum occupies a smaller segment of the wall, and the rostrum a larger. The suture between movable scutum and tergum inside is almost straight, except near the apex.

Carinorostral length at base, 5 mm.; carinorostral length between beaks, 6.5 mm.; diameter at right angles to preceding, 6 mm.; height of fixed tergum, 3.5 mm.

This barnacle agrees with the less spreading forms of *V. floridana* in general shape and pattern of sculpture, but it differs by the steeper walls with obtuse basal edges, the more numerous teeth of the carinorostral suture, the stronger sculpture, the absence of a projecting myophore within the fixed scutum, and the color of the plates, outside and within.

It was seated with the carinorostral axis obliquely transverse to the supporting branch of white coral.

Another specimen has a quite shallow adductor pit in the fixed scutum. The suture between movable scutum and tergum, inside, is bisinuate as in typical *V. xanthia*. The rostrum is very large. Carinorostral length between apices 8 mm.

VERRUCA ENTOBAPTA, new species.

Plate 6, figs. 3, 3a, 3b.

Type.—Cat. No. 32924, U.S.N.M.

Type-locality.—*Albatross* station 2415, east of Fernandina, Florida, north latitude 30° 44′; west longitude 79° 26′, in 440 fathoms, bottom temperature 46°.6 F., or station 2416, north latitude 31° 26′; west longitude 79° 07′, in 276 fathoms, bottom temperature 53°.8 F.

The barnacle is dull red within, tinted with lilac outside, about as wide as long, with the movable plates nearly parallel to the plane of the base. Plates of the wall rather thick, beveled to an obtuse basal edge; their parietal areas with rather weak sculpture of well-spaced grooves roughly parallel to the basal borders.

The movable scutum has four beaded articular ribs and an upper rib, which is extremely short and narrow, forming the upper margin of the tergal edge of the apex. The rest of the plate has strong flat ribs parted by narrower grooves, parallel to the rostral margin. The acute beak curves upward a little. The inner face is plain, a little excavated near the beak. The movable tergum has a strong diagonal rib and three other articular ribs, the second one from the top a little smaller than the others. The acute beak curves upward.

The fixed scutum is tripartite, the upper area sunken below the lower and more strongly sculptured. There is a very small radiiform area in the sutural furrow. Inside there is an ample pit for the adductor, its lower border projecting shortly as a thick adductor ridge or low myophore, concave above. The apex of the plate projects strongly.

The fixed tergum is tripartite externally, the parietal area being strongly raised, beak produced and a trifle recurved. Internally it is calloused.

The carina and rostrum interlock by teeth which terminate several scaly radial ribs in each valve, the upper rib of the rostrum being the largest. These ribs are flattened, somewhat imbricating upward, and are conspicuously scaly. There are no short curved ribs on the upper edge of the rostrum.

Carinorostral length of the base, 5 mm.; between the apices, 5.5 mm.; diameter of the base, 5 mm.; height of fixed tergum, apex to base, 3.9 mm.

Cirrus i with rami of 8 and 12 segments, the shorter about two-thirds the length of the longer. Cirrus ii has subequal rami.

Terminal appendage of 18 long segments, about twice as long as the protopod (pl. 9, fig. 4).

This species, of which three individuals were taken, stands close to *V. calotheca*, from which it is readily separable by the deep pit, bounded below by a low adductor ridge or even a narrow myophore in the fixed scutum; by the rounded callous rim near the beveled basal edge within, and which is best seen in detached valves; and by the upper border of the rostrum. Its upper articular rib stands close to the scutum, from which it is separated by a narrow depression in which a minute thread runs parallel to the margin or curves a little at the end. In *V. calotheca* there is a far wider area bearing curved riblets. The color of the interior also is different in the three specimens by which *V. entobapta* is known.

V. imbricata Gruvel, from near the Canary Islands, seems to be closely related to *V. entobapta*, but it differs by being more depressed and of a pure white color; the fixed tergum projects much farther above the fixed scutum, and both of the movable plates have one more articular rib. The interior of *V. imbricata* has not been described.

This species occurs with *V. xanthia*, from which it differs conspicuously in sculpture.

Section C: CAMERAVERRUCA.

The basal borders of the wall-plates are thin and simple; *the apical cavities of fixed tergum and rostrum are partitioned off, forming recesses of the general cavity.* The fixed scutum has a vertical, partition-like myophore. The parietes of fixed scutum and tergum are separated by a broad ala and a radius. The movable plates slope steeply. Cirri with nearly equal rami; terminal appendages extremely short.

Type.—Verruca englypta.

VERRUCA EUGLYPTA Pilsbry.

Plate 3, figs. 2, 2a.

1908. *Verruca euglypta* PILSBRY, U. S. Nat. Mus. Bull., 60, p. 108, pl. 10, figs. 1, 2, 3.

Type.—Cat. No. 32906, U.S.N.M.

Type-locality.—Albatross station 2415, off Fernandina, Florida, north latitude 30° 44'; west longitude 79° 26', in 440 fathoms, bottom temperature 45°.6 F.; on the coral *Anisopsammia profunda* Pourtalès.

The plates of this barnacle are thin. The basal edge of the wall is thin and simple. The movable scutum is smooth inside, with a shallow, oblong pit for the adductor muscle, and a narrow, well-raised rim along the occludent side and apex.

The rostrum and carina unite in a suture conspicuously zigzag inside as well as out. The cavity of the apex of rostrum is inclosed by a partition (pl. 3, fig. 2). The carina has a very much narrower partition.

The fixed scutum has a vertically depending plate, which from its position must be regarded as an enlarged adductor ridge or myophore; behind it is a deep, narrow cavity. The cavity of the fixed tergum has also a partition like that of the rostrum (fig. 2a, interior of the movable and fixed scuta and terga, the carina and rostrum removed).

Cirrus i has equal rami of 17 joints. Cirrus ii has very unequal rami of 9 and 18 segments, the shorter ramus obtuse at the tip, densely hairy; longer ramus with mainly three pairs of spines on each segment. Cirrus iii has subequal rami, the anterior ramus with four or five pairs of spines, the posterior with three pairs on each segment.

The terminal appendages are very small, shorter than the adjacent protopods, being about 1.6 mm. long, composed of 11 profusely bristly segments (pl. 9, fig. 3).

Penis 1.3 mm. long.

These additions to the description given in my previous paper are made for the reason that the structure of the interior is peculiar. *V. strömia* when immature, and sometimes in the adult stage, resembles *V. euglypta* by having the fixed scutum and tergum vaulted; also, to a less extent, by having the rostrum hollowed out above. In most other respects the two species are widely diverse.

Section D: ALTIVERRUCA.

Form erect, the movable plates very steeply sloping or erect; basal edges of the wall not inflexed, often having a narrow, hemlike border within; fixed scutum with no adductor pit or ridge; no internal partitions; paries of fixed tergum narrow; alæ very wide. Caudal appendages are very short.

Type.—Verruca hoeki.

This group, which is quite distinct by its erect posture, wide alæ of the fixed scutotergal wall, and weak development of the articular ribs, comprises most of the species known from very deep and cold water.

The following forms belong here:

NORTH ATLANTIC SPECIES.[1]

V. obliqua Hoek, off southwestern Spain.
V. longicarinata Gruvel, Sargasso Sea.
V. hoeki Pilsbry, West Indies, 491 fathoms.
V. erecta Gruvel, off Azores.
V. radiata Gruvel, off Canaries, 912 meters.
V. bicornuta Pilsbry, western Atlantic.
V. rathbuniana Pilsbry, western Atlantic.
V. darwini Pilsbry, western Atlantic.

---

[1] *Verruca sculpta, crenata, inermis,* and *cornuta* of Aurivillius probably belong to this section also. They have not been figured, and the internal structure is unknown.

V. gibbosa Hoek, east of Patagonia, 1,863 meters.

V. mitra Hoek, south latitude 70°, west longitude 80° 48′, 555 meters.

V. incerta Hoek, south latitude 32° 34′, west longitude 13° 5′, 2,565 meters.

V. quadrangularis Hoek, south latitude 35° 39′, west longitude 50° 47′, 3,240 meters.

V. sulcata Hoek, near the Kermadec Islands, 950–1,165 meters.

V. nitida Hoek, Malay Archipelago, 915 meters.

V. plana Gruvel, off Andaman Islands, 380–465 meters.

V. cristallina Gruvel, off Andaman Islands, 768 meters.

VERRUCA HOEKI Pilsbry.

1907. *Verruca hoeki* PILSBRY, U. S. Nat. Mus. Bull., No. 60, p. 113, pl. 11, figs. 4, 5, 6.

Type.—Cat. No. 1493, U.S.N.M.

Type-locality.—*Albatross* station 2750, Anegada Passage, in 496 fathoms, bottom temperature 44°.5 F.

In addition to the published description it may be noted that the basal edge of the wall is thin. There seems to be a very thin calcareous lining in the chitinous base.

Cirrus i has subequal, rapidly tapering rami. In cirrus ii the anterior ramus is obtuse and a little shorter than the other. The caudal appendages are as long as the first joint of the pedicel of cirrus vi, 0.6 mm., and one-fifth as long as cirrus vi. Penis is 0.5 mm. long. The posterior cirri have segments with three pairs of spines, the distal pair very long.

Verruca longicarinata Gruvel, from the Sargasso Sea in 3,432 meters depth, resembles *V. hoeki*, but differs by having two contiguous, projecting, articular ribs on the movable scutum; the movable scutum and tergum are larger and narrower; the shape of the fixed scutum is different; and the suture adjoining the fixed tergum is sinuated, not straight as in *V. hoeki*.

V. obliqua Hoek, *V. erecta* Gruvel, and *V. plana* Gruvel also belong to the same group of small, compressed, inornate species.

VERRUCA RATHBUNIANA, new species.

Plate 7, figs. 2, 2a, 2b.

Type.—Cat. No. 11026, U.S.N.M.

Type-locality.—*Albatross* Station 2572, southeast from Cape Cod, 40° 29′ north; 66° 04′ west, in 1,769 fathoms, gravel ooze; bottom temperature 37°.8 F.

The barnacle is cream-white, very high, compressed laterally, the movable plates approaching a vertical position. The apices of the carina and rostrum project. Plates of the wall are rather thin, and have a very narrow inflexed edge, like a hem, at the base.

The movable scutum has two beaded, contiguous, articular ribs, the second reaching the baso-tergal angle; outside of this the plate is flat with sculpture of regular, imbricating, transverse ribs. The tergal area is sunken and densely, finely striate. Inside, the tergal and occludent borders are raised, the middle of the plate sunken. The suture between scutum and tergum is straight except near the apices, where the scutum projects.

The movable tergum divides into two subequal areas by a diagonal beaded rib accompanied by a narrow groove. The scutal area is hollowed out in the upper part. It is sculptured with narrow, curved riblets parallel to the scutal suture. The other area is flat, with sculpture of about 25 flat, imbricating ribs, which denticulate the occludent margin. The interior face is smooth and flat.

The fixed scutum has three areas, a triangular, wide median area or paries, an almost equally large rostral, and a very narrow, radiiform tergal area. The median area has a sculpture of imbricating, shingle-like ribs parallel to the base. The other areas have narrower, steeply ascending ribs. There is no internal myophore.

The fixed tergum is the highest plate. Its raised median area or paries is *narrow*, the two side areas large, and subequal. All are sculptured like the fixed scutum.

The carina curves around the carinal end of the wall. It has regular imbricating sculpture parallel to the basal margin, except on the rostral side, where there is a shallow radial sulcus bordered by vertically costate bands. There is also a very narrow rib running along the scutal border.

The rostrum is higher than the carina, with two radial sulci and three flat, costulate ribs. The carinorostral suture is zigzag by the interlocking of two conic teeth in each plate.

Greatest length of base 7.6 mm.; length between apices of carina and rostrum 9.8 mm.; greatest diameter of base 5.5 mm. Height from base to apex of fixed tergum 10.5 mm.

Cirri substantially as in *V. bicornuta*. Cirrus i has slightly unequal rami of 10 and 11 segments. Anterior ramus of cirrus ii four-fifths the length of the posterior, segments 6 and 11. The caudal appendages are broken, but evidently very short, about as in *V. bicornuta*.

This handsome species is well distinguished by its large size, high, two-horned contour, and the beautiful imbricated sculpture of all the plates.

V. radiata Gruvel has somewhat similar sculpture of the walls. *V. rathbuniana* is closely related to *V. bicornuta*, but there are several differences which we can only consider specific in the present state of our knowledge. In the movable scutum of *V. bicornuta* the second articular rib, parallel to the third or crescentric rib, is wider in *V. rathbuniana*, and the median articular ridge of the movable tergum, distinct in *V. bicornuta*, is represented by a low wave only. The carina and rostrum interlock by more numerous, smaller teeth in *V. bicornuta*. This is a conspicuous difference. The sculpture of the fixed scutum and tergum of *V. rathbuniana* is extremely regular, while in *V. bicornuta* it is uneven and irregular. The difference in total contour is doubtless due to the accident of station, and the same circumstance may possibly have affected the sculpture. The nature of the support is unknown, since both barnacles had been removed from their supports. *V. rathbuniana* evidently sat upon a level surface, while *V. bicornuta* perched upon a small, irregular prominence not admitting of free expansion of the base.

Verruca rathbuniana is one of the largest and finest of the erect forms. It is named for Miss Mary J. Rathbun, of the United States National Museum.

VERRUCA BICORNUTA, new species.

Plate 7, figs. 1–1c; plates 8, figs. 3–3b.

Type.—Cat. No. 11027, U.S.N.M.

Type-locality.—*Albatross* station 2575, east of Nantucket, latitude 41° 07′ north; longitude 65° 26′ 30″ west, in 1,710 fathoms, gray ooze; bottom temperature 37° F.

The barnacle is cream-white, high, with steeply sloping movable plates; laterally compressed. Plates of the wall are not thick and have a narrow hemlike ledge around the base. The apices of rostrum and carina are produced beyond the outlines of the wall, forming short horns.

The movable scutum is thick. There are two contiguous narrow, curved, beaded, articular ribs, the lower one reaching the basi-tergal angle and defining a lunate, sloping tergal area. The tergal edge protrudes weakly near the apex. When the scutum is isolated there is seen to be a deep, narrow, articular furrow below the apex, but this is not visible in complete individuals. The occludent area of the plate has regular, strong, flat, imbricating ribs. The interior face is deeply concave between the articular and outer raised borders (fig. 1c).

The movable tergum is rather thin, divided by a strongly raised diagonal ridge, above which there are two articular ridges, the median one low, wide near the diagonal, the other one stronger, a concavity below it. The area below the diagonal has rib sculpture, like the corresponding area of the scutum. The internal face is slightly concave. The suture between scutum and tergum is nearly straight internally, except near the occludent end, where the tergum has a small projection.

The apices of the fixed scutum and tergum are shortly prolonged and curve toward one another. The paries of the fixed scutum is ridged parallel to lines of growth. The tergal area or radius is very narrow, the rostral area larger than the paries. The interior is smooth, without pit or myophore.

The fixed tergum is the highest plate. It has a very narrow, raised paries, and rather large, subequal scutal and carinal radiiform triangles.

The carina and rostrum are transversely ridged at the ends, but in front interlock by about four subequal teeth in each, these terminating as many strong, imbricate-sculptured radial ribs.

Length between apices of rostrum and carina 9 mm.; height of fixed tergum 8.3 mm.

Cirrus i has subequal rami of about 10 and 11 segments (pl. 8, fig. 3a). Cirrus ii has the anterior ramus three-fourths the length of the posterior, blunt at the distal end; segments 7 and 13 (pl. 8, fig. 3). The rami of other cirri are subequal, and bear three pairs of spines on the segments (pl. 8, fig. 3b, cirrus vi). Terminal appendage of 10 segments, 2.6 mm. long, being a trifle longer than the protopod of cirrus vi, which is 2.4 mm. long (pl. 9, fig. 1).

This fine *Verruca* is known by a single individual, which grew upon a small irregular object, not preserved. This doubtless affected the shape of the walls, which enlarge upward, more I think, than they would on a supporting object of more ample dimensions.

The species is related to *V. rathbuniana* (p. 41), which came from a neighboring station, but its chief affinity is with *V. gibbosa* Hoek, from the *Challenger* station 317, northeast of the Falkland Islands, in 1,035 fathoms, bottom temperature 1°.7 C. I note the following differences between the two forms: (1) In *V. bicornuta* the rostrum and carina interlock by at least four subequal teeth in each plate, terminating as many ribs and fitting into the ends of as many furrows, while in *V. gibbosa* "both valves are furnished with one very distinct and two rather shallow furrows," one upper tooth in each plate therefore predominating conspicuously over the others. The articular rib, next to the lower one, of the movable scutum is better developed in *V. bicornuta*, and separated from the lower rib by a narrow, rather deep and *smooth* furrow. The movable tergum is a little wider in *V. bicornuta*. *V. mitra* Hoek, from about 70° south latitude, is *very closely* related to *V. gibbosa*, and differs from *V. bicornuta* in much the same features.

Another somewhat related but antipodal species is *V. sulcata* Hoek from near the Kermadec Islands.

VERRUCA DARWINI Pilsbry.

1907. *Verruca darwini* Pilsbry, U. S. Nat. Mus. Bull., No. 60, p. 111, pl. 10, figs. 4–8.

Type.—Cat. No. 9015, U.S.N.M.

Type-locality.—*Albatross* station 2042, east from New Jersey, north latitude 39° 33′, west longitude 68° 26′ 45″ in 1,555 fathoms, bottom temperature 38.5 F. Also at *Albatross* station 2573 southeast of Cape Cod, north latitude 40° 34′ 18″, west longitude 66° 09′, in 1,742 fathoms, bottom temperature 37.3 F

This species was described from two examples from the type-locality. Another specimen (Cat. No. 32923, U.S.N.M.) has now turned up from *Albatross* station 2573. It agrees substantially with the type in contour, but has a pair of ribs on the movable scutum like the individual drawn in plate 10, figure 8, of my former paper. This is probably the usual condition. This example from station 2573 measures: Carinorostral length of base 6 mm.; between apices 6.2 mm.; diameter of base 3 mm.; height of fixed tergum from apex to base 4 mm.

Cirrus i has subequal rami of about 8 segments. Cirrus ii has the wide, obtuse, anterior branch two-thirds the length of posterior, both being densely bristly. Cirri iii and iv are nearly similar, composed of segments armed with two pairs of spines on the anterior side (or in a few segments three pairs). Cirrus v has only one pair of bristles on the anterior side of most of the segments. In cirrus vi there are mostly three pairs of bristles, as usual in the genus. The terminal appendage is longer than the protopod of cirrus vi, composed of 11 segments copiously bristly at their distal ends. The penis is 2.8 mm. long, nearly twice the length of protopod. It has a few short hairs near the end, as in all other Verrucæ.

Verruca darwini is closely related to *V. rathbuniana*, from which it differs by the less regular sculpture, especially of the parietal areas of the plates of the wall; by the much lower contour, and finally the less erect movable plates, which in slope form a smaller angle with the plane of the base.

There is a further difference in the basal margin of the wall, which is beveled to a simple sharp edge in *V. darwini*, while in *V. rathbuniana* and *V. bicornuta* there is a sort of inflexed border or hem within the edge. This may, however, be a difference due to age. The reduction in the number of spines on several cirri is notable, because very unusual in this genus.

The cream-white tint and comparative sizes of the plates and the absence of any myophore or pit in the fixed scutum for the scutal adductor muscle are characters in common with *V. rathbuniana*, *V. bicornuta*, and various other deep-water species.

INDO-PACIFIC SPECIES.

VERRUCA HALOTHECA Pilsbry.

Plate 8, figs. 1, 1a.

1907. *Verruca halotheca* PILSBRY, Bulletin of the Bureau of Fisheries, vol. 26, p. 188, pl. 4, figs. 9, 10 (June 29).

1913. ?*Verruca capsula* HOEK, *Siboga*-Expeditie, Cirripedia, p. 130, pl. 12, figs. 1–3; pl. 13, figs. 1–4.

Type.—Cat. No. 32423, U.S.N.M.

Type-locality.—*Albatross* station 4060, off northeast coast of Hawaii, on a volcanic pebble, in 913 fathoms, bottom temperature 36°.5 F. Also taken off Kauai in 228–235 fathoms, a few detached valves.

The barnacle is white, flattened above, with steep sides, almost perpendicular to the base of attachment, which has a rounded contour. Surface weakly corrugated with concentric growth ridges.

Movable scutum small, flat, with an acute apex and three articular ridges, the upper one minute, lower one barely indicated, not raised, the middle one very wide. Movable tergum larger, quadrate, flat, with three strong imbricating articular ridges.

Fixed scutum roughly quadrate, divided by an oblique sulcus into two nearly equal triangles. Fixed tergum of very irregular shape, divided into three triangular areas; its umbo adjacent to that of the movable tergum, but not quite marginal.

The carina articulates with the rostrum by means of three large and several smaller teeth, forming a zigzag suture; each tooth terminates a low ridge. It articulates with the fixed tergum by a single tooth projecting into the tergum near the base.

The rostrum is irregularly cone-shaped, minus a segment, in shape somewhat like the anterior valve of some chitons. It has several radiating ridges on the carinal side.

The basal margins of the wall are inflexed, forming a ledge 1.5 mm. wide. The fixed scutum has a flat, tongue-shaped adductor ridge, depending vertically. The other valves are plain inside. The carina and rostrum articulate by an undulating suture. The lower surface of the movable scutum has two rounded projections into the movable tergum. There is a thin, yellowish, basal membrane.

Greatest rostrocarinal length at base 14 mm., at umbones 12 mm., breadth 12.5 mm. Height from base to apex of rostrum, fixed scutum or carina 7.5 mm.

Length of the straight rostrocarinal hinge of the opercular valves 10 mm. Length of scutum from this line to umbo 5.5 mm. Length of tergum 6 mm.

The first cirrus has equal rami 3 mm. long, of 14 and 12 segments. Cirrus ii has the anterior ramus, of 9 segments, somewhat over half as long as the posterior, of 22 segments. Cirrus iii with rami of 29 and 34 segments. Cirrus vi has rami of about 40 segments, with three pairs of spines on each. The caudal appendages are 2 mm. long, much shorter than the protopod of cirrus vi, composed of 10 segments, and copiously hairy. The cirri and caudal appendages are much like those of *V. euglypta*, but the latter are shorter in comparison to the size of the barnacle.

A single entire specimen of this large *Verruca* was obtained, but several valves were taken at a station at the other end of the archipelago. It is chiefly notable for the flat top, absence of salient umbones, and the generally inornate appearance, somewhat like *V. coraliophila*, which belongs to the same group. It is one of the largest *Verrucas* yet described, and the only one known from the northern Pacific. It is a truly deep-sea species, which may prove to have a wide distribution. *V. capsula* Hoek, 1913, from the Malay Archipelago in 513–1,300 meters seems, from the figures and description, to differ very little from *V. halotheca*. I doubt whether it is specifically distinct. Both of these species are closely related to *V. magna* Gruvel, from the Gulf of Gascoyne.

VERRUCA INTEXTA Pilsbry.

1912. *Verruca intexta* PILSBRY, Proc. U. S. Nat. Mus., vol. 42, p. 292.

Type.—Cat. No. 43468, U.S.N.M.

Type locality.—*Albatross* station 5259, off northwestern Panay, 312 fathoms.

This species belongs to the group of *V. nexa*.

VERRUCA ALBATROSSIANA Pilsbry.

1912. *Verruca albatrossiana* PILSBRY, Proc. U. S. Nat. Mus., vol. 42, p. 292.

Type.—Cat. No. 43472, U.S.N.M.

Type locality.—*Albatross* station 5447, east of Luzon, 310 fathoms.

This species and the preceding will be illustrated in a report on the Cirripedia of the *Albatross* Philippine cruise.

Suborder BALANOMORPHA.

1905. *Operculata*, tribe *Symetrica* GRUVEL, Monographie des Cirrhipèdes, p. 189.

KEY TO FAMILIES AND SUBFAMILIES.[1]

a^1. Rostrum having radii; labrum with an angular notch or cleft in the middle.

Family BALANIDÆ, p. 48.

  b^1. Opercular valves together as large as the orifice, the scutum and tergum articulated together.....................................Subfamily BALANINÆ, p. 49.

  b^2. Opercular valves together not nearly as large as the orifice; basis membranous.

   c^1. Compartments six, but the rostrum is divided into three by fine sutures, visible within; wall porose, or if filled up, having radial lamellæ at the base; the sheath forms the wall of the body chamber, reaching to the base, where it is deeply, irregularly notched; articular ridge of the scutum chitinous.

Subfamily CHELONIBIINÆ, p. 262.

   c^2. Compartments six, the rostrum undivided; scutum and tergum not articulated together, sometimes absent...............Subfamily CORONULINÆ, p. 268.

---

[1] For convenience in identification, the arrangement of the key is artificial.

a^2. Rostrum having alæ, or when united with the rostral latera, the composite compartment has overlapping lateral borders; opercular valves as large as the orifice; labrum with concave edge, not angularly notched in the middle.

Family CHTHAMALIDÆ, p. 290.

Family BALANIDÆ Gray.

1825. *Balanidæ* LEACH, Zoological Journal, vol. 2, p. 209.—GRAY, Annals of Philosophy, new ser., vol. 10, p. 104.[1]
1854. *Balaninæ* DARWIN, Monograph, p. 175.

Sessile barnacles in which the rostrum is concrescent with the rostro-lateral compartments, the composite plate having radii, or overlapping the lateral compartments; sometimes all the compartments are concrescent into one piece. The labrum has a narrow median notch or cleft and is never swollen or "bullate." The cirri of the third pair are more like the second than the fourth in proportions and arrangement of spines. There are no caudal appendages.

The family Balanidæ comprises the most evolved sessile barnacles, understanding by this, those which have departed farthest from the ancestral pedunculate forms. Their progress has been chiefly in reducing the number of compartments of the wall, increasing the complexity of these compartments, and in transforming the cirri of the third pair to agree in form with the second instead of the fourth pair. Such forms as *Pyrgoma* present the extreme of reduction in number of wall-plates, but they are primitive in the structure of the plates. It is rather difficult to decide whether the Coronulinæ, Tetraclita, or the porous Balani are the most evolved, but the Balani have more highly modified cirri. The Verrucidæ have the wall highly specialized, but the rest of the organization is not far removed from the pedunculate *Thoracica*.

The common ancestors of Balanidæ and Chthamalidæ were apparently forms having eight wall-plates, since this number is present in some genera of both families.

M. Gruvel's family Tetrameridæ was proposed for genera of Balanidæ and Chthamalidæ having the compartments reduced to four. The genera *Tetraclita*, *Elminius*, *Creusia*, *Pyrgoma*, and *Pyrgopsis* might be segregated as a subfamily Tetraclitinæ, yet as the group is much more closely related to *Balanus* than are the other subfamilies, and as the compartments of the carino-lateral pair are much reduced or even eliminated in some Balani, I have thought the division unnecessary.

---

[1] Leach and Gray were the first to use the term Balanidæ, but both included various incongruous genera and excluded others belonging here. Gray's Pyrgomatidæ and Coronulidæ are now placed in Balanidæ.

[2] In *Chelonibia* the union is not quite complete, and the sutures are often visible.

Subfamily BALANINÆ Darwin.

1854. *Balaninæ*, First Section, DARWIN, Monograph, p. 175 (exclusive of *Chelonobia*).

Opercular valves together as large as the orifice; scuta articulated with the terga. Sheath distinctly differentiated from and shorter than the inner wall of the body-chamber, its lower edge not cut into teeth.

KEY TO GENERA OF BALANINÆ AND CHELONIBIINÆ.[1]

a^1. Compartments six.

> b^1. Opercular valves much narrower than the orifice, the scutum united to the tergum by a chitinous articular ridge; walls porous, or septate at the base; sheath forming the whole inner wall, deeply notched or reduced to slender pillars at the base; basis membranous.....................*Chelonibia*, p. 262.
>
> b^2. Opercular valves together as wide as the orifice; sheath differentiated from and shorter than the inner wall.
>
>> c^1. Radii wanting or very weakly, indistinctly developed; compartments not porose.
>>
>>> d^1. Alæ conspicuous externally.
>>>
>>>> e^1. Basis calcareous......................................*Pachylasma*, p. 327.
>>>>
>>>> e^2. Basis membranous, at least in part.....................*Hexelasma*, p. 329.
>>>
>>> d^2. Sutures narrow, the alæ not conspicuous externally.........*Balanus*, p. 49.
>>
>> c^2. Radii developed; or if wanting, the compartments are porose..*Balanus*, p. 49.
>>   (Basis calcareous, cup-shaped, or flat; compartments thin, not porose, weakly connected; living imbedded in sponges..........*Acasta*, p. 241.)

a^2. Compartments four, or by calcification of the sutures, united into one piece.

> b^1. Wall conspicuously porose, the sutures visible, at least inside. *Tetraclita*, p. 248.
>
> b^2. Wall-compartments not porose.
>
>> c^1. Basis membranous; four compartments; sessile, on rocks, etc., littoral.
>>   *Elminius*, p. 260.
>>
>> c^2. Basis membranous, produced in form of a short peduncle; wall compartments concrescent into one, as in *Pyrgoma*..............................*Pyrgopsis*.[2]
>>
>> c^3. Basis calcareous, cup-shaped, or cylindric; growing on corals and millepores.
>>
>>> d. Four compartments, with radii...........................*Creusia*, p. 261.
>>>
>>> d^1. Compartments concrescent into one....................*Pyrgoma*, p. 261.

Genus BALANUS E. da Costa.

1758. *Lepas* LINNÆUS, Systema Naturæ, ed. 10, p. 667, in part, and of most early authors.

1763. *Balanus* GRONOVIUS, Zoophylacii Gronoviani, p. 257.[3]

---

[1] For obvious considerations of convenience, this key takes account of the hard parts only. It is therefore somewhat artificial, since provision had to be made for *Pachylasma* and *Hexelasma*, genera of Chthamalidæ which resemble Balanidæ superficially, but differ fundamentally by the shape of the labrum, etc.

[2] *Pyrgopsis* Gruvel, 1907. Mem. Asiatic Soc. of Bengal, vol. 2, No. 1, p. 8, for *P. annandalei* Gruvel, Andaman Islands, on reef. The single species of this genus is not contained in the National Museum.

[3] Gronovius was the first post-Linnæan author to divide the Linnæan genus *Lepas*. He established the genus *Balanus* for several species of *Balanus* and *Chelonibia*. I nominate his species No. 1077 as the type. This is identical with *Balanus balanus* Linnæus.

Gronovius was not a binomial author, except in some pages of *tabularum explicatio* at the end of his work, but his nomenclature was "binary.' His genera were properly proposed, but his species, with the exception already noted, are not named, but are indicated by phrases. According to the ruling of the International Committee on Nomenclature—which I think was in a high degree injudicious—the genera of Gronovius are to be accepted.

1778. *Balanus* EMANUEL DA COSTA, Historia Naturalis Testaceorum Britanniæ,
   p. 248; type by tautonymy, *Balanus porcatus* da Costa new name for *Lepas
   balanus* Linnæus.
1852. *Monolopus* Klein, MÖRCH, Catal. Yoldi, p. 67 (*M. balanus* Linnæus here
   selected as type).
1854. *Balanus* auct., DARWIN, Monograph, p. 177.
1913. *Ortho-Balanus* HOEK, *Siboga*-Expeditie, Monographie 31*b*, p. 158 (*Balanus
   amphitrite* here selected as type).

Compartments six, usually having radii, except the carina; sheath
differentiated from rest of the inner wall. Scutum and tergum interlocked.

Type.—Balanus balanus (Linnæus).

The genus *Balanus* in its Darwinian limits comprises species in
very diverse stages of evolution. Highly evolved stocks, such as
Megabalanus and the *amphitrite* group of *Balanus*, coexist with relatively primitive stocks, like *Solidobalanus* and *Austrobalanus*. It
may be that the groups now ranked as subgenera will in future be considered generic; but I do not think this step can properly be made at
present, if at all. A careful study of the Austral *Balani*, of *Conopea*,
and of certain forms partaking of the characters of more than one
subgenus must be carried out before the desirability of dismember-
ing *Balanus* can be considered intelligently. Recognition of the fact
that pores in the wall may sometimes be closed by secondary filling
does away with some apparent anomalies, but the difficulties mentioned by Darwin [1] have by no means been overcome, especially in the
case of *Conopea*.

For convenience, and from force of habit, modern authors have
retained *Acasta* as a genus separate from *Balanus;* but it is now clear
that Darwin's misgivings on this point were well founded. The distinctions in the cirri, formerly thought to exist, have been broken
down; and it is now known that *Acasta* has no higher rank than some
of the groups still considered to be subgenera of *Balanus*.

It is a remarkable testimony to Darwin's insight and restraint that
every one of the species of *Balanus* admitted by him is still accepted
as valid. Vast collections from coasts but scantily represented in
his collection, or not at all, have confirmed his specific distinctions.

The older conchologists, up to and including Lamarck, defined and
figured a large number of species of *Balanus* by external characters
only. Most of these can never be recognized; but the Lamarck collection at Geneva should be gone over and his species elucidated.
As many are without opercular valves, this could only be done by
one thoroughly acquainted with the species.

---

[1] Monograph, pp. 190, 191.

a^1. Parietes permeated by pores.

  b^1. Radii well developed, permeated by pores parallel to the basis.

                                          Megabalanus, p. 51.

  b^2. Radii not porous, rarely wanting.

    c^1. Basis calcareous, boat-shaped, elongated in the carino-rostral axis.

                                          Conopea, p. 234.

    c^2. Basis calcareous; parietes vertically ribbed within, at least near the base.

                                          Balanus, p. 77.

    c^3. Basis membranous; parietes smooth or with reticulated ridges within; rostrum not especially lengthened ....*Semibalanus*, p. 182.

a^1. Parietes not permeated by pores, solid.

  b^1. Basis membranous; rostrum much longer than the other compartments.

                                  Membranobalanus, p. 229.

  b^2. Basis calcareous, boat-shaped or oblong, only a small part of it attached.

                                          Conopea, p. 234.

  b^3. Basis calcareous, normally flat and attached throughout. Form normal.

    c^1. Radii wanting; tergum with a long spur, but no external furrow. No spinules on the segments of the cirri...........................*Metabalanus*, p. 200.

    c^2. Radii more or less distinctly developed.

      d^1. Tergum with the spur short, $\frac{1}{4}$ to $\frac{1}{3}$ as wide as the base, its end truncate parallel with the base; fourth cirri having some segments armed anteriorly with recurved teeth. Small, solid barnacles, smooth or sharply ribbed.

                                        Armatobalanus, p. 226.

      d^2. Spur of the tergum narrower; cirrus iv without recurved teeth.

        e^1. Scutum with crests for the lateral depressor muscles, and a long, strong, adductor ridge; internal basal edge of parietes roughened with irregular points and ridges (or in *B. vestitus*, strongly ribbed). Often large, and usually colored............................*Austrobalanus*, p. 218.

        e^2. Scutum without crests for the depressor muscles: basal edge of parietes merely ribbed inside.

          f^1. Spur rounded distally, curving into basal margin; tergum externally flat or with a shallow furrow without infolded sides, not bounded by impressed lines; scutum not much thickened within; *a row of spines on lower side of mandible*, which has acute lower teeth. Small or minute, solid barnacles, smooth or with low, broad ribs..*Solidobalanus*, p. 220.

          f^2. Scutum ridged between adductor scar and the high articular ridge; tergum with strong articular ridge, and no external furrow; lower teeth of mandible short, obtuse, its lower edge hairy. Rather small, whitish barnacles............................*Hesperibalanus*, p. 192.

          f^3. Scutum not conspicuously ridged within; tergum with an external furrow, or a spur-fasciole bounded by lines; lower teeth of mandible acute, the lower edge hairy. Barnacles of moderate or large size, colored or white.................................*Chirona*, p. 203.

Subgenus MEGABALANUS Hoek.

1854. *Balanus*, Section A, DARWIN, Monograph, p. 194.
1913. *Mega-Balanus* HOEK, *Siboga*-Expeditie, Monographie 31b, p. 158.

Balani having the parietes, basis *and radii* permeated by pores.

Type.—*Balanus tintinnabulum* (Linnaeus).

Distribution.—World-wide, in tropical and warm temperate seas; into cold seas in the Southern Hemisphere. Low tide to about 30 fathoms.

In *B. tintinnabulum* (various varieties) and *B. algicola* the cirri are rather characteristic. The rami of the third pair are exceptionally short, like those of the second pair, the pedicel being rather long and the first segment extremely broad. The general proportions of the cirri may be seen in fig. 8. In other Balani the rami of the third cirri are decidedly longer than those of the second. Whether this peculiarity characterizes the other species of *Megabalanus* I do not know.

This is a group of littoral barnacles mainly of moderate or large size. With the exception of *B. tintinnabulum*, all of them are restricted to single faunal provinces, and are not especially variable. *B. tintinnabulum*, in the Darwinian sense, has a range almost covering that of the subgenus, but is represented by different races in the several faunal districts. Several of the forms are commonly carried on ships to ports all over the world. In north temperate latitudes

Fig. 8.—BALANUS TINTINNABULUM AZORICUS. CIRRI OF THE RIGHT SIDE, DRAWN FROM PHOTOGRAPH.

the imported forms do not survive long, or at any rate they do not become part of the local faunas. Whether any species of barnacle has been colonized by ships, outside of its natural area, is unknown. No data showing such colonization have been put on record, and the collections before me afford nothing definite.

Observations bearing on this point might easily be made in tropical and subtropical ports. I have found fragments of *B. tintinnabulum* along the water front of Honolulu, where it must be brought very frequently, but no trace of it on the reefs east of the city, or on the *Anomia* beds and rocks of Pearl Harbor, to the west, where other barnacles are abundant.

Many of the forms which are subordinated to *B. tintinnabulum* as varieties or subspecies have a very distinct appearance. I can not but believe that most of the races herein called subspecies (excepting *zebra* and *galapaganus*) will eventually be considered species. Darwin has related his perplexity and repeated reversals of opinion in dealing with them. This was partly due to the wide range of individual variation, including the changes induced in the individual by the incidence of the immediate environment, and partly because many characteristics are common to several of the local forms, each having a different combination of characters, which, singly, are also common to some others. Working with specimens in large part of uncertain habitat, partly taken from ships, which had successively picked up the forms of different ports, an appearance is given of intergradation of characters greater than the actual condition.

The problem can be solved only when well-localized material can be studied, and all parts of the organism compared. My material is fairly competent only for America, and I have therefore not been able to undertake a thorough revision.

KEY TO SPECIES OF MEGABALANUS.[1]

a^1. Apex of the tergum acute but not produced in a beak.
  b^1. Scuta strongly sculptured externally.
    c^1. Basal margin of the tergum forming nearly a straight line on both sides of the spur; no distinct crests for the depressor muscle.
      d^1. Shell extremely massive, often elongated in the carino-rostral diameter.
        B. ajax, p. 74.
      d^2. Shell usually strong but not massive, approaching circular in outline.
        e^1. Shell of moderate or large size; basal breadth of scutum less than its height.
          B. tintinnabulum, p. 54.
        e^2. Shell very small; basal breadth of scutum at least equal to the height; no adductor ridge......................................*B. algicola*, p. 72.
    c^1. Basal margin between spur and basiscutal angle concave, forming an arc.
      d^1. Spur placed half its own width from the basiscutal angle; inner lamina of parietes normal.
        e^1. Pale rose; basal border of scutum somewhat concave...*B. decorus*, p. 77.
        e^2. Whitish; basal border of the scutum convex.................*B. campbelli*.
      d^2. Shell purplish dark brown; inner lamina of the parietes cellular; spur placed about 1½ times its own width from the basiscutal angle......*B. vinaceus*.
  b^2. Scuta marked externally with delicate growth-striæ only, and without an adductor ridge. Shell pale rose, with deeply toothed orifice........*B. tulipiformis*.
a^2. Apex of the tergum produced in a long beak.
  b^1. Adductor ridge of the scutum united with the articular ridge, inclosing a cavity which extends nearly to the apex of the valve.
    c^1. Beak of the tergum purplish; spur placed at less than its own width from the basiscutal angle....................................*B. psittacus*, p. 75.
    c^2. Beak of the tergum white; spur removed from the basiscutal angle by at least its own width....................................*B. maxillaris*, p. 77.
  b^2. Adductor ridge not united with the articular ridge to form a cavity. Shell usually purplish black....................................*B. nigrescens*.

The following species of *Megabalanus* are not represented in the United States National Museum.[2]

B. tulipiformis Darwin. Mediterranean, Madeira.

B. nigrescens Lamarck. Australia.

---

[1] Taken with slight alteration from Gruvel's Monographie des Cirrhipedès.
[2] Specimens of *tulipiformis* and *nigrescens* are contained in the collection of the Academy of Natural Sciences, leaving two species which I have been unable to study, both of them, I believe, known from the original lots only. The specimens of *B. decorus* in the United States National Museum have no opercular valves.

B. campbelli Filhol.[1]   Campbell Island.
B. vinaceus Darwin.   "West Coast of South America."

BALANUS TINTINNABULUM (Linnæus).

1758. *Lepas tintinnabulum* LINNÆUS, Systema Naturæ, ed. 10, p. 668.

1854. *Balanus tintinnabulum* Linnæus, DARWIN, Monograph, etc., p. 194, with varieties *communis, vesiculosus, validus, zebra, crispatus*, p. 195, and varieties *spinosus, coccopoma, concinnus, intermedius, occator, d'orbignyi*, p. 196.

1883. *Balanus tintinnabulum* Linnæus, HOEK, Zool. *Challenger* Exped., vol. 25, Report on the Cirripedia, p. 147.

1897. *Balanus tintinnabulum* Linnæus, WELTNER, Verzeichnis der bisher beschriebenen recenten Cirripedienarten, in Archiv für Naturgeschichte, p. 260.

1903. *Balanus tintinnabulum* Linnæus, GRUVEL, Nouvelles Archives du Muséum d'Histoire Naturelle, ser. 4, vol. 5, p. 125.

1913. *Balanus tintinnabulum* Linnæus, HOEK, The Cirripedia of the *Siboga* Expeditie, Monographie 31*b*, p. 164, with variety *validus*, pp. 164, 166, pl. 16, figs. 16–19; var. *costatus*, p. 165, pl. 14, figs. 5, 6; var. *plicatus*, p. 165, pl. 14, fig. 7.

Distinguished from other species of the same subgenus by the broad, triangular terga, with long spur remote from the basiscutal angle, and without crests for the depressor muscle; the wide radii with the summits usually subhorizontal; the fine, straight, regular sutural septa, which are *denticulate on both sides* (pl. 10, fig. 2). This last character will distinguish large specimens without opercular valves from such similar species as *B. psittacus*, but of course it can be seen only by breaking the compartments apart.

Balanus tintinnabulum may be said to be, in a way, the best known of sessile barnacles, since for three or four hundred years it has constantly been brought into almost every port of deep-sea traffic in the world, is common in museums, and in the last century or two it has frequently been figured and described. But the very circumstances that it is freely carried about, and that most of the specimens accessible to zoologists have been from ships' bottoms, have effectually befogged the zoogeographic study of the races, several of which are known from ships' bottoms only. Published records of distribution are not to be trusted implicitly, since in many cases they were probably based upon specimens from ships, even when not so stated. Moreover, there seems reason to believe that there are many more local subspecies than were known to Darwin, and this may have led to wrong identifications and therefore false locality records of the Darwinian subspecies.

We do not know to what extent the subspecies may hybridize when gathered together by vessels successively entering waters inhabited by different forms. So far as I know, no evidence of hybridism has been found.

---

[1] The systematic position of *B. campbelli* is uncertain, as the characters of walls and basis are unknown. M. Gruvel, who has figured the opercular valves, considers it related to *B. decorus*.

THE SESSILE BARNACLES. 55

From the consistent distribution of American forms, of which large series of carefully localized specimens are available, it may fairly be inferred that most tropical and subtropical coasts are inhabited by one or more subspecies of *B. tintinnabulum*, and that these subspecies are just as definitely local in distribution as most other invertebrates of the littoral faunas. So far as American forms are concerned, the collections of the United States National Museum and Academy of Natural Sciences show the distribution to be as follows:[1]

Antillean Province: *B. t. antillensis*.

Magellanic and Peruvian Provinces: *B. t. concinnus*.

B. t. galapaganus.

Panamic Province: *B. t. coccopoma* (Panama to Mazatlan).

B. t. peninsularis (Cape St. Lucas).

Californian Province: *B. t. californicus*.

The collections before me afford a little information upon the distribution of Old World forms. Some new data are recorded for Japanese and Philippine races; but the distribution of Indo-Pacific, Australasian, and West African races of *B. tintinnabulum* remains in a chaotic condition. For the convenience of American naturalists, descriptions and figures are given of the forms commonly brought by ships to our ports, as well as of a few new subspecies

BALANUS TINTINNABULUM TINTINNABULUM Linnæus.

Plate 10, figs. 1 to 1e.

1758. *Lepas tintinnabulum* LINNÆUS, Syst. Nat., ed. 10, p. 668.
1838. *Balanus dilatatus* SCHLÜTER, Kurzgefasstes systematisches Verzeichniss meiner Conchyliensammlung, p. 38.
1854. *Balanus tintinnabulum*, var. *communis* DARWIN, Monograph, p. 195.

The typical form of this species was called var. *communis* by Darwin. His plan was to give this name to the typical or usual form of all species having several varieties. The name is inadmissible in this connection, as there was a prior *Balanus communis* of Pulteney and Montagu, another of Defrance.

The barnacle is "conic or tubulo-conic, smooth or moderately ribbed longitudinally; colors varying from purplish pink to blackish purple, often in obscure longitudinal stripes; orifice of the shell rounded-trigonal" (Darwin). Size large, the diameter ordinarily 50 to 65 mm. in conic forms. The radii are wide, usually in part transversely grooved. The walls are not very thick, stained inside with livid purple or in part white, the sheath dirty white, with fleshy or purplish gray in the parietes. The interior is slightly ribbed near the base. The basis is white and smooth inside.

The scutum (pl. 10, figs. 1c, 1d) is buff, with dull, dark-purple clouds; basiscutal angle rounded and ascending. Surface is strongly

---

[1] Data are lacking on the forms of the whole east coast of South America; also the continental coasts of the Gulf of Mexico and Caribbean Sea.

ridged, the ridges near the base slightly crenulated by longitudinal striæ, which are very fine or subobsolete in the intervals. The articular ridge is high, flattened and reflexed, not much more than half the length of the tergal margin, its lower end usually overhanging. Adductor ridge confluent with the articular above, continued downwards in a broad, rounded callous ridge or merely a general thickening of the median part of the valve, bounding the depressor muscle scar. Muscle impressions deep; occludent edge folded over near the base.

The tergum (pl. 10, figs. 1*a*, 1*b*) is purplish toward the apex, triangular, broad, delicately ridged, with the groove to the spur closed. The spur is long, and *separated by about twice its width from the basiscutal angle.* The articular ridge and the reflection of the scutal edge are both high and acute. The external ridges denticulate the scutal border.

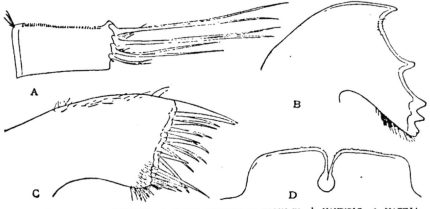

FIG. 9.—BALANUS TINTINNABULUM. *a*, MIDDLE SEGMENT OF CIRRUS VI. *b*, MANDIBLE. *c*, MAXILLA. *d*, LABRUM.

Compartments.—The radii are wide, with level summits. The outer lamina of the wall bears numerous short lamellæ on its inner edge (pl. 10, fig. 1*e*) between the septa. The parietal tubes are entirely open, except quite near the summits, where they have numerous transverse septa. The interlocking septa of the radii and sutural edges are straight, regular, and *denticulate on both sides.*

The labrum has a straight, shortly hairy edge and narrow notch. In the specimen examined there are two small teeth on one side, one on the other (fig. 9*d*).

The mandible has four strong teeth, the fifth tooth small, united with the blunt lower point (fig. 9*b*).

The maxilla has a straight edge and 14 large spines; those below the upper large pair are in two series (fig. 9*c*).

The cirri i to iii are shorter than in other groups of the genus. Cirrus i has rami about 5 mm. long, of 17 and 15 segments, those of the posterior ramus protuberant. Besides the usual long spines, the distal borders of the segments bear minute multifid scales.

Cirrus ii has 15 and 12 protuberant segments, posterior ramus shorter by 5 segments.

Cirrus iii is about one-third longer than ii, with rami of 14 and 13 somewhat protuberant segments, the posterior ramus shorter by 4 segments. They have series of short, erect spinules along the distal borders of the segments.

Cirri iv to vi are nearly similar, composed of a great number of short segments, which bear three pairs of long and a fourth of short spines. There are tufts of small spines on the anterior edge, between the spines of the pairs. A regular row of erect spinules borders each segment distally, wanting on some of the ill-defined basal segments. The anterior distal angles of the pedicel are also spinulose. The median segments of cirrus vi are about twice as wide as long (fig. 9a). Cirrus vi is about 23 mm. long.

Balanus tintinnabulum tintinnabulum (Linnæus) is known in North American waters only as a frequent immigrant on ships. I do not know that it has anywhere established itself in our fauna, but we have no knowledge of the barnacles of the Gulf ports, where such introduction would be expected to occur, if anywhere. The natural habitat of the race remains to be defined, and the inquiry is difficult, because specimens from ports all over the world find their way into museums, without data showing whether they are part of the local fauna or from ship's bottoms; moreover, it is likely that some forms recorded as var. *communis* will prove to be separable races. It has not been found in any Antillean or North American Tertiary or Pleistocene deposits.

Figures 1—1e and the above description were drawn from specimens taken from a ship which arrived at Philadelphia from Hongkong and Java. They were associated with *B. t. zebra* and *B. t. occator*, but no intermediate or transitional forms were seen. The cylindric form with larger orifice is prevalent in other lots, particularly those standing crowded.

The United States National Museum contains numerous specimens referred to *B. t. tintinnabulum*, chiefly collected from ships in English and American ports; others from tropical localities and New Zealand are without opercular valves, and therefore of uncertain subspecific identity.

BALANUS TINTINNABULUM ZEBRA Darwin.

Plate 10, figs. 2 to 3.

1854. *Balanus tintinnabulum,* var. *zebra* DARWIN, Monograph, etc., p. 195, pl. 1, fig. *g.*

Form conical or somewhat tubular; livid purple or dark livid purple, with snow-white ribs; radii wide, colored; *sheath madder brown.* Summits of the alæ oblique.   Opercular valves as in *B. t. tintinnabulum*, the adductor ridge of the scutum often very low, a mere convexity of the median part of the valve, but more emphatic in young individuals.

Typical examples from ship bottoms are symmetrically conic and very conspicuously striped.   Diameter 50 mm.; height 30 mm., more or less (pl. 10, figs. 2a, 2b, from a ship arriving in Philadelphia from Hongkong and Java).

A series collected at Zamboanga, Mindanao, by Dr. E. A. Mearns, show the features assumed in their natural habitat, on a rough support.   These clustered specimens are more cylindrical than those from ships, with larger aperture and less regular ribs, and in some the base is deep, as usual with crowded barnacles.   The color stripes are usually less regular and often the color spreads over the whole parietes toward their bases.   The sheath has the remarkable rich madder-brown color characteristic of the subspecies (pl. 10, figs. 3).

Weltner (*Verzeichnis*, p. 260) reports this variety from Walfisch Bay, southwest Africa.   Various lots in the United States National Museum are without locality or are from ships, like No. 41169, from Dublin Bay (W. H. Dall), and other specimens on a ship from Hongkong and Java.

This form is very closely related to the typical form of *tintinnabulum*.

BALANUS TINTINNABULUM SPINOSUS (Gmelin).

1791. *Lepas spinosa* GMELIN, Systema Naturae, ed. 13, p. 3213.
1798. *Lepas echinata* BOLTEN, Museum Boltenianum, p. 197.
1854. *Balanus tintinnabulum*, var. *spinosus* Gmelin, DARWIN, Monograph, p. 196, pl. 1, fig. i.

Convexly conical; rather thin, the parietes somewhat ribbed, the ribs terminating in *very long, slender, up-curved tubular spines*.   White or violet-tinted toward the summit, the spines usually colored.   According to Darwin the scuta "externally were smooth; the adductor

ridge was rather more distinct from the articular ridge than in any other variety, and the terga more plainly beaked."   The opercular valves are wanting in the specimen figured, from an unknown locality.   In size, this form is one of the smallest, diameter 15 to about 20 mm. (fig. 10).

From its frequent occurrence on ships'

FIG. 10.—BALANUS TINTINNABULUM SPINOSUS × 2.

bottoms associated with *B. t. tintinnabulum*, it may be presumed to be from China or India, but it is certainly west African also, possibly colonized by vessels from India by the Cape route.   Weltner gives the localities Siam, East Indies, and St. Helena for specimens in the Berlin Museum, and Hoek reports small specimens, up to 7 mm. diameter, taken from the screw of the *Challenger* when at St. Vincent, Cape Verdes, on the return voyage. Specimens in the United States National Museum and those in the Academy of Natural Sciences have no locality data.

BALANUS TINTINNABULUM OCCATOR Darwin.

Plate 11, figs. 1 to 1e.

1854. *Bàlanus tintinnabulum*, var. *occator* DARWIN, Monograph, etc., p. 196, pl. 1, fig. *k;* pl. 2, fig. 1b.

1900. *Balanus tintinnabulum* (Linnaeus), var. *occator* Darwin, BORRADAILE, Proc. Zool. Soc. London, p. 799 (Fiji).

Type.—In the British Museum; locality unknown.

Distribution.—Indo-Pacific Province: Zamboanga, Mindanao, E. A. Mearns.

Radii with their summits slightly oblique; parietes smooth, or ribbed, or spinose; very pale bluish-purple, with narrow darker longitudinal lines; sheath, with the internal surface of the rostrum and lateral compartments, dull blue, whilst the corresponding parts of the carina and carinolateral compartments are white. *Scuta with small, sharp, hood-formed points, arranged in straight radiating lines.* Terga with the spur placed at either *its own width, or less than its own width,* from the basiscutal angle. Darwin.

Italics of the foregoing description are mine. The color varies from pale purple to cream color, with white radii, the summit more or less tinged with purple.

The deflected tergal area of the scutum is rather narrow and is bent very abruptly, the angle between that area and the face of the valve being but little greater than a right angle. The whole valve is narrower than in *B. t. tintinnabulum.* The inner face of the scutum is similar to that of *B. t. tintinnabulum,* the adductor ridge being *very weakly developed,* obsolete in the lower half of the valve.

The longitudinal furrow of the tergum is more or less open, and the spur varies in proximity to the basiscutal angle, though always nearer than in *B. t. tintinnabulum.*

The habitat Fiji has been given for this race, but most specimens in collections were from ships. A single specimen was in a lot of *B. t. zebra* collected by Dr. E. A. Mearns at Zamboanga. It has the violaceous coloring on a whitish ground and the narrow ribs of the *occator* from ships, but no spines are developed. The orifice is broad and triangular. Valves typical, the spur of the tergum inserted at half its own width from the basiscutal angle.

Figures 1, 1a, 1c to 1e of Plate 11 represent specimens from the bottom of a ship reaching Philadelphia, 120 days from Sudders Bay, Java. Other examples (pl. 11, fig. 1b) are from a ship arriving in Philadelphia from Hongkong and Java, via India, and associated with *B. t. tintinnabulum* and *B. t. zebra.*

It seems rather likely that *B. t. occator* was the original *Lepas crispata* of Schröter, but as he gave no description or figure of the tergum, I do not see that his form can be identified with certainty.

BALANUS TINTINNABULUM VOLCANO, new subspecies.

Plate 11, figs. 2 to 2*e*.

? *Balanus tintinnabulum*, var. *crispatus* Schröter, DARWIN, Monograph, pp. 195, 201, pl. 1, fig. *h*. Not *Lepas crispata* Schröter.

Type.—Cat. No. 43488, U.S.N.M. Japan, collected by H. Loomis.

A large barnacle with the conic shape of typical *B. tintinnabulum*, nearly smooth except for *minute, irregularly scattered and downwardly projecting acute points* or very short spines on the parietes, most numerous on the rostral and lateral compartments. Purplish lilac, in places deep slate-violet, where worn becoming pale smoke-gray. Radii wide, transversely striate, with level summits. Sheath whitish or pale flesh tinted. Carinorostral diameter 58 mm.; height 47 mm.

Scutum flatter than in *B. t. tintinnabulum*, with the basi-tergal corner but little cut off, *the deflected tergal segment very small;* exterior finely but *strongly ribbed longitudinally*, the ribs prominent on the growth-ridges, which are deeply scalloped by them. The adductor ridge is high and rather massive.

The tergum is similar to that of typical *tintinnabulum*, white with a buff cuticle when unworn, having narrow growth ridges and rather faint traces of fine longitudinal striæ. Spur about twice its own width from the basiscutal angle.

This subspecies is well characterized by the flat scutum, its tergal segment much less deflected than in *B. t. occator*, its surface radially costulate over the growth-ridges. The parietes are rather sparsely armed with minute spines; size large, colors dull. *B. t. occator* is paler, white or violaceous, the size smaller, and the tergum quite different. It is often profusely spinose, the spines larger than in *B. t. volcano*. Probably the latter will be found sometimes without spines.

In two rather large and strong specimens in the collection of the Academy of Natural Sciences, which I refer to *B. t. volcano*, the parietes are somewhat rugose, and all the compartments have minute spines. The adductor ridge of the scutum is moderately developed in one, low and rounded as in typical *tintinnabulum* in the other. They grew on wood, probably ships.

B. t. volcano is probably equivalent to part of Darwin's *B. tintinnabulum* var. *crispatus* Schröter. I do not believe that it can be the *Lepas crispata* of Schröter. This species, as defined by Schröter,[1]

---

[1] *Lepas crispata* Schröter, Einleitung in die Conchylienkenntniss nach Linne, vol. 3, 1786, p. 534, pl. 9, fig. 21.

is a medium-sized barnacle; diameter 1½, height 1 inch; radii shaded bluish and white; parietes vertically striate, lighter than the radii, of a reddish color, thickly beset with spines for halfway up from the base. Smaller opercular plates are white, the larger (scuta) are dark blue with sculpture of serpentine (*geschlängelten*) transverse striæ.

Schröter's figure represents a profusely spinose barnacle very similar to well-developed *B. t. occator*. The blue radii and scuta also favor this variety, which is usually marked with violet. The form of the terga and color of the sheath, characteristic marks of *occator*, are not mentioned or figured by Schröter, so that I do not think we would be justified in substituting the name *crispatus* for *occator*. Unless the type can be found, *crispatus* would better be dropped as not certainly identifiable.

Darwin states of the form (or forms) which he included under var. *crispatus* Schröter, that they have "scuta with their exterior surface either plain or with radiating lines formed of hoodlike projecting points;" and on page 201 he adds that the scutum is "broader and flatter than in var. *communis*, and the adductor ridge is very feebly developed." This last character does not agree with the type lot of *B. t. volcano*, which has scuta with the adductor ridge rather strongly developed and massive, but some specimens before me from ships' bottoms have it only moderately developed. It seems likely that Darwin's specimens with "plain" scuta (that is, with growth-ridges only) belong to another race.

Under the circumstances, it seems best to describe the Japanese form as a new subspecies, in view of the suspicion that at least two and perhaps three races have been known as *crispatus*, and the practical certainty that the form now called *volcano* is not the original *Lepas crispata* of Schröter. I may add that the specimens of Schröter and Darwin were off of ships, and no locality is known for them, though they may be presumed to be of East Indian origin.

Another obscure spinose barnacle is *Lepas echinata* Spengler.[1] While I have not been able to match the figure of this form, it seems rather characteristic, and may prove recognizable when the exact race is encountered again.

BALANUS TINTINNABULUM ROSA, new subspecies.

Type.—Cat. No. 43494, U.S.N.M., from Azabu, Japan.

The barnacle is conic or subcylindric, with a rather large, broadly and acutely ovate aperture; roseate (between pomegranate-purple and Indian-lake of Ridgway's Color Standards), the parietes of rostrum and lateral compartments paler than the carina, the radii a deeper shade of the same color. Parietes smooth. Radii with horizontal summits. Sheath a duller shade of the external color.

---

[1] Skrifter af Naturhistorie Selskabet, vol. 1, 1790, p. 177.

Scutum with simple growth-ridges, at least in young individuals; adductor ridge very weakly developed. Tergum rather long, with relatively *short spur*, separated by nearly twice its own width from the basoscutal angle, the basal margin sloping to it on both sides.

Carinorostral diameter 27 mm.; height 20 mm. (type).

Carinorostral diameter 21 mm.; height 25 mm. (cylindric specimen).

Carinorostral diameter 41 mm.; height 49 mm.

More brilliant than other oriental forms of the species; by its beautiful color and smoothness resembling *B. t. coccopoma*, and readily distinguishable from other Indo-Pacific races of *B. tintinnabulum*. Unfortunately, the large individuals had lost their opercular valves, which were described from one of the small individuals of a group of over 20, from Wakanoura.

Large specimens become quite heavy and strong, and I had, at one time, some suspicion that the race might be referable to *B. ajax* Darwin; but a comparison with Darwin's description and a specimen of that species from Mariveles, Luzon, assures me of their specific difference. The very large rostrum, dark-colored sheath, small orifice, and remarkably thick walls of *B. ajax* are conspicuous differential characters.

Museum No.	Locality.	Donor.
43494	Azabu, Japan	Imperial University of Tokyo.
43493	Wakanoura, Japan	Do.
43495	Kishiu, Japan	Do.
11300	Japan or Bonin Islands	Jon Uchimura.
43497	Japan	
	Yedo Bay, Japan	Rev. H. Loomis.

BALANUS TINTINNABULUM AZORICUS, new subspecies.

Plate 12, figs. 2, 2a, 2b.

Type.—Cat. No. 48126, U.S.N.M., from Crace, Terciera, Azores, growing on *Patella cœrulea;* taken in 1894; collector not recorded.

The barnacle is cylindric in general shape, the orifice rather large, ovate-trigonal. Parietes roughened by numerous small, irregular riblets. Summits of the radii level. Color dull blue-violet or dark hyssop-violet, clouded with white; terga pale yellow externally; scuta marked with the darker shade down the middle and internally. The sheath is pale violaceous with dirty whitish alæ; carinolateral compartments sometimes paler than the others. Height 40 mm.; diameter 29 mm.

Scutum rather flat, the tergal segment but slightly deflected; growth-ridges narrow and prominent, *conspicuously crimped*, intervals deeply striate. Adductor ridge strong and *acute*, much as in *B. t. concinnus.*

Tergum rather narrow, with the spur normal in position, but rather short; furrow nearly or quite closed; growth-ridges much more prominent than in *B. t. tintinnabulum;* radial striæ rather weak or wanting.

The cirri are generally similar to those of *B. t. tintinnabulum*, except that the last three pairs have not nearly so many segments, with compensating far greater length of the individual segments. There are fewer distal spinules on the segments, but the same number (four) of anterior pairs of spines. (See p. 52, fig. 8; p. 67, fig. 11c.)

The penis is as long as the posterior cirri. There are a few sparse hairs near the end, but no basi-dorsal point was seen.

A general view of the cirri and penis is given in figure 8.

The opercular valves of this race are most like those of *B. t. concinnus*, but the slight deflection of the tergal segment of the scutum is a conspicuous differential character. The acute adductor ridge and the conspicuously crimped growth ridges of the scutum serve to separate the Terciera form from *B. t. tintinnabulum*. The rather sharp, irregular ridges of the parietes and especially the *smaller number and much longer segments* of the posterior cirri, are also unlike that race. The color of the sheath is such as one often sees in *tintinnabulum*, and not darkened as in *B. t. zebra*, or specially colored, as in some other races described by Darwin.

The specimens were much overgrown with seaweed and incrusted with lime.

BALANUS TINTINNABULUM ANTILLENSIS, new subspecies.

Plate 13, figs. 1 to 2e.

Type.—No. 2083, A. N. S. P., St. Thomas, R. Swift.
Distribution.—West Indies to Rio Janeiro.

The barnacle is small, somewhat tubular, with irregularly ribbed parietes; white or whitish, with reddish purple lines on the parietes, or the latter may be Indian lake throughout. Radii wide, whitish. Insides of parietes dusky, sheath elsewhere pale.

Diameter 18 mm.; length 28 mm.
Diameter 21 mm.; length 25 mm.
Diameter 26 mm.; length 33 mm.

The opercular valves are formed substantially as in typical *tintinnabulum;* but the spur is somewhat shorter, twice its own width from the basi-scutal angle; the terga are white or nearly so, and are about as wide as the scuta. The adductor ridge of the scutum is better developed, long and narrow, especially in the smaller examples.

The type of this race is in a group (pl. 13, fig. 1e) which grew upon an oyster shell. The largest measurement given above is from the largest individual of the group, evidently an old one. A few *Tetraclita radiata* grew upon the same group. So far as I know, this is the chief if not the only form of the species found in the West Indies, but collections are very meager, and it would occasion no surprise if the large oriental races were found established around ports frequented by deep-sea vessels.

The specimens from Jamaica have waved, transverse, colored bands crossing the stripes on the parietes, and one of them has a deep, pocketlike base and cylindric walls, 47 mm. long, with a greatest diameter of 20 mm. Those from Rio Janeiro are imperfect, and referred to this race with some doubt. Mr. S. Raymond Roberts collected specimens near Havana, Cuba.

A large series from a whaler, Cape Cod, September 3, 1879, collected by Prof. A. E. Verrill, is interesting for its associates and coloration (pl. 13, figs. 2 to 2e). In all probability the vessel was a Provincetown schooner whaling in the West Indies, and the barnacles were gathered in course of the usual short (six months) voyage. The wooden bottom was first rather copiously covered with *Balanus trigonus* up to about 8 mm. diameter. These were then mostly covered by flat, thin oysters (*Ostrea folium* Linnæus), mainly under 25 mm. in length, and by the *Balanus tintinnabulum antillensis*, which seem to have settled down at the same time. Upon these oysters and barnacles *Tetraclita radiata* sits, the specimens reaching a diameter of about 8 mm. There are also a few extremely young *Balanus eburneus*, 1 to 2 mm. diameter, which were clearly the last settlers, after the vessel returned to Massachusetts.

The *B. tintinnabulum antillensis* of this lot measure 15 to 20 mm. diameter, with a height up to 25 mm., and may, perhaps, fall short of their full growth. The parietes are moderately ribbed, rose-pink to Indian lake, nearly uniform or in longitudinal stripes. The very wide *radii are white* or nearly so, very smooth and glossy. Sheath very pale. The base is roughened by the projecting edges of the concentric slips composing it (fig. 2a). Scuta and terga as in *B. tintinnabulum tintinnabulum*, the growth-ridges of the scuta somewhat crimped by the fine longitudinal striæ. The scuta are rose tinted; terga white.

Museum No.	Locality.	Collector.
....	Jamaica..	C. B. Adams.
....	Cape Cod, on whaler from West Indies..............	A. E. Verrill.
43499..............	Rio Janeiro..	

Balanus tintinnabulum, var. *vesiculosus* Darwin [1] was based upon extremely small individuals, scutum about 4 mm. long, and is scarcely comparable with the other forms. Indeed, it seems to have been regarded as a young stage rather than a true variety by Darwin.

---

[1] Monograph, etc., p. 195, pl. 2, fig. 1h. No locality.

There is a single specimen of unknown origin in the United States National Museum collection (Cat. No. 43496), which agrees with Darwin's too brief description. The scutum is 8.5 mm. long, the upper 4 mm. more coarsely ridged than usual in this part of the valve; the intervals between ridges are deepened to form *a series of shallow pits* between the tergal edge and a low rounded ridge or convexity which radiates from the apex, nearer to the occludent than to the scutal margin. The lower half of the valve is ridged as in typical *tintinnabulum*, without pits. The adductor ridge is acute and rather prominent, about as in *B. t. antillensis*. The other scutum of the same individual does not show the pits between growth ridges. The tergum is *decidedly broader than the scutum*, with narrow spur, remote from the basiscutal angle. The orifice is rather large and triangular; parietes weakly striate, the intervals between striæ marked with dark violet lines. The wide radii are pale violet. Carinorostral diameter 16 mm., height 13.6 mm.

This barnacle has a young specimen of *Balanus improvisus assimilis* Darwin embedded in the base, suggesting a West Indian or South American habitat. It may prove to be a form of *B. t. antillensis*, but in the long series of that race I have examined none have pitted scuta.

BALANUS TINTINNABULUM CALIFORNICUS, new subspecies.

Plate 14, figs. 1–3; plate 15, fig. 4.

Type.—Cat. No. 9434a, U.S.N.M., from San Diego, California.
Distribution.—Santa Barbara to San Diego, California.

Conic, or sometimes tubular, with diamond-shaped or angularly ovate orifice. Parietes *rather finely striate, the striæ white on a red (Indian-lake) ground*, or some tint of that color; radii similar or paler, sometimes transversely striate near the level summits. Summits of the alæ subhorizontal.

Scutum similar to that of *B. t. tintinnabulum*, except that the depressor muscle impression is smaller and deeper; adductor impression deep. The external growth ridges show more or less distinct traces of longitudinal striæ, and the outside is largely roseate, not distinctly bicolored as in *B. t. coccopoma*.

Tergum rose or partly white, with faint longitudinal striæ between the growth-ridges, the spur broad, about its own width from the basiscutal angle.

The parietal tubes are extremely narrow and numerous (pl. 15, fig. 4, part of the rostrum, with attached vesicular basis on the right), the septa being very thin and delicate, thereby differing from other forms of *B. tintinnabulum*.

Greatest diameter 57 mm.; height 34 mm. The mouth parts and cirri are unknown, the specimens being preserved dry.

When growing unhampered on a smooth object, this is a handsome barnacle, quite distinct in appearance from *B. t. coccopoma*, by the raised white striæ of the parietes, as well as by the somewhat different opercular valves. The basi-tergal corner of the scutum is less cut off, and the tergal segment is less broadly deflected and less contrasted in color. The tergum has a broader spur. When crowded, and sometimes under other circumstances, the shape becomes cylindric, with deep basis, such a shape as is often assumed by forms of *B. tintinnabulum*. Plate 14, figure 3, represents such a specimen from near Santa Barbara.

The coloration, the *crowded, narrow parietal tubes*, the shorter, broader spur of the tergum, and the somewhat smaller size distinguish it from *B. t. tintinnabulum*. Unfortunately, only dry specimens, from which the body had been removed, are at hand. It appears to be a common barnacle from Santa Barbara to San Diego, at low-water mark, on rocks, oysters, shells, the carapaces of crabs, and on other barnacles, having about the same distribution as *B. aquila*. It will probably be found as far north as Monterey Bay, and may be expected southward along the ocean coast of the peninsula.

So far as is known, this is the only form of *B. tintinnabulum* inhabiting the Californian coast, though no doubt various oriental forms are constantly brought into the deep-water ports.

Museum No.	Locality.	Collector.	Notes.
9434a.........	San Diego, Cal..............	R. E. C. Stearns............	Type; figured.
9435.........	....do.............	C. R. Orcutt................	On Ostrea; figured.
9434.........	....do.............	R. E. C. Stearns............	On *B. aquila.*
11144.........	Santa Rosa Island..........	P. Schumacher..............	Do.
9179.........	San Miguel Island..........	W. H. Dall.................	
43484.........	Santa Barbara..........	....	On rocks; figured.
....	(No label).............	....	On crab.

BALANUS TINTINNABULUM PENINSULARIS, new subspecies.

Plate 15, figs. 1 to 2d.

Type.—Cat. No. 43486, U.S.N.M.

Type-locality.—Cape St. Lucas, Lower California, growing on shells, etc., collected by John Xantus. No other locality is known.

The barnacle is cylindric or conic, with an ovate-triangular orifice. Parietes cinereus, densely covered with lighter spines projecting toward the base; radii from light grayish-olive to fuscous-black, paler toward the rostrad edge, wide, deeply striate transversely, the *summits level, parallel to the base*. Basal edges of the septa rather thick; basal pores about 18 to 21 in the rostrum. Sheath usually long, with the insides of the parietes dark, the strongly oblique alæ pale.

Greatest diameter 20 mm.; height 28 mm. (type).

Greatest diameter 22 mm; height 17 mm. (conic specimen).

Scutum dull purple, with smooth growth-ridges. Adductor ridge strongly developed, rather acute.

Terga white, shaped as in *B. t. tintinnabulum*, with a rather short, acute beak; the external furrow closed; spur narrow; scutal margin smooth.

The labrum has a small median notch and no teeth on the shortly hairy edge.

Mandible with five well-developed teeth, the last united with the lower point (fig. 11a).

Maxilla has 13 large spines, about as in *B. t. tintinnabulum*.

Cirri about as in *B. t. tintinnabulum*, except that the segments of the three posterior cirri are not so short, and the lower pair of spines on each segment is smaller (fig. 11b).

The above description applies to solitary specimens (figs. 2 to 2d) not encrusted by nullipore, algæ, or other marine growths. In the

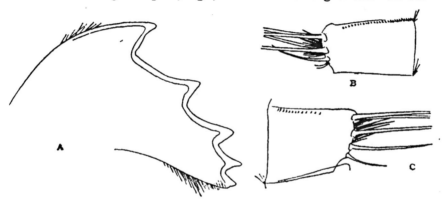

Fig. 11.—*a*, Mandible, and *b*, median segment of cirrus vi, of Balanus t. peninsularis. *c*, median segment, cirrus vi, of B. t. azoricus.

large series comprised in Cat. No. 43487, U.S.N.M., the barnacles grow in clusters (figs. 1, 1a), and are overgrown with algæ, etc. The spines in this lot are less fully developed, usually appearing only on some of the compartments, the others being irregularly ribbed, plicate, or nearly smooth. Some individuals lack spines altogether. The radii are often smooth, rarely striate throughout. The color may be soiled white throughout, or like the type, or lineate and clouded with livid purple, the radii being livid purple, shading into white along one side. The opercular valves are similar to the typical form.

I worked over this race a long time in an attempt to identify it with one or other of Darwin's named forms of *B. tintinnabulum*, finally deciding to give it subspecific rank. Darwin's account of *B. t. dorbignyi* Chenu, and Chenu's figure, resemble *peninsularis* rather closely, yet differ by the oblique summits of the radii. Chenu gives no figure of the opercular valves, and Darwin says that the tergum is like that of *occator*. This does not apply to *peninsularis*, which has the tergum like *B. t. tintinnabulum*. According to Darwin, *B. t. dorbignyi* was taken from a ship from Java.

B. t. spinosus and *B. t. occator* are oriental forms, certainly distinct from the present subspecies. *B. t. crispatus* Schröter, as figured by Schröter, agrees better with our specimens, but it is from an oriental locality, just where being uncertain, as all known examples are from ship's bottoms. There are various discrepancies between our specimens and Darwin's account and figures, which cause me to hesitate to assume their identity. Moreover, it is not at all likely that an oriental form was imported to such an out-of-the-way place as Cape St. Lucas, where it seems to be abundant, growing on native shells, etc. It is equally unlikely that the ship furnishing Schröter's specimens could have picked them up in Lower California prior to 1786.

Nonspinose individuals of *B. t. peninsularis* are a good deal like the Antillean *B. t. antillensis* in color, size, and opercular valves, but the eastern form seems never to become spinose in the lot of several hundred I have seen.

BALANUS TINTINNABULUM COCCOPOMA Darwin.

Plate 16, figs. 1, 1a, 2, 2a.

1854. *Balanus tintinnabulum*, var. *coccopoma* DARWIN, Monograph, etc., p. 196, pl. 1, fig. d; pl. 2, figs. 1f, 1l, 1o.

Type.—British Museum, from Panama.
Distribution.—Panama to Mazatlan.

Convexly conic, with small rounded orifice, or sometimes cylindric, with the orifice large. Walls smooth or weakly striate, the parietes roseate (spinal red or hellebore red of Ridgway), radii vinaceous purple or rarely white. Greatest diameter 30 mm.; height 26 mm.; specimens with a long, cylindric basis up to 50 mm. long.

Scutum vinaceous purple, fading toward the lower margin, the deflected tergal segment broad, cream white; adductor ridge prominent, slightly overhanging the deep pit of the depressor muscle; articular rib terminating in a broad free point; basiscutal angle usually much cut off, but sometimes shaped as in typical *tintinnabulum*; external growth-ridges close, smooth.

Tergum as in *B. t. tintinnabulum* [or "sometimes with a broader spur placed nearer to the basiscutal corner of the valve"].

This small, deep rose-colored race is restricted to the Panamic faunal Province,[1] and appears to be rather a common littoral barnacle. It has a very distinct appearance, but no doubt Darwin was right in

---

[1] Darwin mentions specimens resembling this variety sent him as "from a ship direct from China;" but such data are open to doubt. Possibly he had *B. t. rosa*. The types were on a pearl oyster from Panama "as Mr. Cuming believes;" and I have seen a good many from that place. M. Gruvel has reported it from "California," but if the locality of his specimens is correct, they will probably be found to be *B. t. californicus*.

giving it the same rank as the other races subordinated to *B. tintinnabulum*.

Some specimens in the collection of the Academy of Natural Sciences of Philadelphia, received from Frederick Stearns, are labeled "West coast of Lower California." Part of them are cylindric, with lengthened bases.

Darwin mentions a form of *B. tintinnabulum* from the coast of Mexico and California which is "rugged and of a dull bluish-purple" color, with "opercular valves exactly like those of var. *coccopoma*." I have not seen it.

Locality.	Collector	Museum.
Panama, on oysters	Dr. W. S. W. Ruschenberger, United States Navy.	Academy of Natural Sciences, Philadelphia.
Panama	Samuel N. Rhoads	Do.
Salinas Bay, Costa Rica	Anastasio Alfaro	Do.
Bottom of U. S. S. Portsmouth after leaving Guaymas, Mexico.	Dr. W. H. Jones, United States Navy.	United States National Museum.
Mazatlan, Mexico	Dr. Paul Bartsch	Do.

BALANUS TINTINNABULUM CONCINNUS Darwin.

Plate 16, fig. 3; plate 17, figs. 5–8.

1854. *Balanus tintinnabulum*, var. *concinnus* DARWIN, Monograph, etc., p. 196, pl. 1, fig. *e;* pl. 2, fig. 1*g.*

1903. *Balanus tintinnabulum*, var. *concinnus* GRUVEL, Nouv. Archives du Muséum 4 sér., vol. 5, p. 126.

1909. *Balanus tintinnabulum* Linnæus, PILSBRY, Proc. U. S. Nat. Mus., vol. 37, p. 65, pl. 16, fig. 3; pl. 18, figs. 5–8.

Type.—British Museum.

Distribution.—Straits of Magellan to Peru.

The barnacle is large, cylindric, or somewhat conic, the orifice usually large. The parietes are nearly smooth or a little roughened, sometimes striate, sometimes weakly plicate; with many *longitudinal lines and waved, transverse, narrow streaks of livid purple and livid violet on a whitish ground, producing a finely speckled pattern.* Radii broad, with horizontal summits; violet-plumbeous. Alæ with nearly horizontal summits. Sheath livid purplish with paler alæ.

The scutum (pl. 15, fig. 3; pl. 17, figs. 6, 8) has the basi-tergal corner a good deal cut off, the deflected tergal segment broad; external growth-ridges rather coarse and prominent; *longitudinal striæ usually conspicuous. Adductor ridge acute and prominent, broadly overhanging the deep and large pit for the lateral depressor muscle.* The rostral depressor pit is often bounded by a small rib.

The tergum is substantially as in *B. t. tintinnabulum*, except that it is *conspicuously striated longitudinally* between the narrow growth-ridges, the striæ coarse on the scutal side of the closed furrow, fine on the broader side. Spur separated from the basiscutal angle by twice its own width.

According to Darwin, the segments of the sixth pair of cirri bear six pairs of spines.

The conic form is often not large: diameter 33 mm., height 38 mm. (Pacasmayo). The cylindric forms are larger; diameter 40 mm., height 50 mm. (Payta). The largest individual seen in which the base is flattened measures about 67 mm. in greatest diameter, 85 mm. height. It is from the coast of Peru. Some individuals have a very long base, as in *B. psittacus*. One taken from a wreck at Payta is 150 mm. long, of which the parietes occupy hardly 40 mm.; greatest diameter 42 mm. In these examples the vertical sides of the base are longitudinally plicate, and clouded with white and livid purple. The pocket-like cavity runs down to a point.

B. t. concinnus is well defined by the speckled coloration of the parietes, the sculpture of tergum and scutum, and the acute, overhanging adductor ridge of the latter. According to Darwin, the joints of the last cirrus bear six pairs of spines instead of four. Like *B. t. californicus* it is a strongly individualized form. Possibly both may deserve specific rank.

Darwin gives the locality west coast of.South America. Gruvel records it from the Straits of Magellan, on *B. psittacus*, also Aden and French Congo. The last two records, if really pertaining to *concinnus*, must have been based on specimens taken to those places on ships. The records of *B. tintinnabulum communis* from the west coast of South America may possibly be based on specimens of *concinnus*.

Museum No.	Locality.	Collector.	Notes.
....	Bay of Sechura, Peru......	Dr. R. E. Coker.............	In 5 to 6 fathoms.
9223..........	Pacasmayo, Peru...........	Dr. W. H. Jones.............	On beach.
43491..........	.....do..........	.....do.............	Chain on pier.
43490..........	Coast of Peru.................	W. E. Curtis...............	
43492..........	Payta, Peru.................	Lieut. W. C. Babcock.......	On a wreck.

BALANUS TINTINNABULUM GALAPAGANUS, new subspecies.

. Plate 12, figs. 1, 1*a*, 1*b*.

Type.—Cat. No. 48003, U.S.N.M., from Hood Island, Galapagos, on a rock, *Albatross*, April 7, 1888.

The barnacle is conic with a rather small orifice and smooth or weakly ribbed parietes; white or pink, with red lines on the parietes; radii whitish, usually grooved transversely, their summits level; summits of the alæ very oblique.

Height 10 mm.; diameter 15 mm.

Height 10 mm.; diameter 13 mm.

Scutum pale grayish-pink, flat, the *tergal border not noticeably deflected*. Sculpture of close, sigmoid growth-ridges, no longitudinal striæ. Adductor ridge very small, merely an acute ledge alongside the depressor muscle-impression.

Tergum whitish, striate on the carinal area, with growth-ridges on the scutal area; furrow closed or almost closed; spur narrow, fully double its own width, or more, from the basiscutal angle.

This form differs from *B. t. concinnus* of the mainland by the *flat scutum*. I have compared scuta of *concinnus* of the same size and smaller, and in all of them the tergal segment is broadly deflected, as in the adult stage. The external color reminds one of *B. concavus*.

B. t. coccopoma also has a wide deflected tergal border of the scutum, and the external form and color are different.

In specimens of *B. t. tintinnabulum* a little larger than the Galapagos form, the tergal edge of the scutum is noticeably inflected. Otherwise there seems little difference between them. Possibly the Galapagos specimens may be the descendants of imported examples of this oriental subspecies, though it seems to me rather unlikely: Darwin mentions *tintinnabulum* from the Galapagos, without comment. As he treats rather fully of the West American forms, it would seem likely that if he found "var. *communis*" there he would have made note of it.

Over 60 individuals are grouped on a volcanic rock about 8 inches long. From the nearly equal size of the larger ones, of the bases left by their departed brethren, and the nearly closed furrow of the tergum, it may be inferred that they are nearly or quite adult; yet I feel some doubt on account of the fact that the parietes below the sheath are ribbed. In the fully adult stage, *B. tintinnabulum* has a smoother interior. Some individuals of the smaller subspecies, such as *occator* and *spinosus* I have examined are strongly ribbed within, though doubtless of full size; others, probably older, though not larger, have the interior smooth, except near the base. However this may be, it appears that the Galapagos form differs from other known races of the west coast of the Americas and should be readily recognizable, even if it proves to attain a size greater than the type lot.

There is another West American form of *tintinnabulum* apparently differing from those described above. It was taken by Dr. L. Plate at Cavanche, near Iquique, to a depth of 50 meters, and has been described by Weltner.[1] The shell is white, and rather strongly ribbed, "like *porcatus*," the sheath uncolored or pale rose; radii are very oblique. The scutum has sculpture like *occator*. The size is up to 30 mm. in height. In color it certainly resembles *B. psittacus*.

Other named oriental forms of *B. tintinnabulum* may be mentioned here. Variety *intermedius* Darwin, locality unknown, and var. *dorbignyii* Chenu, which Darwin reports from a ship from Java, are not represented in the United States National Museum collection.

---

[1] Archiv für Naturgeschichte, 61 Jahrg., 1895, p. 291.

Hoek has described two new varieties: var. *costatus* and var. *plicatus*,[1] both taken from the bottom of the *Siboga* and therefore from some part of the Malay Archipelago. Var. *costatus* was based upon one specimen 14 mm. in diameter; var. *plicatus* upon two, the larger of 10 mm. diameter. The open furrow of the tergum probably means that both were young barnacles. Quite possibly both may be the young of var. *zebra* Darwin. In any case, the very great difficulty of reaching a satisfactory understanding of the forms of *B. tintinnabulum* can not be lightened by the description of scanty, immature, and imperfectly localized material.

BALANUS ALGICOLA, new species.

Plate 12, figs. 3 to 3*g*.

Type.—Cat. No. 15063, U.S.N.M., from Cape Town, growing on algæ, collected by Wm. Harvey Brown, United States eclipse expedition, 1889.

Distribution.—South Africa.

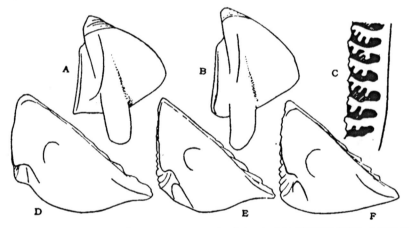

FIG. 12.—BALANUS ALGICOLA *a*, *b*, TERGA OF TWO AND *d*, *e*, *f*, SCUTA OF THREE INDIVIDUALS. *c*, PART OF THE EDGE OF A RADIUS, SHOWING DENTICULATE SEPTA AND OPEN ENDS OF THE RADIAL PORES.

Very small, conic or cylindric, usually growing in crowded clusters; white, or sometimes with faint violet stains, chiefly on the radii; smooth or somewhat ribbed.

Diameter 7 mm.; height 9 mm. (typical, cylindric form).

Diameter 11 mm.; height 6 mm. (solitary, conic form).

Scutum very broad, having widely spaced growth-ridges, alternate ones forming teeth along the occludent margin; no radial striation. A broad, shallow depression runs down the middle of the valve. The tergal border is rather narrowly deflected. The basitergal angle is cut off in varying degree, as shown in figure 12 *d*, *e*, *f*. The articular ridge is moderately high, reflexed, with its lower end trun-

---

[1] Both of these names are preoccupied in *Balanus*.

cated or slightly overhanging. A ridge runs downward from it, bordering the deep pit of the lateral depressor muscle, but *there is no adductor ridge*. Pit for the adductor muscle is well marked.

The tergum has the longitudinal furrow more or less open. Spur rather short, with rounded end, situated about its own width, more or less, from the basiscutal angle. Articular ridge strong. There are no crests for the depressor muscle.

Compartments.—The parietes are typically smooth, but in some conic, solitary individuals they have rather numerous ribs. The radii are wide, with level summits. The lateral edges of the radii and the opposed sutural edges are rather coarsely septate, but the septa are either not distinctly denticulate, merely a little irregular, or there may be a few coarse denticles on one side (fig. 12c). The horizontal pores of the radii are well developed.

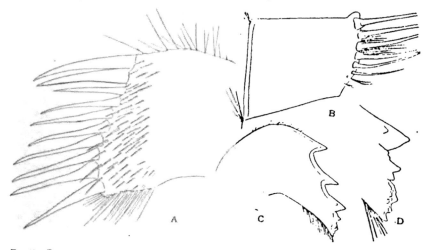

Fig. 13.—Balanus algicola. *a*, maxilla. *b*, 14th segment of cirrus vi. *c*, mandible. *d*, more enlarged third tooth and lower point of the mandible.

The basis is not very thick. It is radially porous, without a cellular under-layer, so far as seen.

The labrum has three minute teeth on each side. The mandible has three strong teeth, the fourth and fifth being quite small and short (fig. 13c, *d*).

The maxilla has 8 to 10 large spines. The margin protrudes somewhat toward the lower border (fig. 13a).

The cirri are purple. The first three pairs are quite short, as in *tintinnabulum;* the later ones are not very long, and have segments a little wider than long. The sixth pair has rami of about 22 segments with from six to eight pairs of spines on the middle segments (fig. 13b). I could find no spinules along the distal borders of the segments, such as other races of *B. tintinnabulum* have.

The penis is more than twice as long as the last cirri, and has a conspicuous, acute, basidorsal point.

Several hundred specimens in the United States National Museum show this to be a distinct species of the *tintinnabulum* group. They have the form and appearance of mature barnacles. Nearly all of those I opened contained large masses of eggs, of the usual elliptical shape, and from 0.12 to 0.14 mm. long, much smaller than the eggs of *tintinnabulum*. While we know that *Balanus* reproduces long before attaining its maximum size, yet the eggs produced by small individuals equal in size those of the larger. The great number of spines on the later cirri is also a feature of maturity. Very young barnacles have fewer spines than old ones. I am therefore convinced that these pygmy barnacles are mature. I believe that Darwin had the same race before him, but mistook it for young *B. tintinnabulum*, when he stated that "in some young specimens from the Cape of Good Hope * * * I found six pairs of spines on the segments of the posterior cirri." (Monograph, p. 200.)

While this barnacle is certainly related to *B. tintinnabulum* by the shape of the terga, it differs in so many characters that I can not rank it as a subspecies. Except the small size, these characters are not directly correlated with its peculiar station. The structure of the walls is that common to species of *Megabalanus*, but special differential features of *B. algicola* are: The small size and pale color; simplified sutural septa (those of *B. tintinnabulum* being denticulate on both sides); the broad scuta; the short lower teeth of the mandible; the numerous spines of the posterior cirri, and the absence of spinules along the distal borders of the segments.

B. algicola grows on algæ, usually in masses mounted upon one another, and is apparently a very abundant form.

BALANUS AJAX Darwin.

1854. *Balanus ajax* DARWIN, Monograph, etc., p. 214, pl. 3, figs. 1a–1d. (Philippine Archipelago.)
1884. *Balanus ajax* Darwin, FISCHER, Bull. Soc. Zool. de France, vol. 9, p. 357.
1907. *Balanus ajax* Darwin, GRUVEL, Bull. Soc. Zool. de France, vol. 32, p. 164.

Locality.—Mariveles, Luzon, Paul Bartsch. Cat. No. 43498, U.S.N.M.

I do not find that any definite locality in the Philippines has been given for this barnacle, which, though related to *B. tintinnabulum*, is characterized by its "excessively strong, massive, and heavy" walls, dark sheath, and large rostral compartment. According to Dr. Paul Fischer, it has been collected by Lambert from reefs south of the Isle of Pines, New Caledonia. Professor Gruvel adds the localities Salomon Island, in the Chagos Archipelago, and Seychelles.

BALANUS PSITTACUS (Molina).

Plate 17, figs. 1 to 4; plate 18, figs. 1 to 3.

1782. *Lepas psittacus* MOLINA, Saggio sulla storia naturale del Chili.[1]
1818. *Balanus tintinnabulum,* var. *c.* RANZANI, Opuscoli Sci., vol. 4, p. 69, pl. 3, figs. 1–4.
1831. *Balanus picos* LESSON, Voyage autour du Monde de la *Coquille,* Zoologie, vol. 2, pt. 1, p. 445 (Concepcion, Talcahuano, S. Vincent, Chili).
1854. *Balanus psittacus* DARWIN, Monograph on the Cirripedia, Balanidæ, p. 206, pl. 2, figs. 3a–d (Arica to Chiloe I., Chili).
1904. *Balanus psittacus* Molina, GRUVEL, Nouvelles Archives du Muséum d'Hist. Nat., sér. 4, vol. 6, p. 103, fig. 9.
1905. *Balanus psittacus* VAYSSIERE, Annales de la Faculté des Sciences de Marseille, vol. 15, fasc. 5, p. 161, pl. 1, figs. 1–4 ("Taleahuana," Chili).
1909. *Balanus psittacus* (Molina) PILSBRY, Proc. U. S. Nat. Mus., vol. 37, p. 66, pl. 16, figs. 1, 4; pl. 18, figs. 1–4.

Distribution.—Strait of Magellan to Pacasmayo, Peru.

The barnacle is pale pink or sometimes soiled white, conic when young, often becoming subcylindric with age, sometimes very large, with a very long tapering basis.

The scutum (pl. 17, figs. 3, 4) is trapezoidal, the basitergal corner being cut off, forming an oblique edge parallel to the occludent margin, and about as long as the rest of the base; tergal third of the valve deflected. Sculpture of rather strong growth-ridges crossed by fine but deeply engraved longitudinal striæ. Articular furrow narrow. Articular ridge high and thin, *continuous with the high, oblique adductor ridge,* which arches over the space between the ridges, leaving *a cavity which penetrates nearly to the apex.*

The tergum is *very narrow* and long, terminating in *a long beak of a pink or purplish color.* The spur is long, narrow, and *less than its own width from the basiscutal angle,* usually very close to it. Groove to the spur closed. External sculpture of growth-ridges and radial striæ, but both are often very weak. Inside, the articular ridge stands upon that running to the spur. Between this ridge and the carinal border there is a short, narrow, longitudinal ridge; these ridges and an oblong space between them being purple or deep pink. There are no crests for the depressor muscles.

Compartments.—The tubes in the parietes are rather large, not filled up above, and not transversely septate. The inside below the sheath is ribbed in young, usually becoming smooth in large individuals. The radii are very wide, with level summits, and permeated by unusually large pores. Their distal edges are wide, with rather coarse, branching laminæ, which are deeply denticulate on their lower sides only. Alæ have oblique summits. Laminæ of the sutural edges denticulate on the upper side.

---

[1] See Proc. U. S. Nat. Mus., vol. 37, p. 66, footnote *a,* for some account of the various editions of the Abbe Molina's Natural History of Chile.

The basis, in the small form, is flat, porous, often with an underlying multicellular layer. In the large form, the basis is lengthened, forming half or three-fourths of the walls, and the cavity usually tapers downward. According to Gruvel, it consists of two portions, the true basis and an intermediate segment which he terms the false wall ("*pseudo-muraille*"), wherein the porous hypodermic layer is reduced to a minimum, the greater part being solid and secreted by the mantle.

The littoral form of *B. psittacus*, which is what the Abbe Molina described, is not a very large barnacle, in shape from conic to cylindric. In a series from Valparaiso the diameter is 35 to 40 mm.; height 40 to 45 mm. The basis is flat or but little built up. The walls are thin or moderately thick; and the parietes are usually ribbed near the summits, but sometimes part or all of them are nearly smooth. A series of varying sizes, down to 2.5 mm. diameter shows that in the early stage, up to about 6 mm. in diameter and height, the parietes are quite smooth. In some individuals a ribbed stage then ensues, to be followed by another smooth stage. In individuals 6 mm. in diameter the opercular valves are exactly as in adults, except that the furrow of the tergum is not closed. At this stage the radii are very narrow.

Some of the specimens from Arica show the best development of the ribs (pl. 18, fig. 3). The inside, below the sheath, is strongly ribbed.

Examples from Chincha Islands, "abundant on the shore rocks," and others from the Pescadores Islands, collected by Dr. R. E. Coker, are small, though clearly adult. They measure 35 to 45 mm. high, 25 to 35 mm. in basal diameter. The shape is conic or vertical-sided; parietes irregularly ribbed, radii rather wide. The orifice is ovate, or angular at the sides and truncate at the rostral end. The color is dull whitish gray, sometimes partly dull pink. The parietes are ribbed lengthwise inside below the sheath. The basis is as flat as circumstances permit, and either forms no part of the side walls or is but slightly excavated. A group from the Chincha Islands, No. 38692 U.S.N.M., is figured[1] of the natural size in plate 16, figure 4, of my paper on Peruvian barnacles.

A very large and massive form of *B. psittacus* is found on the Chilean coast. The lengthened basis forms about one-half of the total height of the side walls. It is irregularly plicate longitudinally, the folds rounded; compartments usually worn, and giving foothold to numerous young of its own kind, *B. lævis nitidus* and *Verruca lævigata.* Orifice nearly as large as the tube. They grow in groups, diverging from the base. The largest in a group from Conception

---

[1] Proc. U. S. Nat. Mus., vol. 37.

Bay measures 20 cm. long, 8.3 cm. in greatest diameter. One from Talcahuano Bay measures 18 cm. long, 8.5 cm. diameter.

A specimen from Pacasmayo, Peru,[1] differs from these by being much thinner, and the basis is longer, forming about two-thirds of the height. Length 16 cm.; greatest diameter 6.2 cm.

Museum No.	Locality.	Collector or donor.
33692	Chincha Islands, Peru, shore..........	R. E. Coker.
....	Pescadores Islands, Peru..............	Do.
15474	Pacasmayo, Peru......................	W. H. Jones, United States Navy.
48124	Arica, Peru..........................	I. Lea collection.
43482	Talcahuano Bay, Chile................	R. E. C. Stearns collection.
48125	Valparaiso, Chile....................	
....	Chile................................	
48123	Port Churruca, Strait of Magellan.....	Albatross.

BALANUS MAXILLARIS Gronovius.

1763. *Balanus maxillaris* GRONOVIUS, Zoophylacii Gronoviani, Iconographia sive Tabularum Explicatio, vol. 5. pl. 19, figs. 3, 4.
1790. *Lepas cylindrica* GMELIN, Systema Naturæ, p. 3213.
1854. *Balanus capensis* Ellis, DARWIN, Monograph, p. 209, pl. 2, figs. 4a, 4b.

Distribution.—Cape of Good Hope (Algoa Bay and Lagulhas Bank).

Cat. No. 3596, Cape Town, U. S. Expl. Exped.; young specimens only.

Ellis, who is usually given as the authority for the species *capensis*, did not make the slightest attempt to use the Linnæan system of nomenclature and certainly can not be quoted for specific names.

BALANUS DECORUS Darwin.

1854. *Balanus decorus* DARWIN, Monograph, p. 212, p. 2, figs. 6a, 6b.

Type.—British Museum, from New Zealand.

Wanganui, New Zealand. S. H. Drew. Chatham Islands, New Zealand, Dr. E. Kershner.

As the opercular valves are wanting, the identification is not positive.

Subgenus BALANUS Da Costa.

= *Balanus* + *Tamiosoma* CONRAD, 1856 + *Ortho-Balanus* HOEK, Siboga-Expeditie, Monographie, 31b, 1913, p. 158, *B. amphitrite* here selected as type.

Balani in which the parietes but not the radii are porous; basis calcareous, either solid or porous; cirrus iii (and sometimes iv–vi) armed with teeth or spinules.

At one time I thought that Hoek's subgenus *Ortho-Balanus* could be maintained for the species with porous basis, Darwin's Section C; but it is clear that *B. nubilis* and *B. flos*, which have the basis incom-

---

[1] Figured in Proc. U. S. Nat. Mus., vol. 37 pl. 16, fig. 1.

pletely porous, are more related to *B. balanus* (with a solid basis) by the characters of the maxillæ and terga. A division founded upon the character of the basis would not be natural. The armature of the cirri, the sculpture of the scuta and the shape of the terga are diversified so much, and in combinations so various, that unless the group is to be divided into at least six sections, it had better be left intact. In this opinion I find myself in agreement with Doctor Hoek.

The interrelations of the species may be shown by a grouping into eight series, of which the first three may be bracketed together, and similarly the last four.

Series of *B. amphitrite.*
Series of *B. trigonus.*
Series of *B. perforatus.*

Series of *B. gregarius.*

Series of *B. aquila.*
Series of *B. nubilis.*
Series of *B. balanus.*
Series of *B. crenatus.*

The following species, not contained in the United States National Museum, belong to this subgenus, part of them being doubtfully distinct from *B. amphitrite.* Some notes on their characters and affinities are appended.

Balanus poecilus Darwin. See p. 110.

Balanus minutus Hoek. Siboga-Expeditie, Cirripedia (p. 177). Entrance of Kwangdang Bay, 80 meters. One specimen on a crinoid pinnule, diameter about 3.7 mm. Pink with reddish stripes. This and *B. alatus* are similar externally to *B. amphitrite,* but differ by wanting an adductor ridge in the scutum. From the color, both may be expected to occur also in shallower water, as the truly deep-sea species are usually white. *B. poecilus, alatus,* and *minutus* are alike in having no adductor ridge.

Balanus hystrix Hoek. *Siboga-*Expeditie, Cirripedia (p. 218). Ambon anchorage, reef. Diameter 5 mm. Third to fifth pairs of cirri armed with recurved teeth on the anterior borders of the segments. It probably stands near *B. perforatus.*

Balanus violaceus Gruvel. Nouv. Arch. du Mus. (ser. 4, vol. 5, 1903, p. 133). Locality unknown; type in British Museum. Near *B. amphitrite.* It is not *Lepas violacea* Gmelin, also a *Balanus.*

Balanus dybowskii Gruvel. Nouv. Arch. du Mus. (ser. 4, vol. 5, 1903, p. 143). Congo. Diameter 6 mm.; no radii. The absence of radii may be due to their removal by the very deep erosion of the surface, which also gives the opercular valves a peculiar shape. It will probably turn out to be closely related to *B. amphitrite* or a variety thereof.

Balanus mirabilis Krüger. Abh. math-phys. Klasse der K. Bayer. Akad. der Wissensch. (vol. 2, Suppl.-Bd., 8 Abhandlg., 1912, p. 11). Japan. Diameter 20.5 mm.; the walls and opercular valves are very deeply eroded, and therefore no radii are visible. The peculiarly hollowed out tergal border of the scutum is due to erosion of the outer layer of the valve, and will not be present when unworn specimens are found. Affinities uncertain, but I fancy that it will turn out to be a form of *B. amphitrite*. It is not *Balanus perforatus*, var. *mirabilis* Darwin.

Balanus patellaris Spengler, Darwin, Monograph (p. 259).

b^2. Ribs of the parietes within all continuous with septa in the wall (pl. 40, fig. 4a).

  c^1. Spur short, near the basi-scutal angle of tergum.

    d^1. Adductor ridge of scutum strongly developed, remote from the pit of the lateral depressor muscle.

      e^1. Radii *narrow*, with *smooth*, oblique summits; walls smooth, white under a yellowish epidermis; spur of tergum one-fourth the width of the basal margin or less......................................*B. improvisus*, p. 84.

      e^2. Radii rather wide; walls white or colored; spur wider.

        f^1. Spur of tergum about one-third the width of the basal margin; basis conspicuously porous; diameter up to about 25 mm., usually much less...*B. amphitrite*, p. 89.

        f^2. Spur nearly one-half the basal width; basis with but few pores; sheath dark colored; diameter up to about 30 mm. Peru.

                                     B. peruvianus, p. 97.

    d^2. Adductor ridge of scutum short, a pit below it (pl. 43, figs. 4, 6, 7); spur of tergum very short, broad, and truncate; basis not porous. West coast of North America....................................*B. glandula*, p. 178.

    d^3. No adductor ridge in the scutum.

      e^1. Basis porous; walls smooth, fragile, dull red, freckled with white. West coast of South America.............................*B. pœcilus*, p. 110.

      e^2. Basis not porous; walls smooth or ribbed, white; opercular valves with strong articular ridges. Northern seas..............*B. crenatus*, p. 165.

  c^3. Spur wide at the base, tapering distally, rather remote from the basiscutal angle, and near the middle of the basal margin. Adductor ridge of scutum close to the pit for the lateral depressor muscle.

    d^1. Opercular valves white, thin; adductor ridge of scutum weakly developed. California...*B. flos*, p. 135.

    d^2. Opercular valves buff, solid; adductor ridge of scutum strong. West Coast.

                                       B. nubilis, p. 131.

NOTE.—*B. regalis*, p. 108, is not included in the above key, as its opercular valves are unknown.

SERIES OF B. AMPHITRITE.

BALANUS EBURNEUS Gould.

Plate 24, figs. 1–1c, 2.

1841. *Balanus eburneus* GOULD, Invertebrata of Massachusetts, p. 15, pl. 1, fig. 6.

1854. *Balanus eburneus* Gould, DARWIN, Monograph, p. 248, pl. 5, figs. 4a–4d.

1874. *Balanus eburneus* Gould, VERRILL, Invertebrate Animals of Vineyard Sound, p. 285, in Report of Commissioner of Fish and Fisheries, p. 579.

1897. *Balanus eburneus* A. Gould, WELTNER, Verzeichnis recenter Cirripedien-arten, p. 266.

1911. *Balanus eburneus* Gould, SUMNER, Bull. Bur. of Fisheries, vol. 31, p. 129, 302, 645, chart 84.

Type-locality.—Boston Bay, Massachusetts.

Distribution.—Massachusetts to the Caribbean coast of South America, low water to about 20 fathoms.

The barnacle is obliquely conic or sometimes shortly cylindric, smooth, with a very acutely ovate orifice. Parietes and opercular valves white, covered with light yellow epidermis, the radii white, without epidermis.

The scutum has rather fine, ripplelike growth-ridges crossed by *clearly cut radial grooves*. The articular ridge is very high and terminates in a free point. Adductor ridge high but short; there is a small ridge running parallel to it, near the depressor muscle insertion. The upper part of the valve is thickened and rough.

The tergum is broad, without an external furrow. The carinal margin is highly arched, having a sort of low appendage built upon it. Spur long, truncate at the end, and separated from the basiscutal angle by about half its own width. There is a deep or shallow bay in the basal margin on the carinal side of the spur, which, when fully developed, gives the valve a *three-pronged outline*, very characteristic of the species in its adult stage. The articular rib is moderately developed, the crests for the depressor muscles usually weak.

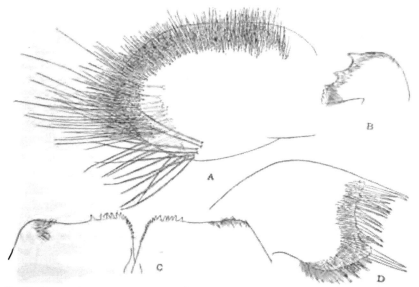

FIG. 14.—BALANUS EBURNEUS. *a*, PALPUS. *b*, MANDIBLE. *c*, LABRUM. *d*, MAXILLA. SMITH'S CREEK, POTOMAC RIVER.

The radii are wide, with oblique, *somewhat crenulated and irregular summits*. (See p. 85, fig. 16*b*.) The parietes have strong, regular internal ribs, the sides of which are usually minutely striated longitudinally. The parietal tubes are copiously provided with transverse septa, down to the base. There are usually 16 to 20 tubes in the rostrum. Hollows behind the sheath are very shallow. The carina stands steeper than the rostrum, and is sometimes recurved. The basis is very porous, pores large near the periphery and having transverse septa.

Labrum armed with numerous teeth, with series of smaller teeth running down the sides of the notch (fig. 14*c*). Palpi densely hairy in a broad band along the upper and distal borders, and having a series of long spines at the distal fourth (fig. 14a).

Mandible with three acute, widely spaced teeth, with three short, blunt teeth below (fig. 14b).

Maxilla has 17 spines, the smaller ones between the upper and lower larger pairs being pectinated. The lower pair stands on a long prominence, below which the margin is densely hairy (fig. 14d). A young specimen from Betterton, Maryland, 7 mm. diameter, has only 10 spines.

Cirrus i has very unequal rami of 31 and 19 segments, those of the shorter ramus very protuberant.

Cirrus ii has unequal rami of 21 and 16 segments, all protuberant.

Cirrus iii has 23 and 20 segments, the anterior ramus longer by six segments. All the segments of the outer ramus are protuberant, the

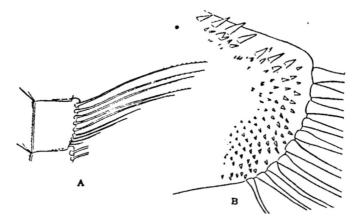

Fig. 15.—BALANUS EBURNEUS. a, 27TH SEGMENT OF CIRRUS VI. b, PROTUBERANT PORTION OF THE 13TH SEGMENT OF ANTERIOR RAMUS, CIRRUS III. SMITH'S CREEK, POTOMAC RIVER.

protuberance armed with a distal row of erect, spike-like spinules, a rather large anterior area set with many short, conic spinules (fig. 15b). The posterior ramus has long spines in place of the anterior patch of spinules, and a double subsutural row of erect spinules.

Cirrus iv has the anterior ramus armed like that of cirrus iii; posterior ramus without spinules.

Cirri v and vi have no spinules. The segments bear 7 to 9 pairs of spines, which as usual are pectinated near the end (fig. 15a).

This is one of the common species along the Atlantic seaboard, to be found wherever suitable situations offer standing room. Probably the scarcity of records from the West Indies and Gulf of Mexico is due to the small amount of shore collecting in those areas. The smooth, neat contour, rather wide radii with jagged summits (but often broken), the longitudinally striate scutum and pronged tergum are such easy recognition marks that no one need mistake the adult

barnacle for any other. Young specimens in which the sculpture of
the scutum and the emargination of the base of the tergum have not
been developed, are perhaps most easily recognized by examination of
the cirri, which differ from those of *improvisus*, *amphitrite* and *crenatus*,
species inhabiting the same waters.

B. eburneus and *B. improvisus* never develop ribs, and are never
colored.

B. eburneus has some superficial resemblance to small specimens
of *B. hameri*. It is closely related to *B. improvisus*, and small or
young individuals in which the tergum has not assumed the bird's-foot
shape, and the striæ of the scutum have not yet appeared, are often
extremely hard to distinguish from that species. Darwin writes:

I for some time mistook the var. *assimilis* of *B. improvisus* for the young of *B.
eburneus*. But I found in the latter that the rami of the first pair of cirri are always,
even in the earliest youth, more unequal in length, and that each segment of the
posterior cirri bears a greater number of pairs of spines, there being, even in very
minute specimens, seven pairs. Moreover, after having examined scores of specimens, I found I could almost always distinguish the two species by the smoothness
and curvature of the summits of the radii of *B. improvisus;* I entertain no doubt
whatever about the distinctness of the two species; indeed, when both are mature,
besides the greater size, striated scuta, etc., of *B. eburneus*, their general aspect is very
different.

B. eburneus varies but little. The basal margin of the scutum is
not always so hollowed out as in the individual figured; and of course
in quite young individuals it is not at all hollowed out. Pleistocene
examples from the Panama Canal Zone are quite similar to recent
ones from Massachusetts.

B. eburneus often lives in brackish water. I found small ones on
the piles at Betterton, near the head of Chesapeake Bay, where the
water is but slightly brackish, the fresh-water snails *Goniobasis* and
Amnicola living in it. "Professor Wyman found it living about 50
miles up the St. Johns River, Florida, where the water was fresh
enough to drink, and the specimens lived well when transferred to a
vessel of perfectly fresh water."

B. eburneus often attaches to ships' bottoms. No doubt the examples in the Jeffreys collection, taken by A. d'Orbigny at Rochelle,
were so transported. It has been reported by Herr Weltner from
Venice and Manila, but these records must have been based upon
ship-carried individuals.

It does not often form crowded or superposed masses, as many
species do, and is far oftener found on wood and oyster shells than on
rocks. Mr. Wm. J. Fox gave me examples taken from the screw of
his launch, in frequent use.

Dr. Benjamin Sharp took specimens 23½ mm. diameter from a
Nantucket boat which had been in the water 98 days, from June 13
to September 21. In a lot in the Museum, from a boat which had

been in water (Quissett Harbor) some 80 days (about July 1 to September 18), the largest are 20 mm. in diameter. Dr. F. B. Sumner has recorded specimens from 20 to 26 mm. in diameter, on the bottom of a whaleboat which had been moored within the inclosure of the pier at Woods Hole from May until November or December, 1908. It appears, therefore, to attain full size in a little over three months.

Locality.	Collector.	Notes.
Rochelle, France	D'Orbigny	Jeffreys coll.
Lynn, Mass	Dr. Prescott	
Boston, Mass	R. E. Griffith	A. N. S. P. coll.
Off Chatham, Mass. (13-20 fathoms)	Fish Hawk	
Nantucket, Mass	Dr. B. Sharp	Do.
"St. George Island"	M. C. M.	Do.
Waquoit Bay, Mass	U. S. Fish Commission	
Woods Hole, Mass	do	Many lots.
Quissett Harbor, Mass	do	
Vineyard Sound, Mass	do	Do.
Off Marthas Vineyard, Mass	do	
Buzzards Bay, Mass	do	
Off Newport, R. I	do	
Noank, Conn	do	
Long Island Sound	do	
Savin Rock, New Haven, Conn	R. Rathbun	
Seaside Park, N. J	H. L. Viereck	A. N. S. P. coll.
Near Port Republic, N. J	H. A. Pilsbry	Do.
Ocean City, N. J	H. W. Fowler	Do.
Sea Isle City, N. J	Wm. J. Fox	Do.
Beasleys Point, N. J	Dr. Benj. Sharp	Do.
Highland Beach, N. J	H. W. Fowler	Do.
Cape May, N. J	Isaac Lea	
Betterton, Md., near head of Chesapeake Bay	H. A. Pilsbry	Do.
St. Georges Island, Md	M. C. M.	
Ocean City, Md	H. W. Fowler	Do.
Smiths Creek, Potomac River, Md	R. D. Evans	Very large.
Chesapeake Beach, Va	H. D. Hance	On drift log.
Ocean View, Va	Helen Winchester	A. N. S. P. coll.
Fort Macon, N. C	Dr. H. C. Yarrow	
Charleston, S. C	I. Lea coll	
Mayport, Fla	M. A. Mitchell	Do.
Near mouth St. Johns River, Fla	Hon. F. E. Spinner	
Indian River, Fla	Dr. E. Palmer	
Tarpon Springs, Fla	Wm. M. Beakley	Do.
Pass Christian, Miss	E. M. Price	
Cuba	Isaac Lea coll	
Jamaica	C. B. Adams	
Near New Hope, Canal Zone (Pleistocene)	Dr. A. P. Brown	Do.

BALANUS IMPROVISUS Darwin.

Plate 24, figs. 3–3b, 5–5d.

1854. *Balanus improvisus* DARWIN, Monograph, p. 250, pl. 6, figs. 1a–1c, with var. *assimilis*, p. 250.

1869. *Balanus improvisus*, var. *gryphicus* MÜNTER, Mittheil. naturwissensch. Verein von Neu- Pommern und Rügen, vol. 1, p. 1. See METZGER, Nachrichtsblatt d. deutschen malak. Ges., vol. 10, 1878, p. 7–9.

1897. *Balanus improvisus* WELTNER, Verzeichnis recenten Cirripedienarten, p. 266.

1870. *Balanus improvisus* Darwin, CZERNIAVSKI, Zool. Record, p. 205 (Black Sea).

Type.—British Museum, from Kent, England.

Distribution.—Scotland to the ocean coast of France; Nova Scotia to southern Patagonia, Guayaquil, west Colombia, attached to wood, shells, rocks and ships' bottoms, from low tide to 20 fathoms depth (Darwin). Black Sea and Red Sea (Weltner).

The original description by Darwin is as follows:

General appearance.—Shell conical, with a rather large diamond-shaped orifice, moderately or but little toothed; very smooth; walls never folded longitudinally; white, with an extremely thin pale-yellow persistent epidermis. The radii are very narrow, with their summits very oblique, rounded, and smooth; the epidermis is generally more persistent on the radii than on other parts, and this is exactly the reverse of what is common with *B. eburneus.* The specimens from nearly fresh water in the River Plata are brownish and have undergone a remarkable degree of corrosion, the outer lamina of the walls having been entirely removed to near the base; hence the external aspect of these specimens is wholly different from ordinary individuals. The var. *assimilis* has also a very different appearance, owing to the dead white of the walls being relieved by narrow approximate longitudinal hyaline lines, corresponding with and caused by the longitudinal parietal septa being externally visible through the outer lamina of the parietes; the epidermis in the radii is

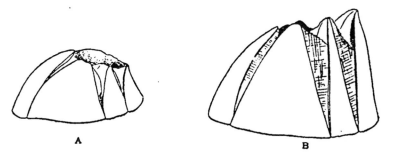

FIG. 16.—*a*, BALANUS IMPROVISUS x 3, QUINNEPIAC, MASS.; *b*, B. EBURNEUS x 2, OCEAN CITY, MD., TO ILLUSTRATE DIFFERENCE IN THE RADII.

also of a rather brighter yellow. The largest specimens which I have seen are those from the Plata and those attached to a ship from the West Indies, and they had a basal diameter of 0.6 of an inch—from 0.4 to 0.5 of an inch is the more usual full average size.

Scuta, with the lines of growth but little prominent; articular ridge prominent but little reflexed; adductor ridge straight and very prominent, varying a little in its distance from the articular ridge; there is scarcely any depression for the lateral depressor muscle; the upper internal surface of the valve is roughened with ridges.

Terga, with a moderately deep longitudinal furrow; spur short, rather narrow, with the end rounded, placed at less than its own width from the basiscutal angle; in the Rio Plata specimens the spur is close to this angle; the basal margin is generally straight on opposite sides of the spur, but sometimes on the carinal side is a little hollowed out. The lines of growth are upturned along the carinal margin, which consequently is a little protuberant, but to a varying degree. The crests for the depressors are extremely distinct and prominent. In the varieties having the basicarinal margin hollowed out, and the carinal margin protuberant, there is a marked resemblance to the peculiar tergum of *B. eburneus.*

Walls: The parietal pores are tolerably large and are crossed by numerous transverse septa; the longitudinal septa are very finely denticulated at their bases, but occasionally almost smooth. The radii are, as stated, extremely narrow, and very remarkable from their smooth rounded edges; their septa are barely denticulated. The alæ are remarkably protuberant; they have their summits much less oblique than those of the radii, and sometimes they are almost parallel to the basis; their sutural edges are coarsely crenated. Basis flat, thin, permeated by pores, but the pores do not generally run to the very center—they are, as usual, crossed by transverse septa. Mouth: The labrum is the most remarkable part. On each side of the central notch there are generally two teeth, and on the two sides of the notch itself nine or eleven smaller teeth, decreasing regularly in size downwards till they become so minute as to be hardly visible even under the compound microscope. Thus, in the two specimens closely examined, there were altogether twenty-two and twenty-six teeth on the labrum. Mandibles with the two inferior teeth reduced to mere knobs; maxillæ with the lower part of the edge bearing two large spines, and generally, but not always, forming a step-formed projection. Cirri: The rami of the first pair are but slightly unequal; in one specimen examined there were fifteen segments in one ramus and twelve in the other; segments very protuberant in front. Second cirrus with the segments only slightly protuberant; segments thirteen. Third cirrus longer than the second pair, with the rami rather unequal in length. There is a tuft of long spines on the basal segment of the pedicel of this cirrus. Fourth cirrus twenty-two segments. Sixth cirrus, in the same individual, thirty-four segments; on each of these segments there are five or six pairs of spines. I may specify that the longer ramus of the first cirrus of a large Rio Plata specimen had twenty-four segments.

English examples examined (pl. 24, figs. 3–3b) have the spur of the tergum more rounded distally than the American, which have the end of the spur obtuse or truncated, as in plate 24, figs. 5–5d. The external furrow of the tergum is variable; sometimes distinctly depressed, and again quite flat, but with grooves at the sides or on one side. On both sides of the Atlantic the shape varies from spreading and quite depressed to cylindric, higher than wide; always smooth, unless vicariously bearing the sculpture of a supporting shell, and always having exceptionally narrow radii, with steeply sloping, smooth summits.

Though widely distributed, this species is not common on the American coast, so far as my experience goes, and it is partial to somewhat brackish water. Darwin found it near Montevideo, in a stream where the running water was wholly fresh at low tide. Specimens were taken by Prof. E. B. Wilson on oyster shells in Quinnipiac River, Massachusetts, "below Grand Street Bridge, where the water is very brackish at low tide." It occurs, however, in pure sea water also.

B. improvisus is closely related to B. eburneus, but the latter differs by its striate scutum and pronged tergum when adult. The young eburneus, before striæ appear on the scutum, and before the characteristic shape of the tergum has developed, is excessively similar to improvisus; but in the latter the narrow radii have smooth, slightly arched summits, the rami of the first cirri are nearly of the same length, or at least not so conspicuously unequal as in B. eburneus and the posterior rami have not so many spines. There is also a conspicuous difference in the third cirri, the segments in B. eburneus being highly protuberant and set with small teeth. White forms of B. amphitrite differ from B. improvisus by their much broader radii, and they may be known by the more unequal rami of the first cirri, the armature of the third cirri, and the teeth of the labrum, which do not form a long, regularly graduated series, as is usual in *B. improvisus*. The spur of the tergum of *B. improvisus* is longer and narrower than that of *B. amphitrite niveus*, and it has the external furrow more developed, or at least distinctly indicated. *B. crenatus* differs from *improvisus* by wanting a distinct adductor ridge in the scutum, among various other differences. There are many lots of *improvisus* and related species which can be determined only by a deliberate examination of the whole animal.

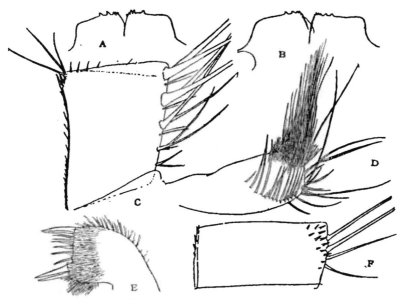

FIG. 17.—BALANUS IMPROVISUS, WINYAH BAY, SOUTH CAROLINA. *a, b,* LABRUM. *c,* MEDIAN SEGMENT OF CIRRUS VI. *d,* PALPUS. *e,* MAXILLA. *f,* OUTER FACE OF A SEGMENT OF CIRRUS III. *a* AND *f* ARE FROM ONE INDIVIDUAL, *b–e* FROM ANOTHER.

In a specimen from Quinnipiac River, Massachusetts, the first cirri have equal rami. Second cirri with subequal rami of 13 and 12 segments. Third cirri with rami of 15 and 12 segments, the longer projecting four segments beyond the shorter; *sides of the segments spinose, without teeth,* such as *B. amphitrite* has. The sixth cirri have five pairs of spines on the segments (fig. 17*c.*) The labrum has about 16 teeth on each side.

Specimens from *Fish Hawk* stations 1641–2, Winyah Bay, South Carolina, are small, though adult, the largest about 5 mm. in diameter, 5 to 7 mm. high, with subvertical walls and large orifice. Some of them show white lines, and in the upper two-thirds the transverse septa also show through. They grew on *Mytilus exustus* and on one another, and some show the sculpture of the shell.

The labrum (fig. 17b) has about 12 teeth on each side of the notch. Mandible as in *B. amphitrite*. Maxilla (fig. 17e), with six spines between the upper and lower pairs. It is like some specimens of *B. amphitrite niveus*, having the lower pair of large spines on a slight projection. The labral palpus (fig. 17d) is like that of *B. amphitrite niveus*, in having an external row of long spines, but the opposite face (not shown in the figure) has a very serried band of short spines directed toward the labrum, instead of a single row, as in *amphitrite*.

The first cirrus has rami of 19 and 14 segments, more unequal than usual, the posterior ramus about three-fourths as long as the anterior. Cirrus ii has slightly unequal rami of 12 and 10 segments. Cirrus iii has 15, 14 segments, but the posterior ramus is but little more than two-thirds as long as the anterior. The longer ramus has few long spines on the lower 9 segments, but there are a few short ones on and adjacent to the anterior margin (fig. 17f); also spines along the posterior outline. The inner faces of these segments have very few spines or none. The shorter ramus has armature like the longer on the lower five segments, but their inner faces are densely covered with long spines. The distal segments of both rami are densely covered with long spines. Cirrus vi has five pairs of spines, with some minute ones near their bases and along the posterior outline.

Another individual of the same lot has cirrus i with 18 and 12 segments, posterior ramus four-fifths the length of anterior. Cirrus ii, 11 segments on both rami, anterior ramus longer by two. Cirrus iii, 14 and 11 segments. The labrum (fig. 17a) has *only five teeth on each side*, so that at first I thought it could not be *improvisus;* but as all other characters are exactly like the others of the same colony examined, I am reluctantly obliged to admit that what was thought to be one of the most tangible differences between *improvisus* and *amphitrite* is not a wholly reliable criterion, though it holds in all other specimens I have dissected.

Locality.	Collector.	Notes.
South Downs	Rev. Mr. Sheldon	Jeffreys coll. Pl. 24, figs. 3-3b.
Rochelle, France	Jeffreys coll	On Solen.
Station 2057, east of Cape Cod (86 fathoms)	*Albatross*	Young only; identification not positive.
Quinnipiac River, Mass	E. B. Wilson	On oyster shells. Pl. 24, figs. 5-5d.
Queen Anne County, Md., opposite Chestertown.	E. G. Vanatta	Fresh-water stream; coll. A. N. S. P.
Chesapeake Beach, Va	Chas. S. Washington	On wood.
Sullivan's Island, S. C.	Wm. G. Mazyck	Coll. A. N. S. P.
Winyah Bay, S. C., Station 1641-2	*Fish Hawk* (1-3-1891)	Bottom temperature 50° F.
Savannah River, Ga	J. S. Raymond	On piles.
Jamaica	C. B. Adams	

BALANUS AMPHITRITE Darwin.

1789. *? Balanus radiatus* BRUGUIÈRE, Encyclopedie méthodique, p. 168.
1790. *? Lepas purpurea* SPENGLER, Skrivter af Naturhistorie Selskabet, vol. 1, p. 172.
1795. *Lepas balanoides* Linnæus, POLI, Testacea utriusque Siciliæ, p. 23, pl. 5, figs. 2–7. Not of Linnæus.
1815. *Lepas radiata* WOOD, General Conchology, pl. 7, fig. 7.
1815. *? Lepas minor* WOOD, General Conchology, pl. 7, fig. 6.
1854. *Balanus amphitrite* DARWIN, Monograph, p. 240, with varieties *communis, venustus, pallidus, niveus, modestus, stutsburi,* and p. 241, var. *obscurus, variegatus,* and *cirratus.*
1897. *Balanus amphitrite* Darwin, WELTNER, Verzeichnis, p. 264.
1907. *Balanus carenatus* GRUVEL, Mem. Asiatic Soc. of Bengal, vol. 2, No. 1, p. 6.
1913. *Balanus amphitrite* Darwin, HOEK, *Siboga*-Expeditie, Monographie 31*b*, p. 167, with var. *malayensis,* p. 172, pl. 14, figs. 8–17.

Distribution.—Tropical and warm temperate seas.

Next to *B. tintinnabulum,* this is the most widely distributed *Balanus,* and it is also variable with numerous races. I have attempted a revision of the American forms only. The concave carina and notched scutum which characterize *B. carenatus* are inconstant features in *amphitrite;* in fact, that form of carina is occasionally assumed by almost any *Balanus.* Whether *carenatus* is valid as a *variety* of *amphitrite* can be ascertained only when a revision of the oriental forms of the species is undertaken.

The typical form of *B. amphitrite* is that which Darwin called var. *communis,* and figured on plate 5, figures 2*e,* 2*h,* 2*l.* This form is a common barnacle in the Philippines.

In some Philippine forms of *amphitrite* the adductor ridge of the scutum is very much reduced, making a close approach to the condition found in *B. alatus* and *B. minutus.* of Hoek. These forms will be illustrated in a report on Philippine barnacles now in preparation.

Locality.	Collector.	Notes.
Sicily	Isaac Lea coll	
Macao, China	Dr. B	
Kowloon, China	Albatross	Shore.
Near Penang	E. Deschamps	
Singapore	...do	
Hull of barque from Straits of Malacca	Jeffreys coll	
Calcutta	Isaac Lea coll	
Dagupan, Luzon	Albatross	
Cavite, Luzon	...do	Ship's bottom.
Manila Bay, Luzon	...do	On shells and ship.
Do.	Dr. Bartsch	Outside breakwater.
Subig Bay, Luzon	...do	On *Strombus.*
Dagupan, Union, Luzon	...do	
Reef opposite Cebu	...do	On twigs.
Oton Beach, Panay	...do	
Mantaguin Bay, Palawan	...do	
Pamubatan, Mindanao	...do	Shore, on bamboo.
Batavia, Java	Bryant and Palmer	
Tamandjaija, Bantam, Java	...do	
Hawaiian Islands	Wm. A. Bryan	On a reed.
Pearl Harbor, Oahu	H. A. Pilsbry	On *Anomia* bed.

BALANUS AMPHITRITE ALBICOSTATUS, new subspecies.

Plate 20, figs. 1 to 4.

1911. *Balanus amphitrite*, var. *communis* Darwin, KRÜGER, Beiträge zur Cirripedienfauna Ostasiens, Abh. math.-phys. Klasse K. Bayer. Akad. Wiss.,
vol. 2, Suppl.-Bd., 6 Abhandlg., p. 51, fig. 102–104; pl. 1, fig. 7; pl. 4, fig. 40
(Hongkong, Dr. Schauinsland; Yokohama, Dr. Haberer). ?Also var. *niveus*
Darwin, KRÜGER, Abh. math.-phys. Klasse K. Bayer. Akad. Wiss., pl. 4,
fig. 35 (Making, Pescadores, Dr. Haberer).

Type.—Cat. No. 32950, U.S.N.M., from Japan.

Distribution.—Yedo Bay to Hongkong.

The barnacle tapers slightly to the ample rhombic orifice. Color
varying from dark Indian red to dark livid purple with *white ribs*,
which may be moderately prominent or barely raised. Sheath short,
purplish. *Radii very broad*, purplish or pink tinted, their summits
not very oblique.

The scutum has only weak traces of growth-ridges and very fine,
faint radial striæ. The articular ridge is half the length of the tergal
margin. The adductor ridge stands rather farther from the articular
ridge than in ordinary *amphitrite*. A sharp little fold, sometimes
doubled, divides the articular furrow.

The tergum is *narrow and long*. There is only a slight depression
running to the spur, which is narrow and typically long, separated
by its own width from the acute basiscutal angle, or nearer in some
lots. The carinal margin is short and arched, the basal margin
typically somewhat excavated on the carinal side of the spur. Crests
for the depressor muscles are strongly developed.

The basis has sharp radial ridges within. Parietal tubes have
numerous transverse septa in the upper part, but in the lower half
they are rather large and open. The longitudinal septa between the
tubes "bifurcate at their bases close to the outer lamina, making an
irregular row of minute pores," the degree of development of this
structure being variable.

Carinorostral diameter 16.5 mm.; height 10 mm.

Carinorostral diameter 14 mm.; height 10 mm.

Carinorostral diameter 12.5 mm.; height 8.5 mm.

The labrum has one very small tooth on one side, two on the other.
The margins of the notch are shortly hairy (fig. 18a).

The mandible (fig. 18b) has three strong teeth and two obtuse short
ones, *the lower point being irregularly spinose.*

The maxilla has nine spines below the upper pair, the lower pair
larger, and standing on a slight projection.

The cirri could be examined very imperfectly, as they were much
broken in the dry specimens. The posterior cirri have five pairs of
spines on the segments. Third cirri not found.

This form is known by several hundred individuals received from H. Loomis with the label Japan and a small lot labelled Yedo Bay. The former grew on small sticks, the base being concave in consequence; the Yedo Bay set lived on stone, and are more strongly ribbed, with flat bases. A small set from Shinagawa Bay, from the Imperial University of Tokyo, Cat. No. 32951, U.S.N.M., has one individual of the typical ribbed form and several having narrower radii and nearly smooth surface, without white ribs, but showing the white septa indistinctly on the purplish parietes. As none of them contain the opercular valves, I do not know whether these smoothish examples represent another subspecies or are a smooth phase of *B. a. albicostatus*.

Very rugged examples, the largest with a diameter of 20 mm., were sent from Hirado, province of Hizen, by Mr. Y. Hirase (No. 1518, A. N. S. P.). None contain the opercular valves. They grew on stone. It appears that the petricolous individuals of this race are more strongly ribbed than those on wood (pl. 20, fig. 4).

FIG. 13.—BALANUS AMPHITRITE ALBICOSTATUS. *a*, LABRUM AND *b*, MANDIBLE.

A group, without locality, from the North Pacific Exploring Expedition, Capt. John Rodgers, United States Navy, consists of strongly ribbed specimens, the largest 19 mm. in diameter, seated on a quartz pebble. The spur of the tergum is decidedly shorter and broader than in the type lot, but the valve has the same elongate shape (pl. 20, fig. 3).

The figures given by Doctor Krüger represent different forms of the tergum, such as are found in different colonies, but probably falling within the latitude of variation which must be allowed for a subspecies of *Balanus*. He figures the labrum with four teeth on each side, but with a hairy margin, as in my preparations. The number of teeth is highly variable in many species of *Balanus*.

I referred the specimens of *albicostatus* at first to *B. amphitrite stutsburi* Darwin, described from West Africa, on account of the narrow terga with long, narrow spurs. Several characters of the Japanese form, however, do not agree with Darwin's account, especially the very wide radii, the ribs of the wall, and the absence of epidermis. Darwin says of his *stutsburi* that the epidermis is persistent and the radii very narrow, and he does not mention any ribs. No other

known form of *B. amphitrite* is in the slightest degree ribbed.   It may
prove to be closely related to, or specifically identical with, *B. violaceus* Gruvel, described from specimens in the British Museum, the
locality unknown; but that form, from the description and figures,
differs from *albicostatus* by several minor details of the internal
structure of the scuta, and particularly by the terga, which "pré-
sentent extérieurement une série de plissements longitudinaux plus
ou moins profonds"—a structure quite absent in *B. a. albicostatus*.
In my opinion, *B. violaceus* would be better as a subspecies of *B.
amphitrite* than as a distinct species.   The name is preoccupied by
Gmelin, his *Lepas violacea* being a *Balanus*.

Whether *Balanus mirabilis* Krüger is an old specimen of *albicostatus* can not now be determined, since its hard parts are so extensively eroded that specific characters are largely obliterated, and
the cirri and other internal parts were destroyed.   There is no evidence that it was ribbed.   The characters of *B. mirabilis*, so far as
made out, are those of *B. amphitrite;* but it may have had other
features, now lost by corrosion.   Until differential features are shown
to exist, *B. mirabilis* may well be considered a synonym of *B. amphitrite*

BALANUS AMPHITRITE NIVEUS Darwin.

Plate 19, figs. 1 to 2e.

1854. *B. a.*, var. *niveus* DARWIN, Monograph, p. 240, pl. 5, fig. 2f.
1867. *Balanus improvisus*, var. *assimilis* DARWIN, and bastard, *B. armatus* and
    B. improvisus, var. *assimilis*, FRITZ MÜLLER, Archiv für Naturgeschichte,
    Jahrg. 33, vol. 1, pp. 329–356, pl. 7, figs. 22, 29–43; pl. 8, figs. 45, 49–51.
1912. *Balanus crenatus* Bruguiere, FOWLER, Crustacea of New Jersey, in Ann.
    Rep. N. J. State Mus. for 1911, pl. 46 (Cape May, N. J.).

Distribution.—Vineyard Sound, Massachusetts, to the Gulf of Mexico; Southern Brazil.   Low water to about 30 fathoms.[1]

"White, with longitudinal hyaline lines; epidermis not persistent."   Radii rather wide, with oblique, somewhat irregular summits.
Parietes smooth, ribbed inside, but slightly hollowed behind the
sheath; the parietal tubes having transverse septa in the upper part,
open below.   Basis thin, porous, except in the center.

Diameter 10 to 12 mm., often smaller.

Scutum finely ridged externally.   Articular ridge somewhat reflexed, more than half the length of the tergal margin, continued
downward in a ridge bounding the lateral depressor muscle pit.
Adductor ridge strong, but short.

Tergum level or with a slight depression running to the spur.
Interior roughened; articular ridge rather strong but not overhang-

---

[1] The distribution here given is what I have been able to verify from specimens in hand.   Darwin
gives some foreign localities; it would be well to confirm them by dissection of specimens.   Fritz Müller's
Balanus improvisus, var. *assimilis*, and his supposed bastard between that and *B. armatus*, are clearly
B. amphitrite niveus.   This extends the range southward to Santa Catharina Island, in southern Brazil.

ing. Spur short, its width over one-third that of the base; crests for depressor muscles strongly developed, projecting below the basal margin.

The labrum has three teeth on each side, one within the notch (fig. 19*f*). Labral palpi have two rows of spines, one of numerous small ones, the other of long spines; also the usual dense terminal covering of spines and bristles (fig. 19*e*).

The mandible has the two lower teeth short and blunt. (Fig. 19*c*.)

Maxilla with a nearly straight edge, and five spines between the upper and lower pairs of large spines (fig. 19*b*).

First cirrus of 18 and 12 segments, the posterior ramus two-thirds the length of the anterior, and having strongly protuberant segments.

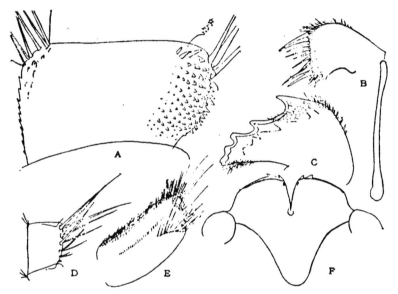

FIG. 19.—BALANUS AMPHITRITE NIVEUS, MARCO, FLORIDA. *a*, SEGMENT OF CIRRUS III. *b*, MAXILLA. *c*, MANDIBLE. *d*, INTERMEDIATE SEGMENT OF CIRRUS VI. *e*, PALPUS. *f*, LABRUM.

Cirrus ii of 13 and 11 segments, strongly protuberant, the posterior ramus three-fourths as long as the anterior. Cirrus iii with the anterior, outward part of the lower nine segments thickly set with short, conic, decurved teeth (fig. 19*a*); the inner faces of these segments having long spines, not shown in the figure. The posterior margins of the segments are also shortly spinose. The outer ramus is two or three segments longer than the inner. The succeeding cirri are much alike. Cirrus vi has 28 segments bearing five pairs of spines, a few median segments having a minute sixth pair (fig. 19*d*). The above description is from specimens from Marco, Florida (pl. 19, figs. 2–2*e*).

The definition of subspecies of *B. amphitrite* is a very intricate problem, demanding more time and material than I can command,

and first of all, the Darwin collection must be restudied and type localities for his varieties selected. Large series from single colonies must be dissected, in order to ascertain the constancy of the peculiar features of the third cirri, which Darwin did not notice. After working more than a week upon the American specimens, my impression is that the armature of the cirri varies a good deal; yet there may possibly be more than one race in the Atlantic coast series I have grouped under *B. a. niveus*, or two or three races may be mingled in a hybrid population. In many lots the gray lines of the parietes are faint, or they may persist only on the carina; sometimes they can not be made out; these variations occurring in the same colony. In most of the northern and some southern examples the epidermis persists over both parietes and radii, as in var. *pallidus* Darwin; and these forms do not agree with Darwin's definition of his var. *niveus;* yet to separate them from others of the same neighborhoods which are nude when adult would be an arbitrary course. In most of the Florida colonies there are a few individuals with lavender or violaceous tinted parietes, or with the lines lavender or plumbeus rather than gray; but these colors do not appear in the lots from north of Delaware. It may be noted that Darwin gives Florida among his localities for variety *niveus*.

A diameter of over 10 mm. is rare north of Hatteras.

B. a. niveus is one of the most abundant barnacles where suitable bottom is found, coating wood and especially shells in prodigious numbers, as far north as Vineyard Sound. It does not go, apparently, north of Cape Cod. The wide radii of these northern examples differentiate them readily from the much rarer *B. improvisus;* but externally they are not readily distinguishable from young *B. eburneus*.

Sarasota Bay, Florida.—Most specimens are white with gray lines and white radii, but scattered among them are individuals of various lavender tints, or with the lines lavender tinted, radii sometimes pink. The colored individuals are connected with the white by others of nicely graduated tints. The scuta are dark in some individuals, whether the walls are dark or light. Epidermis very thin or wanting. Maximum diameter about 12 mm.

Marco, Florida.—A second set from this place has the labrum, palpi, mandible, and posterior cirri as described above. The maxilla has seven spines between the upper and lower pairs. The first cirrus has 18 and 13 segments (fig. 20c). Cirrus ii, 15 and 13 segments, rami subequal. Cirrus iii has 15 and 13 segments, the anterior ramus about three segments longer. The anterior ramus has 10 segments set with short, conic teeth, and some longer twin spines distally (fig. 20b). Posterior ramus with nine armed segments (fig. 20a).

Pine Key, Florida.—Similar to the Marco lots and intermediate between them. The labrum has two and three teeth on the two sides.

Maxilla with six spines between upper and lower pairs. Cirrus iii with a few twin spinules, intermediate between figures 19a and 20b. Cirrus vi has five pairs of spines.

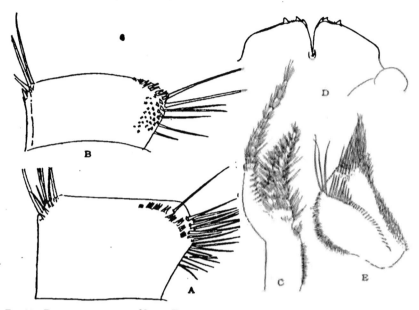

FIG. 20.—B. AMPHITRITE NIVEUS, MARCO, FLA. a, 9TH SEGMENT POSTERIOR RAMUS OF CIRRUS III. b, 6TH SEGMENT ANTERIOR RAMUS CIRRUS III. c, 1ST CIRRUS. d, LABRUM. e, PALPUS.

Cedar Keys, Florida.—Maxilla with five spines between upper and lower pairs, the latter standing on a little projection. Otherwise like Marco *niveus*.

Rehoboth, Delaware.—*Cuticle thin but persistent* on parietes and radii. Gray lines distinct. In some examples the carina has a

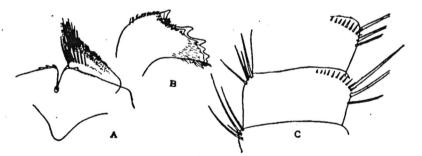

FIG. 21.—B. AMPHITRITE NIVEUS, REHOBOTH, DEL. a, LABRUM AND PALPUS. b, MANDIBLE. c, TWO SEGMENTS FROM THE POSTERIOR RAMUS OF CIRRUS III.

violet tint. Scutum with the ridge below the articular ridge weak, adductor ridge strong and longer than in Marco individuals. Labrum with two-notch-three teeth. Cirrus i, 17 and 11 segments. Cirrus ii, 12 and 10 segments, the posterior ramus three-fourths as long as the anterior. Cirrus iii with 11 and 10 segments, the posterior three-fourths as long as the anterior. The basal seven segments of both rami here are armed with short spines in a row near the distal border (fig. 21c), but there are no scattered teeth.

Vineyard Sound (pl. 19, figs. 1–1e).—The epidermis is persistent. Spur of the tergum usually longer and narrower than in Marco *niveus*, sometimes pointed. Labrum with three teeth on each side. Maxilla with five spines between the upper and lower pairs, edge straight. Cirrus iii as in fig. 20 a, b. Posterior cirri as in Marco *niveus*.

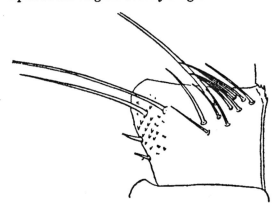

FIG. 22.—B. AMPHITRITE NIVEUS, VINEYARD SOUND. INNER FACE OF THE EIGHTH SEGMENT OF THE OUTER RAMUS OF CIRRUS III, SHOWING THE SHORT TEETH OF THE OUTSIDE BY TRANSPARENCE.

Vineyard Sound, 21553, U.S.N.M. Cirrus iii has few teeth, the posterior ones very minute and in groups of two or three (fig. 22, eighth segment of outer ramus, inner face; showing the short teeth of the outside by transparence).

Locality.	Collector.	Notes.
Off Falmouth, Mass.	*Fish Hawk*	
Woods Hole, Mass.	U. S. Fish Commission	7–13 fathoms.
Do.	F. B. Sumner	
Vineyard Sound, Mass.	U. S. Fish Commission	Several lots.
Stations 2250, 2260, off Marthas Vineyard	*Albatross*	Do.
Station 1177, east of Marthas Vineyard	*Fish Hawk*	3–7 fathoms.
Off Newport, R. I. (12–13 fathoms)	U. S. Fish Commission	Several lots.
Newport, R. I.	Sam Powel	On Crepidula.
Loc. 850, Narragansett Bay, R. I.	*Fish Hawk*	14½ fathoms.
Noank, Conn.	U. S. Fish Commission	On Crepidula.
Cape May, N. J.	C. Le Roy Wheeler	On Fulgur, etc.
Smiths Island, Northampton County, Va.	Chas. W. Richmond	
Beaufort Harbor, N. C.	Wm. Stimpson	
Station 2284–5–6, 2277, 2290, off Cape Hatteras (10–16 fathoms).	*Albatross*	On shells.
Charleston Bay, S. C.	Wm. Stimpson	On Fulgur.
Stations 2274, off St. Johns River, Fla.	*Albatross*	16 fathoms.
Pass-a-Grille reef, Pine Key, Fla.	H. Hemphill	On Fasciolaria.
Pine Key, Fla.	do	On Strombus.
Marco, Fla.	do	On Fasciolaria, Crepidula, and Fulgur perversum.
Sarasota Bay, Fla.	do	On Fasciolaria and Fulgur.
Tampa Bay, Fla.	*Fish Hawk*	On *Portunus gibbesii*.
Clearwater Harbor, Fla.	H. A. Pilsbry	A. N. S. P. coll.
Cedar Keys, Fla.	H. Hemphill	
Do.	*Str. Bache*.	
Station 2369–74, Gulf of Mexico, off Cape San Blas, west Florida.	*Albatross*	25–27 fathoms.
Fergusons Pass, Fla.		
Near Havana, Cuba.	S. R. Roberts	Coll. A. N. S. P.
Honduras.	T. W. Stanton	
10 miles east of north end of Patros Island, Brazil.	*Norseman*	34 fathoms.

BALANUS AMPHITRITE INEXPECTATUS, new subspecies.

Plate 20, figs. 5 to 5e.

A series of about 40 specimens from the Gulf of California, Cat. No. 12398, U.S.N.M., the largest 15 mm. in diameter, was collected by Dr. E. Palmer. They grew on oyster shells. The shape is low-conic, with diamond-shaped orifice, with an even margin. The smooth parietes are of a dull purplish-blue (Ranier blue) color, with many indistinct, whitish, radial lines, the radii white and drab, with summits parallel to the base. The interior is strongly costate. Basis porous throughout, radially grooved inside.

Scutum with the basal margin longer than the tergal; dull dark-purplish, with a white band along the tergal margin, and an irregular whitish ray near the occludent margin. There are minute growth-striæ and faint longitudinal scratches. The articular rib is very high and prominent, terminating downward in a point. Adductor ridge long and strong; *below it is a deep oblong pit,* as if for a muscle-insertion. There is a very small pit for the lateral depressor muscle. The upper part of the valve is conspicuously roughened.

Tergum white, flat externally, the rather broad spur-fasciole defined by grooves. *Spur wide, over one-third the width of the valve,* short, either rounded or truncate distally, separated from the basi-scutal angle by less than half its own width. Crests for the depressor muscles are strong and project below the margin. The inner face of the valve is roughened. Articular ridge high, articular furrow wide and rather deep. Scutal border rather broadly inflected.

Possibly referable to the very inadequately described var. *obscurus* Darwin, which, from the alleged distribution, I suspect to be merely a color-form and not a race; yet as Darwin records no specimens of *amphitrite* from the west coast of the Americas, it is not likely that he had the present race.

BALANUS AMPHITRITE PERUVIANUS Pilsbry.

Plate 24, fig. 4; plate 37, figs. 2–2c.

1909. *Balanus peruvianus* PILSBRY, Proc. U. S. Nat. Mus., vol. 37, p. 69, fig. 1, pl. 19, figs. 1–4 (October 18).

Cotypes.—Cat. Nos. 38691 and 38692, U.S.N.M.

Distribution.—Salt creeks at La Palasada, near Tumbez, Peru, growing on mangroves.

General form conic, with flat or concave base and rather small aperture; dirty purplish white or pale dull purple, radii usually darker; *very solid* and strong. The parietes are smoothish, without ribs, and only minutely roughened. The aperture is pentagonal, with a strongly notched margin. Traces of a thin, pale straw-colored epidermis are visible near the base. The parietes have small pores near the base, and the basis, in large part solid, has some rounded pores near and at the periphery.

The scutum is nearly half as wide as long, dirty white externally, suffused with dark quaker drab toward the apex, with a ray of the same near the tergal margin; sculpture of narrow, shallow grooves, with wider flat intervals, which in the lower part bear membranous borders from former opercular membranes. The articular ridge is very high and oblique, abruptly truncated below, its inner face striate. An acute ridge defining the lateral depressor muscle insertion runs downward from it. Adductor ridge very strong but short, nearer to the occludent than to the tergal margin, confluent above with the articular rib. Adductor muscle insertion deep. Articular furrow deep.

The tergum is bicolored, the carinal half deep quaker drab, scutal half white. Surface marked with superficial grooves of growth and the faintest traces of radial striæ. There is no furrow to the spur, but

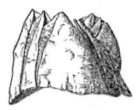

FIG. 23.—BALANUS AMPHITRITE PERUVIANUS, LATERAL VIEW.

the flat fasciole is defined by impressed lines. The scutal border is a little turned up. The spur is short, truncated distally, over one-third the width of the basal margin, and separated from the basi-scutal angle by about half its width. The articular rib is rather strong and runs toward the spur, leaving a broad articular furrow. The scutal margin of the valve is broadly inflexed. The carinal half of the interior is granose-striate. Crests for the depressor muscles are strongly developed, terminating in little teeth projecting at the basal margin.

Compartments: The radii have *strongly oblique summits* and are thick to the edge, which has fine, nearly straight, long, parallel, weakly denticulate septa. The alæ are thin, with oblique summits; sutural edges finely septate, the septa very regular, minutely denticulate. The parietal pores are small, circular, and filled up solidly in the upper part. A transverse section midway of a compartment shows them partially filled, reduced to very small tubes. The inner faces of the parietes below the sheath have strong, rounded, smooth ribs, terminating below in minutely denticulate basal laminæ. The number of internal ribs is smaller than usual, 12 in a rostrum examined, 5 in a carinolateral compartment. The *sheath is purplish gray*, with a darker lower border, strongly ridged transversely, the ridges bearing minute fringes of bristles. Its lower edge overhangs shallow cavities.

The basis clings very firmly to the walls, and can not be parted from them without breaking the interlocking laminæ. It has some pores near the periphery, at least in places, but is *in great part pore-less*. Central portion is thin.

Carinorostral length of the base 31 mm,; width 28.5 mm.; height 23 mm. Length of the scutum 10.5 mm.; width 5 mm. Length of the tergum 8 mm.; width 5 mm.

The labrum has two teeth on each side of the median cleft. Palpi having a distal group of long spines externally. Inside there is a

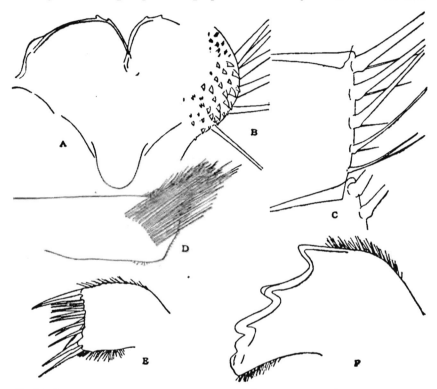

Fig. 24.—BALANUS AMPHITRITE PERUVIANUS. *a*, LABRUM. *b*, ANTERIOR PART OF 8TH SEGMENT OF CIRRUS III. *c*, ANTERIOR PART OF AN INTERMEDIATE SEGMENT OF CIRRUS VI. *d*, OUTSIDE OF PALPUS. *e*, MAXILLA. *f*, MANDIBLE.

long area of short spines, part of them curved or hooked, and a distal tuft of longer spines. It is similar to *B. amphitrite niveus* (fig. 21*a*) in arrangement of the spines (fig. 24*a*, *d*).

The mandible has blunt teeth, the fourth and fifth very short and obtuse (fig. 24*f*).

The maxilla has 12 spines and scarcely any notch below the upper pair of large spines. The lower two spines are longer (fig. 24*e*).

The first cirrus has rami of 26 and 14 segments, those of the posterior ramus strongly protuberant. The posterior ramus is about two-thirds as long as the anterior.

The second cirrus has 23 and 16 segments, protuberant on both rami. The anterior ramus is about 5 segments longer.

The third cirrus has rami of 20 and 17 segments. The anterior ramus has recurved teeth on the anterior side of the first nine segments, and there are some erect spinules near the anterior distal angle on most of the segments. The posterior ramus has very few straight teeth on a few of the lower segments (fig. 24b).

Cirrus iv has no teeth or spinules on the segments.

Cirrus vi has five pairs of spines on the median segments, with a few small spines springing between the large spines of the upper four pairs (fig. 24c). Lowest pair is much smaller than the others. The penis is about equal to the posterior cirri in length.

I at first described this form as a distinct species, but a larger acquaintance with this group of *Balanus* induces me to reduce it to subspecific rank, although it is as distinct from *amphitrite* as several East Indian forms described as species. At present we know very little about west American forms of the *amphitrite* group—only what is contained in this work—and the final status of the several forms existing from Lower California and Peru can not be foreseen.

B. a. peruvianus is closely related to *B. amphitrite*, but it differs in the following characters: (1) It is a much stronger barnacle, with the parietal tubes filled up solidly, except close to the base. (2) The basis clings strongly to the walls and has very few pores. (3) The sheath is dark colored. (4) The tergum is flat outside, and has a wider spur. Finally, it reaches a larger size.

The opercular valves are variegated with dark rays or areas, as in dark forms of *B. amphitrite*. The mouth parts and cirri do not differ materially from those of *B. amphitrite*. The pores of the parietes are filled up except close to the base, and might readily be overlooked. The basis is not solid, as I stated in the original description. It has distinct pores, near the periphery only, which did not appear in the sections I made at first. They may be seen in plate 24, figure 4, which shows part of the basis adhering to the rostrum.

BALANUS CONCAVUS Bronn.

Plate 21, figs. 1–1c.

1831. *Balanus concavus* BRONN, Italiens Tertiär Gebilde und deren organische Einschlüsse, p. 127.

1838. *Balanus concavus* BRONN, Lethæa Geognostica, vol. 2, p. 1155, pl. 36, fig. 12a–e.

1854. *Balanus concavus* Bronn, DARWIN, Monograph, p. 235, pl. 4, figs. 4a–e. Monograph on the Fossil Balanidæ and Verrucidæ of Great Britain, p. 17, pl. 1, figs. 4a–p.

1904. *Balanus concavus* Bronn, G. C. MARTIN, Maryland Geological Survey, Miocene, p. 94, pls. 33, 34 (=*B. c. chesapeakensis*).

1906. *Balanus concavus* Bronn, De Alessandri, Palæontographia Italica, vol. 12, p. 295, pl. 16, figs. 21–25; pl. 17, figs. 1–4.

Type-locality.—Andona Valley, near Asti, Piedmont. Pliocene.

Distribution.—Oligocene to Pleistocene of Italy. Pliocene of England and Portugal. Various races or subspecies in the Miocene and Pliocene of the United States. Other races recent from California to Peru and in the Philippines.

Balanus concavus, in the broad sense, was an abundant barnacle throughout the Neocene in both hemispheres. In the Miocene, when our definite information begins, there were several strongly individualized races, possibly species, but here ranked as subspecies. These continued, in their several areas, into the Pliocene with more or less change; in the Mediterranean basin they endured into the Pleistocene. The total disappearance of the group from Recent Atlantic faunas does not seem explicable at present.

The typical form of *B. concavus*, as figured by Bronn and recently treated in detail by De Alessandri, is conic or convexly conic, with the orifice more or less contracted, or often cylindric with large orifice. The summits of the radii are very oblique, and the parietes are usually ribbed, not very strongly, or variously roughened. Sometimes it is smooth. The Pliocene examples often show color-stripes. De Alessandri, who studied Italian specimens from Oligocene (Tongrian of Sardinia) to Pleistocene, does not record any change throughout the duration of the species in that area—a remarkable constancy if really the fact. I believe, however, that he had not seen the opercular valves of the Oligocene form.

The British Red Crag examples (pl. 21, figs. 1, 1c, from the Jeffreys collection, Cat. No. 12058, U.S.N.M.) are practically typical, but they perhaps vary somewhat from the Italian by having the tergum sometimes narrower, with a longer spur. My plate 21, figure 1b, is very similar to one of De Alessandri's figures (pl. 4, fig. 21) of a topotype.

The scutum has rather coarsely latticed sculpture, the longitudinal striæ often divided, and obsolete on the roundly inflected tergal margin. The basitergal angle is cut off. The adductor ridge is quite short and not very prominent. The inner border of the rather deeply sunken depressor muscle pit is slightly prominent, but not raised into a ridge.

This European form was an abundant Pliocene barnacle of that area, where it seems to have existed almost to the present time. It has not been found in America, where various other races of the species existed, and is noticed here merely for comparison with the latter.

Our definite knowledge of East American barnacles of the *concavus* type begins with the Miocene, continuing to the Pliocene, when the species became extinct in this area.[1] It appears that two phyletic series are represented, strongly differentiated from their first appearance, and both differing from any European forms known to me. In the *glyptopoma* series the scutum is narrower, more strongly sculptured than European *concavus*. In the *proteus* series it is wider, more delicately sculptured. The sequence of known forms is about as follows:

	Europe.	Eastern America.		West America.
Recent.......	....	....	?regalis	pacificus
Pleistocene....	concavus...	....		pacificus
Pliocene.......	concavus	Alligator Creek form	glyptopoma	
Miocene......	concavus	proteus	glyptopoma	? cooaensis
		chesapeakensis		
Oligocene.....	concavus			

BALANUS CONCAVUS GLYPTOPOMA, new subspecies.

Plate 21, figs. 2, 3; plate 22, figs. 2–2c.

In the Yorktown, Virginia, Miocene there is a rugged, small-ribbed form (pl. 21, fig. 3) resembling the typical *B. balanus* superficially, and reaching a diameter of about 25 mm. There are fully 20 pores in the rostrum. The opercular valves resemble those of the following form, which may fairly be considered a direct descendant.

The typical *B. c. glyptopoma* of the Caloosahatchie Pliocene (pl. 21, fig. 2; pl. 22, figs. 2–2c) has rather numerous small ribs on the parietes, sometimes weak or nearly obsolete, and not stronger toward the apices. The orifice is large, the summits of the radii not very oblique. Carinorostral diameter 20 to 37 mm. The scutum is sculptured with strong growth-ridges cut into high, erect nodes by the rather deep longitudinal striæ. This sculpture is coarser than in other subspecies of *B. concavus*. The tergal side is abruptly bent nearly at right angles with the rest of the valve, is deeply grooved, but without nodes. The adductor ridge is strong but rather short.

The tergum has a short, obliquely truncate spur.

---

[1] I have seen some American Oligocene barnacles probably belonging to the *concavus* stock, but without opercular valves.

Prof. Gruvel has recorded *B. concavus* as recent from Rio Janeiro, on the evidence of specimens in the Paris Museum, collected by Delalande 1817. As there is no other Atlantic record, this requires confirmation. See Nouv. Arch. du Mus., ser. 4, vol. 5, p. 136.

BALANUS CONCAVUS PROTEUS Conrad.

Plate 22, figs. 3–3c.

1834. *Balanus proteus* CONRAD, Journal of the Academy of Natural Sciences of Philadelphia, vol. 7, p. 134 (James River, Suffolk; Yorktown, Virginia).

1845. *Balanus proteus* CONRAD, Fossils of the Medial Tertiary of the United States, No. 3, p. 77, pl. 44, fig. 1 (Prince George Co., Virginia).

A large, solid, conic form, with small, angular, and deeply toothed orifice, and very strong, unequal ribs, resembling the *geniculatus* form of *B. balanus*. The summits of the radii slope steeply. The opercular valves are thin and frail for so solid a barnacle. Scutum with *much finer, more delicate external sculpture* than Crag *concavus*, the longitudinal grooves shallower; tergal marginal inflection narrower; articular ridge delicate. Adductor ridge usually somewhat better developed than in Crag *concavus;* and there is a slightly raised edge to the depressor muscle pit. The tergum is wider than that of typical *concavus*. It commonly grows on oysters or the large Pectens, often in very fine groups.

B. c. proteus seems to have persisted to the Pliocene in a somewhat changed form. A barnacle from the Floridian Pliocene of Alligator Creek is very solid and strong; aperture contracted, but less than in *B. c. proteus;* parietes ribbed throughout or near the apices only. Opercular valves not seen. Diameter 50 to 60 mm., height somewhat greater.

BALANUS CONCAVUS CHESAPEAKENSIS, new subspecies.

Plate 22, figs. 1–1c.

1890. *Balanus convexus*, American Naturalist, p. 771 (presumably an error for *concavus;* no description).

1904. *Balanus concavus* Bronn, MARTIN, Maryland Geological Survey, Miocene, p. 94, pl. 33, figs. 1–6; pl. 34, figs. 1–7.

Type.—No. 1143, A.N.S.P.

Distribution.—St. Marys and Choptank formations, Miocene of Maryland.

A large, solid barnacle, with small orifice, the parietes having few, strong ribs near their apices, becoming broader and lower downward until they disappear, and with a peculiar fine sculpture as if shriveled; radii sunken, slitlike in the lower part.

Diameter 57 mm., height 44 mm.

Scutum having fine, unequal, longitudinal striæ over the rather low and wide growth-ridges, about as in *B. c. proteus*. Ridges of the inner face more developed than in *B. concavus* or *proteus;* adductor ridge long, high in the middle. The large and deep pit for the lateral depressor muscle has a strongly raised bordering ridge, which is parallel to the adductor ridge, and nearer it than to the tergal margin.

Tergum triangular, with a long spur more than its own width from the basiscutal angle. The spur is continued as a rounded ridge on the inner face of the valve; borders of the external furrow folded closely together. This appears to be a lateral branch of the *B. c. proteus* stock.

Balanus finchii Lea, from St. Marys, Maryland),[1] may be a very young specimen of this race, but it is smooth, and the opercular valves are unknown. The young of *chesapeakensis* should be strongly costate.

There are probably one or more races of the *concavus* group in the Atlantic slope Miocene, in addition to those already mentioned. Darwin's figures, 4*h*, 4*i*, 4*k*, represent a Maryland form unlike any I have seen. The subject deserves further investigation with much more material than I can command.

BALANUS CONCAVUS PACIFICUS, new subspecies.

Plate 23, figs. 1–2c.

Type.—Cat. 32953, U.S.N.M., from San Diego, California.

Distribution.—Northern California to Callao, Peru; Pliocene and Pleistocene of California.[2]

The barnacle is conical (or cylindric), with a diamond-shaped orifice with the peritreme but slightly toothed; smooth, the wide radii but slightly sunken; striped with vinaceous or deep vinaceous on a much paler or white ground, the radii and sheath vinaceous or white. Epidermis thin and transparent, usually persistent on the parietes. The opercular valves have more or less vinaceous coloring, chiefly inside and near the apices.

Greatest diameter 34 mm.; height 20½ mm. (type, pl. 23, fig. 1).

Greatest diameter 25 mm.; height 55 mm. (cylindric; San Pedro).

Greatest diameter 22 mm.; height 26½ mm. (cylindric; Crescent City).

Greatest diameter 18 mm.; height 9 mm. (conic; Crescent City).

The scutum has rather low growth-ridges and *close, unequal, radial striæ throughout.* The articular ridge is small, reflexed and not much over half as long as the tergal margin. *Adductor ridge high and long,* approaching the basal margin. A thin but high ridge bounds the lateral depressor muscle insertion, its crest usually curving toward it, to form an imperfect tube.

The tergum is broad, triangular, with a nearly closed furrow to the spur. Spur rather long, separated by its own width or less from the basiscutal angle. The scutal border is but slightly inflected. Crests for the depressor muscles are moderately developed, weakening near the basal margin. Articular ridge is low.

---

[1] Contr. to Geol., p. 211, pl. 6, fig. 222.   [2] See Arnold, Mem. Cal. Acad. Sci., vol. 3, 1903, p. 344.

Compartments.—The radii are wide, with the summits making angles of about 45 degrees with the base in young or small individuals, large ones having nearly horizontal summits; sutural edge with the laminæ denticulate below. Interior of parietes ribbed. *Parietal tubes very numerous*, about 20 in the rostrum, *without transverse septa*, but filled up near the apices.

The basis clings very firmly to the walls. It is porous throughout, and in large specimens the lower part is somewhat vesicular, though it is nowhere very thick.

The labrum of *B. concavus* has three teeth on each side of the notch, according to Darwin; but in that from Long Beach (fig. 25c) there

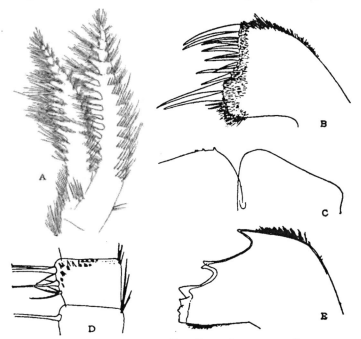

FIG. 25.—BALANUS CONCAVUS PACIFICUS, LONG BEACH, CALIFORNIA. *a*, SECOND CIRRUS OF LEFT SIDE. *b*, MAXILLA. *c*, LABRUM. *d*, 11TH SEGMENT OF THE ANTERIOR RAMUS OF CIRRUS III. *e*, MANDIBLE.

are none on one side and the outer one on the other side is bifid or twinned. Such asymmetry in the labrum is so frequent as to be hardly anomalous. In a specimen from *Albatross* station 2939 there were two excessively minute teeth on one side, none on the other.

The mandible has four teeth, the fifth united with the lower point. The bifid tip of the second tooth in figure 25e is similar in both mandibles of the individual figured. In a specimen from station 2939 (fig. 26b) the second tooth is minutely bifid on one side, simple on the other, and the third and fourth teeth are very obtuse. This tooth is often more or less noticeably bifid in other species of the group.

Maxilla (fig. 25b) with nine spines between the upper and lower large pairs, the lower pair standing on a projection, in a Long Beach individual, but this is scarcely noticeable in that from station 2939.

The first cirrus in a specimen from Long Beach has 18 and 16 segments, the anterior ramus slightly longer, the posterior having extremely protuberant segments. Cirrus ii has subequal rami of 15 and 14 extremely protuberant segments (fig. 25a). Cirrus iii, anterior ramus, has a few long "teeth" or rather short, spikelike spines on the outer face of each segment near its anterior border. Those farther from the anterior border are often twinned. By focusing down, some excessively small spines, in groups of three or four, may be seen close to the distal suture. The posterior ramus has no such armature. The

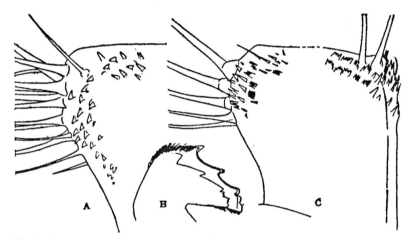

Fig. 26.—BALANUS CONCAVUS PACIFICUS, STATION 2939. a, ANTERIOR PART OF THE 13TH SEGMENT OF THE FORWARD RAMUS OF CIRRUS III. b, MANDIBLE. c, ANTERIOR AND POSTERIOR PARTS OF THE 8TH SEGMENT.

inner faces of the segments of both rami bear long spines. The fourth cirri have no teeth. Later cirri have segments with four pairs of spines.

In a larger example, from *Albatross* station 2939, the third cirrus has its outer face set with curved, conic teeth on the anterior ramus (fig. 26a), and with similar teeth mingled with bifid, trifid, or comb-like teeth (fig. 26c) on the posterior ramus, the teeth grouped near the anterior and posterior distal angles of each segment. The fourth cirrus has a few small erect spinelike teeth on the anterior distal part of the lower segments of the anterior ramus.

One of the large specimens from station 2939 has rather strong rounded ribs in the lower half of the parietes, the upper half being ribless and pink striped. Others of the same lot are typical in sculpture (pl. 23, figs. 2–2c).

Its wide terga and the nearly level summits of the radii give this west coast barnacle the appearance of *B. tintinnabulum*. In these characters it certainly differs widely from the original *B. concavus*, which had a very deeply toothed orifice and narrow terga. No estimate of the relation it bears to the very large barnacle of the Oregon Miocene (*coosensis* Dall) can be formed until the opercular valves of the latter are found. Darwin's plate 4, figures 4a–4c, from Panama, belongs, I believe, to the Californian race, but I have not seen any Panamic or Peruvian specimens.

B. concavus pacificus attains a size much greater than *B. amphitrite;* the scuta differ by their longitudinal striation, the terga by the longer spur and the well-developed, more or less infolded furrow of the exterior. The rami of the first cirrus are but slightly unequal in length, while in *B. amphitrite* they are very unequal. Finally, the armature of the third cirri is less developed in *concavus*.

Of the variations of *B. concavus pacificus* in California it need only be said that when crowded the cylindric form is assumed. The details of the mouth parts and cirri are from a specimen of 15 mm. diameter from Long Beach, one of a group on *Trophon triangularis*. Specimens from Santa Maria Bay, on the western coast of Lower California, are more solid than the type, deep hellebore red with coral pink radii, having some resemblance to *B. tintinnabulum coccopoma*. The opercular valves are wanting.

In the specimens from *Albatross* Station 2939, near Newport, California (pL 23, figs. 2–2c), both scutum and tergum are narrower than in the type. The adductor ridge is more united with the articular ridge above, and the articular furrow is deep, bridging over the pit of the depressor muscle, which thus becomes tubular. While the actual structure has not changed much, the appearance is quite unlike the ordinary form. See page 337.

Darwin has noticed the same tubular structure of the depressor muscle pit in Panamic examples. The tergum in the specimens from station 2939 has a much shorter spur than in the type of *pacificus*, but varies in different examples; its external furrow is not quite closed.

The armature of the cirri varies; the larger individuals from station 2939 examined having more "teeth" on the third cirrus than the smaller one from Long Beach, and also having a few on the fourth cirrus, where I found none in the smaller specimen.

The oriental form or forms of *B. concavus* are unknown to me. As it was not obtained by the *Siboga* or the *Albatross* expeditions, I presume that it is either rare or local.

U. S. F. C. Station.	Locality.	Depth (fathoms).	Collector.	Notes.
4492	Crescent City, Cal.[1]		Unknown	Cat. No. 13111.
	Monterey Bay, Cal.	20	Albatross	
	San Pedro, Cal.		W. M. Gabb	Coll. A. N. S. P.
	Long Beach, Cal.		Mrs. Oldroyd	On Trophon.
2939	Near Newport, Cal.	27	Albatross	
4420	Near San Nicolas Island	33	....do	
	San Diego, Cal.		Dr. Palmer	
4303–4	Near San Diego, Cal.	21–25	Albatross	
	Santa Maria Bay, Lower Cal.		....do	

[1] This locality, if authentic, carries *B. c. pacificus* well north of the greater part of its faunal associates in southern California. The distribution of the species on the coast above Monterey needs further investigation.

BALANUS CONCAVUS COOSENSIS Dall.

1909. *Balanus tintinnabulum coosensis* DALL, The Miocene of Astoria and Coos Bay, Oregon, U. S. Geol. Survey, Professional Paper No. 59, p. 138, pl. 19, figs. 1, 6.

This is a very large form from the Miocene of Coos Bay, Oregon, the greatest diameter 50 mm. Parietes smooth; radii with oblique summits, thereby agreeing with most forms of *concavus*, but differing from *B. tintinnabulum* and *B. concavus pacificus*. The parietal tubes of one of the type lot have no transverse septa. There are about 39 tubes in the rostrum. The radii are not porous. It is therefore not related to *B. tintinnabulum*, which has not been found fossil in America, and is represented in the recent fauna by quite different forms. The opercular valves of *B. c. coosensis* have not been found, so that the reference to *B. concavus*, though probable, is provisional.

A rather strongly ribbed barnacle from the Lower Miocene or Upper Oligocene of Ventura County, California, has been referred to *B. concavus* by Ralph Arnold.[1] It resembles *B. c. glyptopoma* externally, but the opercular valves and structure of the wall are unknown.

BALANUS REGALIS, new species.

Plate 21, figs. 4, 4a.

Type.—Cat. No. 43485, U.S.N.M., from Point Abreojos, west coast of Lower California. *Albatross*, March 14, 1911.

A large, strong barnacle. The walls form a cone strongly bent toward the rostrum. Parietes rather finely, irregularly ribbed and with large folds near the base. Color, from old rose to Vandyke red and dahlia carmine, clouded with white, the sheath and interior pale flesh-tinted. Aperture broadly ovate.

The carina and carinal latera are closely united by linear sutures, externally visible with difficulty. The other sutures are deep, narrow clefts. Radii are extremely narrow, almost wanting, or represented by irregular, roughened ledges, their summits very oblique, their edges very irregularly crenulated, and not in contact with the broad,

---

[1] U. S. Geol. Surv. Bull. 309, pl. 32, fig. 5.

flat, opposed sutural edges, which have fine, irregular, denticulate crenulation. The alæ are narrow, with very oblique summits. The rostrum is short and broad; lateral compartments very broad; carino-laterals very narrow. There are deep, rather roomy hollows behind the lower edge of the sheath.

The interior surface is rather strongly ribbed near the base, becoming smooth above. Each rib is continuous with a septum in the wall, as usual. The parietal pores are large, square, separated by thin septa, which at their junction with the inner plate of the wall are thicker and denticulated, as usual. There are a few small, incomplete septa arising from the outer plate of the wall. The parietal pores are not filled up in the upper part, but transverse septa are rather numerous, from the base up.

The basis is strong, flat, rather well provided with round pores, but there is no underlying cellular layer. It clings very firmly to the walls.

	Carino-rostral diameter.	Lateral diameter.	Height.
a........	60	62	38 mm.
b........	59	65	46 mm.

This large and handsome barnacle is known by two individuals calcified together, which grew on some nearly flat object. The opercular plates and body were not collected. It is remarkable for the absence of radii, which are represented only by irregularly roughened white thickenings along the carinad borders of the lateral compartments; also for the intimate union of the carina and carino-lateral compartments, the sutures being merely linear or wholly obliterated, although the surface is not eroded. The color and the very short rostrum (if the latter is not the result of some unusual situation or position of the individuals), are also notable. The species should be readily recognizable, since there is no west coast barnacle which could be confused with it, to my knowledge.

The affinities of this form can not be worked out until complete specimens come to hand, but the walls suggest relationship with B. concavus and possibly B. nubilis; at all events, it belongs to the same division of the genus, group C of Darwin's classification. The transverse septa of the parietal tubes serve to further distinguish B. regalis from both B. nubilis and B. concavus pacificus. Among the forms of B. concavus, it has some superficial resemblance to B. c. proteus, of the Virginian Miocene. It should be noted also that there is a rare ribbed form of B. c. pacificus, shown in plate 23, figure 2c.

As this is one of the largest and handsomest west coast barnacles, it is hoped that living specimens will be looked for, in order to complete its description.

BALANUS POECILUS Darwin.

1854. *Balanus poecilus* DARWIN, Monograph, p. 246, pl. 5, figs. 3a, 3b.

Type.—British Museum.

Distribution.—West coast of South America, attached to an *Avicula* (Cuming).

Shell fragile, tubulo-conical; fine dark-rose color, freckled with transverse, sharply pointed, fine, zigzag white lines, and obscurely striped longitudinally. Basal diameter one-half inch.

Scuta dull red with a white band along the tergal margin, externally smooth; articular ridge moderately developed, slightly reflexed. *There is no adductor ridge.* There is a distinct pit for the lateral depressor muscle.

Tergum with the scutal margin unusually prominent, toothed; longitudinal furrow shallow, the edges not folded in. Spur short, barely one-third the width of valve, with the *lower end sharply truncated,* parallel to the basal margin.

Walls very fragile; radii fragile, broad, their summits moderately oblique. Basis with an underlying cancellated layer.

Cirri, first pair with one ramus longer by about four segments, the shorter ramus with protuberant segments. Sixth pair with segments much elongated, but bearing only four pairs of spines.

This species is not contained in the United States National Museum, and seems to be known by only one group of specimens, with the indefinite locality recorded above. The above details are abbreviated from Darwin's description. It does not differ much in essential characters from *B. amphitrite,* but the absence of an adductor ridge of the scutum and the sharply truncated spur of the tergum are sufficient to distinguish it.

BALANUS ALATUS Hoek.

1913. *Balanus alatus* HOEK, *Siboga*-Expeditie, Monographie 30b, p. 175, pl. 15, figs. 1–8.

Type.—*Siboga* station 97, latitude 5° 49′ .7″ north, longitude 119° 49′ .6″ east, northeast of the Sulu Archipelago, 564 meters.

B. alatus was founded on two specimens, having a diameter of about 3.25 mm. A few specimens which I refer to this species were taken at *Albatross* station 5163, in the Tawi Tawi group of the Sulu Archipelago, off Observation Island, in 28 fathoms. The basal margin of the scutum is shorter than the tergal margin; maximum diameter of the base about 9 mm.

BALANUS POECILOTHECA Krüger.

1911. *Balanus poecilotheca* KRÜGER, Beiträge zur Cirripedienfauna Ostasiens, Abh. der Math.-Phys. Klasse der K. Bayer. Akad. der Wissenschaften, vol. 2, Suppl.-Bd., 6 Abh., p. 48, pl. 1, figs. 2c–e; pl. 3, fig. 32.

Type-locality.—Okinose bank, Sagami Bay, Japan.

Numerous examples from three *Albatross* stations seem referable to this species, agreeing well with the description, except in having the lower teeth of the mandible blunt.

D. 5134. Sulu Archipelago, near Balukbaluk Island, 25 fathoms.

D. 5135. Sulu Archipelago, vicinity of Jolo, 161 fathoms.

D. 5146. Sulu Archipelago, vicinity of Siasi, 24 fathoms.

BALANUS TRIGONUS Darwin.

Plate 26, figs. 1 to 13*e*.

1854. *Balanus trigonus* DARWIN, Monograph, etc., p. 223, pl. 3, figs. 7*a*–7*f* ("Java; East Indian Archipelago; Peru; West Colombia; California; Sydney; New Zealand ").

1867. *Balanus armatus* MÜLLER, Archiv für Naturgeschichte, Jahrg. 1867, vol. 1, pp. 329–356, pl. 7, figs. 1–21, 23–28; pl. 8, figs. 44, 46–48; pl. 9, fig. 56.

1868. *Balanus armatus* MÜLLER, Ann. Mag. Nat. Hist., vol. 1, p. 392.

1897. *Balanus trigonus* Darwin, WELTNER, Verzeichnis, p. 262.

1911. *Balanus trigonus* Darwin, KRÜGER, Beiträge zur Cirripedienfauna Ostasiens, in Abh. Math.-Phys. Klasse der K. Bayer. Akad. Wissensch., vol. 2, Suppl.-Band, p. 49, figs. 98–100, pl. 1, fig. 6; pl. 3, fig. 33.

Type.—British Museum.

Distribution.—Pacific, from Tokyo Bay, Japan, through the East Indies to Sydney, New South Wales, and New Zealand; Red Sea; West America from Peru to southern California. Atlantic, West Indies to southern Brazil; Madeira and Azores to South Africa.[1]

According to Darwin, it is described as follows:

Parietes ribbed, mottled purplish-red; orifice broad, *trigonal*, hardly toothed. Scutum thick, with from *one to six longitudinal rows of little pits*. Tergum without a longitudinal furrow, spur truncated, full one-third the width of valve.

General appearance: Shell conical, generally depressed; orifice broad, triangular, almost equilateral; walls colored or only mottled with purplish-pink, having either irregularly branching, or regular, longitudinal ribs, which are generally white. The radii are pale pink or nearly white; the opercular valves have either their upper parts, or nearly their whole surface, clouded with pinkish-purple. The epidermis is not persistent; the walls are moderately strong. The largest specimen was one inch, but generally full-grown specimens are about half an inch in basal diameter.

The opercular valves have their lower growth-ridges minutely fringed with bristles when unworn. The membrane lining them is dark purple. When cleaned both valves are in part of a pink color internally.

The scutum has prominent, narrow growth-ridges which cross several deep longitudinal furrows, producing rows of small, deep pits. There may be from two to six such rows in San Diego individuals of one group. Very rarely there are individuals without pits, according to Darwin. The articular ridge is rather long; articular furrow deep

---

[1] The locality "Delaware," given by Weltner (Verzeichnis, p. 262), could refer only to imported specimens, as *B. trigonus* is certainly not found living there.

and narrow. There is a short adductor ridge, not united with the articular, and not extending upon the lower fourth or third of the valve. The lateral depressor muscle lodges in a deep cleft. The width of the scutum varies rather widely, and the tergal side is abruptly deflected.

The tergum is relatively large, wider than the scutum, and a trifle shorter. It is flat, with slight growth-lines and no furrow to the spur; the latter stands close to the basiscutal angle, is very short, truncate, and *broad*, one-half to one-third the width of the valve. Inside there is a moderate articular ridge, defining a broadly open articular furrow; the scutal border is not inflexed. Crests for the depressor muscles are sharp and numerous.

The labrum (fig. 27b) has three rather strong teeth on each side. Palpi substantially as in *B. amphitrite* (See p. 93, fig. 19e).

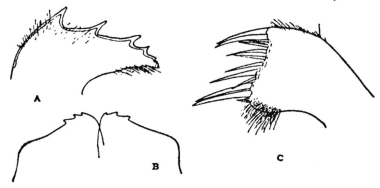

FIG. 27.—B. TRIGONUS, WEST INDIES. a, MANDIBLE. b, LABRUM. c, MAXILLA.

Mandible (fig. 27a) with four teeth and an irregular lower point. Maxilla (fig. 27c) with seven or eight spines between the upper and lower large pairs, which stand upon very slight projections.

Cirrus i has rami of 20 and 9 segments, the *posterior ramus half as long as the anterior*, its segments moderately protuberant. Cirrus ii with 10 and 8 segments (West Indies), or 13 and 9 segments (Cape St. Lucas, Lower California). Cirrus iii having 15 and 12 segments, the anterior ramus 4 segments longer. The lower segment of the pedicel is very broad. The segments of both rami are convex anteriorly, and armed with thorn-shaped teeth. Smaller teeth, grading down to minute tubercles, are on the adjacent outer face of the segment. These may be numerous, as in the West Indian individual figured (fig. 28a), or few, as in that from Cape St. Lucas (fig. 28d). The distal two segments of the anterior ramus, and four of the posterior, have no teeth. The inner faces of the toothed segments of the anterior ramus are smooth, but those of the posterior ramus have some or many long spines. Cirrus iv is long, like the following cirri, but about six segments near the middle of the outer ramus have small teeth on the anterior margin (fig. 28b). The later cirri have four or at most five pairs of spines (fig. 28e). The second joint of the pedicel of cirrus vi has an upwardly directed tooth near the proximal posterior part, usually with a few minute ones above it (fig. 28c.)

B. *trigonus* may usually be readily recognized by the triangular orifice, the ribbed and colored walls, the *rows of little pits in the scutum* (which, however, may rarely be wanting, or in very old specimens they may be obscured or removed by erosion), and the thin, flat tergum with a broad spur. The shape of the orifice varies, two angles

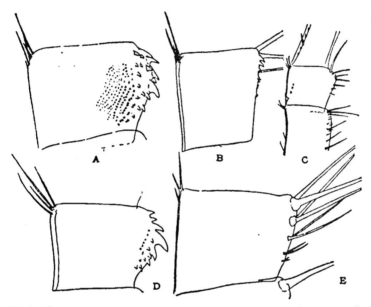

FIG. 28.—BALANUS TRIGONUS. *a*, SEVENTH SEGMENT OF ANTERIOR RAMUS, CIRRUS III. *b*, EIGHTH SEGMENT OF CIRRUS IV. *c*, SECOND SEGMENT OF THE PEDICEL OF CIRRUS VI, WITH PART OF THE LOWER SEGMENT AND BASES OF THE RAMI. *d*, SEVENTH SEGMENT OF ANTERIOR RAMUS, CIRRUS III, CAPE ST. LUCAS. *e*, A MEDIAN SEGMENT OF CIRRUS VI. ALL FIGURES EXCEPT *d* FROM WEST INDIAN SPECIMEN. THE RIGHT SIDE IS ANTERIOR.

of the triangle often being cut off, forming two short facets, changing the triangle to a pentagon with two very long sides.

It is very frequently associated with other barnacles, and is one of the forms often found on ships' bottoms. Sometimes it forms masses on shells, which may be completely covered excepting the aperture. Doctor Krüger, who has given an excellent account, with figures, found it on crabs from Japan, where it is a common species. He also records a group of small individuals embedded *Acasta*-like in a sponge. He independently reached Fritz Müller's idea that the spines on the third cirrus were evolved to break away sponge-spicules from the orifice.

The size and the sculpture of the scutum are variable among individuals, and especially in different colonies, even in the same general region. Thus, a lot of small *trigonus* from Misaki, Sagami, Japan, growing on *Fusus*, has but one row of pits in the scutum, though they were apparently adult. Another Japanese lot from Kagoshima, at the southern extreme of Kyushu, has long, narrow scuta, with several rows of pits. Detailed faunistic studies are needed to determine the significance of such variations.

It is quite possible that the Atlantic form of *B. trigonus* (pl. 26, figs.1–12a) can be separated from the Pacific form (pl. 26, figs. 13–13e) as a race or subspecies. The typical Pacific form of *trigonus*, as figured by Krüger (Japan) and shown in figure 28d, Cape St. Lucas, has the anterior margin of the segments of cirrus iii more protuberant and more coarsely toothed than in Atlantic examples examined (fig. 28a). The tergum is somewhat wider. If these differences prove constant, when a large series is examined, the Atlantic race may be called *B. trigonus armatus*. As most of the specimens at my command are dry, I have been unable to satisfy myself that the differences are sufficiently constant to have racial value.

Balanus armatus Fritz Müller, from Santa Catharina Island, Brazil, has been accepted by subsequent authors as a valid species. It is merely a variety of *B. trigonus*, due to station. It lives on sponges, *Papillina* or *Reniera*, on the polyp *Carijoa*, or rarely on *Purpura*, or on rocks, in that case assuming the ordinary ribbed exterior of *B. trigonus*. According to Müller, who has given a full and beautifully illustrated description, the orifice is pentagonal. The projecting apices of the compartments make the peritreme toothed; surface generally smooth, more rarely having indistinct ribs. Those seated on rocks have stronger ribs. There are sometimes traces of epidermis on the lower parts of the parietes. Müller states of the terga, "Diese stimmen ganz mit der von Darwin für *Balanus trigonus* gegebenen Beschreibung überein," but he figures the spur with a more rounded distal end, quite possibly an oversight in drawing. The narrowness of the tergum, as figured, agrees with Antillean specimens. On the west coast the tergum is broader. The scuta are exactly as in a common Pacific form of *trigonus*. The mouth parts and cirri, as figured by Müller, agree well with those organs in West Indian *trigonus*, even in the small details, which vary more or less in specimens from different localities. Part of Müller's figures of *armatus* are copied photographically in plate 26, figures 1 to 11.

Locality.	Donor or collector.	Notes.
San Diego, California..	R. E. C. Stearns............	On *Tegula*.
Magdalena Bay, Lower California	C. R. Orcutt..............	
Head of Conception Bay, Gulf of California......	Paul Bartsch..............	
Manzanillo, Colima, Mexico	C. R. Orcutt..............	On drifted pile.
Panama..	Dr. W. S. W. Ruschenberger.	Coll. A. N. S. P.
Iyo, Japan....:...........................	Y. Hirase................	Do.
Japan............	Imperial University, Tokyo.	
Hayama, near Kamakura, Sagami........	A. C. Hartshorne..........	Coll. A. N. S. P.
Misaki, Sagami..	Imperial University of Tokyo.	On *Fusus*.
Hirado, Hizen, Japan	Y. Hirase................	Coll. A. N. S. P.
Kagoshima Bay, Japan	North Pacific exploring expedition.	
Kagoshima, Japan	Imperial University of Tokyo.	
Philippines	Walter Hough	No opercular valves.
Cape Cod, on whaler from West Indies	A. E. Verrill	On *Charonia lampas* (*Triton nodiferus*).
St. Michael, Azores		

BALANUS SPONGICOLA Brown.

Plate 25, figs. 2, 3, 4–4c.

1827. *Balanus spongicula* Leach MS., BROWN,[1] Illustrations of the Conchology of Great Britain and Ireland, pl. 7, figs. 6, 14, 15.

1844. *Balanus spongicola* BROWN, Illustrations of the Recent Conchology of Great Britain and Ireland, ed. 2, p. 121, pl. 53, figs. 14, 15, 16.

1854. *Balanus spongicola* Brown, DARWIN, Monograph, p. 225, pl. 4, figs. 1a–1c.

1907. *Balanus spongicola* Brown, GRUVEL, Bull. Soc. Zool. de France, vol. 32, p. 164.

Type.—Present location unknown; from Weymouth, Devon.

Distribution.—Southern England, Wales, and Ireland to the Mediterranean; Lagulhas Bank, Cape of Good Hope; off Patros Island, Brazil (Rathbun); La Guayra and Caracas (Weltner); Chagos Archipelago, and Seychelles (Gruvel).

The barnacle is conic or conic-tubular; pompeian red, deep hellebore red, or varying in tint to nearly white on the rostral side; radii red or white; *walls smooth*, the orifice toothed.

Scutum with unequal *radial grooves*, part of them deeply engraved, cutting the strongly developed growth-ridges into small beads. Articular ridge small; adductor ridge small and short, merely forming a raised border of the adductor pit. There is a rather deep and narrow pit for the lateral depressor muscle.

The tergum has the apex tinted, produced into an acute beak projecting above the scuta; exterior nearly flat, band running to the spur being but very slightly sunken. Spur is about one-third the width of the valve, obliquely truncate at the end, the basal margin on the carinal side sloping into it in a nearly straight or slightly concave line (fig. 30a, b, Exmouth.) Crests for the depressor muscles are rather weakly developed.

---

[1] The original spelling *spongicula* was corrected by Captain Brown in the later edition of his work. We may assume that it was a typographical error.

The radii vary in width, but have oblique summits, so that the orifice, especially in the more tubular examples, is toothed. *The parietal tubes are very numerous*, 29 in the rostrum, and are provided with many transverse septa throughout their length. The interior is ribbed only very close to the base. The sheath is colored like the outside.

The base is porous, but often irregularly, large parts of it being poreless. Darwin states that there are no pores in a South African specimen he examined.

Greatest diameter 20 mm.; height 10 mm. (conic).

Greatest diameter 17 mm.; height 15 mm. (conic).

Greatest diameter 16 mm.; height 18 mm. (tubular).

The labrum has three teeth on each side (fig. 29a).

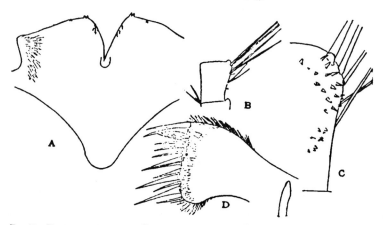

Fig. 29.—Balanus spongicola, Exmouth. *a*, labrum. *b*, 14th segment of cirrus VI. *c*, anterior part of an intermediate segment of cirrus III. *d*, maxilla.

The mandible is like that of *B. concavus*, figured on p. 106, fig. 26b.

The maxillæ (fig. 29d) has eight spines between the upper and lower large pairs. There is also an inserted spine between those of the lower pair, and another below them. The edge is rather even.

Cirrus i has rami of 19 and 12 segments. The posterior ramus is about three-fifths as long as the anterior and has moderately protuberant segments not nearly so long as in *B. concavus*. Cirrus ii has 14 and 15 segments, but the anterior ramus is a trifle longer. Cirrus iii has rami of 15 and 13 segments. On the anterior ramus the third to thirteenth segments are armed as shown in fig. 29c, but vary in the number of "teeth." The posterior ramus has the fourth to eighth segments similarly armed. I see no teeth on cirrus iv. Cirri v and vi have most of the segments with three pairs of spines, but there are four pairs, the lower very small, on a few segments.

The penis is extremely long, as in other species of this group.

The description, figs. 29, 30a, b, and pl. 25, figs. 2, 3, are from south coast of England (Exmouth) specimens, and represent the typical form of the species.

Several specimens taken in 34 fathoms, 10 miles east of the north end of Patros Island, Brazil,[1] presented to the United States National

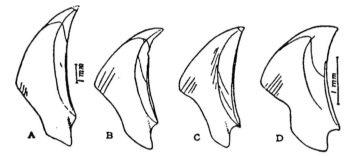

FIG. 30.—TERGA OF BALANUS SPONGICOLA. a, b, EXMOUTH. c, OFF PATROS ISLAND, BRAZIL; ALL DRAWN TO SAME SCALE. d, BALANUS CALIDUS.

Museum by Dr. R. Rathbun, taken by the steamer *Norseman*, Cat. No. 14144 U.S.N.M., grew with *B. amphitrite niveus*. Externally they do not differ from pale examples of the English *B. spongicola*, but the scuta are somewhat narrower, and the terga (fig. 30c) have the basal margin a little more hollowed out on both sides of the spur, which is noticeably narrower. The basal diameter is 13 mm. in the largest example (pl. 25, figs. 4–4c).

The dried bodies of these specimens were much broken, but I note that the mandible is very similar to that of *B. calidus*. It has the fourth tooth conic though short, the fifth very small, and largely united with the obtuse lower point. The maxilla has an even edge, and nine spines between the upper and lower large pairs. The third cirrus has minute bifid and trifid spines near the distal borders of the lower five segments, which alone were preserved. The fourth cirrus

FIG. 31.—BALANUS SPONGICOLA FROM PATROS ISLAND, BRAZIL. ANTERIOR-DISTAL PART OF THE 12TH SEGMENT OF CIRRUS IV.

[1] Unable to locate Patros Island, I applied to Dr. R. Rathbun, who replied as follows: "We exhausted every resource at the Museum in an effort to locate Patros Island, and then I appealed to the Hydrographic Office of the Navy, but they have not met with better success. The facts are these: When I was in Brazil between 1875 and 1878, with headquarters at Rio de Janeiro, I came in contact with the officers of the British steamer *Norseman*, which was the repair steamer for the cable along the Brazilian coast. Small specimens used to be brought up attached to the cable or loose in the apparatus they employed. The doctor of the steamer always brought these to me, and I labeled them in accordance with his information. I do not recall anything from the steamer *Norseman* that did not come from at least moderate depths of water on the coastal platform, and where the name of an island is given, I imagine it simply indicates the approximate locality. I was not the collector of any of the specimens from the *Norseman*, and my name was put on the labels only to show that they came through me."

has a double row of simple, conic, erect spinules near the distal sutures of the sixth to thirteenth segments, where it is broken off (fig. 31, twelfth segment.)

B. spongicola is related to *B. trigonus*, but differs conspicuously by the longitudinally striate and not pitted scuta, and by lacking projecting teeth on the anterior margins of the segments of the third pair of cirri. There are also many other differences. The walls are smooth in the large series examined, except for some specimens growing on *Pecten*, which show traces of sculpture acquired from the shell.

U.S.N.M. Cat. No.	Locality.	Collector.	Notes.
12145	Dublin Bay..........................	J. Gwyn Jeffreys coll.......	On *Pecten*.
12078	Exmouth, South Devon..............	......do......................	On sandstone.
12097	Exmouth............................	......do......................	On sandstone and *Pecten*.
12088	(No locality).......................	......do......................	
14144	10 miles east of north end Patros Island, Brazil.	Steamer *Norseman*..........	34 fathoms.
9198	Farralones [1].......................	Watkins...................	

[1] This can hardly mean the well-known islets off San Francisco Bay, since there is no other Pacific record for the species. The specimen is small, but quite typical *spongicola*, except that the number of pores in the rostrum (14) is smaller than usual.

BALANUS CALIDUS, new species.

Plate 25, figs. 1-1c.

1854. *Balanus spongicola*, var. with the walls slightly folded longitudinally.— DARWIN, Monograph, p. 225, pl. 4, fig. 1d.

Type.—Cat. No. 48193, U.S.N.M., from *Albatross* station 2372, latitude 29° 15′ 30″ north; longitude 85° 29′ 30″ west, 27 fathoms, surface temperature, 64° F., in the Gulf of Mexico southwest of Cape San Blas, western Florida.

Distribution.—West Indies, from St. Vincent to the northern coast of the Gulf of Mexico, 8 to 88 fathoms.

The barnacle is conic, the parietes rather strongly ribbed; purplish-pink with paler ribs, or sometimes pure white. Radii rather narrow, their summits less oblique than in *B. spongicola*. Sheath purplish in colored individuals. Interior strongly ribbed near the base, smooth above. Pores in the bases of parietes rather small, numerous, about 22 in the rostrum. Carinorostral diameter 8 mm.; height, 4.8 mm.

Scutum thick, sculptured externally with crowded growth-ridges and radial striæ, but the latter are weaker than in *B. spongicola*. The articular ridge is larger than in *spongicola*, and ends below in a free point. The adductor ridge is rather strong but short. There is a little pit between its lower end and the tergal margin, as in *B. glandula*. Pit for the depressor muscle is deep and small.

The tergum (fig. 30*d*) is broader than that of *B. spongicola*, with a shorter beak and broader spur. The basal margin is straight on both sides of the spur, which makes angles with it on both sides. In *B. spongicola* the basal margin slopes imperceptibly into the spur on the carinal side. Crests for the depressor muscles well developed.

The labrum has three teeth on each side (fig. 32*f*). Labial palpi having a fringe of short spines along the upper margin, a distal patch of long bristles, and an oblique row of long bristles on the outer face (fig. 32*d*). The inner or labral face has a sigmoid line

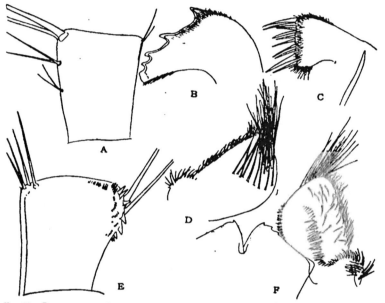

FIG. 32.—BALANUS CALIDUS. *a*, MEDIAN SEGMENT OF CIRRUS VI. *b*, MANDIBLE. *c*, MAXILLA. *d*, OUTER FACE OF PALPUS. *e*, SIXTH SEGMENT OF CIRRUS III. *f*, LABRUM AND PALPUS.

of short bristles, with larger ones, directed downward, above it (fig. 32*f*).

The mandible has four distinct teeth, the fifth concrescent with the blunt lower point (fig. 32*b*). The maxilla has six spines between the upper and lower pairs.

Cirrus i has rami of 20 and 10 segments, the posterior ramus half as long as the anterior, with moderately protuberant segments. Cirrus ii has rami of 11 segments, the anterior ramus longer by about three segments, though having the same number. Cirrus iii has rami of 11 and 10 segments, the anterior ramus longer by about three segments. The third to sixth segments of the anterior ramus have teeth on the anterior border, with others, mainly trifid or multifid, grouped in the anterior distal part of the segments (fig. 32*e*, sixth segment); the eighth and ninth segments have very minute multifid spines near the distal border, but no teeth. The posterior ramus has teeth on six segments. Cirrus iv has a few minute teeth near the distal borders of some segments of the anterior (outer) ramus. Cirri v and vi have two pairs of spines on most of the segments, but on a few there are three pairs, the lower ones small (fig. 32a.)

The penis is extremely long. No point seen on its dorsal base.

This common Antillean form was briefly described but not named by Darwin, who hesitated between describing it as a species and placing it under *B. spongicola* as a variety. His specimens were from St. Vincent, on coral, and others on an *Avicula* without definite locality. Having studied a long series of *B. spongicola* and several hundred *B. calidus*, I do not hesitate to give the latter specific rank. The ribbed wall, the finer and shallower longitudinal striation of the scutum, and the broader tergum, with wider spur, its carinal margin making an angle with the basal margin, are all characteristic. The opercular valves are not only actually but also relatively smaller than in *B. spongicola*. By the distinct "teeth" of the segments of the third cirrus it approaches *B. trigonus*. So far as I know, *B. spongicola* does not have the armature so strongly developed. The spines of the posterior cirri are slightly more reduced than in *B. spongicola*, or in fact than in any *Balanus* I have dissected. The other characters of the barnacle are about as in *B. spongicola*.

B. calidus lives in populous colonies on shells of all kinds, dead echinoderms, and even on the spines of echini (*Cidaris tribuloides*), an unusual station for *Balanus*, though a favorite one for *Verruca*. The largest specimen seen has a diameter of 10 mm., height 8 mm. It is from *Albatross* station 2365.

U.S.F.C. station.	Locality.	Depth (fathoms)	Collector.
2372	Latitude 29° 15′ 30″ north; longitude 85° 29′ 30″ west............	27	*Albatross.*
2405	Latitude 28° 45′ 00″ north; longitude 85° 02′ 00″ west............	30	Do.
2407	Latitude 28° 47′ 30″ north; longitude 84° 37′ 00″ west............	24	Do.
2403	Latitude 28° 42′ 30″ north; longitude 85° 29′ 00″ west............	88	Do.
2365	Latitude 22° 18′ 00″ north; longitude 87° 04′ 00″ west............	24	Do.
2362	Latitude 22° 08′ 30″ north; longitude 86° 53′ 30″ west............	25	Do.
2360	Latitude 22° 08′ 30″ north; longitude 86° 49′ 00″ west............	26	Do.
2363	Latitude 22° 07′ 30″ north; longitude 87° 06′ 00″ west............	21	Do.
6075	Off Boca Prieta, Porto Rico...................................	8½	*Fish Hawk.*

Note.—Station 2372 is in the vicinity of Cape San Blas, or Appalachicola, western Florida. Stations 2405, 2407, 2403 are further offshore in the same region. Stations 2360–2365 are on the Yucatan Bank, north of the northeastern extremity of Yucatan.

SERIES OF B. PERFORATUS.

BALANUS LÆVIS Bruguière.

Plate 27, figs. 1, 1a, 3–3b.

1789. *Balanus lævis* BRUGUIÈRE, Encyclopèdie Méthodique, p. 164, pl. 164, fig. 1.
1818. *Balanus discors* RANZANI, Opuscoli Scientifici, vol. 1, p. 77, pl. 3, figs. 9–13.
1854. *Balanus lævis* Bruguière, DARWIN, Monograph, p. 227, pl. 4, figs. 2–2g, with var. *nitidus*, fig. 2, and var. *coquimbensis*, fig. 2a.

1897. *Balanus lævis* Bruguière, WELTNER, Verzeichnis, p. 263.

1909. *Balanus lævis nitidus* Darwin, PILSBY, Proc. U. S. Nat. Mus., vol. 37, p. 68, pl. 17; pl. 19, figs. 5–9.

Type-Locality.—Cape Horn, on *Mytilus magellanicus*, collected by Dombey.

Distribution.—Cape Horn north to the Rio Negro on the east coast, and to Peru on the west. Shore to 20 fathoms.[1]

The barnacle is white or pale purple, covered with a brown epidermis (or nude in var. *nitidus*). Radii very narrow.

Scutum having growth-ridges and one to three *longitudinal furrows*, varying in width. Inside there is a rather narrow articular rib, *terminating below in a free point*, and a high adductor ridge wholly free from the articular. Pit for the lateral depressor muscle is small but deep.

The tergum has a longitudinal furrow with the edges somewhat folded in. Spur moderately long, wide, with the end obliquely cut off and convex; basicarinal angle very thin; crests well developed.

According to Darwin, "in the cirri none of the segments are very protuberant. In the first pair, one ramus is nearly twice as long as the other. In the posterior pairs the segments are not much elongated, but each supports seven pairs of spines." The more minute structures of the cirri have not been investigated.

Darwin distinguished three varieties, or, as we would now say, subspecies of *B. lævis*, characterized as follows:

a^1. Basis simply porose.
  b^1. Walls covered with yellow or brownish epidermis; scutum usually with one wide external furrow. Southern Chile, including the Straits of Magellan.
  B. lævis Bruguière
  b^2. Walls nude and smooth; scutum usually with two longitudinal furrows or one narrow furrow. Concepcion, Chile, to Peru......*B. l. nitidus* Darwin
a^2. Basis much lengthened, its cavity partially filled with a mass of irregular, superposed septa of papery thinness, forming an openly cellular mass.
  B. l. coquimbensis Sowerby

The distinctive characters of *lævis* and *nitidus* are those of a great majority of the specimens, but subject to exceptions, as Darwin has noted. Some large groups from Gregory Bay, Magellan Strait, though taken alive, had no epidermis. Over 50 individuals examined had one wide furrow on the scuta (pl. 27, fig. 1), and one specimen had an additional small furrow (pl. 27, fig. 1a). Numerous specimens from other localities in the same region agree in having one wide scutal furrow. Two individuals labeled Cape Horn, collector unknown, have the normal yellow cuticle, but the scuta have two small grooves, as in *B. l. nitidus*. A series from Valparaiso is similar, with the epidermis of *lævis*, the scuta of *nitidus*.

---

[1] The locality "California," given by Darwin, was based upon incorrectly localized specimens. The species is confined to the cold water area of South America. Weltner reports specimens without sulci on the scuta from Rio Grande do Sul, Brazil.

BALANUS LÆVIS NITIDUS Darwin.

Plate 27, figs. 2–2d; 4, 5.

Among the very numerous specimens examined from northern Chile (Arica) and Peru, none have the broad scutal furrow of Magellanic *lævis* and the epidermis is wholly or largely wanting. The number of scutal furrows in the two largest series examined is as follows:

	One furrow.	Two furrows.	Three furrows.	
Arica, Chile..........	3	16	1	Pl. 27, figs. 2–2d, 5.
Coast of Peru.........	5	25	1	

The furrows are narrower than in southern *B. lævis*, and often one or both are very lightly impressed. A third furrow when present is only weakly indicated. The pit in the scutum for the lateral depressor muscle is often larger in *nitidus* than in *lævis*.

B. l. nitidus is common on the gastropod *Concholepas concholepas*. Where crowded the usual diameter of the barnacles is 10 to 12 mm. Conic, unhampered individuals of the same group have a basal diameter of about 13 mm. Small pebbles are sometimes completely covered, appearing like balls of barnacles (pl. 27, fig. 4, Callao).

Albatross Station.	Locality.	Depth (fathoms).	Temperature.	Collector.	Support.
....	Rio Negro, Patagonia..........				
2773	East coast Patagonia, lat. 52° 23' south; long. 68° 11' west.	10	51 F.....	Albatross..............	Pebbles.
2777	Magellan Strait, lat. 52° 38' south; long. 70° 10' 30'' west.	19.75	51 F....	......do..............	Do.
....	Gregory Bay, Magellan Strait...	Shore...		......do..............	Stones.
....	Orange Harbor..............			U. S. Exploring Expedition?	Clamshell.
....	Cape Horn..............				
....	Valparaiso, Chile..............			R. E. C. Stearns, coll..	Crepidula.
....	Arica, Chile..............				Concholepas.
....	Talcahuano Bay, Chile..............			R. E. C. Stearns......	On Balanus psittacus.
....	Concepcion Bay, Chile..........			Captain Aulick, U. S. N., coll. A. N. S. P.	Do.
....	San Lorenzo Island, Peru......	Shore...		Dr. W. H. Jones......	
....	Callao, Peru..............				Shells, pebbles.
....	Coast of Peru..............			W. E. Curtis..............	Concholepas.

BALANUS LÆVIS COQUIMBENSIS Sowerby.

Plate 28, fig. 4.

1846. *Balanus coquimbensis* G. B. SOWERBY, in Darwin's Geological Observations, p. 264, pl. 2, fig. 7.

1854. *Balanus lævis* var. *coquimbensis* Sowerby, DARWIN, Monograph, p. 227, pl. 4, fig. 2a.

Type-locality.—Inland from Herradura Bay, Coquimbo, Chile, in a Pleistocene deposit.

Distribution.—Strait of Magellan to Coquimbo.

This barnacle is known to me only by specimens growing in crowded groups, about 32 mm. long, about 11 mm. in diameter. Three-fourths or more of the length is formed by the elongated basis. About two-thirds of the total length is occupied by an openly cellular mass formed of thin, irregular calcareous septa, variously anastamosing and connected with those below and above, often having slender, depending styles, which are frequently superposed in successive septa.

This structure, although confined to this Cirripede, is not so anomalous as might at first be thought, for in most species of the genus, each time that the circumference of the basis is added to, an excessively thin calcified film is thrown down over its whole inner surface; and in any of these species, if the films had been formed thicker and had rested only on certain points, instead of over the whole underlying layer, the cancellated structure above described would have been produced. (Darwin.)

That part of the basis forming the side walls has a single series of large, circular pores and an outer layer of small, irregularly placed pores, resembling the parietal pores of *Balanus cariosus*, but of course homologous with the vesicular, underlying layer of the basis found in many species of *Balanus*.

The peculiar cellular filling of the base is unique among recent barnacles, but it is exactly similar to that of the fossil *Tamiosoma gregaria* Conrad.

Darwin found the scutum to have two furrows, tergum as usual. Opercular valves are wanting in the specimens I have examined.

This subspecies is not contained in the United States National Museum. The specimen figured is No. 2056 A. N. S. P.

BALANUS PERFORATUS Bruguière.

1789. *Balanus perforatus* BRUGUIÈRE, Encyclopèdie Méthodique, p. 167 (Mediterranean coast of Barbary; Senegal).

1854. *Balanus perforatus* Bruguière, DARWIN, Monograph, p. 231, with varieties *angustus* Gmelin, *cranchii* Leach, *fistulosus* Poli, and *mirabilis* Darwin.

The localities given below practically cover the known range of the species, as the localities West Indies and South America are mentioned by Darwin with doubt, and have not been confirmed. Darwin considers it nearest to *B. lævis*, which it often resembles closely in outward form. The scuta, however, have plain, rather fine growth-ridges, and no longitudinal furrows or striæ. The cirri show a close relationship to *B. trigonus*, but differ in some details, especially in having the fourth to sixth cirri more fully armed with teeth along the posterior margins of the proximal segments, as shown in figure 32c.

The armature of the cirri has not been described. Cirrus i has very unequal rami of 30 and 14 segments, the posterior not much more than half as long as the anterior ramus and with very long appendages on the segments.

Cirrus ii is about as in *B. concavus*, with equal rami of about 13 very protuberant segments.

Cirrus iii has unequal rami, not longer than those of cirrus ii, of 14 and 8 segments. All but the lower and terminal segments of both rami bear recurved "teeth" as in figure 33a. These teeth are fewer on the inner ramus and on the distal segments of the outer. Near the base there are some flat multifid scales around the anterior patch of long spines (fig. 33b). The anterior-distal angles of the segments of the pedicel bear some minute, marginal spinules.

Cirrus iv has the outer ramus armed with recurved teeth (fig. 33c). In the lower part there are up-curved teeth on the posterior border. Farther out these disappear, and the great posterior spine

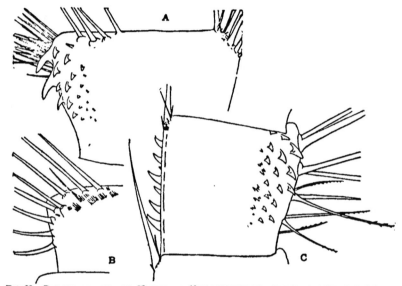

Fig. 33.—Balanus perforatus, Naples. a, 10th segment of anterior ramus of cirrus iii. b, 6th segment of anterior ramus of cirrus iii. c, 7th segment of the anterior ramus of cirrus vi.

is replaced by two smaller ones, finally by several much smaller. The inner ramus has no anterior "teeth," but there are posterior teeth as in the other ramus. It has six pairs of spines on the segments. The segments of the pedicel have no spinules in the fourth to sixth cirri.

Cirrus v is like the inner ramus of cirrus iv. The outer ramus has teeth on the posterior margin toward the base. Cirrus vi has segments much longer than wide, bearing six pairs of spines, which are pectinated toward the ends. The lower segments of both rami are copiously provided with short, up-curved "teeth" along their posterior margins. These teeth gradually become fewer upward.

The penis is longer than cirrus vi and has an acute basi-dorsal point.

In addition to those recorded below there are numerous lots in the Jeffreys collection without definite locality, probably all British. The long series from Exmouth, chiefly seated on sandstone, comprises some small, nearly white examples, with the sheath white, on *Lepas*, *Pecten*, and *Fissuridea*. The var. *cranchii* is well represented, and there are specimens of var. *mirabilis* from Rochelle. The material is not sufficient for an opinion on the status of the named varieties.

Museum No.	Locality.	Collector or donor.	Notes.
....	West Ross, Lough Sheildaig, Scotland.	Jeffreys coll...............	
12098	Cork Harbor, Ireland..............	......do....................	Altitude 19 mm., diameter 29 mm.
....	Fishguard Bay, Wales...........	......do....	Very solid.
....	Tenby, Wales..	......do....	
12061	North Devon, England..........	......do....	
12153	Exmouth, South Devon..........	......do....	On crabs, sandstone rocks, etc.
....	Langland Bay......................	......do....	
12154	Dawlish Warren, near Exmouth.	......do....	
12129	Rosilly Down......................	......do....	
12366	Rochelle, France..................	......do....	Var. *mirabilis* Darwin.
....	Mediterranean Sea...............	C. R. Orcutt...............	
....	Naples.............................	Zoological Station...........	
....	...do..............................	I. Lea coll...................	
....	Guinea.............................	Jeffreys coll...............	From W. Dunker.

SERIES OF BALANUS GREGARIUS.

Large, solid barnacles, in which the basis consists of a thick disk with very few pores, and attached only at one point; this disk typically is surmounted by a cylindric portion with thick walls permeated by many minute pores, and with the cavity filled with a mass of large, thin-walled cells, in old individuals; wall-compartments having porous parietes. Opercular valves unknown.

The structure of the walls and of the cellular filling of the basis in the single species of this group is strictly similar to that of *B. lævis coquimbensis;* but that form has far thinner walls, and the lower part of the basis differs, being attached throughout, while in this species the very thick basis seems to be fixed only by a small initial attachment in all the specimens seen which show the basis; subsequent growth being free. Whether this condition is solely due to attachment to very small objects is a point to be determined.

The cellular filling of the cavity of the base in *B. lævis coquimbensis* and *B. gregarius* is probably due to the production of gas by the mantle lining the floor of the cavity. Bubbles are formed between the solid basis and the mantle, elevating the latter locally. A calcareous film is then secreted on the lower face of the mantle, imprisoning the bubbles of gas. Similar production of gas is known in many aquatic animals, such as fishes and *Nautilus;* but in *Balanus* the resulting buoyancy can hardly have any useful function. Probably the cells merely occupy superfluous space, due to hypertrophic lengthening of the tube.

This series contains only the species *Balanus gregarius* (Conrad), originally described as the type and sole species of the genus *Tamiosoma*. Conrad seems at first to have considered *Tamiosoma* a Rudistid mollusk, and in 1864 he placed its species in the genus *Radiolites*. Gabb, in 1869, took a similar view, looking upon it as a member of the Hippuritidæ In 1876 Conrad recognized the true nature of the fossil, stating that its structure does "not differ essentially from *Balanus lævis* Brug." Dr. W. H. Dall (1902) reached the same conclusion.

BALANUS GREGARIUS (Conrad).

Plate 28, figs. 1–8; plate 29.

1856. *Tamiosoma gregaria* CONRAD, Proc. Acad. Nat. Sci., Phila., p. 315.
1857. *Tamiosoma gregaria* CONRAD, Pacific R. R. Report, vol. 6, p. 72, pl. 4, fig. 18.
1857. *Balanus estrellanus* CONRAD, Pacific R. R. Report, vol. 7, p. 195, pl. 8, fig. 1.
1864. *Radiolites gregaria* CONRAD, Proc. Acad. Nat. Sci., Phila., p. 214.
1869. *Tamiosoma gregaria* Conrad, GABB, Geological Survey of California, Paleontology, vol. 2, p. 61, pl. 18, figs. 22a–d.
1876. *Balanus H. estrellanus* CONRAD, Proc. Acad. Nat. Sci., Phila., p. 273.
1902. *Tamiosoma gregaria* Conrad, DALL, Science, vol. 15, p. 5 (=*Balanus*).

Distribution.—Miocene of California: Estrella; Santa Marguerita ranch, northeast of San Luis Obispo; Tulare Valley (Gabb). Salinas Valley, Monterey County (Homer Hamlin).

In its typical form (pl. 29) this barnacle is columnar or cylindric, with the basis lengthened, occupying nearly three-fourths of the total length; not contracted at the orifice. Externally the basal portion of the tube has low, rounded, unequal, and irregular longitudinal ribs; the compartments are probably almost smooth, but in specimens at hand they are so much corroded that the external sculpture, if any, is not shown. The parietes are porous; radii narrow, and apparently rather deeply sunken if the parietes were not eroded. The sutures are marked by ribs internally. The sheath is from a third to nearly half the length of the compartments, and has a somewhat depending lower edge.

The basis consists of two parts: a disk-like basal plate (pl. 28, figs. 1, 1a), which is rather thick and almost solid, but showing a few pores in places, and many in the peripheral part. *It seems to be attached by a small subcentral point only*, but this may be due to the small size of the supporting object of these specimens, which is not preserved with any of them. Externally the basis is roughened with irregular concentric ridges and with cavities apparently caused by irregularities in the bottom. The vertical portion of the basis has thick walls, copiously porous, the pores small, 0.5 mm. or less in diameter, and crossed by many septa. The cavity of the basis is filled with a mass of cells formed by thin, bubble-like septa which are convex upwardly, often have slender depending pillars, frequently continuous in several or many superposed cells. The upper surface of the cellular mass is irregular, blistered, and hummocky.

The opercular valves are unknown.

Length of specimen figured on plate 29, 198 mm.; diameter about 60 mm.

The specimens figured are from Wild Horse Canyon, Salinas Valley, Monterey County, California, in the San Pablo formation, collected by Homer Hamlin.

In the same lot, but evidently from another bed, there is a turbinate, or more exactly, biconic example, filled with hard matrix, figured in plate 28, figure 2. The patelliform basis was evidently attached by the central point only. It is weakly costate radially. The parietes are not ribbed, but their surfaces are irregular. Radii are deeply sunken with abrupt sides. This specimen measures about 104 mm. in greatest diameter, the figure being reduced.

Several detached bases in the lot, one of them figured, plate 28, figures 1, 1a, upper and lower views, are similar externally to the discoidal part of the basis in the typical form, but they show no traces of the attachment of cell walls on the inside. If they belong to the same species, as seems likely, they are from younger individuals which did not yet have the basal cavity filled with a cellular mass. Figure 1a is natural size.

SERIES OF B. AQUILA.

BALANUS AQUILA Pilsbry.

Plate 31, figs. 1, 2, 4a; plate 32, figs. 2-2c.

1907. *Balanus aquila* PILSBRY, Bulletin of the Bureau of Fisheries vol. 26, Document No. 617, p. 199, pl. 8, figs. 5-8; pl. 10, fig. 2; pl. 11, fig. 2.

Type.—Cat. No. 32403, U. S. N. M., from *Albatross* station 4496,

Distribution.—Monterey Bay to San Diego, California.

The barnacle is large, conic, with a small ovate orifice with toothed margin; white or grayish white, the lower part covered with a straw or naples yellow epidermis. Opercular valves also partly covered with epidermis. Sheath and interior white. Parietes and basis porous, the radii solid.

Greatest diameter 72 mm.; height, 84 mm. Type.

Greatest diameter 63 mm.; height, 42 mm. Santa Barbara.

Greatest diameter 62 mm.; height 38 mm. San Diego.

The scutum is narrow; width less than half the length, strongly convex between the occludent and tergal margins, whitish under a light brown or yellowish epidermis. Tergal margin short, not much over half the occludent length. Sculpture of rounded growth ridges cut into beads by much deeper, closer longitudinal grooves. Inside yellowish, articular ridge rather small, reflexed, about two-thirds the length of the tergal margin, abruptly truncate at the lower end. Articular groove narrow. Adductor ridge well developed, nearly straight, slightly overhanging the pit of the depressor muscle. Toward the basal margin it is longitudinally grooved. The occludent margin is folded inward near the base.

The tergum (pl. 32, figs. 2, 2a) is long and narrow, width less than half the length. It has a long purple beak, one-fourth the length of the whole valve. The exterior is worn in the upper part, elsewhere with fine cancellated sculpture of longitudinal and growth ridges. The longitudinal furrow is wholly closed by infolding of the sides. The basal margin slopes strongly to the spur on both sides. Spur narrow, long, separated from the basiscutal angle by about its own width. The spur continues on the inner face of the valve as a low ridge, with which the very slightly developed articular ridge is concrescent. There is a long purple area in the middle of the inside, which is elsewhere yellow. Crests for the depressor muscles are rather weakly developed. The beak is penetrated by a minute pore from the purple area, and its inner face has transverse arcuate ridges.

Compartments thick and strong. Parietes strongly ribbed; permeated with unequal narrow tubes. Interior of parietes irregularly ribbed, with short depending points in the type (having rather fine ribs near the base only, in other examples). Sheath long, with deep hollows under its depending edge. Radii solid, rather deeply sunken, smooth, with horizontal summits when unworn; very thick, with densely septate edges, the lower side of each septum denticulate. Sutural edges similarly septate, the upper sides of the septa denticulate. Alæ rather wide, the *lateral edge of each ala bifid*, the inner part acute, outer part blunt, somewhat septate.

Basis calcareous, very thick toward the edges, and clinging very firmly to the side walls. In the type-specimen there are very few, irregular pores. Inside smooth except for irregularities of the supporting rock.

The mandible (fig. 34b) has four quite small teeth, the lower one adjacent to several very short, obtuse denticles. There is an extremely short fringe of hair on the upper margin.

The maxilla has a slightly sigmoid edge, receding somewhat but not notched below the upper pair of large spines, about four pairs of smaller spines standing in the concavity. Below this the edge is convex, with very large and smaller spines. There is a long fringe of short hairs on the upper, and a tuft on the lower margin (fig. 34a).

The first cirrus has wide rami, the posterior ramus three-fourths as long as the anterior, with greatly protruding segments, about 22 in number. Segments of anterior ramus less protruding, about 30. The second cirrus has subequal rami, with extremely protruding segments. The third cirrus is but slightly longer than the second. The 21 and 22 segments protrude distally, and bear dense tufts of spines, some of them pectinate near the tips. Fourth to sixth cirri long and slender, of many segments, bearing six pairs of spines, the

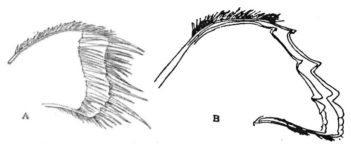

FIG. 34.—BALANUS AQUILA. *a*, MAXILLA, AND *b*, MANDIBLE OF THE TYPE.

lower two pairs quite small. There are also some tufts of minute spines among them, and a rather dense tuft at the posterior distal angles of each segment. Cirrus iv has a regular row of erect spinules along the distal sutures of all but a few extreme proximal and distal segments of the outer ramus. The inner ramus has a feebler development of them. The second segment of the pedicel is minutely spinulose close to the large anterior spines of the distal angle (fig. 35).

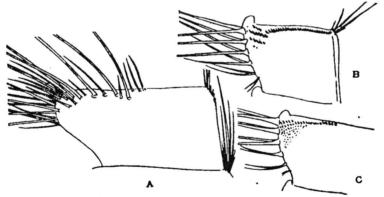

FIG. 35.—BALANUS AQUILA. *a*, ELEVENTH SEGMENT OF CIRRUS III. *b*, TWENTY-EIGHTH, AND *c*, SEVENTEENTH SEGMENTS OF CIRRUS IV, ANTERIOR RAMUS.

The type-specimen, from Monterey Bay in 10 fathoms, was seated upon a rock. The surface is abraded and perforated in places.[1] The

---

[1] The worn condition, together with the peculiar tergum, led me into the error of placing the species in Darwin's Section A in my original account. The examination of additional perfectly preserved examples and a careful reexamination of the type shows that the radii are not in the least porous. It belongs, therefore, to Darwin's Section C.

external ribs are rude, rounded, and very irregular (pl. 31, fig. 4a). Their irregularity is probably in part due to the extremely irregular surface of the stone upon which the barnacle grew. The cone *leans toward the rostrum*, which is much shorter than the carina. Where the parieties are worn externally the very narrow tubes are laid open. They closely resemble those of *B. nubilis*, but have no transverse septa where exposed. The number of tubes is somewhat increased downward by new septa dividing the tubes. The basis is nearly flat. Its substance fills several cavities in the supporting rock, and in only two places a few irregular pores are visible in the section exposed by breaking it across. Elsewhere it is quite solid.

The other examples recorded above, from more southern localities, grew on nearly smooth, flat surfaces, perhaps planks. The cone leans *toward the carina*, which is not much higher than the rostrum. The exterior is perfectly preserved, the ribs stronger and more regular than in the type. The proportions and external sculpture of the compartments are very much as in a large *Balanus balanus* Linnaeus (*B. porcatus* Da Costa). The parietal tubes have transverse septa close to the base, whether farther up was not ascertained. The basis is well provided with rounded or oblong pores in the Santa Barbara specimen, but in places toward the periphery they are solidly filled up. The Santa Rosa Island specimen also is well provided with basal pores. It is not much more than half grown. In the San Diego example (pl. 31, fig. 2) I found regular, rounded pores in one small area of the basis; the rest of the exposure (a section across the base and another near and parallel to the periphery) is quite impervious. It is obvious that in this species there is a good deal of variation in the degree of porosity of the basis; and in some old individuals pores are few and very local, therefore easily overlooked. The opercular valves are identical in the Monterey and Santa Barbara examples, except that in the latter they are less worn externally. The other individuals examined lack opercular valves.

Small examples of *Balanus tintinnabulum californicus* grew on the individuals from San Diego and Santa Rosa Island.

This species and *Balanus nubilis* are the largest shallow-water Balani of North America. When in good condition, *B. aquila* looks like a very large, strongly ribbed *B. balanus;* but it differs from that by the bifid sutural edges of the alæ and by the opercular valves, which—especially the tergum—have a remarkable resemblance to those of *B. psittacus*. The inner structure of the walls is very similar in *B. aquila* and *B. nubilis*, but in the former the compartments cohere far less firmly and the sheath is longer. *B. nubilis* will break through the compartments rather than part at the sutures. The internal organs, so far as I examined them, are remarkably similar, particularly the cirri, but it may be noted that the maxillæ differ. In *B. aquila* there is no distinct notch below the upper pair of spines, and there is an enlarged spine (as in *B. balanus*) on the lower prominence of the edge.

The very narrow, purple-beaked tergum, the whiteness of the very strong walls, and the bifid alæ readily separate *B. aquila* from all varieties of the Protean *B. concavus*. It is a very distinct species.

Besides the specimens recorded below, there is one labeled "Oregon," without definite locality or record of collector. Its occurrence so far north needs further evidence.

Locality.	Collector.	Number of specimens.	Remarks.
Monterey Bay (10 fathoms)	Albatross	1	Type.
Santa Barbara, Cal.	R. E. C. Stearns	1	
Santa Rosa Island	P. Schumacher	1	Rostrum and lateral plates only.
San Diego, Cal.	R. E. C. Stearns	1	

SERIES OF B. NUBILIS.

BALANUS NUBILIS Darwin.

Plate 30, figs. 1–4; plate 31, figs. 3, 3a 4, 5.

1854. *Balanus nubilis* DARWIN, Monograph, etc., p. 253, pl. 6, figs. 2a–2o.

Type.—British Museum, from Monterey Bay, California.

Distribution.—Southern boundary of Alaska to Santa Cruz, California.

Darwin's original description is as follows:

General appearance.—Shell conical, rugged, sometimes furnished with sharp longitudinal ribs; dirty white. Orifice not large, oval, toothed. Radii rather narrow, with their summits oblique, much jagged. Basal diameter of largest specimen 2.1; height only 1.3 of an inch.

Scuta broad, with the lines of growth prominent; internally, articular ridge very little prominent, sometimes hardly developed, but thick, ending downwards in a small free point. Adductor ridge prominent, blunt, produced straight downward, making a deep longitudinal cavity for the lateral depressor muscle; in some specimens this cavity is almost arched over, so as to tend to be tubular, with a short ridge in the middle; in other specimens there is no trace of this tubular structure.

Terga, with the apex beaked, beak triangular, dull purple; the longitudinal furrow is so shallow as hardly to exist. The basal margin slopes down on both sides, with a nearly equable curvature toward the spur; hence the spur is broad in its upper part and narrow at its obliquely truncated lower end. Internally, there is an elongated dark purple patch. The shallow articular furrow is of quite remarkable breadth. The articular ridge is medial, and the inflected scutal margin is not wide. The internal surface of the spur is formed into a ridge, which runs a little way up the valve, and is sometimes partially separated from the spur itself, making the basal extremity toothed or double. The crests for the depressors are pretty well developed.

Walls moderately strong; inner lamina slightly ribbed; the denticuli on the bases of the parietal longitudinal septa are sharp. I could not see any transverse septa in the parietal tubes. The radii are rather narrow, their summits are remarkably jagged and very oblique; the septa are plainly denticulated on both sides, but chiefly on the lower side; each septum itself, toward the inner lamina of the radius, branches and divides; the interspaces are filled up nearly solidly. The alæ have apparently their summits less oblique than those of the radii, their sutural edges are finely crenated. The lower edge of the sheath is hollow underneath. The basis is flat; it is rather thin, and imperfectly porose; in parts it is not at all porose, in others it is traversed only by very minute pores; there is, nevertheless, in some parts, even where the upper layer is not porose, an underlying, cancellated layer.

The labrum is deeply notched, with the edge almost plain, but showing one very minute tooth in the specimen dissected (fig. 36a).

The mandible has four short spines and a lower cutting edge. The hairs on the upper and lower edges are extremely short (fig. 36d).

The maxilla has a deep notch below the upper pair of spines, which are smaller than usual. There are about 22 spines below the upper pair, and no enlarged one near the lower angle, such as the related species have (fig. 36c).

The first pair of cirri has very unequal rami of 32 and 17 segments, those of the shorter ramus strongly protuberant.

Cirrus ii has subequal rami of 17 and 16 strongly protuberant segments.

Cirrus iii has the anterior ramus a little longer, segments of both rami moderately protuberant, and armed with long spines, as figured for *B. aquila*. It has decidedly longer and more slender rami than cirrus ii, both of about 20 segments.

Cirrus iv has small groups of erect spinules on the distal anterior parts of the lower segments, and a distal row of spinules, as in the following cirri.

Cirri v and vi have both segments of the pedicel densely spinulose near their distal anterior borders, and the median segments have six pairs of spines and a distal row of erect spinules (fig. 36b).

Part of the spines of the cirri—especially those inserted on their inner faces—are beautifully pectinated on one or both sides.

Darwin's description, quoted above, applies to the small or moderate-sized examples of California. The mouth parts and cirri are described from a Monterey Bay specimen. In the northern waters of Oregon to the southern boundary of Alaska, and especially in Puget Sound and communicating waters, *B. nubilis* grows to a very large size, and is remarkable for its thick, solid, yellowish, opercular valves and the tendency to deepen the base, somewhat after the manner of *Megabalanus*, whereas the species related to *B. nubilis* gain room by lengthening the compartments. The shape of the tergum is especially characteristic, the spur being wide at the base, tapering to the narrow end, and standing rather remote from the basiscutal angle. Only *B. flos* among our species has a similar tergum. *B. balanus* has some affinity to *B. nubilis* by the tapering spur and the colored beak of the tergum.

B. nubilis has a certain external likeness to *B. aquila*, but the opercular valves are very different, and I have never seen a specimen with any trace of epidermis. It is closely related to *B. flos*, yet here again the valves differ widely in the structure of their inner faces.

The opercular valves vary in the tint of the inner faces from light or warm buff to cinnamon buff; never white. The purple color of the beak and median spot of the tergum is not invariable, being absent in

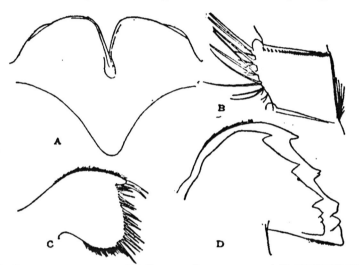

Fig. 36.—BALANUS NUBILIS, STATION 4496, MONTEREY BAY. *a*, LABRUM. *b*, 32D SEGMENT OF CIRRUS VI. *c*, MAXILLA. *d*, MANDIBLE.

an example from Santa Cruz. The tergum varies a good deal in the ratio of width to length. Except in the very young stages, the occludent border is worn away in its upper part, but in the lower part it is broadly inflexed in the adult stage.

The scutum varies chiefly in the degree of concrescence of the adductor and articular ridges, as shown in the figures. The occludent side is conspicuously folded in, forming an inclosed cavity near the base. The little ridge which divides the cavity of the lateral depressor muscle varies in prominence and position, and at times may be hardly noticeable. Sometimes it is carried up on the side of the adductor ridge, when it may readily be overlooked altogether. The growth-ridges of the exterior are very minutely and closely crossed by fine longitudinal striæ, but in old examples, such as shown in plate 31, figures 3, 3*a*, the whole surface is removed.

The basal pores are irregular (pl. 30, fig. 1*b*). The basis is copiously porous at the periphery (pl. 30, fig. 1*c*).

The young barnacle, sometimes up to a diameter of 25 mm. or more, is more or less strongly ribbed (pl. 30, fig. 2a, Puget Sound) ; but old ones, by wear of the summit, lose this sculpture wholly or to a great extent. Plate 30, figure 1a, Straits of de Fuca, shows about the maximum size of specimens preserving the external surface unworn. Rarely a diameter of 60 mm. is attained before the walls become worn. Some specimens of *B. nubilis*, when young, imitate *B. rostratus* superficially, having abruptly sunken radii and a similar shape and habit of growth.

Large individuals, such as are common in Puget Sound, are as a rule deeply eroded, showing the crowded, thin-walled parietal tubes, which are seen to have but few transverse septa. These old specimens are often riddled by boring animals, so that all external characters of a barnacle are lost. The orifice is usually very ample, and the sheath rather short, the wall always hollow below it (pl. 30, fig. 4, · four-fifths natural size).

Young specimens are deeply ribbed inside the parieties. The flat basis is thin and poreless in the middle, but thicker, with numerous pores, toward the periphery. Old ones become *entirely smooth* inside and usually have a deep, pocketlike basis. In one group from Port Orford, Oregon, the base is very deep, the total length 152 mm., of which the compartments form only one-third or less; diameter, 75 to 100 mm. The greatest diameter is around the junction of basis and wall. A more usual size is, height, 85 mm.; greatest diameter, 80 mm. (near Port Townsend). A very low individual from Puget Sound measures, height, 55 mm.; greatest diameter, 100 mm. The basis in this example is nearly flat. Another large example measures, height, 105 mm.; rostrocarinal diameter, 103 mm.; length of orifice, 64 mm.

To increase the capacity by deepening of the basis is unusual among the species most nearly related to *B. nubilis*. Some other species, such as *B. crenatus*, become elongated by lengthening of the compartments. The serried spinules, standing in saw-tooth like row along the posterior sutures of the segments of the last three pairs of cirri are a very characteristic feature of *B. nubilis*, but *B. aquila* has almost exactly the same structure. In *B. flos*, which is otherwise closely related, this arrangement of spinules is seen only in an incipient stage.

B. nubilis lives on rough, rocky or shelly bottoms in water of no great depth, but probably always well below low tide. The greatest depth recorded is 37 fathoms. It was not taken in deep water off the California coast by the *Albatross*, and probably does not exist much below the depth mentioned. Santa Cruz is probably at or near its extreme southern range, and it can hardly be expected much farther north than the southern boundary of Alaska. The extensive collections made by Dall and others, on shore and in moderate depths, and those of the *Albatross* in deeper water, show that it does not extend to the Alaskan Peninsula, or even, so far as we know, to Sitka.

Locality.	Collector.	Notes.
Fort Tongass, Alaska	F. M. King	
Pent Strait	Com. L. A. Beardslee, U.S.N.	
Vancouver Island [1]		
Juan de Fuca Strait	U. S. exploring expedition	
Neah Bay, Wash	J. G. Swan	
Port Townsend Bay, Wash	do	
Point Hudson, Port Townsend	do	
Bellingham Bay, Whatcom County, Wash	Dr. Buckley, 1856	
Puget Sound	J. G. Swan	
Station 3593, latitude 48° 11′ 30″ north; longitude 122° 48′ west (37 fathoms).	*Albatross*	Bottom temperature 46°.
Port Orford, Oreg	F. W. Crosby	
Farralone Islands, Cal	C. H. Townsend	Height, 47 mm., diameter, 50 mm.
Station 4496, Monterey Bay, Cal. (10 fathoms)	*Albatross*	Diameter, 50 mm.
Santa Cruz, Cal		

[1] Specimens in British Museum and Academy of Natural Sciences of Philadelphia.

BALANUS FLOS Pilsbry.

Plate 32, figs. 1–1 *f*.

1907. *Balanus flos*, PILSBRY, Bull. Bureau of Fisheries, vol. 26, p. 201, pl. 9, figs. 1–7; p. 202, fig. 3.

Type.—Cat. No. 32405, U.S.N.M., from *Albatross* Station 4558, near Point Pinos Lighthouse, Monterey.

Distribution.—Coast of California, surface to 338 fathoms.

The general form is tubular, the base about as wide as long; walls steep, sometimes flaring above; parietes faintly pink, sheath pink, opercular valves white. Surface smoothish, without an epidermis. Orifice large, very deeply toothed.

The scutum is concave between apex and base; length over twice the width; external sculpture of shallow, spaced grooves parted by flat growth-ridges, of which alternate ones crenulate the occludent margin. Inside there is a very low articular ridge half the length of the tergal margin, and hardly any articular furrow. *The adductor ridge is low and inconspicuous*, near and parallel to the tergal margin; very weak in the lower half, where it bounds the narrow pit for the depressor muscle.

The tergum has an acute apex, triangular in section, but is not "beaked." Scutal border concave, thin, and acute throughout. Articular ridge is rather strong, overhanging toward the carinal border, crescentic, extending from apex to basiscutal angle. Articular furrow extremely broad and shallow. Crests for the depressor muscles feebly developed. Externally it is flat, marked with growth-lines, and faintly traced longitudinal striæ near the carinal margin. No furrow to the spur, which is wide at the base, tapering to the narrow distal end, and remote from the basiscutal angle.

Compartments.—The parietal tubes are filled up in the upper part, rather large and square toward the base, where some short lamellæ from the outer lamina of the wall project into the lumen much as in *B. balanus.* The tubes have no transverse septa. The inner lamina of the wall is ribbed below the sheath, each rib crenulated at the base, terminating in a septum to the outer lamina. The sheath is long, smooth, and lies close to the wall, only very narrow hollows in places below its edge. The radii are smooth, rather wide, with *extremely oblique, minutely jagged summits;* lateral edges narrow, rather deeply denticulate. Alæ have also very oblique, smoothish summits. Sutural edges deeply denticulate, the denticles hardly crenulated.

The basis is concave externally in the specimens seen. It is of moderate, nearly equal thickness, distinctly porous, and in places has

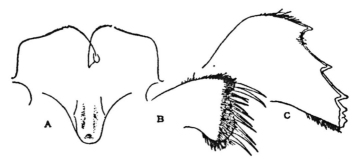

Fig. 37.—Balanus flos. *a*, labrum of specimen from Humboldt Bay. *b*, maxilla. *c*, mandible of a paratype.

an underlying cellular or spongy layer in some specimens. It clings rather firmly to the walls.

Height 16 mm.; rostrocarinal diameter of base 12 mm., lateral diameter 11.5 mm.; rostrocarinal length of orifice, 10 mm. Height 12 mm.; rostrocarinal diameter 11.5, lateral diameter 12 mm.; rostrocarinal length of aperture 8.5 mm.

The labrum (fig. 37*a*) has a finely hairy edge with two small teeth on each side. There are no hairy tracts on its lateral faces.

The mandibles (fig. 37*c*) have three rather slender teeth and a blunt or divided fourth one partly united with the lower point. The maxillæ (fig. 37*b*) have two strong spines above, the margin notched below them, then becoming convex, the lower angle being broadly rounded. The edge bears about 10 spines, the lower ones stronger, and there is a tuft of fine bristles below the lower extremity.

The first pair of cirri has very unequal rami, the anterior branch of about 23 segments, and about twice the length of the shorter ramus, of 11 segments, which are strongly protuberant on the forward side. Another individual has 21 and 12 segments in the rami of the first cirrus. The second pair of cirri has rami of 13 and 12 joints, respectively, also strongly protuberant in both rami. The third cirri have longer and more slender rami of 16 and 15 joints, which protrude moderately in front. The anterior ramus is the longer by about 3 segments. First joint of the peduncle is broad. Most or all the segments have some minute multifid spinules, and toward the base there are some simple spinules near the anterior margin (fig. 38c, seventh segment). The fourth to sixth cirri have patches of spinules near the distal anterior angles of both segments of the pedicel. Cirrus iv has a few spinules on part of the segments of both rami (fig. 38b). Cirri v and vi have a few short, erect, spike-like spinules along the distal borders of part of the segments (fig. 38a, seventeenth segment of cirrus vi), and four pairs of anterior

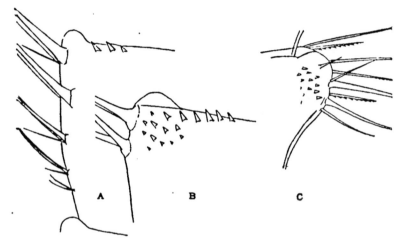

Fig. 38.—Balanus flos. a, 17th segment of cirrus vi, outer ramus. b, 14th segment of outer ramus cirrus iv. c, 7th segment anterior ramus of cirrus iii. a, and b from a paratype; c from Humboldt Bay.

spines. A few median segments of cirrus vi have a minute fifth pair. There are about 36 segments in the rami of cirrus vi. The posterior distal angles of the segments have a group of unequal spines, the longest about two-thirds the length of the segment.

Some of the spines on all of the cirri are pectinated near the end, but the pectination is best developed on the third cirri. In figure 38c the pectinated ends of some spines of the posterior ramus of cirrus iii may be seen projecting beyond the anterior ramus.

The penis is rather short, as in *B. balanus*, less than half as long as the sixth cirri, not hairy, and has a small projection near the dorsal base.

In some individuals the sculpture of the scutum has more the appearance of narrow, very low ridges, separated by much wider flat intervals. Under a strong lens there are very faint traces of radial striation, not visible in all cases.

By the shape of the tergum, which has a tapering spur, wide at the base, and remote from the basiscutal angle, this species is related to *B. nubilis;* but the far less deeply sculptured exterior of the opercular valves, and the very weak development of ridges on the inner faces of the valves, readily distinguish *B. flos* from its larger, coarser companion at all stages of growth. The color of walls and valves, the smaller size, the very deeply toothed orifice, and the armature of the cirri are further differential features.

In *B. spongicola* Brown, the spur of the tergum is wider, shorter, and nearer the basiscutal angle; the scutum has much more deeply cut growth ridges, which are distinctly beaded, and the articular and adductor ridges are stronger. The summits of the radii are more oblique in *B. flos,* and the apices of the opercular valves diverge. There are important differences in the cirri.

B. flos seems to have an unusually great range in depth, but possibly the example from *Albatross* Station 4420 had been washed into deep water from somewhere near the surface.

Albatross station.	Locality.	Depth (fathoms).	Collector.	Notes.
4558	Near Point Pinos Lighthouse, Cal.	40	*Albatross*	On polyzoan colony.
4420	Off east point San Nicolas Island, Cal.	338	......do........................	On seaweed.
	Off Humboldt Bar, Cal.........	....	Leland-Stanford University	On buoy.

SERIES OF B. BALANUS.

Balani with the ribs on the inner face of the parietes more numerous than the septa in the wall; basis not porous; maxilla with one spine near the lower angle much larger than its neighbors.

This boreal group extends into the cool Temperate Zone. It is prolific in races and local forms, especially in Bering Sea and the North Pacific—probably its center of radiation. There are only two clearly defined species, distinguished as follows:

Parietal pores without transverse septa, though usually filled up above

B. balanus, p. 149.

Parietal pores having transverse septa, at least in the upper half__*B. rostratus.*

BALANUS ROSTRATUS Hoek.

Plate 36, figs. 1, 2, 2a.

1854. *?B. porcatus* * * * some fine, brilliantly white specimens (without opercula) from the coast of China, DARWIN, Monograph, p. 259.

1883. *Balanus rostratus* HOEK, *Challenger* Report, Zoology, vol. 8, p. 152, pl. 13, figs. 16–22.

1900. *Balanus porcatus* Da Costa, WELTNER, Fauna Arctica, vol. 1, p. 296, pl. 8, fig. 13.

1911. *Balanus rostratus* Hoek PILSBRY, Bull. Bur. of Fisheries, vol. 29, p. 73, pl. 12, fig. 6 (issued Feb. 17).

1911. *Balanus rostratus* Hoek, KRÜGER, Beiträge zur Cirripedienfauna Ostasiens, Abh. math.-phys. Klasse der K. Bayer. Akad. der Wissenschaften, Suppl.-Bd. 2, p. 52.

1911. *?Balanus crenatus* Bruguière, KRÜGER, Beiträge zur Cirripedienfauna Ostasiens, Abh. math.-phys. Klasse der K. Bayer. Akademie der Wissenschaften, Suppl.-Bd. 2, p. 52, figs. 105–107; pl. 4, figs. 36 (Sagami Bay and Yokohama).

Type.—British Museum, from Kobe, Japan, in 8–50 fathoms.

Distribution.—North Pacific: Ocean coast and Inland Sea of Japan; varieties in Bering Sea and Puget Sound.

The barnacle is strong and rather thick, conic, with a rather small, ovate orifice, moderately wide, *deeply sunken radii*, very narrow carinolateral compartments, and broad lateral and rostral compartments. Surface smooth or somewhat folded, not regularly or distinctly ribbed; partially covered with a very thin pale-buff epidermis.

The scutum is like that of *B. balanus* externally. There are narrow, prominent ridges of growth, somewhat imbricating downward, and crenulated by the fine, deep longitudinal striation which runs over ridges and intervals. The articular ridge is very low; articular furrow very narrow and shallow. The adductor ridge is low, often weak; it stands free of the articular ridge, and bounds the rather deep pit of the depressor muscle.

The tergum is *white*, flat, with sculpture of growth-ridges and weak longitudinal striæ. A *narrow* fasciole runs to the spur. The spur is wide at the base, but tapers to a narrow, obliquely truncate end. The scutal margin is only narrowly inflected. Articular ridge moderate. No ridge runs to the spur. Crests for depressor muscles are weak or wanting (fig. 39*a*).

Compartments.—The parieties are angular along the deeply sunken radii, which have the appearance of slits made with a knife. The summits of the radii are level or somewhat oblique and jagged when perfect, but they are usually broken; edges irregularly laminate. Alæ narrow, with very oblique summits. The sheath lies very close to the wall, leaving scarcely any hollows below it. Parieties below the sheath are strongly ribbed. Between the ribs which terminate in septa there are usually from one to four ribs ending in points on the inner lamina of the wall, exactly as in *B. balanus*. Tubes of the parieties large and square, about 14 in number in the rostrum. They *have many transverse septa* down to the base, as shown in plate 36, figure 2*a*. Outer lamina with many extremely small, short lamellæ within the margin.

Basis thin, radially grooved, without any pores.

Carinorostral diameter, 42 mm.; height, 36 mm.

Carinorostral diameter, 34 mm.; height 26 mm. (Tokyo Harbor).

By the shape and sculpture of the opercular valves, the wholly solid basis, the square tubes of the parietes, and the development of accessory ribs on the inside, between those corresponding to septa, this species is extremely similar to *B. balanus;* but it differs in the important character of having transverse septa in the parietal tubes. In very long series of *B balanus*, examined from all parts of its range, there are never any transverse septa, and near the apices of the parietes the tubes become filled up solidly. There are also some differences in the opercular valves, as noted under *B. balanus*. The mouth parts could not be distinguished from those of *B. balanus*. The cirri of the Bering Sea races have more spines than Atlantic *B. balanus;* Bering Sea specimens of *balanus*, however, have as many. The penis is much longer in *B. rostratus*.

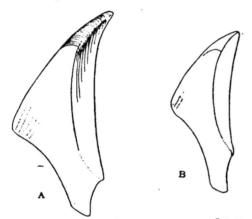

FIG. 39.—SCUTA OF *a*, BALANUS ROSTRATUS, JAPAN, No. 1814, AND *b*, B. R. APERTUS, POPOFF STRAIT, ALASKA.

Originally described from quite young specimens collected by the *Challenger*, this species has been found to reach about the size of *B. balanus*. While the typical form is only known from a few localities between Kobe and Tokyo Bay, it will probably turn out to have a much wider range northward, continuous with the range of the following race.

Like *B. balanus*, it usually grows on shells. It is often overgrown with *Serpula*, the young of its own kind, and in one case with *Balanus trigonus*.

The barnacle recorded from Japan as *B. crenatus* by Doctor Krüger agrees with some forms of *rostratus* in the details figured, but as nothing is said of the radii or cirri, I dare not make a positive identification. It is certainly not *B. crenatus*.

Plate 36, figure 1, is from a specimen in the museum of the Academy of Natural Science, Philadelphia, from Tokyo Harbor. A lot of the typical form in United States National Museum from H. Loomis is labeled Japan, without exact locality (pl. 36, figs. 2, 2*a*).

The large development of *rostratus* forms in the north, where other related species exist, seems to indicate that *B. r. heteropus* and typical *B. rostratus* are peripheral southern forms derived from the north. No related species are found farther south.

In the far north, *B. rostratus* appears in various forms differing from the typical Japanese form of much warmer waters. Just what status these races, if such they are, will eventually be given, can not be decided until many hundreds are collected and studied. They have no regional differentiation, and it may be a matter of station. At present it seems to me desirable to advertise the differentiation of the group by giving names to the leading forms, which have more tangible characters than the forms of *B. balanus.* Their most obvious characters are as follows:

a^1. Transverse septa of parietal tubes extending nearly or quite to the base.
  b^1. Radii conspicuously sunken; about 14 tubes in the rostrum____*B. rostratus*
  b^2. Radii but slightly sunken; about 18 or more tubes in the rostrum.
    c^1. Large Alaskan form, diam. 60–70 mm.; four or five pairs of spines on
      each segment of the posterior cirri_____*B. r. alaskensis*
    c^2. Smaller Puget Sound form, diam. about 18 mm.; at most four pairs of
      spines on segments of posterior cirri_____*B. r. heteropus*
a^2. Transverse septa confined to the upper half of the parietal tubes; usually
  about 18 tubes in the rostrum.
  b^1. Radii but slightly sunken.
    c^1. Rather thin, wall spinose or somewhat rugose; basis typically concave;
      usually on sponges, sometimes on shells_____*B. r. apertus*
    c^2. Large and solid, walls smooth_____*B. r. dalli*
  b^2. Radii conspicuously sunken, walls thick_____*B. r. suturalis*

BALANUS ROSTRATUS ALASKENSIS, new subspecies.

Plate 38, figs. 4, 4a, 5.

Type.—Cat. No. 3415, U.S.N.M., from Kodiak, Alaska, 50 feet, collected by W. H. Dall.

The barnacle is white, conic, very solid, with narrow radii; outer lamina of the wall smooth where preserved, but extensively eroded, exposing the large parietal tubes, which are crossed by *many transverse septa, down to the base.* Between the septa, several longitudinal threads are seen on the inner lamina. The rostrum has 18 tubes. Interseptal ribs on the inside numerous, sometimes 6 or 9 in one interval. Adductor ridge of the scutum prominent. Both tergum and scutum have a faint pink tint toward their apices.

Carinorostral diameter, 61 mm.; height, 53 mm. (Kodiak).

Carinorostral diameter, 70 mm.; height, 46 mm. (Unalaska).

The labrum in the type-specimen is toothless on one side, with one tooth on the other. Mandibles as usual in the species. Maxillæ (fig. 40c) with the three major spines about twice as long as the others, the discrepancy in size being greater than usual.

The penis is not so long as in the type of *B. r. apertus*, but is longer than in *B. balanus.*

Cirrus i has rami of 34 and 16 segments; cirrus ii nearly equal rami of 19 and 17 segments; cirri iv to vi have five pairs of spines on part of the segments of one ramus, four on the rest and on those of the other ramus. A general view of the cirri of one side is given on page 8, figure 6. The spines do not show in the photograph. The cirri are pigmented, so that spinules are hard to see. There are subsutural multifid spinules on cirri iv and v, and numerous simple spinules on the segments of cirrus iv.

A rather thin, smooth specimen (Cat. No. 48026, U.S.N.M.), which had grown on a large *Mytilus*, was taken at Cape Douglas, Alaska, by T. W. Stanton during the Shelikof Strait exploration in 1904. The radii are but slightly sunken and rather narrow. The interior is very closely and sharply ribbed up to the sheath. The rostrum has part of the tubes subdivided, so that there are 45 parietal tubes, an extraordinary number. This is evidently correlated with the thinness of the wall, bringing the inner and outer laminæ close together, so that the lamellæ, which form imperfect septa in ordinary *rostratus*, become concrescent, forming complete septa. The transverse septa occur nearly to the basal edge (pl. 38, fig. 5). Opercular valves wanting.

All of the localities for this subspecies are along the Aleutian chain and the southern coast of the Alaskan Peninsula.

U.S.N.M. Cat. No.	Locality.	Collector.	Notes.
	Marmot Island, Alaska..............	Dr. W. N. Jones......	45 fathoms; collection A. N. S. P.
48026	Cape Douglas, Alaska...............	T. W. Stanton........	Dead, on beach.
3415	Kodiak, Alaska.....................	W. H. Dall............	8 fathoms; type-specimen.
	Cold Bay, Shelikof Strait............	T. W. Stanton........	
9182	Unalaska, Aleutian Islands..........	W. H. Dall............	Dead, on beach.

BALANUS ROSTRATUS HETEROPUS, new subspecies.

Plate 36, figs. 7, 7a, 8.

Type.—Cat. No. 48022 U.S.N.M., from *Albatross* Station 2864, latitude 48° 22' north, longitude 122° 51' west; Puget Sound, Washington, in 48 fathoms; bottom temperature, 47°.7 F.

Other localities.—San Juan Islands, Puget Sound, between 10 and 50 fathoms; Homer Wheeler, in collection of the Academy of Natural Sciences of Philadelphia.

The barnacle resembles *B. r. apertus*, being steep-walled, with large orifice. It is rather thin, the parietes smoothish, not ribbed or spinose; radii wide, only slightly sunken, with level summits when unbroken. The parietal tubes are small (18 to over 30 in the rostrum), with many transverse septa, which extend nearly to the base.

Greatest carinorostral diameter, 18 mm.; height, 20 mm.

Greatest carinorostral diameter, 17 mm.; height (of rostrum, the longest compartment), 27 mm.

The scutum has longitudinal striæ in the intervals between the growth-ridges, but they do not crenulate the latter. The adductor ridge is rather strong in some individuals, very weak in others.

Tergum is nearly as in *B. r. apertus*. The spur is rather short and *narrower than in B. balanus pugetensis*. The inflexed scutal margin also is narrower (pl. 36, fig. 7).

Mouth parts.—The labrum is very shortly hairy, with a single almost obsolete tooth on each side (fig. 40*b*). Mandibles as in *B. r. apertus*. Maxilla with the three major spines nearly twice as long as the minor spines, of which there are 13.

Cirri.—Cirrus i has rami of 13 and 24 segments; cirrus ii has very slightly unequal rami of 15 segments each; cirrus iii has more unequal rami of 18 and 15 segments, those of the anterior ramus armed with a few spinules. Cirrus vi has about 40 segments. There are at most four pairs of spines, the lower pair very small (fig. 40*a*).

The penis is long, but shorter than in *B. r. apertus*, about as in *B. r. alaskensis*.

With the external form of *B. rostratus apertus*, this race has transverse septa in the lower as well as the upper part of the parietal tubes,

FIG. 40.—BALANUS ROSTRATUS HETEROPUS, TYPE.   *a*, 27TH SEGMENT OF CIRRUS VI.   *b*, LABRUM AND PALPUS.   *c*, B. R. ALASKENSIS, MAXILLA.

and the posterior cirri have *few spines*, like *B. balanus pugetensis*. The numerous and small parietal tubes, well furnished with transverse septa, are characters like *B. rostratus apertus*, or perhaps more like *B. r. alaskensis*, since there are septa in the lower parts of the tubes. It should be noted that in the reduced number of spines on the posterior cirri, *B. r. heteropus* and *B. r. alaskensis* resemble one another.

Figures 5, 7*a*, 8, 9 and 10 of plate 36 have the outer lamina of the parietes partly filed away, to show the parietal tubes and septa.

B. r. heteropus and *B. b. pugetensis* occur together in both localities given above, sometimes growing upon the same shell or upon one another. They are exceedingly similar externally, and can not be separated without thorough examination. In the large series I have studied there are no individuals suggesting intergradation or hybridism.

The specimens from the San Juan Islands approach the size of *B. r. apertus*, the largest measuring 23 mm. in carinorostral diameter,

24 mm. high. The scutum is deeply striated longitudinally, just as in
B. r. apertus, and all the opercular valves are faintly tinged with
pink toward the apices. The parietal tubes are small and numerous,
36 in the rostrum of one individual.

BALANUS ROSTRATUS APERTUS Pilsbry.

Plate 36, figs. 3–6; pl. 37, figs. 1–1c.

1911. *Balanus rostratus apertus* PILSBRY, Bull. Bur. Fisheries, vol. 29, p.
74, fig. 6, pl. 12, fig. 4, 7; pl. 13, fig. 1, 2, 8, 9 (issued Feb. 17).

Type.—No. 38667, U.S.N.M., from *Albatross* Station No. 4778,
Bering Sea, north latitude 52° 12′, east longitude 179° 52′ in 43
fathoms; embedded in a sponge.

Distribution.—Bering Sea.

The shell is white under a very thin marguerite-yellow epidemis,
often deciduous; subcylindric or conic, with a large, triangular-ovate
orifice, frequently almost or quite as large as the base. The parietes
are marked with minute growth-striæ, usually showing lines of
minute granules at considerable intervals; there are some irregularities but rarely any ribs, some specimens (including the type) bearing
a few short, acute spines projecting downward, each terminating
a short rib. The radii are much wider than in *B. rostratus*, with
the upper edges parallel to the base. They are only *very little*
sunken below the parietes. Internally the parietes are deeply,
closely, and sharply ribbed. Parietal tubes square, crossed by many
transverse septa in the upper part, but without septa near the base.
The tubes are more numerous than in *B. rostratus*, about 18 (16 to
over 20) in the rostrum. The wall is thin in the typical form, the
tubes therefore compressed.

Opercular valves as in *B. rostratus* except that the tergum (pl.
37, figs. 1a, 1c) is narrower, and often has well-developed crests for
the depressor muscles. The terga of both forms are drawn in
figure 39.

The basis is concave, often deeply so, in specimens growing on
sponges, the typical station of the subspecies. It is rather thin, without pores.

Height 46 mm., greatest diameter 33 mm., length of aperture 19
mm., length of tergum 22 mm. (Station 4778).

Height 45 mm., greatest diameter 31 mm., diameter of base 24
mm., length of aperture 26 mm. (Station 4778).

Height 27 mm., greatest diameter 26 mm. (Captains Harbor).

Height 44 mm., greatest diameter 31 mm. (Unalaska).

Height 33 mm., greatest diameter 21 mm., length aperture 29 mm.
(Station 2849, on *Terebratulina*).

Height 73 mm., greatest diameter 36 mm., diameters of base 27 and 28½ mm. (Unalaska, on a sponge).

The labrum has two minute teeth on each side. Palpi similar to those of *B. balanus.*

The mandibles of No. 38667 have three rather stout short teeth, then a minute tooth and an obtuse lower angle. The upper and lower borders are densely and very finely hairy, as are also the intervals between the teeth (fig. 42*b*).

The maxillæ do not differ materially from those of *B. rostratus* as figured by Hoek, except that there are several small spines above

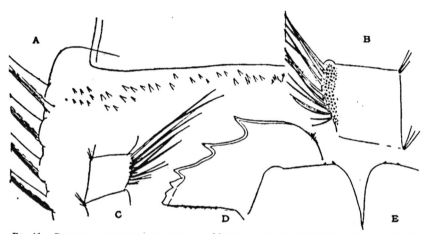

Fig. 41.—Balanus rostratus apertus. *a*, 14th segment of anterior ramus cirrus iv, much enlarged to show distal spinules. *b*, 27th segment of anterior ramus cirrus vi, both from Cat. No. 38667. *c*, form suturalis, No. 48025, 37th segment cirrus vi. *d*, mandible. *e*, labrum.

the two great spines (fig. 42*c*). There is a large spine in the middle of the lower border, as in all of the *B. balanus* group.

The first cirrus (fig. 42*a*) has very unequal rami of 15 and 27 segments, those of the posterior branch strongly protuberant at the anterior side, with dense hair-tufts. The second and third cirri also have unequal branches, the segments of both strongly protuberant, with dense tufts. Cirrus ii has 15 and 19 segments; cirrus iii, 12 and 19. Both rami are rather well provided with spinules except in the distal third. In cirrus iv, both rami have spinules along the distal borders (fig. 41*a*, part of the fourteenth segment of anterior ramus). Cirrus v has one or two rows of spinules near the distal sutures of the segments. Cirri iv to vi are of the usual slender and elongate shape, with subequal branches of about 35 segments. These segments are convex anteriorly, each with 6 or 7 pairs of spines, with some minute accessory spines at their bases, and having the usual posterior sutural groups of small spines (fig. 42*d*, fifteenth and sixteenth segments of cirrus v). There are also some spines along the distal sutures of the segments of the outer ramus of cirrus vi (fig. 41*b*).

The penis is very long, over 20 mm., purplish, densely and conspicuously annulated, with a very few short hairs near the end. There is a blunt projection on the dorsal base.

A paratype of *apertus* examined has numerous simple bifid and trifid spinules on the segments of cirrus iii, also a band formed of several rows of minute, flat, fimbriated spines on the distal borders of the segments. Cirrus iv has a row of sutural spinules, but none

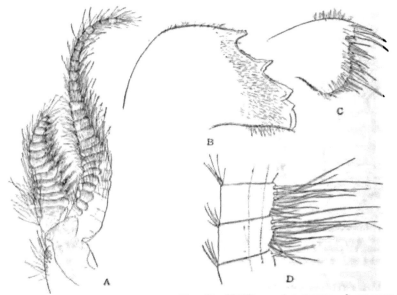

FIG. 42.—BALANUS ROSTRATUS APERTUS (CAT. NO. 38667). *a*, 1ST CIRRUS. *b*, MANDIBLE. *c*, MAXILLA. *d*, 15TH AND 16TH SEGMENTS OF CIRRUS V.

were seen on vi. The palpi are similar in structure to those of *B. balanus*, except that the bristles are all very much smaller and shorter.

Typical *B. r. apertus* is readily distinguishable from typical *B. rostratus* by the thinner wall, cylindric form, with large orifice, the wider, not sunken radii, and especially by having more tubes in the parietes, about 18 in the rostrum, without transverse septa in the lower part, against about 14 in *B. rostratus*, where the septa extend close to the base. The tergum is narrower for its length, and, while usually white, it sometimes has a beautiful pink (vinaceous) tint, which also colors the apices of the scuta in some of the specimens taken by Dall at Unalaska. The only tangible differences between the appendages of this form and *B. balanus* is that the number of spines on the segments of the cirri is greater in *B. r. apertus*, and the penis is decidedly longer.

The most profusely spinose examples of *B. r. apertus* were taken from a "hermit crab sponge," Captains Bay, Unalaska (pl. 36, fig. 6). The base is very concave, and the spines remind one of spinose varieties of *B. tintinabulum.* Opercular valves, pink-tinted. The sponge which these barnacles grow in is a very close-grained, soft and friable species. The typical form of *apertus* is almost always on sponge, but sometimes on shells. One from *Pecten* (Captains Bay, Unalaska, 10 fathoms, Dall) reproduces the ribs of the shell and has no spines (pl. 36, fig. 4). Another, growing on *Terebratulina* (pl. 36, figs. 3, 5), *Albatross* Station 2849, is unusually thin, with smooth walls and very large orifice. A ground specimen is figured to show the transverse septa of the upper half of the parietal tubes, and their absence in the lower half. A rostrum of one of this lot has 18 tubes; there is a single accessory rib in each interseptal interval. In the specimens growing on shells the base is less concave than when growing on sponges, conforming, of course, to the contour of the shell.

When growing on a sponge, it appears that the pressure of the growing basal edges of the wall tends to cut into the sponge, so that the periphery penetrates deeper than the initial point of fixation, causing the base to be dome or cone shaped. In *Acasta* the exactly opposite condition obtains; the growing periphery of the barnacle yields to the pressure of the living sponge and is forced upward, the base becoming an inverted cone, or bowl-shaped.

U. S. F. C. Sta. No.	Locality.	Depth (fathoms).	Bottom temperature °F.	Collector.
	10 miles west of Franklin Point, Arctic Ocean, Alaska.	13½	....	Point Barrow expedition.
	Latitude 66° 12′ 00″ north; longitude 168° 54′ 00″ west.	....	....	Lieut. Geo. M. Stoney.
3232	Latitude 58° 31′ 30″ north; longitude 157° 34′ 15″ west.	10½	47	*Albatross,*
	Constantine Harbor, Amchitka Island..	....	....	W. H. Dall.
4777	Near Semisopochnoi Island.............	52	....	*Albatross.*
4778	Latitude 52° 12′ 00″ north; longitude 179° 52′ 00″ east.	43	....	Do.
	Captains Harbor, Unalaska.............	10	....	W. H. Dall.
	Unalaska (several lots).................	5–15	....	Do.
	Popoff Strait, Shumagin Island........	....	....	Do.
	East coast Nague, Shumagin Island.....	....	....	Do.
2849	Latitude 56° 16′ 00″ north; longitude 160° 28′ 00″ west.	69	43	*Albatross.*
2856	Latitude 58° 07′ 00″ north; longitude 151° 36′ 00″ west.	68	44	Do.
	Middleton Island, Alaska...............	Low tide.	....	W. H. Dall.

BALANUS ROSTRATUS DALLI, new subspecies.

Plate 38, figs. 1–1c, 2.

This form attains a large size and is quite solid; external surface smooth; radii very little sunken, moderately wide. Parietal tubes large and square, with one or two interseptal ribs on the inner lamina;

these tubes having transverse septa about half way down, the lower half being open. Inside of the parietes sharply ribbed to the sheath (or in some old individuals, becoming nearly smooth above).

Carinorostral diameter, 55 mm.; meight, 43 mm. (type).

Greatest basal diameter, 47 mm.; height, 62 mm. (No. 48023).

The type of this variety was taken by Dall at Unalaska (Cat. No. 9202, U.S.N.M.). It is on a very large valve of *Placunanomia*.

It differs from *B. r. alaskensis* by having septa in the upper part of the parietal tubes only, as in *B. r. apertus*, which is a much thinner, smaller, and generally rougher barnacle. There are 21 tubes in the rostrum of this specimen.

The mouth-parts of the largest specimen in group No. 38670 (figured in my former paper, pl. 12, fig. 4), agree with *B. r. apertus* No. 38667. The third cirrus has no spinules, but there are some minute fimbriated flat spines and slender sutural bristles as in *B. balanus*. Some of the flat spines were seen on cirrus v, but none on vi. The largest individual in this group of seven on the shell of a *Pecten* measures 55 mm. high, 45 mm. in greatest diameter of the base.

Cat. No.	Locality.	Collector.	Notes.
9202	Unalaska....................................	W. H. Dall.............	Type. Pl. 38, figs. 1–1c.
48023	.....do...................................	....do.................	Pl. 38, fig. 2.
	Plover Bay, Siberia......................	....do.................	In 25 fathoms.
38670	*Albatross* Station 4779, near Semisopochnoi Island, Aleutians (54 fathoms).	*Albatross*	Bull U. S. Bureau of Fisheries, vol. 29, pl. 12, fig. 4.
9187	Kyska Harbor............................	W. H. Dall.............	

Form *suturalis* (pl. 38, fig. 3). The *Corwin* took a peculiar form in Alaska, exact locality not noted, in 1884. It is externally a good deal like typical *B. rostratus*, as the shape is conic, with small orifice, radii are sunken, parietes with angular edges. Otherwise it is more like *dalli*. The wall is thick, with large square tubes, 17 in one rostrum examined. Interseptal ribs, usually one or two. The tubes are open a long way up; no septa visible from below. The labrum (fig. 41e) has no teeth. The teeth of the mandibles are unusually acute, but typical in arrangement (fig. 41d). Cirri and penis are substantially as in *B. r. apertus*, the posterior cirri having segments with seven pairs of spines (fig. 41c).

The type is Cat. No. 48025, U.S.N.M.

I have some doubt whether this form will prove separable from *B. r. dalli* when large series are obtained. A specimen of *dalli* from Kyska Harbor and one from Plover Bay have very narrow radii, but they are not sunken as in *suturalis*.

BALANUS BALANUS (Linnæus).

Plates 33, 34, 35.

1758. *Lepas balanus* LINNÆUS, Systema Naturæ, ed. 10, p. 667 ("*ad littora oceani Europaei*"); see HANLEY, Ipsa Linnæi Conchylia, 1855, p. 18.

1778. B[*alanus*] *porcatus* DA COSTA, Historia Naturalis Testaceorum Britanniæ, p. 249.

1780. *Lepas balanus* Linnæus, BORN, Testacea Musei Caesarei, p. 8, pl. 1, fig. 4 (good).

1789. *Balanus sulcatus* BRUGUIÈRE, Encyclopedie Méthodique, p. 163, pl. 164, fig. 1.

1803. *Lepas costatus* MONTAGU, Testacea Britannica, p. 11.

1804. *Lepas balanus* Linnæus, DONOVAN, Natural History of British Shells, pl. 30, fig. 1.

1804. *Lepas costata* DONOVAN, Natural History of British Shells, pl. 30, fig. 2.

1815. *Lepas scotica* WOOD, General Conchology, p. 40, pl. 6, fig. 3.

1818. *Balanus tessellatus* SOWERBY, Mineral Conchology, pl. 84.

1830. *Balanus geniculatus* CONRAD, Journal of the Academy of Natural Sciences of Philadelphia, vol 6, p. 265, pl. 11, fig. 16.

1844. *Balanus communis* BROWN, Illustrations of the Recent Conchology of Great Britain and Ireland, p. 120, pl. 53, fig. 23.

1844. *Balanus costatus* Montagu, BROWN, Illustrations of the Recent Conchology of Great Britain and Ireland, p. 120, pl. 54, figs. 2, 3.

1854. *Balanus porcatus* E. da Costa, DARWIN, Monograph, p. 256, pl. 6, figs. 4a–4e; Monograph on Fossil Balanidæ, p. 21, pl. 1, figs. 5a–5g.

1878. *Balanus porcatus* Da Costa, MIERS, Narrative of a Voyage to the Polar Sea, by Capt. S'r G. S. Nares, vol. 2, p. 247 (Cape Louis Napoleon, lat. 79° 38′ N., 50 fathoms; Richardson Bay, lat 80° 2′ N., 70 fathoms).

1897. *Balanus porcatus* Da Costa, WELTNER, Verzeichnis der bisher beschriebenen recenten Cirripedienarten, Archiv f. Naturg., Jahrg. 1897, p. 267 (exclusive of Japanese records).

1900. *Balanus porcatus* Da Costa, WELTNER, Fauna Arctica, vol. 1, pp. 292–297, 303, pl. 8, figs. 1–12 (distribution and variation).

1911. *Balanus porcatus* Costa, SUMNER, Biol. Survey Woods Hole and Vicinity, Bull. Bur. Fisheries, vol. 31, p. 646.

Type.—Collection of the Linnean Society of London.

Distribution.—Arctic and North Atlantic Oceans, from 80° North latitude, Franz Josef Archipelago to the English Channel, and in America south to Long Island Sound. Bering Sea; a variety in Puget Sound. From low tide (in northern localities) to about 90 fathoms. English Pliocene; Pleistocene of Sweden, Canada, and Maine.[1]

According to Darwin its characters are as follows:

Shell white, generally sharply ribbed longitudinally; radii with their summits almost parallel to the basis. Scutum longitudinally striated; tergum with the apex produced and [usually] purple.

---

[1] The records of this species from Campbell and Stewart Islands, New Zealand, were undoubtedly based upon erroneous identifications. Weltner states that it does not exist in the Mediterranean.

General appearance.—Shell conical, somewhat convex; white, sometimes tinted yellowish, from the thin investing membrane; the produced tips of the terga are purple; the parietes of each compartment have from two to four strong, prominent, sharp, straight, longitudinal ribs; these are sometimes irregular, and rarely, as will presently be described, they are absent. The radii are smooth and of considerable breadth; their summits are nearly parallel to the basis or only slightly oblique; hence the orifice is entire; it is rather small and ovate, being broad at the rostral end and very sharp and narrow at the carinal end.

The scutum is more or less concave from end to end, with sculpture of narrow, *prominent growth-ridges, crossed by fine longitudinal striæ* which crenulate the ridges. The articular ridge is low, rather abruptly terminated below. Usually there is no distinct adductor ridge, but the callous occupying its place has a slightly raised, acute border, bounding the very deep pit for the lateral depressor muscle, and the border of the adductor muscle pit is slightly prominent and angular. Sometimes these prominences stand in line and are weakly connected, forming thus a rather ill-defined adductor ridge.

The tergum is very much narrower than the scutum, its length nearly twice the width. Its pointed beak, of a purplish or pale-pink tint, or sometimes white, *projects well above the scutum.* Externally it is marked with somewhat coarse growth-lines. There is no longitudinal furrow, but a wide spur-fasciole is defined by impressed lines. Spur close to the basiscutal angle, truncate distally, the basal margin sloping to it on both sides. The articular ridge is rather low; scutal margin is sharply inflexed in the lower part. Crests for the depressor muscles are irregular, not very strong.

Darwin says:

The parietes have large, square parietal tubes; in the upper part these are filled up solidly *without transverse septa;* the longitudinal septa are finely denticulated at their bases, and the denticuli extend unusually close to the outer lamina. In very young specimens the inner lamina of the parietes is ribbed in lines corresponding with the longitudinal septa, as is the case with most species of the genus; but in medium and large-sized specimens there are *between the ribs, thus produced, from one to four smaller ribs,* which do not correspond with any longitudinal septa; they are finely denticulated at their bases and may be considered as the representatives of longitudinal septa which have not been developed and reached the outer lamina. I have seen no other instance of this structure, namely, the presence of a greater number of ribs, on the inner lamina of the walls, than there are longitudinal septa. [*B. rostratus* is similar in this respect.] The radii have their summits generally parallel to the surface of attachment, as is usual in the first section of the genus, but sometimes they are slightly oblique; the septa sometimes rudely branch a little, but they exhibit scarcely a trace of denticuli; the interspaces are filled up quite solidly. The alæ have their summits very oblique; their sutural edges are finely crenated.

Basis rather thin, translucent, not permeated by pores; obscurely furrowed in lines radiating from the center; the circumference is marked in a peculiar manner by the longitudinal septa and by the tips of those intermediate denticulated ribs which occur on the inner lamina of the parietes.

Mouth.—Labrum with six teeth; mandibles with the fourth and fifth teeth small and rudimentary. Maxillæ, with a small notch under the upper pair of spines; in the lower part there is a single large spine. Cirri, dark brownish purple, making a singular contrast with the white operculum and shell; first pair, with one ramus having 26 segments, and about twice as long as the shorter ramus having 12 or 13 segments, with their front surfaces protuberant. In the second pair of cirri the segments are but little protuberant; third pair about one-third longer than the second pair; sixth pair elongated, having in the same individual 46 segments; these segments have shield-shaped fronts bearing 5 pairs of spines, with some minute intermediate bristles. There is the usual point at the dorsal base of the penis.[1] (See p. 152, fig. 43.)

The third (fig. 43*e*) and fourth (fig. 43*c*) pairs of cirri have minute spinules on the outer faces of part of the segments.

Nomenclature.—Darwin accepted da Costa's name *Balanus porcatus* for this species in order to avoid tautonymy, the earlier specific name *Lepas balanus* becoming *Balanus balanus* in the new combination. This custom, sanctioned by the general usage of Darwin's time, has long ago been discarded. The specific name is now held to be the permanent part of the binomial combination. Most of the early authors correctly identified the species Linnæus described as *Lepas balanus*. His original specimen is preserved in the collection of the Linnean Society of London, and is figured on plate 33, figures 1, 1*a*.

Affinities and differential characters.—*B. balanus* is very distinct from all other Atlantic species. The long-beaked terga, with a wide but rather long spur, the fine longitudinal striation of the scuta, the square tubes of the wall, which has *more numerous ribs on the internal surface than there are septa in the basal edge*, and, finally, the solid, never porous, calcareous basis, are amply diagnostic characters. Any single wall compartment or opercular valve will serve to identify it. Usually it may be known also by the wide, level-topped radii and strongly ribbed walls. Some specimens of *B. crenatus* resemble *B. balanus* superficially. In the Pacific it is different. There we have a very closely related species in *B. rostratus*, which occurs with *B. balanus* in Bering Sea; but the two differ in several important details of structure, as follows:

B. balanus.	*B. rostratus.*
Parietal tubes without transverse septa.	Parietal tubes having numerous transverse septa.
Spur of tergum wide at the end, its fasciole broad.	Spur narrow distally, its fasciole narrower.
Adductor ridge of the scutum wanting or weakly developed.	Adductor ridge distinct, and, though often rather weak, it stands free of the articular ridge.
Penis short.	Penis long.

[1] It is not known whether Darwin's description of the mouth and cirri were from the strong or the rather weak ribbed form of the species, both of which occur in the British Islands.

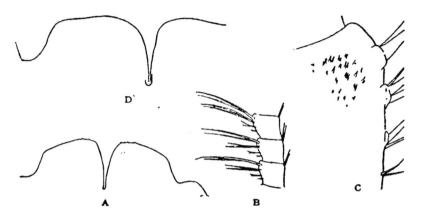

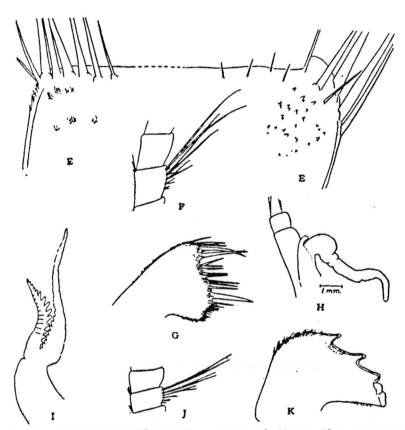

FIG. 43.—BALANUS BALANUS (LINNÆUS). *a*, LABRUM. *b*, 16TH TO 18TH SEGMENTS OF
CIRRUS VI, ENGLAND. *c*, PART OF THE 16TH SEGMENT OF CIRRUS IV. *d*, LABRUM.
e, DISTAL PART OF A SEGMENT OF THE ANTERIOR RAMUS OF CIRRUS III. *f*, INTERMEDIATE
SEGMENTS OF CIRRUS VI. *g*, MAXILLA. *h*, PENIS. *i*, FIRST CIRRUS. BAR HARBOR,
MAINE. *j*, 17TH AND 18TH SEGMENTS OF CIRRUS VI. *k*, MANDIBLE. BAY OF FUNDY.

The first and last of these differences are the most definite, and in my experience they are invariable characters in each species. *B. rostratus* is rarely ribbed, and never ribbed so strongly as the common forms of *B. balanus*. In the latter species the inflexed scutal border of the tergum terminates basad in a lobe, while in *B. rostratus* it is straight or obliquely cut off, and the spur stands nearer the basiscutal angle.

B. balanus, like its Pacific relative *B. rostratus*, is far from being a homogeneous species. In going over large numbers from several regions one gains the idea that there are several subordinate races. Differences in the sculpture, the structure of the walls, the dentation of the labrum, and the number of spines on the cirri are readily found. Yet, without making a great number of dissections and devoting several weeks or perhaps months to the problem, I do not feel competent to distinguish between fluctuating variation, variation due to the effect of station on the individual, on the one hand, and heritable variation of racial import on the other. It would be an ill service to science to attempt the diagnosis of local races without such an investigation as I have indicated. The results of my work so far as I have gone, are briefly given below.

Station.—*B. balanus* usually makes its home on shells, probably because they are the most abundant solid objects available in the depths it inhabits. When growing on objects with an even surface, such as *Pecten magellanicus* or *Modiolus modiolus*, they reach their ideal development; but on the banks they are also common on *Buccinum, Tritonifusus, Aporrhais, Terebratulina*, on pebbles, or more rarely growing on one another. *B. balanus* is frequently associated with *B. hameri* and *B. crenatus*. It is rather common in from 20 to 90 fathoms, but seems to drop out of the fauna rather abruptly at the latter depth, as it would surely have been taken if present at some of the very numerous *Albatross* stations in deeper water. South of Cape Cod it seems exceptional above 18 or 20 fathoms, where *B. eburneus* and *B. amphitrite niveus* are the prevalent species. Farther north, on the Maine coast and northward, *B. balanus* is sometimes taken at depths of only a few fathoms. On Coffin Island, Magdalen Islands, in the Gulf of St. Lawrence, Mr. Bayard Long found it at low water, on *Mytilus edulis*.

Variations in the structure of the wall.—The figures on plate 35 show the chief variations in the basal septa of the walls. Figure 5, from Georges Bank, is the normal and most frequent condition. There are from one to four ribs on the inner lamina between the complete septa; outer lamina has several or many very short lamellæ within the margin. The rostrum here figured has 14 tubes.

Plate 35, figure 3, represents portions of two rostra from Eastport, Maine; strongly ribbed form. Here the inner and outer laminæ of the wall are more separated and the septa are irregularly spaced, the internal ribs are more numerous, and the lamellæ within the outer lamina are stronger. Rostrum has 13 tubes. There is an extraordinary development of the interseptal lamellæ within the outer lamina of the wall in a specimen from Portland, Maine (pl. 35, fig. 6). In one example from Cork, Ireland, the interseptal lamellæ within the outer lamina of the wall are similarly lengthened (pl. 35, fig. 7, Cat. No. 12092). These lamellæ are minutely crenulate; many of them almost reach the inner lamina.

Plate 35, figures 2, 2a, *Albatross* Station 2079, Georges Bank, in 75 fathoms. Wall thin, the tubes compressed. Inner lamina of wall with one to four ribs terminating in strong, denticulate teeth. Outer lamina bordered with crowded, short lamellæ. The rostrum has 13 tubes.

Plate 35, figure 1a, Aberdare Channel, Franz Josef Land, above north latitude 80°. *Very few* interseptal ribs or lamellæ; 14 tubes in the rostrum, which is very narrow. It appears that the number of tubes (about 14 in the rostrum) is rather constant, but their shape and the development of interseptal ribs and lamellæ depend upon the thickness of the walls and the shape of the compartment, whether spreading, as in conical individuals, or narrow, as in cylindric forms of the species.

There are never any transverse septa in the tubes.

Individuals growing on *Pecten* are often beautifully fluted, in harmony with the ribs of the shell (pl. 33, fig. 2a), while others in the same group may be unaffected. Often the *Pecten* specimens have only traces of ribs, the surface being minutely shagreened, as though the conflict between the ribs of the barnacle and those induced by the *Pecten* had resulted in a general flattening of sculpture (pl. 35, fig. 2). The scutum is thick, often strongly curved; pit for the depressor muscle narrow, deep, almost tubular from the prominence of the tergal border and the adductor callous. In the single British specimen of the typical form I was able to dissect, the six teeth of the labrum (fig. 43a) are exceedingly small. The sixth cirrus has four pairs of spines on the segments (fig. 43b) instead of five, as stated by Darwin, but it is likely that more distad segments would show another pair. In the dry example examined, the cirri were broken at the eighteenth segment. The mandibles and maxillæ are substantially alike in the numerous forms of *B. balanus* and *B. rostratus* examined, merely differing a little in the proportions and number of the spines of the maxillæ.

Regional distribution and variation.—European specimens (pl. 33, figs. 1–6b) rarely attain 30 mm. in diameter, and are more frequently 20 to 25 mm., judging by a considerable series in the museum, brought together by the conchologist J. Gwyn Jeffreys.

There seem to be two chief races among the British specimens. The typical form (pl. 33, figs. 1-2a, 6-6b) is rather high with steep walls, which have the ribs only moderately prominent and usually irregular; radii wide. The external sculpture is readily modified by the irregularities of the supporting object.

The type-specimen [1] is represented in plate 33, figures 1, 1a. The surface is irregularly roughened by the laminæ of the *Pecten*, and the ribs are irregular.

The other European race or "form" (pl. 33, figs 4, 5) is conic, spreading and very rugged; rostrum with four strong ribs, laterals and carina, three or four, carinolaterals with one strong rib; radii rather narrow. Opercular valves as in typical *B. balanus*. The ribs in this race seem very little affected by the irregularities of the support. Examples from Belfast Bay, growing on *Pecten opercularis* (fig. 5), are similar to those growing on the smooth mussel *Modiolus modiolus* (fig. 4).

Donovan's *Lepas balanus* is this form. His *Lepas costata* seems to be the young stage of a similar form which I have seen from Scarborough (fig. 4), and which differs only by having more ribs; in a specimen 19 mm. in diameter there are seven ribs on the rostrum, five on the lateral compartments.

Northward *B. balanus* becomes larger than in England and Ireland. Darwin records a specimen 2.1 inches in diameter from the Shetland Islands, and others equally large from glacial deposits of the Isle of Bute.

Arctic Ocean.—The highest latitude for *B. balanus*, or so far as I know, for any cirripede, is Aberdare Channel, east of Alger Island, latitude 80° 21' 21" north, longitude 56° 08' east, in the Franz Josef Land Archipelago. Here the Baldwin-Ziegler Expedition obtained a series of rather peculiar specimens, Cat. No. 48195, U.S.N.M., illustrated on plate 35, figures 1, 1a, 1b. The form is cylindric or barrel shaped, the orifice as large as the base. The parietes usually show weak ribs in the upper part, and sometimes they persist irregularly to the base. Radii very broad. Interior strongly striate, the septa between outer and inner laminæ about as numerous as in the typical form, but with fewer interstitial points than in typical *balanus*. The scutum is thin, with even less trace of an adductor ridge than usual. The tergum is remarkably narrow, its carinobasal angle rounded off, and the long, free apex is not tinted (fig. 44).

The mouth parts are normal, but the posterior cirri have an additional pair of spines. First cirrus with 23 and 10 segments, second with 17 and 13. The third cirrus has many spinules on the segments of the anterior ramus, as far as the twelfth segment. On the posterior ramus there are fewer spinules, and fewer segments. On the fourth cirrus there are a few spinules, chiefly of the flat multifid form, in a row near the distal sutures of the segments. There

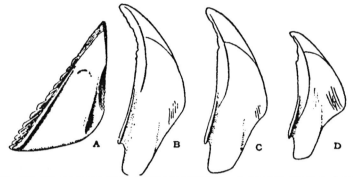

FIG. 44.—BALANUS BALANUS FROM ABERDARE CHANNEL. *a*, SCUTUM AND *b, c, d*, TERGA OF THREE INDIVIDUALS. × 2½.

are many erect, mainly simple spinules on the second segment of the pedicel. Cirrus iv has minute, flat multifid spinules on the distal parts of the segments of both rami. In cirrus vi the segments of the pedicel have many minute, multifid spinules, but there are none on the segments of the rami. These have 46 segments, bearing *six pairs of spines*. The fourth and part of the segments of the fifth cirri have five pairs of spines. The penis is typical except that I can find *no trace of the point near the base*, characteristic of *B. balanus*. The individual dissected is certainly adult, the largest of a considerable series (fig. 45).

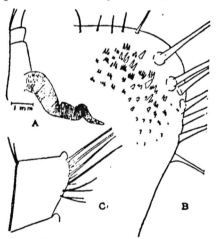

FIG. 45.—BALANUS BALANUS, ABERDARE CHANNEL. *a*, BASE OF CIRRUS VI WITH PENIS. *b*, PART OF 7TH SEGMENT OF ANTERIOR RAMUS OF RIGHT CIRRUS III. *c*, 32D SEGMENT OF CIRRUS VI.

The habit of this colony is to grow in branching groups, unlike the usual colonies of *B. balanus*.

Greenland (Upernavik) specimens attain a good size, 44 mm. in diameter and height. Ribs as in typical *B. balanus* but weaker, often hardly noticeable. Tubes of the parietes large. Beak of the tergum white. Darwin also has noted that in Arctic specimens the terga have white beaks.

Labrador specimens from 60 fathoms are deficient in ribs, with the aperture as large as the base. The terga and sometimes the scuta are faintly pink tinted. Others from 7 and 45 fathoms have the usual ribs. All are rather small.

A lot taken by Mr. O. Bryant 20 miles south of Nain, Labrador, have the terga hardly beaked, and white. The longitudinal striation of the scutum is very faint. They are small, measuring 8 mm. in diameter.

Specimens externally similar to typical *B. balanus*, but frequently larger, are common on the American coast, and on Georges Bank (pl. 35, figs. 2, 2a.) A usually larger form from Bar Harbor, Maine (pl. 34, figs. 1, 1a, 6), has six ribs on the rostrum, four and five on the latera. Others may have as many as eight ribs on the rostrum. The ribs are not nearly so strong as in the form called *B. geniculatus* by Conrad. The individual figured has the posterior ramus of the first cirrus two-thirds as long as the anterior, segments 25 and 13 (fig. 43i). Rami of second cirrus somewhat unequal, of 18 and 14 segments. The anterior ramus of cirrus iii has a few spinules, most numerous about the tenth segment (p. 152, fig. 43e). There are also some delicate spines near the distal sutures of the segments. Most of the segments of this cirrus have no spinules. Cirrus iv has a few spinules on some of the median segments (p. 152, fig. 43c, sixteenth segment of anterior ramus). The sixth cirrus has 50 segments bearing four or five pairs of spines (p. 152, fig. 43f), agreeing thus with British *B. balanus*. The *labrum* (p. 152, fig. 43d) *has no teeth*, thereby agreeing with some West American forms. Penis (p. 152, fig. 43h) has a basidorsal point. In some lots from the banks, on *Pecten islandicus*, *Albatross* stations 2079 and 2080, the diameter does not exceed 16 or 20 mm.; ribs not very strong. The walls are thin, very elaborately denticulate around the parietal tubes at the base (pl. 35, figs. 2, 2a).

An individual from Portland, Maine (pl. 34, fig. 2; pl. 35, fig. 6), collected by J. W. Mighels (Cat. No. 48016, U.S.N.M.) illustrates the mutations sometimes encountered in *Balanus*. The rostrum and lateral compartments are many-ribbed and symmetrically spreading. Their bases rested upon the shell of *Pecten magellanicus*. The carina and carinolateral compartments rested upon some irregular object on the *Pecten*, and have the vertical, rugose, obsoletely ribbed walls of the ordinary cylindric form of *B. balanus*. The basal edges of the spreading compartments are remarkably wide between the inner and outer plates of the wall, and the incomplete septa springing from the outer plate are very long, almost reaching to the inner plate. This peculiarity I have seen elsewhere only in one individual from Cork. The lateral diameter of the base is 59 mm.

Plate 34, figure 4, growing on a smooth pebble, and figure 5, on *Pecten magellanicus*, further illustrate the forms of the fishing banks.

In a specimen growing on an oyster, taken at *Fish Hawk* station 1595, Long Island Sound, 1890, the scutum has the adductor ridge almost as well developed as in the Pacific *B. rostratus.* The external characters and tergum are as in typical *B. balanus.* The diameter of the base is about 21 mm.

On the coasts of Nova Scotia and Maine, and the fishing banks offshore, we find, together with subtypical *B. balanus,* a large, very strongly ribbed, thick-walled form, which Conrad called *B. geniculatus.* It has the same rib arrangement as the Belfast form *costatus,* but the aspect is different; size larger, ribs high and angular, intervals wide, concave. Conrad's type-specimen is figured (pl. 34, fig. 3), No. 2105 A.N.S.P. A group of smaller, higher specimens from the Bay of Fundy, growing on a smooth stone, is shown in plate 34, figure 7, Cat. No. 2303 U.S.N.M. The size is often considerable. Carinorostral diameter, 44 mm.; lateral diameter, 42 mm.; height, 30 mm. (Eastport). Carinorostral diameter, 50 mm.; lateral diameter, 39 mm.; height, 32 mm. (Georges Bank).

The very strongly ribbed form from the Bay of Fundy (pl. 34, fig. 7) has cirri differing in several respects from British examples. The sixth cirrus has 49 segments, which are decidedly shorter than usual, and bear six pairs of spines (fig. 43*j*). Penis short, as usual. As *in all American specimens examined, the cirri are light yellow,* not dark as described by Darwin. The mandible is figured (fig. 43*k*).

Long Island Sound is the extreme southwestern point for *B. balanus* on our coast. Offshore it reaches a little farther south. Latitude 40° 13′ 15″ north, near the southern edge of the continental shelf, in about the latitude of Asbury Park, New Jersey, but farther east than Nantucket, is the extreme southern range known for *B. balanus* in the western Atlantic. The total range in latitude is therefore slightly over 40 degrees.

The temperatures recorded are mainly between 40° and 55° F., but at one station in Vineyard Sound, 69° F. (Aug. 27, 1887).[1]

A remarkable peculiarity in the distribution of *B. balanus* is its absence from the Great Banks of Newfoundland, where the companion species *B. crenatus* is abundant.

Alaska and Bering Sea.—B. balanus is known from latitude 57° 18′ north to the Aleutian Islands, and a form occurs in Puget Sound, widely separated from the northern herd, probably because we have few near-shore collections from intermediate points.

There is no feature of the hard parts differentiating Bering Sea specimens from some of those of the western Atlantic, but

---

[1] At 18 fathoms in Vineyard Sound there is a difference of at least 22° F. between the winter and summer bottom temperature at one station. See Sumner, Biological Survey of Woods Hole and Vicinity (Bull. Bur. of Fisheries, vol. 31, 1911).

they seem to have a constantly greater number of spines of the cirri. The tergum is narrow, as usual in New England, with a longer carinal margin than in English *balanus*. Plate 33, figure 6*c*, is the tergum of a Bering Sea specimen, rather straighter than some others.

Externally the wall may be strongly ribbed (pl. 35, fig. 4, from *Albatross* station 3289, Bering Sea), or cylindric with smaller ribs like typical *B. balanus* (pl. 35, fig. 8, Cape Prince of Wales, Alaska). Opercular valves of this lot are similar to plate 34, figures 1*a* to 1*c*. Pores of the wall like plate 35, figure 5. There is also a thin, smoother form (pl. 38, fig. 2*a*, Unalaska). The parietal tubes are compressed, approaching the condition seen in plate 35, figure 2*a*.

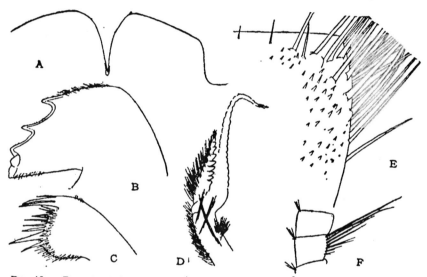

Fig. 46. — BALANUS BALANUS FROM ALASKA. *a*, LABRUM. *b*, MANDIBLE. *c*, MAXILLA. *d*, RIGHT CIRRUS I. *e*, 8TH SEGMENT OF THE ANTERIOR RAMUS OF CIRRUS III. *f*, MEDIAN SEGMENTS OF CIRRUS VI.

They are solidly filled up near the summits, as in Atlantic specimens. In the specimens from *Albatross* station 3289 the tubes are larger, but are also filled up in the upper fourth or third. They have no transverse septa in any part.

The largest Bering Sea specimen seen measures 41 mm. in greatest diameter. A cylindric specimen measures 33 mm. diameter, 30 mm. high. The large, boldly sculptured New England forms, such as plate 34, figures 1, 2, 3, are wanting in Bering Sea collections.

A specimen from Alaska, collected by the *Corwin*, has typical mouth parts, except that *the labrum has but one tooth*. The first cirrus has rami of 22 and 10 segments, the posterior ramus hardly half the length of the anterior. Second cirrus with unequal rami of 18 and 16 protuberant segments. Cirrus iii has rather numerous simple spinules on the anterior ramus, very few on the posterior. Long spines are copiously developed on both rami. Cirrus iv has a small group of mostly simple spinules on the anterior distal part of the segments. The sixth cirrus has rather short segments bearing six to seven pairs of spines. Penis about half as long as sixth cirrus, with the usual point near the base. The great inequality of the rami of cirrus i and the large number of spines on the later cirri differentiate this form from Atlantic specimens (fig. 46).

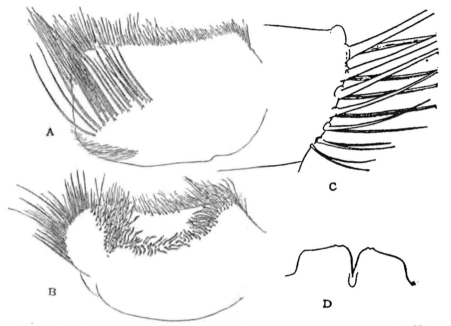

Fig. 47.—Balanus balanus, St. Pauls Island. *a*, *b*, both sides of a palpus. *c*, 22d segment of cirrus vi. *d*, labrum.

In a specimen from St. Pauls Island, Bering Sea, the labrum has two small teeth on each side, mouth parts otherwise typical. First cirrus with rami of 24 and 12 segments. The third and fourth cirri have very few small spinules, not so many as in the Bar Harbor form. The sixth cirrus has six to seven pairs of spines, as in the preceding form, from which this differs by having teeth on the labrum. The penis has the usual point near the base, and is less than half as long as the sixth cirrus (fig. 47).

By the numerous spines of the cirri the Bering Sea *B. balanus* resemble *B. rostratus*, yet the characters of the opercular valves, the absence of septa in the parietal tubes, and the more ribbed external wall are characters which surely indicate that they belong to the Atlantic species.

Herr Weltner[1] records *B. porcatus* (=*balanus*) from various points in Japan—Hakodate, Enoshima, and Yokohama—but on the following page he inserts *B. rostratus*, without locality record, as one of the species not contained in the Berlin collection. In *Fauna Arctica* (p. 296) these specimens are discussed and one of them is figured. It is, without doubt, *B. rostratus*. It may be surmised that all of his Japanese records for *porcatus* really pertain to *B. rostratus*. This mistake on the part of a zoologist expert in the determination of barnacles is readily understood, for the really diagnostic character of *B. rostratus*—the presence of transverse septa in the parietal tubes—was not mentioned in Hoek's description and can be seen only by filing the wall or looking into the pores at the base.

EUROPEAN.

Locality.	Collector.	Notes.
Aberdare Channel, east of Alger Island, Franz Josef Land.	Baldwin-Ziegler Polar Expedition.	1901.
Spitsbergen	Ernest Williamson, U.S.N..	1882.
Shetland Islands	J. Gwyn Jeffreys	
Loch Shieldag, West Ross, Scotland	...do...	
Oban, Scotland	...do...	On *Astarte*, *Pecten*, and *Terebratulina*.
Northumbrian coast	...do...	
Scarborough, England	...do...	On *Pecten*.
Mouth of the Thames	...do...	
Sandwich	...do...	
Swansea Bay, Wales	...do...	On *Mytilus*.
Rosilly Down	...do...	
Exmouth, south Devon	...do...	
Langland Bay	...do...	On *Buccinum*.
Bridlington Crag	...do...	Pliocene.
North of Ireland	...do...	
Bantry Bay, Ireland	...do...	
Cork Harbor, Ireland	...do...	On *Pecten* and *Pinna*.
Kiel Bay	Karl Möbius	

EAST AMERICAN.

U.S.F.C. Station.	Locality.	Depth (fathoms).	Bottom temperature. °F.	Collector.
	Barden Bay, Inglefield Gulf	10–40		Princeton Expedition.
	Upernavik, Greenland			
	Latitude, 70° 20′ north; longitude, 56° west, off Hare Island, Greenland.	90		C. S. McClain.
	Arctic Ocean			Capt. Rogers.
	Greenland			N. P. Scudder.
	Rittenbank, Greenland			H. G. Drexel.
	Davis Strait	40		N. P. Scudder.
	Labrador			Storer.
	Off Hebron, Labrador	60		O. Bryant.
	Egg Harbor, Labrador	7		Do.
	20 miles south of Nain, Labrador			Do.
	Anticosti Island			J. Schmitt.
	Off Halifax, Nova Scotia			U.S.F.C.
	14 miles south of Cape Sable, Nova Scotia	45		O. Bryant.
	Bay of Fundy			U.S.F.C.
2500	Latitude, 44° 28′ north; longitude, 60° 15′ 15″ west.	36		*Albatross*.
	Between La Have and western banks			J. Allen.
	Grand Manan			W. Stimpson.
	Eastport, Me			Rathbun.
	Casco Bay, Me			Do.
	Portland, Me			J. W. Mighels.

[1] Verzeichnis, p. 258.

EAST AMERICAN.[1]

U.S.F.C. Station.	Locality.	Depth (fathoms).	Bottom temperature.	Collector.
			°F.	
32	Gulf of Maine	90		U. S. F. C.
	Brunswick, Me., pleistocene			
	Northeast edge Georges Bank	50		Schooner *Otis P. Lord.*
2520	Latitude, 42° 41' 00" north; longitude, 64° 55' 30" west.	62	40.6	*Albatross.*
2066	Latitude, 42° 19' 40" north; longitude, 65° 49' 30" west.	65	43.5	Do.
2525	Latitude, 41° 49' 00" north; longitude, 65° 49' 30" west.	72	43.6	Do.
2079	Latitude, 41° 13' 00" north; longitude, 66° 19' 50" west.	75	45	Do.
2081	Latitude, 41° 10' 20" north; longitude, 66° 30' 20" west.	50	46	Do.
2082	Latitude, 41° 09' 50" north; longitude, 66° 31' 50" west.	49	46.5	Do.
2057	Latitude, 42° 01' 00" north; longitude, 68° 00' 30" west.	86		Do.
21B	Latitude, 42° 49' 00" north; longitude, 68° 50' 00" west.	52–90	43	*Bache.*
2260	Latitude, 40° 13' 15" north; longitude, 69° 29' 15" west.	46	50.2	*Albatross.*
2253	Latitude, 40° 34' 30" north; longitude, 69° 50' 45" west.	32	52.9	Do.
	West part of Georges Bank			E. P. Wonson.
158	Off Cape Ann, Mass.	38		*Speedwell.*
216	North Thatchers Island, Massachusetts Bay	35		Do.
135	do	25	40.5	Do.
219	Massachusetts Bay	32	55.5	Do.
23,28–32	do	35–48		Do.
22	Off Salem, Mass.			Do.
	Lynn, Mass.			Dr. Prescott.
348	Off Cape Cod, Massachusetts Bay	16½	46	*Speedwell.*
322	Off Cape Cod	67	40.5	Do.
321	do	29½	44.5	Do.
269	do	53	39.5	Do.
981	Off Chatham, Cape Cod	43	49	*Fish Hawk.*
1084	Off Cape Cod	37½	38	Do.
370	Off Chatham, Cape Cod	18		*Speedwell.*
240	Off Cape Cod	18	64.5	Do.
972	Off Chatham, Cape Cod	16	52	*Fish Hawk.*
983	do	36	42	Do.
984	Vineyard Sound, off Chatham, Mass.	33	41.5	Do.
1222–26	Vineyard Sound off Nobska Light	11½–13	68–69	Do.
	Noank, Conn.			U. S. F. C.
	Fishers Island Sound, Conn	9–11		Do.
	Long Island Sound			J. E. Benedict.

WEST AMERICAN AND ASIATIC.

	Cape Prince of Wales, Alaska			E. M. Kindle.
	St. Paul Island, Pribiloff Islands	Beach		H. W. Elliott.
	do			Wm. Palmer.
3482	Latitude, 57° 18' 00" north; longitude, 170° 42' 00" west.	42	38.9	*Albatross.*
3558	Latitude, 56° 58' 00" north; longitude, 170° 09' 00" west.	25	42.9	Do.
3289	Latitude, 56° 44' 30" north; longitude, 159° 16' 00" west.	16		Do.
3600	Latitude, 55° 06' 00" north; longitude, 163° 28' 00" west.	9	40	Do.
	Unalaska			W. H. Dall.
	Iliuliuk Harbor, Unalaska	10		Do.
	Kyska Harbor	10		Do.
	Bering Island			L. Stejneger.
	Ochotsk Sea			Capt. Stevens.

[1] Records of many specimens from Georges Bank, donated by fishermen who catch the barnacles on cod lines, are omitted, as that region is well covered by the more exact *Albatross* records. Most of the Maine and Massachusetts localities are represented by several or many lots, from as many collectors, only one from each place being cited here, unless details of temperature or depth are given.

All of the specimens from Bering and Ochotsk Seas, except a few detached ones, grew upon *Buccinum*, *Chrysodomus*, and *Placunanomia.*

BALANUS BALANUS PUGETENSIS, new subspecies.

Plate 36, figs. 9, 10–10b.

Type.—Cat. No. 2040, A. N. S. P., San Juan Islands, Puget Sound, between 10 and 50 fathoms, on *Pecten*, collected by Homer Wheeler, 1910.

The barnacle is rather small and thin, with steep walls and a large orifice, *not ribbed*, dirty whitish, the parietes dull, more or less roughened, radii usually glossy, with the summits slightly oblique and jagged, level in the rostrum. Parietes have rather large tubes,

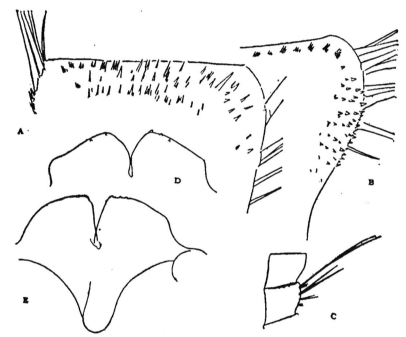

Fig. 48.—BALANUS BALANUS PUGETENSIS. *a*, 15TH SEGMENT OF THE ANTERIOR RAMUS OF CIRRUS IV. *b*, 9TH SEGMENT OF ANTERIOR RAMUS OF CIRRUS III. *c*, 21ST AND 22D SEGMENTS OF CIRRUS VI. *d*, LABRUM; ALL OF THE TYPE. *e*, LABRUM OF SPECIMEN FROM STATION 2864.

not septate, and filled up solidly in the upper part (pl. 36, fig. 9). Rostrum with 11 to 16 tubes.

Carinorostral diameter of base 21 mm.; height, 18 mm.

Opercular valves as in the typical form, except that the longitudinal striæ of the scutum are delicate and weak, and the growth ridges have an appearance of imbricating, like shingles. The valve is curved between apex and base, and has a rather deep, narrow pit for the depressor muscle.

The labrum has two and three small teeth in the type-specimen (fig. 48d). In one from *Albatross* station 2864 there are three very minute but acute denticles on one side, one barely perceptible prominence bearing several minute points and short hairs on the other (fig. 48e). Mandibles and maxillæ as usual in *B. balanus*.

Cirri.—Cirrus i with rami of 19 and 12 segments; ii with 14 and 13 segments in the type. In a specimen from *Albatross* Station 2864 there are: Cirrus i, 21 and 12; cirrus ii, 15 and 12 segments. Cirrus iii has both rami provided with numerous spinules (fig. 48b) wanting on the distal segments. Cirrus iv has many spinules near the distal sutures of the segments (fig. 48a). Cirrus v has similar but fewer spinules. Cirrus vi has four pairs of spines, the third pair small, fourth pair minute, wanting on part of the segments. There are a few minute accessory spines at the bases of the pairs, and some small ones near the distal sutures (fig. 48c).

The penis is longer than in *B. balanus*, but not so long as in *B. rostratus*. It has the usual point near the base.

By the small number of spines on the posterior cirri, this form approaches some British specimens of typical *B. balanus*.[1] It has decidedly shorter spines on the posterior sutural angles of the segments, and the penis is longer. The parietes are not ribbed, in considerable numbers seen. In the series of *B. balanus* from Bering Sea, the parietes are rugose or ribbed, and the cirri are conspicuously more spinose.

A long series growing on *Pectens*, from which the type lot was selected, was submitted by Dr. Homer Wheeler. A small lot, probably from the same locality, is in the United States National Museum collection, received from the University of Kansas; and a lot was taken by the *Albatross* at station 2864, latitude 48° 22′ north, longitude 122° 51′ west, in 48 fathoms, bottom temperature 47.7° F. (Cat. No. 48021, etc., U.S.N.M.)

It lives mingled with *B. rostratus heteropus*, and the two can not be discriminated externally. The easiest and most reliable way to tell them apart is to file the parietal face enough to expose the tubes, which are large and unobstructed in *B. b. pugetensis*, much smaller and transversely septate in *B. r. heteropus*.

SERIES OF B. CRENATUS.

White Balani, with the basis poreless; terga not beaked, not projecting conspicuously above the scuta, and without a furrow to the spur; scuta without longitudinal striation. Maxilla with one longer or larger spine near the lower angle.

Near the group of *B. balanus*, differing chiefly by the opercular valves and by the absence of spinules on the segments of the peduncles

---

[1] On the segments of *B. r. pugetensis* corresponding to those I have figured for *B. balanus* there are only three pairs of spines. Another pair appears nearer the distal end, as usual in *Balanus*.

of the cirri. As in the *B. balanus* group, there is one larger spine near the lower angle of the maxilla, instead of a pair, such as the *B. amphitrite* group has.

It is a boreal group, extending into the Temperate Zone.

Three of the commonest west American species, *B. crenatus*, *B. glandula*, and *B. hesperius*, agree in the rather small size, the dirty white ribbed or smooth wall with ribbed interior, the calcareous, poreless base, and the short spur of the tergum. The parietes have tubes in *B. crenatus*, none in *B. hesperius*, while *B. glandula* has tubes in some specimens, but wholly filled up in others. They are most easily distinguished by the scuta.

In *B. crenatus* there is no adductor ridge, the upper part of the valve being calloused, smooth or roughened.

In *B. glandula* a short adductor ridge branches downward from the articular ridge, and there is a pit below their confluence.

In *B. hesperius* the thick callous between adductor scar and articular ridge is cut into sharp little ridges.

B. balanoides is distinguished from these species by its membranous basis, but detached, fragmentary or fossil specimens may be known by the scuta. There is a convexity or rounded callus down the middle of the valve (pl. 45); moreover, the parietes are not longitudinally ribbed inside, but have some low anastomosing ridges near the basal edge.

BALANUS CRENATUS Bruguière.

Plates 39, 40.

1789. *Balanus crenatus* BRUGUIÈRE, Encyclopèdie Méthodique, p. 168.
1790. *Lepas plicata* SPENGLER, Skrivter af Naturhistorie Selskabet, vol. 1, p. 167.
1790. *Lepas fistula* SPENGLER, Skrivter af Naturhistorie Selskabet, vol. 1, p. 176.
1791. *Lepas elongata* GMELIN, Syst. Nat., ed. 13, p. 3213.[1]
1799. *Balanus rugosus* PULTENEY, Catalógue of the Birds, Shells,. etc., of Dorsetshire, p. 25 (tubular form).
1819. *?Balanus glacialis* GRAY, Suppl. to Parry's Voyage, p. ccxlvi.
1841. *Balanus rugosus* Pulteney, GOULD, Invertebrata of Massachusetts, p. 16, fig. 10.
1854. *Balanus crenatus* Brugulère, DARWIN, Monograph, etc., p. 261, pl. 6, figs. 6a–6g.
1913. *Balanus arcnatus* Brugulère, STEPHENSEN, Meddelelser om Groenland, vol. 51, p. 71 (North Stroemfjord).

Type-locality.—Coast of England.

Distribution.—Arctic Ocean; North Atlantic south to Long Island Sound; Bering Sea and North Pacific, south to Santa Bar-

---

[1] I am not sure that *L. elongata* and *L. fistula* belong to this species. They ·may be *Balanus balanoides.*

bara, California, and Northern Japan.[1]   British Pliocene; Pleistocene of Norway, Canada, Maine, and Alaska.

Darwin's description is as follows:

General appearance.—White, usually of a dirty tint, from the yellowish or brownish persistent epidermis; conical, generally with the parietes rugged and irregularly folded longitudinally, but sometimes much depressed and extremely smooth; often cylindrical and very rugged; occasionally club shaped, the upper part being much wider than the lower; specimens in this latter condition sometimes have extremely narrow parietes, like mere ribs, and wide radii. The orifice in the cylindrical varieties is often most deeply toothed. The radii are generally narrow, and have jagged, oblique summits, but not infrequently they are so narrow as to form mere linear borders to the compartments. The orifice is rhomboidal, passing into oval, either very deeply or very slightly toothed.

Scuta: The lines of growth are but little prominent; the surface is generally covered by disintegrating membrane. The upper ends are usually a little reflexed, so that the tips project freely as small flattened points. Internally the articular ridge is highly prominent and somewhat reflexed; there is no adductor ridge, but a very distinct impression for the adductor muscle; the depression for the lateral depressor muscle is small but variable. The terga are rather small, the spur is short and placed at rather less than its own width from the basiscutal angle, the basal margin slopes a little toward the spur of which the lower end is rounded or bluntly pointed in a variable degree. There is no longitudinal furrow, hardly even a depression. Internally the articular ridge is very prominent in the upper part; the crests for the tergal depressors are well developed but variable.

Compartments.—The internal carinal margin of each compartment from the sheath to the basis, generally, but not invariably, projects a little inward beyond the general internal surface of the shell in a manner not common with the other species of the genus; the basal edge of this projecting margin rests on the calcareous basis and is crenated like the basal edges of the longitudinal parietal septa. The whole internal surface of the shell is ribbed, but the ribs are not very prominent. The parietal tubes are large and are crossed in the upper part and often low down by transverse thin septa; the longitudinal parietal septa are only slightly denticulated at their bases; occasionally they divide at the basis close to the outer lamina of the parietes, making some short outer subordinate pores. In the circular furrow beneath the lower edge of the sheath there are sometimes little ridges dividing it into small cells; sometimes, however, this furrow is filled up by irregular knobs of calcareous matter. The radii are always rather narrow, and often they form mere linear ribbons of nearly uniform width along the edges of the compartments. Their summits or edges are always more or less irregular and jagged, they form an angle with the horizon of generally above 40°. Their septa are fine, and barely or

---

[1] I do not know the southern limit of *B. crenatus* in the eastern Atlantic. Darwin gives the localities Mediterranean; Algoa Bay, South Africa; also Jamaica. Gruvel states that specimens in the Paris Museum are labeled Île King (an island in Bass Strait) and Perou (Nouv. Arch. du Mus. (4), vol. 5, p. 139); and he has also recorded it from Wasin, British East Africa (Bull. Soc. Zool. France, vol. 32, p. 164). I hesitate to accept these extensions of the range of *crenatus* into and past the Tropics until confirmed by fresh material. There seems a possibility that ballast or ship-carried specimens have been picked up, or there may have been a mixture of material in some of the old museum specimens.

For the details of the range of *B. crenatus* in European and Arctic Seas, Weltner's Verzeichnis and his article on cirripedes in *Fauna Arctica* (vol. 1, p. 303) may be consulted.

not at all denticulated. The alæ have oblique summits; their sutural edges are rather thick and distinctly crenated. Basis flat, calcareous, very thin, with the surface slightly marked by radiating furrows, which furrows answer to the radiating pores that occur in the bases of most species.

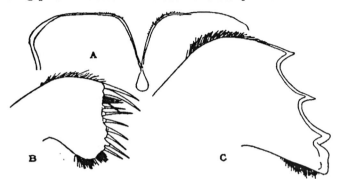

FIG. 49.—BALANUS CRENATUS, INGLEFIELD GULF, GREENLAND. *a*, LABRUM. *b*, MAXILLA. *c*, MANDIBLE.

According to Darwin:

Mouth: Labrum with six teeth. Mandibles with the fourth tooth minute or rudimentary, and the fifth generally confluent with the inferior angle. Maxillæ with generally, but not invariably, a small notch under the upper pair of great spines. Cirri, first pair with the rami very unequal in length, one

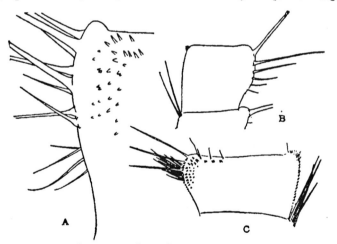

FIG. 50.—B. CRENATUS, INGLEFIELD GULF, GREENLAND. *a*, ANTERIOR PART OF THE FIF-TEENTH SEGMENT OF OUTER RAMUS OF CIRRUS IV. *b*, MEDIAN SEGMENT OF CIRRUS VI. *c*, TENTH SEGMENT OF OUTER RAMUS OF CIRRUS III.

ramus being nearly twice the length of the other; in a large specimen having a cylindrical shell the proportional numbers of the segments in the two rami of the first cirrus were 10 to 23; in a small conical specimen the members were only 8 to 13. The second cirrus has only two or three more segments than the shorter ramus of the first pair. The third cirrus has one or two more segments than the second; but it is nevertheless decidedly longer than the second. On the dorsal surfaces of both segments of the pedicel of the third cirrus, there is a tuft of fine spines. The segments of these three pairs of cirri are not much protuberant in front. The segments of the posterior cirri have four, or five, or six pairs of spines. Penis, with a straight, sharp, short point on the dorsal basis.

It may be added to Darwin's description of the cirri, quoted above, that there is a small area of short spinules on part of the segments of the third pair of cirri, and in some large forms there are a few on the fourth cirri also. The peduncle of the third cirrus is very broad. There is a group of small slender spines below the upper great pair of the maxilla, and another group of small spines just above the lower angle. These are characteristic of all forms of the species examined (fig. 50).

Bruguière describes this barnacle as depressed-cónic, smooth, crenulated or sometimes plicate toward the base. This is a common English form, figured on plate 39, figure 1 from specimens on a potsherd, mouth of the Exe River. The diameter is usually up to 16 or 18 mm. The opercular valves of one of these patelliform specimens are drawn in figure 51, a, b.

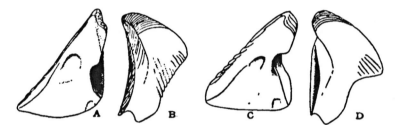

FIG. 51.—BALANUS CRENATUS. a, b, SCUTUM AND TERGUM OF AN UNWORN PATELLIFORM INDIVIDUAL FROM EXMOUTH, SOUTH DEVON. c, d, SCUTUM AND TERGUM OF A RUGGED, DEEPLY CORRODED INDIVIDUAL FROM EXMOUTH.

A rugged, deeply-worn individual, in which the articular ridges are more broadly reflexed, supplied the valves drawn in figure 51 c, d.

These specimens will serve to show the typical form; but it will be understood that there is great variation among English specimens, from depressed and quite smooth to cylindric and very rugged. Various forms from American waters differ more or less. In some cases, as on the Newfoundland Banks, the divergence is probably racial; yet as I have not seen deep-water specimens from Europe I merely note here the chief American forms, leaving the question of racial differentiation in abeyance.

Greenland specimens are rather large and solid, cylindric, short or long or tubular, often having rude, rounded ribs distally, varying from weak to nearly as strong as in the form of the Newfoundland Bank. The scutum, as usual in long specimens, is rather lengthened; the upper part roughened inside in a lot from Davis Strait (pl. 39, figs. 4, 4a), but smooth in those from Inglefield Gulf (pl. 40, figs. 4, 4a). See also fig. 52a, b.

The first cirrus in a specimen from Inglefield Gulf (pl. 40, figs. 4, 4a, Cat. No. 24911, U.S.N.M.), has rami of 15 and 10 segments. Cirrus ii has 12 and 10 segments, the anterior longer by 3 or 4. Cirrus iii has 15 and 16 segments, the anterior ramus one-quarter longer than the inner. Both rami have areas of short spinules on the anterior part of the segments, and others along the posterior borders. The latter are more developed than in specimens from any other locality examined. Cirrus iv has a few minute spinules near the anterior margins of some segments of the outer ramus and some erect spinules near the posterior margin (fig. 50).

Sixth cirrus with segments bearing five pairs of spines, and usually some minute ones at the bases of the two larger pairs. The spines

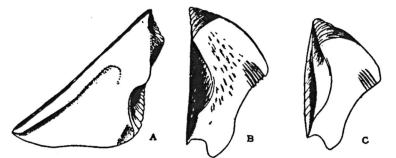

FIG. 52.—BALANUS CRENATUS. a, b, SCUTUM AND TERGUM OF A GREENLAND SPECIMEN, CAT. No. 24911. c, TERGUM OF A SPECIMEN FROM THE GRAND BANK, ALBATROSS STATION 2462, WALL SIMILAR TO PLATE 40, FIGURE 6.

at the posterior distal angles are about as long as the segments. Penis is longer than the posterior cirri.

The maxilla (fig. 49b) has no notch under the superior pair of large spines; below them there are nine subequal spines, with two brushes of bristles at and below the rounded lower angle. The labrum (fig. 49a) has two exceedingly small teeth on each side.

The form from the Grand Banks of Newfoundland (pl. 40, fig. 1) is characteristic. The walls taper but little upward, leaving a large orifice, which is deeply toothed in the young, but in old specimens the points are often broken or worn off. The parietes have massive, irregular, rounded ribs. There are generally three or four ribs on rostrum and lateral compartments, one on the carinolateral, two to four on the carina, in the half-grown stage (pl. 40, fig. 6, Cat. No. 9215); but in old ones the number is increased by division of the ribs. The tergum is broader than in English crenatus, with its carinal margin longer. It is broader than the scutum. Often the spur is shorter than in Greenland crenatus. There are also columnar (pl. 40, fig. 2) and tubular forms, flaring toward the orifice (pl. 40, figs. 5-5b), quite like those from Greenland. Two specimens of the columnar form out of the lot from Albatross station 2462, Grand Banks,

39 fathoms, measure: length 58 mm., diameter 12 mm., and length 40 mm., diameter 17 mm. The radii are narrow.

In a few specimens from *Albatross* station 2462 the spur of the tergum is quite narrow (fig. 52c). The scutum is of the usual narrow form of Newfoundland Bank *crenatus*.

In a series from Sable Island, off Nova Scotia, on bark (probably from a stake or pile) the form and size are similar, but the ribs are split into numerous irregular riblets. The peritreme is acutely toothed. The articular ridge of the scutum projects beyond the tergal margin more than in the Grand Banks form, and the spur of

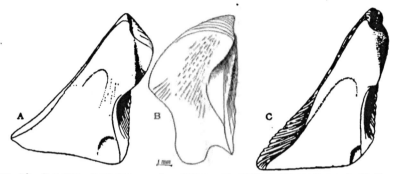

Fig. 53.—BALANUS CRENATUS. *a*, *b*, SCUTUM AND TERGUM OF SPECIMEN FROM SABLE ISLAND, FROM GROUP PL. 40, FIG. 3. *c*, SCUTUM OF SPECIMEN FROM THE FISHING BANKS.

the tergum is a little longer, but otherwise the opercular valves are similar (pl. 40, fig. 3; text fig. 53a, b).

The common forms from shallow water on the New England coast are not distinguishable from English examples. A group from Vineyard Sound is figured (pl. 39, figs. 2–2c, 3, 5, Cat. No. 48027–8, U.S.N.M.) showing the columnar form, growing on a pebble, and the conic form, on *Mytilus edulis*. The opercular valves of the columnar form do not differ materially from those of the smooth form figured, except that they are larger and thicker, the interior of the tergum (fig. 3) being extensively granulated. Specimens, growing on *Mytilus*, from an iron buoy, Gay Head, Marthas Vineyard (pl. 39, figs. 2–2c), are beautifully smooth and white, with thin walls and regular, square tubes, 12 in the rostrum of one counted. The opercular valves are rather thin, and the spur of the tergum is farther, from the basiscutal angle and narrower than is usual in European *crenatus*. The scutum is concave externally, with a broadly reflexed articular ridge.

On the Newfoundland Banks, this species is most abundant on *Buccinum humphreysianum, donovani*, etc., but also occurs in *Chrysodomus, Tritonifusus, Pecten islandicus, Cyrtodaria, Serripes*, on crabs (*Hyas*), and on bowlders. It has been found in the stomachs of cod. On Georges Bank it is common on *Pecten magellanicus* and *Buccinum undatum;* and in the shallow waters of Vineyard Sound it occurs commonly on *Balanus hameri, Cyprina islandica Fulgur, Polinices, Pecten, Cytherea, Mytilus edulis,* on bark, etc., Darwin notes that *B. crenatus* sometimes incrusts vessels, and that it never occurs above low-water mark, while *B. balanoides* is strictly limited to the intertidal zone, and does not extend into the zone of *B. crenatus.* Sometimes the two are found growing together where their zones meet.

Most of the American records are from low tide to 50 fathoms, but in some cases it has been taken in deeper water, up to 98 fathoms. The absence of *B. crenatus* from the great number of dredgings off our coast in 100 fathoms and over is good evidence that its vertical range is limited rather sharply.

The temperature records show a wide range from 30° F., on the Grand Banks, to 67° F. in Vineyard Sound, 9 fathoms, in July, but no doubt individuals from low-tide stations experience greater extremes of temperature in the course of a year.

In the estuary of the Exe River, Channel coast of Devon, *B. crenatus* lives where there is some admixture of fresh water, below low tide, according to the labels in the Jeffreys collection. Specimens on potsherds (pl. 39, fig. 1) are patelliform, also those on *Mytilus,* where it occurs with similarly shaped *B. balanoides.* On *Pecten,* doubtless in deeper water, the usual steeply conic form is found.

In Alaska and on the Pacific coast *B. crenatus* seems to be restricted to much shallower water than in the Atlantic. Nearly all the records are from collections made on shore or in shallow water, while it is conspicuously absent from most of the *Albatross* hauls in deeper water.

Pacific and Bering Sea forms.

The occidental forms of *crenatus* do not differ materially from those of the North Atlantic. There is the same range in size. The smooth form (pl. 41, figs. 2, 2a, 2b, Tacoma, Washington, Cat. No. 48033) and the rudely plicate form (pl. 41, figs. 3, 3a, Bering Sea, and pl. 41, fig. 5, Alaska, *Corwin,* Cat. No. 48035), with various intermediate stages are of common occurrence. The opercular valves resemble those of Newfoundland and Vineyard Sound specimens. The articular ridges of both valves vary in the degree of reflection; that of the tergum sometimes stands vertical to the plane of the valve, or sometimes is reflexed or hooked in varying degree over the articular furrow. The articular ridge of the scutum is usually shorter in Pacific forms.

A smooth, conic form with rather wide radii was taken by the *Albatross* in Union Bay, Bayne Sound, British Columbia, on shore, the specimen figured having a basal diameter of 14 mm. The labrum has a wide notch, with three teeth on each side; only the upper one marginal (fig. 54).

In the elongated and club-shaped forms the radii become wide, especially those of the rostrum. This is also the case in many Atlantic specimens. Plate 41, figures 6 to 6e, are from *Albatross* station 2851, near the Shumagin Islands, in 35 fathoms. The scutum is long, its tergal margin decidedly longer than the basal margin. The callus between the adductor pit and the articular ridge is but slightly roughened, the interior being unusually smooth. The articular ridge of the tergum is moderately recurved. On the borders of the crowded colonies there are often transitions to the normal conic form shown in figure 6a.

The labrum has two teeth on each side, larger than those of the Greenland specimen figured. Maxilla with a very slight notch and

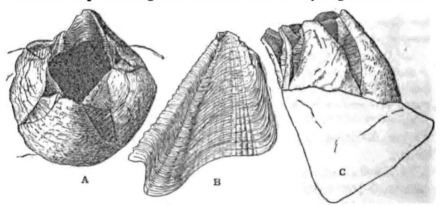

Fig. 54.—B. CRENATUS, UNION BAY, BAYNE SOUND. TOP AND LATERAL VIEWS X3, AND TERGUM.

seven subequal spines below the upper great pair, otherwise as in the Greenland form. First cirrus has rami of 17 and 8 segments, the posterior ramus half the length of the anterior. Second cirrus with slightly unequal rami of 13 segments. Third cirrus with 15 and 13 segments, the posterior ramus two-thirds as long as the anterior. Sixth cirrus having segments with six pairs of spines and sometimes a minute seventh pair. Penis exceedingly long, with an acute point dorsally near its base, the end with a pencil of short bristles.

Similar but much smaller examples were taken by the U. S. R. S. *Corwin* in the Arctic Ocean, on *Chrysodomus heros*, the contour varying from conic and short to columnar.

Southward on the Pacific coast we know little of the range of *B. crenatus*, as the smaller barnacles of California have been neglected by collectors. At Point Richmond, San Franciso Bay, numerous specimens were taken on *Thais plicata septentrionalis* (Reeve) by Mr.

C. H. Townsend in 1890. The walls are smooth; radii rather narrow; parietes having an unusually large number of tubes, 13 to 17 in the rostrum. Spur of the tergum short. The scutum is about typical. The largest examples have a basal diameter of 8 mm. It has the external appearance of *B. improvisus*.

The farthest south known for *B. crenatus* in the Pacific is Santa Barbara, California. A few opercular valves and detached compartments were found in débris washed from *Balanus tintinnabulum californicus* and the rock it grew upon. The valves seem nearly typical, but the compartments are thin with smooth outer surface. Complete specimens are needed to show the characters of the race.

Pleistocene specimens of this species are in the United States National Museum from Lawlors Lake, St. John County, New Brunswick, Brunswick, Maine, and Douglas Island, near Juneau, Alaska, where they were collected by Dr. Wm. H. Dall "200 feet above tidewater, in a trench of the pipe line near old mill in bowlder clay." The specimens do not differ from recent forms found in neighboring waters.

EUROPEAN.

Locality.	Collector.	Notes.
Iceland		
Shetland Islands	J. G. Jeffreys	
Oban, Scotland	do	On *Pecten*.
Cork Harbor, Ireland	J. G. Jeffreys (Geo. Barlee).	1846.
Arran Isles, west coast of Ireland	J. G. Jeffreys	
Bantry Bay, Ireland	do	
Irish Channel	do	On *B. hameri* and *Fusus contrarius*.
Scarborough, England	J. G. Jeffreys (Turton)	
Swansea Bay, Wales	J. G. Jeffreys	
Milford, South Wales	W. Stimpson	
English Channel, near Guernsey	Jeffreys collection	On *Pecten*.
Exmouth, south Devon	do	
Langland Bay	do	
Portsmouth	do	
Sandwich	do	
Off Caswell Bay	do	On *Aporrhais*, etc.
Helgoland. North Sea	Royal Biological Station	On *Mytilus edulis*.

EAST AMERICAN.

U. S. F. C. Station.	Locality.	Depth (fathoms).	Bottom temperature.	Collector.
			°F.	
	Barden Bay, Inglefield Gulf, Greenland	10–40		Princeton expedition.
	Godthaab, Greenland			
	Greenland [1]			N. P. Scudder, Cornell expedition.
	Near Egg Harbor, Labrador			O. Bryant.
	St. Michael, Labrador			Turner.
	Northeast part Grand Bank of Newfoundland [2]	45		Schooner *Henry Wilson*.
	North part Grand Bank of Newfoundland			Gloucester fisheries.
	Grand Bank of Newfoundland:			
2449	Latitude, 46° 37′ 00″ north; longitude, 49° 50′ 30″ west.	39	33	*Albatross*.
2448	Latitude, 46° 28′ 00″ north; longitude, 49° 39′ 30″ west.	40	33.9	Do.
2447	Latitude, 46° 26′ 00″ north; longitude, 49° 42′ 00″ west.	39	34.8	Do.

[1] Greenland specimens without nearer indication of locality are in the museum from the J. G. Jeffreys and Isaac Lea collections, with others from unknown source.
[2] Many specimens, some very fine groups, the gifts of Gloucester fishermen, are in the United States National Museum from the Grand Bank of Newfoundland, the Banquereau and Georges Banks. As these areas are fairly covered by the exactly located stations of the Fish Commission, the lots designated by banks only are not entered here.

EAST AMERICAN.

U. S. F. C. Station.	Locality.	Depth (fathoms).	Bottom temperature.	Collector.
	Grand Bank of Newfoundland—Continued.		°F.	
2445	Latitude, 46° 09' 30'' north; longitude, 49° 48' 30'' west.	39	33.5	Albatross.
2444	Latitude 45°, 59' 00'' north; longitude, 49° 45' 30'' west.	39	34.4	Do.
2441	Latitude, 45° 27' 00'' north; longitude, 49° 42' 00'' west.	34	33	Do.
2462	Latitude, 45° 45' 30'' north; longitude, 54° 20' 30'' west.	41	30	Do.
2463	Latitude, 45° 44' 00'' north; longitude, 54° 27' 00'' west.	45	30	Do.
2465	Latitude, 45° 35' 00'' north; longitude, 55° 01' 00'' west.	67	30	Do.
2468	Latitude, 45° 11' 30'' north; longitude, 55° 51' 30'' west.	42	33	Do.
2467	Latitude, 45° 23' 00'' north; longitude, 55° 41' 00'' west.	38	35.8	Do.
2443	Latitude, 45° 44' 00'' north; longitude, 49° 45' 00'' west.	35	34.9	Do.
2440	Latitude, 43° 38' 00'' north; longitude, 49° 49' 30'' west.	33	38.3	Do.
2438	Latitude, 43° 36' 00'' north; longitude, 50° 03' 30'' west.	37	36.8	Do.
2439	Latitude, 43° 37' 50'' north; longitude, 49° 56' 30'' west.	36	37.8	Do.
2436	Latitude, 43° 36' 00'' north; longitude, 50° 06' 30'' west.	36	34	Do.
2437	Latitude, 43° 36' 00'' north; longitude, 50° 05' 00'' west.	37	35.8	Do.
	Misiane Bank:			
2493	Latitude, 45° 19' 00'' north; longitude, 58° 51' 15'' west.	45	32.3	Do.
2498	Latitude, 44° 54' 00'' north; longitude, 59° 46' 45 west.	65	....	Do.
2500	Latitude, 44° 28' 00'' north; longitude, 60° 15' 15'' west.	36	....	Do.
	Banquereau Bank ¹....................	75	....	Capt. McKimmon.
	Banquereau Bank, off Nova Scotia...........	50	....	Do.
	Banquereau Bank, northwest part.	....	....	Gloucester fisheries.
	Latitude,44° 28' north; longitude,59° 20' west...	....	....	Wm. Hutchings.
	Sable Island.............................	....	....	
	Nova Scotia.............................	....	....	Willis.
	Bay of Fundy.............................	....	....	U. S. F. C.
	East of Georges Bank.....................	50	....	Bache.
	Georges Bank:			
2079	Latitude, 41° 13' 00'' north; longitude, 66° 19' 50'' west.	75	45	Albatross.
2080	Latitude, 41° 13' 00'' north; longitude, 66° 21' 50'' west.	55	46	Do.
2244	Latitude, 40° 05' 15'' north; longitude, 70° 23' 00'' west.	67	52.9	Do.
2245	Latitude, 40° 01' 15'' north; longitude, 70° 22' 00'' west.	98	50.9	Do.
2250	Latitude, 40° 17' 15'' north; longitude, 09° 51' 45'' west.	47	51.4	Do.
2580	Latitude, 41° 25' 30'' north; longitude, 69° 01' 00'' west.	83	42.4	Do.
2251	Latitude, 40° 22' 17'' north; longitude, 69° 51' 30'' west.	43	50.9	Do.
2256	Latitude, 40° 38' 30'' north; longitude, 69° 29' 00'' west.	30	52.9	Do.
	Georges Bank, northwest part.............	....	....	Schooner Clytie.
	Lawlor's Lake, St. Johns County, New Brunswick.	....	....	Matthews.
	Grand Manan.............................	....	....	W. Stimpson.
	Gulf of Maine.............................	....	....	U. S. F. C.
	Eastport, Me.............................	....	....	R. Rathbun.
	Casco Bay, Me.............................	....	....	
	Brunswick, Me. (in Leda clay).............	....	....	
	Nantucket.............................	....	....	U. S. F. C.
972	Off Chatham, Cape Cod.............	16	52	Fish Hawk.
983	.....do.	17	51	Do.
370	.....do.	18	....	Speedwell.
	Vineyard Sound.........................	Shore.	....	
861	.....do.	17	61	Fish Hawk.
984	Vineyard Sound, off Chatham, Mass.........	33	41.5	Do.
	Woods Hole, Mass.	....	....	U. S. F. C.
	Off Marthas Vineyard	....	....	Do.
	Gay Head, Marthas Vineyard	Buoy.	....	
	Buzzards Bay, Mass.	....	....	Do.
856	Off Newport, R. I.............	11	67	Fish Hawk.
	Saybrook, Conn.............	Shore.	....	

NORTH PACIFIC, BERING SEA, AND ARCTIC OCEAN.

U. S. F. C. Station No.	Locality.	Depth (fathoms).	Collector.
	Point Barrow, Alaska		E. A. McIlhenny.
	Arctic Ocean		U. S. R. S. *Corwin.*
	Latitude, 66° 12' north; longitude, 168° 54' west		Lt. Geo. M. Stoney.
	Bering Strait		Dr. Robert White.
	Latitude, 63° 37' north; longitude, 165° 19' west		Lieut. Geo. M. Stoney.
	Latitude, 60° 16' north; longitude, 167° 41' west, off Monroe Island.		Do.
	Plover Bay, Siberia	8–20	W. H. Dall.
	Ochotsk Sea		Capt. Stevens, North Pacific exploring expedition.
	Bering Island		L. Stejneger.
	Adak Island, Aleutians		W. H. Dall.
	Unalaska		Do.
	Iliuliuk, Unalaska		Do.
3232	Latitude, 58° 31' 30'' north; longitude, 157° 34' 15'' west.	10½	*Albatross.*
2851	Latitude, 54° 55' north; longitude, 159° 52' west	35	Do.
	Belkofski, Alaska	2½–4	W. H. Dall.
	Cold Bay, Shelikof Strait		T. W. Stanton.
	Alaska		U. S. R. S. *Corwin.*
	Douglas Island, near Juneau (Pleistocene)		W. H. Dall.
	Loring, Revillagigedo Island, Alexander Archipelago.		*Albatross.*
	Quarantine Station, Port Townsend, Wash.		Do.
	Tacoma, Wash.		Mrs. W. B. Hare.
	Point Richmond, San Francisco Bay		C. H. Townsend.
	Santa Barbara, Cal.		Not recorded.

BALANUS CRENATUS CURVISCUTUM, new subspecies.

Plate 41, figs. 1, 4; plate 42, figs. 1–1*b*, 2–2*d*.

Type.—Cat. No. 48037, U.S.N.M., from Bristol Bay, Alaska, collected by C. L. McKey. Growing on *Mytilus.*

Form usually cylindric, the walls thin, weak, or fragile, white, formed of *very thin outer and inner laminæ* joined by delicate septa forming square or irregular pores, of which there are 10 to 12 in the rostrum. Parietes smooth or nearly so. Radii rather narrow usually, but sometimes wide in the rostrum. Basis very thin, poreless.

Size rather small, the largest 14 mm. in diameter, with a height of 11 mm. The figured type measures, diameter 10 mm., height 11.4 mm. Another of the same group measures, diameter 9.5 mm., height 12.3 mm.

The scutum is usually warped strongly, externally concave between base and apex. It has *an unusually long basal margin,* equal to or exceeding the tergal margin, is thin, and smooth inside, without callouses or distinct muscle impressions. The articular ridge is thin and well reflexed.

The tergum has *the spur narrower than in crenatus,* the articular ridge forms a triangular projection overhanging the furrow and scutal margin. The scutal border is rather broadly inflected at a right angle with the face of the valve.

The maxilla has a notch below the upper pair of great spines, several small spines standing in it. The edge advances below the notch, and bears five large spines, the *next to the lower one largest* (as in the *B. balanus* group). The rounded, receding lower extremity bears a group of 9 or 10 small straight spines, and the lower edge has rather long bristles (fig. 55c).

The first cirrus has rami of 14 and 10 segments, the posterior ramus about two-thirds the length of the anterior. Cirrus ii with slightly unequal rami of 12 and 11 segments. Cirrus iii with more unequal rami of 12 segments. I see no spinules on the segments (yet a few may be there, as the preparation is not very clear). Cirrus vi has five pairs of spines on the median segments (fig. 55b). The penis is longer than the sixth cirrus.

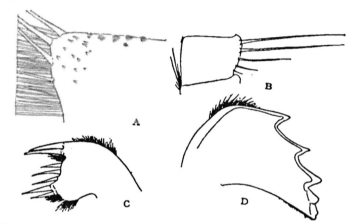

Fig. 55.—BALANUS CRENATUS CURVISCUTUM. *a*, FIFTH SEGMENT OF OUTER RAMUS OF CIRRUS III, SPECIMEN FROM STATION 3232. *b*, MEDIAN SEGMENT OF CIRRUS VI, TYPE. *c*, MAXILLA. *d*, MANDIBLE OF THE TYPE.

The shape of the plain, uncalloused scuta, the narrow spur of the terga, the thin, weak walls, and the maxillæ are all characteristic. The characters vary in different colonies, about as much as in *B. crenatus*, and in the limits of this work it is impossible fully to discuss or illustrate the local variations. Two of the forms may be noticed.

Specimens from Unalaska (pl. 41, figs. 1, 4) are typical in external form, but the tergum has a much longer carinal margin than in the type lot.

Numerous specimens (Cat. No. 32948, U.S.N.M.) from *Albatross* station 3232, Bristol Bay, 10½ fathoms, have a remarkable resemblance to *B. balanoides*. The opercular valves and general form are shown in plate 42, figures 2–2d. They grew in crowded groups which are very fragile, the compartments parting readily, so that it is hard to handle them without breaking. The summits are deeply toothed, the *form tubular or club-shaped;* parietes having thin-walled tubes, as in similarly shaped Atlantic forms of *B. balanoides*.

Tips of the terga and scuta diverge conspicuously, as in typical *curviscutum*, and the scutum is very concave between apex and base. The articular ridge is longer and more widely reflexed than in the type. The tergum is wider, with longer carinal margin, but the spur is narrow.

The labrum has three acute teeth on each side of the notch. Maxilla about as in typical *curviscutum*.

The posterior ramus of the first cirrus is about three-fifths the length of the anterior. Cirrus ii with subequal rami of 8 segments. Cirrus iii has slightly unequal rami of 10 and 9 segments. Part of the segments of the outer ramus have a few spinules and flat, multifid scales near the anterior and distal borders (fig. 55a). The last cirri have 24 segments, bearing 5 pairs of spines. The spines at the distal posterior angles are nearly or quite as long as the segments, or sometimes longer.

The specimens measure from over 20 mm. long, $5\frac{1}{2}$ mm. wide near the upper end, to about 8 mm. long, 4 mm. wide.

U. S. F. C. Station No.	Locality.	Depth (fathoms).	Collector.	Notes.
	St. Michael, Norton Sound, Alaska.		R. Kennicott.	
3506	Latitude, 58° 33' north; longitude, 164° 49' west.	23	Albatross.	Bottom temperature, 42° F.
	Bristol Bay, Alaska.		C. L. McKey.	On *Mytilus*.
	Unalaska, Alaska.		W. H. Dall.	
	....do.		....do.	On *Thais*.
	Elder village, Unalaska.		....do.	
4268	Afognak Bay, Afognak Island, Alaska.	16	Albatross.	50.9° F.
	Naha Bay, Revillagigedo Island, Alexander Archipelago, Alaska.		Allen, 1904.	In mouth of starfish.
	Sitka Harbor, Alaska.	10–25	W. H. Dall.	
	Tongass, Alaska.		H. E. Nichols, U. S. N.	
	Quarantine Station, Port Townsend, Wash.		Albatross.	
3780	Off Kamchatka.	12	....do.	With *B. hesperius*.
5003	Off southwest coast Saghalin Island.	35	....do.	42.4° F.
3760	Off Suno Saki, Honshu Island, Japan.	83; 50	....do.	

BALANUS CRENATUS DELICATUS, new subspecies.

Plate 42, figs. 3, 3a, 3b.

Type.—Cat. No. 48039, U.S.N.M., from a buoy on Humboldt Bar, California, received from Leland Stanford Junior University; associated with *Balanus flos*.

The walls are *thin*, as in *B. c. curviscutum;* not ribbed; parietes covered with a thin epidermis of very pale yellow tint; *radii wide*, white. Parietal tubes square, rather numerous, 16 in the rostrum of the type-specimen; septa very thin, not crenulated. No transverse septa in the lower half of the tubes.

Opercular valves thin, much as in *B. c. curviscutum*, but the scutum is higher, not so wide, and the spur of the tergum is truncate at the end.

Carinorostral diameter of base, 7.5 mm.; height, 13 mm.

The maxilla has five spines below the upper great pair, about as in *B. c. curviscutum*.

Labrum (fig. 56d) with three teeth on each side.

First cirrus with rami of 14 and 9 segments, the shorter ramus about half as long as the longer. Cirrus ii has nearly equal rami of 10 segments. Cirrus iii with unequal rami of 11 and 9 segments. All but the first and last segments of the outer ramus bear short

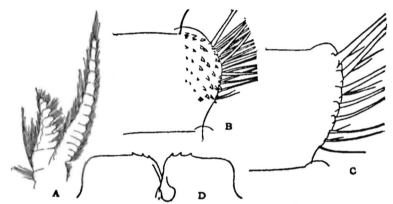

Fig. 56.—BALANUS CRENATUS DELICATUS, TYPE. *a*, 1ST CIRRUS. *b*, FIFTH SEGMENT ANTE-
RIOR RAMUS OF CIRRUS III. *c*, 18TH SEGMENT OF CIRRUS VI. *d*, LABRUM.

recurved spinules near the anterior or distal borders. (Fig. 56b, part of fifth segment of cirrus iii). The segments of the inner ramus are not so copiously spinose. The sixth cirrus has *8 pairs of spines* on the median segments (fig. 56c).

The penis is nearly twice as long as the posterior cirri, and has a few hairs near and at the end. There is an acute basidorsal point.

This race resembles *B. c. curviscutum* in the main, but differs by the greater number of spines on the posterior cirri, and of spinules on the third cirri, as well as by the wider truncate spur of the tergum.

BALANUS GLANDULA Darwin.

Plate 43.

1854. *Balanus glandula* DARWIN, Monograph, Balanidæ, p. 265, pl. 7, figs. 1a, 1b.

1909. *Balanus crenatus* Bruguière, PILSBRY, Bulletin of the Bureau of Fisheries, vol. 29, p. 75, pl. 14, figs. 4–9.

Type.—British Museum, from California.

Distribution.—Southern California to the Aleutian Islands; shore, chiefly in the intertidal zone.

The barnacle is conic or cylindric-conic, rarely elongated, columnar; dirty white, with the surface generally ribbed or plicate closely and deeply, without epidermis, and often eroded. The orifice is typically small, but is large in some lots. Usual diameter 14 mm., height 7 to 8 mm.; often smaller.

The scutum has fine growth-ridges on the flat exterior. The articular ridge is very prominent, articular furrow wide and deep. The adductor ridge is very short, united above with the articular ridge, *a pit below their junction.* Adductor pit deep. Pit for the depressor muscle small, marginal, and usually deep. The upper part of the interior is not striate.

The tergum is flat or has a slight depression leading to the spur. The articular ridge and inflexed scutal margin are very prominent, the articular furrow deep. Spur short, occupying nearly half of the lower margin, truncate, and standing *very close to the basiscutal angle.* Crests for the depressor muscles are conspicuous. The lining membrane of the valves is black.

The *radii are narrow or very narrow*, not conspicuously differentiated from the parietes. Their summits are very oblique and smooth. The articulating edges are broad and very finely laminate. The opposed sutural edges also have a broad, minutely laminate band. The alæ are rather wide with the edges simple. Sheath pale yellow, with transverse raised lines. Below its depending edge there is a rather broad, shallow excavation. The inside of the parietes is smooth above in adults, becoming very strongly ribbed near the base, where the ribs are conspicuously crenulated. *The pores in immature individuals are small and irregular, and in most adults they are nearly or entirely wanting*, being filled up with calcareous material; but sometimes traces of them may be seen at the worn summits of the parietes.

The basis is flat, thin, and without pores, its inner face finely grooved radially.

It was described by Darwin, as follows:

Mouth: Labrum with the central notch rather widely open, with four teeth on each side of it. Palpi with very short spines along their inner margins. Mandibles with the fourth and fifth teeth forming mere knobs. Maxillæ small, with a mere trace of a notch under the two great upper spines. Cirri: First pair with the rami unequal by three or four segments, the longer ramus being only one-quarter of its own length longer than the other ramus. Second pair short, with the segments (and those of the shorter ramus of first pair) somewhat protuberant. Third pair with the rami one-third longer than those of the second pair. Sixth pair with the upper segments elongated, and bearing six or seven pairs of spines.

The cirri are densely pigmented in some of the specimens I have examined. The third pair have no short spinules on the segments, but their place is taken by long spines, as in *B. balanoides*. This differentiates *B. glandula* from *B. crenatus*, which has the anterior part of the segments of the third cirri set with short spinules.

B. glandula may most easily be distinguished from *B. crenatus* by the presence of a short adductor ridge in the scutum, with *a conspicuous pit*, like that for a muscle, below the confluence of the adductor ridge with the base of the articular ridge. The very short broad spur of the tergum is also characteristic. In *B. hesperius* there is a prominent rugosity between the adductor muscle pit and the articular ridge, which is wanting in *B. glandula*. All of these species, together with *B. balanoides*, have terga of the same general appearance, and the mouth parts and cirri do not differ very conspicuously.

The pores in the basal edges of the parietes are irregular, not developed between all of the ribs of the interior; when developed the inner lamina of the wall does not reach quite to the base. In fullgrown barnacles a few narrow pores may usually be found deep between some of the basal ends of the ribs, which are crenulated and unequal; but in some specimens they are wholly filled up, as in *B. balanoides*.

I take San Diego to be the type-locality. Plate 43, figures 1 to 3*a*, represent specimens from there. The shape is conic or convexly conic, and the aperture is small in all the specimens seen.

At La Jolla, California, I found *B. glandula* on rocks near hightide mark, with *Mitella polymerus* and *Chthamalus fissus*.

In a group of nine individuals from San Francisco the shape is more cylindric, and the walls are much more weakly ribbed, or in some not at all ribbed. Aperture larger.

A Puget Sound series, on valves of *Mytilus*, contains strongly ribbed, typical individuals, with others of a more cylindric shape, with very weak ribs and large orifice. One is 13 mm. in basal diameter, 12 mm. high.

At Union Bay, Bayne Sound, British Columbia, elongated columnar individuals occur with a shorter, obliquely conic form, growing upon the large ones. In some of the shorter individuals the opercular valves are unusually long, the tergal margin of the scutum decidedly surpassing the basal margin, as in figure 57*g*. The radii are rather wide in some of this lot, but the compartments are thin and weak (fig. 57).

At Sitka the strongly ribbed conic and the smoother, short, cylindric forms occur. The largest individual measures 16 mm. in basal diameter, 13 mm. high. Cirri and mouth parts as described by Darwin. See plate 43, figs. 5, 7, 7*a*.

Unalaska specimens are strongly ribbed, with *decidedly wider radii* than those of southern California. The bases of the parietes show no pores, but traces of them may be seen externally in some compartments. Opercular valves (pl. 43, figs. 6, 6a) like Sitka specimens.

Atka specimens are similar to those of Unalaska in the walls, but the opercular valves are peculiar, unlike any other lot examined. The scutum is very wide and short, the tergum is unusually narrow in contour, but this is largely due to corrosion (pl. 43, figs. 4 to 4c).

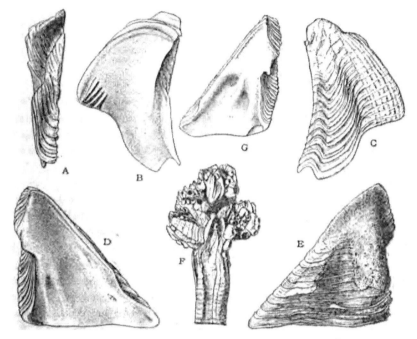

Fig. 57.—BALANUS GLANDULA FROM UNION BAY, BAYNE SOUND, BRITISH COLUMBIA, a, b, c, SCUTAL, INTERNAL AND EXTERNAL ASPECTS OF THE TERGUM, AND d, e, INTERNAL AND EXTERNAL ASPECTS OF SCUTUM OF THE LONG INDIVIDUAL IN THE GROUP f. g, SCUTUM OF A SHORT INDIVIDUAL IN THE SAME LOT.

The individual I dissected from Atka has the first cirri quite unequal, posterior ramus of 10 segments not quite two-thirds as long as the anterior of 16. Second pair subequal, of 10 and 11 segments. The posterior cirri have six pairs of spines on a segment. Penis long, with a dorsal point near the base.

Balanus glandula has been reported from the "southern Pacific Ocean attached to *Pollicipes polymerus*" (Darwin, Monograph, p. 266), on the evidence of specimens in the British Museum labeled as having been collected by Sir James Ross in course of his Antarctic Expedition. Such distribution seems highly improbable. Until confirmed by new records it may be put in the doubtful list.

U.S.N.M. Cat. No.	Locality.	Collector.	Notes.
11151	San Diego, Cal...............................	O. N. Sanford.........	On indurated sand.
	.....do.	C. R. Orcutt...........	Do.
	.....do.	H. Hemphill...........	On jetty.
	.....do....	E. A. Mearns...........	On *Mytilus*
	San Francisco, Cal.....................	U. S. Exploring Expedition.	
12333	Puget Sound, Wash......................	R. E. C. Stearns......	Do.
	Gordon Head, 7 miles from Victoria, British Columbia.	J. E. Benedict........	
38672	Union Bay, Bayne Sound, British Columbia	*Albatross*.............	Shore.
12316	Sitka, Alaska............................	J. J. McLean..........	On *Mytilus*.
32934	Naha Bay, Revillagigedo Island, Alexander Archipelago, Alaska.	Allen, 1904...........	"In mouth of starfish."
	Unalaska, Alaska.......................	Dr. B. Sharp..........	Coll. A. N. S. P.
	Nazan Bay, Atka, Alaska...............	*Albatross*.............	Shore.
	Chasina Bay, Prince of Wales Island, Alaska.	T. H. Street..........	
	Adak, Alaska............................	Wm. H. Dall..........	

SEMIBALANUS, new subgenus.

The basis is membranous; parietes porous, or with the pores filled up; *interior not longitudinally ribbed*, but usually having small anastomosing wrinkles near the basal edge; rostrum not prolonged downward below the other compartments. No spinules or "teeth" on the cirri.

Type.—Balanus cariosus.

I do not regard *B. balanoides* and *B. glandula* as transitional between the Balani with solid and those with porous walls. They are porous forms which have filled up the pores more or less completely, in some individuals. While related to the typical group of *Balanus*, this subgenus is strongly individualized. The membranous basis and the profusely bristly third cirri, without spinules on the outer faces of the segments, are primitive characters, but the closing of the parietal pores in *B. balanoides* and their multiplication in *B. cariosus* are relatively more evolved features than the ordinary types of porous wall.

KEY TO SPECIES.

Parietes copiously ribbed externally with several rows of unequal pores; tergum very narrow, with long, narrow spur and a more or less closed external furrow_____ *B. cariosus.*

Parietes coarsely folded or smooth, the pores normal or obsolete; tergum with short spur and no trace of an external furrow_____ *B. balanoides.*

BALANUS BALANOIDES (Linnæus).

Plate 44.

1766. *Lepas balanoides* LINNÆUS, Systema Naturæ, ed. 12, p. 1108.
1789. *Balanus fistulosus* BRUGUIÈRE, Encyclopèdie Méthodique, p. 166.
1790. *?Lepas elongata* Gmelin, Syst. Nat., ed. 13, p. 3213.
1799. *Balanus clavatus* PULTENEY, Catalogue of the birds, shells, and some of the more rare plants of Dorsetshire, p. 25.
1818. *Balanus palmulatus* LAMARCK, Anim. sans Vert., vol. 5, p. 394.

1839. *Balanus fissus* ANTON, Verzeichniss meiner Conchyliensammlung, p. 108, No. 3292.

1841. *Balanus palmulatus* Lamarck, DELESSERT, Receuil de Coquilles décrites par Lamarck, pl. 1, fig. 12.

1841. *Balanus ovularis* Lamarck, GOULD, Invertebrata of Massachusetts, p. 17, 1st pl., fig. 7.

1841. *Balanus elongatus* Linnæus, GOULD, Invertebrata of Massachusetts, p. 18, 1st pl., fig. 8.

1844. *Balanus interruptus* DE KAY, Zool. of New York, Mollusca, p. 252 (Long Island Sound, on rocks).

1847. *Chthamalus germanus* and *C. philippii* FREY and LEUKART, Beiträge zur Kenntniss Wirbelloser Thiere, p. 167 (Heligoland).

1854. *Balanus balanoides* Linnæus, DARWIN, Monograph, p. 267, pl. 7, fig. 2a–2d.

1863. *Balanus balanoides* Darwin, STIMPSON, Proc. Acad. Nat. Sci. Phila., p. 140 (Port Foulke).

1882. *Balanus balanoides* Linnæus, LEIDY, Proc. Acad. Nat. Sci. Phila., p. 224 (variation at Bass Rocks, Mass.).

1897. *Balanus balanoides* Linnæus, WELTNER, Verzeichnis, p. 269.

1892. *Chthamalus europæus* PHILIPPI, MS., according to WELTNER, Zoologischer Jahrbücher, vol. 6, p. 454.

Type.—Lost; from the coast of Sweden.

Distribution.—From latitude 66° 34' north, in the Arctic Ocean, to the ocean coast of France, and to Delaware Bay;[1] in the Pacific from Unalaska to Sitka. *Station,* between tides, chiefly on stones, wood, and shells (*Mytilidæ*).

The barnacle varies in form from a rather low cone with small orifice, and more or less ribbed or folded walls, to cylindric or club-shaped and much lengthened; dirty white. Conic forms are rather solid, but the lengthened varieties are often fragile. The opercular valves are sunken very little below the peritreme.

The opercular valves are very similar to those of *B. crenatus*, but in the scutum there is a callus running downward from the lower end of the articular ridge. The tergum has a very strong triangular articular ridge, and the inflection of the scutal margin is unusually broad. The spur is short, rounded distally, and about half its own width from the basiscutal angle.

The inner faces of the parietes are smoothish, or have low, irregular, or branching ridges, but *no ribs*, and there is never any denticulation at the base. The parietal pores are small, rounded, or irregular; the septa between them sometimes branching near the outer lamina of the wall; or sometimes they are entirely filled up, the wall appearing to be solid when viewed from the base. If the outer lamina is eroded or ground down, it will be seen that there are numerous parietal tubes, transversely septate, or sometimes in part filled up

---

[1] Darwin gives the locality Delaware. I have not myself taken it south of Ocean City, New Jersey. Northward the United States National Museum has specimens from Cumberland Gulf or Sound, a little short of the high latitude given by Darwin and quoted above.

solidly.   In much worn individuals the tubular layer may be entirely
removed.   The sheath is very short.   Radii narrow or almost obsolete.
The basis is wholly membranous.

Darwin further describes it as follows:

Mouth: Labrum with the teeth on each side of the central notch unusually variable in number; I have seen specimens with only two on each
side, with four on each side, with five on one side and four on the other,
with five on one side and none on the other, and with six on both sides;
hence the total number ranges from four to twelve.   Mandibles, with the
fourth and fifth teeth small, or quite rudimentary.   Maxillæ, with scarcely
even a trace of a notch under the upper pair of spines.   Cirri: First pair,
with one ramus one-third or one-fourth longer than the other; in one specimen the number of segments were 9 and 16 in the two rami; second and

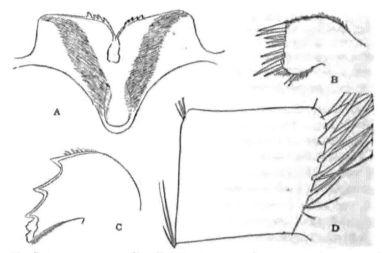

Fig. 58.—Balanus balanoides, New Haven. a, labrum. b, maxilla. c, mandible. d, intermediate segment from cirrus VI. Figures a, b, d from a conic specimen, No.
32946. Fig. c from a tubular specimen, No. 32947.

third rami short, very nearly equal in length, having in the first-mentioned
specimen respectively 10 and 11 segments.   The sixth cirrus in this same specimen had 25 segments, each segment being about as long as broad and supporting six pairs of spines.   In the singular variety (a) the posterior cirri are
more elongated, and each segment supports 7 or 8, and in one case even 10
pairs of spines.   The third pair is also in this variety proportionally rather
longer; at the base of the third pair there is a tuft of fine spines.   The penis
has not, as in B. crenatus, a point at its dorsal basis.

The membranous basis amply distinguishes B. balanoides from
species of the region otherwise similar.   When the barnacle is detached, it may be known by the wall which is *not ribbed within*, thus
differing from B. crenatus.   Conic, depressed forms have not the
well-developed tubes and septa of most other species, and in most of
the lengthened, cylindric, or club-shaped forms the tubes are mainly
closed at the basal edge.   I believe that the scuta may be recognized

by the callus below the articular ridge. The callus between the adductor pit and the articular ridge is sometimes grooved, somewhat as in *B. hesperius*, but much less strongly. The tips of the opercular valves do not diverge as they frequently do in *B. crenatus*. When the surface has been at all disintegrated, the tips of the scuta form a square projection locked into the terga. The first and third cirri differ from those of *B. crenatus*.

In the walls, but not the opercular valves, *B. balanoides* often has very much the appearance of *Chthamalus stellatus*. The name *Chthamalus europæus* Philippi seems to have been applied to Helgoland specimens by some authors.

In patelliform and tubular specimens from New Haven and a high conic specimen from Nahant, I found six pairs of spines on the segments of the later cirri, and rarely a seventh minute pair. In a patelliform individual cirrus i has 13 and 9 segments, cirrus ii 10, cirrus iii 12 and 10, and cirrus vi 30 segments. *There are no spinules or " teeth " on cirri iii and iv*, such as are found in *B. crenatus*. The bristles at the posterior distal angles of the segments are always *very short*. In a tubular specimen the labrum has four teeth on each side. In a conical one from the same place there are four teeth on one side, five on the other. In all, the mandibles and maxillæ could not be distinguished from some *B. crenatus;* but there is *never a notch below the upper pair of spines* of the maxillæ in *B. balanoides* (fig. 58).

The elongated, tubular, or trumpet-shaped form (*fistulosus* Bruguière) is in no sense a race, as it is commonly found in the same group with patelliform individuals, as in the group figured from Savin Rock, New Haven, Connecticut. Usually the shape may be attributed to crowding, but, as both Gould and Darwin have noted, extremely lengthened, club-shaped individuals are often found growing solitary, under such circumstances that neither crowding nor the nature of the supporting object can be responsible for the shape of the barnacle. Plate 44, figure 4, represents such a solitary specimen from Loch Fyne, Scotland, 61 mm. long, 11 mm. in greatest diameter, the tube smallest (5.5 mm. diameter) near the base.

Small cylindric crowded specimens from sandstone rocks near Exmouth, England, measure 8 to 18 mm. long, the tube near the base 2 to 5 mm. in diameter.

Figures 1–1*b*, plate 44, represent the rostrum, interior and exterior of a conic specimen from a buoy at Exmouth, channel coast of Devon, diameter 22 mm., height 8.5 mm.

A series from Arctic Island, Cumberland Gulf, consists of patelliform individuals only. Another from Cumberland Gulf contains transitions from the patelliform to cylindric, the latter solitary and mainly of large caliber, height 21 mm., diameter 12 mm. (pl. 44, figs. 3, 3*a*).

Labrador specimens seen are rather small, all of the patelliform shape, and like those of New England.

In New England *B. balanoides* is an exceedingly abundant barnacle, on rocks between tides, on piles and buoys, and on the mussels growing there; in such places they often become larger than those on shore rocks in the same vicinity.

The low-conic form may be either sharply, strongly ribbed, as in plate 44, figure 5, from New Haven, Connecticut, on *Mytilus edulis*, or it may be moderately folded as in plate 44, figure 2, on bark of a pile, New Haven, Connecticut. The less-ribbed form is the commonest and closely resembles European specimens. When they stand crowded the walls become subvertical and higher than the conic form, yet often with no tendency toward the tubular form. Another lot from the same locality, growing on oyster shells, vary from shortly cylindric to hourglass shaped.

The tubular form, growing in crowded masses (pl. 44, figs. 2, 7–7d, Savin Rock, New Haven, Connecticut), is excessively variable in shape. The individuals cohere rather weakly, and may usually be separated without breaking. The compartments are often calcified together in the lower part. Parietal tubes square, the septa thin, but usually they are closed at the basal edge. Two very slender individuals measure:

Length 46 mm.; greatest diameter 8.8 mm.; least 3.3 mm.

Length 26 mm.; greatest diameter 4 mm.; least 1.5 mm.

In the Savin Rock colony the tergum is slightly narrower than usual, but it is identical in shape in the patelliform and the tubular (pl. 44, fig. 6) forms. I have noted above that the mouth parts and cirri are practically identical in patelliform and tubular individuals. In some groups one may trace all transitions of contour from the low-conic to the tubular.

Plate 45, figures 2, 2a, represent tergum and scutum of a small, deeply corroded form of *balanoides*, growing in the vicinity of the following form.

Variety with a narrow spur and numerous spines on the later cirri.—This form, figured on plate 45, figures 1 to 1c, has been noticed by Darwin as var. *a.* I have seen it from Nahant, Massachusetts, collected by Prof. A. S. Pearse. It is somewhat conic with rather large orifice, weak, the walls smooth, thin, compartments readily separable, the parietes having *regular square tubes* not obliterated at the base, and separated by thin septa, but the interior is not ribbed. The scutum does not differ from that of normal *B. balanoides*, but the tergum (pl. 45, fig. 1, 1c) has the spur narrow, longer, and pointed, unlike the ordinary form in *B. balanoides*. The segments of the posterior cirri have *seven pairs of spines* (p. 190, fig.

59*d*). Darwin notes that specimens he examined had 7, 8, and even 10 pairs of spines. The lower two points of the mandible are longer than usual, but I noticed no other differences in the cirri and mouth parts.

Darwin found various of these characters in other combinations with characters of normal *B. balanoides*, in some European individuals, and therefore did not segregate the form as a new species. My experience with the variety is too limited to enable me to form an opinion as to its status. It does not seem to be a form due to any direct reaction to environment, as it occurs in the immediate proximity of normal *B. balanoides*.

Alaskan forms of B. balanoides.—Specimens from Unalaska, Cat. No. 58063, growing on *Balanus cariosus*, with *Chthamalus dalli*, are small, diameter 5 to 6 mm., rugged, resembling plate 43, figure 4*c*, or with more ribs. The tergal and basal margins of the scutum are of equal length, and the valve is curved between apex and base, concave externally, as in *B. crenatus curviscutum*. The tergum has a peculiarly concave scutal margin, very broadly inflected below. Free apex is unusually long. The spur is shorter than normal for the species. The apices of the opercular valves diverge somewhat when in the occluded position.

The labrum has three strong teeth on either side of the median notch. Maxilla has a very small notch, in which several small spines stand, below the two upper spines, and a rather prominent pair of spines near the lower angle.

The first cirrus has 15 and 9 segments, the posterior ramus three-fourths as long as the anterior. Second cirrus with subequal rami of 10 segments. Third cirrus of 10 and 9 segments, the posterior ramus three-fourths as long as the anterior, and without spinules on the segments. The later cirri have segments with, at most, 7 pairs of spines.

This is the only West American lot referable to *B. balanoides* which I have seen, and here the terga and maxillæ differ somewhat from all Atlantic specimens examined. Other Alaskan forms seen may be segregated as a subspecies.

EUROPEAN.

Locality.	Collector.	Notes.
Belfast Bay, Ireland	W. T. Thompson	Coll. A. N. S. P.
Portmarnock, Ireland	Jeffreys coll	
Loch Fyne, Scotland	do	
Scarborough, England	Turton, Jeffreys coll	
Fishguard, Wales	Jeffreys coll	
Swansea Bay	do	
Exmouth, south Devon	do	On buoy.
Do	do	On sandstone rocks.
Estuary of Exe River	do	
Langland Bay	do	
Rochelle, France	Orbigny, Jeffreys coll	
Heligoland	Royal Biological Station	On *Mytilus*.

ARCTIC AND WEST ATLANTIC.

Cumberland Sound	Mintzee	
Arctic Island, Cumberland Sound	L. Kumlien	
Rigolet, Labrador	L. M. Turner	
Nain, Labrador	O. Bryant	
Labrador	Storer	
Ligby, Nova Scotia	Mary J. Rathbun	On *Mytilus*.
Nova Scotia	Jeffreys coll	
Passamaquody Bay	Isaac Lea coll	
Frenchman's Bay, Me	Wm. H. Seaman	On granite pebbles.
Nahant, Mass	A. F. Pearse (in tidal pools)	
Provincetown, Cape Cod, Mass	U. S. F. C	On piles.
Do	do	On *Modiolus dermissus*.
Nantucket, Mass	Benj. Albertson	
Vineyard Sound	U. S. F. C	On bark.
Vineyard Haven, Martha's Vineyard	do	On piles.
Do	S. R. Roberts	On pebbles, coll. A. N. S. P.
Ten Pound Island	A. E. Verrill	Low water.
Newport, R. I	U. S. F. C	On piles.
Do	Dr. E. A. Mearns	On rocks and *Modiolus*
New Haven, Conn	Richard Rathbun	On *Mytilus*.
Savin Rock, New Haven, Conn	do	On piles.
Ocean City, N. J	H. A. Pilsbry	On pile.

PACIFIC.

Unalaska, Alaska	W. H. Dall	On clam shell; very young.
Do	Albatross	On *B. cariosus*.
Cold Bay, Shelikof Strait, Alaska	T. W. Stanton	Var *calcaratus*.
Sitka, Alaska	Dr. B. Sharp	Coll. A. N. S. P.; var. *calcaratus*.

BALANUS BALANOIDES CALCARATUS, new subspecies.

Plate 45, figs. 3–3c; 4–4c.

Type.—Cat. No. 32949, U.S.N.M., from Cold Bay, Shelikof Strait, Alaska, collected by T. W. Stanton, 1904.

The specimens are tubular, thin, very fragile, and grow in crowded groups. When a group is broken, the break is usually through a barnacle, so loosely are the compartments cemented. The length varies from 9 to 20 mm., but fragments indicate that it attains over double this size; diameter at orifice 5 to 8 mm. It is like the form of *B. crenatus* from *Albatross* station 3282, except that the parietes are smooth inside. The scuta are nearly flat, the apices not diverging. Articular ridge short, broadly reflexed, with a callus between its lower end and the adductor pit. Tergum with a long and *extremely narrow spur.* Cirri not examined, as the body has been destroyed by insects, the specimens being preserved dry. It occurred with *B. crenatus*, and therefore probably below low-water mark.

A single individual from Sitka (pl. 45, figs. 4–4c) is conic, strongly ribbed, with small, irregular marginal pores, most of them filled up, at the basal margin. *The wall is excessively thick* and the sheath much longer than in patelliform specimens from the Atlantic. The scutum resembles that of the Shelikof Strait lot. It is flat, the articular ridge strongly developed, basal and tergal margins about equal. The tergum has a decidedly narrow tapering spur.

The body was not preserved. It occurred with *B. crenatus*, one of which grew upon the specimen figured. Though the opercular valves resemble those of *calcaratus* from Shelikof Strait, the walls are very different. It appears that this west American race has the same wide variation in external form long known in Atlantic *balanoides*.

BALANUS CARIOSUS (Pallas).

Plate 46; plate 47, figs. 1–1c.

1788. *Lepas cariosa* PALLAS, Nova Acta Academiæ Scientiarium Imperialis Petropolitanæ, vol. 2, p. 234, pl. 6, figs. 24A, 24 B.

1854. *Balanus cariosus* Pallas, DARWIN, Monograph, p. 273, pl. 7, figs. 3a–3c.

1897. *Balanus cariosus* Pallas, WELTNER, Verzeichnis, p. 270.

1903. *Balanus cariosus* Pallas, GRUVEL, Nouvelles Archives du Muséum, ser. 4, vol. 5, p. 140, pl. 4, fig. 13. "Golfe de Géorgie, Amérique (Agassiz), et de Cochinchine."

1911. *Balanus cariosus* Pallas, KRÜGER, Beiträge zur Cirripedienfauna Ostasiens, Abhandl. der Math.-phys. Klasse der K. Bayer. Akademie der Wissenschaften, Suppl.-Bd. 2, p. 54, figs. 108–111, pl. 1, fig. 8; pl. 4, fig. 37 (Iterup, Kuril Is., Doctor Haberer, and Todohokke, Hokkaido, Doctor Doflein).

Type-locality.—The Kuril Islands.

Distribution.—Bering Sea south to Oregon and to northern Japan; in the littoral zone.

Darwin's diagnosis:

Parietes thick, formed by several rows of unequal-sized pores. Tergum narrow, with the apex beaked and the spur sharply pointed.

The form is usually steeply conic, with a small orifice, but sometimes cylindric with the orifice large; dirty white. Sculpture of many narrow, deeply cut, irregular ribs, usually provided with occasional projecting points—"from the manner in which these overlap each other the shell almost appears as if thatched with straw." The upper part in old individuals is generally eroded, irregularly rugose, and pitted. Radii usually very narrow, often scarcely distinguishable as such; but in some cylindrical examples, such as plate 46, figures 2, 2a, they become very wide, with strongly oblique summits. The wall is ordinarily very thick, permeated with many unequal rounded and angular tubes (pl. 46, figs. 1, 8). They have transverse septa and become filled up and then eroded away in the upper part of the cone. Sometimes the pores are almost filled up, in large part obliterated, at the base. Within the basal edge the inside is peculiarly roughened or has irregularly branching wrinkles. The sheath is long, often over half the height of the cone, the space between it and the wall usually filled up solidly, and the opercular valves lodge far within the orifice.

The scutum has low growth ridges, the lower ones fringed with the remains of former opercular membranes, and usually a very minute, weak, longitudinal striation. Inside there is a rather small, well-reflexed articular ridge, which is continued downward in a sharp, high, curved adductor ridge in some specimens; in others the adductor ridge is very weak. The pit for the depressor muscles is deep, and rather large, and often is divided by one or two inconspicuous ridges. There are several very oblique, coarse teeth on the occludent margin.

Tergum is *very narrow*, beaked, the beak often purplish. *Furrow to the spur narrow or closed.* The articular ridge is long and acute. *Spur very narrow and long*, acute, continued upward as a raised

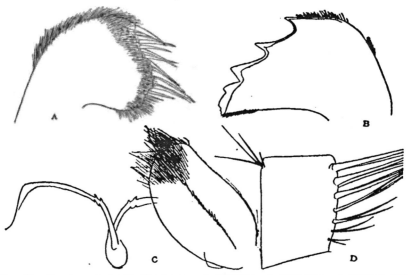

FIG. 59.—BALANUS CARIOSUS, UNALASKA. *a*, MAXILLA. *b*, MANDIBLE. *c*, LABRUM AND PALPUS. *d*, BALANUS BALANOIDES, MIDDLE SEGMENT OF 6TH CIRRUS (SEE P. 186).

ridge on the inside of the valve. Crests for the depressor muscles are strongly developed.

The basis is wholly membranous.

The size is rather variable. Unalaska specimens measure:

Diameter, 56 mm.; height, 32 mm. (largest conic example).

Diameter, 57 mm.; height, 37 mm.

Diameter, 30 mm.; height, 24 mm. (conic).

Diameter, 35–40 mm.; height, 50 mm. (cylindric).

Diameter, 35 mm.; height, 100 mm. (cylindric, longest seen).

The first measurement is very close to that of Pallas's figures of the type. The third measurement is a more usual size.

The labrum has two teeth on each side of the median notch; outer angles are more abrupt than usual. Palpi nearly covered with short hairs. The mandible has three strong conic teeth and a short fourth one, the fifth tooth very low and obtuse, united with the lower point.

The maxilla is notched below the upper spines. Margin advancing below the notch, bearing about 8 spines, the lower two larger. Lower angle and upper margin are profusely hairy.

The cirri are nearly black. First three of nearly equal length, not half as long as the following three. Posterior ramus of cirrus i, of 17 segments, about three-fourths as long as the anterior, of 21, and having extremely protuberant segments. Rami of cirrus ii subequal, of about 15 rather strongly protuberant segments. Cirrus iii having nearly equal rami of about 15 segments; both rami very densely hairy. Cirrus vi has about 40 segments, the median ones bearing 7 pairs of spines (fig. 59).

Penis is nearly as long as cirrus vi, sparsely hairy near the end.

The young of about 5 or 6 mm. diameter are beautiful, starlike barnacles, with two or three ribs on the carina, one on the carino-lateral, and three or four on the lateral and rostral compartments. The number of ribs soon increases by intercalation in the intervals. The pores of the parietes are much less numerous in young than in old individuals, but they are already somewhat subdivided and irregular at the 5 mm. stage. I have seen old specimens from a narrow support in which the membranous basis is reduced to very small area, and the pores are closed at the basal edge.

Balanus cariosus has a superficial resemblance to *Tetraclita* due to its membranous basis and porous wall. It is related to *B. bala-noides*, but not closely, as the opercular valves are very different. Darwin has called attention to points of resemblance (not, I think, relationship) between the present species *B. flosculus* and *B. nubilis*, but there are also important differences; altogether it is an isolated species.

B. cariosus is a shallow-water and shore species, commonly growing on pebbles, shells, such as living *Mytilus*, *Pecten*, and other cast-up shells. The single example from a deep-water station (*Albatross* station 2871) has evidently been dead a long time and probably drifted into deep water from the shore. All of the rest of the series was taken by collectors from the shore.

Plate 46, figures 1, 2, 2a, 4, 6, 8, are from Unalaska specimens; figures 3 and 7 are from Nazan Bay, Atka; figure 5 from Neah Bay, Washington. Figures 1 and 8 are slightly enlarged, the others natural size.

Rarely *B. cariosus* grows on sponges which almost bury the barnacle. The group shown partly cleared of the sponge in plate 46, figure 9, is from Sanborn Harbor, Nagai Island, Shumagins. The parietes are narrow, radii wide in the lower part, narrow above, the alæ forming the greater part of the walls between the parietes. The

compartments are thin and part very easily. Without the opercular
monly harbors *Balanus rostratus apertus*.

The sponge is the same friable species of soft texture which commonly harbors *Balanus rostratus apertus*.

The United States National Museum collection is rich in specimens
from the Aleutian Islands, and as far south as Puget Sound, but
the southern limit of the species remains to be ascertained. Darwin
records it from the Columbia River. It probably occurs in northern
California. The locality " Golfe de Géorgie " (Paris Museum, Gruvel) also quoted by Krüger, evidently means the Gulf, or more properly Strait of Georgia, east of Vancouver Island, British Columbia,
where Dr. A. Agassiz collected many years ago. On the west, it extends as far south as Hakodate in southern Yesso (Hokkaido), and
probably farther south, as it was taken by Mr. H. Loomis, whose
material is chiefly from Jedo Bay, in middle Japan. The record
Cochin China, in the Paris Museum, can hardly be accepted without
confirmation. It seems most improbable.

U. S. N. M. Cat. No.	Locality.	Collector.	Notes.
	St. Paul Island, Pribilof Islands	William Palmer.............	
	Bering Island......................	L. Stejneger..................	
	Nazan Bay, Atka....................	W. H. Dall..................	On shore.
3507	Attu...............................	.....do........................	
3509			
9178	Sarana Bay, Attu...................	.....do........................	
	Dutch Harbor, Unalaska...........	*Albatross*........................	
823, 9172			
9174–9176			
9180–9181	Unalaska...........................	W. H. Dall..................	Very fine series.
9200, 9226			
3501, 3505			
3489			
	Amaknak Islands, Unalaska.........	.....do........................	Beach.
	Nikolski Bay, Umnak Island........	*Albatross*........................	
3511	Sanborn Harbor, Shumagins........	W. H. Dall.................	In sponge.
	Coal Harbor, Shumagins.............	.....do........................	
	Cold Bay, Shelikof Strait...........	T. W. Stanton.............	
	Fort Wrangell, Alexander Archi-pelago.	W. H. Dall.................	
	Kloosta village, Parry Passage, Graham Islands, British Columbia.	Jas. G. Swan...............	
	Port Townsend, Wash..............	....	
	Fort Steilacoom, Puget Sound.......	Dr. Geo. Buckley, U. S. A...	
	Neah Bay, Wash...................	J. G. Swan..................	
	Puget Sound, Wash................	.....do........................	On stone.
	Station 2871, off northwestern Washington.	*Albatross*........................	Long dead; 559 fathoms
	Oregon............................	....	
	Japan.............................	H. Loomis..................	

HESPERIBALANUS, new subgenus.

Balani with poreless walls and basis, the radii with thick, septate
edges; opercular valves as in the *Balanus crenatus* group. Mandible
with the fourth and fifth teeth short and broad, lower edge shortly
hairy. Maxilla with few spines.

Type.—B. hesperius.

The single west American species composing this group resembles *Solidobalanus* in the hard parts, but has the mandibles and maxillæ formed as in the typical *Balanus,* and unlike those of any poreless group of the genus. It is possible that we have to do with a secondarily simplified group descended from some ancestor of the *B. crenatus* stock. At all events, *Hesperibalanus* is not at all closely related to *Solidobalanus, Armatobalanus, Chirona,* or any other poreless subgenus.

BALANUS HESPERIUS, new species.

Plate 49, figs. 1–1*d,* 7–7*b,* 8.

Type.—Cat. No. 32935, U.S.N.M., from *Albatross* Station 3483.
Distribution.—Alaska, Bering Sea.

The barnacle is small, conic or shortly cylindric, white or buff, typically ribbed in the adult stage, but sometimes smooth; epidermis very thin, pale yellow, usually fugacious.

Greatest basal diameter of type 15.7 mm.; height, 7.2 mm. The largest specimen seen is from Attu, Aleutians, measuring 22 mm. in greatest diameter; the longest compartment 17 mm. high. The ordinary size is 12 to 16 mm. diameter.

The scutum (pl. 49, figs. 1*b,* 1*c,* 1*d*) is shaped like that of *B. crenatus;* tergal border slightly inflected, longer than the basal; the occludent border often slightly convex, *thick.* Sculpture of close, sharp growth-ridges, every alternate one more prolonged and higher on the occludent edge; over the ridges there is a very minute longitudinal striation. The articular ridge is very high, reflexed, and usually ends in a point; adductor ridge very short, passing upward into a heavy callus between the articular ridge and the deep pit of the adductor muscle, *this callus being cut into several sharp ridges,* which typically terminate downward in teeth. Articular furrow deep. Pit for the lateral depressor muscles very small but sunken.

The tergum (pl. 49, fig. 1*a*) has a rather short carinal margin. Articular ridge well developed, triangularly overhanging the upper part of the broad articular furrow. Spur short, one-fourth the width of the valve or less, rounded or subtruncate, and *standing very close to the basiscutal angle.* The external face is flat, with a very slight depression running to the spur. Growth-ridges delicate, mainly epidermal, stronger on the scutal side. There are some weak radial striæ near the carinal margin.

Compartments.—*The parietes have no pores or tubes whatever.* Their inner faces are very strongly and deeply ribbed, the ribs more or less crenulated at the base, and generally unequal. The sheath is extremely short, the opercular valves, therefore, lodged high in the orifice. *Radii broad;* their summits making angles of about 45° with the base, edges laminate, the laminæ often somewhat irregular, branching, but not very distinctly denticulate. Alæ broad, with nearly horizontal summits.

The basis is calcareous, thin, not porous, its inner face deeply grooved radially, the periphery being denticulate, with deep pits for the basal septa of the parietes.

The labrum (fig. 60c) usually has three teeth on each side.

The palpus (fig. 60a, c) has an irregular longitudinal row of pectinated bristles on the labral face and two dense groups of spines at the distal end.

Mandible (fig. 61a) substantially as in *B. crenatus*.

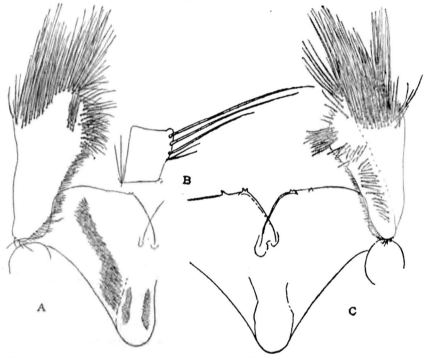

Fig. 60.—Balanus hesperius, Albatross station 3483, Bering Sea. *a, c*, both sides of the labrum and of one palpus. *b*, 27th segment of cirrus VI.

Maxilla (fig. 61b, c) is slightly notched under the two great spines. there are nine spines below the upper pair in the type, seven in another specimen, one of them stouter, as in *B. balanus*.

Cirri, first and second pairs injured in the type-specimen. The posterior ramus of cirrus i has 9 or 10 segments; anterior segment had been decidedly longer. Cirrus iii with the pedicel expanded as in *B. crenatus;* posterior ramus of 12 segments two-thirds the length of the anterior of 15 segments. The segments are densely bristly, without any spinules or teeth. The posterior cirri have segments with three or four pairs of spines, the lower pair minute; the posterior distal angle of each segment has a group of spines at least as long as the segment; both rami of cirrus vi have 34 segments (fig. 60b).

The penis is longer than the cirri, with very few hairs, and so far as I can see, no point at its dorsal base.

Examples from other lots examined vary in the armature of the labrum and maxilla, and relative length of the rami of cirrus i, but all are practically alike in other respects.

As in other ribbed species, the early stages are smooth; the ribs appear when it is 3 or 4 mm. in diameter, sometimes later, up to 7 mm. The type is one of a very strongly ribbed lot. The ribs are not quite so deeply cut in most lots, and they vary, as in all ribbed Balani. It seems never to become elongated, club shaped, or columnar, as in *B crenatus*, *B. balanoides*, and rarely *B. glandula*. The small

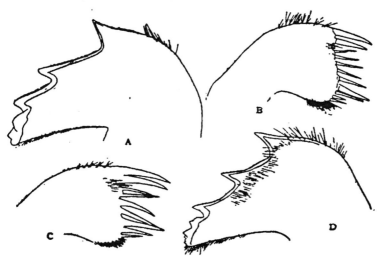

Fig. 61.—BALANUS HESPERIUS, STATION 3483. a, MANDIBLE. b, MAXILLA. c, MAXILLA OF SPECIMEN FROM STATION 3540. d, B. H. NIPPONENSIS, MANDIBLE.

number of spines on the posterior cirri distinguishes *B. hesperius* from all of these species. *B. glandula* occasionally has almost or quite poreless parietes, but the scutum is unlike that of *B. hesperius*. It is almost exclusively seated on shells, especially gastropods, in the collections at hand, but this may be because stones are less likely to be taken by the collector.

Plate 49, figure 8, represents a large typical specimen growing on the anterior part of a *Chrysodomus*. Diameter 18 mm. This seems to be the maximum size.

In specimens from *Albatross* station 3540 the wall resembles that shown in plate 49, figure 3. The labrum has one tooth on one side, three on the other. Mandible and maxilla about as in the specimen dissected from Station 5003, except that there is no notch below the upper pair of spines of the maxilla. Cirrus i has 12 and 8 segments, the posterior ramus over three-fourths the length of the anterior. Cirrus ii has slightly unequal rami of 9 segments. Posterior cirri with three pairs of spines on the segments. By the proportions of the rami of the first cirrus, this form differs strongly from *B. h. nipponensis* (station 5003), but otherwise is much like it.

U.S.N.M. Cat. No.	U.S.F.C. Sta. No.	Locality.	Depth (fathoms).	Bottom temperature.	Collector.
				°F.	
10038	....	Latitude, 60° 16′ north; longitude, 167° 41′ west, off Monroe Island.	....	....	Lieut. Geo. M. Stoney.
		Cape Prince of Wales, Alaska.....	....	....	E. M. Kindle.
		Bering Sea:			
32942	3302	Latitude, 57° 45′ 45″ north; longitude, 160° 12′ 15″ west.	30	40.2	*Albatross.*
32944	3482	Latitude, 57° 18′ 00″ north; longitude, 170° 42′ 00″ west.	42	33.9	Do.
	3487	Latitude, 57° 10′ 00″ north; longitude, 173° 45′ 00″ west.	81	37.6	Do.
32935	3483	Latitude, 57° 18′ 00″ north; longitude, 171° 18′ 00″ west.	56	36.8	Do.
32940	3540	Latitude, 56° 27′ 00″ north; longitude, 166° 08′ 00″ west.	51	36	Do.
	3231	Latitude, 56° 14′ 00″ north; longitude, 161° 41′ 15″ west.	36	....	Do.
	3542	Latitude, 56° 10′ 00″ north; longitude, 163° 26′ 00″ west.	40	39.2	Do.
32937	3537	Latitude, 54° 45′ 00″ north; longitude, 169° 06′ 00″ west.	40	38	Do.
	3548	Latitude, 54° 44′ 00″ north; longitude, 165° 42′ 00″ west.	91	39.5	Do.
32938	....	St. Paul Island, Pribiloff Islands..	Beach.	....	H. W. Elliott.
3508	....	Attu, Aleutian Islands..........	....	....	W. H. Dall.
32939	3674	(Record missing)............	....	....	*Albatross.*
32936	3675	....do...........	....	....	Do.
	A.N.S.P.	Mary Island, Alexander Archipelago.	....	....	J. G. Malone.
32945	....	Kloosta village, Graham Island, Parry Passage, British Columbia.	....	....	

Several other lots are labeled Alaska, without nearer indication of locality.

BALANUS HESPERIUS form LÆVIDOMUS, new form.

Plate 50, figs. 1–1*f*; 2–2*b*.

Type.—Cat. No. 2106, Acad. Nat. Sci. Phila., from San Juan Islands, Puget Sound, collected by Homer Wheeler.

Distribution.—Monterey, California, to Alaska.

The shape varies from broadly conic to shortly cylindric. The external walls are smooth in the typical form of the subspecies; the ribs on the inner faces of the parietes are regular. The scutum has fewer, more widely spaced growth-ridges than in *hesperius;* they are often low, or very weak. The basal margin of the scutum is usually longer.

I segregate this form with some hesitation, yet after going over the material repeatedly there seems to be a constant difference in the external sculpture of the scuta, which it would be a fault to ignore.

As the geographic ranges of the two forms overlap in the north and there are some transitional specimens, I do not call it a subspecies.

The greater number of lots having widely spaced growth-ridges on the scuta also have smooth parietes; yet this association is not invariable. A lot from Port Townsend, growing on *Pecten caurinus*, is as strongly ribbed externally as most *hesperius*, but in the lower part only, the upper part of the cone being smooth. They reach a basal length of 17 mm. (pl. 49, fig. 2). In another lot from *Albatross* station 2869, off northern Washington, there are faint traces of ribs close to the base, thus connecting the strongly ribbed and smooth forms. Some fine groups, growing on *Natica*, at *Albatross* station 3675, are also transitional in external sculpture (pl. 49, figs. 3, 3a).

Figures 1 to 1*f* are from very regular, smooth, solitary specimens growing on the interior of *Pecten*. They are not mature, measuring 7.25 mm. in greatest diameter, 2.5 mm. high. Other regular, low-conic specimens were dredged by the *Albatross* in 32 fathoms off the northwestern coast of Washington (station 2869). The largest measures 13 mm. diameter, 5.8 mm. high, probably about maximum size. Close to the base there are traces of ribs.

The cylindric form from Puget Sound (pl. 49, fig. 5, on the shell of *Thais*) is similar to the low-conic form except in shape of the wall. Diameter 11.5, height 8 to 11 mm.; orifice 9.5 mm. long.

Californian specimens seen are very small. One of the shortly cylindric form from *Albatross* station 4457, Monterey Bay, 15 fathoms, is 7 mm. in greatest diameter. Others from Albatross station 4561, Monterey Bay, 15 fathoms, and 3096, off Oregon, in 33 fathoms (pl. 50, figs. 2, 2a, 2b) are still smaller, the largest 6 mm. in diameter; shape conic with large orifice, or cylindric, the orifice as large as the base; *radii more oblique* than in the usual *B. hesperius*. Scutum having very low, widely spaced growth-ridges, and internally simpler than ordinary *hesperius;* the callus between articular ridge and adductor pit smooth, raised into an acute ridge along the pit.

Most of the characters are those of young *hesperius*, but the appearance of the specimens, which are very numerous, is that of adult barnacles. Possibly a small race inhabits the coast from Oregon to Monterey Bay, but further shore collections are needed to demonstrate this. Both lots grew on twigs.

In Alaska the smooth form with convexly conic shape has been taken at Sitka; diameter 15.5 mm., height 7 mm., growing on *Tegula pulligo* (pl. 49, fig. 4). Further north, in the waters where typical *B. hesperius* is abundant, the variety *lævidomus* seems to be rare. There are a few specimens up to diameter 6 mm., from Chagafka Cove, Kodiak, and from the mouth of Port Clarence, which, by the smooth exterior and low, widely spaced growth-ridges of the scuta, seem to belong here. Both grew on small gastropods. Smooth individuals seen from other Alaskan localities may be, at least in part, immature stages of the ribbed *B. hesperius*.

The form *lævidomus* often has a strong superficial resemblance to *Balanus æneas* Lanchester,[1] from the Malay Peninsula, but the following differences may be noted: In *B. hesperius* the spur of the tergum is wider and very much closer to the basiscutal angle. The articular and adductor ridges of the scutum are shorter and differ in shape. Finally the radii are much better developed.

U. S. F. C. station.	Locality.	Depth (fathoms).	Bottom temperature.	Collector.
			° F.	
4561	Monterey Bay, Cal............................	15	60	Albatross.
4457	.....do............................	46		Do.
3096	Off Oregon, latitude, 42° 45′ north; longitude, 124° 36′ 15″ west.	33	46. 7	Do.
	Puget Sound, Wash...........................			Kennerley.
	San Juan Island, Puget Sound, Wash........			Homer Wheeler; coll. A. N. S. P.
	Raft Island, Puget Sound, Wash............			John Allen, coll. A. N. S. P.
	Sitka, Alaska...........................			F. Bischoff.
	Chagafka Cove, Kodiak Island.................	15–20		W. H. Dall.
	Mouth of Port Clarence, Alaska...............	7–12		Do.

Somewhat doubtful records are *Albatross* stations 2869, 2872, 3508, and 3282. These may be the young of either *hesperius* or *lævidomus*.

Ribbed forms of B. hesperius, from the Asiatic coast. A series from *Albatross* station 3780, attached to egg-capsules of *Chrysodomus*, taken off Kamchatka in 12 fathoms, is externally of the typical ribbed form; basal diameter 9 to 11 mm. (pl. 49, figs. 7–7b). The scuta differ by having growth-ridges decidedly *more widely spaced*, as in Puget Sound *hesperius*. In most individuals the valve has the shape of a right-angled triangle with basal and tergal margins subequal; but sometimes the angle is slightly greater, and the tergal margin longer. The spur of the tergum is longer than usual.

A similar form was taken at *Albatross* Station 5003, off southwestern Saghalin Island, growing on a *Turritella*, in 35 fathoms, bottom temperature 42.4° F. In this lot the labrum (fig. 62c) has three teeth on one side of the median cleft, one on the other. The palpi differ from those of typical *B. hesperius*. The longitudinal row of bristles on the labral side (fig. 62c) is short, with similar pectinated bristles scattered above it. The patch of bristles near its distal end is situated near the upper margin. All of these spines are pectinated. There is no distal patch of long spines on this side of the palpus. The outer side of the palpus has a very dense distal patch of long, simple bristles (fig. 62d).

The mandible does not differ materially from that figured for *hesperius*. Maxilla (fig. 62e) is notched under the upper pair of great spines, a pair of short spines in the notch. There are five

---

[1] On the Crustacea collected during the Skeat expedition to the Malay Peninsula, Proc. Zool. Soc., London, 1902, vol. 2, p. 370, pl. 34, figs. 4, 4a.

spines between the upper pair and the large lower spine, and two below the latter.

First cirrus (fig. 62a) with rami of 18 and 8 segments, the posterior ramus less than half the length of the anterior. Cirrus ii short, with rami of 9 and 8 segments. Cirrus iii with slightly unequal rami of about 10 segments each. There are some minute trifid, multifid and rarely simple spinules on the anterior distal part of all the segments of both rami (fig. 62b); also a few observed on the anterior ramus of cirrus iv. Posterior cirri have three pairs of spines on the segments, with some minute ones near the bases of the pairs.

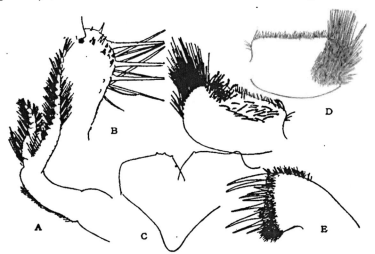

FIG. 62.—BALANUS HESPERIUS, OFF SAGHALIN ISLAND. a, 1ST CIRRUS. b, 3D SEGMENT OF ANTERIOR RAMUS OF CIRRUS III. c, LABRUM AND PALPUS. d, REVERSE SIDE OF PALPUS. e, MAXILLA.

Another lot having broad scuta and a ribbed wall was taken by Lieut. Geo. M. Stoney in latitude 60° 22′ north, longitude 168° 45′ west.

BALANUS HESPERIUS NIPPONENSIS, new subspecies.

Plate 49, fig. 6.

Type.—Cat. No. 48194, U.S.N.M., from *Albatross* station 3768, off Daikohu Saki, main island of Japan, 25 to 27 fathoms, surface temperature 64° F., June 5, 1900.

Parietes smooth; walls otherwise as in the smooth form of *B. hesperius.* Scutum having the basal margin about as long as the tergal margin or longer; the external growth ridges close. Tergum narrow toward the spur. Both opercular valves are very thick (fig. 63).

The labrum has three teeth on one side, two on the other.

Mandible (fig. 61d) having the teeth acute. Maxilla hardly notched under the two great spines, and with six other spines, one of which is large. There is a group of small spines above the lower angle, as in other forms of the species. The third cirrus has *very few* irregular spinules situated as in figure 61*b*. The posterior cirri have three pairs of spines on the segments, the lower pair very minute, or sometimes wanting.

This form differs from that of northern Asiatic waters by the longer basal margin and finer external sculpture of the scutum, the smooth parietes, and some reduction in the spines of the later cirri. Whether these differential features will hold good when the Japanese barnacle fauna is studied from adequate materials remains to be determined. The characters are variable in *B. hesperius*. However, it has been thought desirable to signalize by

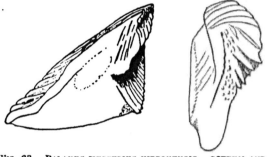

Fig. 63.—BALANUS HESPERIUS NIPPONENSIS. SCUTUM AND TERGUM OF THE TYPE.

name the presence of a modified form of the species in the much warmer waters of Japan.

METABALANUS, new subgenus.

Parietes and basis not porous; radii wanting; scutum having a very weak articular and no adductor ridge; tergum with a rather long spur and no external furrow. Third cirri like the second, armed with densely spinose areas and no small spinules.

Type.—Balanus hoekianus.

The single species composing this group was formerly placed by me in Hoek's section G of *Balanus*. It has been enumerated by Doctor Hoek in his genus *Hexelasma*. The form of the mandible, the ribbed interior of the wall, the overhanging lower edge of the sheath, the long spur of the tergum, and especially the form and chætotaxy of the third cirri are all Balanid characters and make it certain that the species is not a *Hexelasma*. Not having the specimens at hand, I have been unable to examine the labrum, but the description of the cirri is amplified below from the slide mounted when I described the species. Whether the absence of radii is sufficient to distinguish *Metabalanus* from *Chirona* is somewhat doubtful.

BALANUS HOEKIANUS Pilsbry.

Plate 52, figs. 2 to 2f.

1911. *Balanus hoekianus* PILSBRY, Bulletin of the Bureau of Fisheries, vol. 29, p. 77, fig. 8 (mouth parts and cirri) ; pl. 13, figs. 3–7 ; pl. 15, figs. 1, 2.

Type.—No. 38666, United States National Museum.

Type-locality.—*Albatross* Station 4778, Bering Sea, latitude 52° 12′ north, longitude 179° 52′ east, in 43 fathoms, seated on a gastropod shell (*Buccinum*).

The shell and opercular plates are white throughout. Shape shortly subcylindric, flaring outward at the large triangularly ovate orifice. Compartments solid, without pores; no radii. The parietes are slightly roughened but not distinctly ribbed or sulcate, with no chitinous cuticle and no hairs. The alæ are smooth, with extremely oblique upper margins, so that the peritreme is deeply serrate. Internally the compartments have a long glossy sheath below which they are somewhat sulcate, chiefly near the base.

The rostrum is much the largest plate. Externally, while it is finely, indistinctly rugose longitudinally, there is no distinct costation, and no trace of radii. Inside, the sheath is tripartite. The carina is strongly concave. The lateral plate is wide, triangular, with a well-developed ala but no radius. The carinolateral plate is narrow, recurved, with the ala wider than the parietal area. Inside the sheath is bipartite.

The basis is an excessively thin transparent film, calcareous at the edges, membranous in the middle.

Height of the shell 8 mm.; diameter of the base 8 mm.

The scutum is moderately thick. It flares outward and is twisted toward the apex. Externally it is indistinctly marked with fine, weak growth-striæ and rather widely spaced growth-arrest lines which are scarcely raised. Inside there is a short but well-developed articular ridge, about one-third the greatest length of the plate. The articular furrow is narrow and distinct though not deep. There is no adductor ridge, though a noticeable thickening extends downward from the lower end of the articular ridge, representing a vestigeal adductor ridge. A shallow oblong pit marks the insertion of the depressor muscle.

The tergum is very thick for so small a plate, white, the scutal margin concave, carinal margin short, strongly convex. The spur is long and narrow, separated from the scutal margin by nearly its own width. A smooth depressed band runs to it. The area on the scutal side of this band is marked with widely spaced, strongly arched, linear growth-ridges. The wide area on the other side has very oblique linear growth-ridges, and an interstitial sculpture of very weak, fine, longitudinal striæ. There are some minute hairs

on the cuticular ridges along the scutal border, but none on the
outer surface of the plate. Internally the upper or beak portion
of the plate is transversely striated. The articular ridge is high and
massive, arcuate; the articular furrow wide but not very deep. The
crests for the depressor muscle are short and sharp.

Mandible (fig. 64b) has four principal teeth. The upper two
are rather long and acute, the second one in the middle of the
edge. The third and fourth teeth are blunt, and there are two
denticles between them. The lower point is short and slightly
bifid. The lower edge of the mandible is heavily bearded. The
two mandibles are exactly similar.

Maxilla (fig. 64c) has an even edge except for a notch below
the upper two large spines. There are six or seven large spines,

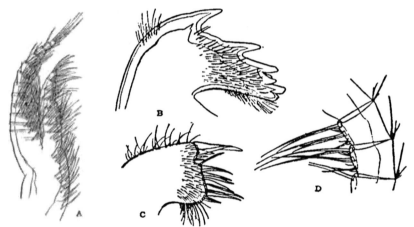

Fig. 64.—Balanus hoekianus, type. a, cirrus i. b, mandible. c, maxilla. d, segments
of cirrus vi.

two near the lower angle being longer, and a few smaller ones
below the notch. A band along the edge of the maxilla and below
the lower angle is bristly, and there are a few hairs along the upper
edge.

The first cirrus has rami of 9 and 13 segments, the anterior ramus
two-thirds as long as the posterior. The segments are rather densely
hairy and spinose, and in the terminal tuft of the shorter segment
there are some bipinnate spines (fig. 64a). Cirrus ii has rami of
10 and 9 segments, the anterior longer by three segments. The segments have the usual bands of spinules on the distal part, widening
toward the anterior side.

Cirrus iii has 14 and 13 segments, the anterior ramus longer by
five segments. Spines as in cirrus ii.

Cirri iv to vi are longer, with segments bearing two large and one
small pair of spines, and some short spines on the anterior edge, between the pairs (fig. 64d).

By the absence of radii and the shape of the opercular valves, this is a rather isolated species. The cirri do not differ much from those of *Chirona*, except that the rami of the forward pairs are decidedly unequal, and there are no patches of minute spinules on the segments of any of the cirri.

The relationship I formerly thought I saw with species of *Hexelasma* was in the superficial character of the absence of radii. Everything else about this barnacle shows it to be a *Balanus*.

Subgenus CHIRONA Gray.

1835. *Chirona* Gray, LYELL, Philosophical Transactions of the Royal Society of London, for 1835, pt. 1, p. 37, monotype *Balanus tulipa* Müller = *B. hameri* Ascanius.

1913. *Striato-Balanus* HOEK, Siboga-Expeditie, Monographie 31b, Cirripedia, p. 159, type *B. amaryllis* Darwin.

Large or moderate sized Balani, with thin, poreless walls and calcareous basis; orifice conspicuously toothed; radii narrow or wide, with thin, smooth, or sometimes weakly crenulated sutural edges. Scuta without crests for the depressor muscles. Tergum with the spur moderately long, not tapering. Cirri without " teeth " on the anterior borders of the segments. Mandibles with the lower teeth well developed, basal margin hairy.

Type.—B. hameri.

Chirona[1] comprises two groups of species, the most important structural differences being in the cirri. Of more significance, perhaps, is the difference in habitat, the one group being boreal in distribution, the other tropical.

Part of the characters of this subgenus are evidently correllated with the rather deep-water station of most of the species. The weakly connected compartments, the absence of transverse, interlocking septa on the thin sutural edges (except in the littoral *B. amaryllis*), and the usual absence of color tell of a long existence in quiet waters, with degeneration of the structures which give strength to the ordinary shore barnacles.

KEY TO SPECIES.

a[1]. Boreal group (*Chirona s. str.*). The substance of walls and valves is invariably white; *compartments cohere feebly to each other and to the basis;* sutural edges of the radii and the opposed surfaces smooth, without septa or denticles; basis solid. *Rami of first pair of cirri subequal, the segments not protuberant.* Cirri iv to vi have many minute erect spinules on the distal outer portion of part of the segments, and there is a dense group of short spines on the anterior edge of the segments, between the paired spines. *Maxillæ with many crowded spines, without an enlarged pair of spines on the lower part.*

---

[1] The derivation of the name *Chirona* is unknown. Gray coined many names of uncertain or undiscoverable etymology, which must be accepted as they stand. Nobody has the right to assume that *Chirona* is etymologically identical with Chiron or Chironia.

b^1. Scutum longitudinally striate; an angle near the lower end of the thin articular ridge. Radii very wide; within the base the crests of the parietal ribs are sharp or rounded, and their tapering lower ends are crenulate _____ *B. hameri.*

b^2. Scutum not striate longitudinally; its articular ridge very low and broad, not angular. Radii rather narrow; within the base the crests of the parietal ribs are flattened, and their tapering lower ends are smooth *B. evermanni*

a^2. Tropical group (*Striatobalanus*). Substance of walls either pink or white; *compartments strongly united with the basis;* sutural edges of radii feebly crenulated or smooth; basis solid or porous. *First pair of cirri with decidedly unequal rami, the segments of the shorter ramus protuberant.* Spinules, when present on the later cirri, are not numerous. *Maxillæ have an enlarged lower pair of spines.*

b^1. Spur of the tergum very short and broad, half the width of the valve; scutum strongly striate longitudinally, with a strong adductor ridge. Entirely white; basis not porose_____*B. krügeri.*

c^1. Scutum strongly striate longitudinally; walls usually more or less roseate.

d^1. Radii rather wide. Basis porose. Scutum with a distinct adductor ridge; tergum with a longitudinal furrow; median segments of cirri vi wider than long, with 2 pairs of spines_____*B. amaryllis*

d^2. Radii extremely narrow. Adductor ridge of scutum rather small, in the upper part of valve only; tergum without a furrow to the spur; median segments of cirri vi longer than broad.

e^1. Median segments of cirrus vi with three parts of spines__*B. bimæ.*

e^2. Median segments with four pairs of spines_____*B. maculatus.*

c^2. Scutum finely or delicately striate longitudinally; tergum with a spur fasciole but no furrow. Walls and valves entirely white. Deep water species.

d^1. Radii narrow; adductor ridge of scutum only feebly developed.
B. albus.

d^2. Radii rather wide; no adductor ridge_____*B. tenuis.*

B. amaryllis has the subgeneric characters less fully developed than the other forms. It is also the only really littoral species, and the most brilliantly colored one. The colored deep-water species or varieties are probably rather recent derivatives of *amaryllis.* The *hameri* group lives only well below low-water mark.

In addition to the species contained in the United States National Museum the following East Indian forms belong to this subgenus, all of them described in the report on Cirripedia of the *Siboga* expedition:

Balanus bimæ Hoek.   13 to 31 meters.

Balanus maculatus Hoek.   69 to 73 meters.

Balanus albus Hoek.   90 to 522 meters.

Plate 53.

1765. *Lepas balanus uddewallensis* LINNÆUS, Reisen durch Westgothland, Erklärung die Figuren, pl. 5, fig. 1, 1b.

1767. *Lepas hameri* ASCANIUS, Icones rerum naturalium, vol. 1, p. 8, pl. 10.[1]

1776. *Lepas tulipa* O. F. MÜLLER, Zoologiæ Danica Prodromus, p. 251, No. 3026.

1790. *Lepas foliacea* SPENGLER, Skrivter af Naturhist. Selskabet, vol. 1, p. 173.

1798. *Lepas rosata* BOLTEN, Museum Boltenianum, p. 197.

1827. *Balanus scoticus* BROWN, Illustr. Conch. Great Britain and Ireland, pl. 6, figs. 9–12.

1835. *Balanus tulipa* Müller, LYELL, Philos. Trans., p. 37, pl. 2, figs. 34–39 (Uddevalla, west coast of Sweden).

1835. *Balanus uddevallensis* auct., LYELL, Philos. Trans., p. 37.

1844. *Balanus candidus* BROWN, Ill. Rec. Conch. Gt. Brit., ed. 2, p. 121, pl. 54, figs. 9–12.

1854. *Balanus hameri* Ascanius, DARWIN, Monograph on the subclass Cirripedia, Balanidæ, p. 277, pl. 7, figs. 5a–c; Monograph of the fossil Balanidæ and Verrucidæ of Great Britain, p. 24, pl. 1, figs. 7a–d; pl. 2, figs. 1a, b.

1866. *Balanus hameri* Ascanius, LEIDY, Proc. Acad. Nat. Sci. Phila., 1866, p. 237 (Bangor, Maine, *Leda* clay).

1872. *Balanus hameri* Ascanius, DAWSON, Canadian Naturalist, vol. 6, p. 402.

1889. *Balanus hameri* Ascanius, DAWSON, Canadian Record of Science, vol 3, p. 287 (distribution in the Pleistocene of Canada).

1900. *Balanus hameri* Ascanius, WELTNER, Fauna Arctica, vol. 1, p. 303, pl. 8, figs. 14, 15. (Distribution).

1913. *Balanus hameri* Ascanius, STEPHENSEN, Medelelser om Groenland, vol. 51, p. 71 (North Stroemfjord, Greenland).

Type-locality.—Finmark.

Distribution.—Northern Europe, south to the English Channel; Nova Scotia to off the mouth of Chesapeake Bay, 16 to 167 fathoms; southward only in deep water.

The barnacle is large, cylindrical, or somewhat tapering, sometimes enlarging upward; the walls white, under a yellow cuticle which covers parietes and radii; compartments *smooth, very weakly cemented together* and to the strong calcareous basis. Orifice large, deeply toothed, radii very broad, covered with epidermis, with smooth, strongly oblique, straight summits and smooth sutural edges. Alæ broader with arched summits, the edge with a narrow longitudinal groove in some individuals, obsolete in others. Sutures not in the least septate or denticulate. Sheath smooth, its lower edge overhanging, leaving very narrow cavities. The parietes below the sheath are *longitudinally finely and sharply ribbed throughout,*

---

[1] I have been unable to consult the original edition of the first part of the *Icones* of Ascanius, and quote the reference from the reprint of 1772.

the bases of the ribs minutely and very weakly denticulate. Basis solid, denticulate at the edge, radially striate in the young (pl. 53, fig. 2).

The scutum is noticeably warped in large specimens. It has strong, somewhat unevenly spaced growth ridges and close, rather weak or deep longitudinal striæ. Inside there is a moderately prominent, *thin, articular ridge* and a narrow articular groove. The adductor

FIG. 65.—BALANUS HAMERI. *a,* MAXILLA. *b,* MANDIBLE. *c,* LABRUM.

ridge is wholly confluent with the articular rib above, running straight to the basal margin, where it defines a rather large depressor muscle pit. *It is often weak* or almost obsolete in American specimens.

The tergum has less coarse growth-ridges than the scutum, and there are a few longitudinal striæ near the carinal border. A furrow leads to the spur, its sides more or less folded in in old specimens. The spur is rounded at the end, moderately long, typically separated by its own width from the basiscutal angle, but more distant in most American specimens, in which it is sometimes separated from the basiscutal angle by nearly double its own width. Articular ridge short, sharp, and moderately high. Crests for the depressor muscle sharp and numerous.

The labrum has a very shallow notch and two teeth on each side (fig. 65c).

The mandible has four primary acute teeth, with smaller ones between the third and fourth and below the fourth (fig. 65b).

The maxilla has a notch below the upper large spines, and many crowded spines on the edge below it. The upper edge is bearded for a long distance (fig. 65a).

Cirrus i has subequal rami of 16 and 14 segments.

Cirrus ii with 17 and 19 segments, the rami subequal.

Cirrus iii with 15 and 14 segments, the anterior ramus slightly longer. The external anterior faces of the segments have many long spines, and there are some short, slender spines near the distal sutures.

Cirri iv–vi are similar, the segments wider than long, each with three pairs of large spines and one small pair. There is a dense tuft of small spines between the first and third pairs. The posterior distal angles of the segments have groups of three or four unequal spines, the longest as long as the segment. On cirrus iv the segments of the pedicel have narrow areas of minute, erect spinules on the distal anterior part (fig. 66a). Following segments have increasingly more extensive spinulose areas anteriorly and along the distal margin (fig. 66c). The inner ramus has fewer spinules. The fifth and

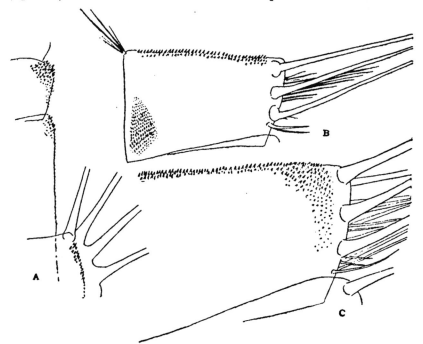

Fig. 66.—BALANUS HAMERI. a, SECOND SEGMENT OF THE PEDUNCLE AND TWO LOWER SEGMENTS OF ONE RAMUS OF CIRRUS IV; ONLY THE ANTERIOR MARGIN SHOWN. b, TWENTY-FOURTH SEGMENT OF CIRRUS VI. c, NINETEENTH SEGMENT OF CIRRUS IV, OUTER RAMUS.

sixth pairs of cirri have fewer spinules than the fourth. The fifth pair has spinules on the pedicel. The sixth pair has densely spinulose areas on the posterior proximal parts of the segments (fig. 66b, twenty-fourth segment of cirrus vi), but none on the pedicel.

The penis is as long as the posterior cirri.[1]

B. hameri is easily known from other Atlantic barnacles by its readily separable, thin, externally smooth compartments, poreless

---

[1] The above details and figures of mouth parts and cirri are from a specimen 43 mm. in basal diameter, from Georges Bank. A young one 13 mm. in diameter is very similar, but with fewer segments—10 and 9 in the rami of cirrus i—and with the spinules far less developed.

when broken across or viewed from the base; by the poreless, calcareous basis, the longitudinally striate scutum, and the narrow spur of the tergum. It is closely related to the north Pacific *B. evermanni*, but differs by the *distinct longitudinal striation* of the scutum, which invariably, in a vast number of specimens I have particularly examined, has a thin, well-raised articular ridge, culminating below in an obtuse but very distinct angle, below which it tapers downward. In *B. evermanni* the exterior of the scutum is flat, without longitudinal striation, and the articular ridge is extremely low, rounded, and not angular. The spur of the tergum is narrower in *B. evermanni*. There are also important differences in the compartments. The wall is thinner than in *B. evermanni*, its inner surface more ribbed; the basal edge has fewer septa, which are subequal, more spaced and different in shape.

The size and shape are variable. The following measurements of American specimens give the maximum and the usual size attained in our waters.

Altitude.	Greatest basal diameter.	Locality and notes.
mm.	*mm.*	
35	50	Off Cape Cod, 33½ fathoms; truncato-conic; solitary.
90	50	Woods Hole; tuliplform; growing on one another.
35	45	Woods Hole; maximum size in ordinary colonies.
63	50	New England, on *Pecten magellanicus*.
53	56	Do.
67	68	New England, on *Pecten magellanicus*; scuta 37.3 by 17.3 mm.
62	58	*Speedwell* Station 41, off Nova Scotia, 82 fathoms.
75	61	Do.
64	61	Off Chatham, Cape Cod.

Darwin mentions specimens from Scarborough 2 inches in diameter, 1¾ inches high, and 1.6 inches diameter, 3 inches high. The usual dimensions are therefore about the same in northern European and American waters. Pleistocene specimens from Uddevalla, Sweden, are said to be nearly 4 inches long, therefore about equal to the largest American individuals.

They grow upon any available object, usually on shells and upon one another. The commonest situs in our waters is on *Chrysodomus decemcostatus*, *Buccinum undatum*, *Pecten magellanicus*, *Modiolus modiolus*. More rarely I have seen them on *Terebratulina septentrionalis*, the carapax of *Hyas*, and on stones.

By far the greatest number of specimens in the museum are from between 30 and 55 fathoms. It is abundant on the fishing banks, and is frequently brought up on cod lines. Like *B. balanus*, it is wanting on the Newfoundland Bank, and none have been obtained in a greater depth than 167 fathoms. The recorded temperatures are from about 39° to 58°.

Whether the American area of the species is continuous in the north with the European is not positively known, but from what we know of the limitations of the species, such continuity at the present time does not seem likely.

In the Pleistocene this was an abundant barnacle in northern Europe and Canada, New Brunswick, and Bangor, Maine. Linnæus was the first to notice the species. He found it in the pleistocene deposits of Uddevalla, but in the text of his work (p. 198) he seems to have taken it for the Uddevalla form of *B. balanus*, and not a distinct species.

EUROPEAN.

Locality.	Collector.	Remarks.
Faroe Islands	Isaac Lea collection	
Shetland Islands	J. Gwyn Jeffreys	
Larne, Ireland	do	
Dublin Bay, Ireland	do	
Irish Channel	do	On *Chrysodomus antiquus.*
Bantry Bay, Ireland	do	
Swansea Bay, Wales	do	
Scarborough, England	do	
Mouth of Thames, England	do	
Off Margate, England	do	
Sandwich, England	do	

AMERICAN.

U.S.F.C. Station No.	Locality.	Depth (fathoms).	Bottom temperature.	Collector.
			°F.	
	La Have Bank	45		Gloucester fisheries.
41	Latitude, 42° 49′ north; longitude, 66° 19′ west.	82		*Speedwell.*
	Sable Island, Nova Scotia			Unknown.
	Off Nova Scotia	55		Gloucester fisheries.
2518	Latitude, 43° 05′ north; longitude, 64° 40′ 30″ west.	60	38.7	*Albatross.*
40	Latitude, 42° 46′ north; longitude, 66° 27′ west.	75		*Speedwell.*
2063	Latitude, 42° 23′ north; longitude, 66° 23′ west.	141	46	*Albatross.*
2522	Latitude, 42° 20′ north; longitude, 65° 07′ 30″ west.	104	46.7	Do.
2067	Latitude, 42° 15′ 25″ north; longitude, 65° 48′ 40″ west.	122	46	Do.
2060	Latitude, 42° 10′ north; longitude, 66° 46′ 15″ west.	123	55	Do.
2059	Latitude, 42° 05′ north; longitude, 66° 46′ 15″ west.	41		Do.
2057	Latitude, 42° 01′ north; longitude, 68° 00′ 30″ west.	86		Do.
	Lawlors Lake, St. Johns County, New Brunswick.			Pleistocene.
	Off Grand Manan			Fishermen.
	New England coast			Steamer *Spray.*
	Jeffreys Bank			Schooner *Paul Revere.*
	East of Georges Bank			Schooner *Alice G. Wonson.*
82B	Latitude 41° 25′ north; longitude 65° 58′ 03″ west.	60	58	*Bache.*
	Northeast edge Georges Bank	50		Schooner *Otis P. Lord.*
	Georges Bank (many lots)			Fishermen.
	Northwest part of Georges Bank			Schooner *Clytie.*
	West part of Georges Bank			Schooner *E. P. Wonson.*
2525	Latitude, 41° 49′ north; longitude, 65° 49′ 30″ west.	72	43.6	*Albatross.*
2580	Latitude, 41° 25′ 30″ north; longitude, 69° 01′ west.	83	42.4	Do.

AMERICAN—Continued.

U.S.F.C. Station No.	Locality.	Depth (fathoms).	Bottom temperature.	Collector.
			°F.	
2579	Latitude, 41°23′ north; longitude, 68° 47′ west.	83	42.2	Albatross.
2080	Latitude, 41°13′ north; longitude, 66°21′ 50″ west.	55	46	Do.
2079	Latitude, 41°13′ north; longitude, 66° 19′ 50″ west.	75	45	Do.
2081	Latitude, 41° 10′ 20″ north; longitude, 66° 30′ 20″ west.	50	46	Do.
2082	Latitude, 41° 09′ 50″ north; longitude, 66° 31′ 50″ west.	49	46.5	Do.
2256	Latitude, 40° 38′ 30″ north; longitude, 69° 29′ west.	30	52.9	Do.
2253	Latitude, 40° 34′ 30″ north; longitude, 69° 50′ 45″ west.	32	52.9	Do.
2251	Latitude, 40° 22′ 17″ north; longitude, 69° 51′ 30″ west.	43	52.9	Do.
2250	Latitude, 40° 17′ 15″ north; longitude, 69° 51′45″ west.	47	51.4	Do.
2249	Latitude, 40°11′ north; longitude, 69° 52′ west.	53	51.4	Do.
326	Off Cape Cod			F. C., 1879.
984	Off Chatham, Cape Cod	33	41.5	Fish Hawk.
964-983	Vineyard Sound to Cape Cod			Do.
269	Off Cape Cod	53	39.5	Speedwell.
1081	.....do	33½	39	F. C., 1882.
972	Off Chatham, Cape Cod	16	52	F. C.
983	.....do	36	42	Do.
981	Southwest of Chatham Light	43		Fish Hawk.
991	Latitude, 40°39′ north; longitude, 70°46′ west.	34	47.5	F. C.
	Off Marthas Vineyard			Albatross.
	Woods Hole			F. C., 1888.
519	Off Block Island	11	55	F. C.
2016	Latitude, 37°31′ north; longitude, 74°52′ 36″ west.	19	54.5	Albatross.
2264	Latitude, 37° 07′ 50″ north; longitude, 74° 20′ west.	167	46.8	Do.

BALANUS EVERMANNI Pilsbry.

Plate 54.

1907. *Balanus evermanni* PILSBRY, Bulletin of the Bureau of Fisheries, vol. 26, p. 203, fig. 4, pl. 7, figs. 7–14; pl. 8, figs. 1–4; pl. 10, fig. 1; pl. 11, fig. 1 (June 29).

1911. *Balanus evermanni* Pilsbry, KRÜGER, Zoologischer Anzeiger, vol. 38, 7A, B. (Feb. 17).

1911. *Balanus evermanni* Pilsbry, KRÜGER, Zoologischer Anzeiger, vol. 38, pp. 460, 463.

Type.—Cat. No. 41840, U.S.N.M., from *Albatross* station 4239, at the junction of Clarence Strait and Behm Canal, Alaska.

Distribution.—Southern Alaska through Bering Sea to the Kuril Islands, in 72 to 248 fathoms, bottom temperature 37°.1 to 48°.8 F.

The barnacle is tubular, tulip-shaped, enlarging upward, usually with the summits of the compartments, except the carina, curving inward at the aperture, which is large, quadrangular and very deeply toothed. White, with traces of a thin, pale primrose-yellow epidermis, which is deciduous in large part, often wholly lost, and more persistent on the radii than on the parietes. The opercular valves are white under a similar epidermis. The parietes have low, transverse, well-spaced growth-ridges or merely some irregular rugæ, and usually show fine, irregular, longitudinal striæ; next to the radii and

especially along the alæ, there is often an acute ridge, sometimes overhanging, or a strong longitudinal rib. The strong, calcareous basis
is flat or irregular, and never forms part of the wall.

The scutum is flat, with well-developed growth-ridges; faint, irregular and rather close longitudinal scratches may be seen between
the ridges. The articular ridge is very low, narrowly reflexed, its
contour gently rounded from end to end; it is confluent with the
adductor ridge, which is represented by a low callous, rounded or
angular along the depressor muscle scar.

The tergum is more delicately ridged than the scutum, and there
may be a few weak longitudinal striæ near the sides. The furrow is

Fig. 67.—Balanus evermanni, one-half natural size. *a*, near Bering Island. *b*, near
Simushir Island, No. 38662.

deep and narrow, the sides partly folded in. The spur is narrow,
separated from the basiscutal angle by twice its own width. Articular ridge moderate. There are small crests for the lateral depressor
muscles.

The compartments are strong, rather thick, but very weakly cemented together. The carina is recurved, but the other compartments
usually curve inward at the orifice. The parietes of the carinolaterals
are always very narrow—less than half as wide as those of the laterals.
The radii are wide or moderate, with very long, steeply sloping, smooth
summits; sutural edges not denticulate. The alæ are extremely
wide, summits strongly oblique; their surfaces are smooth and nude,
except for the distal triangles, which often retain the epidermis;
edge without septa or denticles. The sheath is glossy above, its
lower edge hanging close to the wall, leaving narrow cavities. Below it the parietes are almost smooth, except close to the base, where
they become very closely and acutely ribbed, the ribs flattened and

striate (somewhat T-shaped in section), but not in the least denticulate at the basal edge. There are many accessory short lamellæ on the inner edge of the outer lamina of the wall.

The basis is strong, white, poreless, with only very weak, obtuse traces of peripheral denticles.

Greatest carinorostral diameter 67 mm.; lateral diameter 66 mm.; height 150 mm. (station 4253).

Height 88 mm.; length of scutum 41 mm., breadth 18.7 mm.; length of tergum 33 mm., breadth 13 mm.

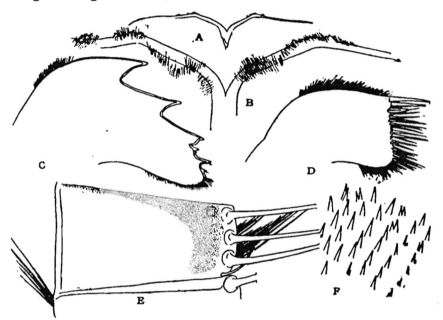

Fig. 68.—Balanus evermanni. *a*, labrum. *b*, more magnified central part of same. *c*, mandible. *d*, maxilla. *e*, intermediate segment of cirrus vi. *f*, spinules of the area indicated on fig. *e*.

The labrum (fig. 68*a*, *b*) has a wide, shallow notch, with several unequal teeth and numerous short hairs on each side.

Mandible (fig. 68*c*) has four acute teeth and a rounded lower point, which is densely hairy. There is a small tooth between the third and fourth large teeth and another above the lower point.

Maxilla (fig. 68*d*) has a nearly straight edge, very slightly notched below the upper pair of spines. It is set with many crowded spines, in pairs.

Cirrus i has equal rami of about 16 segments. Cirrus ii longer, with rami of 26 and 24 segments. Cirrus iii has rami of about 32 segments, which have a few minute, multicuspid spinules distally. Cirrus iv has segments set with spike-like spinules as figured for *B. hameri*, but covering a larger portion of the segments, closely and evenly arranged, and continuing nearly to the end of the rami. Cirrus vi has the segments much wider than long, bearing three long pairs and one short pair of spines, with an intermediate dense group of rather long bristles. There is a narrow band of minute, erect spinules along the distal suture, widening into a large patch anteriorly. These spines are very minute.

The penis is about 30 mm. long, not quite as long as the sixth cirri, and has the usual basi-dorsal point.

This is the north Pacific representative of *B. hameri* of the north Atlantic. While closely related, the two species differ in many details, and no annectant individuals have been found among the very long series of each which I have examined. The chief differences are as follows: *B. evermanni* is more solid, more roughened, and attains a far greater size than *B. hameri*. The summits of the radii are very much longer and more oblique. The parietes are not ribbed internally below the sheath, and the ribbing at the base is of a wholly different character. The basal lamellæ are not in the least denticulate, and are very much more numerous. The periphery of the basal plate is smooth, or only very indistinctly denticulate. The scutum is flatter, not longitudinally striate, and the articular ridge is lower and not angulate. The spur of the tergum is narrower, the furrow running to it deeper and narrower, and the scutal edge of the valve is much straighter. The maxilla has no notch below the upper pair of spines, and the segments of cirrus vi have no posterior lateral patches of spinules.

B. evermanni is a distinctively cold-water barnacle, the data in hand indicating a range of only about 13°, from 35.9° to 48.8°[1] F. It is probably to be regarded as a member of the Bering Sea fauna, which spreads southward on both sides, in the cold waters of the Kuril Islands and the inside passages of southern Alaska, which are colder than the ocean outside.

In habit of growth it resembles the large forms of *B. hameri*, growing solitary or in branching candelabral forms, one barnacle upon another. In Bering Sea nearly all were upon dead gastropod shells or on others of their own species. No other species of *Balanus* was found associated in the same groups, except that on one or two individuals from Bering Sea I found a few very minute, recently attached barnacles, which I suspect to be infants of *Balanus crenatus*.

In the type lot of *B. evermanni*, from the inland waters of southern Alaska, the radii are wide in the adult stage, and the spur of the scutum is about one-fifth the total length of the valve. In those

---

[1] The bottom temperature was not given for Station 4792, but as the surface temperature was 42° F., it probably falls under 40° F. Only in the inland passages of southern Alaska was the temperature above 40° F.

from Bering Sea and the Kuril Islands (Simushir) the radii of the lateral compartments are narrower, and the spur of the tergum is longer, about one-fourth the total length of the valve, which is slightly narrower (pl. 54, fig. 1; p. 211, fig. 67b).

The specimens from Bering Sea do not reach the length of those from southern Alaska. One of the largest, from station 3602 is 105 mm. in height, 61 mm. rostrocarinal diameter. Another, from station 3487, has a height of 53 mm., diameter 45 mm. These differences apparently indicate incipient racial differentiation of the northern forms (fig. 67a).

The youngest individual seen, from station 3487, has a diameter of 10 mm., height 7 mm. It is almost as wide at the aperture as at the base, *and there are no radii;* alæ very wide. This is unlike *B. hameri,* which is somewhat contracted above at this size, and has well-developed radii. In *evermanni* of 13 mm. diameter the radii appear as extremely narrow borders. In those of 20 to 25 mm. they are still very narrow. Thus, a rostrum 25 mm. long, 15 mm. wide, has radii only 1.5 mm. wide in the widest place.

U. S. N. M. Catalogue No.	Station No.	Locality.	Depth (fathoms).	Bottom temperature.	Collector.
				° F.	
41840-32404	4239	Junction Clarence Strait and Behm Canal, Alaska.	206-248	48.8	Albatross.
	4253	Stephens Passage. Alaska...................	131-183	40.9	Do.
	3487	Bering Sea, latitude, 57° 10' north; longitude, 173° 45' west.	81	37.6	Do.
	3488	Bering Sea, latitude 57° 05' north; longitude, 173° 47' west.	106	37.3	Do.
	3602	Bering Sea, latitude, 56° 32' north; longitude, 172° 40' east.	81	37.1	Do.
	3675	Record missing..................	....	....	Do.
38661	4792	Near Bering Island, latitude, 54° 36' 15'' north; longitude, 166° 57' 15'' east.	72	....	Do.
38659-38662	4804	Cape Rollin, Simushir Island, Kuril Islands, latitude, 46° 42' north; longitude, 151° 47' east.	229	35.9	Do.
38658	4803	2' west of preceding.........................	229	35.9	Do.

BALANUS KRÜGERI, new species.

Plate 52, figs. 1–1f; pl. 51, figs. 2, 2a, 2b.

Type.—Cat. No. 38700, U.S.N.M., from *Albatross* station 3707, near Ose-Zaki, in the upper part of Suruga Gulf, Japan, 63–75 fathoms; surface temperature 65° F. Seated on a branch of coral.

Distribution.—Japan, Suruga Gulf to Kagoshima, 63–103 fathoms.

A barnacle with thin solid walls, the base calcareous, without pores, and flat. Orifice rather large, deeply toothed. Exterior nearly smooth, the parietes marked with faint growth lines and weak, unevenly developed longitudinal striæ. White, under a thin, pale-yellow epidermis, covering both parietes and radii.

Rostrocarinal diameter, 13 mm.; height, 15 mm.

The scutum is flat, and externally has close, cordlike growth-ridges beautifully cut by deeply engraved longitudinal striæ. Toward the base there are very minute fringes of fine hairs. Inside there is a rather low articular ridge fully three-fourths the length of the tergal margin. Articular furrow very narrow and rather deep. The adductor ridge is high and narrow, stands close to but deeply separated from the articular ridge. Its acute continuation downward does not reach to the basal margin. Adductor and depressor muscle impressions rather deep.

The tergum is flat, thin, delicately and regularly marked with growth-striæ. The spur is very short, half the width of the plate, and truncate at the end. There is no longitudinal furrow or depres-

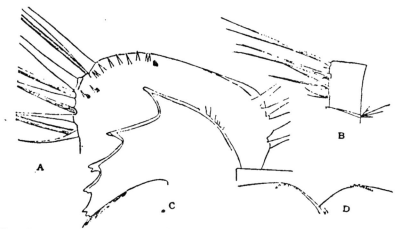

FIG. 69.—BALANUS KRÜGERI. *a*, 8TH SEGMENT OF CIRRUS III.   *b*, 12TH SEGMENT OF CIRRUS VI.   *c*, MANDIBLE.   *d*, MEDIAN PART OF THE LABRUM.

sion externally, but slight grooves define the broad spur-fasciole. Inside there is no articular ridge or furrow; the crests for the depressor muscle are few and short; and under a strong lens the middle and upper part appear minutely granose.

Compartments are only weakly cemented together, but cling firmly to the basis. The parietes of the carinolateral compartments are extremely narrow (pl. 52, figs. 1*e*, 1*f*). The radii are narrow, with very oblique, smooth, straight summits. Alæ are not very wide, their summits extremely oblique, smooth. Sutural edges smooth. The interior surfaces of the parietes have regular, rounded longitudinal ribs in the lower half, but are smooth above. The basal laminæ are continuations of the ribs, without intermediate laminæ or denticles, but they are firmly interlocked with the basis, and not to be extricated without breaking. The sheath is conspicuously and closely ridged transversely.

The mandible (fig. 69*c*) has five rather slender teeth and a short one above the lower point.

The labrum has a rather shallow but wide median notch. There is a group of five small denticles on one side, about nine on the other (fig. 69d). The first cirrus has unequal rami of 8 and 13 segments. The longer ramus is over one and one-half times the length of the shorter, and has slightly protuberant segments. Cirri ii and iii have also slightly protuberant segments; cirrus iii has groups of erect spinules near the distal anterior borders of the segments. Cirri iv to vi have four pairs of spines on each segment, the lower pair very small (fig. 69a, b).

The penis is rather short, tapers rapidly and is very densely, indistinctly annulated. The distal half bears delicate, rather sparse hairs, and there is a terminal pencil. The basi-dorsal point is blunt but well developed.

This is a small and delicate form of the group of B. hameri, closely resembling that species, B. evermanni and B. amaryllis, in the form and structure of the compartments of the wall and the basis. It differs from all of these by the well-developed adductor ridge of the scutum, which stands quite separated from the articular ridge, though close to it, and also by the very broad and short spur of the tergum, which has no longitudinal furrow and no infolding of the sides of the spur fasciole, and resembles the tergum of Armatobalanus. The rami of the first cirrus are subequal in B. hameri and B. evermanni, but strongly unequal in B. krügeri. The cirri and the external sculpture of the scutum are somewhat similar in B. amaryllis and B. krügeri. The articulating edges of the radii are smooth in B. krügeri, crenulated in B. amaryllis. By the shape of the tergum B. krügeri resembles B. cepa Darwin; but the scutum is narrower, the spur of the tergum longer, not so wide; the base is not in the least porous, the aperture is large and the color white. The numerous small teeth of the labrum are a special feature of this species.

At Albatross station 4935, off Kagoshima Gulf, southern Kiusiu, 103 fathoms, a few small specimens were brought up with B. amaryllis. The opercular valves are somewhat wider than in the type, and the adductor ridge of the scutum is more curved (pl. 51, figs. 2-2b).

B. krügeri is named for Dr. Paul Krüger, who has given us several excellent papers on cirripedes.

BALANUS TENUIS Hoek.

1883. Balanus tenuis HOEK, Challenger Report, vol. 8, Cirripedia, p. 154, pl. 13, figs. 29–33 (Challenger Station 204, lat. 12° 43′ N., long. 122° 10′ E.; 100 and 115 fathoms).

1913. Balanus tenuis HOEK, Cirripedia of the Siboga Expeditie, monographie 31b, p. 190, pl. 17, figs. 14–19; pl. 18, fig. 1 (Siboga station 105, lat. 6° 8′ N.; long. 121° 19′ E.; 275 meters).

Type.—British museum.

Distribution.—China Sea and Philippine Archipelago, in deep water.

This species was originally taken by the *Challenger* in the China Sea west of Mindoro, and again by the *Siboga* in the Sulu Sea east of northern Borneo. Its range is considerably extended by the *Albatross* collections, recorded below. It is a truly deep-water species, all of the records being between 100 and 244 fathoms. Though described from quite young and small examples, it attains a considerable size, up to 35 mm. in rostrocarinal diameter, with a height of 50 mm. In some places it is evidently abundant.

U. S. N. M. No.	Station.	Locality.	Depth (fathoms).	Bottom temperature.	Collector.
				° F.	
	D. 5325	Near Hermanos Islands, off Northern Luzón..	224	53.2	*Albatross.*
	D. 5294	China Sea, near Escarceo Light, southern Luzon	244	48.4	Do.
	D. 5265	China Sea, near Malocot Point, southern Luzon	135	....	Do.
	D. 5290	.....do..	214	....	Do.
	D. 5298	.....do..	140	....	Do.
	D. 5289	.....do..	172	....	Do.
	D. 5520	Near Point Tagolo, northern Mindanao......	102	61.3	Do.
	D. 5551	Off Jolo Island, near Jolo Light..............	193	53.3	Do.

BALANUS AMARYLLIS Darwin.

1854. *Balanus amaryllis* DARWIN, Monograph, p. 279, pl. 7, figs 6*a*–6*c*.

1902. *Balanus amaryllis dissimilis* LANCHESTER, Proc. Zool. Soc., p. 369, with var. *clarovittata* (p. 370).

1905. *Balanus amaryllis* Darwin, GRUVEL, Monographie des Cirrhipèdes, p. 250, with var. *roseus* and *niveus.*

1913. *Balanus amaryllis* Darwin, HOEK, *Siboga* Exped., Cirripedia, Monogr. 31*b*, p. 179, pl. 15, figs. 17–21; pl. 16, figs. 1–4.

Type.—British Museum.

Distribution.—Southern Japan and India to northern Australia, shore to over 100 fathoms.

This species has an unusually great range in depth. The colored form with cirri of characteristic short segments bearing two pairs of large spines in the sixth cirrus is certainly found living from low tide to over 100 fathoms (*Albatross* station 4935), probably to 150 fathoms; but the specimens from stations 5313, 5398, and from the Verde Island Passage came up dead and empty, and may have floated or drifted into deep water, especially those from the last locality, which were seated upon bark.

B. amaryllis is quite variable, as Darwin recognized. This would be expected in a common form which has a wide geographic and bathymetric range. It appears to me possible that the forms described by Dr. Hoek as *B. bimœ* and *B. maculatus* are varieties or subspecies of *B. amaryllis*, since their small differences in various details are such as one finds variable in all of the well-known species, and indeed in the specimens of *B. amaryllis* which I have dissected. *B. albus* and *B. tenuis* seem to be sufficiently distinct for specific separation. Unfortunately, the sutural edges and the basis have not been sufficiently investigated in the small species closely related to *B. amaryllis*, obtained by the *Siboga* Expedition. We know that in *B. amaryllis* the basis is porous, and the edges of the radii are crenulated; but these characters are unknown in *B. bimæ*, *B. maculatus*, and *B. albus*. *B. tenuis* has a poreless basis and smooth, thin edges of the radii, and is therefore quite distinct from *B. amaryllis*.

Albatross Station.	Locality.	Depth (fathoms).	Collector.	Notes.
D4935	Off Kagoshima Gulf, Japan.....	103	*Albatross*	
	Shanghai, China..............	....	E. Deschamps.........	
	Hongkong, China..............	....	Wm. Stimpson........	North Pacific exploring expedition.
D5311	China Sea, vicinity of Honkong..	88	*Albatross*	
D5313	China Sea, vicinity of Hongkong, off Pratas Island.	150	....	Dead; no opercular valves.
	Philippine Islands.............	....	Dr. E. A. Mearns.....	
D5345	Malampaya Sound, Palawan, near Cliff Island.	7	*Albatross*	
D5181	Off northeast Panay............	26	.....do.....	White; var. *albus?*
	Catbalogan, Samar.............	....	.....do.....	On reef.
	Off Malocot Point, Verde Island Passage.	135	.....do.....	On bark.
	Off Mantacao Island, west coast Bohol.	Shore.	.....do.....	
D5398	Off Gigantangan Island, between Leyte and Masbate.	114	.....do.....	Dead.
	Siet Lake beach, Sulu Island....	....	E. A. Mearns..........	
D5142	Vicinity of Jolo, Sulu Archipelago	21	*Albatross*	
D5143	.....do.....	19	.....do.....	
D5141	Off Sirun Island, Tawi Tawi group, Sulu Archipelago.	24	.....do.....	
D5147	Vicinity of Siasi, Sulu Archipelago.	21	.....do.....	
	Scarborough, England..........	....	Bean..................	Jeffreys coll.; from a ship.
	Dublin Bay, Ireland...........	....		With Cat. No. 1169.

AUSTROBALANUS, new subgenus.

Walls solid, poreless, their basal edges roughened with irregular points and ridges (except in *B. vestitus*); basis calcareous, sometimes extremely thin; radii narrow or wanting; the sutural septa irregular. Scutum with the adductor ridge long and strong, and usually with crests for the lateral depressor muscle.

Type.—Balanus imperator Darwin.

The species composing this subgenus are very distinct from one another. Further investigation of the cirri is needed.

KEY TO SPECIES.

a¹. Interior of walls and valves of a fine violet color, the basal edge of wall thick, with dense sculpture of fine ridges and points. Scutum with irregular crests for both rostral and lateral depressor muscles; spur of tergum rounded distally; rather large_____*B. imperator* Darwin.

a^2. Color purplish or white; scutum with crests for the lateral depressor muscle.
  b^1. Basal and internal edges of parietes roughened by irregular points and
    ridges. Tergum very narrow, with a rather long, pointed spur.
    c^1. Exterior smooth_____B. flosculus Darwin.
    c^2. Exterior with sharp longitudinal ribs_____B. f. sordidus Darwin.
  b^2. Externally covered with an orange epidermis. Lower internal surface
    of parietes subregularly ribbed. Tergum with a short spur, obliquely
    truncate distally_____B. vestitus Darwin.

BALANUS IMPERATOR Darwin.

1854. *Balanus imperator* DARWIN, Monograph, p. 288, pl. 8, figs. 4a–4c.

Type.—British Museum.

Distribution.—Eastern Australia, Sydney, New South Wales, to Moreton Bay, Queensland (Darwin).

A very distinct species by its beautiful dark violet or dusky-violet interior and the peculiar base of the wall, formed of a mass of depending points, and by the long third pair of cirri.

The United States National Museum possesses specimens without locality.

BALANUS VESTITUS Darwin.

1854. *Balanus vestitus* DARWIN, Monograph, p. 286, pl. 8, figs. 3a–3b.

Type.—British Museum.

Distribution.—New Zealand, New South Wales (Darwin).

Dry specimens are in the United States National Museum from the Bay of Islands, New Zealand.

BALANUS FLOSCULUS Darwin.

Plate 51, Figs. 1–1f.

1854. *Balanus flosculus* DARWIN, Monograph, p. 290, pl. 8, figs. 5a, 5c–5f,
    with var. *sordidus* DARWIN, Monograph, p. 290, pl. 8, fig. 5b.

Type.—British Museum.

Distribution: Peru and Chili; var. *sordidus* from Tierra del Fuego; attached to littoral shells, wood, and rock (Darwin).

The specimens in hand from Chili, on the gastropod *Concholepas*, are small, up to diameter 8.5 mm., altitude 3.5 to 4 mm. Form convexly conic, with small aperture, its margins not toothed. The walls are thick, *solid*, externally with strongly, irregularly ribbed parietes; radii very narrow. *Internal basal edges rough, with coarse, irregular points and ridges,* extending nearly up to the sheath, behind which there are small cavities (pl. 51, fig. 1b, carina). The basis is calcareous and usually so excessively thin that it is hardly noticeable.

The scutum is strongly *convex* externally, finely marked with growth ridges. Inside salmon tinted, concave, the free apex long. Articular ridge small but rather long. Adductor ridge acute and strongly curved, terminating at the middle of the basal margin. Lateral depressor muscle attached to one or two short crests below the adductor ridge in some individuals, but these crests are entirely wanting in others.

The tergum is long and narrow, with a furrow running to the spur. Internally the articular ridge is continuous with the straight ridge running to the spur. Spur rather long, bluntly pointed, separated by about half its width from the basiscutal angle.

These specimens differ from the types figured by Darwin by the weakness or absence of the crests for the depressor muscles on the scuta and by the distinctly wider terga. They are also rather small, Darwin giving six-tenths of an inch as the maximum diameter observed.

By its solid wall, with irregular, roughened basal edge and inner surface, this species is related to the Australian *B. imperator*, but both seem to be very distinct species.

Subgenus SOLIDOBALANUS Hoek.

1913. *Solido-Balanus* Hoek, *Siboga*-Expeditie, Monographie 31b, pp. 159, 192.

Small or minute barnacles with solid, rather thick wall compartments, the parietes smooth or having few low ribs, the basis calcareous, radially grooved (or perhaps sometimes porous); usually with wide, transversely grooved radii, which have septate sutural edges. Opercular valves lodged high, projecting above the lateral compartments. Scutum without longitudinal striation, the adductor ridge weak or wanting. Tergum with the spur rather narrow, rounded at the end, its sides curving into the basal margin. Mandible with the lower teeth acute, lower point spinose, a *single series of spines on the lower edge*. Maxilla having few spines; a lower pair enlarged. Outer surfaces of some segments of the third cirrus, or the third and fourth, sometimes bearing small spinules.

Type.—*B. auricoma.*

Distribution.—Indo-Pacific faunal province, chiefly in deep water.

This group is rather hard to define succinctly, for want of conspicuous differential characters. The small size, the shape of the terga, and the mandible, with spinose lower point and a series of long spines (in place of numerous hairs) on the lower border are its chief diagnostic features in the series of nonporose Balani. It has not the very wide tergal spur or conspicuously armed cirri of *Armatobalanus*.

B. maldivensis and *B. socialis* (including *B. æneas*) probably occur nearly up to low-water mark, as well as in deeper waters. The others are known from deep water only.

The following species are not contained in the United States National Museum:

B. socialis Hoek (?including *B. æneas* Lanchester).

B. maldivensis Borradaile.

B. auricoma Hoek.

B. ciliatus Hoek.

B. compressus Hoek.

Before proceeding with the descriptions of species, I may be permitted some remarks on *Balanus æneas* Lanchester,[1] of which I have been able to examine the type material, through the courtesy of Mr. C. Forster Cooper, in charge of the University Museum of Zoology, Cambridge.

The type as preserved consists of both scuta and terga of one individual (pl. 47, figs. 2, 2a, 2c, 2d) and a scutum and tergum (pl. 47, fig. 2b) of another. I have therefore not been able to add anything to Mr. Lanchester's account of the walls, basis, or internal anatomy.

The scutum has narrow, very little raised and widely spaced growth ridges, much like some forms of *B. amphitrite*. The articular ridge is prominent and somewhat reflexed. The adductor ridge is very narrow and low, and there is a smaller ridge parallel with it, nearer the articular rib; these two ridges are connected above by a semicircular ledge, bounding the flat, depressed interval between them; and in suitable light they appear to form a narrow inverted U. The pit for the lateral depressor muscle is small but distinct. The tergum has a distinct though quite shallow depression running to the spur, varying in depth in the two individuals. The carinal margin is arched, and shorter in one of the examples, and it bears numerous delicate hairs. The crests are well developed.

It will be noted from the above details, together with Mr. Lanchester's account, that this form agrees very closely with *Balanus socialis* Hoek.[2] I can find no tangible differences; and unless the cirri (which are not described in *B. æneas*) are shown to differ, I would suggest that *B. æneas* be written as a synonym of *B. socialis*.

I may further remark that *B. socialis* and *B. æneas* differ from the other forms of *Solidobalanus* by having very narrow, smooth radii, with steeply oblique summits, whereas the other species have wide, transversely grooved radii, with summits far less oblique; yet from Doctor Hoek's account of the mouth parts of *B. socialis*, it appears to belong with the other Solidobalani rather than with the *B. amaryllis* group.

---

[1] *Balanus æneas* Lanchester, Proc. Zool. Soc., London, 1902, vol. 2, p. 370, pl. 34, figs. 4, 4b. Malay Peninsula, on the shells of *Strombus* and *Natica* inhabited by the hermit crab *Pagurus hessii* Miers (Proc. Zool. Soc., London, 1902, vol. 2, p. 364). Collected by the Skeat expedition.

[2] *Balanus socialis* Hoek, *Challenger* Report, Zoology, vol. 8, Report on the Cirripedia, p. 150, pl. 13, figs. 23–28 (1883). *Siboga*-Expeditie, Cirripedia, p. 192, pl. 18, figs. 2–12 (1913). Arafura Sea, type locality; also Malay Archipelago, in 9 to more than 69 meters.

Type.—Cat. No. 43474, U.S.N.M.

Distribution.—Hawaiian Islands, 21 to 222 fathoms, on spines of the sea-urchin *Phyllacanthus thomasi* Agassiz and Clark; collected by the *Albatross* Hawaiian Expedition, 1902.

A very small, strong, and firmly attached barnacle, with a solid, calcareous basis and rather thick, solid (poreless) walls. Radii pink; parietes white, or sometimes having some pink stains.

The form is oval, conical, with strongly ribbed parietes; carinal latera have a single strong rib, the rostrum usually three, and the other compartments two ribs. The radii are rather wide and rather deeply, regularly grooved transversely, their summits strongly oblique. The alæ have straight or arched and smooth summits when unbroken, and are nearly level, so that the margin of the aperture is nearly regular. The aperture is ovate, angular at the carinal end. The sheath is very short and its lower border does not overhang. Below it the inner surface of the parietes is smooth, becoming ribbed near the base. Basal edges of the wall plates are thick and crenulated. The articulating borders of the radii are finely crenulated, as are the opposed sutural surfaces. The basis is thick.

Length of base 3.2 mm., width 2.8 mm., height 1.5 mm.

Length 5 mm., width 3.5 mm., height 2.2 mm., largest specimen.

The white opercular plates lodge close to the aperture and project above it. The scuta are sculptured with flat, regular growth-ridges, about every second or third one forming a tooth on the occludent margin. These teeth, interlocking in the closed barnacle, produce a crenellated occludent suture. There is a rather prominent, acute, somewhat reflected articular ridge, nearly the whole length of the tergal margin, and a narrow articular groove. There is no trace of an adductor ridge. The scar of the adductor muscle is small and distinct.

The terga are nearly twice as long as wide. Externally there are very weak ridges of growth except on the band leading to the spur, where the ridges are stronger and arcuate. This band is not depressed, but is separated from the rest of the surface by a slight radial depression. The spur is very short, tapering to a rounded end. Its outline passes imperceptibly into that of the basal margin. Inside there is a moderate articular ridge about one-third the length of the plate. There are about five rather strong crests for the depressor muscles.

The labrum has three short, conical teeth on each side of the deep, narrow median notch (fig. 70b).

Palpi armed with very long hairs (fig. 71c).

The outer maxillæ are oval, rather densely covered with long hairs.

Maxilla (fig. 70a) has a small notch below the upper pair of large spines, a short spine in the notch. Below it the straight margin bears five principal spines, the lower two largest. The distal fourth of the face and the lower margin have some delicate spines and the upper margin several pairs of hairs.

Mandible (fig. 70c) with four teeth above the pointed, bispinose or trispinose lower angle. Lower margin bears a close series of delicate regular spines. The distal part of the inner face is hairy, and there are five pairs of long hairs on the upper margin.

Cirri.—First pair with very unequal branches of 6 and 11 segments, the shorter branch about two-thirds as long as the longer, with strongly convex segments.

Second pair, branches slightly unequal, of 8 segments which protrude somewhat, and are densely hairy.

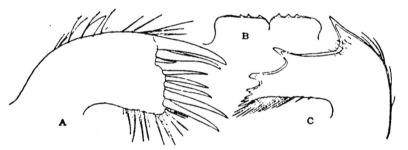

Fig. 70.—BALANUS HAWAIIENSIS. *a*, MAXILLA. *b*, UPPER EDGE OF LABRUM. *c*, MANDIBLE.

Third pair, branches somewhat unequal, of 8 and 9 segments, which protrude a little and bear fewer hairs than the second pair.

Fourth to sixth cirri much longer, of long segments, with four or five pairs of spines on each segment, the proximal one or two pairs short (fig. 71a, fifth segment of cirrus vi). Cirrus vi has rami of 19 and 20 segments. The terminal segments have the distal pair of spines very long (fig. 71b). None of the cirri have any "teeth" or spinules on the segments.

The penis is extremely long, closely annulate, and very sparcely hairy.

Specimens from six localities indicate that this small barnacle inhabits the entire Hawaiian ridge, in the warm water (60° to 69° F.) of moderate depths, down to 212 fathoms. It is usually seated lengthwise on the rough spines of the sea-urchin *Phyllacanthus thomasi*, and is very uniform in the size attained, and in other characters, throughout its range of about 1,700 miles. It is sometimes abundant. On one spine 6 cm. long from Station 4064 there are about 108 individuals.

B. hawaiensis is a species of the subgenus *Solidobalanus*, nearest, I believe, to *B. auricoma* Hoek, from Ternate. It differs from *B. auricoma* in the following characters: The wall is strongly ribbed externally. There are no hairs on the opercular plates. The articular ridge of the tergum is much shorter, and the tergum is wider toward the spur, which is shorter. The teeth of the labrum are more separated. The outer maxillæ have a regularly oval shape. The palpi have a row of long spines instead of a patch. The greatest

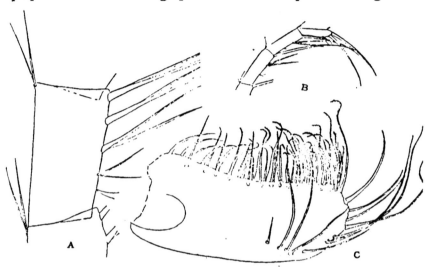

FIG. 71.—BALANUS HAWAIENSIS. *a*, 5TH SEGMENT OF CIRRUS VI. *b*, THREE TERMINAL SEGMENTS OF INNER RAMUS OF CIRRUS VI. *c*, PALPUS.

number of spines on cirrus vi is five pairs, without short hairs at their bases.

Albatross Station No.	Locality.	Depth (fathoms).	Bottom temperature.	Museum No.
			°F.	
4062	Off northeast coast of Hawaii	88–113		43474
4064	....do.	63–107	69	43475
3863	Pailolo Channel, between Maui and Molokai	127–154	60–61	43476
3838	South coast of Molokai	92–212	67	43477
3823	....do.	78–222	69	43478
4162	Off Bird Island (Modu Manu)	21– 24		43479

BALANUS TANTILLUS, new species.

Plate 48, figs. 2–2e.

Type.—Cat. No. 48202, U.S.N.M.

Distribution.—*Albatross* station D5153, near Tocauhi Point, Tawi Tawi group of the Sulu Archipelago, 49 fathoms.

The barnacle is minute, oval, tapering slightly to the broad summit, between cartridge buff and white; solid, the walls and base not porous; rostrum and lateral compartments usually parted into two or three broad, low, rounded ribs near the base, by one or two shallow furrows. Radii broad. Orifice pentagonal, with two long sides; closed by the scuta, which lodge high and project above the lateral compartments.

Scutum (pl. 48, figs. 2c, d) slightly arched from base to apex, the outer face with a longitudinal flattening or slight depression, marked with low growth-lines but no longitudinal striæ; occludent edge crenated; a tergal segment rather deeply deflected. Inside there is a moderately high articular ridge, about three-fourths the length of the tergal border, and a moderate articular furrow. There is no ad-

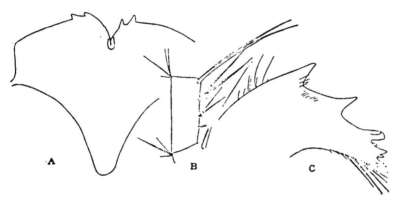

Fig. 72.—BALANUS TANTILLUS. a, LABRUM. b, 12TH SEGMENT OF CIRRUS VI. c, MANDIBLE.

ductor ridge whatever. Pit for the lateral depressor muscle is small, deep, and upon the basal margin.

The tergum (pl. 48, figs. 2, 2b) is flat externally, with very fine growth-striæ. No trace of a band or depression leading to the spur, which is rather narrow and rounded distally, and passes gradually into the basal margin. A basiscutal angle is hardly perceptible, the spur forming a continuation of the scutal margin. Inside there is a high but short articular ridge and a rather broad articular furrow. Crests for the depressor muscle are strongly developed.

Compartments.—The walls are thick and massive for so small a barnacle. Inside irregularly ribbed close to the thick base, smooth above. Sheath short, not overhanging, though the wall is somewhat hollowed below it. Radii wide, transversely grooved, with the summits oblique; edges thick and septate, as are the opposed sutural edges. Alæ wide.

Basis rather thin, calcareous, poreless.

Greatest diameter, 3.3 mm.; height, 1.6 mm. (largest example).

Greatest diameter, 2.5 mm.; height, 1 mm. (usual size; type).

The labrum has two stout teeth on each side of the median notch (fig. 72a).

The palpi closely resemble those of *B. hawaiensis*

The mandible has four rather long teeth, and a trifid lower point. There are small teeth above and below the fourth tooth. The lower margin bears a few long spines. There are a few hairs on the upper margin (fig. 72c).

Cirrus i has very unequal rami of 8 and 5 segments, the anterior ramus nearly twice as long as the posterior. The segments are slightly convex, but not protuberant.

Cirrus ii has rami of 8 and 7 segments, the anterior ramus longer by two segments. They are not protuberant.

Cirrus iii is slightly longer than ii, but otherwise similar.

Cirri iv to vi are much alike. Cirrus vi has rami of 16 segments, which bear four pairs of spines (fig. 72b).

The penis is longer than the posterior cirri, closely annulated, not hairy. I see no basidorsal point.

About 40 presumably adult individuals, besides numerous young ones, are seated upon a large sea-urchin spine. From the nearly uniform size of the larger barnacles, and the remains of dead ones, I conclude that they are adult. They are with one or two exceptions seated with the long axis conforming to that of the spine, and all but five are headed the same way.

The species has some resemblance to the much larger *B. maldivensis* Borradaile,[1] but that species, as well as all the other East Indian species of *Solidobalanus*, has a distinct basiscutal point on the tergum, while in the present form the spur is confluent with the scutal margin. The low, broad ribs of the parietes are also characteristic. There are fewer spines than usual on the lower border of the mandible.

Subgenus ARMATOBALANUS Hoek.

1913. *Armato-Balanus* HOEK, *Siboga*-Expeditie, Monographie 31b, Cirripedia, pp. 159, 162, 207.

Small, conic Balani with calcareous basis; walls solid, poreless, sharply and deeply costate within. Sutural septa present. Scutum with the articular ridge long, tapering below, adductor ridge moderate or subobsolete; no crests for the lateral depressor muscle. Tergum without distinct external furrow, the spur wide, occupying one-third to over half the basal margin, short, the end obliquely truncated.

[1] *Balanus maldivensis* Borradaile, in The Fauna and Geography of the Maldive and Laccadive Archipelagoes, vol. 1, 1903, p. 442, fig. 118. South Nilandu Atoll, Maldive group, on a twig of wood. See also Hoek *Siboga*-Expeditie, Monographie, 31b, p. 195, pl. 18, figs. 13–19.

Maxilla with a pair of larger spines near the lower angle. First cirri with unequal rami; fourth cirri having recurved teeth on the anterior margins of parts of the segments.

Type.—*Balanus quadrivittatus* Darwin.

Distribution.—Japan to the Great Barrier Reef of Australia.

By its peculiarly armed fourth cirri, this group resembles some species of *Acasta, Membranobalanus* and *Balanus;* yet this character is variable, and may merely indicate homoplastic modifications of structures present in most groups of the genus. The opercular valves, however, show great resemblance to those of *Acasta* and *Membranobalanus*, and I think indicate an actual affinity to both groups, more especially the former. The shape of the tergum will serve to separate the group from *Solidobalanus*.

Besides the species recorded below, the following, not contained in the United States National Museum, belong to the group:

Balanus terebratus Darwin. Key Islands.

Balanus quinquevittatus Hoek. Latitude 1° 42′ 30″ south; longitude 130° 47′ 30″ east.

Balanus hystrix Hoek, placed by its author in this subgenus, has the porous parietes and armed cirri of the *amphitrite* and *trigonus* groups of *Balanus*. It differs from the present group also in the form of the terga. See p. 78.

KEY TO SPECIES OF ARMATOBALANUS.

a^1. Scutum with the growth-ridges crenulated, or showing longitudinal striæ in the intervals; pit for the lateral depressor muscle well marked.

b^1. Radii broad, with level summits; basis concave or flat, poreless; scutum with the adductor ridge very indistinct or wanting. Tergum moderately curved, its spur short, depending below the basiscutal angle about one-fourth of its own width_____*B. allium.*

b^2. Similar, but with the tergum deeply concave on the scutal margin _____*B. arcuatus.*

b^3. Radii narrow; parietes strongly ribbed; tergum with the spur longer, depending below the basiscutal angle about half its own width. Scutum with a weak adductor ridge_____*B. cepa.*

a^2. Scutum with the growth-ridges smooth; no longitudinal striæ.

b^1. Exterior smoothish; basis thin, smooth, or not distinctly ribbed.

c^1. Four gray bands forming a cross, on rostrum, carina and lateral compartments; scutum without a distinct pit for the lateral depressor muscle_____*B. quadrivittatus.*

c^2. Five brownish spots, on rostrum and latera; six small apertures above the base in the sutures of the compartments. Scutum with a pit for the lateral depressor muscle_*B. quinquevittatus.*

b^2. Exterior white, strongly ribbed longitudinally, the ribs projecting at the periphery; basis with corresponding projections, concave, radially ribbed, with little pits between the ribs. Tergum with a sharp chitinous beak_____*B. terebratus.*

BALANUS ALLIUM Darwin.

1854. *Balanus allium* DARWIN, Monograph, p. 281, pl. 7, figs. 7a–7d.

Type.—British Museum.

Distribution.—Raines Island, Great Barrier Reef.

Besides the locality given above, Darwin had specimens on *Porites* of unknown origin. The Museum has specimens, locality unknown, growing on a coral with *Pyrgoma.* The size varies from basal diameter 12.5 mm., altitude about 6 mm., to basal diameter 7 mm., altitude 5 mm.

BALANUS ARCUATUS Hoek.

1913. *Balanus arcuatus* HOEK, *Siboga*-Expeditie, Cirripedia, Monographie 31*b*, p. 210, pl. 21, figs. 4–14 (Banda, 9–13 meters).

Distribution.—Banda to the Sulu Archipelago (Hoek). *Albatross* station D5156, near Tinakta Island, in the Tawi Tawi group of the Sulu Archipelago, 18 fathoms.

Three specimens grew on a calcareous plate of organic origin, nature not determined. The largest is 10 mm. in greatest diameter. They were dead when collected, but from one I obtained the opercular valves, embedded in mud. They agree with Doctor Hoek's account, particularly in the peculiarly arcuate shape of the terga; but the spur is wider. The scutum has somewhat more closely placed growth-ridges than his figure shows, and the articular ridge is longer, nearly the whole length of the tergal margin. It is certainly related very closely to *B. allium*, if indeed it can be held distinct. In the features in which the *Albatross* specimens vary from Hoek's description, they approach *B. allium*.

BALANUS CEPA Darwin.

1854. *Balanus cepa* DARWIN, Monograph, p. 283, pl. 7, figs. 8a–8c.

Type.—British Museum, from Japan.

Distribution.—Japan to the Philippine Islands on other barnacles, shells, and *Isis.*

Mogi, Japan, from the Imperial University of Tokyo; on *Balanus trigonus.* Zamboanga, Mindanao, collected by Dr. E. A. Mearns; on *Balanus tintinnabulum zebra.* Jolo, Jolo Island, on oysters and pearl oysters, *Albatross* Expedition, 1908.

Darwin says of this that the basis is " flat, obscurely permeated by pores." In the specimens from Jolo, which could be removed entire, the basis shows radial white and gray lines, as in *B. amphitrite;* but these are caused by rather strong little ridges on the inside or upper surface of the basis, which is not really permeated by pores, at least in the examples I examined. It may be that some of the radial furrows become closed over in some individuals.

BALANUS QUADRIVITTATUS Darwin.

1854. *Balanus quadrivittatus* DARWIN, Monograph, p. 284, pl. 8, fig. 1.
1913. *Balanus quadrivittatus* Darwin, HOEK, *Siboga*-Expeditie, Cirripedia, Monographie 31*b*, p. 213, pl. 21, figs. 15–20; pl. 22, figs. 1, 2.

Type.—British Museum, East Indies or Philippines.
Distribution.—Philippines and Malay Archipelago. Taken by the *Albatross* at Catbalogan, Samar, growing, associated with small *B. amaryllis*, on a living *Euchelus* found on the reef.

Subgenus MEMBRANOBALANUS Hoek.

Membrano-Balanus HOEK, The Cirripedia of the Siboga-Expedition, *Siboga*-Expeditie, Monographie 31*b*, pp. 159, 205, May, 1913.

Walls thin, impervious, the compartments weakly united; sutural edges of the radii not septate; basis membranous; rostrum boat-shaped, about twice as long as the other compartments; spur of the tergum very short and broad. First cirri with very unequal rami. Fourth cirri having teeth on part of the segments. Sixth cirri composed of long segments bearing few pairs of spines (4 in known species). Living embedded in sponges.

Type.—*Balanus declivis* Darwin.

This group, as proposed by Hoek, "corresponds to Darwin's Section E and contains the species with a membranous basis." As the only species mentioned are *B. longirostrum*, new species, and *B. declivis* Darwin, the latter being a member of Darwin's Section E, I restrict the new section to this aberrant group, selecting *B. declivis* as its type. The poreless walls and armed cirri of these forms show that they are not directly related to other species having the basis membranous, and I believe that the two series should be widely separated in a natural classification. *Membranobalanus* is related to *Armatobalanus* and to *Acasta*.

KEY TO SPECIES OF MEMBRANOBALANUS.

a¹. Small, fragile, rostrum less than 10 mm. long; radii present; tergum about as wide as scutum, the spur occupying half the basal margin; scutum with the adductor ridge very weak or wanting.

    b¹. Rostrum convex throughout, its lower half broadly rounded. Fourth cirri with the segments of outer ramus armed with erect distal teeth and with large, recurved teeth on the anterior protuberance. West Indies_____*B. declivis* Darwin

    b². Rostrum grooved by a median longitudinal furrow; its lower half narrower, tapering; scutum with two shallow longitudinal depressions externally. Fourth cirri armed with erect teeth near the distal margin of the lower 10 segments. East Indies.

                                    B. longirostrum Hoek [1]

---

[1] *Balanus longirostrum* Hoek, Cirripedia of the *Siboga*-Expeditie, Monographie 31*b*, p. 205, pl. 20, figs. 8–16, 1913. Off Dongola, Palos Bay, Celebes, 36 meters, and east of Dangar Besar, Saleh Bay, 36 meters. This species is not represented in the collection of the United States National Museum. It seems to be closely related to *B. declivis*, but is clearly a distinct species by reason of the marked difference in the armature of the fourth cirri, the protuberant segments of the shorter ramus of the first cirri, and various minor details of structure. An undetermined form similar to *B. declivis* has been reported from the Black Sea by Czerniavski. See Zoological Record, 1870, p. 205.

a^3. Much larger, rostrum about 18 mm. long; radii extremely narrow or wanting; tergum much wider than scutum, the spur occupying two-thirds of the basal margin; scutum with a well-developed adductor ridge; sheath long, two-thirds the length of the lateral compartments. West America.

B. orcutti Pilsbry

BALANUS DECLIVIS Darwin.

Plate 55, figs. 1–1d.

1854. *Balanus declivis* DARWIN, Monograph, p. 275, pl. 7, figs. 4a–4d.
1901. *Balanus declivis* Darwin var. *cuspidatus* VERRILL, Trans. Connecticut Academy, vol. 11, p. 22.

Type.—British Museum.

Distribution.—Antillean faunal province, known from the following localties: *Fish Hawk* Station 7369, off Cape Sable, Florida, 11½ feet, in a sponge. Bermuda, Louis Mowbray. It has also been reported by Darwin from the West Indies (British Museum) and Jamaica, in a sponge (Cuming collection, now in British Museum).

The barnacle is fragile, the compartments being very weakly cemented together; walls thin, not porose, basis membranous; rostrum boat-shaped, about twice as long as the other compartments. Aperture toothed. Parietes smooth except for faint growth-lines and in places some fine, oblique wrinkles or scalelike tuberculation; gray or white under a very thin cartridge-buff epidermis, which also covers the opercular valves. Greatest diameter 6 mm., length of rostrum 9 mm. in the largest specimens.

The scutum is somewhat convex externally, but with a slight longitudinal depression in some examples, with sculpture of close, fine growth-ridges, which are all continued on the occludent edge. The ridges are very finely crenulated by longitudinal striæ, sometimes very faint, and in the best-preserved specimens are minutely bristly. There is a narrowly triangular area or radius built out on the apical half of the occludent edge. The articular ridge is rather strong, two-thirds as long as the tergal edge or less, its lower end oblique. There is the mere trace of an adductor ridge, or none, and a small, rather deep depression for the lateral depressor muscle at the lower margin.

The tergum is about as wide as the scutum, somewhat beaked, ciliated along the carinal border, which is well arched. Articular ridge moderate, articular furrow wide. The spur is very short, truncate, half as wide as the basal margin or slightly more. It stands very close to the basiscutal angle.

Compartments.—The paries of the lateral compartment is wider, sometimes three times as wide, as that of the carinolateral. The radii are usually narrow but sometimes wide, not sunken or conspicuous, but whiter than the parietes by lacking epidermis; summits oblique. The alæ are rather wide with oblique summits and smooth edges.

The sheath is short, about half the length of the carina and sides, one-fourth that of the rostrum, with fine horizontal ridges bearing short fringes of golden bristles. Its lower edge is continuous with the interior of the walls. The parietes are nearly smooth within, but sometimes very weak ribs are visible. The basal edges of the compartments are smooth and beveled. The base of the rostrum is broadly rounded, the upper end tapering a little. Sides nearly in a plane.

The labrum has three teeth and is minutely hairy on each side of the deep notch (fig. 73b).

The mandible (fig. 73a) has five teeth, the lower two small, lower one united with the lower point. The maxilla (fig. 73c) has a slight notch below the upper pair of spines. There are seven spines below the upper pair, the lower two slightly larger.

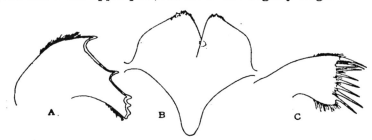

FIG. 73.—BALANUS DECLIVIS. a, MANDIBLE. b, LABRUM. c, MAXILLA.

The first cirrus has rami of 25 and 9 segments, the posterior ramus about one-third as long as the anterior. The segments do not protrude. Both rami are very slender.

The second cirrus has slightly unequal rami of 13 and 10 segments. The third is somewhat longer, with rami of 18 and 15 segments, the outer slightly longer. There are a few minute spinules near the distal borders of some segments. In the remaining cirri the first joint of the pedicel is very long. Cirrus iv has unequal rami of 18 and 24 segments, the outer ramus shorter, with protuberant segments (fig. 74a). Both segments of the pedicel have series of small, erect spinules at the distal anterior angles (fig. 74b). The lower segments of the outer ramus have a short distal series of erect teeth, and an anterior series of large recurved teeth. The latter appear on the lower 12 segments, but the teeth become fewer above (fig. 74c, d). The inner ramus has three pairs of spines on the segments. The sixth cirrus has rami of 36 segments, bearing three pairs of spines, some median segments with a very minute fourth pair (fig. 74e).

The penis is nearly as long as the sixth cirrus, with a few short hairs near the distal end. Near the proximal end there is a minute point on the dorsal side.

Specimens from Bermuda which I have seen agree with Darwin's description. The irregular, strongly marked ridges of growth on the lower part of the rostrum show that individuals 8 to 9 mm. long are old. The maximum length of rostrum given by Darwin is .3 of an inch, or about 7.5 mm.

Professor Verrill's var. *cuspidatus*, from Bermuda, is described as follows:

Our specimens differ as a variety from the typical form described by Darwin, in having the summit of the rostrum divided into four or six acute denticles;

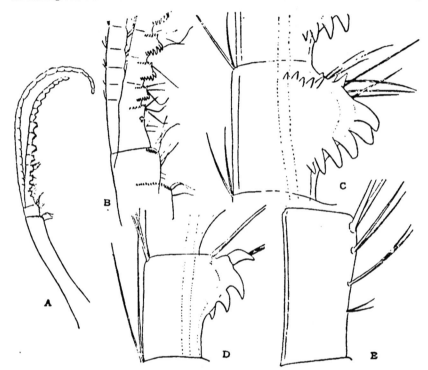

Fig. 74.—BALANUS DECLIVIS. *a*, CIRRUS IV, THE SPINES OMITTED. *b*, LOWER PART OF THE SAME. *c*, FIFTH SEGMENT, AND *d*, TENTH SEGMENT OF CIRRUS IV. *e*, 22D SEGMENT OF CIRRUS VI.

It is very convex and considerably incurved. The summit of the carina is bilobed by a narrow incision. The base is membranous and very obliquely placed, owing to the downward prolongation of the rostrum, as in the type. Long Bird Island, on the flats, embedded in a blackish massive keratose sponge (*Spongia*, sp.), which often lives half buried in the calcareous sand at low tide, and which also harbors a small *Alpheus* and several isopod crustaceans.

The denticles at the summit can only be produced by breakage or erosion, and their presence in Professor Verrill's specimens is probably accidental—an individual and not a racial character. Some specimens I have seen show faint gray and white longitudinal stripes near the summit of the rostrum, possibly indicating differences in the density of the wall, which might sometimes result in apical denticulation, though in all individuals I have seen the summits of rostrum and carina are irregularly worn.

In one specimen the rostrum and lateral compartments on one side have been injured when the barnacle was half grown. Perfect repair followed, but the rostrum was stunted, projecting very little below the bases of the other compartments. The opercular valves are normal.

B. declivis is described here in some detail because it was known to Darwin by but few examples not containing the soft parts, and except for Verrill's brief note, its characters have not been noticed by any other author. In view of the description of allied species from west America and the East Indies, it does not seem superfluous to confirm the characters assigned to *B. declivis* by the description of other specimens.

B. declivis is known from the Antillean faunal province only, since it is likely that Weltner's record from Batjan [1] pertains to the closely similar East Indian species *B. longirostrum* Hoek.

BALANUS ORCUTTI Pilsbry.

Plate 55, figs. 2–2*d*.

1907. *Balanus orcutti* PILSBRY, Proc. Acad. Nat. Sci. Phila., p. 361, pl. 29, figs. 1–7, September 28, 1907.

Type.—No. 1783 A.N.S.P. *Topotypes* in the United States National Museum.

Distribution.—San Ysidro, Lower California, embedded in sponges, collected by C. R. Orcutt.

The walls are thin, impervious, the compartments not firmly cemented together; basis membranous; rostrum boat-shaped, twice as long as the rest of the wall, strongly arcuate and convex; the other compartments nearly straight. Aperture small, oblong, toothed. Parietes marked with growth-lines, and minutely, densely wrinkled, the rugæ transverse or oblique, in some places interrupted, forming a pattern of long granules.

Greatest diameter 11 mm., lateral diameter 9.2 mm., length of rostrum 18 mm.

The scutum is decidedly less than half as wide as long. It is sculptured with close, irregular, deeply cut ridges of growth. Articular ridge high and angular, about half as long as the tergal margin, its lower end oblique. Articular furrow is very narrow. The adductor ridge stands free of the much higher articular ridge. It is strong and straight, running to the basal margin, close to and slightly overhanging the pit for the lateral depressor muscle, which is oblong and deep. Adductor scar well marked.

---

[1] Verzeichnis, p. 270.

The tergum is triangular, *much wider than the scutum*. It is flat externally and sculptured like the scutum. Articular ridge is very short and acute; articular furrow wide. The spur is extremely short, two-thirds as wide as the basal margin, extremely close to and curving into the basiscutal angle. The whole inner face is roughened with lengthened tubercles. There are no crests for the depressor muscle.

Compartments.—The carinolateral compartment is about half as wide as the lateral. *There are no radii*, merely a slight thickening along the radial edges. The alæ are wide, with thin, oblique summits. The sheath is about two-thirds the length of the carina and lateral compartments, over one-third the length of the rostrum. It bears many fine horizontal ridges closely set with short, golden bristles. The parietes are not hollowed out below the sheath and are distinctly ridged longitudinally. The basal edges of the compartments are blunt and nearly smooth. The lower part of the rostrum tapers to a rounded extremity (appearing more obtuse in the foreshortened figure 2b).

None of the dry specimens examined contained the body and limbs.

This species is known by numerous specimens, more or less perfect, collected by Mr. Orcutt in 1889. It is twice the size of the largest specimens of *B. declivis* Darwin and differs from that West Indian species in the following respects: The radii are practically absent. The sheath is much longer. The interior is much more strongly ribbed. The scutum is constantly much narrower relative to its length. Its articular ridge is shorter, and there is a *well-developed adductor ridge*. The tergum is much wider, with a wider, shorter spur, and roughened interior.

The external sculpture of the parietes is essentially similar in the two species, but the minute wrinkling is more fully developed in *B. orcutti*. The type-specimen is figured.

Fragments of a small, delicate species of *Membranobalanus* were found in a sponge from Cape St. Lucas, Lower California. The rostrum is much narrower than that of *B. orcutti;* Cat. No. 32933 U.S.N.M.

Subgenus CONOPEA Say.

1822. *Conopea* SAY, Journal of the Academy of Natural Sciences of Philadelphia, vol. 2, p. 323.

1825. *Conoplea* GRAY, Annals of Philosophy, new ser., vol. 10, pp. 98, 108.

1839. *Balaninus* O. G. COSTA, Corrispondenza Zoologica, vol. 1, p. 181; Fauna del Regno di Napoli, Molluchi, Cirropedi, p. 19, monotype *B. galeatus*.

1854. *Balanus, Section B*, DARWIN, Monograph, p. 216.

1913. *Patella-Balanus* HOEK, *Siboga*-Expeditie, Monographie 31b, Cirripedia sessilia, pp. 160, 162, 221 (Type *Balanus calceolus* Ellis, Darwin).

"Parietes and basis sometimes permeated by pores, sometimes not; radii not permeated by pores. *Shell elongated in its rostrocarinal axis; basis boat-shaped* [or compressed conic]. Attached to Gorgoniæ and Milleporæ." (Darwin). Radii well developed.

Type.—C. elongata Say=*Balanus galeatus* (Linnaeus) Darwin.

Distribution.—Tropical and warm temperate seas in both hemispheres, from above low tide to over 200 fathoms.

This group was thought by Darwin to have affinities with the subgenus now called *Megabalanus*, and with *Acasta*. Hoek places it at the end of *Balanus*, after the groups with poreless compartments. The characters of the cirri favor this view. The segments of the first and second cirri are not protuberant, and in some species the fourth cirrus bears some short spinules, reminiscent of those of *Acasta*.

I have been unable to decide whether the species of *Conopea* with poreless compartments are secondarily so by reason of the filling up of pores solidly, or whether, like *Acasta*, parietal pores have never been evolved. It is possible, though it does not appear probable, that the group is diphyletic, composed of one series of species related to the poreless *Balani* and *Acasta*, and another related to the porous *Balani*. I have been able to study only *B. galeatus*, *B. calceolus*, and *B. scandens*.

B. cornutus is remarkable for the abortion of the carinolateral compartments. It is the only *Balanus* having but four compartments.

Lepas cassis Spengler[1] is a *Balanus* growing on a gorgonian as the Conopeas grow. It can probably be recognized if found again.

Conopea contains nine species, enumerated below. They are not well-known barnacles, as excepting *B. galeatus*, the species are known by but few specimens in museums. The Malay Archipelago is the center of speciation. Only two species are known to occur in the Atlantic. Those represented in the United States National Museum are starred in the following list.

B. stultus Darwin, 1854. Singapore.

* *B. calceolus* Darwin, 1854. West coast of Africa; Tuticorin; Malay Archipelago; Coralline Crag of Britain.

B. investitus Hoek, 1913. Flores Sea.

* *B. galeatus* Linnæus. West Indies; Southern California.

B. navicula Darwin, 1854. Tuticorin; Malay Archipelago.

B. cornutus Hoek, 1913. Malay Archipelago.

B. cymbiformis Darwin, 1854. Tuticorin, near Madras.

B. proripiens Hoek, 1913. Malay Archipelago.

* *B. scandens* Pilsbry. Japan.

---

[1] Skrivter af Naturhistorie Selskabet, vol. 1, 1790, p. 184, pl. 6, fig. 3a, b.

a^1. Parietes porous.

    b^1. Tergum with an external furrow, closed except on the spur, which is nearly its own width from the basiscutal angle. Scutum with strong growth-ridges and sinuous base, prominent in the middle; adductor ridge moderately developed_____*B. stultus.*

    b^2. Tergum sometimes with a depression but no furrow; spur near the basiscutal angle.

        c^1. Scutum with the basal margin prominent in the middle, and having a moderate adductor ridge_____*B. investitus.*

        c^2. No adductor ridge in the scutum; spur of tergum ¼ to ⅓ width of valve, usually having small teeth or points at the end_____*B. calceolus.*

a^2. Parietes not porous.

    b^1. Carinolateral compartments wanting; laterals bearing hornlike processes_____*B. cornutus.*

    b^2. Carinolateral compartments present, as usual.

        c^1. Rostrum produced, its end reaching the supporting stem.

            d^1. Apex of tergum square, by projection of the articular ridge.

                B. galeatus.

            d^2. Apex of tergum acute; carinal margin forming an acute angle with the scutal margin; scutum longitudinally striate; carinolateral compartments very narrow_____*B. navicula.*

            d^3. Carinal margin of tergum at a right angle with the scutal margin.

                B. cymbiformis.

                B. proripiens.

        c^2. Rostrum scarcely produced, not extending to the supporting twig, which is clasped by the base only_____*B. scandens.*

BALANUS GALEATUS (Linnæus).

Plate 56, figs. 1–1d.

1771. *Lepas galeata* LINNÆUS, Mantissa Plantarum altera, p. 544.

1822. *C.[onopea] elongata* SAY, Journal of the Academy of Natural Sciences of Philadelphia, vol. 2, p. 324 (inlets of Charleston Bay). Not *Lepas elongata* Gmelin=*Balanus crenatus.*

1854. *Balanus galeatus* Linnæus, DARWIN, Monograph, p. 220, pl. 3, figs. 4a–c.

1907. *Balanus (Conopea) galeatus* Linnæus, PILSBRY, Bull. Bureau of Fisheries, vol. 26, pl. 7, figs. 5, 6; pl. 9, figs. 8–11.

Type.—Lost; from the West Indies.[1]

Distribution.—South Carolina to the West Indies and Central America; southern California.

The barnacle is more or less lengthened in the rostrocarinal axis, the rostrum being produced in a point which at its tip clasps the supporting gorgonian; the carina either short, or similarly prolonged in a point, which is usually free, but sometimes clasps a

---

[1] Linnæus gave no locality, but according to Spengler *Lepas galeata* was on a West Indian gorgonian. See Skrifter af Naturhistorie Selskabet, vol. 1, 1790, p. 184.

branch. There is an angle where the compartments join the basis. Surface smooth, pinkish, or with the parietes faintly striped with pink when cleaned. The radii are rather broad, very little sunken.* Parietes not porous. The basis is boat-shaped or in form of a compressed cone. It clasps the gorgonian from the lowest point of the cone to its rostral end. It is permeated by small, rounded pores in some examples, but solid except very close to the edge in others. The barnacle is usually covered with the outer layer of the gorgonian, but in most museum specimens this has been removed, leaving the slender axis of the gorgonian and the barnacle nude, except for the rather strong epidermis of the latter.

Rostrocarinal length 20 mm., height 9½ mm.

Rostrocarinal length 10 mm., height 8 mm.

Rostrocarinal length 24 mm., height 8 mm.

The scutum is somewhat concave externally, the apex obtuse or truncate; sculpture of rather prominent growth-ridges. Articular ridge prominent, terminating in a short, rounded point. No adductor ridge.

The tergum has a peculiar square apex, due to the prominence of the upper end of the articular rib. This is the distinctive mark of *B. galeatus*. The spur is short, truncate, and about half the width of the valve. Crests for the depressor muscles are scarcely indicated.

The first cirrus has rami of 12 and 7 segments, the anterior ramus nearly twice as long as the posterior. Second cirrus with 9 and 8 segments, the anterior ramus two segments longer. Neither of these cirri have protuberant segments. Third cirrus similarly proportioned, having 10 and 9 segments. The fourth to sixth cirri are alike. The segments bear three pairs of spines and unusually long tufts at the posterior sutures, the largest spines usually much longer than the segments and nearly as long as the anterior pairs. I see no spinules or "teeth" on any of the cirri.

This is the only *Conopea* known to be American. It was a great surprise to receive it from California, where a couple of dead specimens were taken by the *Albatross* in deep water. These are shown in figure 75.

It appears that *B. galeatus* is an old species, which has existed since the Panamic connection between the two oceans.

Locality.	Donor or collector.	Notes.
South Carolina	I. Lea collection	From Ravenel.
Do.		
Nassau, N. P., Bahamas	I. Greegor	
Brockway Point, Santa Rosa Island, Cal., Station 4432	Albatross	272 fathoms.

Specimens in collection of the Academy of Natural Sciences of Philadelphia are from inlets of Charleston Bay (T. Say, type of *C.*

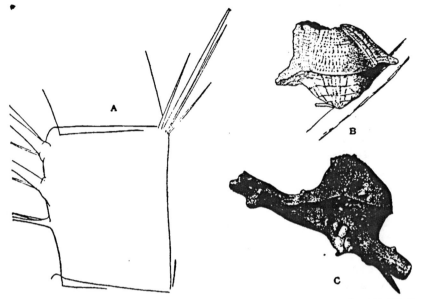

FIG. 75.—BALANUS GALEATUS. *a*, SEVENTEENTH SEGMENT OF CIRRUS VI. *b, c*, WALLS OF TWO INDIVIDUALS ; ALL FROM ALBATROSS STATION 4432, SANTA ROSA ISLAND, CAL.

elongata) ; Edisto Island, South Carolina (Edw. Hopkinson) ; southwest coast of Florida (Joseph Willcox).

BALANUS CALCEOLUS Darwin.

1854. *Balanus calceolus* DARWIN, Monograph, p. 218, pl. 3, figs. 3*a–e*.

Distribution.—West coast of Africa; Tuticorin, near Madras; Coralline Crag, England (Darwin).

Specimens from *Albatross* station 5145, latitude 6° 04′ 30″ north; longitude 120° 59′ 30″ east, vicinity of Jolo, Sulu Archipelago, in 23 fathoms, agree in the main with Darwin's description, and I have no doubt belong to the same species. I could find no pores in the basis, but in *B. galeatus* I have found this character variable.

Conoplea ovata Gray,[1] which Darwin places as a synonym of *B. calceolus* with a mark of doubt, was defined only by the words "The base ovate, Africa," and nothing further is known of it. Ellis, who is quoted as authority for *B. calceolus*, was polynomial in his nomenclature, and although he published in 1758 his work gives no evidence that he understood the Linnæan system of nomenclature. The species attributed to him should be ascribed to Darwin, who first used the names in binomial combinations.

---

[1] Annals of Philosophy, new ser., vol. 10, 1825, p. 103.

Lepas calceolus was merely mentioned by Pallas as adhering to *Gorgonia verrucosa*, and covered by its bark. Since there is no description whatever, and no reference to a figure, or to Ellis, the name is absolutely nude, and does not prejudice Darwin's subsequent use. It may or may not be Darwin's species.[1]

BALANUS SCANDENS, new species.

Plate 56, figs. 2–2d.

Type.—Cat. No. 48048 U.S.N.M., from *Albatross* station 3716, off Ose-Zaki, Honshu Island, Japan, in 65 to 125 fathoms.

The barnacle has rather thin, impervious compartments and basis and is oval in peripheral contour, the outlines rounded below, obliquely conic above the periphery, which is angular at the sides and rostral end, rounded at the carinal end. The surface is smooth. The carina is steep, almost vertical, rostrum sloping, but not produced in a point, and not clasping or approaching the supporting stem, which is clasped only by the bottom of the basal cup. When cleaned, the compartments are lilac tinted with whitish vertical lines, fading to white below, the radii rather narrow and white, basis whitish. The carinolateral compartments have narrow, bandlike parietes, nearly as wide at apex as at the base. Inside, the parietes are ribbed below the sheath; basis also ribbed very close to the periphery, elsewhere smooth. The sheath is very long, about three-fourths the length of the compartments, and of a dull lilac tint.

The scutum has distinct but not prominent growth-ridges; alternate ridges appearing on the inflected occludent margin as prominent, oblique teeth. The articular ridge is rather low, somewhat reflexed, about two-thirds the length of the tergal border and truncate at the end. Articular furrow rather deep but narrow. There is no adductor ridge. Pit for the lateral depressor muscle small and very close to the edge.

The tergum is broad, flat, with fine, sinuous growth-ridges externally, the carinal margin much shorter than the scutal, and making with it an angle decidedly less than a right angle. Articular ridge low and close to the scutal margin. Spur short, very close to the scutal border, more than half the width of the valve, its end obliquely truncate.

The labrum has three teeth on each side of the median notch (fig. 76a).

The palpi have an irregular row of long spines on the face and a double or triple series of short ones along the upper margin (fig. 76c).

The mandibles have five teeth, the lower one more or less united with the lower point (fig. 76b).

---

[1] See P. S. Pallas, Elenchus Zoophytorum, 1766, p. 198.

The maxilla has an even edge, armed with eight large spines, below the last a group of short spines. There are unusually long bristles behind the spines (fig. 76d).

The first cirrus has strongly unequal rami, the shorter ramus of seven segments (longer ramus broken).

The second cirrus has rami of 10 and 7 segments, the anterior ramus longer by about 4 segments.

The third cirrus has 12 and 9 segments, unequal as in the second.

Fourth to sixth cirri are similar. The sixth has segments with four pairs of spines, lower pair quite small. None of the cirri have any "teeth" or spinules.

The penis is decidedly longer than the last cirri, closely annulated, with a very few short hairs near the end. There is no basi-dorsal point.

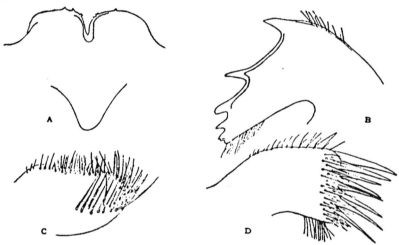

Fig. 76.—Balanus scandens. a, labrum, b, mandible. c, palpus. d, maxilla.

This species stands near B. cymbiformis Darwin and B. proripiens Hoek. In both of these species the carinal margin of the tergum makes a right angle with the scutal margin. In B. scandens the angle is acute and the valve is narrower. In B. proripiens and presumably in B. cymbiformis the rostrum is elongated and touches the supporting stem, as usual in Conopea, whereas in B. scandens the rostrum is not especially lengthened and is lifted high above the support. B. proripiens has "teeth" on the third and fourth cirri, but there are none in B. scandens. The cirri of B. cymbiformis are unknown. These characters seem sufficient ground to forbid a reference of the Japanese species to any of the described forms.

B. cymbiformis and B. proripiens seem to be very closely related to one another. The latter has a somewhat less broad tergum and the articular ridge of the scutum is better developed. B. proripiens and *B. scandens* are known from single specimens, *B. cymbiformis* by three.

Genus ACASTA Leach.

1817. *Acasta* LEACH, Journal de Physique, vol 85, p. 69.
1854. *Acasta* Leach, DARWIN, Monograph, p. 302.

Compartments six, thin, not porous, weakly attached together and to the basis; all except the carina provided with radii. Base not porous, calcareous, flat, or cup-shaped; form globose or acorn-shaped, the basal contour rounded or oval, not produced in the carinorostral axis; opercular valves and mouth parts as in *Balanus;* fourth cirri armed with stout, short, erect spinules or recurved teeth. Living embedded in sponges or cœlenterates.

Type.—Acasta spongites.[1]

Acasta is to be regarded as a group derived from *Armatobalanus*, from which it differs by adaptations consequent upon life in sponges. These adaptive features are of quite secondary value, as Darwin recognized; but they are nevertheless conspicuous, and have secured for it recognition as a genus. So long as we recognize that *Acasta* is of no greater taxonomic rank than the subgenera of *Balanus*, I agree with such good authorities as Darwin, Gruvel, and Hoek that it is an advantage to retain it as a genus; the more because *Balanus* will sooner or later be dismembered to form several genera.

The armature of teeth on the fourth cirri was first observed by Darwin, and supposed to be peculiar to *Acasta;* but it is now known that many *Balani* are similar in structure. *Membranobalanus* has entirely homologous structures, and those of *Armatobalanus* and the *Balanus trigonus* group are similar, though in some forms it is the third cirrus which is chiefly modified. It would not be amiss to speak of *Membranobalanus* as an *Acasta* with membranous basis, just as *Semibalanus* is a *Balanus* with membranous basis.

Darwin described nine species, of which one is known only as a fossil of the British Crag. Twelve species and one subspecies have been described since his monograph appeared.[2] The following 21 species are now known, those represented in the United States National Museum marked with an asterisk:

A. spongites (Poli), 1795. Europe; Mediterranean; South Africa.

A. sulcata Lamarck, 1818. Australia.

A. cyathus Darwin, 1854. Madeira; West Indies.

A. undulata Darwin, 1854. Coralline Crag, Sutton.

---

[1] Leach gave an unmistakable diagnosis of *Acasta*, but mentioned no type. Subsequently he described *A. montagui* (=*A. spongites*).

[2] *Amalthea corl* Sowerby, Proc. Malac. Soc. London, vol. 8, p. 17, pl. 1, figs. 9–11, seems to be the basis of an *Acasta*. See Hedley, Proc. Linn. Soc. N. S. Wales, vol. 33, 1908, p. 468.

A. *fischeri* Locard Miocene, Corsica.

A. *muricata* Seguenza Pliocene, Sicily.

A. *sarda* De Alessandri, 1895. Oligocene, Sardinia.

A. *formæ* De Alessandri, 1897. Miocene, Italy.

A. *schäfferi* De Alessandri, 1910. Miocene, Austria.

A. *glans* Lamarck, 1818. Australia.

A. *lævigata* Gray, 1825. Red Sea; Philippines.

A. *fenestrata* Darwin, 1854. Philippines.

A. *purpurata* Darwin, 1854. East Indies.

A. *sporillus* Darwin, 1854. Sulu Islands.

A. *scuticosta* Weltner, 1887. Carthagena, Spain.

A. *striata* Gruvel, 1901. Atlantic, 400 meters.

A. *funiculorum* Annandale, 1906. Gulf of Manaar, Ceylon.

*A. *japonica* Pilsbry, 1911. Japan.

*A. *dofleini* Krüger, 1911. (Japan ?); Philippines.

*A. *pectinipes* Pilsbry, 1912. Philippines (+ A. *nitida* Hoek, 1913. Java Sea).

*A. *idiopoma* Pilsbry, 1912. Philippines.

A. *conica* Hoek, 1913. Macassar.

Besides the species starred in the above list, I have been able to study specimens of A. *glans*, A. *sulcata* and A. *lævigata*, in the collection of the Academy of Natural Sciences.

The distribution of the genus will probably be much extended when the sponges of some extensive coasts are examined for barnacles—such as east and west Africa and west America. Most of the species now known inhabit the shores and archipelagos between Japan and South Australia, with the most intense speciation about the middle of this region.

ACASTA SPONGITES (Poli).

1795. *Lepas spongites* POLI, Testacea utriusque Siciliæ, p. 25, pl. 6, figs. 3–6.
1854. *Acasta spongites* Poli, DARWIN, Monograph, p. 308, pl. 9, figs. 1a–1d.
    (See for synonymy.)

Distribution.—British Islands to the Mediterranean; Cape of Good Hope (Darwin).

The tergum of a specimen from Exmouth is figured (fig. 77).

U. S. N. M. Cat. No.	Locality.	Collector or donor.
....	West Ross, Lough Shelldaig, Scotland..........................	J. G. Jeffreys, 1843.
12086	Exmouth, south coast of Devon..................................	J. G. Jeffreys, 1831.
12074	Cornwall..	Do.
....	Weymouth..	Do.
12101 12107 12135	No locality, probably English.................................	Do.
....	Sicily...	I. Lea collection.

ACASTA JAPONICA Pilsbry.

1911. *Acasta spongites japonica* PILSBRY, Bull. Bur. of Fisheries, vol. 29 (Document No. 739), p. 80, pl. 16, figs. 1–9.

Type.—Cat. No. 38681, U.S.N.M., from *Albatross* station 4936, off Kagoshima Gulf, Japan, in 103 fathoms, embedded in a sponge.

In the absence of specimens of *A. spongites* for direct comparison, I described this as a subspecies of that European form. Having now studied a long series of the latter, I have reconsidered the matter and believe that the Japanese form is specifically distinct. It is larger than *A. spongites;* the shape of the tergum is quite different and it

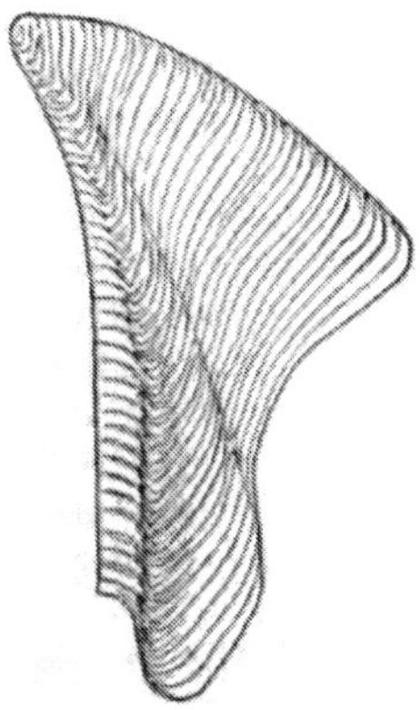

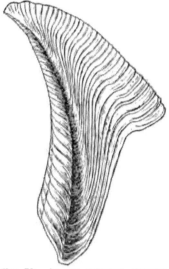

FIG. 77.—ACASTA SPONGITES, EXMOUTH, TERGUM.

FIG. 78.—ACASTA JAPONICA, TERGUM OF TYPE.

has an external depression or furrow to the spur. In *A. spongites* there is no furrow, but the flat spur-fasciole is bounded by lines. As there seems to be no figure of the exterior of the tergum of *A. spongites* I am illustrating it here for comparison with that of *A. japonica*, both figures being drawn to the same scale. The sculpture of the scutum is stronger in *A. spongites*, the longitudinal grooves more emphatic. In *A. japonica* the longitudinal sculpture is of narrow raised threads. Finally, the proportions of the valves are different. In *A. spongites* the length of the tergum is but slightly more than three-fourths that of the scutum. In *A. japonica* it is seven-eighths. The breadth of the tergum is less than that of the scutum in *A. spongites*, but in the Japanese species both valves have the same maximum breadth (fig. 78).

ACASTA CYATHUS Darwin.

Plate 57, figs. 1–3.

1854. *Acasta cyathus* DARWIN, Monograph, p. 312, pl. 9, figs. 3a–3c.
1906. *Acasta cyathus* Darwin, ANNANDALE, Supplementary Report No. 31,
on the Cirripedia, in Herdman's Rep. Pearl Oyster Fisheries of the
Gulf of Manaar, p. 144.

Distribution.—Madeira; West Indies, west coast of Florida, and near Colon.

Darwin's description of this species is as follows:

Carinolateral parietes about one-fourth of width of lateral parietes; radii
wider than the parietes; basis nearly flat, small; tergum with the spur truncated, half as wide as valve.

General appearance.—Color pale pink, or that of flesh; basis remarkably flat
and rather small, with the walls above bulging out a little. The radii are very
wide, being wider than the parietes to which they belong; the orifice is generally rather large. The parietes of the carinolateral compartments vary from
one-third to one-fourth of the width of the parietes of the lateral compartments. Basal diameter of largest specimen .35 of an inch. Internally, the
parietes are generally more strongly ribbed than *A. spongites.*

The opercular valves are large, owing to the form of the shell. The scuta
present no particular character, and are not distinguishable from those of *A.
sulcata*, but the adductor ridge is perhaps rather more developed. The terga
[pl. 57, figs. 1b, 2a] are nearly as large as the scuta, and this is an unusual circumstance; the spur is more than half as wide as the valve; it is placed not
quite close to the basiscutal angle; on the carinal side the basal margin of the
valve slopes a little toward the spur. I may mention that in several specimens
from Madeira the scuta and terga, on one side, had grown to a monstrous
thickness.

Cirri: These resemble in every respect those of *A. spongites*, with the remarkable exception that on the anterior ramus of the fourth cirrus several segments
were furnished with the beautiful downward curved mandiblelike teeth, as in
A. sulcata; but differently from in that species, there were none on the upper
segment of the pedicel. I should have thought this an excellent specific character had not these teeth been so extremely variable in *A. sulcata.*

Two American specimens which I dissected show considerable variation in the armature of the cirri; one from near Colon (pl. 57, figs. 1
to 1b; text figs. 79, 80a to 80d), the other (pl. 57, fig. 3; text figs. 80e
to 80h), from near the Dry Tortugas, Florida.

The labrum has two teeth on one side of the median notch, none on
the other (fig. 79a).

The mandible has four teeth and a truncated or denticulate lower
point (fig. 79b).

Maxilla has a straight edge, armed with 10 spines below the upper
great pair, three near the lower angle are larger than the others.
There is a tuft of small, short spines below the lower large one
(fig. 79c).

The first cirri have slender rami of 17 and 9 segments, the anterior
ramus nearly double the length of the posterior.

The second cirri have 10 and 7 segments, anterior ramus longer by about three segments. The segments do not protrude.

Third cirri similar to the second, with slightly unequal rami of 11 and 10 segments.

The fourth cirri are longer (fig. 80d). The pedicel is rather long. The anterior ramus has recurved teeth on the anterior margins of the first to tenth segments, varying in number and size as shown in the figures. There are also several smaller, erect spinules near the anterior distal part of each toothed segment. These segments bear two or three spines, which arise behind the teeth or toward the inner face of the cirrus, except the upper one, which stands on the front margin.

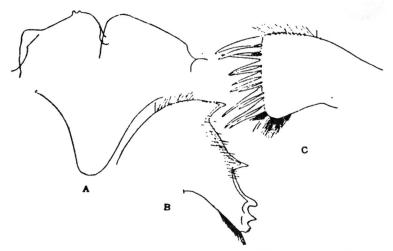

Fig. 79.—ACASTA CYATHUS FROM ALBATROSS STATION 2146. *a*, LABRUM. *b*, MAXILLA. *c*, MANDIBLE.

Beyond the tenth segment the anterior ramus is similar to the posterior, which has no teeth, the segments bearing three to four pairs of spines.

The individual from near the Dry Tortugas (figs. 80e to h) differs from the preceding by having the segments of the fourth to sixth cirri longer, about twice as long as wide.

The teeth are not so large, and there are three instead of two on part of the segments. There is also some difference in the number of erect spinules, as shown in the figures, although the general arrangement is not very different. The sixteenth and last toothed segment of the anterior ramus is drawn in figure 80e.

The largest individuals seen are from St. Thomas, collected by Robert Swift, in the museum of the Academy of National Sciences. Greatest diameter 12 mm., height 11.8 mm. The color is pale pink. The hollow spines are often forked at the end.

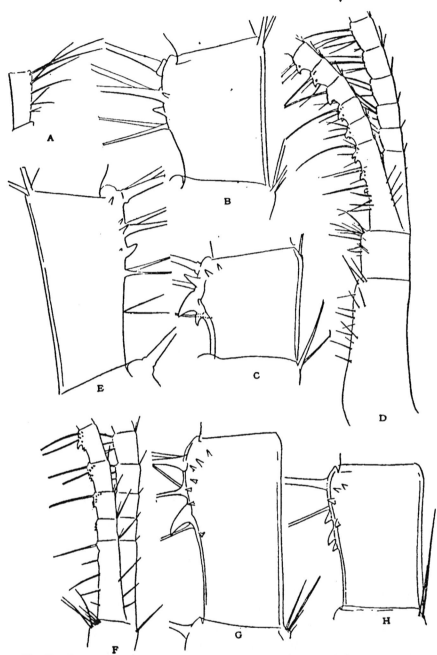

FIG. 80.—ACASTA CYATHUS. *a*, INTERMEDIATE SEGMENT OF CIRRUS VI. *b*, TENTH SEGMENT
OF CIRRUS IV, ANTERIOR RAMUS. *c*, FIFTH SEGMENT OF SAME. *d*, LOWER PART OF CIRRUS
IV; ALL FROM ALBATROSS STATION 2146. *e*, SIXTEENTH SEGMENT OF CIRRUS IV, ANTERIOR
RAMUS. *f*, LOWER PART OF CIRRUS IV. *g*, SEVENTH AND *h* FIFTH SEGMENTS OF CIRRUS IV,
ANTERIOR RAMUS; ALL FROM ALBATROSS STATION 2414.

A specimen (pl. 57, fig. 3) from *Albatross* station 2414 is 8.7 mm. in diameter, 9 mm. high, and another from the same station is 7 mm. in diameter, 9 mm. high. Both of them have profusely spinose parietes, and are pale cream, with a pinkish suffusion on parts of the carina and carinolaterals.

Cat. No. 7842, from near Colon, is very short, diameter 9.5 mm., altitude 8 mm., and the wall is abruptly contracted near the base (pl. 57, figs. 1–1b).

Locality.	Collector or donor.
Station 2414, near the Dry Tortugas, Fla. (26 fathoms).	*Albatross.*
Station 2146, latitude 9° 32′ north, longitude 79° 54′ 30″ west, near Colon, C. Z. (34 fathoms).	Do.
St. Croix	Dr. Griffith, in I. Lea collection.
No locality	(Unlabeled specimens.)

Doctor Annandale has reported *A. cyathus* from the Gulf of Manaar, the shell longer and less spheroidal than the one figured by Darwin, and white instead of pink. He does not mention whether his specimen has the characteristic teeth on the fourth cirri.

ACASTA DOFLEINI Krüger.

1911. *Acasta dofleini* KRÜGER, Beiträge zur Cirripedienfauna Ostasiens, in Abh. K. Bayer, Akad. Wissensch, Suppl.-Bd. 2, 6 Abhandl., p. 56, pl. 4, fig. 39a–d.

Doctor Krüger does not give the locality of his type, but it was apparently collected by Doctor Doflein, whose chief collecting was in Sagami Bay, Japan. The *Albatross* obtained numerous examples from sponges at station D5147, in the Sulu Archipelago, near Saisi, in 21 fathoms.

ACASTA PECTINIPES Pilsbry.

1912. *Acasta pectinipes* PILSBRY, Proc. U. S. Nat Mus., vol. 42, p. 294.
1913. *Acasta nitida* HOEK, *Siboga*-Expeditie, Monographie 31b, p. 237, pl. 24, figs. 17–19; pl. 25, figs. 1–3.

Type.—Cat. No. 43473, U.S.N.M., from *Albatross* station 5276, near Malavatuan Island, off southern Luzon, 18 fathoms.

ACASTA IDIOPOMA Pilsbry.

1912. *Acasta idiopoma* PILSBRY, Proc. U. S. Nat. Mus., vol. 42, p. 294.

Type.—Cat. No. 43466, U.S.N.M., from *Albatross* station 5254, Gulf of Davao, Mindanao, 21 fathoms.

This species and the two preceding will be fully illustrated in a report on barnacles of the *Albatross* Philippine Expedition.

Genus TETRACLITA Schumacher.

1817. *Tetraclita* Schumacher, Essal d'un nouveau Système des Habitations des Vers testacés, p. 91, type *T. squamulosa* Schumacher=*T. squamosa* Bruguière.

1817. *Conia* Leach, Journal de Physique, vol. 85, p. 69, monotype *C. porosa*. (*Monolopus* Klein stated to be the same.)

1817. *Asemus* Ranzani, Opuscoli scientifici, vol. 1, p. 275, no species mentioned; also vol. 2, 1818, p. 64, for *A. porosus* (=*Lepas porosa* Gmelin).

1822. *Polytrema* Férussac, Dictionnaire classique d'Histoire Naturelle, vol. 2, p. 144 (*Balanus stalactiferus* Lamarck and *squamosus* Bruguière).

Balanidæ with four compartments, sometimes externally calcified together; parietes permeated by pores, generally forming several irregular rows; radii either developed or obsolete. Basis flat, irregular, calcareous, or thin or membranous. Labrum notched in the middle.

Type.—T. squamosa (Bruguière).

*Distribution.—*All tropical and warm temperate seas, in the littoral zone.

Tetraclita and the allied genera *Elminius*, *Creusia*, and *Pyrgoma* are apparently to be regarded as Balanoid barnacles which have lost the carinolateral compartments. These compartments tend to disappear in some hexamerous barnacles. They are very narrow and do not reach the base in some species of *Acasta* and *Conopea*, and are wanting in *Balanus* (*Conopea*) *cornuta*. In *Tetraclita* and several other tetramerous genera it appears that a parallel modification has taken place. There is a striking resemblance between *Tetraclita* and *Semibalanus*, possibly indicating some affinity. Both have a tendency to subdivide the parietal pores, and in both the internal lamina of the wall is ribless.

When radii are undeveloped there are still vermiculate ridges representing the septa of the radial edges. These are represented in plate 61, figure 1e.

Schumacher, Leach, and Ranzani recognized and gave names to this generic group in the same year. It is not known which actually published first, but the name given by Schumacher has been preferred by all subsequent zoologists mentioning the group.

My field experience with *Tetraclita* is limited to southern Florida, Cuba, and California, where it is an intertidal barnacle, living in a zone above any *Balanus* of the same localities. From its frequent association with *Chthamalus* I presume that it is also a surf barnacle elsewhere. *Tetraclita* has its greatest development in the Philippines and Malay Archipelago.

The following three forms are not represented in the National Museum collections:

T. squamosa patellaris Darwin (*T. porosa* var. *patellaris* Darwin, Monograph, p. 330). The type was from a ship in Boston Bay. One specimen in the collection of the Academy of Natural Sciences, Philadelphia, was from a ship from the East Indies. It is volcano-shaped, with very small orifice; scutum thin, with rather weak crests for the lateral depressor muscle; tergum small and extremely narrow.

T. mitra (*Lepas mitra* Spengler, Skrivter af Naturhistorie Selskabet, vol. 1, 1790, p. 192, pl. 6, fig. 5. From "Niquebar").

T. serrata Darwin (Monograph, p. 334), South Africa. Close to *T. squamosa*, but the articular and adductor ridges are united above, inclosing a "cavity which runs to the apex of the valve." Weltner and Krüger state that there are forms intermediate between *serrata* and *squamosa*. This species could not be distinguished by the characters given in the keys of Hoek and Gruvel. These keys are also otherwise impracticable.

T. purpurascens Wood (Darwin, Monograph, p. 342). Synonyms: *Balanus plicatus* Lamarck. *Conia depressa* Gray. Australia; New Zealand.

TETRACLITA SQUAMOSA (Bruguière).

1789. *Balanus squamosus* BRUGUIÈRE, Encyclopèdie Méthodique, p. 170.

1790. *Lepas fungites* SPENGLER, Skrivter af Naturhistorie Selskabet, vol. 1, p. 189.

1791. *Lepas porosa* GMELIN, Systema Naturæ, ed. 13, p. 3212.

1817. *Tetraclita squamulosa* SCHUMACHER, Essai d'un nouv. Syst. Vers Testac., p. 91.

1854. *Tetraclita porosa* Gmelin, DARWIN, in part, Monograph, p. 329, pl. 10, figs. 1a–1m, with varieties *communis, nigrescens, viridis, rubescens,* and p. 330, var. *elegans, patellaris.*

1900. *Tetraclita porosa* (Gmelin) var. *viridis* Darwin, BORRADAILE, Proc. Zool. Soc., London, p. 799 (Rotuma).

Distribution.—World-wide in tropical and subtropical seas; distribution of the typical form, Japan, coast of China, Philippines, and the Malay Archipelago.[1]

Six varieties of this species were defined by Darwin. As in the cases of *Balanus tintinnabulum* and *B. amphitrite,* he at first thought to rank several of them as distinct species, but was deterred by finding various forms uniting characters of two varieties. After studying some hundreds of specimens I am much disposed to rank as species *T. rubescens* and *stalactifera* in America, and *T. squamosa, japonica,* and *rufotincta* in the Old World. While they are variable, I have no reason to think that any of these races intergrade. Yet as the forms of India, South Africa, and Australia are unknown to me, such a course might be premature. Moreover, I have not been able to find time for a thorough examination of the cirri and mouth parts of the several races.

---

[1] Doctor Krüger has reported *T. porosa* var. *viridis* from Sagami Bay, Japan, and the Pescadores, and has figured the tergum and six scuta. The form of the tergum is somewhat unlike the Chinese and Philippine specimens I have seen.

My studies in the group show that the distribution of the races as here defined conforms to that of mollusks and other littoral animals, each of the marine faunal provinces having its race of *Tetraclita.* They are not scattered haphazard, as one might suppose from the existing literature.

We have no direct means of knowing the type-locality of Bruguière's type of *squamosus.* His references, so far as they can be localized, pertain to oriental forms. The terms of his description apply to either the Panamic or the Chinese and Philippine forms, not to the West Indian. He states that the orifice is small, that there is no trace of radii, and " l'épaisseur de ces valves est très-considérable, elle égale à la base la moitié du diamètre inférieur de la coquille." The opercular valves were wanting in his specimen. It seems far more likely that Bruguière would have an East Indian than a Panamic barnacle, as oriental shells and barnacles were common in Europe long before his time.

The type-specimen was probably lost, for the illustrations published in the Encyclopédie several years later (pl. 165, figs. 9, 10) were copied from Chemnitz. Under these conditions it has seemed best to consider the common form of China and the Philippine Islands as typical *T. squamosa.*

Gmelin's *L. porosa* was also of oriental origin, so far as can be determined. His very brief account was compiled. *Lepas fungites* and *T. squamulosa* were also from eastern sources. Darwin did not assign typical localities for the varieties he described, but incidentally he mentioned having var. *communis* from Pernambuco and the Galapagos Archipelago; var. *rubescens* from the Philippine Archipelago, and var. *elegans* from California. The Galapagos form may be what is herein described as *milleporosa.* The Philippine record for *rubescens* must have been based upon specimens with an erroneous locality, or upon some oriental form which I have not seen. It may be noted here that some obvious errors among localities given for barnacles by Darwin may be traceable to specimens from Cuming's collection, which is known to have been the source of numerous erroneous localities in the literature of mollusks. It is well known that Cuming trusted to his memory for localities, instead of recording them on the labels at the time the specimens were collected or received.

KEY TO SUBSPECIES OF T. SQUAMOSA.

a^1. Inflected occludent margin of the scutum having few (one to three) oblique teeth or folds. Tergum narrow, its width not much over one-third its length, the basal margin sloping to, and almost in line with, the carinal border of the spur. California.

b^1. External wall eroded, reddish; sheath and interior of tergum reddish-purple or tinted_____*T. s. rubescens*

b^2. External wall not eroded, whitish_____*T. s. rubescens,* form *elegans.*

a^2. Inflected occludent margin of the scutum broad, with four or five very coarse teeth. Scutum white with purplish clouds and stains, the crests at base strongly developed. Spur of the tergum tapering to a narrow end. Sheath somewhat purplish _____*T. s. japonica*

a^3. Inflected occludent margin of scutum having rather small and close oblique teeth (one to every second growth-ridge of the exterior), their number depending upon the degree of erosion of the valve.

    b^1. Exterior and sheath, pink; scutum, pinkish or white within; tergum with the basocarinal angle very prominent, the basal margin nearly at right angles with the carinal edge of the rather narrow spur___*T. s. rufotincta*

    b^2. Exterior usually dark, the sheath generally of a greenish shade. Scutum dusky bluish-green, with narrow, multidentate, occludent border; crests in the base weak. Tergum narrow_____*T. squamosa squamosa*

    b^3. Exterior nearly white, gray, or blackish; sheath blackish. Scutum wide, violet-black and white, with strong crests for the depressor muscles.

        c^1. Pores of the wall rather coarse and not extremely numerous; tergum about half as wide as long, with the spur wide at the end,

                                           T. s. stalactifera

        c^2. Similar, but tergum narrower_____*T. s. stalactifera* form *confinis*

        c^3. Pores of the very thick wall small and very numerous.

            d^1. Width of tergum decidedly less than half its length—*T. s. panamensis*

            d^2. Tergum as in *T. s. stalactifera;* scutum white with a purple stain on tergal margin _____*T. s. milleporosa*

TETRACLITA SQUAMOSA SQUAMOSA (Bruguière).

I am using this name as synonymous with *T. porosa* var. *viridis* Darwin. It is a rather low, spreading, circular barnacle when growing on a flat surface, the orifice small, sutures obliterated or nearly so, the outer lamina of the wall dark colored or gray, eroded, exposing the filling of the parietal tubes, producing fine, more or less interrupted ridges, which are *usually beaded finely*. The wall is thick, pores very numerous and small. The sheath usually has a decidedly greenish hue. The radii are represented by very irregular or vermiculate crenulations on the flat radial faces.

The scutum is *dusky bluish-green*, fading on the crest of adductor ridge and toward the basitergal border. Articular ridge and furrow small, in comparison with the West Indian subspecies. Adductor ridge very long, extending nearly to the apex and to the base, not confluent with the articular ridge. *Inflexed occludent border narrow*, set with many small teeth. Crests for the lateral depressor muscle simple; the crests on the occludent side of the base *very weak or wanting*.

Tergum very narrow, the basal margin sloping toward and nearly in line with the carinal border of the spur. Spur narrow and long, with the end rounded or pointed.

This seems to be a very distinct form. I have seen a large number without any tendency whatever to grade into either the Japanese or the East African subspecies. Unfortunately, I have not been able to compare the Tetraclitas of the *squamosa* group inhabiting India or those of Australia.

The outer lamina of the parietes is pitted internally, as may be seen by looking in the outer row of basal pores. This produces the distinctly beaded riblets of the worn exterior. The same structure is found in some other subspecies of *T. squamosa*, but much less distinctly developed.

Locality.	Collector.	Notes.
China	Doctor Emerson	I. Lea collection.
Kowloon, China	Albatross	
Philippine Islands	Dr. E. A. Mearns	
Balayan Bay, Luzon	Albatross	Shore.
Jamelo Bay, Luzon	do	
Tibi and Pili Hot Springs, Albay, Luzon	Dr. E. A. Mearns	
Port Binanga, Subig Bay	Albatross	
Pucot River, Mariveles	do	
Catbalogan, Samar	do	On reef.
Port Cuyo	do	
Damerug Point, Masbate	Dr. Paul Bartsch	
Maricaban Island	Albatross	On shore.
Siasi Island, Jolo	do	
Moronga Island, Jolo	do	
Rapatag Island, Tawi Tawi group	do	Shore.
West Africa [1]		A varietal form.

[1] A form from West Africa in the National Museum, and Cape Palmas in the collection of the Academy of Natural Sciences of Philadelphia, closely resembles the oriental *T. s. squamosa*. The specimens seen, about 20, are small, the largest 16 mm. in diameter. The radii are generally distinct, though narrow, and the eroded ribs of the parietes are conspicuously beaded. The pores are coarse, in two or three irregular rows, and the wall is not very thick, thus differing from typical *squamosa*. The sheath is green. The long adductor ridge of the scutum unites with the articular ridge above, but there is no cavity perforating to the apex, such as is described for *T. serrata*.

TETRACLITA SQUAMOSA JAPONICA, new subspecies.

Plate 58, figs. 1 to 3a.

1911. *Tetraclita porosa* var. *nigrescens* KRÜGER, Beiträge zur Cirripedienfauna Ostasiens, p. 61, pl. 4, fig. 41c.

Type.—Cat. No. 58060, U.S.N.M., from Ayukawa, Japan.

The surface is wholly removed in adults, deep or dark purplish-gray or deep mouse-gray; sutures distinct or obliterated; no crenulation on the flat radial faces; pores of medium or small size; sheath generally of unusual length, but sometimes short, vinaceous slate to dull violet black. Orifice usually rather large in adults.

Scutum with rather inconspicuous growth-ridges. Inside varying shades of slate-violet. Articular ridge small and projecting or reflexed very little. Articular furrow small. The adductor ridge is strong and extends nearly to base and apex; a deep but narrow furrow separates it from the articular ridge throughout. The crests for the depressor muscles are strongly developed. The rather broadly inflexed occludent border has four or five strong, oblique teeth (pl. 58, fig. 3a).

The tergum is rather narrow, its median width contained two and one-third to two and one-half times in the length. Externally it has a slight depression running to the spur, which is removed a little from the scutal border; growth-ridges narrow and rather conspicuous. Inside nearly white, not bicolored. Basal margin oblique, but making a wide angle with the spur. The spur is long and tapers to a narrow end. The scutal border is very narrowly inflexed.

The compartments may be separated readily in some individuals, but in others the sutures are calcified and the wall will break through the parietes rather than part at the sutures. The sutural edges, in individuals which part there, are flat and smooth without the irregular crenulations representing radii in *T. s. squamosa.*

In this race the articular ridge of the scutum is longer than in *T. s. squamosa,* and not united above with the adductor ridge; the crests at the base are much stronger, the teeth of the more broadly inflexed occludent border are larger and less numerous, and the external sculpture is more effaced. There are also differences in the terga and walls. The color is toward purple instead of green. The opercular valves are larger relative to the size of the walls than in *T. s. squamosa.*

I have seen a good many specimens. It seems to be the prevalent form of the species in Japan. Doctor Krüger reports it (as var. *nigrescens*) from Tokyo and Sagami Bays and the Pescadores.

Locality.	Collector.	Notes.
Ayukawa, Japan	*Albatross*	Type lot.
Yokohama, Japan	H. Loomis	
Ana, Japan	....do.	
Wakanoura, Kishiu	Imperial University of Tokyo	

TETRACLITA SQUAMOSA RUFOTINCTA, new species.

Plate 58, figs. 5 to 6a.

Type.—Cat. No. 48055, U.S.N.M., from Aden.
Distribution.—Gulf of Suez to Zanzibar.

The surface is eroded, showing fine short ridges or raised lozenges; *pink* (hydrangea pink to pinkish vinaceous of Ridgway); sutures often scarcely or not visible; sheath colored like the outside. Wall very thick, with many rows of small pores. Diameter 30 to 44 mm.

Scutum livid brown and whitish within, adductor ridge well developed, but low, and in the upper part it is low, close to and united with the articular ridge by a callous partly filling the groove. In the lower half of the inflected occludent margin there are 6 to 10 or more short, oblique teeth.

Tergum with the *basocarinal angle very prominent, the basal margin nearly transverse to the adjacent margin of the spur.* Scutal margin only narrowly inflected.

This race is readily recognized by the pale color of exterior and sheath, the small pores, the shape of the tergum, and the numerous "teeth" of the occludent border of the scutum.

I have seen two apparently typical specimens, said to be West Indian, one from " St. Crux, Doctor Griffith, I. Lea collection," the other from St. Thomas, R. Swift, in the collection of the Academy of Natural Sciences, Philadelphia. As both were associated in trays with ordinary West Indian *stalactifera*, it seems possible that there has been a mixture or exchange of specimens in the 50 years or more they have been in collections. Without further evidence I hesitate to add *West Indies* to the range of the subspecies, as its known habitat is the Red Sea and East Africa.

A single large example from Prison Island, Zanzibar, collected by Sir Charles Eliot, 1901, is in the collection of the Academy of Natural Sciences. It differs from the Aden examples by having the opercular valves white within. The scutum is wider, with a deeper and wider articular furrow. The tergum has the angle between basal margin and spur less deeply entering, and the scutal margin is broadly inflected below (pl. 58, figs. 6, 6a).

Locality.	.	Collector.	.	Notes.
Aden, Arabia..		Ward's natural science establishment.		Two groups.
Do..		L. M. McCormick......		
Gulf of Suez..		McAndrew............		
"St. Crux"..		Doctor Griffith........		I. Lea collection.

TETRACLITA SQUAMOSA STALACTIFERA (Lamarck).

Plate 59, figs. 1 to 5b.

1818. *Balanus stalactiferus* LAMARCK, Animaux sans Vertèbres, vol. 5, p. 394 (Habite les mers de St. Domingue).
1854. *Tetraclita .porosa* var. *communis* DARWIN, Monograph, p. 329, pl. 10, fig. 1a (? and 1i, 1k).
1854. *Tetraclita porosa* var. *nigrescens* DARWIN, Monograph, p. 329, pl. 10, fig. 1b.

Type.—Presumably in Musée d'Histoire Natural de Genève, from the island of Haiti.

Distribution.—West Indies and American mainland, Florida to southern Brazil; west coast of Mexico.

The surface is typically eroded, dull, and variable in color, dirty white, cream, pale olive-buff, or plumbeous-black, the sheath plumbeous-black (never green or pink even in forms externally light colored). Pores larger and fewer, in the average, than in *T. s. squamosa* or *T. s. rufotincta.* Usual diameter of adults from 24 to 30 mm.

The scutum is dusky slate-violet, dull violet-black, or raisin black or clouded with these colors internally, with paler or whitish borders and adductor ridge. The adductor ridge is very strongly developed, deeply undercut, rather well removed from the articular ridge, but sometimes the space between them is partly filled up above. The articular ridge is rather broad. There are usually five or six strong, oblique teeth on the lower part of the occludent margin, those above having been removed by erosion.

The tergum is typically about half as wide as long. The carinal half is dark or dark-tinted, like the scutum, the scutal half and spur white within. The basal margin forms an angle with the spur. The spur is moderately wide, with a very obliquely truncate end.

The great variation in color led Darwin to define a var. *nigrescens*—" Outer lamina of shell almost wholly removed; the portion preserved and the exposed parietal tubes very dark purple or inky black." I have been unable to satisfy myself that this form is racially distinct from the light colored and gray forms. The opercular valves are similar in all.

Form *floridana:* The only deviation of note observed among the specimens seen is in a large lot from the rocks at Lake Worth Inlet, Florida. In these the young individuals, sometimes up to 20 mm. diameter, preserve the surface, which is finely and evenly ribbed. The largest individuals, 25 mm. in diameter, have lost the outer layer. The scuta are pale, only tinted with violet, and the terga, also pale, are decidedly narrower (pl. 59, figs. 6–6b).

On the Pacific coast there is a form of *T. s. stalactifera* ranging from Cape St. Lucas, Lower California, to Nicaragua (pl. 59, figs. 5–5b, Mazatlan). The color, rather coarse pores, and characters of the opercular valves seem to be the same as in Antillean examples.

There is a good deal of variation in the size of the pores, even between individuals of the same group and having the opercular valves practically identical. Plate 59, figure 4, from San Juan del Sur, Nicaragua, illustrates this variation. In an old stock, such as this, which has been separated from its Antillean relatives without much change since the Oligocene or Miocene, it is natural that there should exist a number of collateral varieties, resulting in heterogeneous colonies. There are also several incipient geographic races.

Form *confinis:* A lot taken by the *Albatross* at St. Georges Island, in the Gulf of California (pl. 60, fig. 2), resembles *T. s. milleporosa* and the Lake Worth Inlet form *floridana* by having the terga decidedly narrower than in typical *stalactifera* and the spur projects very shortly below the basiscutal angle. The articular ridge of the scutum is narrower, and the articular furrow makes a shallower bay below it. The eroded exterior is gray or cream. This is probably a local race of the Gulf, which may be called form *confinis* (fig. 81).

Locality.	Collector.	Notes.
Bahamas	B. A. Bean	
Lake Worth Inlet, Fla	H. A. Pilsbry	Form *floridana*.
Porto Rico	U. S. F. C	
St. Thomas		
Barbados	Lieut. C. L. Fitzgerald, R. A.	
Santa Marta, Colombia	Dr. Amos P. Brown	Coll. A. N. S. Phila.
Santa Catherina, Brazil		I. Lea collection.
Cape St. Lucas, Lower California	Dr. E. Palmer	
Do	J. Xantus	
San Benedicito, Lower California	do	
St. George's Island, Gulf of California	*Albatross*	Form *confinis*.
Mazatlan, Mexico	P. Bartsch	

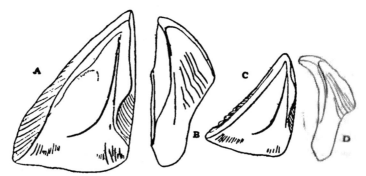

FIG. 81.—TETRACLITA SQUAMOSA STALACTIFERA FORM CONFINIS. *a, c*, SCUTA AND *b, d*, TERGA OF TWO INDIVIDUALS FROM ST. GEORGES ISLAND, GULF OF CALIFORNIA.

TETRACLITA SQUAMOSA PANAMENSIS, new subspecies.

Plate 60, figs. 3–3*b*.

1909. *Tetraclita porosa* (Gmelin) PILSBRY, Proc. U. S. Nat. Mus., vol. 37, p. 64, pl. 16, fig. 2.

Type.—Cat. No. 58061, U.S.N.M., from Panama.

Distribution.—Panama to Peru.

Form, *thick wall*, small orifice and *fine pores* as in *T. s. milleporosa*, the external color gray or tea green with light purplish-gray stains, the sheath slate-violet to dusky slate-violet. Diameter 30 to 40 mm.

Scutum, very similar to that of *T. s. stalactifera;* often whitish in the middle. Articular ridge and furrow narrow and small. Adductor ridge strongly developed, arcuate and long.

Tergum decidedly narrower than in *stalactifera* or *milleporosa*.

I have seen a considerable number from Panama. While related to *T. s. milleporosa* and *T. s. stalactifera*, it has a rather distinct aspect, somewhat like typical *T. squamosa*.

Locality.	Collector.	Notes.
Panama	C. B. Adams	
Ecuador or Peru	Dr. W. H. Jones, U. S. Navy	
Payta, Peru	do	Figured, Proc. U. S. Nat. Mus., vol. 37, pl. 16, fig. 2.

TETRACLITA SQUAMOSA MILLEPOROSA, new subspecies.

Plate 60, figs. 1 to 1d.

Type.—Cat. No. 58059, U.S.N.M., from Albemarle Island, Galapagos.

The form is often lower, more spreading than usual, the orifice very small. External lamina wholly eroded, exposing the fine, short, scalelike upfilled pores; sutures usually wholly obliterated externally, calcified. Walls very thick, the pores very small and numerous. External color ivory yellow or with a grayish tone, the sheath dark varley's gray or violet-slate. Diameter 46 mm., height 16½ mm.

The opercular valves are very small. Scutum short and broad, white within, stained with dull purple on the articular rib and at the base of the occludent margin. Articular rib not so strong as in *stalactifera.* Adductor ridge strong, parallel to the rounded basitergal border, approaching the articular ridge above, and separated from it by a superficial groove only.

The tergum is shaped much like that of *T. s. stalactifera,* the spur being wide with oblique end; but the carinal side of the valve is somewhat narrower than *stalactifera,* the scutal side wider.

Related to *panamensis* by the unusually thick wall, which is so calcified that it can not be broken along the sutures; but the tergum is shaped like that of *stalactifera.*

TETRACLITA SQUAMOSA RUBESCENS Darwin.

Plate 61, figs. 1 to 1e.

1854. *Tetraclita porosa* var. *rubescens* DARWIN, Monograph, p. 329, pl. 10, fig. 1b (? and 1l, 1m).
1854. *Tetraclita porosa* var. *elegans* DARWIN, Monograph, p. 330, pl. 10, fig. 1d.

Distribution.—Farallones, California, to Cape St. Lucas, Lower California.

The surface is dull, eroded, roughened like thatch, varying from deep hellebore red to livid brown, sometimes with a gray-white zone at the base, where it is less deeply eroded in some specimens; sheath colored like the exterior. The pores are larger than in typical *squamosa.*

Scutum but little cut off at the basitergal angle, and with the adductor ridge strongly developed; white below the adductor ridge, corinthian purple or deep hellebore red above it. The occludent margin has only one to three very long, very oblique teeth.

Tergum is extremely narrow, its greatest width but little exceeding one-third of the length; carinal part of the base steeply sloping, nearly in line with the adjacent border of the long spur. Crests for the depressor muscles strongly developed. Corinthian red, fading to white at end of the spur.

Large specimens reach a diameter of 42 mm. I have seen others, containing eggs, not more than 11 mm. in diameter.

Darwin did not give the distribution of *rubescens*, but his figure and description apply perfectly to the Californian race defined above, for which I use his name in a restricted sense. Reports of *rubescens* from other regions were doubtless founded on other races of somewhat similar color or upon erroneously localized specimens. *T. s. rufotincta* is paler, with finer pores, producing finer external sculpture; it has a differently shaped tergum and numerous short teeth on the occludent border of the scutum. It is not closely related to the Californian race.

Form *elegans* Darwin (pl. 61, fig. 2). Outer layer of the wall preserved, except sometimes near the summit; white under a cream-color or cream-buff epidermis, which, when perfectly preserved, bears close concentric fringes of short, delicate hairs; strongly ribbed, the ribs crossed by fine concentric growth-ridges. Sheath reddish in some examples, and these usually show reddish spots where eroded near the orifice, and if filed, a red layer is found under the white, caused by the colored filling of the pores. Some individuals, however, are truly albino, without red in the sheath or pores, and others show only a few small red spots on the sheath. The opercular valves are like those of *rubescens*. The largest specimens seen are 20 mm. in diameter.

The form described as var. *elegans* by Darwin does not seem to be separable from *rubescens*, as there are some transitional individuals. It appears to be a form, perhaps an incipient race, in which the cuticle, with the underlying whitish outer layer, are persistent up to a certain size, as in the Lake Worth Inlet form of *squamosa*, noticed on p. 255. It is not a stage passed through by all individuals of *T. s. rubescens*, as I have seen typically eroded and colored specimens only 11 mm. in diameter. The exact status of *elegans* must be determined by observations by those who have opportunity to study and collect them.

Locality.	Collector.	Notes.
Farallone Islands, Cal.		
Pacific Grove, Cal.	J. E. Benedict.	
San Pedro, Cal.		
San Diego, Cal.	C. R. Orcutt.	
Do.	Dr. Palmer.	
South end Cerros Island, Lower California.	*Albatross*.	With form *elegans*.
"West Coast".		
Catalina Island, Cal.		Form *elegans*.
Point Loma, San Diego, Cal.	C. R. Orcutt.	Do.
No locality; on *Mytilus californianus* Conrad		Do.
Cape St. Lucas, Lower California.		Do.

TETRACLITA RADIATA (Blainville).

Plate 61, figs. 3–3c, 4.

1854. *Tetraclita radiata* Blainville, DARWIN, Monograph, p. 343, pl. 11, figs. 5a–5d.

Distribution.—West Indies (? also New South Wales and Sumatra).

This was described by Darwin as follows:

Shell white, with numerous approximate longitudinal ribs; radii broad, with their summits slightly oblique, internally porose; tergum with the articular ridge extraordinarily prominent, with the spur not joined to the basiscutal angle.

The white color, the narrowly and closely ribbed parietes, and the broad radii give this species an aspect by which it can be easily recognized.

The large size of the tergum in comparison with the scutum is a further characteristic mark of this species. Unlike most Tetraclitas, it has often been found on ships.

Specimens in the United States National Museum were found growing on *Balanus tintinnabulum antillensis*, Cat. No. 2031, taken from the bottom of a Cape Cod whaler from the West Indies. There are others in the collection of the Academy of Natural Sciences of Philadelphia from St. Thomas.

TETRACLITA COSTATA Darwin.

1854. *Tetraclita costata* DARWIN, Monograph, p. 339, pl. 11, figs. 2a–2c.

Type.—British Museum, from the Philippine Archipelago.

Specimens are in the collection from " East Indies," Isaac Lea collection, and Tataan Island, Tawi Tawi group of the Sulu Archipelago, *Albatross.*

TETRACLITA CŒRULESCENS (Spengler).

1790. *Lepas cærulescens* SPENGLER, Skrivter af Naturhistorie Selskabet, vol. 1, p. 191.

1854. *Tetraclita cærulescens* Spengler, DARWIN, Monograph, p. 342, pl. 11, figs. 4a–4d.

Tataan Island, Tawi Tawi group of the Sulu Archipelago, *Albatross.* Zamboanga, Mindanao, E. A. Mearns.

TETRACLITA VITTATA Darwin.

1854. *Tetraclita vittata* DARWIN, Monograph, p. 340, pl. 11, figs. 3a–3e.

Tataan Island, Tawi Tawi group, Sulu Archipelago, *Albatross.*

TESSEROPORA, new subgenus.

Tetraclita with a single row of parietal pores.

Type.—*T. rosea* Krauss.

Darwin has noted that the pores in the walls of Tetraclitæ become more numerous with age, and at a very young stage there is but one row. The recent species for which this subgenus is proposed, is to be regarded as an unprogressive form, which retains characters of the ancestral stock of the genus, elsewhere found only in an early stage of development.

The Italian Oligocene species, *Tetraclita isseli* De Alessandri,[1] belongs to this group and is closely related to *T. rosea*.

TETRACLITA ROSEA (Krauss).

Plate 58, fig. 4.

1848. *Conia rosea* KRAUSS, Die Südafrikanischen Mollusken, p. 136, pl. 6, fig. 28.

1854. *Tetraclita rosea* Krauss, DARWIN, Monograph, p. 335, pl. 10, figs. 3a–3d.

Distribution.—South Africa; Australia.

A single large specimen of this species in the National Museum is labeled "Orange Harbor," no doubt erroneously. No collector given. This specimen is figured (pl. 58, fig. 4) to show the features of the pores. It is 25 mm. in diameter. There is a series in the collection of the Academy of Natural Sciences of Philadelphia from Richmond, near Melbourne, Victoria, collected by Mrs. Agnes F. Kenyon.

Genus ELMINIUS Leach.

1825. *Elminius* LEACH, Zoological Journal, vol. 2, p. 210.

1854. *Elminius* Leach, DARWIN, Monograph, p. 345.

Barnacle conic or cylindric; compartments four; parietes not porous; basis membranous.

Type.—*E. kingii* Gray.

Distribution.—Austral in both hemispheres; littoral.

Elminius differs from *Tetraclita* by the absence of pores in the parietal walls. It holds such a relation to *Tetraclita* as *Chirona* to the typical *Balani*. *Tetraclita* is a more evolved genus. Leach did not mention a species in his table defining this genus. In fact no species had then been described. I am selecting *E. kingii*, the first species described, as the genotype.

ELMINIUS KINGII Gray.

1831. *Elminius kingii* GRAY, Zoological Miscellany, p. 13.

1831. *Elminius leachii* KING and BRODERIP, Zoological Journal, vol. 5, p. 334.

1854. *Elminius kingii* Gray, DARWIN, Monograph, p. 348, pl. 11, figs. 6a–6e.

1911. *Elminius kingii* Gray, ORTMANN, Princeton Patagonian expedition, p. 637.

1914. *Elminius kingii* Gray, STEBBING, Proc. Zool. Soc., London, p. 376.

Distribution.—Falkland Islands, Tierra del Fuego, Chiloe (Darwin). Darwin describes it as follows:

Shell smooth, gray, or dirty white; radii broad, smooth edged. Scutum without an adductor ridge. Tergum with the spur distinct from the basiscutal angle. Scutum and tergum sometimes calcified together.

---

[1] Palæontographia Italica, vol. 12, 1906, p. 318.

The barnacle is thin, the compartments rather easily separated. They are sometimes more or less roughened, but not ribbed or plicate. The thin basal edge is not crenulated, but there are sometimes some fine vertical striæ within the edge. "The scuta are remarkable for not having any adductor ridge or crests for the depressor muscles."

There is a cylindrical specimen in the United States National Museum from the Isaac Lea collection, without locality.

ELMINIUS PLICATUS Gray.

1854. *Elminius plicatus* Gray, DARWIN, Monograph, p. 351, pl. 12, figs. 2a–2f.

Distribution.—New Zealand. Two specimens without opercular valves. Also two from "Orange Bay," with *Tetraclita rosea;* no collector given, and locality doubtless erroneous.

Two other species of *Elminius* have been described from New Zealand, *E. sinuatus* and *E. rugosus* Hutton,[1] and two from Australia, *E. simplex* and *E. modestus* Darwin. Professor Gruvel has described a very small form from the breakwater at Ponta Delgada, San Miguel, Azores, as *E. cristallinus.* This is the only species known in the Northern Hemisphere.

Genus CREUSIA Leach.

1854. *Creusia* Leach, DARWIN, Monograph, p. 375.

Darwin describes this genus as consisting of—

Compartments four, furnished with radii; basis cup-formed; attached to corals.

This genus is represented in the United States National Museum by five small specimens on a bit of coral, I. Lea collection. No locality is recorded.

Darwin records the single species recognized by him, *Creusia spinulosa* Leach, from both the West and East Indies. No definite West Indian locality is given.

Genus PYRGOMA Leach.

1854. *Pyrgoma* Leach, DARWIN, Monograph, p. 354 (see for synonymy, etc.).
1838. *Duplocona* SCHLÜTER, Kurzgefasstes systematisches Verzeichniss meiner Conchyliensammlung, p. 38, for *D. lævigata* Schlüter (=*Balanus duploconus* Lamarck).

According to Darwin, this genus possesses a "shell formed of a single piece; basis cup-formed or subcylindrical, attached to corals."

Pyrgoma is considered a further development of *Creusia,* in which the four compartments have become wholly concrescent.

---

[1] Trans. N. Z. Inst., vol. 11, 1879, p. 328.

Few of these barnacles are in the National Museum, evidently because the corals and millepores of the collection have not been examined for them. No species is positively known from American seas, but *P. stokesii* (Gray) Darwin has been found upon *Agaricia agaricites*, believed to be West Indian, and *P. cancellatum* Leach was found on a *Gemmipora*, probably West Indian, but perhaps Pacific.

PYRGOMA ANGLICUM Sowerby.

Cat. No. 12072. Exmouth, England, from the Jeffreys collection.

PYRGOMA CRENATUM Sowerby.

Jeffreys collection and I. Lea collection; one specimen in each; no locality.

Subfamily CHELONIBIINÆ Pilsbry.

Balanidæ, in which the sheath extends to the base and forms the whole inner wall of the body-chamber. The sutures uniting rostral latera and rostrum into a composite rostral compartment are usually discernible. Compartments essentially porose, though often secondarily filled up, always conspicuously lamellate at the basal edge. Basis membranous. The opercular valves are much smaller than the orifice; the articular ridge of the scutum is chitinous.

This seems to be a group of at least as high systematic rank as the Coronulinæ. It has a primitive character in the incomplete concrescence of the elements of the composite rostrum, but in other respects is decidedly specialized. The reduced opercular valves resemble those of the Coronulinæ superficially, but differ in their articulations, so that no direct relationship is to be predicated from them. It appears that this reduction is connected in some unexplained way with their habits, since it occurs in all genera living on vertebrate animals. The specialization of the wall is also adaptive, but the resemblance to the whale barnacles is merely superficial, as Darwin has shown.

The retention of a primitive character—the incomplete union of the rostrum and rostral latera—is of much greater systematic value in the highly evolved family Balanidæ than the same feature is in the more primitive Chthamalidæ.

Genus CHELONIBIA Leach.

1817. *Chelonibia* LEACH, Journal de Physique, vol. 85, p. 68.
1818. *Coronula* LAMARCK (part), Animaux sans Vertèbres, vol. 5, p. 385.
1825. *Astrolepas* Klein, GRAY, Annals of Philosophy, new ser., vol. 10, p. 105.
1854. *Chelonobia* DARWIN, Monograph, p. 382.

Compartments generally extremely thick, six, but the rostrum is composed of three very intimately united compartments, the sutures visible internally and in worn specimens also on the outside. Parietes porous (septate), but sometimes filled up solidly nearly to the bases of the septa. Basis flat, membranous; opercular valves narrow, not nearly closing the orifice, the scuta and terga united by a chitinous articular ligament (pl. 62, fig. 6). Labrum having a long row of teeth and a median notch in the margin. Third pair of cirri long, but structurally like the second; later cirri long, having segments with two pairs of spines, with little tufts of fine spines between.

Type.—C. testudinaria (Linnæus).

Distribution.—Tropical and temperate seas, on turtles, crabs, and manatees. Pliocene of Grand Canary and Italy.

This group retains a primitive character in the incompletely concrescent rostrum and rostro-lateral compartments. The sutures may be traced on the inside and in worn individuals externally. It is a transition from the octomerous stage to the hexamerous. In other respects it is rather highly specialized. In the least modified species, *C. patula*, the structure of the wall reminds one of *Balanus*, but I venture the opinion that the resemblance is probably due to convergence, the structures being homoplastic. The more specialized species are admirably adapted to the rough conditions of existence on the backs of sea turtles, the walls being enormously thickened and the stature low. They have a superficial resemblance to the whale barnacles, *Coronula*.

C. testudinaria is attached superficially, and when removed the turtle shell is found quite smooth and uninjured. It is the same with *C. patula* on crabs. In *C. caretta* the growing peripheral edge cuts into the turtle shell, which commonly covers or curves up over the edges of the barnacle. Darwin quite appropriately compares this penetrating power of the barnacle to that of growing roots.

Chelonobia patella (Ranzani)[1] is evidently a pen error for *C. patula*.

The following fossil species have been described: *C. hemisphærica* Rothpletz and Simonelli,[2] Pliocene of Grand Canary; *C. emisphærica* De Alessandri, 1906. *C. depressa* Seguenza, 1875, Pliocene of Sicily. *C. capellinii* De Alessandri,[3] Miocene and Pliocene, Italy.

All of them are of the *testudinaria* type, and therefore afford no information on the phylogeny of the genus. The recent *C. patula* is the most primitive of the known species in structure.

---

[1] Zoologischer Anzeiger, vol. 38, p. 461, November, 1911.
[2] Zeitschrift deutsch. Geol. Ges., vol. 42, 1891, p. 724, pl. 36, fig. 2.
[3] Palaeontographica Italica, vol. 12, 1906, p. 313.

a^1. Walls heavy, the compartments thick and strong; radii narrow; septa very
numerous; living on turtles or on the manatee.

b^1. Radii rather narrow and well sunken; cavities in the parietes between
the basal septa rather deep.

c^1. Radii usually notched on the sides, sometimes smooth; parietes not
ribbed or longitudinally folded, the peripheral edge not lobed or in-
cised_____C. testudinaria.

c^2. Parietes ribbed or folded, at least near the edge; radii usually quite
without notches.

d. Parietes with coarse ribs, subdivided near the periphery___C. manati.

d^2. Lower part of parietes plicate; periphery lobed_____C. m. lobatibasis.

d^3. Parietes plicate at the edge, showing a few small, loop-like incisions
in the base_____C. m. crenatibasis.

b^2. Radii not developed, or narrow; parietes solidly filled up nearly to the
base, the septa much interrupted. Shell extremely massive and
heavy _____C. caretta.

a^2. Thin and light, the outer lamina and septa of the wall very thin, cavities
between septa not at all filled up with calcareous matter. Shell steeply
conic, the orifice generally exceeding half the basal diameter; radii broad,
smooth, only slightly depressed. Usually living on crabs_____C. patula

CHELONIBIA TESTUDINARIA (Linnæus).

Plate 62, figs. 1–4.

1758. *Lepas testudinaria* LINNÆUS, Systema Naturæ, ed. 10, p. 668.

1778. *Balanus polythalamius* BOCK, Der Naturforscher 12tes Stück, p. 170,
pl. 4, figs. 9a, 9b.

1825. *Astrolepas rotundarius* J. E. GRAY, Annals of Philosophy, new ser.,
vol. 10, p. 105.

——. *Coronula testitudinaria* Lamarck, CHENU, Illustr. Conchyl., pl. 2,
fig. 2.

1854. *Chelonobia testudinaria* Linnæus, DARWIN, Monograph, p. 392, pl.
14, figs. 1a–1d, 5; pl. 15, fig. 1.

1911. *Chelonobia testudinaria* Linnæus, KRÜGER, Die Cirripedien fauna
Ostasiens, p. 57, figs. 121–125 (mouth-parts of specimens from Sagami
Bay, Japan).

Distribution.—All tropical and warm temperate seas. Pliocene
of Tuscany.

This species is very widely distributed in tropical and temperate
seas, probably wherever its usual host, the loggerhead turtle, occurs.
It is common on our Gulf coast and in the Atlantic as far north as
Delaware Bay, but is not often taken farther north.

The distinct, star-like radii, usually toothed along the edges, and
the rather deep excavation of the parietes between the parietal septa
will readily separate this species from *C. caretta*, which must be rare
on our eastern coast. The parietes are not folded or ribbed longi-

tudinally, and there are no incisions or lobes in the periphery, unless the two varieties placed under *C. manati* belong to this species.

There seems to be but little racial differentiation in *C. testudinaria*, though very large series might show more than I can see at present. The Atlantic specimens, as a general rule, have fewer and coarser transverse sutural ridges than those of the Pacific. Rarely they are almost obsolete. When old the wall is usually higher, especially the rostrum, which has a more arched profile; but this is not obvious in smaller examples. The basal septa are often, but not always, thicker. The orifice is sometimes longer, but varies from about one-third to nearly one-half the total length. A specimen of about the maximum size reached on our coast measures 48 mm. in carinorostral diameter, height 18 mm. (pl. 62, fig. 2).

The only one I have seen from the Galapagos is very large and low, 78 mm. long, 19 mm. high. The body-chamber is less than half of the basal diameter (pl. 62, fig. 1). A similar specimen 60 mm. long was taken in San Bartholome Bay, Lower California.

In the Gulf of California and at Cape St. Lucas there may be a small race. At all events, in three lots, about 25 specimens, the maximum length is about 28 mm. (pl. 62, fig. 3). In these, and all west American specimens seen, the transverse ridges in the radii are narrower and slightly more numerous than in Atlantic examples.

Locality.	Collector.	Notes.
Newport, R. I.	Dr. Edgar A. Mearns.	On loggerhead.
Point Pleasant, N. J.[1]	Witmer Stone.	
Delaware Bay, N. J.[1]	H. J. Mitchell.	On turtle.
Beaufort, N. C.[1]	L. R. Gibbes.	
East Coast of Florida.	F. E. Spinner.	
Pensacola, Fla.	Silas Stearns.	
Key West, Fla.	*Albatross*	
Progreso, Yucatan	Heilprin expedition.	
Point Patuca, Honduras.	W. H. Sligh.	On loggerhead.
Cape Frio, Brazil.		Do.
Albemarle Island, Galapagos.	Stanford University.	On turtle; diameter 28 mm.; largest 29 mm. diameter.
Gulf of California.		
San Luis Gonzales Bay, Gulf of California.	*Albatross*	Diameter 27½ mm.
Cape St. Lucas, Lower California.		
Magdalena Bay, Lower California.	C. R. Orcutt.	
San Bartholome Bay, Lower California.	*Albatross*	
Hawaiian Islands.	Wm. Alanson Bryan.	
Pearl Harbor, Oahu.	*Albatross*	
Carolina Island, Central Pacific[1]	C. D. Voy.	
Ana, Japan.	H. Loomis.	
Do.		Up to 68 mm. diameter.

[1] Specimens in the collection of the Academy of Natural Sciences of Philadelphia, the records inserted here to show its occurrence in the Middle States, etc.

CHELONIBIA MANATI Gruvel.

1903. *Chelonobia manati* GRUVEL, Nouvelle Archives du Muséum d'Histoire Naturelle, ser. 4, vol. 5, p. 116, pl. 2, figs. 14, 17, 18; pl. 4, figs. 15, 16.
1905. *Chelonobia manati* GRUVEL, Monographie des Cirrhipèdes, p. 267, fig. 297b.

Type.—Muséum d'Histoire Naturelle de Paris, from the Congo coast, abundant on skin of *Manatus senegalensis*.

This species is related to *C. testudinaria*, from which it differs by having the sides of the well developed radii not dentate, the parietes having salient longitudinal ribs which subdivide toward the base, and the basal septa are fewer.

I do not know that typical specimens of this species exist in any American museum, but there are certain barnacles in the series before me which, while possibly referable to *C. testudinaria* as varieties, have some characters of the West African species, and may be noticed here.

I am giving names to these forms in order to call attention to their characters which might otherwise be overlooked by those having opportunity of seeing large numbers of turtle barnacles. Their status as races can not yet be considered established.

C. m. lobatibasis, new variety. A specimen from Osprey, Florida (pl. 62, figs. 7, 7a), on *Caretta caretta*, No. 2107, Academy Natural Sciences, Philadelphia, has a large orifice and steep walls, which are irregularly plicate or ribbed in the lower half, producing an irregularly lobed periphery. The radii are rather wide, without "teeth." The basal septa are less numerous than in *C. testudinaria*, and there are rather small, deep cavities between them. Base of sheath as in *C. testudinaria*, with many breaches, leaving only wide and narrow pillars. Diameter 23 mm., height 9½ mm.

C. m. crenatibasis, new variety. A group of three old specimens (pl. 62, figs. 5, 5a, Cat. No. 48196, U.S.N.M.), from the Isaac Lea collection, locality and station unrecorded, have the orifice very large, the radii partly simple, but a few show very weak traces of teeth. Very close to the base there are numerous inconspicuous folds, and the interstices between these, or part of them, form minute loops, projecting into the septate base. (Seen on the right side in fig. 5.) This rather inconspicuous character is not present in any of the large series of ordinary *testudinaria* which has passed under my eye. The parietal cavities are particularly large and evenly developed. The parietal septa are distinctly of four lengths—those extending to the inner wall, those extending half across the cavities, others extending to the inner border of the outer wall, and the shortest series at the peripheral margin. Specimens measure, diameter 43 mm., height 18 mm.; diameter 37 mm., height 13 mm.

The battered summits of the compartments testify to a life of hard knocks, such as falls to the lot of most turtle barnacles. Moreover, some thin laminæ adhering to the base are probably from the loggerhead turtle.

CHELONIBIA CARETTA (Spengler).

Plate 63, figs. 5, 5a.

1790. *Lepas caretta* SPENGLER, Skrifter af Naturhist, Selskabet, vol. 1, p. 185, pl. 6, fig. 4.
1825. *Astrolepas testudinaria* GRAY, Annals of Philosophy, vol. 10, p. 105.
1840. *Balanus chelytrypetes* HINKS, Annals of Natural History, vol. 5, pp. 333–4.
——. *Coronula sulcata* CHENU, Illustrations Conchyliologiques, pl. 1, fig. 1.
1854. *Chelonobia caretta* DARWIN, Monograph, p. 394, pl. 14, fig. 2.

According to Darwin—

The descending sheath and radiating septa are of very variable thickness and have their basal edges finely dentated. The septa are not continuous from the circumference to the sheath in unbroken plates, but are irregularly divided into separate, often short, portions and even occasionally into mere points. The sheath differs from that of the other two specimens in having loopholes for the entrance of ribbons of corium only on the eight lines of suture, and not, with rare exceptions, in the middle of each compartment. This is evidently due to fewer filaments of corium being here sufficient to supply the less deep interspaces between the radiating septa, for in this species there are no flattened cavities or tubes running far up the shell. The inner lamina of the walls can not be here distinguished, for a solid, flat calcareous surface extends from the circumference between the radiating septa to the sheath. The sheath, had it not been from the light thrown on this part by the other species, would have certainly been mistaken for the inner lamina of the walls. *The absence of the flattened cavities or tubes extending up the parietes seems to be the least varying character* and serves to distinguish this species from those worn and massive specimens of *C. testudinaria,* which have narrow and not-notched radii.

The opercular valves hardly present any essential difference, compared with those of the other species, but the occludent margin of the scutum is apt to be more sinuous and its rostral end blunter and squarer. The carinal end of the tergum is also squarer than in any common variety of *C. testudinaria,* the external furrow or spur near the carinal margin is very indistinct, and even sometimes is quite absent.

Distribution.—Darwin had this species from the west coast of Africa and northern Australia. Doctor Weltner reports it from Venezuela, Massaua, and Torres Strait. The Paris Museum has specimens from Cape of Good Hope and Saigon. Specimens are in the collection of the Academy of Natural Sciences, Philadelphia, from St. Thomas, West Indies, taken by Robert Swift, and from a loggerhead turtle from Delaware Bay, New Jersey, taken by myself. These examples are very small and flat, 13 mm. long, and nearly covered by the shell of the turtle. Equally small examples of *C. testudinaria* on the same turtle were not at all embedded. Those in the United States National Museum are from "East Indies," I. Lea collection, and Cape Frio, Brazil, collector not recorded. It appears to be chiefly tropical. Records from the central and eastern Pacific are lacking.

CHELONIBIA PATULA (Ranzani).

Plate 63, figs. 4, 4a.

1818. *Coronula patula* RANZANI, Opuscoli Scientifici, vol. 2, pl. 3, figs. 25–28.
1822. *Coronula dentulata* SAY, Journal of the Academy of Natural Sciences of Philadelphia, vol. 2, p. 325.
1825. *Coronula denticula* Say, GRAY, Annals of Philosophy, new ser., vol. 10, p. 105.
1825. *Astrolepas lævis* GRAY, Annals of Philosophy, new ser., vol. 10, p. 105.
1854. *Chelonobia patula* Ranzani, DARWIN, Monograph, p. 396, pl. 14, figs. 3a, 3b, 4.

Distribution.—Mediterranean and both sides of the Atlantic in tropical and subtropical waters; Australia; Japan.

The pale buff or nearly white shell is very light and fragile in contrast with the preceding species. The outer lamina of the wall is thin, the radiating septa are thin, with delicately crenulated edges. The interseptal pores are not filled up, but penetrate to the summits of the parietes. The lower edge of the sheath is reduced to mere pillars. The opercular valves are somewhat narrower than in the other species. Greatest diameter 22 mm., height 8 mm.

All of the specimens I have seen attached and others bearing data are or were seated on crabs or *Limulus*. The types of Say's *Coronula dentulata*, in the collection of the Academy of Natural Sciences of Philadelphia, are labeled Florida. The single specimen seen from Port Townsend (presumably Washington) was without record of the collector. It has been reported by Gruvel from the Hawaiian Islands, specimens collected by M. Bailleu, 1875. Ranzani's type was from the Adriatic, on a crab.

Locality.	Collector.	Notes.
Cedar Keys, Fla.	Steamer Bache.	On *Callinectes sapidus* Rathb.
Cameron, La.	L. R. Cary.	On crab.
Texas.	J. D. Mitchell.	On *Callinectes sapidus*.
Tarpon, Tex.	University of Kansas.	On *Callinectes sapidus*.
Cape Cajon, Cuba.	Tomas Barrera expedition.	Cat. No. 48830.
Rio Bayamon above Palo Seco, Porto Rico.	U. S. F. C.	On *Callinectes*.
Port Townsend.	(Not stated).	Locality seems doubtful.

Subfamily CORONULINÆ.

1825. *Coronuladæ* LEACH, Zoological Journal, vol. 2, p. 209 (exclusive of *Chelonibia*).
1854. *Second section of the subfamily Balaninæ,* DARWIN, Monograph, p. 397.
1905. *Coronulinæ* and *Xenobalaninæ* GRUVEL, Monographie des Cirrhipèdes, p. 8.

Compartments six. Scutum and tergum, when present, not overlapping or articulated together; the terga or both scuta and terga sometimes wanting and always much smaller than the orifice they protect. Parietal pores, when developed, in the outer layer only. Basis membranous. Each branchia is composed of two plicated folds. Living attached to marine vertebrates.

This group of genera was recognized by Leach and Gray, but they included *Chelonibia* with the whale barnacles. Darwin eliminated *Chelonibia*, showing that its resemblance to the others is merely adaptive and superficial. We owe to him a discussion of the morphology of the group so lucid that no subsequent student has been able to add anything of importance. Darwin did not consider the group of enough systematic importance for subfamily rank; but systematic values throughout zoology have risen, and the group is now generally held to be a subfamily. Professor Gruvel has separated *Xenobalanus* as another subfamily, Xenobalaninæ; but while this genus shows great modification, it is essentially Coronulid, with many characters in common with *Tubicinella*. It appears to me that its affinities are obscured by segregating it in a separate subfamily. The number of genera of Coronulinæ has been doubled since Darwin's monograph was published.

It is somewhat remarkable that with the exceptions of *Coronula*, *Platylepas*, and possibly *Stomatolepas*, all of the genera of Coronulinæ are monotypic.

The wall in Coronulinæ is essentially poreless; or at least there are no pores homologous with those of the Balaninæ, which arose, as already explained, by the concrescence of lateral processes on internal ribs. In many Coronulinæ there are pores in the *outer* layer of the parietes, which are wholly independent in genesis from those of *Balanus*, and apparently were formed by the deepening and closing over of external striæ.

The body-chamber of the shell has the conic form of more normal Balanidæ only in the genus *Platylepas*. In other genera the chamber is cylindric or contracted at the base, reducing the size of the membranous basis. A basis of large area would doubtless be pressed inward by the skin of the host.

The genera of Coronulinæ form two collateral series, indicating an early split in the stock. The differences between the two series, as well as nearly all those characterizing the genera, are adaptive, being directly related to the modes of strengthening the shell to withstand impacts.

In the Coronulid series the parietes have no median sulcus or change of sculpture, and there is never any trace of props or midribs projecting into the body chamber; the oral borders of the integument are produced, forming a "hood." The species are singularly conservative in the selection of hosts. They are known only from Cetacea.

The Platylepadid series is composed of genera having a midrib within each compartment, produced by a median infolding; or when this is not present there is externally a median longitudinal smooth area, or interruption of the sculpture, which may be regarded as the vestige of a former mesial infolding which has left this permanent mark upon the external sculpture after the fold itself has utterly disappeared. So far as known there is no oral "hood." In the selection of hosts the species show catholic tastes. While chiefly (and probably in the beginning) turtle barnacles, they also live on mammals (Sirenia), sea-snakes, and fishes, but not one has yet been found on a cetacean.

The genera of these two series follow, closely related groups being bracketed together.

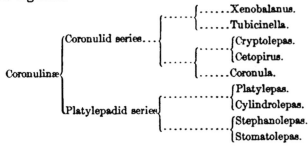

KEY TO GENERA OF CORONULINÆ.

a^1. Body lengthened, having the appearance of a naked pedunculate cirripede, not contained in the cavity of the wall, which is minute, star-shaped, and embedded in the skin of the host. Opercular valves wanting.
--*Xenobalanus*, p. 282.

a^2. Body contained in the cavity formed by the walls; opercular valves present.

  b^1. Parietes having similar sculpture throughout, the median part not longitudinally sulcate, smoothed, or otherwise differentiated from the rest of the parietes; compartments without internal midribs. Whale barnacles.

    c^1. Wall of the body-chamber having external radial ribs or folds, visible at least on the base; radii well developed, triangular.

      d^1. Radiating ribs having T-shaped terminal loops which unite to form an outer and upper wall__*Coronula*, p. 271.

      d^2. Radiating ribs not forming an outer wall; sheath transversely grooved_____*Cryptolepas*, p. 278.

    c^2. Tubular, annulate, without longitudinal ribs; radii narrow; opercular valves well developed_____*Tubicinella*, p. 281.

  b^2. Parietes not sculptured evenly throughout, but having a longitudinal sulcus, smooth area, or change in the direction of the sculpture, or having midribs in the compartments within. Turtle, manatee, and snake barnacles.

    c^1. Basal edges of the compartments ribbed or toothed.

      d^1. Form conic, the orifice decidedly smaller than the basis; each compartment having a midrib within, serving to support the basis; inner and basal edges acutely ribbed_____*Platylepas*, p. 284.

d^2. Form cylindric (hexagonal), the orifice and basis of
equal size; basal edges of compartments having small
teeth, the median one largest____*Cylindrolepas*, p. 287.

c^2. Orifice much larger than the basis; basal edges of compartments
simple.

d^1. Cup-shaped, subspherical or shortly cylindric, the
parietes with annular ridges interrupted in the middle
of each compartment by a smooth longitudinal area;
inner edges of the compartments not forming a lobed
rim around the orifice_____*Stephanolepas*.[1]

d^2. Bowl-shaped, with a cellular outer layer; inner layer
of each compartment forming a thin, rounded lobe at
the orifice_____*Stomatolepas*, p. 288.

CORONULID SERIES. *Borders of the mantle produced around the
oral opening to form a hood over the cirri; plates of the wall without
a median longitudinal sulcus or impression. Living on Cetacea.*

Genus CORONULA Lamarck.

1802. *Coronula* LAMARCK, Annales du Muséum Nationale, vol. 1, p. 464,
for *Balanus diadema, Balanus balænaris,* and *Balanus testudinarius.*

1817. *Diadema* SCHUMACHER, Essai d'un nouveau Système Vers Testacés,
p. 90; monotype, *D. vulgaris = Lepas diadema* Linnæus.

1817. *Diadema* RANZANI, Opuscoli Scientifici, vol. 1, fasc. 4, p. 276. No
species mentioned.[2]

1817. *Cetopirus* RANZANI, Opuscoli Scientifici, vol. 1, fasc. 4, p. 276. No
species mentioned.[2]

1825. *Polylepas* Klein, GRAY, Annals of Philosophy, new ser., vol. 10, p. 105
(*P. diadema* here selected as type).

1833. *Coronulites* PARKINSON, Organic Remains of a Former World, vol. 3,
p. 240; monotype, *C. diadema* Parkinson (=*C. barbara* Darwin?).

1852. *Polylopas* Klein. MÖRCH, Catalogus Conchyliorum quæ reliquit D. A.
d'Aguirra et Gadea, Comes de Yoldi, p. 66; monotype, *P. diadema.*

1852. *Ceteopirus* Ranzani, MÖRCH, Catalogus Conchyliorum quæ reliquit
D. A. d'Aguirra et Gadea, Comes de Yoldi, p. 67; monotype, *C. complanatus* Chemnitz.

1854. *Coronula* DARWIN, Monograph, p. 397.

1895. *Flabelcorona* DE GREGORIO, Annales de Géologie et de Paléontologie,
17 livraison, p. 5; monotype, *Coronula (Flabelcorona) ficarazzensis*
De Gregorio.

Barnacles with six equal compartments around the small body-
chamber, the parietes bearing four radiating lamellar folds, simple
or branching, and terminating in T-shaped flanges, which, being in
close contact, form an outer wall and inclose cavities open below, occupied by the skin of the host. Radii wide. Basis membranous. Oper-

[1] *Stephanolepas* will not be considered further in this work, since the single species is
not contained in the collection of the National Museum. For description see H. Fischer,
Actes de la Société Linnéenne de Bordeaux, vol. 40, 1886, p. 193. Further notes and figures
are given by A. Gruvel, Nouvelles Archives du Muséum, ser. 4, vol. 5, 1903, p. 149. Type
and sole species *S. muricata* Fischer, Pulo Condor, Cochin China, in the interstices of the
dermal plates of *Thalassochelys imbricata.*

[2] In his paper of 1818 Ranzani supplied types to the genera proposed in the previous
year. He described *Cetopirus balænaris* (=*Coronula complanata*), and *Diadema candidum*
(=*Coronula diadema*). No other species of these genera were mentioned.

cular valves much smaller than the orifice of the shell, the terga vestigial or absent, scuta connected by a chitinous ligament. Oral borders of the opercular integument projecting hood-like.

Type—Coronula diadema (Linnæus).

*Distribution—*All seas; living on whales. .

The whale barnacles are admirably adapted to resist the impacts incident to their station, the radially symmetrical and buttressed wall being ideally constructed for strength. The morphology of *Coronula* has been discussed by Darwin with characteristic insight and clarity. It will suffice here to direct attention to the fact that the partitions seen in the base are not homologous with the parietal septa of *Balanus*, but with external parietal ribs. These ribs are narrow, much lengthened, and looped T-like at the ends, thus forming an external wall, analogous to the fly of a tent. The cells partitioned off by the ribs, and filled by the skin of the whale, are therefore external to the barnacle, though inclosed except on the bottom by processes of its walls.

Further features of note are the minute longitudinal striæ of the parietes, producing beads where they cross circular ripples or wrinkles; a structure common also to *Tubicinella* and *Platylepas.* The hood-like oral border of the sack, shown in plate 65, figure 4, occurs also in *Xenobalanus, Tubicinella,* and *Cryptolepas.*

C. diadema lives only slightly embedded in the skin, and it very frequently affords support to the stalked barnacle, *Conchoderma auritum. C. reginæ* is about one-fourth or more covered by the skin, or in other words, the edges of the barnacle cut into and embed themselves in the skin of the host. Coronulæ are disliked by whalers because they dull the knives used in "cutting in."

C. diadema is a common and long known barnacle, but *C. complanata,* while known since 1705 or earlier, is comparatively rare in collections, and we have little information as to its distribution, and none upon its station or soft anatomy. *C. reginæ* has been the rarest species, as no author except Darwin seems to have seen it; but we now know that its station is on the lip of the humpback whale, in both the North Atlantic and the North Pacific Oceans. It is probably not very rare, though being inconspicuous it has not often been collected.

KEY TO SPECIES OF CORONULA.

a^1. Body-chamber shaped like a teacup, the orifice much larger than the basal opening; sheath running nearly to the base of the inner wall; branches of the sutural ribs not symmetrically arranged, the ribs sometimes without branches; opposed sides of the terminal flanges of the ribs crenulated; radii less than half the thickness of the compartments, leaving a cavity between radii and alæ. Subgenus *Coronula.*

b^1. Crown-shaped, elevated, the parietes convex, with convex ribs.

C. diadema, p. 273.

b^2. Convexly conic, depressed, the parietal ribs flat, beautifully beaded; ribs in the base having few, not symmetrical branches_____$C.\ reginœ$, p. 275.

a^2. Body-chamber very shortly barrel-shaped or cylindric, the basal opening at least as large as the orifice; sheath decidedly shorter than the inner wall, its basal edge not overhanging; ribs along the sutures, in the base, having several symmetrically arranged branches in adult individuals; radii almost as thick as the compartments; opposed edges of the terminal flanges of the ribs roughened but not crenulate; form depressed. Subgenus *Cetopirus*.

$C.\ complanata$, p. 276.

Pliocene species of Coronula.

Coronula barbara Darwin (Monograph, p. 421), of the British Red Crag, is related to *C. diadema*, but the spaces below the radii are solidly filled up.

Coronula bifida[1] has not been very clearly distinguished from *C. barbara*.[2] *Diadema diluviana* O. G. Costa[3] appears from the figures to be either *C. bifida* or *C. barbara*.

Coronula ficarazzensis De Gregorio, referred to above under the perfectly useless subgenus *Flabelcorona*, is a form very close to *C. reginœ* Darwin; whether identical or not requires a comparison of specimens to tell.

CORONULA DIADEMA (Linnæus).
Plate 65, figs. 3, 4.

1767. *Lepas diadema* LINNÆUS, Systema Naturæ, ed. 12, p. 1109 (see Hanley, The Shells of Linnæus, p. 20).

1776. *Lepas balœnaris* O. F. MÜLLER, Zoologiæ Danica Prodromus, p. 250, No. 3024.

1778. *Balanus balœna* DA COSTA, Hist. Nat. Test. Brit., p. 251.

1780. *Lepas balœnaris* O. FABRICIUS, Fauna Grœnlandica, p. 425.

1790. *Lepas balœnaris* GMELIN, Systema Naturæ, ed. 13, p. 3208.

1817. *Diadema vulgaris* SCHUMACHER, Essai d'un nouveau Syst. Vers Testaces, p. 91.

1818. *Diadema candidum* RANZANI, Opuscoli Scientifici, vol. 2, p. 88.

1818. *Coronula diadema* Linnæus, LAMARCK, Hist. Nat. Anim. sans Vert., vol. 5, p. 387.

1825. *Polylepas (Diadema) kleinii* GRAY, Annals of Philosophy, new ser., vol. 10, p. 105.

——. *Coronula diadema* Lamarck, CHENU, Illustration Conchyliologiques, pl. 1, fig. 3; pl. 2, fig. 3; pl. 3, fig. 5.

1854. *Coronula diadema* Linnæus, DARWIN, Monograph, p. 417, pl. 15, figs. 3, 3a, b; pl. 16, figs. 1, 2, 7.

1870. *Coronula biscayensis* VAN BENEDEN, Bull. de l'Acad. Roy. des Sci. des Lettres, et des Beaux-Arts de Belgique, ser. 2, vol. 29, p. 349. No description.

1870. ? *Diadema japonica* VAN BENEDEN, Bull. de l'Acad. Roy. des Sci. des Lettres, et des Beaux-Arts de Belgique, ser. 2, vol. 29, p. 354. Named, but not described, from a Japanese drawing.

[1] Bronn, Italiens Tertiär-Gebilde, 1831, p. 126.
[2] de Alessandri, Palæontographica Italica, vol. 12, 1906, p. 315.
[3] Di alcuni Balanidi app. al Regno di Napoli, in Atti Accad. Sci. Napoli, vol. 5, pt. 2, 1843, p. 120, pl. 1, fig. 7.

1870. *Diadema californica* Van Beneden, Bull. de l'Acad. Roy. des Sci. des Lettres, et des Beaux-Arts de Belgique, ser. 2, vol. 29, p. 355. No description.

1874. *Coronula diadema* Linnæus, Scammon, The Marine Mammals of the Northwest Coast of North America, p. 47, pl. 10, fig. 5.

1897. *Coronula diadema* Linnæus, Weltner, Verzeichnis, Archiv für Naturgeschichte, vol. 1, p. 254 (distribution).

1900. *Coronula diadema* Linnæus, Weltner, Fauna Arctica, vol. 1, p. 302 (distribution).

1903. *Coronula diadema* Linnæus, Stead, Proc. Linn. Soc. New South Wales, vol. 28, p. 944 (on Balænoptera, off Cavalli I., N. Z.).

The barnacle is crown-shaped, or formed like a short cask, having convex ribs, crossed by narrow, minutely beaded rugæ, the opposed lateral edges of the ribs not crenated. Radii very broad, and seen to be very much thinner than the compartments, leaving a large space filled by branches of the ovary between the radii and alæ, visible only when the compartments are separated. Orifice very much larger than the basal opening. Terga wanting, or rarely present as minute vestiges.

Diameter, 86 mm.; height, 67 mm (Tonga Island).

Diameter, 75 mm.; height, 59 mm. (Monterey, California).

Diameter, 63 mm.; height, 31 mm. (Unalaska).

Diameter, 44 mm.; height, 36 mm. (Unalaska).

Diameter, 57 mm.; height, 36 mm. (Bering Sea).

The lamellar parietal folds or ribs branch much less freely than in *C. complanata*. Individuals up to 45 mm. in diameter and evidently adult sometimes have all of the ribs simple, though usually some are forked. The branches appear first on the rostral sides of the sutures; they are not symmetrically developed on both sides of the sutures, as in *C. complanata;* nor are the branches arranged symmetrically on the two sides of the barnacle. As a general rule, the more spreading individuals have more branches, thus keeping the buttresses evenly spaced at the periphery.

The elaborately denticulated radii (pl. 65, fig. 3), are much wider than in *C. reginæ*, but they leave a far larger cavity than in *C. complanata.*

Only a small part of the total height of the barnacle is embedded in the skin of the whale. They are often seated upon it about as close as they can stand. One piece of dried whale skin in the United States National Museum, 26 inches long and averaging nearly 5 inches wide, supports 118 individual Coronulas of all sizes.

This is the common whale-barnacle of the Northern Hemisphere. It is the "whale louse" of the humpback whales, *Megaptera.* I have found no record of it from other genera of whales. In the Arctic and Atlantic I have seen specimens from Spitzbergen and Disco south to St. Bartholomew, but it is certainly much less abundant southward.

There are no records from the equatorial and southern Atlantic, Antarctic, or Indian Oceans.

In the Pacific *C. diadema* is widely spread from Bering Sea, Japan, and California south to New Zealand, Tonga,. and Chili—practically the whole Pacific Ocean.[1]

Dr. W. H. Dall notes that " this species has been obtained from the Humpback (*Megaptera versabilis*) from Bering Strait to the Gulf of California. It is especially abundant on the flippers and on the underlip of these animals." Captain Scammon in his interesting book on Marine Mammals has given a figure of the humpback whale showing the areas chiefly infested with barnacles—the underlip and throat, front edges of the fins, and the flukes. The opercular membrane in the living barnacle is brown, the " hood " slightly purplish.

Locality.	Collector.	Notes.
Godhaven, Disco Island, Greenland.........		
Shetland Islands..........................	J. G. Jeffreys..............	
Snooks Arm, Newfoundland...............	F. W. True.................	On lip of humpback; alcoholic.
Nova Scotia..............................		
St. Bartholomew, West Indies.............		
Bering Island............................	L. Stejneger...............	
Igognak Point, Unalaska..................	Wm. H. Dall...............	
Unalaska................................	....do.....	On *Megaptera versabilis* Cope.
Alaska..................................	Mrs. E. H. Harriman.......	
Neah Bay, Wash........................	J. G. Swan..............	
Mouth of Umpqua River, Oreg...........	Doctor Holbrook...........	In alcohol.
Near Pigeon Point, Cal..................	Stanford University........	From whale; in alcohol.
Monterey, Cal...........................	Taylor...................	
Do.................................	Captain Scammon..........	On humpback.
Magdalena Bay, Lower California..........	*Albatross*	Dry and in alcohol.
Tonga Island............................	Ward's natural science establishment.	
(No locality)............................	Vinal Edwards.............	On whale skin; in alcohol.
(No label)..............................		On whale skin.

CORONULA REGINÆ Darwin.

Plate 64.

1854. *Coronula reginæ* DARWIN, Monograph, p. 419, pl. 15, fig. 5; pl. 16, fig. 4.

Distribution.—Northern Atlantic and Pacific Oceans, on humpback wales (*Megaptera*).

Shell convexly-conic or depressed-conic, with flattened parietal ribs having crenated edges and beautifully striated and granulated surfaces (pl. 64, figs. 1, 3). Radii not exceeding one-fifth the thickness of a compartment (pl. 64, fig. 1). Body-chamber cup-shaped, the basis much smaller than the orifice. Ribs in the base branching irregularly, as in *C. diadema*, not symmetrically on both sides of the sutures as in *C. complanata*. Terga wanting.

Diameter 65 mm.; height 19 mm. (Unalaska).

[1] Weltner has materially enlarged our knowledge of the southern range of this barnacle, from the rich series in the Berlin Museum.

Diameter 48 mm.; height 19 mm.

Diameter 53 mm.; height 13 mm.

By its depressed contour and the flattened ribs of the upper surface this species has a superficial resemblance to *B. complanata*,[1] but the narrow radii with a large cavity under them, the crenulated edges of the terminal flanges of the ribs, and their irregular branching, and especially the shape of the body chamber, are characters certainly allying it to *C. diadema*. The sculpture is remarkably delicate. From one-fourth to one-third of the whole diameter is embedded in the skin of the whale, so that the barnacle projects very little. The oral opening has a "hood" as in *B. diadema*.

It was supposed by Darwin to be a Pacific species, but the only definite locality he had was Iquique, Peru, on Mr. Cuming's authority. Mr. Gruvel gives the locality Chonos Archipelago, Chile, for a single example in the Paris Museum. It occurs on the lip and perhaps other parts of the whale where the skin is thin and light colored. It appears to be perfectly distinct from both of the old species. About 20 specimens seen.

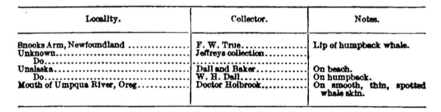

Locality.	Collector.	Notes.
Snooks Arm, Newfoundland	F. W. True.................	Lip of humpback whale.
Unknown...................................	Jeffreys collection..........	
Do.		
Unalaska..................................	Dall and Baker.............	On beach.
Do.	W. H. Dall.................	On humpback.
Mouth of Umpqua River, Oreg.............	Doctor Holbrook...........	On smooth, thin, spotted whale skin.

CORONULA COMPLANATA (Mörch).

Plate 63, figs. 1, 2, 3, 3*a*.

1790. *Lepas balenaris* SPENGLER, Skrivter af Naturhistorie-Selskabet, vol. 1, p. 187.

1802. ? *Coronula balænaris* DUFRESNE, Annales du Muséum Nationale, vol. 1, p. 473, pl. 30, figs. 2–4.[1]

1818. *Cetopirus balænaris* RANZANI, Opuscoli Scientifici, vol. 2, p. 87.

1818. *Coronula balænaris* LAMARCK, Hist. Nat. des Animaux sans Vertèbres, vol. 5, p. 387.

1823. ? *Lepas quinquevalvis* MAWE, The Linnæan System of Conchology, p. 5, pl. 2, fig. 3.[2]

1824. *Coronula balanarum* BLAINVILLE, Dictionaire des Sciences Naturelles, vol. 32, p. 380 (obvious error for *balænaris*).

---

[1] It is quite possible that the figures published by Dufresne as *C. balænaris* are really *C. reginæ*; but their identity would have no effect upon nomenclature.

[2] I have been unable to decide whether *Lepas quinquevalvis* Mawe is *C. complanata* or *C. reginæ*, as the upper view, when partly covered with the whale's skin, shows no clearly diagnostic features in the drawing. The specific name must be dropped as indeterminate. This individual and a specimen of *Chelonibia testudinaria* mentioned by Darwin (Monograph, p. 384, footnote) are the only cases I have seen recorded of the abortion of one compartment in any sessile barnacle. They seem singularly exempt from meristic variations.

1825. *Polylepas (Cetopirus) vulgaris* GRAY, Annals of Philosophy, new
ser., vol. 10, p. 105, based upon *Coronula balænaris* Lamarck. Not
Diadema vulgaris Schumacher, 1817.

1848. *Coronula balænaris* Lamarck, KRAUSS, Die Südafrikanischen Mollusken, p. 135 (Table Bay).

——. *Coronula balænaris* CHENU, Illustrations Conchyliologiques, pl. 2,
figs. 1, 4; pl. 3, figs. 1–4.

1852. *Ceteopirus complanatus* Chemnitz, MÖRCH, Catalogus Conchyliorum,
Comes de Yoldi, p. 67.

1854. *Coronula balænaris* DARWIN, Monograph, p. 415, pl. 15, figs. 2–2b;
pl. 16, figs. 3, 5.

1910. *Coronula darwini* STEBBING, Annals of the South African Museum,
vol. 6, pl. 4, p. 572, based upon *C. balænaris* Darwin.

Distribution.—Amboina (Rumphius); New South Wales (Darwin); South Africa (Krauss, Darwin); West Africa and Valparaiso
(U. S. N. M.); Coquimbo and coast of Norway (Paris Museum).

C. complanata differs from the other recent species by the broad
base of the body-chamber and the very thick radii, in which the beautifully laminate edge covers almost the whole sectional area of the
compartment, while in the others the laminate edge is restricted, and
there is a hollow below it occupied by branches of the ovaries. (See
pl. 63, figs. 3, 3a). The terminal flanges of the parietal ribs do not have
crenulated edges. The parietal ribs bordering the sutures seen in the
base bear several branches in large specimens, usually symmetrical on
the two sides of each suture, having a tree-like or candelabral appearance; the two intermediate ribs of each compartment being simple or
forking near the end. Externally the ribs are flattened and subdivided. Near the periphery they are crossed by narrow close wrinkles,
which are beaded by the fine radial striæ. The contour varies, but I
believe it is rarely if ever so high as the lowest *C. diadema.*

Greatest diameter 74 mm.; height 28 mm.

Greatest diameter 53½ mm.; height 12 mm.

Greatest diameter 33 mm.; height 14 mm. (compressed young specimen).

The scuta are contiguous, small; terga much smaller.

I have seen a considerable series of this species, but only three lots
bear locality data. One in the collection of the Academy of Natural
Sciences, Philadelphia, is labeled California, but as it was purchased
in London many years ago, the label is probably apocryphal. One
of the lots in the United States National Museum is labeled West
Africa, and another is in a box with the label Valparaiso, but these
specimens have been in the collection many years, and the collector
is not stated. I can not find that any definite records have been published since Darwin's Monograph, except those given by Gruvel for
specimens in the Paris Museum, from collectors of the first half of the
last century.

Mr. Stebbing has shown that Darwin followed Lamarck and others blindly in using the name *balænaris* Gmelin for this species. That name was introduced by Müller in 1776 for a Danish form identical with *C. diadema*. Gmelin's account was wholly compiled from Fabricius, who gave an excellent and unmistakable description of *C. diadema*, under the name *Lepas balænaris*. Lamarck in 1802 first used the name *balænaris* for the present species, mentioning *Balanus balænaris* as one of the species of his new genus *Coronula*,[1] though he did not make this perfectly clear until 1818. Mörch, the Danish conchologist, ascribed the name *complanatus* to Chemnitz, who had given a description and characteristic figures;[2] but Chemnitz was heterodox in his nomenclature, and therefore Mörch must be given as sponsor for the name. The type-specimen is that figured by Chemnitz. The name *C. balanarum* Blainville seems to me to have been merely a careless slip for *balænaris*, for we can hardly suppose that so scholarly a naturalist would intentionally coin a false and inapplicable name to replace an appropriate one which was certainly well known to him. All codes of nomenclature provide for the elimination of such obvious errors.

Genus CRYPTOLEPAS Dall.

1872. *Cryptolepas* DALL, Proceedings of the California Academy of Sciences, vol. 4, p. 300.

Depressed Coronulinæ with the body-chamber shortly cylindric, the parietes bearing radial lamellar folds which are irregularly branched in adults, and are not united into a continuous wall at the ends and above; sheath grooved transversely; radii moderately developed; basis membranous. Opercular valves and oral hood as in *Coronula*.

Type.—*C. rachianecti* Dall.

Distribution.—North Pacific, living embedded in the skin of the California gray whale, *Rhachianectis glaucus* Cope.

Cryptolepas is very closely related to *Coronula*, more especially to *Coronula* (*Cetopirus*) *complanata*, which is similar in the contour of body-chamber and exterior; but the present genus differs by lacking terminal flanges uniting the radial lamellæ into a solid outer wall, though there is sometimes a suggestive approach to that structure. The number of radial lamellæ or folds is greater than in *Coronula;* there are four complete and two (sutural) half folds on each compartment, as a rule, but exceptional individuals have the number reduced by one or two folds. The branches of the lamellæ

---

[1] Ann. du Mus., vol. 1, p. 464.

[2] "*Lepas complanata polythalamia. Balanus polythalamius complanatus,*" CHEMNITZ, Systematisches Conchylien Cabinet, vol. 8, 1785, p. 325, pl. 99, figs. 845, 846.

are irregular in occurrence and arrangement, and many of them do not reach the periphery. Finally, the sheath is grooved transversely, as in *Tubicinella* and *Xenobalanus.*

With the exception of the grooves of the sheath, nearly all of these differences from *Coronula* are degenerative changes apparently correlated with the protected station of the animal embedded in the skin of the host. An outer wall is no longer needed. The branches of the ribs, which in *Coronula* serve as buttresses, have become short and extremely variable. In fact, the form and size of the ribs themselves vary remarkably. The increase in number of parietal ribs or folds over that in *Coronula complanata* probably took place through the accelerated branching of sutural folds, bringing the lower branches down to the circumbasal border, where they appear as primary folds. The circumstances are similar in many phyletic series of shells, in which external ribs become emarginate, then bifid, and finally separate ribs.

It may be concluded, therefore, that *Cryptolepas* is a derivative of the *Cetopirus* branch of *Coronula* and that its differential characters are mainly due to the degeneration of protective and strengthening structures, now useless because of its deep embedment in the skin of the host.

But one species of *Cryptolepas* is known. *Cryptolepas ophiophilus* Krüger is a member of the genus *Platylepas.*

CRYPTOLEPAS RACHIANECTI Dall.

Plate 66, figs. 1–5a.

1872. *Cryptolepas rachianecti* DALL, Proc. California Academy of Sciences, vol. 4, p. 300.
1874. *Cryptolcpas rachianecti* DALL, in SCAMMON, The Marine Mammals of the Northwestern Coast of North America, p. 22, pl. 10, fig. 6.
1903. *Cryptolepas rachianectis* Dall, GRUVEL, Nouvelles Archives des Muséum, ser. 4, vol. 5, p. 153, pl. 2, figs. 4–10; pl. 3, figs. 10, 11.
1905. *Cryptolepas rachianectis* Dall, GRUVEL, Monographie des Cirrihipèdes, p. 274, fig. 299.

Type.—Cat. No. 9192 U.S.N.M., from Monterey, California.

Distribution.—Bering Island to Lower California; Hawaiian Islands.[1]

The barnacle is almost wholly embedded in the whale's skin, "usually on the head and fins," only the opercular membrane and parts of the radii or sometimes the more prominent ribs being exposed. When the skin is removed, four to six ribs are seen on each compartment above. These ribs are denticulate along both sides. In basal view the ribs are seen to be loops of the wall, as in *Coronula.*

[1] The last locality is given on the authority of Professor Gruvel, who found specimens in the Paris Museum.

They are finely striate vertically and crenulated at the basal edges. In young specimens the ribs are simple, but in old ones they branch more or less freely, most of the branches not reaching to the periphery. Normally there are 30 ribs and 30 lobes of the basal margin of the body-chamber. Rarely an individual may have one or more compartments with only three or four loops of the inner wall, with branches parallel with and close to the upper side, so that an incomplete outer wall, analogous to that of *Coronula*, is formed.

In section it is seen that the inner wall is very dense and solid, but has a friable outer layer, which is closely porous, and which forms the greater part of the substance of the ribs.

The radii are as thick as the compartments and their edges are intricately sculptured with crimped sutural laminæ (pl. 66, figs. 5, 5a). The sheath is transversely grooved, a little shorter than the body-chamber, and its lower margin is not overhanging or prominent.

The scuta are juxtaposed as in *Coronula*. Their upper layers scale off. Terga very small.

" Color of membranes, when living, sulphur yellow; hood extremely protrusile."

It is excessively variable in size, proportion of diameter to height, and shape of the ribs or lamellæ, which may be short, with a rounded (semicircular) outline, or long, and triangular in outline. The ribs may have many or very few branches. Apparently adult individuals measure as follows:

Greatest diameter, 55 mm.; height, 15 mm.
Greatest diameter, 49 mm.; height, 16 mm.
Greatest diameter, 37 mm.; height, 18 mm.

In young specimens the shape is that of a thick disk with rounded periphery, and the folds are simple. At all stages their free edges are beautifully crenulated.

Plate 66, figure 3 represents the usual appearance in the skin of the whale, the hood contracted. In figures 2, 2a the lateral compartment of a cylindric individual, with very short parietal ribs, is drawn. The usual forms have the wall triangular (fig. 5) or irregularly convex (fig. 5a) in section. Figures 1, 3, 4 are top views, 1a, 4a basal views.

The porous, friable texture of the radial lamellæ make this barnacle extremely hard to disengage from the skin of the whale. Probably the best way would be to macerate fresh specimens, or have them cleaned by ants or *Dermestes*. After being in alcohol the whale skin becomes extremely hard and tough, and treatment with caustic soda loosens part of the lamellæ, besides separating the compartments.

Upon the opercular membrane, and especially in the shallow cavities of the eroded radii, one often finds the little parasite *Cyamus* clinging.

According to Dr. W. H. Dall:

This species is found sessile on the California gray whale, *Rhachianectis glaucus* Cope. I have observed them on specimens of that species hauled up on the beach at Monterey for cutting off the blubber, in the bay whaling of that locality. The superior surfaces of the lateral laminæ, being covered by the black skin of the whale, are not visible; and the animal removed from its native element—protruding its bright yellow hood in every direction, to a surprising distance, as if gasping for breath—presented a truly singular appearance.

U.S.N.M. Cat. No.	Locality.	Collector.	Notes.
14312 14313	Bering Island.............	Grebnitzky...........	
11609	Neah Bay, Wash.............. California...............	Lockington...........	On gray whale.
12040	....	Chas. H. Townsend...	
9192	Monterey, Cal...............	Wm. H. Dall.........	Dry collection.

Genus TUBICINELLA Lamarck.

1802. *Tubicinella* LAMARCK, Annales du Muséum Nationale, vol. 1, p. 461.
1854. *Tubicinella* Lamarck, DARWIN, Monograph, p. 430.

Shell tubular, wider at the top in adults, composed of six equal compartments, belted by several or many rounded ridges, the parietes longitudinally striated, the outer layer porose; radii narrow; sheath nearly as long as the tube, marked with circular grooves; lower layer of the opercular membrane lining the shell nearly to the base; opercular valves four, rather large.

Type.—Tubicinella major Lamarck.

Tubicinella may be described as an elongated *Coronula* without radial ribs. It is also related to *Xenobalanus* by the very long opercular membrane. It lives embedded nearly to the top in the skin of the whale. With growth the shell and opercular valves wear off at the top, so that the length of an adult individual represents but a small part of the shell formed during growth.

TUBICINELLA MAJOR Lamarck.

Plate 65, fig. 5.

1802. *Tubicinella* (*major*), and *Tubicinella* (*minor*) LAMARCK, Annales du Muséum, vol. 1, p. 463, pl. 30, fig. 1.
1806. *Lepas trachealis* SHAW, Shaw and Nodder's Naturalist's Miscellany, vol. 17, pl. 726.
1815. *Lepas tracheæformis* WOOD, General Conchology, p. 31, pl. 4, figs. 1–3.
1818. *Tubicinella anulata* RANZANI, Opuscoli Scientifici, vol. 2, p. 89.
1818. *Tubicinella balænarum* LAMARCK, Anim. sans Vert., vol. 5, p. 385.
1821. *Tubicinella balænae* OKEN, Naturgeschichte für Schulen, p. 659.
1824. *Tubicinella lamarckii* LEACH, Encycl. Brit. Suppl., vol. 3, pl. 57 (not seen).
1824. *Coronula tubicinella* Lamarck, BLAINVILLE, Dict. des Sci. Nat., vol. 32, p. 380, pl. 117, fig. 5.

1854. *Tubicinella trachealis* Shaw, DARWIN, Monograph, p. 431, pl. 17, figs. 3a–3c.

1900. *Tubicinella trachealis* MARLOCH, Trans. South African Philos. Soc., pp. 1–6, figs. (mode of growth).

1903. *Tubicinella trachealis* Shaw, GRUVEL, Deutsch Südpolar-Expedition, 1901–1903, vol. 11, p. 216.

1910. *Tubicinella "striata* Lamarck" STEBBING, Annals of the South African Museum, vol. 6, p. 573.[1]

Of the three specimens contained in the United States National Museum, one is labeled Isle of France, Isaac Lea collection. The others, without data, are rather remarkable for the wide spacing of the annuli. That shown in plate 65, figure 5, is 50 mm. long, 17¼ mm. in greatest diameter. The series in the collection of the Academy of Natural Sciences in Philadelphia is without locality. I do not know that it has been found on any whale in North American waters. Darwin gives the localities: Southern Pacific Ocean, western South America, New South Wales, Cape of Good Hope. Gruvel, Marloch, and Stebbing have given South African localities. It lives on the southern right whale *Balæna australis*, on the upper jaw, forehead, and over the eye.

In the year 1650, specimens of *Tubicinella* were observed on the head of a whale found dead on the coast of Syderoe, one of the Faroe Islands, according to Doctor Olao Worm, who gives two characteristic figures in his Museum Wormianum, page 281, published in 1655. This is the only reference I have found to the occurrence of *Tubicinella* in the Northern Hemisphere.

Genus XENOBALANUS Steenstrup.

1851. *Xenobalanus (globicipitis)* STEENSTRUP, Videnskabelige Meddelelser fra den naturhistoriske Forening i Kjöbenhavn, pl. 3, figs. 11–15.

1852. *Xenobalanus* STEENSTRUP, Oversigt over det Kongelige danske Videnskabernes Selskabs Forhandlinger, Februar, 1852, pp. 158, 161.

1852. *Siphonicinella* (Darwin), STEENSTRUP, Oversigt over det Kongelige danske Videnskabernes Selskabs Forhandlingar, Februar, 1852, p. 160.

1852. *Xenobalanus* STEENSTRUP, Videns. Meddel., p. 62.

1852. *Siphonicella* DARWIN, Monograph on the Lepadidæ, p. 156.

1854. *Xenobalanus* DARWIN, Monograph on the Balanidæ, p. 438.

It is described by Darwin as having " shell almost rudimentary, star-formed, composed of six compartments; with a long peduncle-formed body rising from the middle; opercular valves none."

This animal has a striking superficial resemblance to *Conchoderma (Otion) auritum*, which is also found on cetacea, though never attached directly to the skin.

---

[1] Mr. Stebbing has, in my opinion, taken the first word of Lamarck's *diagnosis* for a specific name. That the words inclosed in parentheses in Lamarck's paragraphs are the real specific names is demonstrated by his following paragraph, where he says that " Le citoyen Faujas * * * m'a dit que le *tubicinella major* a été découvert dans les mers du sud de l'Amérique."

The morphology of *Xenobalanus* has been very fully discussed by Darwin, who has demonstrated its relationship to other Coronulinæ, and especially to *Tubicinella*. He writes:

In the shell the affinity is almost equally close to *Coronula* and *Platylepas*, but considering the whole animal, the affinity is somewhat closer to *Tubicinella*. *Xenobalanus* may indeed be described as a *Tubicinella* without opercular valves—with the opercular membrane thickened down to the basis—and with the shell, excepting the few last-formed basal zones of growth, almost wholly removed by the breakage of its upper end; this remnant of a shell, however, presenting some strong points of resemblance to *Coronula*.

The tendency toward degeneration of the opercular valves, noticeable in *Coronula*, culminates in *Xenobalanus*, where they are entirely wanting; but the hoodlike borders of the oral orifice are developed more than in the other genera.

XENOBALANUS GLOBICIPITIS Steenstrup.

Plate 65, figs. 2, 2a, 2b.

Distribution.—Northern Atlantic, near the Azores between Madeira and England, and the Faroe Islands; New England, on the fins of the blackfish, *Globiocephalus*.

It is described by Darwin as follows:

General appearance.—The shell is in an almost rudimentary condition, and appears like a small white irregular star, embedded up to its top in the skin of the porpoise. Out of this thin, star-shaped shell a cylindrical flexible, peduncle-formed body springs, which forms the main part of the animal; it is narrow where coming out of the central cavity of the star, but soon acquires its full diameter; at the upper end it has a reflexed hood, and hence is broader, and this has the appearance of forming a capitulum, like that of a pedunculated Cirripede. This pseudo-capitulum is formed by a membranous reflexed collar or hood, which is very narrow at the lower end of the orifice, close under the mouth, and becomes wider and wider toward the upper and carinal or posterior end of the orifice; hence the lower reflexed edge of the hood is only slightly oblique or even nearly transverse. The orifice leading into the sack is large and nearly in the same straight line with the peduncle; it is a little hollowed out in the middle at the upper end, and on each side of this medial hollow there is a small, rounded projection or horn, not perforated, but hollow, as may be seen by turning up the hood and looking at its under side. These two little horns curiously bring to mind the ear-like appendages in *Conchoderma aurita* (*Otion*), but these latter are perforated, open into the sack, and point outward. The peduncle-formed body answers, as we shall presently see, to the main part of the shell in *Tubicinella*, and the hood, as it would appear, to the lips of the sack-aperture, which project between its scuta and terga; of these valves there is not here a trace. The whole surface is smooth and is formed by rather thin membrane of an orange color; but from the color of the underlying corium the whole appears of a dark chocolate red, the reflexed hood being rather lighter colored.

The part forming the hood apparently answers to the protuberant lips of the operculum, and the lower part to the subcylindrical shell of *Tubicinella;* both shell and peduncle in the two genera being wider at top than at bottom.

If in imagination we chip away (an action always in progress) the whole upper part of the shell of *Tubicinella*, leaving only two or three zones of growth at the base, we shall convert it into a *Xenobalanus*, with every internal part and organ occupying the same relative position; for it should be borne in mind that the shell of *Tubicinella* is lined close down to the basis by the opercular membrane, and this is strictly comparable with the outer membrane of the pseudo-peduncle of *Xenobalanus*. The body, as in *Tubicinella*, is attached in a vertical position, with the longer axis of the thorax and of the much elongated prosoma extending in the direction of the longitudinal axis of the pseudo-peduncle.

So far as I can see, the American specimens do not differ from European. The color (in alcohol) is nearly black, and the ordinary length is from 30 to 40 mm. They grow in close groups. The localities represented in the United States National Museum are North Dennis and Woods Hole, Massachusetts, on the tips of the flippers of *Globiocephalus intermedius*, and *Albatross* station 2424, 36° 41′ 37″ north latitude; 74° 42′ 15″ west longitude, on porpoise.

A form which may be called variety *pallidus* is represented by a group of similar individuals, No. 2390, from the Fish Commission, 1875, labeled in Professor Verrill's hand " from tips of flippers of *Globiocephalus intermedius*." The locality is doubtless New England. They are light buff on one side, tinted with russet on the other. Length 43 mm., diameter of shell 5 mm. (pl. 65, fig. 1).

PLATYLEPADID SERIES. *Oral opening not protected by a hood. Each of the wall compartments has a median longitudinal sulcus or impression.*

Genus PLATYLEPAS Gray.

> 1825. *Platylepas* GRAY, Annals of Philosophy, new ser., vol. 10, p. 105, monotype *P. pulchra* Gray (=*P. bissexlobata* Blainville, according to Darwin).
>
> 1832. *Columellina* BIVONA, Effemeridi Sci. e Lit. Sicilia, type *C. bissexlobata*, pl. 3, fig. 1 (not seen).
>
> 1854. *Platylepas* Gray, DARWIN, Monograph, p. 424.

Form conic, the base being decidedly larger than the orifice. Compartments six, each bilobed, at least inwardly, and produced so as to form six midribs, which support the outwardly convex, membranous basis. Sheath short. Basal and inner edges of parietes sharply ribbed. Opercular valves occupying the whole length of the orifice, their upper surfaces scaling off with growth.

Type.—*P. hexastylos* (Fabricius).

Distribution.—Tropical and warm temperate seas, partly embedded in turtles, manatees, sea-snakes, and fishes.

This genus consists, at present, of four species, of which only one can be considered at all well known. The others are known by single or very few lots. The essential feature of *Platylepas* is that its membranous basis is supported by proplike midribs formed by the infolded median parts of the parietes. These props also support the low dome of the wall, which without them would easily be stove in by the impacts incident to its station on turtle shells. In other embedded barnacles the base is smaller relative to the size of the body-chamber. In some species the outer layer of the parietes is permeated with minute pores, as in many other *Coronulinæ*.

Only *P. hexastylos* is known from eastern American waters. The other species described are:

Platylepas decorata Darwin,[1] Galapagos Islands, etc.

Platylepas ophiophilus Lanchester,[2] Malay Peninsula, on the sea-snake *Enhydris curtus*.

Platylepas krügeri, new name for *Cryptolepas ophiophilus* Krüger.[3] Bangkok, Siam, on the sea-snake *Distira;* Gwadar, Beluchistan, on the tail of *Hydrophis*.

Though rather incompletely described, this species seems to be quite distinct from *P. ophiophilus* Lanchester and *P. decorata* Darwin. It certainly is not a *Cryptolepas*.

PLATYLEPAS HEXASTYLOS (O. Fabricius).

Plate 67, figs. 1–1c, 3.

1798. *Lepas hexastylos* O. FABRICIUS, Skrivter af Naturhistorie-Selskabet, vol. 4, Heft 2, p. 35, pl. 10, figs. 1, 2.

1824. *Coronula bisexlobata* DE BLAINVILLE, Dictionaire des Sciences Naturelles, vol. 32, p. 379, pl. 117, fig. 1 (republished in Manuel de Malacologie, p. 600, pl. 86, fig. 1).

1825. *Platylepas pulchra* GRAY, Annals of Philosophy, new ser., vol. 10, p. 105 (Corsica).

1825. "*C. bisexloba* Ranz," GRAY (not of Ranzani), Annals of Philosophy, new ser., vol. 10, p. 105.

——. *Coronula californiensis* CHENU, Illustrations Conchyliologiques, pl. 1, fig. 4 (sur les Cétacés, Californie).

1854. *Platylepas bisexlobata* DARWIN, Monograph, p. 428, pl. 17, figs. 1a–1d. (Mediterranean, on turtles; River Gambia and Honduras, on manatee; Moreton Bay, Australia, "apparently attached to the dugong of that coast").

1884. *Platylepas bisexlobata* Blainville, P. FISCHER, Bull. Soc. Zool. de France, vol. 9, p. 359 (New Caledonia, on *Halicore dugong*).

1903. *Platylepas bisexlobata* Blainville, GRUVEL, Nouv. Ann du Muséum, ser. 4, vol. 5, p. 151, pl. 3, fig. 13 (Sicily; type of *Coronula concentrica* Valenciennes MS.).

1912. *Platylepas bisexlobata* (de Blainville) KRÜGER, Abhandl. K. Bayer. Akad. Wissensch., Suppl.-Bd. 2, 8 Abhandl., p. 13 (Timor Sea, on *Chelone imbricata*).

Type.—Probably lost; from the Mediterranean.

---

[1] 1854, Monograph, p. 429.
[2] Proc. Zool. Soc., London, 1902, pt. 2, p. 371; pl. 35, figs. 5–5b.
[3] 1912, Abhandlungen der math.-phys. Klasse der K. Bayer, Akademie der Wissenschaften, Suppl.-Bd. 2, 8 Abhandl., p. 12, figs. 6–10; pl. 3, figs. 7, 8.

Distribution.—Tropical and subtropical seas, on turtles (*Caretta caretta* and *Thalassochelys imbricata*); also on the African and American manatees, the dugong, and a variety on *Lepisosteus*.

The barnacle is much depressed and broadly oval or circular; orifice oval. Each compartment is divided by a median radial sulcus, which does not reach to the orifice in small individuals. Surface elegantly sculptured with close concentric ridges, and sometimes (especially where worn) showing fine radial striæ. The outer layer is permeated by fine pores. Radii rather narrow, transversely crenulated near and at their edges. Basal and inner margins sharply septate. Sheath not over half the length of the compartments, hollowed out beneath. Each compartment bears an internal buttress or prop, the membranous basis being stretched over them.

Darwin says of it:

Scuta oblong, about twice as long as broad, with the rostral end rounded, rather narrower than the other end, and curled a little inward. Terga of nearly the same shape and nearly as long as the scuta; the carinal end is rather more pointed than the scutal end of the valve, and when viewed internally, the growing surface of this end is seen to be bluntly pointed. In both valves the upper layers of shell usually scale off.

The distribution of this species is wide, as would be expected from the wandering habits of the sea turtles it lives upon. Moreover, it appears to have a variety of hosts. All of the localities I have seen reported are given in the reference paragraphs above. So far as I know, it has not been reported from our west coast except by Chenu, an authority of no great weight.

There is a series of the typical form, agreeing well with Fabricius's figures, in the collection in the Academy of Natural Sciences from Osprey, Florida, taken from *Caretta caretta* by Mr. Baker (pl. 67, fig. 3). They measure up to 17 mm. in diameter. In profile view the base is seen to be as convex as the upper surface in most small examples, but less so in the larger. I took a series of smaller specimens from a loggerhead turtle captured in Delaware Bay (pl. 67, figs. 1–1c). The form is very much depressed; diameter, 9 to 10½ mm. The median sulci of the exterior are far less sharply impressed than in the Florida examples, and the sharp septa within the basal edge are longer. Both of these peculiarities, as well as the considerable length of the internal props, may be due to immaturity, but from the worn condition and nearly uniform size of the largest examples, I imagine that they are full grown, and represent a slightly different race.

Of the synonyms cited above, the names *hexastylos*, *bisexlobata*, *californiensis*, and *concentrica* were based upon the depressed form figured in plate 67, figure 3, and are therefore, I believe, exactly synonymous. *P. pulchra* Gray has not been described, but Darwin, who had seen the type, placed it in the synonymy of *U. bisexlobata*.

Darwin seems to have included barnacles varying a good deal in shape in this species, though the existing descriptions and illustrations give only an inadequate idea of the forms seen by him. There is a small individual in the Isaac Lea collection, United States National Museum, from Sicily, which probably represents a subspecies (pl. 67, fig. 4). It has steep, convex sides, deep median clefts in the compartments, but the internal midribs are slender and project but little. The septa are very numerous, sharp, and close; greatest diameter, 8.5 mm.; height, 4.8 mm. From the appearance of this barnacle I suspect that it did not live on the shell of a turtle. There is some orange-colored skin adhering in the furrows of the lower part of the parietes.

P. h. ichthyophila, new variety, plate 67, figure 2. Specimens taken by Mr. Joseph Willcox from a *Lepisosteus* caught in brackish water in Hernando County, Florida, are small, very thin, and delicate, oval or rounded, 7 to 8 mm. in diameter. The rugæ of growth are reduced, and on some compartments absent. Median sulci of the compartments shallow, probably on account of immaturity. The internal midribs or props are more slender than in *P. hexastylos*, scarcely sculptured. Internal septa of the edge *much less numerous* than in *hexastylos*, and projecting toothlike at the edge. There are four or five principal septa on each side of the midrib in the rostrum (pl. 67, fig. 2).

So far as I know this is the only record of a barnacle attached to a fish. It was identified as *Platylepas decorata* Darwin by Dr. John A. Ryder.[1]

CYLINDROLEPAS, new genus.

Form cylindric, the orifice and base of equal size; bases of the compartments obtusely dentate, the median tooth of each compartment larger, slightly inflected; sheath very long, not quite reaching to the base. Basis and opercular valves as in *Platylepas*. Living embedded up to the orifice in the skin of turtles.

By its deep embedment and small size this barnacle resembles *Stephanolepas*, but it differs by the strictly cylindric shape and the denticulation of the bases of the compartments; *Stephanolepas* being cup-shaped, the base much smaller than the orifice, and the basal edge not dentate. The prominent midribs of the compartments of *Platylepas* are represented in *Cylindrolepas* by slight prominences of the basal borders—vestigeal structures, now useless in consequence of the altered shape of the barnacle. Unlike *Platylepas*, the sheath is nearly as long as the compartments.

Type.—Cylindrolepas darwiniana, new species.

[1] American Naturalist, vol. 13, July, 1879, p. 453

CYLINDROLEPAS DARWINIANA, new species.

Plate 68, figs. 3–3b.

Type.—No. 2057 A.N.S.P.

Locality.—West Indies? embedded in the skin (not the shell) of sea turtles (Robert Swift).

The barnacle is hexagonal, the carinorostral diameter a little larger than the lateral, of about equal diameter from base to summit; whitish, with fine sculpture of close transverse wrinkles, and on the carina and carinolateral compartments a few low, coarse vertical ribs. The compartments when isolated are square. Their summits are beveled and polished, apparently by wear. A median fold or filled sulcus is indicated on the polished summit by a small depression filled with the softer and dull substance of the outer layer; and on some compartments a slight, mesial sulcus is visible externally. The radii are represented by narrow sulci; their edges are distinctly septate. The lower edges of the compartments have about three short, vertical, blunt teeth on each side of a larger median tooth, which bends slightly inward, and is homologous with the prop or midrib in typical forms of *Platylepas*. The sheath is delicately striate transversely, and stops a little short of the basal edges of the compartments. The scuta are in contact with the terga, and together they stretch from end to end of the orifice. Carinorostral diameter, 4 mm.; lateral diameter, 3.8 mm.; height, 3 mm. Some individuals are slightly larger, greatest diameter 5.3 mm.

These barnacles were in the collection of Robert Swift, one time United States consul in St. Thomas. His collection was almost wholly of West Indian mollusks—few, if any, from any other region. He also collected West Indian barnacles. It is likely therefore that this species, which had no locality, was found in the West Indies. In any case, the species differs so widely from those described that it should be easily recognized.

The specimens of *Cylindrolepas* were embedded in a very hard yellowish substance showing but little structure. Dr. Thomas Barbour, of the Museum of Comparative Zoology, to whom I applied, concluded that it is the salt-water cured, sun-dried skin of either a loggerhead or green turtle, probably from between the neck and flippers or around the base of the tail.

On account of its small size and deep embedment *Cylindrolepas* is likely to escape notice. It may turn out to be common and widely distributed.

Genus STOMATOLEPAS Pilsbry.

1910. *Stomatolepas* PILSBRY, American Naturalist, vol. 44, p. 304.

Wall bowl-shaped, the orifice far larger than the base; compartments six, sulcate down the middle, with the outer layer composed of imbricating calcareous scales arranged in chevron pattern; inner layer projecting above, finger-nail like, beyond the outer, its basal edge thin and simple; sheath very long, transversely grooved, without a distinct lower edge. Opercular valves long and narrow, thin, the outer layer not deciduous. Basis membranous.

Type.—Stomatolepas prægustator.

Station.—In the mucous membrane of the gullet of sea turtles.

Stomatolepas and *Stephanolepas* form a little division in the group of turtle barnacles, characterized by the simple, thin basal edges of the compartments, which are without teeth, ribs, or laminæ. The presence of an external shallow median sulcus in each compartment shows that their ancestors were *Platylepas*-like barnacles, since this sulcus is doubtless the vestige of an infolding of the wall. The elaborate sculpture of the exterior of *Stomatolepas* seems to be a development of the sculpture of *Platylepas*, which is formed of concentric wrinkles cut into beads by radial striæ. In *Stomatolepas* the wrinkles assume an oblique direction and the beads are prolonged to form scalelike processes.

STOMATOLEPAS ELEGANS (O. G. Costa).

Plate 68, figs. 2, 2a.

1838. *Coronula elegans* Costa, Di alcuni Balanidi app. al Regno Napoli, 1838 (p. 17 of separate copy), in Atti Accad. Sci. Napoli, vol. 5, 1843, pt. 2, p. 117, pl. 1, figs. 1, 2, 3.

1839. *Chelonibia elegans* Costa, Fauna del Regno di Napoli, Cirropedi, p. 14.

Distribution.—Taranto, Italy, the host unknown.

It is described by Costa, as follows:

Coronula with the tube conic-truncate, prominent areas bipartite, elegantly scrobiculate, the scales coriaceous, depressed areas smooth, internal lamina having naillike projections. Opercular valves four, smooth, subequal; color orange. Breadth 4 lines, altitude 2 lines.

I am giving copies of Costa's description and figures in order to direct attention to this lost species, which will probably be found again in the throat of sea turtle. I suspect that it may be identical with *S. prægustator*, yet the differences in the color and the external sculpture of the parietes, *if not due to careless drawing*, may indicate a distinct species.

STOMATOLEPAS PRÆGUSTATOR Pilsbry.

Plate 68, figs. 1, 1a, 1b.

1910. *Stomatolepas prægustator* Pilsbry, American Naturalist, vol. 44, p. 304, fig. 1.

Type.—Cat. No. 1851 A.N.S.P., from Tortugas, Florida, partially embedded in the mucous membrane of the upper end of the gullet of *Caretta caretta*. Edwin Linton.

General form is that of a broad, shallow bowl, the diameter of the base about half that of the oral orifice. The inner layer of the compartments is thin, white and glossy, and projects well above the outer layer, the upper ends of the compartments being smooth, sharp, and arched. The outer layer is chamois colored, and scaly. There is a groove down the middle of each compartment, and a triangular smooth area, where the outer layer is wanting, at the base. A slight ridge encircles the wall above the middle, marking the limit of the portion of the barnacle embedded. The scaly surface is produced by delicate ribs bearing series of flat lobes or digitations, the ribs being arranged *en chevron* on each compartment, and the lobes or scales of one rib imbricating upward over the bases of the next. Upon the upper-part, above the encircling ridge, the scales are larger and arranged in nearly horizontal rows.

The sheath covers fully two-thirds the height of the compartments, is glossy, white, and regularly grooved transversely. Its lower edge is continuous with the smooth inner surface. The basal edges of the wall plates are thin and smooth.

The basis is entirely membranous and flat.

Rostrocarinal diameter, 6.7 mm.; lateral diameter, 6 mm.; height 3 mm.

The opercular valves protect less than half the area of the orifice, but extend nearly its whole length. They are very thin, glossy, white, and smooth both outside and within. They are long and narrow, the terga in contact with the scuta but not articulated or interlocking in any way. The scuta are longer than the terga, tapering to a point at the rostral end, obliquely rounded at the tergal end.

Costa's paper of 1838, describing and figuring *Coronula elegans*, was not contained in our library at the time I described *Stomatolepas*, and his species has never been mentioned by any other author so far as I know. While it seems likely that the Mediterranean and American forms are specifically the same, there are certain differences which influenced me to leave them apart until an actual comparison of Mediterranean examples can be made with our form. Costa describes *elegans* as orange in color, but this might be on account of the dry tissues of the host adhering to the barnacle. His figure shows the parietes evenly scaled, while in our form the squamation of the upper part differs rather conspicuously from the lower portion. This would be an important distinction if confirmed, but it might easily be due to insufficient observation on the part of Costa's artist.

Family CHTHAMALIDÆ.

1854. *Chthamalinæ* Darwin, Monograph, p. 446.

Sessile barnacles in which the walls are not porous; *the rostrum has alæ;* or when concrescent with the rostrolateral compartments, the composite plate has radii, or overlaps the lateral compartments. The rostrolateral compartments (when not fused with the rostrum) are without alæ on either side. The labrum has a *concave, not notched edge,* and is often swollen or " bullate " externally. The lower angle of the mandible is pectinated. The cirri of the third pair resemble the fourth and later pairs of cirri, or are of intermediate character between the second and fourth.

Every Balanoid barnacle in which both rostrum and carina have alæ belongs to this family; but it includes also one genus—*Pachylasma*, with the satellite or subgeneric groups *Hexelasma* and *Bathybalanus*—in which some species have the rostrolateral compartments wholly concrescent with the rostrum in the adult stage, thus having a wall like that of *Balanus*.

This family is more primitive than the Balanidæ, and in most of its departures from Balanid organization it approaches or is like the *Lepadomorpha*. The labrum is like that of Verrucidæ and the pedunculate groups; also the mandibles and to a less extent the maxillæ. The third pair of cirri is like the succeeding pairs, and not, as in Balanidæ, modified to resemble the second pair. Caudal appendages are often present (never in Balanidæ). The rostrolateral compartments are often retained as separate plates, but in Balanidæ they are always concrescent with the rostrum.

The genera differ a good deal in the degree in which old characters, such as the caudal appendages, have been retained. Advance has been in the simplification of the wall by reduction of the number of compartments. In *Catophragmus* all of the compartments of the ancestral *Balanomorpha* may be presumed to be present. In *Octomeris* the outer whorls have been lost, leaving eight. Two phyletic series lead from this point: (1) *Pachylasma* and *Hexelasma*, culminating in a hexamerous wall, and (2) *Chthamalus* and *Chamæsipho*, the latter tetramerous.

There has been parallel and of course totally independent reduction of wall-compartments in the two families Balanidæ and Chthamalidæ, as shown in the following table, in which the leading genera of both families are grouped to show the number of compartments and the relationship within each series:

	8 compartments with accessory plates.	8 compartments.	6 compartments.	4 compartments.	4 compartments concrescent into one.
Chthamalid series.	Catophragmus.	Octomeris.	Hexelasma. Pachylasma. ...... Chthamalus...	Chamæsipho.	
Balanid series.		Chelonibia.	Balanus. Poreless Balani. Coronulinæ.	Tetraclita. Elminius. Creusia........	Pyrgoma.

Structurally, the Chthamalidæ stand between the Balanidæ and the pedunculate cirripedes, but the most primitive members now existing of the two families are as unlike as the highest in essential structure. In fact, the nearest approximation is found in some of the more evolved members of each series, such as *Pachylasma* and *Balanus*—forms which have been similarly remodeled. The common ancestor of the two families may be presumed to be a Mesozoic genus approximating *Catophragmus* or *Octomeris* in structure of the wall.

Chthamalidæ are very rare as fossils, but it is evident that they arose well down in the Mesozoic. *Chthamalus darwini* Bosquet of the upper cretaceous is a typical species, so far as the walls are concerned, and *Hexelasma* appears in a gigantic species in the Miocene. As neither of these can be considered primitive, it is obvious that the family has had a long history. Indeed, it is probably now decadent. Characteristics suggesting this view are the strikingly discontinuous distribution of the species of most of the genera; the small number of species and their strong differentiation. These peculiarities are most marked in the most primitive and presumably oldest genera. *Chthamalus*, a relatively evolved genus, is the only one which is generally distributed. The others have the appearance of disconnected fragments lingering like *Limulus*, the Dipnoi, or the struthious birds, from an earlier time of wider distribution. As yet there is no palæontological evidence for this view.

In the stations chiefly occupied by Balanidæ—that is, from low-water mark to the edge of the continental shelf, at about 100 fathoms—the Chthamalidæ seem to have been almost crowded out of the race. *Chthamalus*, the only prolific and generally distributed genus, mainly inhabits a higher zone on the shore than *Balanus*. *Pachylasma* and the closely related *Hexelasma* are mainly inhabitants of deep water, where *Balanus* is rare. Other genera have very few species. Only two species of *Octomeris*, two of *Chamæsipho*, and two of *Catophragmus*—all very local and most of them rare— inhabit the shore zone, where they compete with *Balanus* and, more especially, *Tetraclita*.

We owe the establishment of this family solely to the taxonomic genius of Darwin, who first brought the genera together and demonstrated their relationships. I have examined and dissected many more species, I suppose, than anyone else, and I find all of the evidence supports Darwin's views. I have not found any facts favoring Professor Gruvel's distribution of the genera into the three families Octomeridæ, Hexameridæ, and Tetrameridæ, among Balanid genera.

KEY TO GENERA OF CHTHAMALIDÆ.

a^1. Four compartments, the carina and rostrum having alæ; sutures more or less obliterated _____*Chamæsipho.*[1]

---

[1] This genus is not contained in the United States National Museum.

a^2. Six compartments.

b^1. Rostrum having alæ like the carina, the adjacent rostrolateral compartment without alæ on either side_____*Chthamalus* (p. 293).

b^2. Rostrum overlapping the adjacent lateral compartments, which have alæ on the rostral side.

c^1. Basis calcareous.

d^1. Compartments, except the carina, having distinctly differentiated radii _____*Bathybalanus*.[1]

d^2. Radii wanting or not distinctly differentiated from the parietes.

Pachylasma (p. 327).

c^2. Basis membranous, at least in the center; no radii___*Hexelasma* (p. 329).

a^2. Eight compartments at least.

b^1. Rostrum and rostrolateral compartments closely united by linear sutures _____*Pachylasma* (p. 327).

b^2. Rostrolateral compartments as distinct as the others; rostrum with alæ.

c^1. No accessory compartments outside the eight composing the wall.

Octomeris (p. 334).

c^2. Wall surrounded with short accessory compartments outside.

Catophragmus (p. 334).

Genus CHTHAMALUS Ranzani.

1817. *Chthamalus* RANZANI, Opuscoli Scientifici, vol. 1, p. 276 (no species mentioned.)

1818. *Chthamalus* RANZANI, Opuscoli Scientifici, vol. 2, p. 83 (for *C. glaber* and *C. stellatus*).

1837. *Euraphia* CONRAD, Journ. Acad. Nat. Sci. Philadelphia, vol. 7, p. 261, monotype *E. hembeli*.

1854. *Chthamalus* Ranzani, DARWIN, Monograph, p. 447.

Compartments six; rostrum similar to the carina in being provided with alæ; rostrolaterals triangular, without alæ, the sheath having a narrow projection. Carinolaterals wanting. Basis membranous or covered with a calcareous layer formed of the inflected basal edges of the compartments.

Labrum with the concave or straight edge toothed or hairy. Mandible with the lower part pectinated. First two pairs of cirri short, densely spinose, the third pair much longer and bearing spines like those of the later pairs.

Type.—Chthamalus stellatus (Poli).

*Distribution.—*Nearly world wide, in the littoral zone.

Chthamalus is one of the most distinct genera, really forming a subfamily of the Chthamalidæ, distinguished by the persistence of the rostrolaterals as distinct compartments and the loss of carinolaterals. It differs essentially, therefore, from other hexamerous Chthamalidæ, in which the rostrolaterals are concrescent with the rostrum, and the carinolaterals persist as separate compartments. The shape of the rostrolateral compartments, which have no alæ, is extremely characteristic of the genus (pl. 73, fig. 2e; pl. 75, fig. 1).

---

[1] This genus is not contained in the United States National Museum.

The *Chthamali* are exclusively littoral barnacles, many of them living higher up the beach than most Balani. They rarely, if ever, live below low tide. They are usually attached to stones, other barnacles, and molluscan shells, but I have seen one species on rushes, evidently from some inside bay or passage. Sometimes they occur on other barnacles attached to floating objects. The walls and valves are particularly subject to corrosion, owing partly to their exposure to the buffets of the surf, partly to the unusually large amount of animal matter they contain—chitinous films and pores occupied by filaments from the mantle. This corrosion obscures the external characters so much that scarcely any sample can be identified without a deliberate examination of the opercular valves. Even these are subject to great alterations in outline, the effect of erosion of their outer layers. In corroded individuals the sutures of the opercular plates form a figure the shape of the Greek letter Ψ.

The valves and compartments of alcoholic or fresh specimens may be isolated and cleaned under the dissecting microscope, but dry samples must be boiled or soaked in caustic potash to free them of the adherent tissues. After that I have found it convenient to mount the opercular valves with glue or mucilage on slips of black card, so that they may be examined under the microscope without risk of loss—nearly all of them being diminutive objects of only a few millimeters' extent.

Taking the characters of the mouth parts and cirri into account, and making due allowance for distortion and corrosion, and the frequent tendency to become cylindric, the species are not very hard to determine, after one becomes accustomed to *Chthamali*, except in the group of forms typified by *C. stellatus*, and widely spread in the Atlantic and communicating seas, and in the oriental seas. I believe that the definition and full illustration of a number of subspecies will materially simplify the study of this group, and a partial revision has been attempted. A very large amount of oriental material must still be collected and overhauled before we can claim to have a fairly complete knowledge of the tropical Indo-Pacific species.

Thanks to their paltry and insignificant appearance, *Chthamali* are apt to be overlooked, and our collections would be much poorer than they are were it not that they may often be found on the larger barnacles and shells in museums.

The supposed difficulty of the genus has probably deterred naturalists from undertaking serious study of the group. Only one recent species has been described in more than 60 years since Darwin's monograph appeared.

I have not seen *C. dentatus* Krauss (South Africa), or *C. stellatus* var. *depressa* Poli (Mediterranean, etc.). *C. antennatus* Darwin is in the collection of the Academy of Natural Sciences from Richmond,

Victoria. *C. ligusticus* De Alessandri, of the Italian Pliocene and *C. darwini* Bosquet, of the upper Cretaceous of Vaels, Belgium, are fossil species not known to me by specimens. All other described species are in the United States National Museum and are noticed below.

With the exception of the Hawaiian *C. hembeli*, all of the species are small, rarely exceeding 12 or 15 mm. in diameter, and more often half that size. They are generally conic or depressed, but sometimes cylindric. The opercular valves are deeply locked or mortised together. The tergum never has a long or distinctly formed spur.

In many species of *Chthamalus* the terminal segments of the second pair of cirri have one or several broad or lanceolate spines with conspicuously serrate edges, as in figures 82*b*, *e*. I have not dissected enough individuals of any one species to determine the value of these spines as specific characters. They may perhaps vary with the age of the individual. They are somewhat similar to the spines from the first two pairs of cirri of *Mitella* figured by Krüger, and supposed by him to have a sensory function. This appears to me doubtful. Throughout the Balanomorph cirripedes one often notices that some of the spines become delicately pinnate toward the end, but I have not noticed such a specialization of this structure in any genus but *Chthamalus*.

In the maxilla the spines are arranged in three groups: An upper group of two or three large and several small spines, followed by a notch; a middle group partly of rather large spines, and a lower group of mainly smaller spines. The species differ among themselves in the number and length of the hairs on the upper and lower borders of the maxilla and in the shape of the spinose edge, but with a few exceptions the maxillæ are a good deal alike throughout the genus.

The mouth parts and cirri of *Chthamalus* deserve a much more extended examination than I have been able to find time for.

The modifications of the mandible, etc., may be found to give the best characters for subdivisions of the genus, but its structure is unknown in some of the species, so that I have been unable to use these characters in the key to species. There are two main groups:

I. Mandible having four teeth followed by an even, comblike row of narrow spines, below which the lower extremity is trispinose. The upper tooth is much larger than the other three; the third and fourth are usually bifid at the tips. Spines of the lower extremity are usually unequal.

 a¹. Spines between the fourth tooth and lower point are very numerous, narrow, and crowded. (See p. 303, fig. 84*d*.)

  b¹. Cirrus iii with one ramus far longer and more slender distally than the other_____*C. cirratus*.

  b². Rami of cirri iii not very unlike: *C. stellatus*, *C. s. angustitergum*, *C. fragilis*, *C. dalli*, *C. anisopoma*, *C. challengeri*, *C. scabrosus*.

a^2. Spines between the fourth tooth and lower point are fewer, comparatively coarse, and distinct, easily counted (fig. 90)_____*C. malayensis.*

II. Mandible having three large teeth and a broad lower extremity set with many spines, which are largest at the end, decreasing above and below it.

    a^1. Without caudal appendages.

        b^1. Anterior ramus of cirrus III much longer than posterior, with spines in circles on the distal segments_____*C. antennatus.*[1]

        b^2. Third pair of cirri much longer than second, second pair having coarsely pectinated terminal spines_____*C. dentatus.*[1]

        b^3. Third pair of cirri having a few basal segments thickly covered with spines, like the second pair_____*C. intertextus.*[1]

        b^4. Maxilla and cirri normal_____*C. withersi* (fig. 91).

        b^5. Maxilla densely crowded with subequal spines. Posterior ramus of cirrus II long, like the following cirri; dense short tufts between the spines of the later cirri_____*C. hembeli* (fig. 97).

    a^2. Having long caudal appendages_____*C. caudatus* (fig. 92).

KEY TO SPECIES OF CHTHAMALUS.

The keys for the determination of specimens constructed by Hoek and Gruvel from Darwin's descriptions will not work in actual practice. Gruvel's key is workable with the most perfect specimens, but not with much of the material one encounters, since the characters used are often corroded away. The following key is highly artificial and not very satisfactory:

a^1. Very large, solid and strong, with zigzag sutures; base calcareous in adults; tergal margin of the scutum longer than the basal_____*C. hembeli* (p. 324).

a^2. Smaller, diameter usually 5 to 15 mm.; not so strong.

    b^1. Right and left opercular valves very unlike in size and shape.

                                C. anisopoma (p. 317).

    b^2. Opercular valves nearly or quite alike on the two sides in normal specimens.

        c^1. Interior of a uniform very dark (purplish) color.

            d^1. Interior rich violet, the basal margin inflexed; sutures, when unworn, of interfolded laminæ. Tergum very narrow in the lower half, calcified to the scutum_____*C. intertextus* (p. 324).

            d^2. Interior blackish violet, without basal ledge; sutures simple. Tergum narrow, with a short, rounded spur, not calcified to the scutum, which has a very low articular ridge and no pits for the muscle-insertions_____*C. imperatrix* (p. 320).

        c^2. Interior not uniformly very dark.

            d^1. Adductor ridge of scutum distinct.

                e^1. Tergum broad in the lower part, its basal margin not distinctly sinuated below the depressor crests.

                    f^1. Tergum triangular, equilateral; tergal margin of the scutum short, its adductor ridge small_____*C. fissus* (p. 317).

                    f^2. Tergum longer than wide; tergal margin of scutum longer, the adductor ridge long and strong_____*C. dalli* (p. 316).

---

[1] I have not dissected *C. scabrosus, C. antennatus, C. dentatus,* or *C. intertextus,* included in the above table, the details being taken from Darwin. As none of the mandibles have been figured, it is possible that some of these species are incorrectly grouped.

e². Tergum narrower in the lower half, the basal margin distinctly sinuated or incurved below the depressor muscle crests.
   f². Crests of the tergum on a little plate raised from the valve; sutures interfolding when perfect_____C. scabrosus (p. 323).
   f³. Crests of tergum normal; sutures simple___C. challengeri (p. 307).
d². Scutum without a distinct adductor ridge.
   e¹. Greatest prominence of articular ridge of the scutum below middle of tergal margin, its lower end abruptly truncate.
      f¹. Occludent margin of scutum making a right angle with edge of articular ridge; tergum very broad above, triangular, its basal margin not sinuated below the crests_____C. stellatus (p. 301).
      f². Occludent margin of scutum making less than a right angle with the tergal margin.
         g¹. Tergum triangular, broad above, the basal margin straight.
            C. antennatus Darwin.
         g². Basal margin of tergum distinctly sinuated below the crests.
            h¹ Tergum very narrow and thick___C. s. augustitergum (p. 305).
            h². Tergum moderately narrow, having a long furrow next to the crests_____C. s. bisinuatus (p. 306).
            h³. Tergum wide above, narrow at the base.
               C. s. punctatus (p. 304).
            h⁴. Tergum wide at the base_____C. moro (p. 311).
   e². Greatest prominence of the articular ridge of the scutum about median or above, the lower end gradually sloping.
      f¹. Sutures zigzag.
         g¹. Exterior ribbed_____C. dentatus (p. 294).
         g². Exterior nearly smooth_____C. caudatus (p. 314).
      f². Sutures simple.
         g¹. Tergum broad and rounded at base; wall usually not corroded, smooth or with rounded ribs_____C. fragilis (p. 297).
         g². Tergum almost equally wide above and below, with an external furrow; adductor scar of scutum deep__C. panamensis (p. 319).
         g³. Tergum narrow in the lower half.
            h¹. Scutum slender, its greatest width about half the length, the tergal and basal margins about equal; articular ridge very small; tergum triangular in section____C. withersi (p. 312).
            h². Tergal margin of scutum decidedly shorter than the basal.
            C. malayensis (p. 310) ; C. cirratus (p. 321).

ATLANTIC AND MEDITERRANEAN SPECIES.

CHTHAMALUS FRAGILIS Darwin.

Plate 70, figs. 1 to 4.

1854. *Chthamalus stellatus* var. *fragilis* DARWIN, Monograph, p. 456, pl. 18, fig. 1d.
1909. *Chthamalus stellatus* var. *fragilis* Darwin, SUMNER, Science, vol. 30, pp. 373-374.

Type.—British Museum, from Charleston, South Carolina, on oysters.

Distribution.—West Indies, and on the mainland north to Woods Hole, Massachusetts.

The barnacle is conical, rounded or oblong, thin, smooth, or with rounded ribs, not eroded, or but very slightly worn, covered with a thin cuticle; compartment easily separable from one another and from the surface of attachment; radii developed, narrow. Color very light bluish gray or olive brown.

Carinorostral diameter, 5 mm.; lateral diameter, 3.5 mm. Carinorostral diameter, 5.5 mm.; lateral diameter, 3.3 mm.

Scutum rather broad, the apical angle less than a right angle; the articular ridge has a rounded outline, *gradually tapering downward* and upward. The adductor muscle pit is smaller than in *stellatus*, but deep; its tergal margin is straight and very slightly

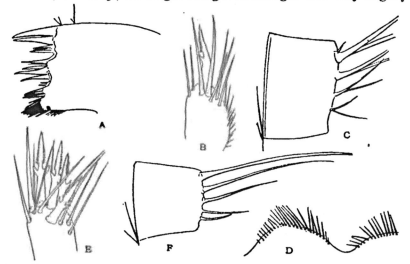

FIG. 82. — CHTHAMALUS FRAGILIS. *a*, MAXILLA. *b*, TERMINAL SEGMENT OF SHORTER RAMUS OF CIRRUS II. *c*, ELEVENTH SEGMENT OF CIRRUS VI. *d*, PART OF THE LABRUM, ALL FROM ALBATROSS STATION 2004. *e*, TERMINAL SEGMENT OF SHORTER RAMUS OF CIRRUS II, OCEAN CITY, N. J. *f*, CHTHAMALUS STELLATUS, NAPLES, TENTH SEGMENT OF CIRRUS VI.

raised, so that there is the trace of an adductor ridge in some specimens. The exterior has conspicuous but very low growth-ridges, and usually a fine longitudinal striation.

Tergum not varying much from that of typical *stellatus*, except that on account of the nearly perfectly preserved scutal margin, the articular ridge appears less prominent. There is a short, rounded and broad spur, decidedly more developed and broader than in *stellatus*.

The labrum is strongly concave in the middle, and on both sides the edge is spinose (fig. 82*d*).

The mandibles, palpi, and maxillæ do not differ materially from those of *C. stellatus*, figured on page 303.

Cirrus i has slightly unequal rami of 7 and 6 segments, armed with simple spines. Cirrus ii has slightly unequal rami of 7 and 5 segments. In a specimen from station 2004 the terminal tuft of spines on each ramus contains one broad, serrate spine with a pair of large teeth (fig. 82b). The specimen dissected from Ocean City has rami of 9 and 6 segments, the terminal tufts having several serrate spines (fig. 82e), and there are others of less characteristic shape on several of the later segments.

The cirri iii to vi have segments with four pairs of spines (fig. 82c).

This species differs from *C. stellatus* by its smoother wall, usually covered with an epidermis, by the shape of the articular rib of the scutum, and the much broader lower part of the tergum. In the specimen of *stellatus* I dissected there are no such strongly modified spines on the second cirri, and the later cirri have five pairs of spines, *fragilis* having four.

The specimens growing on rushes (pl. 70, figs. 1–1d, 4) are usually elongated, and sit with the carinorostral axis lengthwise of the rush. In hundreds examined, the parietes are never ribbed.

In a group on an oyster (*Ostrea parasitica* Gmelin) from Varadero Park, near Cardenas, Cuba, collected by Dr. J. W. Ross, the contour is usually shorter and the surface is either smooth or furnished with round radial ribs. There are also transitional forms. The scutum has a longer basal and shorter tergal margin than in the Florida examples on rushes, and the opercular valves are beautifully rose colored inside. Exterior dull olive or olive brown, not corroded, length 6, width 5 mm. (pl. 70, figs. 3–3c). I did not examine the mouth parts and cirri.

Another group, on a pebble from Charlotte Amalie, St. Thomas, collected by Mr. Silas L. Schumo, consists of smaller but similar specimens.

A large series from Jamaica (C. B. Adams) is on the shell of an *Atrina*, and on broken coconut shells. They agree with the Cuban lot in form and color and are mainly smooth, but with some individuals having low, rounded ribs. The opercular valves are white within, but otherwise like the Varadero Park lot. Some *Balanus amphitrite* grow among them.

In the large series from Esperanza, Cuba, the adults have many strong, unequal ribs, and measure up to 13 mm. in diameter, 4.3 mm. high. The walls are thick, and the basal margins are deeply folded. Individuals of half that size resemble the rougher examples in plate 70, figure 3c. The opercular valves are considerably eroded.

At Ocean City, N. J., this species was found by Mr. Fowler growing on *Balanus balanoides*, the largest specimens 5 mm. in greatest diameter (pl. 70, fig. 2). The contour is more rounded than in those growing on reeds and the surface is not so smooth. The basiscutal angle of the tergum is somewhat cut out, the articular ridge short and tapering below. The articular ridge of the tergum is very small, and the articular furrow is narrow. The bilateral asymmetry of the opercular valves, though not conspicuous, is noticeable in some of this lot (fig. 83). I have often observed such asymmetry in this and other species of *Chthamalus*, but never in any other genus of *Balanidæ* or *Chthamalidæ*. The specimen I dissected from Ocean City differs a little from that taken at station 2004 in the second cirri, as I have noted above, but not in any other character of the mouth or cirri.

Excepting Darwin's Charleston record for *fragilis*, the only published notice of *Chthamalus* on our Atlantic coast is contained in an article by Dr. F. B. Sumner (1909). Specimens identified by Doctor Sumner as *C. stellatus* var. *fragilis* were found

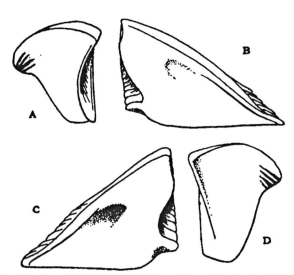

FIG. 83.—CHTHAMALUS FRAGILIS, OCEAN CITY, N. J. OPERCULAR VALVES OF ONE INDIVIDUAL, SHOWING SLIGHT BILATERAL ASYMMETRY.

to occur in considerable numbers on Penzance Point, along the shore of Woods Hole Passage. Further search has revealed its presence on the piles of piers at Woods Hole, New Bedford, and Vineyard Haven, and on rocks at Nobska Point, Nonamesset Island, and the shore of Buzzards Bay near Woods Hole. It is probable, indeed, that its local distribution is very general. At the last-named point this species seems to be particularly abundant. It extends considerably higher up on the bowlders than does *Balanus balanoides*, with which however, it is associated at a lower level. It thus occurs at points which must be uncovered by the tide for the greater part of the time. In local waters, so far as I have seen, *Chthamalus* never grows in such dense clusters as does *Balanus balanoides*, and indeed it appears unable to compete very successfully with the latter in its proper zone. Like its associate, it is a strictly littoral form and probably does not extend below tidal limits.

The local examples, in large part at least, seem to belong to the variety *fragilis* of Darwin, as did the specimens received by the latter author from "Charlestown" (=Charleston ?). A characteristic of this variety is the smooth, delicate appearance of the valves, referred to above as distinguishing local specimens. At Woods Hole I have found few having the rugosity, the weathered aspect, or even the whiteness of *Balanus balanoides*.

Our local representatives of the species are so much darker in color and so much smoother in appearance than the associated *Balanus* as to be plainly distinguishable from the latter, even at considerable distance. Thus, the confusion of the two, said to have been commonly made by English collectors, seems incredible here. The largest specimens which I have seen have not exceeded 10 mm. in diameter at the base.

I am treating this form as a species because many specimens from localities scattered over a wide area agree fully in the characters differentiating it from *stellatus*. These specimens, moreover, are seated upon widely diverse materials—stones, shells, coconuts, and rushes—indicating that their peculiarities are not due to a special environment. The rounded prominence of the articular ridge of the scutum, tapering downward, and the broader spur of the tergum are characteristic.

It is quite possible that the specimens from *Albatross* station 2004 were picked up by the trawl at the surface, for one could not expect *Chthamalus* on a rush from a depth of 102 fathoms. If really from the bottom, the rush on which they were seated certainly floated there and sunk, through becoming water-logged. The barnacles were living when collected. The station is at the edge of the continental plateau, where flotsam brought by the Gulf Stream might naturally be expected to settle. The specimens agree entirely with those figured in plate 70, figures 1–1*d*, 4.

Locality.	Collector.	Notes.
Albatross station 2004, latitude 37° 19′ 45″ north; longitude 74° 26′ 06′ west, east of Cape Charles.	*Albatross*	102 fathoms, on a bit of rush.
"United States coast"	Newberry	On a rush.
Clearwater Harbor, Fla	W. H. Abbott	On rushes.
Jamaica	C. B. Adams	On Atrina and coconut shells.
Esperanza, Cuba	*Tomas Barrera* exped.	On wood.

CHTHAMALUS STELLATUS (Poli).

1791. *Lepas stellatus* Poli, Testacea utriusque Siciliæ, vol. 1, p. 29, pl. 5, figs. 18–20.

1803. *Lepas punctatus* Montagu, Testacea Britanica, p. 8, pl. 1, fig. 5.

1818. *Chthamalus stellatus* Poli, Ranzani, Opuscoli Scientifici, vol. 2, p. 84, pl. 3, figs. 21–24.

1839. ? *Chthamalus vitreus* Costa, Fauna di Napoli, Cirropedi, p. 27 (on pumice, from Lipari?)

1854. *Chthamalus stellatus* Darwin, Monograph, p. 455, with var. *communis*, pl. 18, figs. 1*a*, *c. e. f. h;* var. *fragilis*, fig. 1*d;* var. *depressus* Poli, figs. 1*b, g, h.*

1905. *Chthamalus stellatus*, var. *fistulosus* Gruvel, Monographie des Cirrhipèdes, p. 201.

Distribution.—Eastern coast of the North Atlantic and Mediterranean; type-locality, the Bay of Naples. Littoral, on rocks and shells.

In the Darwinian limits, this species is widely spread in the eastern and western Atlantic and the oriental region.[1] It is a group of

---

[1] Darwin also mentions "Oregon or northern California" among the localities for *C. stellatus*.

local races or "little species" like *Balanus tintinnabulum* or *Tetraclita squamosa.* My present study concerns American barnacles. I have not taken the time to dissect, mount, and illustrate long series of European individuals. Without such an investigation one would not care to revise the master's conclusions.

CHTHAMALUS STELLATUS STELLATUS (Poli).

Plate 71, figs. 1–4a.

This is equivalent to *C. stellatus* var. a, *communis* of Darwin, illustrated in his figures 1a, 1f.[1] It is here figured from specimens from the Bay of Naples, which I take to be the type locality. The broadly oval or subcircular wall is conic, variable in height, often depressed. It is corroded more or less extensively, but usually shows traces at least of radiating ribs; sutures moderately plain or obliterated; radii not developed; orifice rounded-oval. The color is an uneven, soiled pale gray, usually showing black specks under a lens. Diameter 5 to 10 mm.

The scutum is somewhat terra-cotta tinted within. The apex is a right angle. Articular ridge strong, nearly straight, *abruptly truncate* near the basitergal angle, above the deep articular furrow. *The pit for the adductor muscle is large and deep,* those for the depressor muscles generally distinct. No adductor ridge.

The tergum is very broad above, *narrow below.* The upper margin is arched. Articular ridge is very broadly reflexed, triangular. Articular furrow wide. No spur. The strong crests for the depressor muscles barely crenulate the margin of the valve. The external corrosion has carried away most of the original scutal margin, leaving the articular rib projecting.

The palpi (fig. 84b) have very long spines in a straggling group at the distal end, and a band of much smaller ones running down the edge.

Mandible has four teeth, followed by a long, even series of very small, crowded spines; the lower point terminating in one large, stout spine, with two small spines below it. The third tooth is bifid at the tip, the fourth more conspicuously so. There are long bristles at the lower border (fig. 84d).

The maxilla has two large spines above, followed by three small ones; the margin then advances and bears a group of moderately strong spines, occupying the middle third of the edge. The lower third has much smaller, slender, crowded spines. There are some long spines on the basal border, and shorter ones on the upper border (fig. 84c).

Cirrus i has rami with seven and five densely hairy segments.

---

[1] As noted elsewhere, Darwin applied the name "var. *communis*" to the typical form of every species having several varieties.

Cirrus ii has seven and six segments. Among the terminal spines of the shorter (posterior) ramus there is one broader lanceolate spine having two closely toothed edges, but without larger teeth below the serrate portion (fig. 84a). There are three such spines at the distal end of the longer ramus.

Cirri of the third to sixth pairs much longer than those preceding, and bearing five pairs of spines on the median segments (p. 298, fig. 82f).

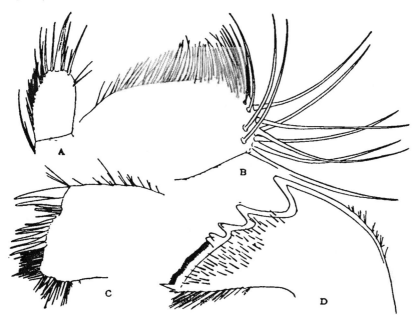

Fig. 84.—CHTHAMALUS STELLATUS, NAPLES. a, TERMINAL SEGMENT OF THE SHORTER RAMUS OF CIRRUS II, SHOWING ONE LANCEOLATE, SERRATE SPINE. b, PALPUS. c, MAXILLA. d, MANDIBLE.

The penis is much longer than the last cirri. It is slender, closely ringed, and has a delicate pencil of hairs at the end.

As this species is the type of the genus, and has been reported from many places all over the world, including our own shores, it has been thought best to give an account of the typical form. Figures 1 to 1b represent topotypes from Naples, which agree fully with Darwin's plate 18, figures 1a (locality not given) and 1f (Madeira); also with De Alessandri's figures of Italian Pleistocene examples. The opercular valves are highly characteristic. My figure of the entire animal shows only deeply corroded specimens.

Small specimens up to 3 mm. diameter, but evidently adult, from Fayal, Azores, growing on *Purpura hæmastoma* have 10 to 12 very conspicuous ribs. The opercular valves are thin, but typical in form (pl. 71, figs. 4, 4a).

It appears, then, that this typical form of the species is known from the Mediterranean, Madeira, and the Azores; whether it occurs in northern Europe is still uncertain.

Darwin figures (pl. 18, fig. 1*h*) a peculiar form which I have not seen, from St. Iago, Cape Verde Islands.

Northern Europe.—Form *punctatus* Montagu (pl. 71, figs. 2–2*b*, 3, 3*a*). In English specimens there is a good deal of variation from the characters given above. The external form is often typical, as in plate 71, figures 3, 3*a*, from Exmouth; but when crowded they become cylindric, as in plate 71, figures 2, 2*a*, 2*b*, exceedingly like the cylindric form of *Balanus balanoides.* This tubular form is what Professor Gruvel has called var. *fistulosus.* There are many transitional specimens between the tubular and the depressed forms, in the same groups.

The scutum, in all of the English examples I have closely examined, is longer than in the Mediterranean form, with the apical angle acute, the tergal margin shorter, and the adductor muscle pit smaller. The tergum also differs by having a sinuation in the basal margin near the depressor muscle crests. I have not taken time to compare large series—the cleaning is somewhat tedious—but according to Darwin these characters of the valves vary so much that he included all of them in var. *communis.* If the form in question proves to be racially distinguishable from typical *stellatus* it will be called *punctatus* Montagu. Eroded specimens usually have a punctate or peppered appearance. My plate 71, figures 2–2*b*, 3, 3*a*, and Darwin's plate 18, figure 1*e*, are from British specimens of this race.

U.S.N.M. Cat. No.	Locality.	Collector.	Notes.
12066 12098	England (?)....................	Clark, in Jeffreys collection..	On *Patella vulgata* and on rocks.
12108	.....do......................	Jeffreys......................	
12148	Exmouth, England............	.....do......................	
12095	England(?)....................	.....do......................	Tubular variety.
	Fayal, Azores................	Lewis Dexter................	
	Port Cuyo, Philippines........	*Albatross*	Not typical. On *Mitella mitella.*

CHTHAMALUS STELLATUS DEPRESSUS (Poli).

1791. *Lepas depressa* POLI, Testacea utriusque Siciliæ, vol. 1, p. 27, pl. 5, figs. 12–17.[1]

1818. *Chthamalus glaber* RANZANI, Opuscoli Scientifici, vol. 2, p. 83, based upon *Lepas depressa* Poli.

1854. *Chthamalus stellatus* var. *depressus* Poli, DARWIN, Monograph, pl. 18, fig. 1*b* (locality not given), 1*g* (Mediterranean).

[1] The name *Lepas depressa* has page priority over *L. stellata,* but subsequent authors have preferred the latter, *depressa* being a far less common and local form.

This subspecies is described by Darwin as follows:

Shell much depressed, surface much corroded, smooth; alæ largely exposed, marked by lines of growth; radii not present; parietes on the under side often supported by pillars; orifice subhexagonal. Diameter up to three-quarters of an inch. Tergum very narrow.

This variety or subspecies is known from the Bay of Naples (type-locality), Straits of Gibraltar, and St. Iago, Cape Verde Islands, where it occurs associated with *stellatus*. It is not present in the museum, and is included here for comparison with the following form, which is rather similar in the shape of the opercular valves.

CHTHAMALUS STELLATUS ANGUSTITERGUM, new subspecies.

Plate 71, figs. 5–5b.

Type.—Cat. No. 48199, U.S.N.M., from the Bahamas.

The walls are deeply corroded above, irregularly ribbed near the base, as in *stellatus;* interior roughened, more or less purple-tinted.

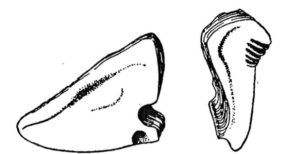

The scutum has a straight articular rib, truncate at the lower end. The adductor muscle pit is very *shallow;* no adductor ridge. Pit for the lateral depressor deep. *The tergum is very narrow and thick.* There is a

FIG. 85.—CHTHAMALUS STELLATUS ANGUSTITERGUM. SCUTUM AND TERGUM OF THE TYPE.

small but distinctly developed spur, much narrower than in *fragilis;* basal margin concave; crests very strong. From its thickness the tergum is triangular in transverse section. It is seen rolled toward the right in plate 71, figure 5b, showing the broad scutal articulating face. In figure 85 a direct view of the inner face is given.

The opercular valves are white or pink inside.

The labrum has a concave edge with teeth along the median portion (fig. 86b).

The mandible and maxilla are very similar to those of *C. stellatus,* shown in figures 84c, d.

Cirrus i has rami of 7 and 5 segments, the anterior longer by two segments.

Cirrus ii has 6 and 5 segments, the anterior ramus longer by two. There are no large pectinated spines.

Cirrus iii has rami of 12 and 14 segments, the lower ones having six pairs of spines, the rest five pairs.

Cirrus vi has rami of 15 segments, most of them bearing five pairs
of spines (fig. 86a).

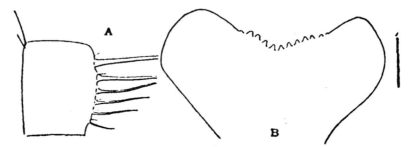

FIG. 86.—CHTHAMALUS STELLATUS ANGUSTITERGUM, ABACO. a, INTERMEDIATE SEGMENT
OF CIRRUS VI. b, LABRUM.

This is the race of the Bahamas and Florida Keys. It is probably
a species distinct from *Ch. stellatus.*

Locality.	Collector.	Notes.
Bahamas	B. A. Bean	Type lot.
Abaco, Bahamas	*Albatross,* 1886	
Boca Chica Key, Fla	H. A. Pilsbry	Coll. A.N.S.P.

CHTHAMALUS STELLATUS BISINUATUS, new subspecies.

Plate 71, figs. 6, 6a.

Type.—Cat. No. 48085, U.S.N.M., from Santa Catharina Island,
Brazil.

Articular ridge of the scutum prominent in the middle, hollowed
out above and abruptly terminated below; the articulating margin
therefore being bisinuate. Pit for the adductor muscle is deeply
excavated, as in typical *stellatus,* and there is no adductor ridge.

The tergum is wider than in *C. s. angustitergum.* The scutal
margin of the articular ridge is prominent. There is a small spur,
as in *angustitergum.* The crests for the depressor muscle are strong
and long, and there is a deep fissure or furrow next to the lower crest,
running far up the central part of the valve. This furrow is present
in both of the specimens I examined, and has not been found in any
other species. Whether it is a constant character of this race remains to be determined.

The dingy, corroded wall measures about 7.5 mm. in diameter.

Darwin has given some notes on specimens from Gorriti Island,
Uruguay, probably belonging to this race.

The specimens in the United States National Museum are from
Brazil; Rio de Janeiro, collector unknown, and Santa Catharina
Island, Isaac Lea collection. Both lots are preserved dry.

ORIENTAL SPECIES.

CHTHAMALUS CHALLENGERI Hoek.

Plate 72, figs. 1–4a.

1883. *Chthamalus challengeri* HOEK, *Challenger* Reports, Zoology, vol. 8, p. 165, pl. 13, figs. 35–38.

1911. *Chthamalus challengeri* Hoek, KRÜGER, Beiträge zür Cirripedienfauna Ostasiens, p. 46, pl. 3, fig. 30.

Distribution.—Japan; Matsushima.

The barnacle has rounded ribs, rather strong, white throughout, not corroded, and smooth inside. The radii are very narrow. Carino-rostral diameter 7.6 mm.

The scutum is lengthened. Articular ridge prominent, its edge bisinuate, being excavated above, tapering below the median promi-

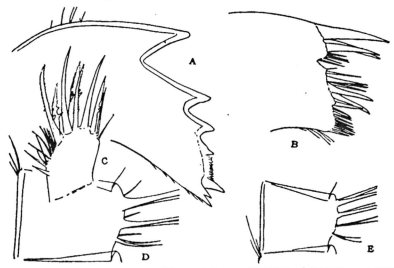

FIG. 87.—CHTHAMALUS CHALLENGERI, MATSUSHIMA. *a*, MANDIBLE. *b*, MAXILLA. *c*, TERMINAL SEGMENT OF THE SHORTER RAMUS OF CIRRUS II. *d*, SEVENTH SEGMENT OF CIRRUS VI. *e*, INTERMEDIATE SEGMENT OF CIRRUS VI OF THE VARIETY FROM AYUKAWA, JAPAN.

nence. Adductor muscle pit small and rather deep, with a raised rim forming *a strong adductor ridge*. Lateral depressor muscle pit is very indistinct.

The tergum is wide above, narrow below. Upper free portion conspicuously laminate. Articular ridge strong, the articular furrow wide. There is no real spur, as the basiscutal angle is terminal. The basal margin is deeply sinuated below the depressor muscle crests, the strongly developed crests being borne on a triangular lobe of the valve, as in many other species.

The mandible is of the *stellatus* form, but the three points at the lower extremity are much more strongly developed and the finely pectinated space above them is shorter (fig. 87*a*).

The maxilla has three large spines and a group of small ones above the rather deep notch (fig. 87b).

Cirrus i has rami of 8 and 6 segments, the posterior ramus three-fourths the length of the anterior. The posterior border of the basal segments of the anterior ramus bears some very short, stout, slightly curved spines, much as figured for *C. cirratus*, but not noticed in any other species.

Cirrus ii has rami of 6 segments, the posterior ramus shorter by the length of one segment. The terminal segments of both rami have several simply serrate spines and a few broad ones with two coarse teeth below the finely serrate portion, as shown in figure 87c.

Cirrus iii has rami of 12 segments; cirrus iv of 14 and 15 segments· cirri v and vi of 16 segments. The segments of these cirri have three pairs of spines (fig. 87d).

Chthamalus challengeri differs from *stellatus* by the well developed adductor ridge of the scutum. The articular ridge is shorter than in *C. stellatus* and differs in shape, its greatest prominence being near or above the middle of the tergal margin, with lower end tapering, not terminated abruptly as in *stellatus*. Some forms still referred by authors to *stellatus* have a tergum resembling that of *challengeri*.

The description and figures 1, 1a of plate 72 represent the valves of a Matsushima specimen. Figure 3 is a group from Yokohama growing on *Tetraclita s. japonica*, borne by a living *Helcioniscus eucosmius*. The largest in this group reach 6 mm. in diameter.

Specimens from Ayukawa, Japan (pl. 72, figs. 2, 2a), have some small crests crossing the lateral depressor pit *in some specimens*, others having it simple. There is the slight rudiment of a spur on the tergum. The mandible is like that of typical *stellatus*. Maxilla as figured for *challengeri*. Cirrus ii has rami of 5 segments, the terminal segments having dense groups of spines, *none of them pectinate*. The posterior cirri have *four* pairs of spines. Cirrus vi with 13 segments (fig. 87e). Whether these peculiarities of the cirri have racial significance remains to be investigated.

Specimens collected in Japan by Mr. Loomis, seated on *Balanus cariosus*, are corroded, with rather short valves, the adductor ridge of the scutum strong but very short, pit for the lateral depressor muscles well marked (pl. 72, figs. 4, 4a). Exterior white.

Doctor Krüger has figured two Japanese forms of *Chthamalus*. According to his account there are no differences in the mouth parts, and the scuta of both are figured with an adductor ridge. I am therefore disposed to suggest that the form he calls *C. stellatus* is more closely related to *challengeri* than to the Atlantic species, which has no adductor ridge.

Locality.	Collector.	Notes.
Yokohama, Japan	H. Loomis	On *Helcioniscus eucosmius* and *Tetraclita* growing thereon.
Japan	do	On *Balanus cariosus*.
Ayukawa, Japan	*Albatross*	
Matsushima, Japan Sea	do	On *Mitella mitella*.

CHTHAMALUS CHALLENGERI NIPPONENSIS, new subspecies.

Another form of *C. challengeri* is represented by Cat. No. 48092. The deeply eroded, conic wall is gray above, light brown near the

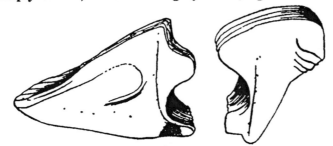

FIG. 88.—CHTHAMALUS CHALLENGERI NIPPONENSIS. SCUTUM AND TERGUM.

base, where it is sculptured with *many narrow ribs*, sometimes branching. The interior is *purplish brown and whitish*, with deep

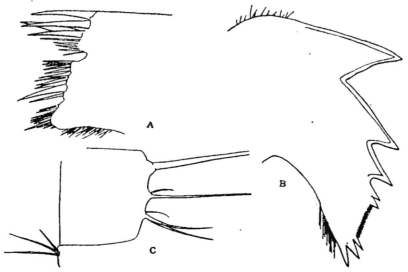

FIG. 89.—CHTHAMALUS CHALLENGERI NIPPONENSIS. *a*, MAXILLA. *b*, MANDIBLE. *c*, AN INTERMEDIATE SEGMENT OF CIRRUS VI.

furrows corresponding to external ribs, punctate in the furrows. Diameter, 9 mm.

The scutum has a very prominent articular ridge and a narrow adductor. The tergum has a carinal margin higher than in *Challengeri* (fig. 88).

The mandible and maxilla do not differ materially from those of *C. challengeri* (fig. 89*a*, *b*).

Cirrus i has rami of 8 and 7 segments, the anterior ramus longer by two and one-half segments.

Cirrus ii has rami of 6 and 5 segments, the anterior ramus longer by two segments.

Both rami have several serrate spines in the terminal tufts, but these spines have not the large lower teeth seen in *C. challengeri*.

Cirrus iii has equal rami of 14 or 15 segments.

Cirrus vi has three pairs of spines, as in *C. challengeri* (fig. 89*c*).

The first and second cirri are black pigmented; also the first joint of the pedicel in the other cirri, the amount of pigment decreasing backward.

CHTHAMALUS MALAYENSIS, new species.

Plate 72, figs. 5, 5*a*.

Type.—Cat. No. 48084, U.S.N.M., from the Malay Peninsula, collected by E. Deschamps.

The barnacle is depressed, strongly ribbed, more or less corroded, and brownish gray externally. The interior is punctate in old individuals; border, pale, within which there is a dull purple band; the remainder flesh tinted. Sheath is extremely short.

The opercular valves are deeply corroded externally, nearly white within, punctate. The articular ridge of the scutum is very prominent in the middle, tapering both above and below. Adductor pit rather deep, and there is a very small rudiment of an adductor ridge.

The tergum is triangular, very narrow at the lower end. Articular ridge broadly reflexed. Scutal border broadly inflexed. Basal border nearly straight.

The mandible has four teeth, as usual, the third and fourth being bifid. The lower extremity is trifid, having three large, stout, equal spines. Between the fourth tooth and the lower spines there are about six subequal small spines, but very much larger than those of *C. stellatus* or *C. challengeri* (fig. 90*b*).

The maxilla has a more irregular edge than *C. challengeri*, but is similar in arrangement of spines. There are three large spines above, as in the Japanese species (fig. 90*a*). The palpi are like those of *C. stellatus*.

The first cirrus has rami of 8 and 6 segments, the posterior ramus about four-fifths as long as the anterior.

Cirrus ii has slightly unequal rami of 7 and 6 segments. The spines of the terminal segments are as described and figured for *C. stellatus*. There are no large-toothed spines, as in *C. challengeri.*

Cirrus vi has 16 segments, bearing four pairs of spines, as in the specimens from Ayukawa drawn in figure 87*e*.

I had thought this a race of *C. stellatus* or *C. challengeri* until I examined the mouth parts. The mandible is so different, however, that in the present state of our knowledge I think it best to rank it as a species. In place of the even, fine, comblike pectination of the space below the fourth tooth of the mandible, which many species

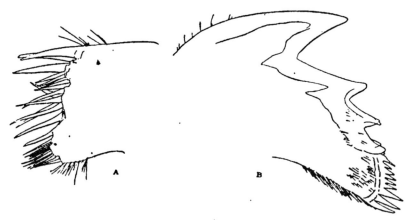

Fig. 90.—Chthamalus malayensis. *a*, maxilla, and *b*, mandible.

of *Chthamalus* have, there is a series of coarse teeth. The equality of the three spines at the lower angle of the mandible is a less important difference. The mouth parts of this species and *C. challengeri* are drawn to the same scale.

The status of this form depends upon the constancy of the features of the mandible, which can be determined only by the examination of a larger series of specimens.

CHTHAMALUS MORO, new species.

Plate 72, figs. 6, 6*a*, 6*b*.

Type.—Cat. No. 48197, U.S.N.M., from Zamboanga, Mindanao, on *Tetraclita squamosa*, collected by Dr. E. A. Mearns.

The barnacle is strongly ribbed, whitish, conic; radii narrow, the alæ rather wide; sutures distinct, simple.

The tergal margin of the scutum is nearly equal to the basal; articular ridge straight, long, obliquely truncate below, not projecting beyond the tergal border of the valve. Adductor muscle pit not deep. There is no adductor ridge. Pit for the lateral depressor muscle deep. Interior white.

Tergum with moderately developed articular ridge and narrow articular furrow. Spur broad, rounded, and short. Carinal lobe, bearing the crests, rather large, making an angle with the rest of the basal margin.

This species has valves much like those of the American *C. fragilis*, but the articular ridges of both valves are weaker. It differs from *C. challengeri* by the much less broadly reflexed articular ridge of the scutum, the absence of an adductor ridge, and the broader lower part of the tergum. It is also unlike the specimen referred to *C. stellatus*, figured in the *Siboga* report, but it probably belongs close to *stellatus*.

Besides the type lot from Zamboanga collected by Dr. E. A. Mearns, there is a beautiful group seated together with *Tetraclita squamosa* upon a mangrove oyster collected by the *Albatross* in the Philippines, exact locality not noted. The specimens were preserved dry, and I have not worked out the mouth parts and cirri.

CHTHAMALUS WITHERSI, new species.

Plate 73, figs. 2 to 2e.

Type.—Cat. No. 48088, U.S.N.M.

Locality.—Reef opposite Cebu, Philippine Islands, in a group of *Balanus amphitrite*. *Albatross*, April 7, 1908.

Specimens not distorted by crowding are depressed with a rather large, wide orifice; cinnamon brown, becoming bluish where the epidermis is worn off; the surface smooth, but little worn, the lower part showing growth-striæ. Alæ broad, with arched, subhorizontal summits, and sculptured with growth-striæ stronger than on the parietes. Interior smooth, without basal rugosity or inwardly growing ledge, dull brown, shading into white; sheath short. Sutures smooth, not plicate or crenulated. Diameter, 9.5 mm.; height, 3 mm.

The scutum is thin, triangular, convex between apex and base, more than twice as long as wide, the basal margin somewhat surpassing the tergal. In the lower part there are fine growth-lines. Inside dull brown and white, smooth. The articular ridge is a very feebly developed median lobe, not extending beyond the scutal border. The articular furrow is shallow but sharply incised. There are no pits for the adductor or depressor muscles.

The tergum is very narrow, club-shaped, very thick (not eroded in the specimens seen). The articular ridge is rather high but not much reflexed. Articular furrow shallow. The lower half of the valve is narrow, but thick, very convex externally, forming a sort of spur, which is wholly united with the basiscutal angle. The carinal lobe is narrow, situated high, and shows a few short crests for the depressor muscle.

The labrum has a broad, nearly straight edge, the middle fourth having a series of 18 strong teeth (fig. 91d). The mandible has three large teeth and a pectinated lower point having eight slender teeth (fig. 91a).

The maxilla has a pair of large upper spines followed by two smaller spines above the small notch. The median part bears a group of about 8 rather large spines. The lower third protrudes, and bears about 10 large and small spines. There is a group of short spines on the lower edge. The prominence of the lower part is a chief feature (fig. 91c).

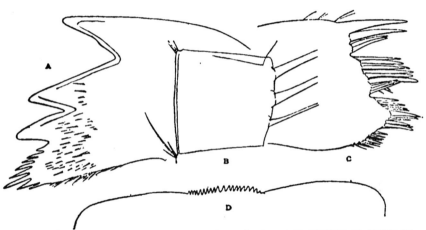

Fig. 91.—CHTHAMALUS WITHERSI. a, MANDIBLE. b, ELEVENTH SEGMENT OF CIRRUS VI. c, MAXILLA. d, UPPER MARGIN OF THE LABRUM.

The first cirrus has rami of 9 and 5 segments, the posterior branch two-thirds as long as the anterior.

Cirrus ii has 9 and 8 segments, the rami proportioned as in cirrus i. None of the spines in the distal segments are pectinated or plumose.

Cirrus iii has rami of 19 segments, bearing three pairs of spines.

Cirrus vi has rami of 23 segments, also with three pairs of spines (fig. 91b).

The chief characteristic of this species is the weak articulation of the scutum and tergum; the articular ridge of the scutum is short and extremely weak, and the articular furrow is shallow. The shape of the tergum is peculiar. These features will at once separate C. withersi from the smooth, unworn forms of C. stellatus. The absence of pits for the adductor and depressor muscles is also notable. In the mouth-parts, the labrum and mandible differ widely from most of the species, and the small number of spines on the posterior cirri is noteworthy.

Named in honor of Mr. T. H. Withers, whose brilliant studies of Mesozoic cirripedes have materially extended our knowledge of the phylogeny of the group.

CHTHAMALUS CAUDATUS, new species.

Plate 73, figs. 1, 1a, 1b.

Type.—Cat. No. 48087, U.S.N.M.

Locality.—Catbalonga, Samar, Philippines, on terga of *Mitella mitella* taken on the reef. *Albatross* Philippine expedition.

The barnacle is rather narrow, oblong, corroded, gray, in places showing yellow laminæ; weakly ribbed near the margins; the radial borders zigzag where not too deeply eroded. The orifice is ovate.

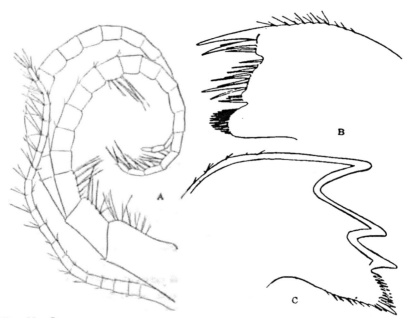

FIG. 92.—CHTHAMALUS CAUDATUS. *a*, CIRRUS VI AND CAUDAL APPENDAGE. THE SPINES ARE OMITTED FROM MOST OF THE SEGMENTS OF THE CIRRUS. *b*, MAXILLA. *c*, MANDIBLE.

Carinorostral diameter, 10 mm.; lateral diameter, 6 mm.; height, 2.7 mm.

The scutum has a rounded articular ridge, most prominent in the middle, sloping downward. No adductor ridge; adductor muscle pit shallow. A rather strong ledge along the occludent border.

The tergum is rather narrow in the lower half, not very wide above.

The crests for the depressor muscles are short but project well over the basal margin.

The mandible has three large teeth and a pectinated lower point (fig. 92c). The maxilla has spines in the usual three groups; those of the lower group are very fine and close (fig. 92b).

Cirrus i has unequal rami with 8 and 6 segments, the posterior ramus slightly over half as long as the anterior.

Cirrus ii has rami of 10 segments, the anterior ramus about two segments longer than the posterior. Posterior ramus is much more slender than the anterior; about half as wide. A few spines in the terminal segment of the anterior ramus are lanceolate with minutely serrate edges, somewhat as figured for typical *C. stellatus*, but more slender.

The remaining cirri have subequal rami, the segments bearing four pairs of spines. I note a minute fifth pair on a few segments.

The caudal appendages are about three-fourths as long as the cirri, slender, each composed of 21 segments bearing some delicate spines. They are closely similar (fig. 92a).

The special features of this species are in the appendages. The rami of the first cirri are *more unequal in length* than usual; the second are *unequal in width*, and there are *long caudal appendages*. The form of mandible is common to several other species.

Before dissecting *C. caudatus* I thought it a form of *C. dentatus* Krauss, which I know only from the published accounts. The hard parts agree in the main with that species, as described by Darwin, but several minor differences may be noted. The parietes are not ribbed, though there is a trace of such sculpture near the bases of some compartments.

The crests of the tergum project more over the basal margin. In *C. dentatus*, according to Darwin, the "tips of the second pair of cirri have many coarsely pectinated spines," and there are but six segments in the shorter ramus. Both of these characters differ from *C. caudatus*. The mandible of *C. dentatus* has not been figured, but it appears from the description to be like that of *caudatus*. The chief difference is in the long and well-developed caudal appendages of *C. caudatus*. Darwin had an abundance of material of *C. dentatus*, and it does not seem likely that structures so conspicuous and remarkable could have escaped his acute observation, if they were present in that species.

C. caudatus is the only species of *Chthamalus* in which caudal appendages have been seen. I could find no trace of them whatever in *C. hembeli* and *C. withersi*, which have the same form of mandible as *C. caudatus*.

SPECIES OF THE WEST COAST OF NORTH AND SOUTH AMERICA.

CHTHAMALUS DALLI, new species.

Plate 73, figs. 3, 3a, 3b.

Type.—Cat. No. 48064, U.S.N.M.

Locality.—Unalaska, Alaska, growing together with *Balanus crenatus* on *Balanus cariosus*. Also Oyster Bay, Washington, on *Balanus glandula.*

The barnacle is conic, with a small oblong orifice; parietes having few unequal ribs, more or less obliterated by the corrosion of the surface; sutures simple. Where corroded the surface is pale gray; in a narrow basal band, where the very thin cuticle remains, it is buff. The interior is whitish, stained more or less with flesh or a livid tint. Opercular valves similarly tinted.

Greatest basal diameter of the type 6.2 mm., height 2.3 mm.

The scutum (pl. 73, fig. 3a) has a moderately developed but short articular rib, extending about to the middle of the tergal margin and tapering downward. Articular furrow is broad. The pit for the adductor muscle is very shallow. *There is a long and strong adductor ridge.* Pit for the lateral depressor muscle is crossed by several crests.

The tergum is broad, its width about three-fourths of the length, the basal margin strongly convex below, straightened in its carinal half. Upper margin well arched. The articular ridge is not very prominent, articular furrow narrow. Crests for the depressor muscle are quite long.

The labrum (fig. 93d) is set with small, rather irregular teeth.

The mandibles, palpi, and maxillæ do not differ materially from those of *C. stellatus* from Naples.

Cirrus i has rami of 7 and 6 segments, the posterior ramus about three-fourths as long as the anterior.

Cirrus ii has 6 and 5 segments, the anterior ramus longer by about 1½ segments. There are no serrate spines.

Cirrus iii has rami of 12 segments bearing four pairs of spines.

Cirrus vi has rami of 20 segments, bearing five pairs of spines, some of them having single short basal bristles.

This is a small species, but as the specimens contained many eggs they may be presumed to be full grown. It differs from *C. stellatus* and its varieties by the strong development of the adductor ridge of the scutum. It is most nearly related to *C. fissus*, but differs by the crests in the scutum for the lateral depressor muscle, the far stronger adductor ridge, and by the different proportions of the valves; in *C. fissus* the length of the tergal margin of the scutum is half of the basal margin; in *C. dalli* it is two-thirds.

This species is named for Dr. William H. Dall, who collected a large part of the Alaskan barnacles in the United States National Museum.

CHTHAMALUS FISSUS Darwin.

Plate 74, figs. 1, 1a, 1b.

1854. *Chthamalus fissus* DARWIN, Monograph, p. 462, pl. 18, figs. 6a, 6b.

Type.—British Museum, from California, on "*Lottia grandis.*"

The barnacle is convexly conic or irregular, with the walls rather strongly folded near the base, smooth in the younger stages, covered when unworn with an olive or olive-brown cuticle. Radii, when present, very narrow. Orifice varying from narrow and lengthened, about twice as long as wide, to oval, the length about one and one-half times the width. Diameter about 5 mm.

The scutum is long; articular ridge not projecting beyond the tergal margin of valve when that is unworn, tapering downward. The adductor muscle pit is deep. Adductor ridge rather strong but short. Pit for the lateral depressor muscle deep.

The tergum is roughly an equilateral triangle in outline, nearly as wide as long, the basal and carinal borders convex. Articular ridge moderate; spur extremely short and wide, merely a convexity of the base.

This species is readily known by the shape of the tergum, which is more shortened than in any other species. I have found it at La Jolla, California, growing on bowlders, *Mytilus*, and on other barnacles (*Mitella*), in the intertidal zone.

Locality.	Collector.	Notes.
San Diego, Cal..	C. R. Orcutt......	On *Mytilus californianus*.
Do..	.....do.........:..	On *Balanus glandula*.

CHTHAMALUS ANISOPOMA, new species.

Plate 74, figs. 2 to 2f.

Type.—No. 48198, U.S.N.M., from San Luis Gonzales Bay, Gulf of California, on a stone (*Albatross*, 1889).

The barnacle is depressed-conic with a rather long, elliptical orifice, closed by the left (rarely the right) scutum and tergum only; radii undeveloped, the sutures distinct and narrow, with *finely crenulated sutural edges*. Parietes strongly, irregularly ribbed. Interior whitish, with a fleshy margin, the basal edges either slightly or copiously roughened with irregular crests (pl. 74, fig. 2e, carina), or quite smooth, except for the fluting caused by the ribs. Diameter, 5 mm.

The opercular valves are peculiar from the conspicuous disparity in size and shape between the right and left valves. In a very great majority of the specimens examined the left valves are larger than the right and assume the position of the free valves of *Verruca.* Plate 74, figures 2 to 2*d*, are drawn to the same scale, and represent valves of one individual.

The larger scutum has nearly the shape of an isosceles triangle. The exterior has conspicuous, not very close laminæ of growth and a shallow radial sulcus which divides off the tergal third. The articular ridge is well developed, with a rounded outline. Articular furrow rather deep. The adductor muscle impression is small and not very deep. No adductor ridge. Pit for the lateral depressor muscle is crossed by delicate crests.

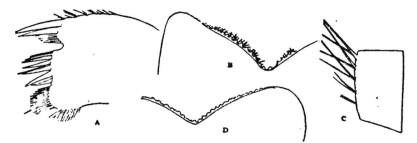

Fig. 93.—CHTHAMALUS ANISOPOMA. *a,* MAXILLA. *b,* LABRUM. *c,* INTERMEDIATE SEGMENT OF CIRRUS VI. *d,* CHTHAMALUS DALLI, LABRUM.

The smaller scutum is long and very narrow, the tergal margin much less than half of the basal. Articular rib well developed, long. The deep pit for the lateral depressor muscle is upon the basal edge of the valve.

The larger tergum is irregularly oblong. Articular ridge angular, strongly produced over the scutal margin. Spur very short and rounded. Basal margin straight. Crests for the depressor muscle usually developed strongly.

Smaller tergum triangular, shaped somewhat like that of *Chthamalus fissus,* but broader; basal margin somewhat sigmoid; articular ridge small.

The labrum has a very broadly V-shaped edge, set with teeth, and many short hairs (fig. 93*b*).

The mandible is like that of Naples *C. stellatus.*

The maxilla (fig. 93*a*) also resembles that of *C. stellatus.*

Cirrus i has 6 and 5 segments.

Cirrus ii has 5 and 7 or 6 and 8 segments, the posterior shorter by two segments.

Cirrus vi has rami of 20 segments, bearing five pairs of spines (fig. 93*c*). Both cirri and spines are quite slender.

This species is known by several hundred individuals upon a stone, probably picked up on the shore. It is very remarkable for the asymmetry of the valves, giving it somewhat the aspect of *Verruca*. The closing apparatus is indeed like that of *Verruca*, since the smaller pair of valves does not extend nearly to the summits of the larger pair, is not visible externally, and takes no part in the closing of the orifice. The summits of the larger valves close against the opposite border of the orifice, the smaller valves then standing vertically along the same border, lower down. It is doubtless on account of the altered pose of the smaller valves that the depressor muscle pit has moved from the face to the lower edge of the valve.

I have found the forms of the valves very constant in a large number of individuals. Having an impression at first that I was dealing with a pathologic barnacle, I was led to go over a greater number in detail than one would otherwise take time for. By the smaller valves it seems related to *C. fissus*. The tergum of the larger pair is more like that of *C. panamensis*.

The slight asymmetry of the opercular valves in some other species of *Chthamalus* has been noted elsewhere in this report. Darwin has remarked upon the occasional asymmetry of *C. scabrosus*. In *C. anisopoma*, however, the asymmetry is much more pronounced and has become a constant character.

CHTHAMALUS PANAMENSIS, new species.

Plate 75, figs. 2 to 2c.

Type.—No. 2008, A.N.S.P., from Quarantine Island, Panama, on *Siphonaria gigas*, collected by Samuel N. Rhoads, 1911.

The barnacle is conic with a small orifice, sometimes corroded and dirty gray, but when well preserved, covered with an olive brown cuticle; varying from weakly folded to strongly, irregularly plicate near the lower border. Interior white and nearly smooth; some of the compartments pitted behind the rather long sheath. Sutures distinct, simple. Radii extremely narrow or undeveloped. Diameter 5 to 7 mm.

The scutum is closely, finely ridged with growth striæ. Inside it has a narrowly reflexed articular ridge, its edge convex, not projecting beyond the finely serrate tergal border of the valve. No adductor ridge. Adductor pit rather deep; that for the lateral depressor distinct.

The tergum is irregularly oblong, widest in the middle, the scutal margin straight, opposite margin arched, the apical end a little narrower than the lower. Exterior finely marked with growth-striæ, and having *a deep furrow from apex to spur*, and traces of one or two other very faint, short radial furrows. Articular ridge prominent but not reflexed over the scutal margin. Spur extremely short and broad. Basal margin straight. Crests for the depressor muscle are weak.

The free apices of both scutum and tergum are unusually long in unworn specimens. If eroded, the outlines of the valves would be considerably altered. The specimens were preserved dry, and I have not examined the internal organs.

This seems to be a strongly individualized species. Unworn examples may be recognized readily by the external furrow of the tergum. The shape of the tergum and the small development of the articular ridge in both tergum and scutum are also characteristic. The external sculpture of the opercular valves is much finer and closer than in *C. anisopoma*.

There is a very slight difference in the size of the opercular valves of the two sides, at least in the individuals I have particularly examined, but this is hardly noticeable unless the cleaned valves are laid side by side.

CHTHAMALUS IMPERATRIX, new species.

Plate 75, figs. 1 to 1e.

Type.—Cat. No. 48200, U.S.N.M.
Distribution.—Panama, on stones. C. B. Adams.

The barnacle is conic, depressed, spreading, the slopes even and showing waved gray lines etched into low relief on the surface;

FIG. 94.—CHTHAMALUS IMPERATRIX. SCUTUM OF AN UNWORN INDIVIDUAL, TO SHOW THE STRAIGHT TERGAL BORDER; LENGTH, 2.6 MM.

when unworn it is set with small granules, or in the early stages of growth it is smooth. The orifice is large and ovate; alæ broad, with horizontal summits. Sutural edges smooth; radii not differentiated. The compartments are moderately thick. The interior of wall and valves is dull-violet black or blue-violet black. The basal edges of the wall are roughened by some scattered tubercles, or sometimes rather close, fine rugosites and asperities. There is no trace of an ingrowing ledge. The sheath is very short (pl. 75, figs. 1, 1a, 1e, interior or rostrolateral, lateral, and carinal compartments).

Diameter, 14 mm.; height, 3 mm.

Diameter, 13 mm.; height, 2.5 mm.

The opercular valves are thick, deeply eroded in adults, and are colored inside like the wall. The scutum is of the usual triangular shape, about twice as wide as high. The tergal border is very thick. The articular rib is not very prominent; articular furrow forms a rather wide and deep notch. Occludent margin inflexed, a rather deep crease under it for the adductor muscle. No pits or scars for depressor muscles are visible. Length 4.5 mm. (pl. 75, fig. 1c; also fig. 94).

The tergum is extremely thick, narrow, with a rather shallow articular furrow. There is a sort of short spur united with the basi-scutal angle and projecting below it. The carinal lobe of the valve appears pushed upward. Crests for the depressor muscle are rather strong and irregular.

The numerous specimens of this species have been in the collection many years, and the body was entirely destroyed in those opened. The uniform violet black color of the interior is unusual and characteristic. *Chthamalus intertextus* Darwin, a Philippine species, is purple within, but other known species are lighter colored or clouded with some dark shade on a lighter ground.

CHTHAMALUS CIRRATUS Darwin.

1854. *Chthamalus cirratus* DARWIN, Monograph, p. 461, pl. 18, figs. 4a, 4b.
1909. *Chthamalus cirratus* Darwin, PILSBRY, Proc. U. S. Nat. Mus., vol. 37, p. 71, fig. 2.

Distribution.—Pescadores Islands, Peru, to the northern Chonos Islands.

The barnacle is either depressed-conic, 10 to 13 mm. in diameter, corroded above, ribbed and crenate at the base, when not crowded,

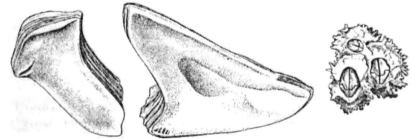

FIG. 95.—CHTHAMALUS CIRRATUS. SAN LORENZO ISLAND, PERU. INSIDE VIEWS OF TERGUM AND SCUTUM ENLARGED, AND GROUP OF THREE ENTIRE ANIMALS, NATURAL SIZE.

or when crowded the walls become vertical, and the orifice and the opercular valves are large. There is also a smooth form. According to Darwin, large specimens from Coquimbo and Valparaiso have a height of 1 inch with a basal diameter of half as much. All of those I have seen from Peru are depressed. The interior is usually dull purplish (fig. 95).

The opercular valves are corroded. The scutum has a *long, strongly projecting articular rib*, which has a long, nearly straight or sometimes convex slope to the deep articular furrow, unlike any form of *C. stellatus*. The adductor muscle pit is deep. The lateral depressor muscle pit is generally but not always crossed by *short crests*, as in several other West Coast species.

The tergum is concave within. *The spur projects in a blunt point below the basiscutal angle.* There is a narrow, basicarinal lobe, with a few short crests for the lateral depressor muscle.

The labrum is concave in the middle, and has many long hairs at the sides.

The mandibles and maxillæ (fig. 96*b*) do not differ materially from those of *C. stellatus*.

Cirrus i has rami of 7 segments, the anterior ramus longer by two. The posterior edge of the lower segment of the anterior ramus

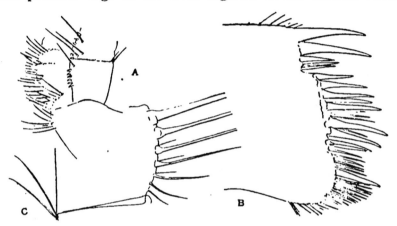

Fig. 96.—Chthamalus cirratus, San Lorrenzo Island. *a*, basal segments of the rami of cirrus ii, the anterior margin toward the left. *b*, edge of the maxilla. *c*, eleventh segment of cirrus vi; only the outer spine of each pair is drawn.

bears a series of about six obliquely conic teeth, reminding one of those of *Acasta*.

Cirrus ii has rami of 8 and 6 segments. The anterior ramus is longer by about two segments, and on its lower segment bears a series of conic teeth directed toward the posterior ramus (fig. 96*a*). Several succeeding segments have one or two similar teeth.

Cirrus iii has *very unequal rami* of 16 and 30 segments. Those of the distal third of the longer ramus are very slender and bear only a few slender spines near their distal ends. The other segments are armed with six pairs of spines. Darwin states that he found the rami equal in one specimen. The later cirri have subequal rami, the segments bearing six pairs of spines (fig. 96*c*).

There is not much variation in the opercular valves, but much more in the wall. In one specimen from San Lorenzo Island the wall is rather thin, *not ribbed*, and *covered with a dark olive-brown cuticle* in the lower part. The upper part is corroded. The interior is smooth, and the sutures are distinct. The long slope of the articular ridge of the scutum is decidedly convex, and the basicarinal lobe of the tergum is less produced.

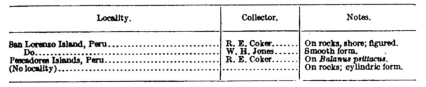

Locality.	Collector.	Notes.
San Lorenzo Island, Peru	R. E. Coker	On rocks, shore; figured.
Do.	W. H. Jones	Smooth form.
Pescadores Islands, Peru	R. E. Coker	On *Balanus psittacus*.
(No locality)		On rocks; cylindric form.

CHTHAMALUS SCABROSUS Darwin.

Plate 73, figs. 4, 4a.

1854. *Chthamalus scabrosus* DARWIN, Monograph, p. 468, pl. 19, figs. 2a–2d.

Distribution.—Peru to Tierra del Fuego and the Falkland Islands (Darwin).

The wall is conic, dirty gray when corroded, "dull purplish brown" or pale purplish vinaceous when well preserved; sometimes retaining traces of the cuticle near the base. Radii usually narrow or scarcely developed; rarely well developed, and then consisting "of small laminæ or ridges placed on both sides of the sutures, and interfolded or interlocked together; usually only a trace of this structure is exhibited." Alæ rather wide, striate. Parietes more or less ribbed. Interior either nearly smooth or roughened, often greenish, the edges of the compartments projecting inward. Diameter about 11 mm.

The scutum is long and narrow. The articular ridge is very prominent, forming a lobe in the middle of the tergal margin. This is more conspicuous in the usual worn examples than in the nearly perfect one figured. An oblique ridge, like an adductor ridge, bounds the adductor pit, which is not very deep.

"The terga are very narrow; they are remarkable in two respects, namely, in the depressor muscle being attached to a plate formed apparently by the union of the usual crests, parallel to the outer lamina of the valve itself, a deep narrow cavity being thus formed; and secondly, in the far more extraordinary circumstance of the existence of a small pit at the extreme basiscutal corner of the valve, in which about half of the scutal lateral depressor muscle is attached." Sometimes this basiscutal pit is very shallow or even entirely wanting, as in the specimen here figured. There is a rounded spur projecting below the basiscutal angle.

The opercular valves, especially the tergum, are very characteristic.

Specimens in the United States National Museum from Valparaiso (Cat. No. 48089) are seated upon a rock and are of the conic form, not strongly sculptured.

According to Darwin:

This species is the commonest cirripede on the shores of the Falkland Islands. Many of the specimens are there crowded together, and rendered elongated and cylindrical, with the walls very thin and the sutures often obliterated; as the opercular membrane is very narrow, the opercular valves are much influenced both in their outline and in their crests and articulations by the varying form of the shell. I have even seen specimens with the scutum and tergum on one side twice as large as on the other side.

HAWAIIAN SPECIES.

CHTHAMALUS INTERTEXTUS Darwin.

1854. *Chthamalus intertextus* DARWIN, Monograph, p. 467, pl. 19, figs. 1a, 1b (Philippine Archipelago, Cuming).

1913. ?*Chthamalus intertextus* Darwin, HOEK, *Siboga*-Expeditie, Cirripedia, p. 269 (Bay of Kankamaraän, south coast of Kangeang).

Diamond Head, Oahu, near the lighthouse, on a reef of volcanic rock covered at high water; abundant. H. A. Pilsbry, 1913. These specimens have the scuta and terga calcified together, the basal edges of the compartments inflected, and the interior of a beautiful violet color (petunia violet or anthracene violet of Ridgway). The sutures are interfolded when unworn. Though far from the original locality, they seem to be quite typical.

CHTHAMALUS HEMBELI (Conrad).

Plate 76.

1837. *Euraphia hembeli* CONRAD, Journal of the Academy of Natural Sciences, vol. 7, p. 261, pl. 20, fig. 13.

1854. *Chthamalus hembeli* Conrad, DARWIN, Monograph, p. 465, pl. 18, figs. 5a–5c.

1897. *Chthamalus hembeli* (Conrad) WELTNER, Verzeichnis, p. 272.

1905. *Chthamalus hembelli* Conrad, GRUVEL, Monographie des Cirrhipèdes, p. 205.

Distribution.—Hawaiian Islands.

The barnacle is large, conic, with a large quadrangular orifice; very solid and strong; parietes pale grayish vinaceous, the alæ and sheath seal brown (or grayish if worn); exterior somewhat folded or but very slightly so. Sutures, when not obliterated by corrosion, formed of interlocking teeth. Radii narrow. Alæ very wide. The sheath is long. The lateral angles of the orifice are somewhat hollowed out for the basitergal corners of the scuta. The interior below the sheath is smooth, pale buff. "Basis membranous, but surrounded by a ledge formed by the inflected basal edges of the parietes," or in old individuals the inflected edges of the compartments cover the whole base with a strong, whitish calcareous layer. The false basis does not, of course, show radial furrows or lines, but is quite smooth.

The scuta and terga are firmly cemented, but not calcified, together, and may be separated by boiling in potash. The articulating faces are very thick. Scutum with a deeply bisinuate tergal margin, the articular ridge in the middle. The occludent edge is broad and flat, obliquely ridged in the lower part. Groups of intricately branching crests at the two basal angles serve for the attachment of the depressor muscles. The outside is regularly ridged transversely when unworn and has one or more shallow radial impressed grooves.

The tergum has a bisinuate scutal border; basal margin formed of two subequal arcs, the posterior one occupied by the deeply cut lateral depressor muscle crests, which in basal view are seen to be intricately branching and pectinated. The exterior is seal brown, with some lighter rays. The low growth-ridges are worn smooth except along the carinal margin, where they are sharp and oblique.

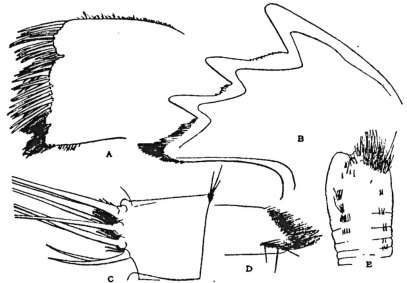

Fig. 97.—CHTHAMALUS HEMBELI. NAPILI HARBOR, MAUI. a, MAXILLA. b, MANDIBLE. c, ELEVENTH SEGMENT OF CIRRUS VI. d, PALPUS. e, END OF THE PENIS.

An old individual measures, carinorostral and lateral diameters 75 mm.; height of carina, 41 mm.; length of scutum, 45 mm.

Carinorostral diameter, 76; lateral, 64 mm.; height of carina, 49 mm.

Labrum has a simply concave edge, not toothed or spinose.

The mandible has three strong teeth and a closely pectinated lower point (fig. 97b).

The maxilla is very closely set with rather slender spines, not varying much in size on the upper two-thirds, but shorter and narrower on the lower third (fig. 97a).

The palpi are closely set with rather small spines near the distal end. There is no group of long spines as in the other species (fig. 97d).

The cirri are densely pigmented, the pigment in dots, chiefly at the bases of the spines and along the carinal borders of the segments.

The general proportions of the cirri may be seen in the photograph (pl. 76, figs. 1, 1a).

Cirrus i has extremely short, conic rami of 10 and 8 segments.

Cirrus ii has very unequal rami, of 10 and 17 segments, the anterior ramus not two-thirds the length of the posterior, covered with fine spines. The posterior ramus has long spines on the anterior edge, similar to those of cirri iii–vi—four spines on the lower, three on the intermediate, and two on the distal segments.

Cirrus iii has rami of 19 segments. Segments of the distal half have three main pairs of spines, the rest having four pairs. There are dense groups of short spines on the anterior side, as in subsequent cirri.

Cirrus iv has rami of 23 and 25 segments, spines as in cirrus iii. Cirrus v is similar.

Cirrus vi has rami of 26 segments, with four pairs of spines (fig. 97c) on the lower half, three pairs on the segments of the distal part. As in the other cirri, there are bunches of short spines between the insertions of the paired spines.

The penis (pl. 76, fig. 1a) is short for a *Chthamalus*—scarcely as long as the sixth cirri. It is very densely annulated, and from this I presume that it is capable of considerable lengthening. The extremity is emarginate, with a dense patch of short hairs on one side near the end (fig. 97e).

This species is readily known by the size—gigantic for a *Chthamalus*—by the solidity of all the parts, and the serrate sutures, when these are not obscured by corrosion. The cirri and mouth-parts are equally characteristic, especially the second pair of cirri, in which the posterior branch is like the third and later cirri. There are more short bristles between the pairs of spines on the cirri than in any other species. The maxilla has more numerous spines than in other species.

The articulating face of the scutum is very broad, being greatly foreshortened in figure 2a. The equally broad opposed face of the tergum is well shown in figure 2.

The specimen from Maui consists of the body, the scuta, and one tergum. It was probably obtained by a landing party, reported at that station.[1] The valves are very deeply corroded, livid pink and white externally. Length of scutum, 33 mm.

The type-specimen of *C. hembeli* seems to be lost, or at all events I have not found it in the collection of the Academy of Natural Sciences. The locality was given by Conrad, on Thomas Nuttall's authority, as "near Sta. Diego." This seems to be incorrect, not only in the gender of the saint, but also in the habitat of the barnacle.

---

[1] Rep. U. S. Fish Commissioner for 1902, p. 408.

No further specimens have been found in California, but we have positive records from the Hawaiian Islands. It is well known that the localities of some of Nuttall's Hawaiian and Californian shells were confused. Doctor Weltner has recorded *C. hembeli* from Nagasaki, collected by the eminent conchologist Eduard von Martens; but I do not know that the specimens have been compared with typical Hawaiian examples.

Chthamalus hembeli is a rare barnacle in collections. I know only of those in the British and the National Museums, unless the Japanese specimens in the Berlin Museum are correctly identified.

Locality.	Collector.	Notes.
Hilo, Hawaii....................................	U. S. Exploring Expedition?	Figured on plate 76, figs. 2–2c.
Napili Harbor, Maui, *Albatross* Station 3881.	*Albatross*	Body and three opercular valves. Plate 76, figs. 1, 1a.

Genus PACHYLASMA Darwin.

1854. *Pachylasma* DARWIN, Monograph, p. 475.

Chthamalidæ having a wall of eight compartments, in which the rostrum and rostral latera are united by inconspicuous, linear sutures, or are wholly concrescent in the adult stage, the barnacle thus becoming virtually six-valved. Radii wanting or very narrow and not well differentiated from the parietes. Wall-plates without pores, not ribbed within in adults. Basis calcareous. Scutum without an adductor ridge. Caudal appendages present.

Type.—P. giganteum (Philippi).

These are barnacles of rather deep water, down to more than 200 fathoms, in the Mediterranean, oriental, and Australian seas. They are at present rare in museums; except *P. giganteum*, each species is known by a single lot from one locality. The several forms sit upon stones, millipores, other barnacles, crinoid stems, and sponges, but to what extent the species are restricted in station remains to be determined. Two species were known to Darwin, and three more have been taken by the *Albatross*. All are well differentiated specifically.

It may be expected that with the progress of deep water exploration the number of species of *Pachylasma* and *Hexelasma* will be very considerably augmented; and I suspect that the division into two genera will become increasingly difficult. The differential characters found in the caudal appendages, the labrum, and the basis are less important than might at first be supposed. In *Pachylasma darwinianum* the caudal appendages are reduced to a single, minute joint, the basis is extremely thin, and the labrum is not bullate, though it is thicker than in *Balanus*. In *Hexelasma callistoderma* the basis is partially calcified and the labrum a little thickened. By its completely concrescent rostrum and rostrolateral compartments, *Hexelasma* is like *Pachylasma giganteum*. It remains to be seen whether these plates are separate in the very early sessile stage of *Hexelasma*, as Darwin has found them to be in *P. giganteum*, up to the time the wall attains a diameter of about 1 mm.

Another question remaining to be worked out is the position of *Bathybalanus* Hoek.[1] It is evidently no Balanid barnacle, but closely related to *Hexelasma* and *Pachylasma*, differing from *Hexelasma* by its distinctly calcareous basis, from *Pachylasma* by the absence of caudal appendages, and from both it differs by having well-developed radii. None of these characters are of very great importance; yet, in the present condition of our knowledge of deep-water barnacles, a union of the groups would be premature.

KEY TO THE SPECIES OF PACHYLASMA.

a^1. Rostrum and rostrolateral compartments completely concrescent in the adult stage (distinct and united by linear sutures for a very brief period after fixation) ; the other compartments having well-developed alæ. Scuta having growth ridges cut by a few longitudinal furrows or impressed lines. Mediterranean_____*P. giganteum* (Philippi).

a^2. Rostrum and rostrolateral compartments closely united by linear sutures, which are sometimes obliterated externally but visible inside.

  b^1. Lateral and carinolateral compartments closely united by a linear suture; only the carina and the lateral compartments showing alæ externally; sheath long; scutum having wrinkled growth-ridges cut by slight radial grooves, its width less than half the length. New South Wales.

                                                  P. aurantiacum Darwin.[2]

  b^2. Carinolateral compartments having conspicuous alæ.

    c^1. Scuta about twice as long as wide, having sinuous or puckered growth-ridges; tergum with no spur; carinolateral compartments much more than half as wide as the lateral. Philippines.

                                         P. darwinianum Pilsbry.

    c^2. Scuta having sculpture of smooth, even, transverse growth-ridges, not cut by longitudinal grooves or striæ; carinolateral compartment half as wide as the lateral; tergum having a very short, wide spur.

      d^1. Scutum convex, its width contained two and one-half times in its length; tergum with no longitudinal depression externally, its articular ridge not projecting beyond the scutal border. China Sea.

                                         P. chinense Pilsbry.

      d^2. Width of scutum contained twice in its length; tergum having a longitudinal depression externally, its articular ridge projecting a little beyond the scutal border. Japan____*P. crinoidophilum* Pilsbry.

---

[1] *Bathy-Balanus* Hoek, *Siboga*-Expeditie, Monographie 31b, p. 160, monotype *Balanus pentscrini* Hoek.

[2] *P. aurantiacum* is not contained in the United States National Museum.

PACHYLASMA GIGANTEUM (Philippi).

1854. *Pachylasma giganteum* Philippi, DARWIN, Monograph, p. 477, pl. 19, figs. 5a–5d.

Cat. No. 12060. Strait of Messina. Seguenza, in Jeffreys collection.

PACHYLASMA DARWINIANUM Pilsbry.

1912. *Pachylasma darwinianum* PILSBRY, Proc. U. S. Nat. Mus., vol. 42, p. 293.

Type.—Cat. No. 43465, U.S.N.M., from *Albatross* Station 5168, Tawi Tawi group of the Sulu Archipelago, 80 fathoms.

PACHYLASMA CHINENSE Pilsbry.

1912. *Pachylasma chinense* PILSBRY, Proc. U. S. Nat. Mus., vol. 42, p. 293.

Type.—Cat. No. 43471, U.S.N.M., from *Albatross* Station 5301, China Sea, near Hongkong, 208 fathoms.

PACHYLASMA CRINOIDOPHILUM Pilsbry.

1911. *Pachylasma crinoidophilum* PILSBRY, Bull. Bureau of Fisheries, vol. 29, p. 81, fig. 11; pl. 17, figs. 1–11.

Type.—Cat. No. 38675, U.S.N.M., from *Albatross* Station 4934, off Kagoshima Gulf, in 152 fathoms.

Genus HEXELASMA Hoek.

1913. *Hexelasma* HOEK, *Siboga*-Expeditie, Monographie 31*b*, pp. 157, 244.

Hoek described this genus as follows:

Compartments six; carina, carinolateral and lateral compartments with alæ, but without radii, the rostrum having neither radii nor alæ. Parietes not porous and without longitudinal ribs on their inner surfaces. Basis membranous. Opercular valves subtriangular. Mouth with the labrum not notched in the middle; mandibles with 4 to 5 sharply pointed teeth; maxillæ with numerous spines beneath the notch. Third pair of cirri resembling more those of the fourth than of the second pair. No caudal appendages. Species living in deep water.

By the texture of the compartments and valves, the absence of radii and the absence of an adductor ridge in the scutum, *Hexelasma* resembles *Pachylasma;* but it differs by having no trace whatever of caudal appendages, and in the typical species by having a membranous basis. In *H. americanum* and *H. callistoderma* the basis is calcareous, but very thin in the center, so that in specimens removed from the support the very thin, filmlike central region adheres partly to the support, so that I formerly described *callistoderma* as having the central part of the basis membranous. There is an inflected rim at the bases of the compartments very much thicker than the true basis.

The absence of terminal appendages is perhaps a more important character, differentiating *Hexelasma* from *Pachylasma;* yet these vary a good deal in *Pachylasma.* In *P. crinoidophilum* the appendages have eight joints; in *P. darwinianum* only one extremely minute joint, with minute terminal bristles.

Since the rostrum of *Hexelasma* overlaps the adjacent latera, which have alæ, it is certainly a composite plate formed of the concrescent rostrum and rostral latera, exactly as in *Pachylasma giganteum.* Young specimens, when found, should be examined for traces of the sutures. Darwin found them at the apex in a *Pachylasma* slightly over 1 mm. in diameter.

The form of the labrum and of the third cirri show at once that *Hexelasma* belongs to the *Chthamalidæ,* and not to the *Balanidæ.* The armature of mandible and maxilla, the form of the lower edge of the sheath, and the texture are also characters pointing in the same direction.

Hexelasma now contains seven species, as follows:

H. velutinum Hoek.   Malay Archipelago, 204 to 390 meters.

H. arafuræ Hoek.   Malay Archipelago, 560 meters.

H. corolliforme Hoek.   Near Kerguelen Island.   270 meters.

H. hirsutum Hoek.   Faroe Channel, 930 meters.

H. aucklandicum Hector.[1]   New Zealand, Miocene.

And the following collected by the *Albatross:*

HEXELASMA AMERICANUM, new species.

Plate 69.

Type.—Cat. No. 14559, U.S.N.M.

Type-locality.—*Albatross* station 2663, off South Carolina, latitude 29° 39′ north; longitude 79° 49′ west; 421 fathoms, bottom temperature 42°.7 F., seated on a branch of coral.

The barnacle has a membranous basis with narrowly inflected calcareous borders; strong, solid compartments which are only weakly cemented together, are without pores, and have no radii. Light buff or delicately salmon tinted under a very thin pale corneous cuticle, which extends over the parietes and part of the alæ. The orifice is rather small and deeply notched. The alæ are broad, regularly obliquely striated, and have very oblique, smooth summits. The parietes have distinct, spaced linear growth-marks, which on some of the plates show an indistinct and minute puckering (possibly indicative of deciduous hairs); the surface between growth-marks being minutely rippled and longitudinally a little roughened. The sheath is salmon buff, smoothly grooved transversely, less than half as long as the

---

[1] T. H. Withers, Proc. Zool. Soc. London, 1913, p. 841, pl. 85. The detached compartments of this gigantic species were originally referred to *Scalpellum*. Its proper generic reference is due to Mr. Withers. It attained a length of 19 cm.

wall, its lower margin not in the least overhanging. The interior is not in the least grooved below the sheath, and at the basal edge the compartments are very narrowly inflexed or have a slight rim around the membranous basis.

The carina is longer than the rostrum, longer than wide, triangular in outline. The carinolateral compartments have very narrow, band-like parietes, hardly one-fourth as wide as that of the rostrum. The rostrum is normally about as high as wide, and triangular in shape. The base is modified in shape by the cylindrical coral, which serves as support, and upon which the barnacle is seated with the carino-

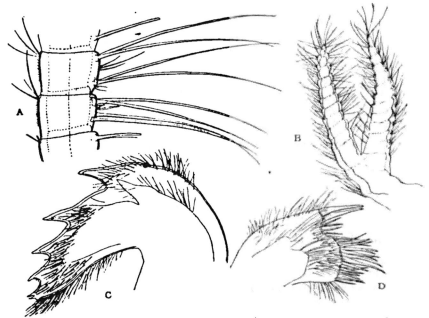

Fig. 98.—HEXELASMA AMERICANUM. *a*, INTERMEDIATE SEGMENTS OF CIRRUS VI. *b*, FIRST CIRRUS. *c*, MANDIBLE. *d*, MAXILLA.

rostral axis transverse to the long axis of the coral-branch in all but one of the specimens seen.

Greatest carinorostral diameter, 17 mm.; basal diameter at right angles to preceding, 18 mm.; height of carina, 21 mm.

The scutum is at least two and one-half times as long as wide, sculptured with regular growth-ridges, which unite by pairs to form oblique teeth along the occludent edge. There are no longitudinal striæ. Inside there is a very low, rounded, rather massive articular ridge, and a deep, very narrow articular furrow, but no adductor ridge whatever. There is a small pit with a couple of short crests for the lateral depressor muscle. The occludent border of the plate is bent up along its lower half.

The tergum is nearly flat, weakly striate transversely, the carinal half slightly convex and scored with a few longitudinal lines. A weakly impressed line runs to the carinal base of the spur, which has no furrow. The spur is very short, occupying about one-third of the basal margin. It is close to the basiscutal angle, and its end is obliquely truncate. Inside there is a rather low but long articular ridge, and numerous sharp but short crests for the depressor muscle.

The mandible has four rather acute teeth and a spinose lower point.

The maxilla has two large spines followed by a notch in which there are several small ones. Median third is armed with long but unequal spines and the lower fourth with shorter spines (fig. 98d).

This peculiar barnacle is obviously related to *Hexelasma callisto-derma* (Pilsbry) of the western Pacific, agreeing with that in the structure of the walls and opercular plates, the slender teeth of the mandible, the strongly annulate, rather short and hairless penis, and the structure and spines of the cirri. It differs from the Pacific species by having a narrower scutum, while the tergum is somewhat wider, with longer basal and shorter carinal margins; the spur is shorter and scarcely separated from the basiscutal angle of the valve. The external sculpture of the compartments is also less developed in the Atlantic species, which moreover differs by the flattened side walls and various other peculiarities of the wall plates, such as their minute sculpture.

The material examined consists of one perfect individual (Cat. No. 14559) from the type-locality, and parts of at least three incomplete ones (detached plates of the wall) from a lot labeled as from *Alba-tross* stations 2662–3–9, 2671–2 and registered as Cat. No. 48093, U.S.N.M.

The remains of two individuals in No. 48093 show carinæ similar to that of the type, except that they are a little less bowed, the roof being flattened (pl. 69, fig. 3).

In the third individual (pl. 69, fig. 2) the carina is almost straight, narrow, and nearly parallel-sided, with the roof very convex. From the shape of the basal margin it is clear that this one grew upon a narrow branch of the coral, with its carinorostral axis parallel to that of the branch. The whole contour of the barnacle was doubtless modified by the narrow support.

HEXELASMA CALLISTODERMA (Pilsbry).

1911. *Balanus callistoderma* PILSBRY, Bull. Bureau of Fisheries, vol. 29, p. 78, fig. 10, pl. 12, fig. 5; pl. 15, figs. 3–7.

Type.—Cat No. 38690, U.S.N.M., from *Albatross* station 5068, Suruga Gulf, Japan, in 77 fathoms.

To the description of this species may be added that the labrum has a rather deep median concavity but no notch. The edge is densely set with minute spines, and below the edge there are shorter spines set in groups. There are no " teeth " (fig. 99).

The palpus has a series of long spines on the face, as usual in *Balanus* and some *Chthamali*, running into a group on the distal end. Upper margin densely covered with much shorter spines.

The third cirrus has long rami like the fourth. The lower segments are densely bristly, like those of the second cirri, but the

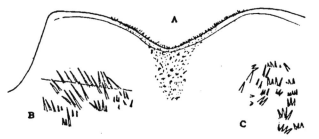

Fig. 99.—Hexelasma callistoderma. *a*, edge of the labrum. *b*, small part of the edge magnified to show the spines. *c*, spines from the central part of the labrum, some distance below the margin.

median and distal segments bear two pairs of long spines as in the later cirri. Dense tufts of hair rise from the inner faces of the median segments.

None of the cirri have " teeth " or spinules. The penis is not much more than half as long as the sixth cirri, and has no basi-dorsal point. There is no trace whatever of terminal appendages.

The basis is entirely membranous in young individuals, and the compartments are longitudinally ribbed inside and at the basal edges. In the adult stage the basal edges of the compartments grow inward, as in some species of *Chthamalus*, forming a ledge, thick outwardly, but thin at its inner edge, which is often somewhat scalloped or lobed. The true basis is partially calcified, there being an extremely thin calcareous film over large parts of it in old individuals, but, so far as I have seen, not complete. It is not easy to observe, since parts of this calcareous film adhere to the peripheral ledge and the body when the barnacle is removed from its support, and parts of it remain upon the support. The calcification is therefore less complete than in *Pachylasma*.

Albatross Station.	Locality.	Depth, fathoms.	Bottom temperature.	Collector.
5068	Suruga Gulf, Japan	77		*Albatross.*
3741	Ose Zaki, Japan	63–68		Do.

Genus OCTOMERIS Sowerby.

1825. *Octomeris* SOWERBY, Zoological Journal, vol. 2, p. 244. Monotype, *O. angulosa.*

1854. *Octomeris* Sowerby, DARWIN, Monograph, p. 282.

Chthamalidœ with eight compartments; edges of the radii crenated; basis membranous.

Darwin describes two species, *O. angulosa* Sowerby, from Algoa Bay, South Africa, and *O. brunnea* Darwin, from the Philippines. No others have been described since his monograph. They inhabit the littoral zone.

OCTOMERIS ANGULOSA Sowerby.

1854. *Octomeris angulosa* Sowerby, DARWIN, Monograph, p. 483, pl. 20, figs. 2a, 2b.

Locality.	Collector.
Cape of Good Hope	Wm. Stimpson, North Pacific Exploring Expedition.
Cape Town...................	U. S. Eclipse Expedition, 1889.
(Not stated).................	Isaac Lea collection.

The Cape Town specimens have deeply cut, continuous ribs, such as are shown in Chenu's figures of "*Octomeris augubra.*" This form may, perhaps, be separable from the typical *O. angulosa*, but my material is not abundant enough for a decision. Chenu's name was probably an error of the engraver and not intended as a new name.

Genus CATOPHRAGMUS Sowerby.

1827. *Catophragmus* SOWERBY, Genera of Recent and Fossil Shells.

1854. *Catophragmus* Sowerby, DARWIN, Monograph, p. 485.

Interior compartments eight, provided with alæ but no radii; their bases concealed by one or several exterior whorls of small, supplemental compartments; basis either membranous or calcareous; scutum without an adductor ridge, the articular ridges of both valves strongly developed. Caudal appendages present in some species.

The three species of this genus are about as widely separated as possible, one littoral species on the eastern coast of Australia, another in the West Indies, and the third in deep water of the Hawaiian Archipelago. They are evidently the remnants of an ancient group. In structure they are rather divergent. I have not seen *C. imbricatus*, but the other two species differ markedly in texture. *C. polymerus* has a great deal of chitin in the compartments, and the calcareous material is partly purplish. *C. darwini* is conspicuously porcellanous and dead white.

KEY TO SUBGENERA AND SPECIES.

a¹. Caudal appendages wholly wanting; basis membranous; basal edges of the inner compartments beveled outside, the outer layer not extending to the base; supplementary compartments numerous, carinate, imbricating over the sutures of each preceding whorl. Subgenus *Catomerus* (new subgenus)_____*C. polymerus* Darwin.

a². Caudal appendages present.

   b¹. Basis calcareous; supplementary compartments not keeled, not very numerous, imbricating over the sutures; white; caudal appendages very small. Subgenus *Catophragmus*_____*C. imbricatus* Sowerby.

   b². Basis unknown; basal edges of the inner compartments not beveled outside, the outer layer extending to the base; supplementary compartments in a single series, not restricted to the sutures of the inner wall, and of several forms, with or without one or two alæ; white and porcellanous in texture; caudal appendages well developed. Subgenus *Chionelasmus* Pilsbry_____*C. darwini* Pilsbry.

CATOPHRAGMUS IMBRICATUS Sowerby.

1827. *Catophragmus imbricatus* SOWERBY, Genera of Recent and Fossil Shells.

1854. *Catophragmus imbricatus* Sowerby, DARWIN, Monograph, p. 490.

1901. *Catophragmus imbricatus* Sowerby, VERRILL, Trans. Conn. Acad., vol. 11, pt. 1, p. 22, pl. 8, figs. 8, 9.

Type.—British Museum, from Antigua.

Distribution.—Antillean faunal province; Antigua and Bermuda.

This species is not contained in the National Museum. It is distinguished from *C. polymerus* by the white color, the calcareous basis and the caudal appendages, which, according to Darwin, are short, equaling only the lower segment of the pedicel of the sixth cirrus, and consisting of three joints, in a young specimen 5 mm. in diameter. It attains a diameter of three-quarters of an inch, according to Darwin. Professor Verrill remarks of those found by him in Bermuda:

Several specimens of this interesting barnacle were found on littoral rocks. They are all young (about 5 to 8 mm. in diameter) and agree well with the young one described by Darwin from Antigua. The eight primary mural plates are pointed and surrounded and partially concealed by about three alternating whorls of smaller, pointed plates; rapidly decreasing in size exteriorly. The opercular scuta are strongly concentrically ribbed and have a deep, median radial sulcus. The base is calcareous, but thin. The color is pure white.

CATOPHRAGMUS DARWINI Pilsbry.

1907. *Catophragmus darwini* PILSBRY, Bulletin of the Bureau of Fisheries, vol. 26, p. 188, fig. 4, pl. 5, figs. 1–8.

1911. *Catophragmus (Chionelasmus) darwini* PILSBRY, Bull. Bur. of Fisheries, vol. 29, p. 82.

Type.—Cat. Nos. 32407, 32408, U.S.N.M.

Distribution.—Hawaiian Islands: *Albatross* station 3998, vicinity of Kauai, in 228 to 235 fathoms.

CATOPHRAGMUS POLYMERUS Darwin.

1854. *Catophragmus polymerus* DARWIN, Monograph, p. 487, pl. 20, figs. 4a–4c.

Type.—British Museum, from Twofold Bay, New South Wales. Richmond, near Melbourne, Victoria, on shells and stones, collected by Mrs. Agnes Kenyon. The shape of the opercular valves varies a good deal. In low, spreading individuals the scutum is broad, as figured by Darwin, but in high ones with steep walls it is narrower, the basal margin shorter than the tergal, and the articular furrows of both valves are more oblique, so that the articulating borders are much less deeply notched than Darwin's figures show. It appears to be a strictly littoral species, living with *Tetraclita*, *Chthamalus*, etc.

Balanus concavus pacificus Pilsbry (p. 104). Specimens from between Venice and Rocky Point, California, collected by the *Anton Dohrn* for the Venice Marine Biological Station, agree with those from Newport, California (pl. 23, figs. 2–2c), in the form of the opercular valves. This particular race may be denoted as form *brevicalcar*. See page 107 for description.

Balanus eburneus Gould (p. 80). The following synonym should be added:

B.[alanus] democraticus DeKay, Zoology of New York, Mollusca, 1844, p. 252.

337

EXPLANATION OF PLATES.

PLATE 1.

FIG. 1. *Verruca coraliophila* Pilsbry. Top view of type. C., carina; F. Sc., fixed scutum; F. T., fixed tergum; Rs. rostrum. Page 21.

1a. *Verruca coraliophila.* Basal view. A. R., adductor ridge.

2, 4. *Verruca coraliophila.* Carinorostral views of two individuals, the movable plates lacking.

3. *Verruca coraliophila.* Interior views of fixed tergum and scutum.

5. *Verruca coraliophila.* Interior views of movable tergum and scutum.

PLATE 2.

FIGS. 1–1b. *Verruca alba* Pilsbry. Pourtales Plateau, near Key West, Florida. Top, carinorostral and basal views. Page 25.

2. *Verruca alba.* Basal view of a *Blake* specimen.

3, 3a. *Verruca alba barbadensis* Pilsbry. Top and rostrocarinal views of the type. Page 28.

4. *Verruca alba caribbea* Pilsbry. Colony on a sea-urchin spine.
Page 28.

PLATE 3.

FIGS. 1–1c. *Verruca nexa,* Darwin. Top, scutotergal, and carinorostral walls and base. Page 29.

2. *Verruca euglypta* Pilsbry. Interior view of rostrum.

2a. *Verruca euglypta* Pilsbry. Interior view of fixed and movable scuta and terga. Page 39.

PLATE 4.

FIGS. 1–1c. *Verruca floridana* Pilsbry. Top, base, rostrocarinal and scutotergal walls. Page 31.

2. *Verruca floridana.* Movable plates of a more sculptured individual.

3. *Verruca floridana.* Carinorostral view of an individual which sat transversely upon an echinoid spine.

4. *Verruca calotheca* Pilsbry. Basal view of type. Page 83.

4a, 4b. *Verruca calotheca.* Interior of movable scutum and tergum.

PLATE 5.

FIGS. 1, 1a. *Verruca calotheca heteropoma* Pilsbry. Top and carinorostral walls of the type. Page 35.

2, 2a. *Verruca calotheca flavidula* Pilsbry. Carinal and top views of the type. F. T., fixed tergum; M. T., movable tergum. Page 34.

PLATE 6.

PLATE 7.

PLATE 8.

PLATE 9.

PLATE 10.

PLATE 11.

PLATE 12.

Figs. 1–1b. *Balanus tintinnabulum galapaganus* Pilsbry. Hood Island, Galapagos. Tergum and scuta of the type. Cat. No. 48008, U.S.N.M.
Page 70.
2, 2a, 2b. *Balanus tintinnabulum azoricus* Pilsbry. Terceira, Azores. Scuta and tergum of the type. Cat No. 48004, U.S.N.M. Page 62.
3–3d. *Balanus algicola* Pilsbry. Cape Town. Groups and solitary individuals growing on various algæ. Cat. No. 15063, U.S.N.M.
Page 72.
3e, 3f, 3g. *Balanus algicola.* Tergum and scuta of type, in group 3a.

PLATE 13.

Figs. 1–1e. *Balanus tintinnabulum antillensis* Pilsbry. St. Thomas, West Indies. Type and paratype group, with opercular valves. Page 63.
2–2b. *B. t. antillensis* from bottom of a Cape Cod whaler from the West Indies. Lateral and basal views. Cat. No. 48005, U.S.N.M. In fig. 2b a small specimen of *Tetraclita radiata* is seen attached.
2c, 2d, 2e. Tergum and scuta of the same.
Figs. 1e, 2–2b, natural size.

PLATE 14.

Balanus tintinnabulum californicus Pilsbry.

Fig. 1. Type and paratypes, San Diego, California. Cat. No. 9434a, U.S.N.M.
Natural size. Page 65.
1a–1d. Opercular valves of type.
2. Group on an oyster, San Diego. Cat. No. 9435, U.S.N.M. Natural size.
3. Group showing the form with lengthened basis, near Santa Barbara, California. Cat. No. 43484, U.S.N.M.

PLATE 15.

Figs. 1, 1a. *Balanus tintinnabulum peninsularis* Pilsbry. Groups. Cat. No. 43487, U.S.N.M. Natural size. Page 66.
2–2d. *B. t. peninsularis.* Cape St. Lucas. Type with its opercular valves, and a smaller specimen. 2b, 2c natural size. Cat. No. 43486, U.S.N.M.
3. *Balanus tintinnabulum concinnus* Darwin. Inside of scutum.
Page 69.
4. *Balanus tintinnabulum californicus* Pilsbry. Basal edge of the wall of one of the type group. The spongy basis is seen near the left side. Page 65.

PLATE 16.

Figs. 1, 1a. *Balanus tintinnabulum coccopoma* Darwin. Tergum and scutum of specimen from Panama. Page 68.
2, 2a. *Balanus tintinnabulum coccopoma* Darwin. Group and outside of scutum. Bay of Panama. Fig. 2 natural size.
3. *Balanus tintinnabulum concinnus* Darwin. Payta, Peru. Cat. No. 12417. Natural size. Page 69.

PLATE 17.

FIGS. 1-4. *Balanus psittacus* (Molina). Talcahuano Bay, Chile.   Page 75.
5-8. *Balanus tintinnabulum concinnus* Darwin. Peru.   Page 69.

PLATE 18.

Balanus psittacus (Molina). Page 75.

FIG. 1. Adults from Talcahuano Bay, Chile. Cat. No. 43482. Length of right-hand specimen about 18 cm. Small barnacles growing on the larger ones are *Balanus lævis nitidus* Darwin and *Verruca lævigata* Sowerby.
2. Young individual from Valparaiso. Cat. No. 48007. Showing transient ribbed stage. Natural size.
3. Young individuals from Arica. Cat. No. 48006, U.S.N.M. Ribbed form, in lateral and obliquely rostral views. Natural size.

PLATE 19.

Balanus amphitrite niveus Darwin. Page 92.

FIGS. 1, 1a, 1b, 1e. Vineyard Sound, Massachusetts. Terga and scuta of an individual of group 1c.
1c. Vineyard Sound, Massachusetts. Cat. No. 38313, U.S.N.M. Group growing on a pebble.
1d. Vineyard Sound, Massachusetts. Tergum of another specimen of group 1c, having the spur rounded distally.
2. Marco, Florida. Cat. No. 48008, U.S.N.M. Group growing on the back of a *Crepidula*.
2a, 2b, 2c. Marco, Florida. Terga of three individuals of same group.
2d, 2e. Marco, Florida. Scuta of individuals of same group.
Figs. 1c and 2 natural size.

PLATE 20.

FIG. 1. *Balanus amphitrite albicostatus* Pilsbry. Yedo Bay, Japan. Cat. No. 48011, U.S.N.M. Lateral view.   Page 90.
2-2b. *B. a. albicostatus.* Type. Cat. No. 32950, U.S.N.M. Lateral view, tergum and scutum.
3. *B. a. albicostatus.* Group on a quartz pebble, from the North Pacific Exploring Expedition. Cat. No. 48008, U.S.N.M.
4. *B. a. albicostatus.* Hirado, Hizen. No. 1518, A.N.S.P. Rugged form.
5-5e. *Balanus amphitrite inexpectatus* Pilsbry. Gulf of California. Cat. No. 12398, U.S.N.M. Type-specimen, growing on an oyster, with terga and scuta.   Page 97.
5c. Tergum of a smaller individual, showing variation in shape of the spur.

PLATE 21.

FIGS. 1-1c. *Balanus concavus* Bronn. Typical form from British Red Crag (Pliocene). Cat. No. 12058, U.S.N.M. Page 100.

2. *Balanus concavus glyptopoma* Pilsbry. Caloosahatchie Pliocene. Cotype, Academy Natural Sciences of Philadelphia. Page 102.

3. *Balanus concavus glyptopoma* Pilsbry. Miocene, Yorktown, Va.

4. *Balanus regalis* Pilsbry. Interior view of rostrum and part of the basis of a cotype. Page 108.

4a. *Balanus regalis* Pilsbry. Point Abreogos, Lower California. Cotypes. Cat. No. 43485, U.S.N.M.

Figs 1b, 2, 3, 4a about natural size.

PLATE 22.

FIGS. 1-1c. *Balanus concavus chesapeakensis* Pilsbry. Chesapeake Bay, Maryland, Miocene. Type, with tergum and scuta. Page 103.

2, 2a, 2b, 2c. *Balanus concavus glyptopoma* Pilsbry. Caloosahatchie River, Florida, Pliocene. Scuta and tergum, cotype, Academy Natural Sciences of Philadelphia. Page 102.

3-3c. *Balanus concavus proteus* Conrad. Virginia, Miocene. Scuta, tergum, and apical view of typical examples, collected and labeled by Conrad. Page 103.

Figs. 1 and 3c natural size.

PLATE 23.

FIGS. 1-1d. *Balanus concavus pacificus* Pilsbry. Lateral view, scuta and terga of the type, San Diego, California. Cat. No. 82953, U.S.N.M. Page 104.

2-2c. *Balanus c. pacificus* form *brevicalcar* Pilsbry. Specimens from *Albatross* station 2939. Page 337.

PLATE 24.

FIGS. 1-1c. *Balanus eburneus* Gould. Smith's Creek, Potomac River, Maryland. Page 80.

2. *B. eburneus*. Vineyard Sound, Massachusetts, off Martha's Vineyard.

3, 3a, 3b. *Balanus improvisus* Darwin. South Downs, England. Cat. No. 48009, U.S.N.M. Tergum and apical view. Page 84.

4. *Balanus amphitrite peruvianus* Pilsbry. Rostrum with part of the basis of a paratype. Page 97.

5-5d. *Balanus improvisus* Darwin. Quinnipiac River, below Grand Street Bridge. Cat. No. 48010, U.S.N.M. Group on an oyster, and opercular valves. Page 84.

Figs 1, 2, 3b, and 5 natural size.

PLATE 25.

FIGS. 1–1c. *Balanus calidus* Pilsbry. *Albatross* station 2372, off western Florida. Opercular valves and lateral view of type-specimen. Cat. No. 10069, U.S.N.M.   Page 118.

2. *Balanus spongicola* Brown. Dublin Bay, Cat. No. 12145, U.S.N.M. Lateral view of specimen seated on *Pecten opercularis*. Natural size.   Page 115.

3. *B. spongicola*. Exmouth, Devon. Cat. No. 12078, U.S.N.M. Lateral view of specimen seated on a sandstone pebble. Natural size.

4–4c. *B. spongicola*. Patros Island, Brazil. Cat. No. 14144, U.S.N.M. Lateral view of group, and opercular valves.

PLATE 26.

Balanus trigonus Darwin. Page 111.

FIGS. 1–9. Type figures of *Balanus armatus* F. Müller, copied photographically from Müller's plate. *c*, carina ; *r*, rostrum.

10, 10a. Internal and external views of the tergum, from the same source.

11. External view of the scutum, from the same source.

12, 12a. Lateral view of wall and inside of tergum of a West Indian specimen, taken from the bottom of a Cape Cod whaler. Cat. No. 21550, U.S.N.M. Length, 8.3 mm.

13–13c. Group covering the shell of a *Tegula*, and opercular valves. San Diego, California. Cat. No. 11153, U.S.N.M.

PLATE 27.

FIGS. 1, 1a. *Balanus lævis* Bruguière. Gregory Bay, Strait of Magellan. Cat. No. 48012, U.S.N.M. Scuta.   Page 120.

2–2d. *B. l. nitidus* Darwin. Arica, Chile.   Page 122.

3, 3a, 3b. *B. lævis*. *Albatross* station 2773, east coast of Patagonia. Cat. No. 48013, U.S.N.M. Groups and spongy bases of specimens which grew on pebbles.   Page 120.

4. *B. l. nitidus*. Callao. Cat. No. 9209, U.S.N.M. Specimens forming a ball, wholly concealing the original supporting object. Page 122.

5. *B. l. nitidus*. Arica, Chile. Scutum with groove much reduced. Figs. 3–4 about natural size.

PLATE 28.

FIGS. 1, 1a. *Balanus gregarius* (Conrad). San Pablo formation, Salinas Valley, Monterey County, California. Detached basis, upper and basal views, the latter natural size.   Page 126.

2. *B. gregarius*. Lateral view of a biconic example 104 mm. in greatest diameter.

3. *B. gregarius*. Section about midway of the basis of an elongated example, viewed from above. Natural size.

4. *Balanus lævis coquimbensis* Sowerby. Opened longitudinally to show the septa of the basis. Somewhat enlarged.   Page 122.

The specimens illustrated in figs. 1–3 are property of the United States Geological Survey.

PLATE 29.

FIGS. 1, 1a. *Balanus gregarius* (Conrad). San Pablo formation, Salinas Valley, Monterey County, California. Median longitudinal section through the carinorostral axis, and external lateral view of the same individual. Length, 198 mm. Property of the United States Geological Survey.   Page 126.

PLATE 30.

Balanus nubilis Darwin.   Page 131.

FIGS. 1–1c. Straits of Juan de Fuca, Washington. Cat. No. 48014, U.S.N.M.
1, Inside of scutum; 1a, group, natural size; 1b, part of the basal edge of the carina; 1c, segment of basis, showing spongy structure of the lower layer.
2, 2a. Puget Sound. Cat. No. 48015, U.S.N.M. Tergum and lateral view of wall, the latter natural size. A young specimen.
3, 3a. Admiralty Inlet, near Port Townsend, Washington. Natural size. Valves of the same individual are shown enlarged in plate 31, figs. 3, 3a.
4. Group, Cat. No. 4669, U.S.N.M., the largest individual having partly lost the outer lamina, exposing the parietal tubes. Four-fifths natural size.

PLATE 31.

FIG. 1. *Balanus aquila* Pilsbry. Santa Barbara, California. Cat. No. 9432, U.S.N.M. Lateral view of a perfect individual. Page 127.
2. *B. aquila.* San Diego, California. Cat. No. 9434, U.S.N.M. Internal view to show strongly bifid alæ of the carina and lateral compartment.
3, 3a. *Balanus nubilis* Darwin. Tergum and scutum of very deeply corroded specimen from Admiralty Inlet; 1½ natural size. Page 131.
4, 5. *Balanus nubilis* Darwin. Tergum and scutum of well-preserved individual, Cat. No. 48014, U.S.N.M., from the Straits of Juan de Fuca.
4a. *Balanus aquila* Pilsbry. Monterey Bay, California. Cat. No. 32403, U.S.N.M. Lateral view of the type, seated upon a rock which is partly concealed by worm-tubes.   Page 127.

PLATE 32.

FIGS. 1–1f. *Balanus flos* Pilsbry. Monterey Bay, California. Cat. No. 32405, U.S.N.M. Lateral and apical views, and opercular valves of the type.   Page 135.
2–2c. *Balanus aquila* Pilsbry. Valves of the type individual figured on plate 31, fig. 5. Reproduced from the Bulletin of the Bureau of Fisheries, vol. 26, plates 8 and 9; drawn by Helen Winchester.   Page 127.

PLATE 33.

Balanus balanus (Linnæus). Page 149.

FIGS. 1, 1a. Tablet bearing Linnæus's specimens, and profile view of the type-specimen, from the collection of the Linnean Society of London.

2. Large English specimen of the typical form. Cat No. 12077, U.S.N.M. This individual grew on *Pecten opercularis*.

2a. Specimen growing on *Pecten opercularis* and showing its sculpture. Cat. No. 12077, U.S.N.M. England.

4. Strongly ribbed form, growing on a smooth mussel. Scarborough, England.

5. Strongly ribbed form, growing on a smooth mussel. Belfast, Ireland.

6, 6a, 6b. Opercular valves of the typical English specimen shown in fig. 2.

6c. Tergum of specimen from Bering Sea, *Albatross* station 3289. See also plate 35, fig. 4.

PLATE 34.

Balanus balanus (Linnæus). Page 149.

FIGS. 1–1c. Bar Harbor, Maine, lateral view of specimen from a smooth shell, with opercular valves.

2. Portland, Maine. Cat. No. 48016, U.S.N.M. Specimen showing normal development of carina and carinal latera, and broadly spreading latera and rostrum. See also plate 35, fig. 6.

3. Maine. Type-specimen of *Balanus geniculatus* Conrad. Coll. A.N.S.P. Page 158.

4. Fish Commission Station 134, off Thatchers Island. Rostral view of specimen growing on a smooth pebble.

5. Georges Bank, in 40 fathoms. Cat. No. 3522, U.S.N.M. Specimens growing on *Pecten magellanicus*.

6. Bar Harbor, Maine. Specimen growing on a small pebble, collected with fig. 1.

7. Bay of Fundy. Cat. No. 2308, U.S.N.M. Group on a smooth pebble.

Figs. 1a–1c enlarged, the others reduced.

PLATE 35.

Balanus balanus (Linnæus). Page 149.

FIGS. 1–1*b*. Aberdare Channel. Two groups, natural size, and basal view of rostrum.

2, 2*a*. Georges Bank, *Albatross* station 2079. Lateral view of group and basal margin, typically sculptured form with thin wall.

3. Off Eastport, Maine. Basal view of the lateral compartments of two specimens growing together. The exterior is like plate 34, fig. 1.

4. *Albatross* station 3289, Bering Sea. Cat. No. 48017, U.S.N.M. Growing on *Chrysodomus.* See also plate 33, fig. 6*c*

5. Georges Bank. Basal view of part of the rostrum.

6. Portland, Maine. Part of the base of specimen figured in plate 34, fig. 2, to show long lamellæ depending from outer lamina of the wall.

7. Cork, Ireland. Cat. No. 12092, U.S.N.M. Basal view of lateral compartment to show long lamellæ of the outer lamina.

8. Cape Prince of Wales, Alaska. Cat. No. 48018, U.S.N.M. Lateral and carinal views of specimens seated on *Chrysodomus.* Height of right-hand specimen, 27 mm.

Figs. 1, 1*b*, 2, 4, and 8 about natural size, the others enlarged.

PLATE 36.

FIG. 1. *Balanus rostratus* Hoek. Tokyo Harbor, Japan, No. 1814 A.Ñ.S.P.

2, 2*a*. *Balanus rostratus* Hoek. Japan. Cat. No. 48019, U.S.N.M. Lateral view and basal view of part of the rostrum. Page 138.

3, *Balanus rostratus apertus* Pilsbry. *Albatross* station 2849. Cat. No. 48020, U.S.N.M. Smooth specimen growing on *Terebratulina.*

4. *Balanus rostratus apertus* Pilsbry. Captains Bay, Unalaska. Cat. No. 9191, U.S.N.M. Growing on *Pecten,* and reproducing its sculpture. Page 144.

5. *Balanus rostratus apertus.* *Albatross* station 2849, on *Terebratulina.* Cat. No. 48020, U.S.N.M. Outer lamina of the lateral compartment filed, showing the parietal tubes. Page 144.

6. *Balanus rostratus apertus* Pilsbry. Captains Harbor, Unalaska. Typical spongicolous form, spinose and with deeply concave basis. Cat. No. 9190, U.S.N.M. Page 144.

7, 7*a*, 8. *Balanus rostratus heteropus* Pilsbry. *Albatross* station 2804. Puget Sound, Washington. Cat. No. 48022 U.S.N.M. Type and paratype. Tergum and lateral view of wall, the lateral compartment filed to show the parietal tubes. Page 142.

9. *Balanus balanus pugetensis* Pilsbry. *Albatross* station 2864. Cat. No. 48021, U.S.N.M. Filed to show parietal tubes. Page 163.

10, 10*a*, 10*b*. *Balanus balanus pugetensis* Pilsbry. San Juan Islands, Puget Sound. Type No. 2040 A.N.S.P. Lateral view, filed to show parietal tubes ; tergum, and scutum. Page 163.

PLATE 37.

FIGS. 1–1. *Balanus rostratus apertus* Pilsbry. Opercular valves of the type.
Page 144.

2–2c. *Balanus amphitrite peruvianus* Pilsbry. Opercular valves of the
type. Page 97.

Figs. 1–1c reproduced from the Bulletin of the Bureau of Fisheries. Figs. 2–2c
from the Proceedings of the United States National Museum. Drawn by
Helen Winchester.

PLATE 38.

FIGS. 1–1b. *Balanus rostratus dalli* Pilsbry. Unalaska. Cat. No. 9202, U.S.N.M.
Type. Lateral view, basis and basal edge of the rostrum.
Page 147.

1c, portion of rostrum filed to show parietal tubes.

2. *B. r. dalli.* Unalaska. Cat. No. 48023, U.S.N.M.

2a. *Balanus balanus* L. Unalaska. Cat. No. 48024, U.S.N.M. Growing on *B. r. dalli*, Cat. No. 48023, U.S.N.M. Page 159.

3. *Balanus rostratus suturalis* Pilsbry. Alaska. Cat. No. 48025,
U.S.N.M. Page 148.

4, 4a. *Balanus rostratus alaskensis* Pilsbry. Kodiak. Cat. No. 34515,
U.S.N.M. Lateral view and scutum. Page 141.

5. *Balanus rostratus alaskensis* Pilsbry. Cape Douglas, Alaska.
Cat. No. 48026, U.S.N.M. Basal edge of the rostrum. Page 141.

PLATE 39.

Balanus crenatus Bruguière. Page 165.

FIG. 1. Estuary of the Exe River, England. Group on a potsherd.

2, 2a, 2b, 2c. Gay Head, Massachusetts. On *Mytilus edulis*, growing on an iron
buoy. Cat. No. 48027, U.S.N.M.

3. Vineyard Sound, Massachusetts. Tergum of a tubular specimen.
Cat. No. 48028, U.S.N.M.

4, 4a. Davis Strait, Greenland. Scutum and tergum.

5. Vineyard Sound, Massachusetts. Cat. No. 48028, U.S.N.M. Group
of the tubular form growing on a pebble.

PLATE 40.

Balanus crenatus Bruguière. Page 165.

Fig. 1. Newfoundland Bank, in 35 fathoms. *Albatross* station 2443. Cat. No. 48029, U.S.N.M. Characteristic group, growing on shell of *Buccinum*.

2. Newfoundland Bank, 39 fathoms. *Albatross* station 2449. Solitary columnar form. Cat. No. 48030, U.S.N.M.

3. Sable Island, Nova Scotia. Growing on bark. Cat. No. 48031, U.S.N.M.

4, 4a. Inglefield Gulf, Greenland., Cat. No. 24911, U.S.N.M. Lateral compartment and interior view of rostrum.

5, 5a, 5b. Newfoundland Bank. Cat. No. 48032, U.S.N.M. Flaring and bell-shaped solitary specimens, one having the lateral compartments removed on one side to show the strong sutural ridges in the cavity.

6. Fishing banks. Cat. No. 9215, U.S.N.M. Growing on the shell of *Cyrtodaria*, which also supports a coral (gift of Gloucester fisherman).

All figures except 4 and 4a are natural size.

PLATE 41.

Fig. 1. *Balanus crenatus curviscutum* Pilsbry. Unalaska. Cat. No. 9201, U.S.N.M. Interior of tergum, showing narrow spur. See fig. 4.
Page 175.

2-2b. *Balanus crenatus* Bruguière. Tacoma, Washington. Cat. No. 48033, U.S.N.M. Nearly smooth specimen on a smooth pebble. Page 171.

3, 3a. *Balanus crenatus* Bruguière. Bering Sea. *Albatross* station 2462. Cat. No. 48034, U.S.N.M. Ribbed form, on gastropod. Page 171.

4. *B. c. curviscutum* Pilsbry. Unalaska. Cat. No. 9201, U.S.N.M. Entire individual and bases of four others, on *Mytilus edulis*. See also fig. 1. Page 175.

5. *B. crenatus* Bruguière. Alaska. Cat. No. 48035, U.S.N.M.
Page 171.

6-6e. *B. crenatus* Bruguière. Alaska. *Albatross* station 851. Cat. No. 48036, U.S.N.M. Smooth cylindric or liliaceous forms, with wide radii when crowded; more conic, with narrow radii when growing alone (fig. 6). Page 172.

PLATE 42.

Figs. 1-1b. *Balanus crenatus curviscutum* Pilsbry. Bristol Bay, Alaska. Cat. No. 48037, U.S.N.M. Fig. 1 is 11.5 mm. high. Page 175.

2-2d. *B. c. curviscutum*. *Albatross* station 3232, Bristol Bay, Alaska. Cat. No. 32948, U.S.N.M. Crowded, cylindric form. Fig. 2c represents specimen 20 mm. long. Page 175.

3-3b. *Balanus crenatus delicatus* Pilsbry. Humbolt Bar, California. Cat. No. 48039, U.S.N.M. Altitude of fig. 3, 13.25 mm. Page 177.

PLATE 43.

Balanus glandula Darwin. Page 178.

Figs. 1–1b. San Diego, California. Cat. No. 48002, U.S.N.M.
 2. San Diego, California. Cat. No. 11151, U.S.N.M. Rostrum.
 3, 3a. San Diego, California. Cat. No. 48040, U.S.N.M. Exterior nearly
 perfectly preserved.
 4–4c. Nazan Bay, Atka. Cat. No. 48001, U.S.N.M. Exterior and opercular valves deeply corroded, the outline of the tergum much
 changed thereby.
 5. Sitka, Alaska. Cat. No. 12316, U.S.N.M. Group on shell of *Mytilus*.
 6, 6a. Unalaska. Opercular valves of crowded examples.
 7, 7a. Sitka.

PLATE 44.

Balanus balanoides (Linnæus). Page 182.

Fig. 1. Exmouth, England. Cat. No. 12156, U.S.N.M. Rostrum of a worn
 specimen showing parietal pores and transverse septa.
 1a, 1b. Lower and upper views of a perfect example of the same lot.
 2. Savin Rock, New Haven. Cat. No. 4791, U.S.N.M. Group growing
 on a pile, showing transition from low-conic form (above) to the
 cylindric form caused by crowding (below). One of the latter is
 shown detached at A.
 3, 3a. Cumberland Gulf. Cat. No. 32946, U.S.N.M. Cylindric and conic
 forms.
 4. Loch Fyne, Scotland. Cat. No. 12150, U.S.N.M. Tubular, solitary
 form, supporting several conic individuals.
 5–5b. New Haven, Connecticut. Cat. No. 48041, U.S.N.M. Patelliform
 ribbed specimens growing on *Mytilus*, with scutum and tergum.
 6. New Haven, Connecticut. Cat. No. 32947, U.S.N.M. Tergum of a
 tubular individual.
 7–7d. Savin Rock, New Haven. Cat. No. 32947, U.S.N.M. Individuals
 and groups taken from a densely crowded colony.
 Figs. 1, 5a, 5b, 6 enlarged; the others about natural size.

PLATE 45.

Figs. 1–1c. *Balanus balanoides,* "var. a." Nahant, Massachusetts. No. 2051,
 A.N.S.P. Terga and scuta.	Page 186.
 2, 2a. *Balanus balanoides* (Linnæus). Nahant, Massachusetts. No. 2052,
 A.N.S.P. Tergum and scutum of small, deeply corroded speci-
 mens.	Page 186.
 3–3c. *B. b. calcaratus* Pilsbry. Cold Bay, Alaska. Cat. No. 32949.
 U.S.N.M. Group of entire animals, natural size. Scutum, both
 sides, and inner view of tergum.	Page 188.
 4, 4a. *B. b. calcaratus.* Sitka, Alaska. No. 2058, A.N.S.P. Lateral and
 basal views of an extremely thick and solid individual, 19 mm. in
 greatest diameter. The depression shown in fig. 4 is where a
 specimen of *B. crenatus* sat.	Page 188.
 4b, 4c. Tergum and scutum of same individual.

PLATE 46.

Balanus cariosus Pallas. Page 189.

FIG. 1. Unalaska. Cat. No. 9226, U.S.N.M. Part of basal edge of lateral compartment and rostrum.

2, 2a. Unalaska. Cat. No. 48042, U.S.N.M. Lateral views of cylindric specimens, the larger one deeply corroded. Natural size.

3. Nazan Bay, Atka. Cat. No. 48045, U.S.N.M Young, natural size.

4. Unalaska. Cat. No. 48043, U.S.N.M. Lateral view, natural size. Basal edge of same specimen shown in fig. 8.

5. Neah Bay, Washington. Cat. No. 43044, U.S.N.M. Natural size.

6. Unalaska. Cat. No. 9226, U.S.NM Colony of young specimens on a clam shell Natural size.

7. Nazan Bay, Atka. Cat. No. 48045, U.S.N.M. Immature stage, not corroded. Natural size.

8. Unalaska. Cat. No. 48043, U.S.N.M. Part of the basal edge of the rostrum.

9. Sanborn Harbor, Shumagin Islands. Cat. No. 8511, U.S.N.M. Two specimens which grew upon and in a sponge, part of which remains on the right side, the rest removed to show the barnacles. Natural size.

PLATE 47.

FIGS. 1–1c. *Balanus cariosus* (Pallas). Scutum and tergum of specimen from Unalaska. Page 189.

FIGS. 2–2d. *Balanus aeneas* Lanchester. Scutum and terga of the type, and tergum of a paratype. Page 221.

PLATE 48.

FIGS. 1–1g. *Balanus hawaiensis* Pilsbry. Interior view of rostrum; interior and outside views of tergum and scutum; an isolated individual, and two groups. All enlarged. Page 222.

2–2e. *Balanus tantillus* Pilsbry. Interior and exterior views of the opercular valves; group on a sea-urchin spine, and more enlarged view of three individuals of the same group. Page 224.

Figures 1c, 1g, 2c × 2¼

PLATE 49.

FIGS. 1–1d. *Balanus hesperius* Pilsbry. Bering Sea, *Albatross* station 3483.
Cat. No. 32935, U.S.N.M. Type. 1d, Scutum viewed from the
basal edge, the articular ridge projecting to the left.   Page 193.
2. Port Townsend, Washington. Form *lævidomus*, ribbed in the
lower part, growing on *Pecten caurinus*. Greatest diameter
17 mm.   Page 197.
3, 3a. *Albatross* station 3675. Cat. No. 32936. Form *lævidomus*, growing
on smooth shells of *Natica*, and varying from smooth to ribbed.
4. Sitka, Alaska. Cat. No. 12418, U.S.N.M. Form *lævidomus* on shell
of *Tegula*.
5. Puget Sound. Cat. No. 48067, U.S.N.M. Form *lævidomus*, growing
on shell of *Thais*.
6. *B. h. nipponensis*, Japan, *Albatross* station 3768. Type-specimen,
growing on shell of *Natica*.   Page 199.
7–7b. *B. hesperius*. Off Kamchatka. *Albatross* station 3780. Cat. No.
48066, U.S.N.M. Growing on egg capsules of *Chrysodomus*,
containing embryos.   Page 193.
8. *B. hesperius*. Alaska. Cat. No. 48065, U.S.N.M. Growing on anterior end of a *Chrysodomus*. Diameter 18 mm.   Page 195.

PLATE 50.

Balanus hesperius Pilsbry. Page 196.

FIGS. 1–1f. San Juan Island, Puget Sound. Form *lævidomus*. Upper view,
opercular valves, rostrum (fig. 1c) and a carinolateral compartment (fig. 1f).
2–2b. *Albatross* station 3096. Cat. No. 48068, U.S.N.M. Opercular valves
and lateral view, the latter from specimen 5.5 mm. in diameter.

PLATE 51.

FIG. 1. *Balanus flosculus* Darwin. Chile. Cat. No. 48050, U.S.N.M.
Group on shell of *Concholepas*. Diameter of individual specimens about 7 mm.   Page 219.
1a, 1c. Terga of specimens from the same group.
1b. Carina of specimens from the same group.
1d, 1e, 1f. Scuta of specimens from the same group.
2, 2a, 2b. *Balanus krügeri*, variety. Off Kagoshima Gulf, *Albatross* station
4935. Cat. No. 48051, U.S.N.M. Two views of tergum and inside
of scutum.   Page 214.

PLATE 52.

FIGS. 1–1f. *Balanus krügeri* Pilsbry. Type. Opercular valves, lateral view of
walls, and two views of the carinolateral compartment. A small
portion of the basis adheres in fig. 1f.   Page 214.
2. *Balanus hoekianus* Pilsbry. Inside of rostrum of the type.
Page 201.
2a, 2b. Top and lateral views of the wall.
2c–2f. Opercular valves.
Figs. 2–2f, reproduced from Bulletin of the Bureau of Fisheries.

PLATE 53.

Balanus hameri (Ascanius). Page 205.

FIG. 1–1*d*. Off Nova Scotia, 82 fathoms, U. S. F. C. loc. 41, 1877. Cat. No. 9044, U.S.N.M. Opercular valves and lateral view of a large specimen. Length of rostrum, 74 mm.

    2. *Albatross* station 2057. Cat. No. 48049, U.S.N.M. Basis of specimen growing on *Pecten magellanicus.*

    3. *Albatross* station 2251. Cat. No. 9163, U.S.N.M. Group on *Buccinum undatum*, natural size.

PLATE 54.

Balanus evermanni Pilsbry. Page 210.

FIG. 1. Tergum of a specimen from the Kuril Islands.

    2–2*c*. Scutum and tergum of the type-specimen. Junction of Clarence Strait and Behm Canal, Alaska. Cat. No. 41840, U.S.N.M.

    3–3*e*. Carina, 3*b*; lateral, 3, 3*d*; carinolateral, 3*c*; rostrum, 3*a*, 3*e* of a paratype. Half natural size.

PLATE 55.

FIGS. 1–1*d*. *Balanus declivis* Darwin, Bermuda. Cat. No. 48052, U.S.N.M. Lateral view and opercular valves. Page 230.

    2–2*d*. *Balanus orcutti* Pilsbry. Type. Lower California. Cat. No. 1783, A.N.S.P. Lateral and carinal views, and opercular valves.

Page 233.

PLATE 56.

FIGS. 1–1*c*. *Balanus galeatus* (Linnæus). South Carolina. Cat. No. 48047, U.S.N.M. Page 236.

    1*d*. *B. galeatus*. South Carolina. Cat. No. 48046, U.S.N.M. Length of right-hand specimen 19.5 mm. Page 236.

    2–2*d*. *Balanus scandens* Pilsbry. Japan. Type. Cat. No. 48048, U.S.N.M. Lateral view and opercular valves, all much enlarged. Page 239.

PLATE 57.

Acasta cyathus Darwin. Page 244.

FIGS. 1, 1*a*, 1*b*. Near Colon, *Albatross* station 2146. Cat. No. 7842, U.S.N.M.

    2, 2*a*, 2*b*, 2*c*. West Florida.

    3. Near the Dry Tortugas, *Albatross* station 2414.

PLATE 58.

FIG. 1. *Tetraclita squamosa japonica* Pilsbry. Wakanoura, Kishiu. Cat. No. 48053, US.N.M. Page 252.

    2, 2*a*. *T. s. japonica*. Japan. Cat. No. 48054, U.S.N.M. Page 252.

    3, 3*a*. *T. s. japonica*. Ayukawa, Japan. Cat. No. 48060, U.S.N.M. Opercular valves of the type. Page 260.

    4. *Tetraclita rosea* Krauss. Page 260.

    5, 5*a*, 5*b*. *Tetraclita squamosa rufotincta* Pilsbry. Aden. Cat. No. 48055, U.S.N.M. Opercular valves and group. Type. Page 253.

    6, 6*a*. *T. s. rufotincta*. Prison Island, Zanzibar. Opercular valves.

PLATE 59.

Tetraclita squamosa stalactifera Lamarck. Page 254.

Figs. 1. Abaco, Bahamas. Cat. No. 48056, U.S.N.M.
1*a*, 1*b*. Tergum and scutum of the same, Cat. No. 48056.
2. St. Thomas. Cat. No. 48057, U.S.N.M.
3. Porto Rico. Cat. No. 26360, U.S.N.M.
4. San Juan del Sur, Nicaragua, A.N.S.P.
5, 5*a*, 5*b*. Mazatlan, Mexico. Cat. No. 48058, U.S.N.M.
6, 6*a*, 6*b*. Form *floridana* Pilsbry. Type. Lake Worth, Florida. No. 1444, A.N.S.P. Page 255.

PLATE 60.

Figs. 1–1*d*. *Tetraclita squamosa milleporosa* Pilsbry. Albemarle, Galapagos. Cat. No. 48059, U.S.N.M. Type. Page 257.
2. *Tetraclita s. squamosa* form *confinis* Pilsbry. St. Georges Island, Gulf of California. Cat. No. 48089, U.S.N.M. Page 255.
3, 3*a*, 3*b*. *Tetraclita squamosa panamensis* Pilsbry. Panama. Cat. No. 48061. U.S.N.M. Type group in lateral and basal views, and a tergum. Page 256.

PLATE 61.

Fig. 1. *Tetraclita squamosa rubescens* Darwin. California. Cat. No. 6652, U.S.N.M. Group on a piece of sandstone. Page 257.
1*a*, 1*b*. *T. s. rubescens*. Cat. No. 6652, U.S.N.M. Basal view of entire specimen and lateral compartment of another.
1*c*, 1*d*. *T. s. rubescens*. Cat. No. 6652, U.S.N.M. Tergum and scutum.
1*e*. *T. s. rubescens*. Cat. No. 6652, U.S.N.M. Articulating face of a radius.
2. *T. s. rubescens*, form *elegans* Darwin. Cat. No. 58062, U.S.N.M. Page 258.
3–3*c*. *Tetraclita radiata* (Blainville). Opercular valves of a specimen from St. Thomas, West Indies. All drawn to same scale. Page 259.
4. *T. radiata*. Apical view of specimen from a Cape Cod whaler. Diameter of largest individual of the group, 7.5 mm.

PLATE 62.

Fig. 1. *Chelonibia testudinaria* (Linnæus). Iguana Cove, Albemarle, Galapagos. Cat. No. 48069, U.S.N.M. Page 264.
2. *C. testudinaria*. Florida. Cat. No. 48070, U.S.N.M.
3. *C. testudinaria*. San Luis Gonzales Bay, Gulf of California.
4. *C. testudinaria*. Brentons Point, Newport, Rhode Island. Cat. No. 48071, U.S.N.M.
5, 5*a*. *Chelonibia manati crenatibasis* Pilsbry. Cat. No. 48072, U.S.N.M. Page 266.
6. *Chelonibia testudinaria*. Scutum and tergum, the chitinous articular ridge removed. Enlarged. Page 263.
7–7*a*. *Chelonibia manati lobatibasis* Pilsbry. Type. Osprey, Florida. Fig. 7*a* enlarged. Page 263.

PLATE 63.

FIG. 1. *Coronula complanata* Mörch. Specimen in coll. A.N.S.P. Page 276.
2. *Coronula complanata.* Cat. No. 48075, U.S.N.M.
3, 3a. *Coronula complanata.* Cat. No. 48076, U.S.N.M. Edge of the radius (3a) and recipient sutural face (3).
4, 4a. *Chelonibia patula* Ranzani. Cedar Keys, Florida. Cat. No. 48074, U.S.N.M. Page 268.
5, 5a. *Chelonibia caretta* Spengler. Cat. No. 48073, U.S.N.M. Page 267.

PLATE 64.

Coronula reginæ Darwin. Page 275.

FIG. 1. Cat. No. 48078, U.S.N.M. Edge of a radius of the rostrum.
2. Unalaska. Cat. No. 9189, U.S.N.M. Basal view of largest specimen seen.
3, 4. Oregon. Cat. No. 48077, U.S.N.M. Part of rostrum, enlarged, and basal view. Diameter of specimen, 36.5 mm.
5. Snooks Arm, Newfoundland. Cat. No. 23326, U.S.N.M. Specimens embedded in skin of the whale's lip.
6. Unalaska. Cat. No. 3506, U.S.N.M.
7. Mouth of Umpqua River, Oregon. Cat. No. 48079, U.S.N.M. Shown in skin of whale.
Figures 1 and 8 enlarged.

PLATE 65.

FIG. 1. *Xenobalanus globicipitis* var. *pallidus* Pilsbry. Types. Cat. No. 23900, U.S.N.M. Page 284.
2, 2a. *X. globicipitis* Steenstrup. Chesapeake Bay. Cat. No. 48080. U.S.N.M. Page 283.
2b. *X. globicipitis.* North Dennis, Massachusetts. Basal view of walls.
3. *Coronula diadema* (Linnæus.) Alaska. Cat. No. 48081, U.S.N.M. Edge of radius. Page 273.
4. *Coronula diadema.*
5. *Tubicinella major* Lamarck. Cat. No. 48082, U.S.N.M. Form with unequal, widely spaced annuli. Page 281.

PLATE 66.

Cryptolepas rachianecti Dall. Page 279.

FIGS. 1–1b. Neah Bay, Washington. Cat. No. 48083, U.S.N.M. Upper, lower, and profile views of a large specimen.
2, 2a. Neah Bay. Cat. No. 48083, U.S.N.M. Lateral compartment of a cylindric specimen, outside and edge of radius.
3. Bering Island. Cat. No. 14313, U.S.N.M. Apical view of specimen embedded in whale skin.
4, 4a. Monterey, California. Cat. No. 9192, U.S.N.M. Paratype, upper and basal views.
5, 5a. Cat. No. 11609, U.S.N.M. Edge of the radius, two individuals, the right-hand one having the periphery broad and obtuse.

PLATE 67.

FIGS. 1-1b. *Platylepas hexastylos*. Delaware Bay. Top, profile, and basal views, the basis removed. Page 285.

1c. *P. hexastylos*. Basal view of one of the same lot, the basis in place.

2. *P. h. ichthyophila* Pilsbry. Rostrum of type. Page 287.

3. *P. hexastylos*. Osprey, Florida. Typical Rostrocarinal diameter of largest specimen, 17 mm. Page 286.

4. *P. hexastylos*, variety. Sicily. Diameter, 8.5 mm. Page 287.

PLATE 68.

FIGS. 1-1b. *Stomatolepas praegustator* Pilsbry. Dry Tortugas, Florida. Type. Upper, lateral, and basal views. Page 289.

2, 2a. *Stomatolepas elegans* (O. G. Costa). Photographic copies from Costa's plate. Page 289.

3-3b. *Cylindrolepas darwiniana* Pilsbry. Type. Inside of rostrum; lateral and top views. Page 288.

PLATE 69.

Hexelasma americanum Pilsbry. Page 390.

FIGS. 1-1g. Opercular valves, penis, and three views of the walls of the type.

2. Carina of another specimen.

3-3b. Carina, lateral compartment, and rostrum of other specimens.

PLATE 70.

Chthamalus fragilis Darwin. Page 297.

FIGS. 1a, 1b. Clearwater Harbor, Florida. Dorsal and lateral views of specimen which grew on a reed.

1c, 1d. Scutum and tergum of same.

2. Ocean City, New Jersey. Dorsal view of specimen taken from a *Balanus balanoides*.

3-3c. Varadero Beach, Cuba. Opercular valves and group growing on an oyster.

4. Clearwater Harbor, Florida. Part of a group on a reed.

PLATE 71.

FIGS. 1, 1b. *Chthamalus stellatus* (Poli). Scutum, tergum, and a group of corroded specimens on a stone, enlarged. Naples. Page 302.

2, 2a, 2b. Scutum, tergum and a group of tubular specimens. England.

3, 3a. Two conic individuals from Exmouth.

4, 4a. Scutum and group of specimens on a living *Thais haemastoma*. Fayal, Azores.

5, 5a, 5b. *Chthamalus stellatus angustitergum* Pilsbry. Group of six specimens of different ages, × 3; scutum and tergum. Bahamas. Page 305.

6, 6a. *Chthamalus stellatus bisinuatus* Pilsbry. Scutum and tergum of the type. Santa Catharina Island, Brazil. Page 306.

PLATE 72.

Figs. 1, 1a. *Chthamalus challengeri* Hoek. Scutum and tergum. Matsushima.
Page 307.

2, 2a. Scutum and tergum. Ayukawa.

3. Group growing on *Tetraclita*. Yokohama.

4, 4a. Scutum and tergum. Japan, on *Balanus cariosus*.

5, 5a. *Chthamalus malayensis*. Malay Peninsula. Scutum and tergum.
Page 310.

6, 6a, 6b. *Chthamalus moro*. Zamboanga, Mindanao. Group on *Tetraclita
scabrosa*. Scutum and tergum. Page 311.

PLATE 73.

Figs. 1, 1b. *Chthamalus caudatus* Pilsbry. Scutum, tergum, and top view of
the wall on the tergum of *Mitella*. Catbalonga, Samar. Cat. No.
48087, U.S.N.M. Page 314.

2. *Chthamalus withersi* Pilsbry. Top view. Page 312.

2a–2d. Opercular valves of the type-specimen.

2e. Rostrolateral compartment, inside view.

3–3b. *Chthamalus dalli* Pilsbry. Top view, scutum and tergum. Unalaska. Cat. No. 48069, U.S.N.M. Page 316.

4, 4a. *Chthamalus scabrosus* Darwin. Scutum and tergum of a specimen
from Valparaiso. Cat. No. 48089, U.S.N.M. Page 323.

PLATE 74.

Figs. 1, 1b. *Chthamalus fissus* Darwin. Scutum, tergum, and group on the
shell of *Mytilus californianus*, San Diego, California. Page 317.

2, 2a. *Chthamalus anisopoma* Pilsbry. Left tergum and scutum of the
type. Gulf of California. Page 317.

2b, 2c. Right scutum and tergum of the same individual, drawn to the
same scale as figs. 2, 2a.

2d. Exterior of scutum of an unusually well-preserved individual.

2e. Carina, interior view.

2f. Part of the group, enlarged.

PLATE 75.

Fig. 1. *Chthamalus imperatrix* Pilsbry. Interior of rostrolateral compartment. Page 320.

1a. Interior of lateral compartment.

1b. Group, seated on a stone; a nearly unworn individual in the lower
median part.

1c, 1d. Scutum and tergum, interior.

1e. Carina, interior view.

2. *Chthamalus panamensis* Pilsbry. Exterior of scutum. Page 319.

2a, 2b. Two individuals of the typical lot.

2c. Exterior of tergum.

2d, 2e. Interior of scutum and tergum of the type.

PLATE 76.

Chthamalus hembeli Conrad. Page 324.

Figs. 1, 1a. Napili Harbor, Maui. Cirri and penis.

2, 2a. Hilo, Hawaii. Tergum and scutum of right-hand specimen, fig. 2b.

2b. Pair of old specimens.

2c. Scutum and tergum united, inside view; same specimen.

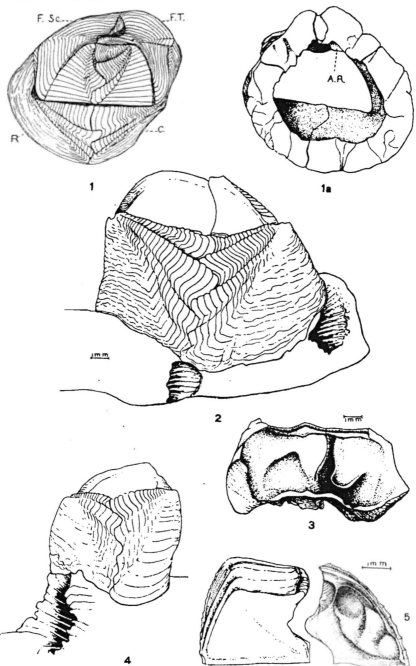

VERRUCA CORALIOPHILA.

FOR EXPLANATION OF FIGURES SEE PAGE 339.

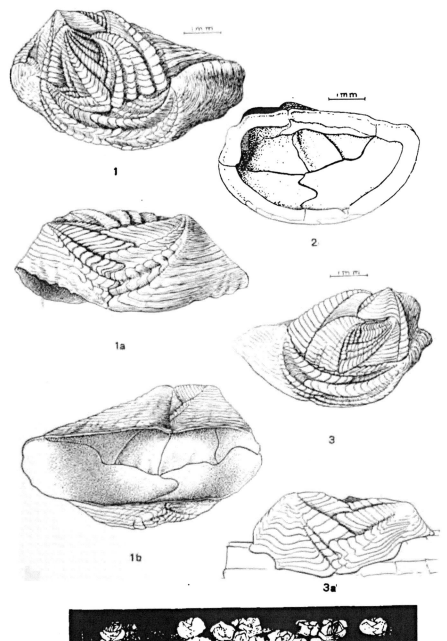

1-2, VERRUCA ALBA; 3, 3A, V. A. BARBADENSIS; 4, V. A. CARIBBEA.

FOR EXPLANATION OF FIGURES SEE PAGE 339.

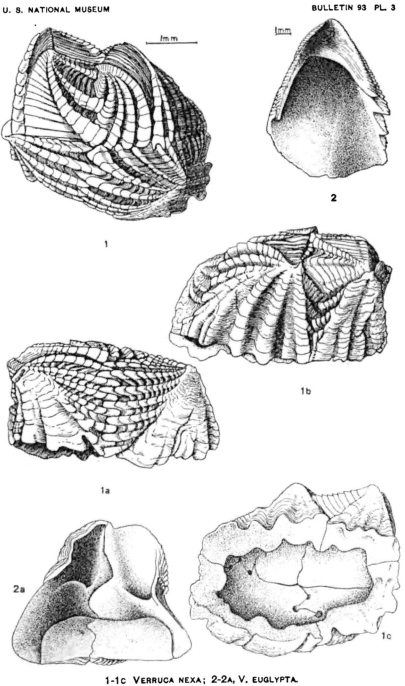

1-1c VERRUCA NEXA; 2-2A, V. EUGLYPTA.

FOR EXPLANATION OF FIGURES SEE PAGE 339.

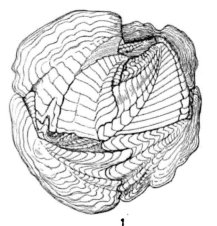

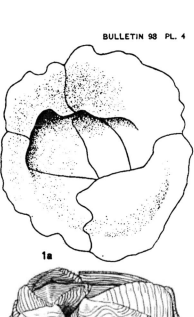

1a

1

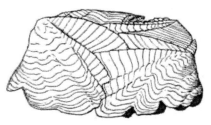

1b

1c

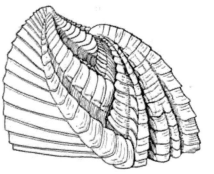

2

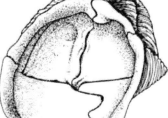

4

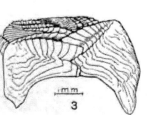

3

4a   4b

1-3 VERRUCA FLORIDANA; 4–4B V. CALOTHECA.

FOR EXPLANATION OF FIGURES SEE PAGE 339.

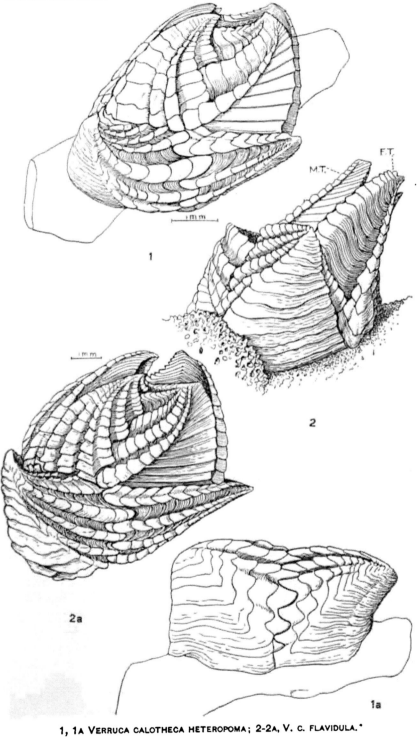

1, 1A VERRUCA CALOTHECA HETEROPOMA; 2-2A, V. C. FLAVIDULA.

FOR EXPLANATION OF FIGURES SEE PAGE 339.

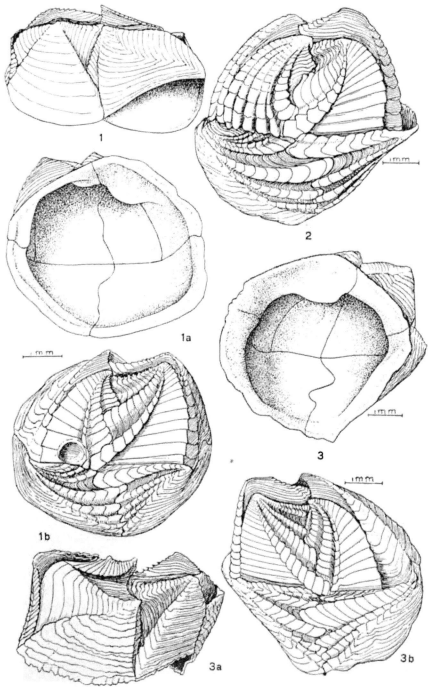

1-1B, VERRUCA XANTHIA; 2, V. X. INSCULPTA; 3-3B, V. ENTOBAPTA.

FOR EXPLANATION OF FIGURES SEE PAGE 340.

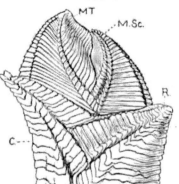

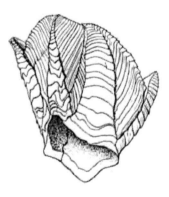

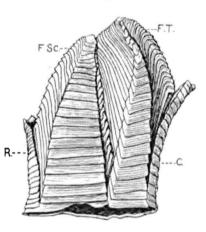

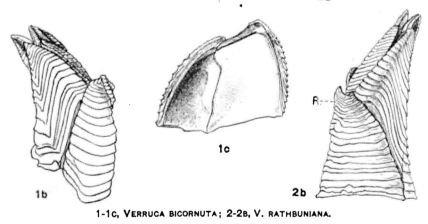

1-1c, VERRUCA BICORNUTA; 2-2b, V. RATHBUNIANA.

FOR EXPLANATION OF FIGURES SEE PAGE 340.

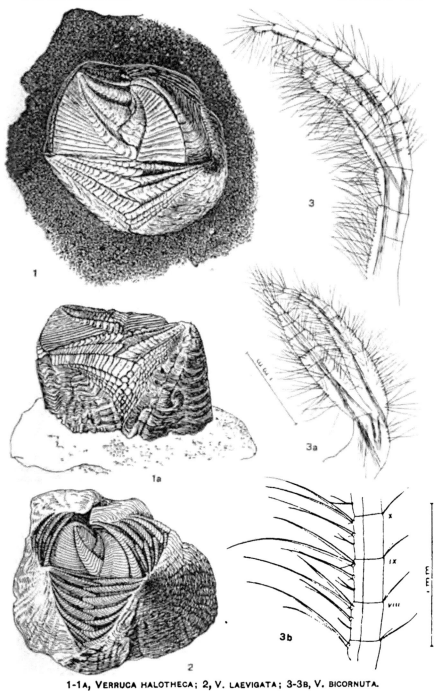

1-1A, VERRUCA HALOTHECA; 2, V. LAEVIGATA; 3-3B, V. BICORNUTA.

FOR EXPLANATION OF FIGURES SEE PAGE 340.

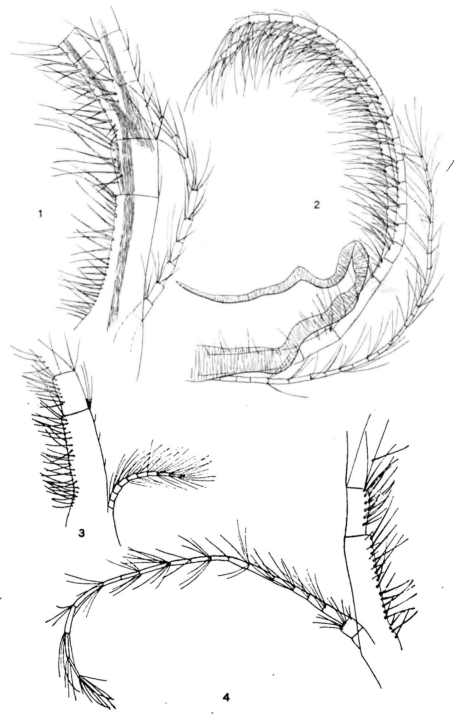

1, VERRUCA BICORNUTA; 2, V. ALBA; 3, V. EUGLYPTA; 4, V. ENTOBAPTA.

FOR EXPLANATION OF FIGURES SEE PAGE 340.

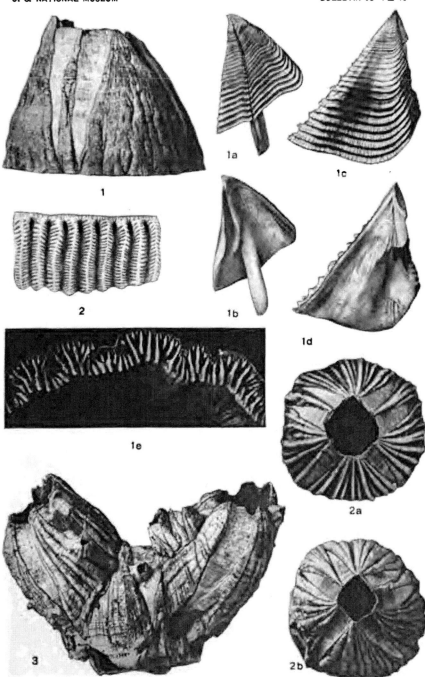

1-1E, BALANUS TINTINNABULUM; 2-3, B. T. ZEBRA.

FOR EXPLANATION OF FIGURES SEE PAGE 340.

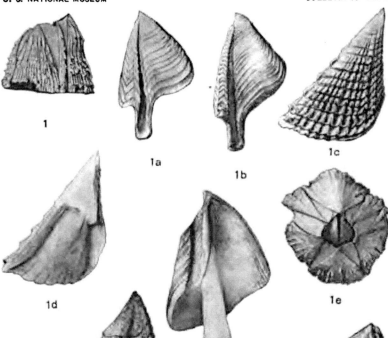

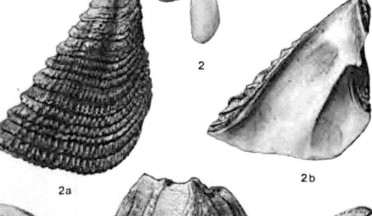

1-1E, BALANUS TINTINNABULUM OCCATOR; 2-2E, B. T. VOLCANO.

FOR EXPLANATION OF FIGURES SEE PAGE 340.

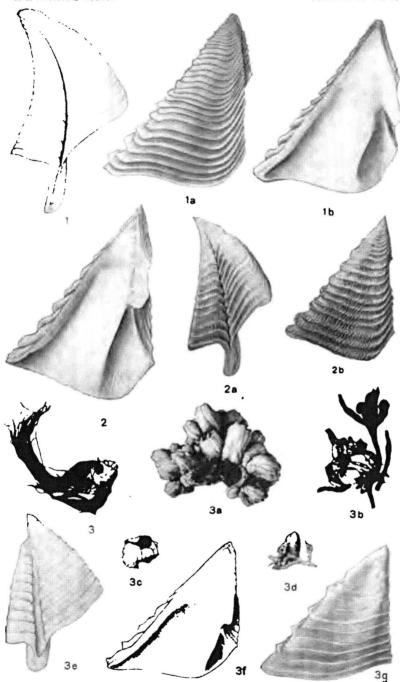

1-1B, BALANUS TINTINNABULUM GALAPAGANUS; 2-2B, B. T. AZORICUS; 3-3G,
B. ALGICOLA.

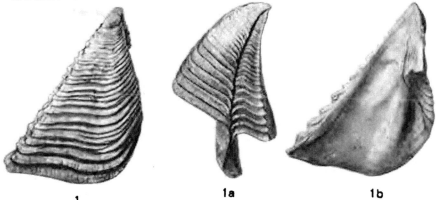

1

1a

1b

1c

1e

2

1d

2b

2a

2c

2d

2e

BALANUS TINTINNABULUM ANTILLENSIS.

FOR EXPLANATION OF FIGURES SEE PAGE 341.

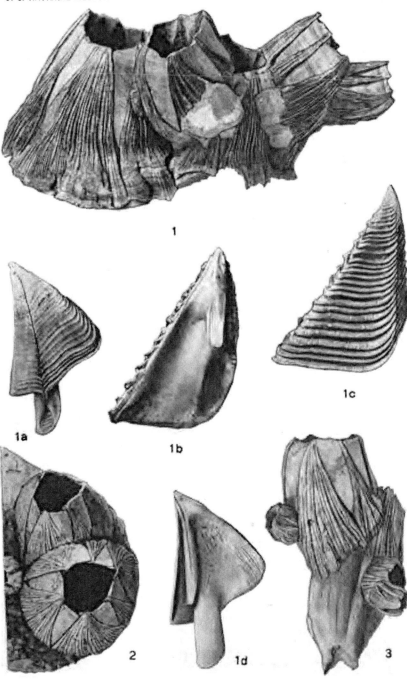

BALANUS TINTINNABULUM CALIFORNICUS.

FOR EXPLANATION OF FIGURES SEE PAGE 341.

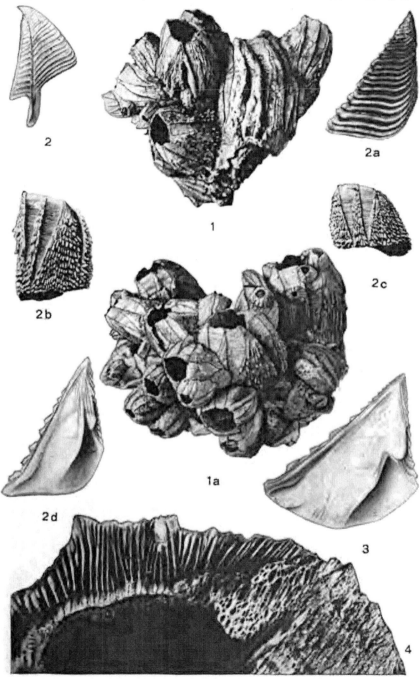

1-2D, BALANUS TINTINNABULUM PENINSULARIS; 3, B. T. CONCINNUS; 4, B. T. CALIFORNICUS.

FOR EXPLANATION OF FIGURES SEE PAGE 341.

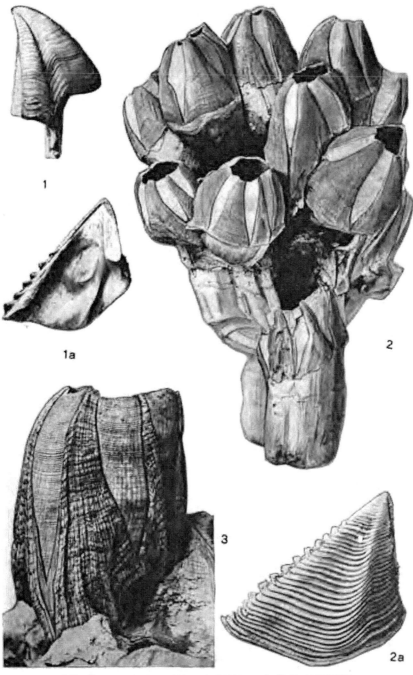

1-2A, BALANUS TINTINNABULUM COCCOPOMA; 3, B. T. CONCINNUS.

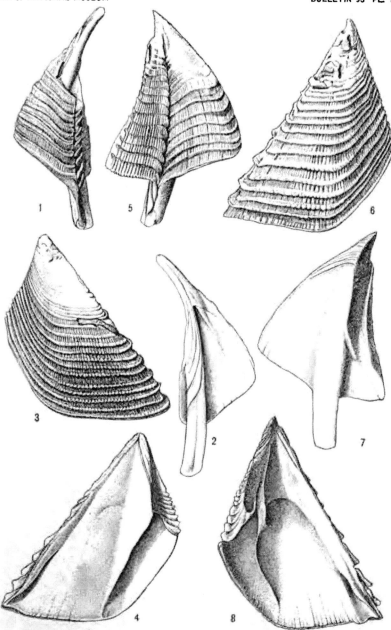

1-4, BALANUS PSITTACUS; 5-8, BALANUS TINTINNABULUM CONCINNUS.

FOR EXPLANATION OF FIGURES SEE PAGE 342.

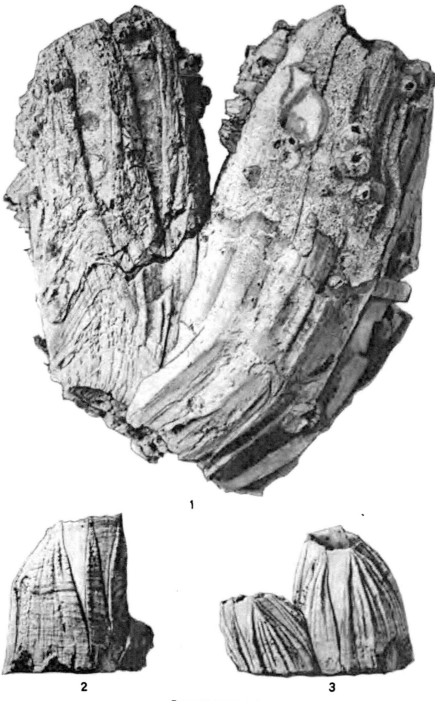

1

2   3

BALANUS PSITTACUS.

FOR EXPLANATION OF FIGURES SEE PAGE 342.

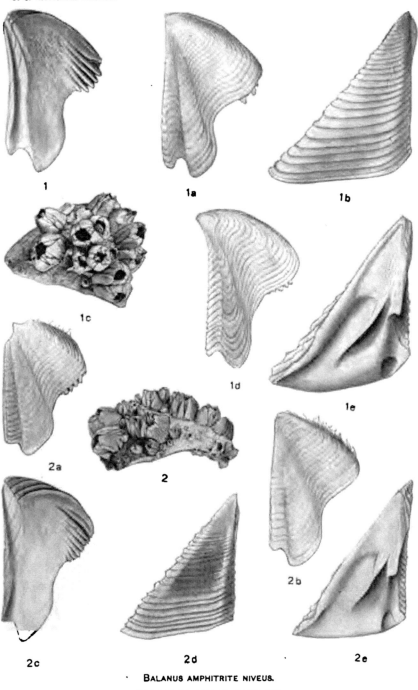

1

1a

1b

1c

1d

1e

2a

2

2b

2c

2d

2e

BALANUS AMPHITRITE NIVEUS.

FOR EXPLANATION OF FIGURES SEE PAGE 342.

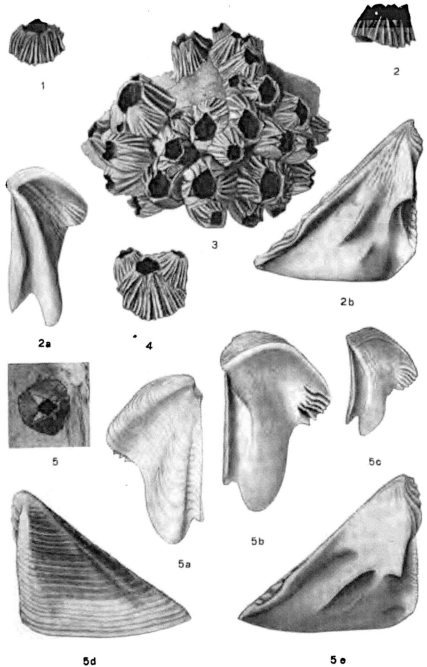

1-4, BALANUS AMPHITRITE ALBICOSTATUS; 5-5E, B. A. INEXPECTATUS.

FOR EXPLANATION OF FIGURES SEE PAGE 342.

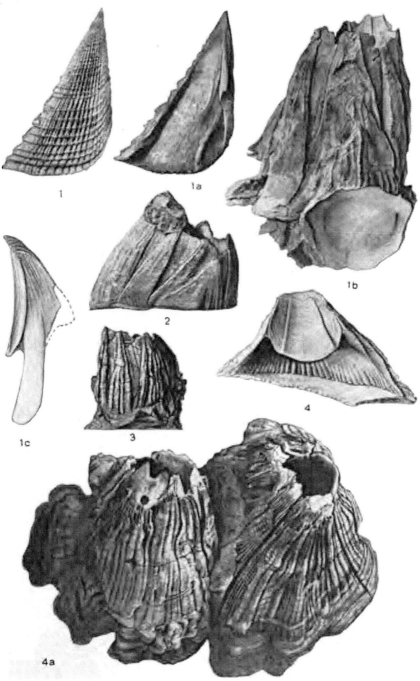

1-1c, BALANUS CONCAVUS; 2, 3, B. C. GLYPTOPOMA; 4, 4A, B. REGALIS.

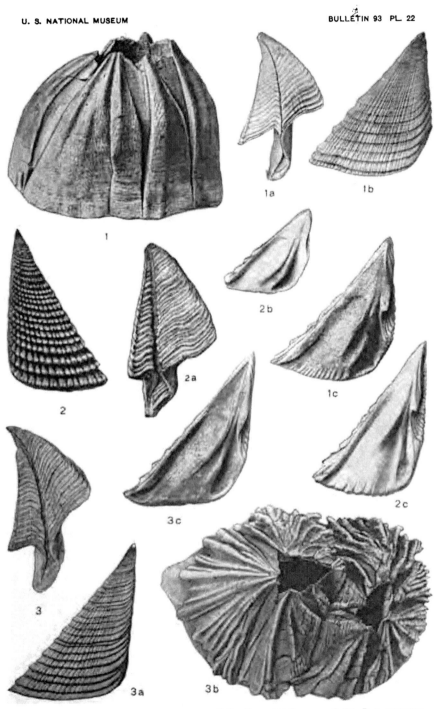

1-1c, BALANUS CONCAVUS CHESAPEAKENSIS; 2-2c, B. C. GLYPTOPOMA; 3-3c, B. C. PROTEUS

FOR EXPLANATION OF FIGURES SEE PAGE 343.

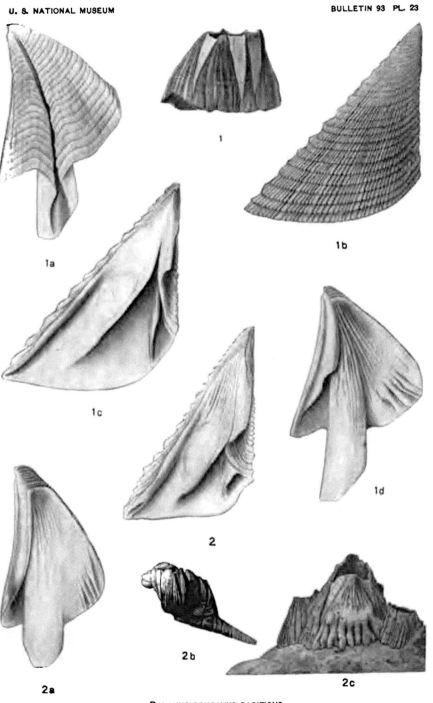

1

1a

1b

1c

2

1d

2a

2b

2c

BALANUS CONCAVUS PACIFICUS.

FOR EXPLANATION OF FIGURES SEE PAGE 343.

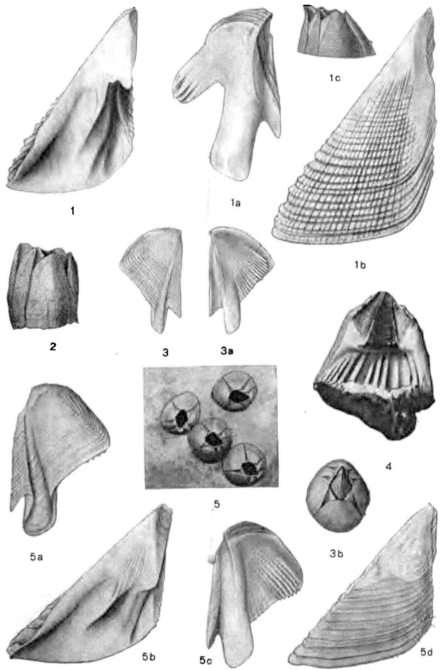

1-2, BALANUS EBURNEUS; 3-3B, 5-5D, B. IMPROVISUS; 4, B. AMPHITRITE PERUVIANUS.

FOR EXPLANATION OF FIGURES SEE PAGE 343.

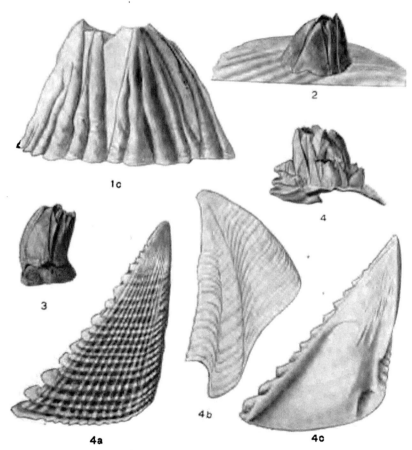

1-1c, BALANUS CALIDUS; 2-4c, B. SPONGICOLA.

FOR EXPLANATION OF FIGURES SEE PAGE 344.

10

10 a

13

12

11

13a

12 a

13b

13c

13d

13e

BALANUS TRIGONUS.

FOR EXPLANATION OF FIGURES SEE PAGE 344.

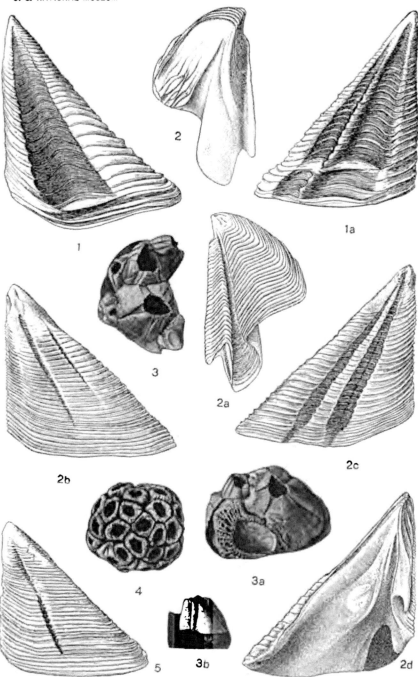

1-1A, 3-3B, BALANUS LAEVIS; 2-2D, 4, 5, B. L. NITIDUS.

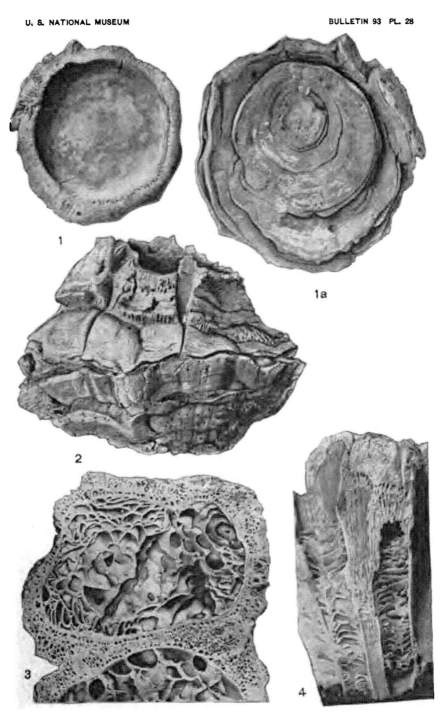

1-3, BALANUS GREGARIUS; 4, B. LAEVIS COQUIMBENSIS.

FOR EXPLANATION OF FIGURES SEE PAGE 344.

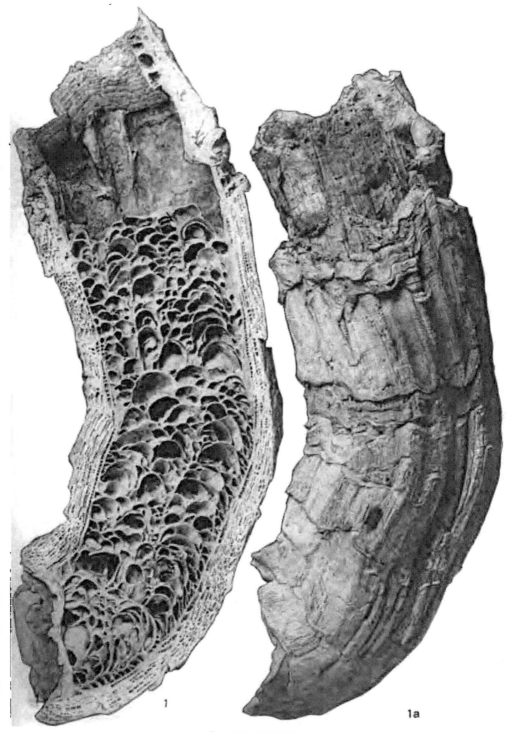

1

1a

BALANUS GREGARIUS.

FOR EXPLANATION OF FIGURES SEE PAGE 345.

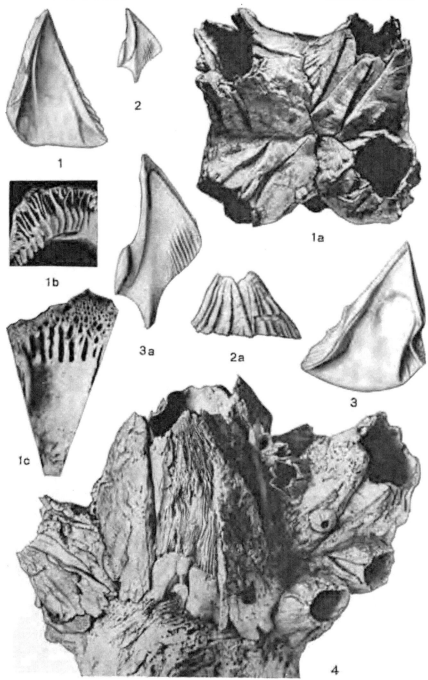

BALANUS NUBILIS.

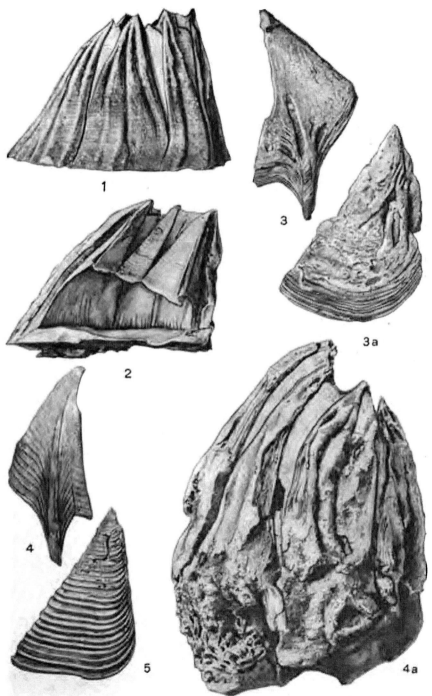

1, 2 4A, BALANUS AQUILA; 3, 3A, 4, 5 B. NUBILIS.

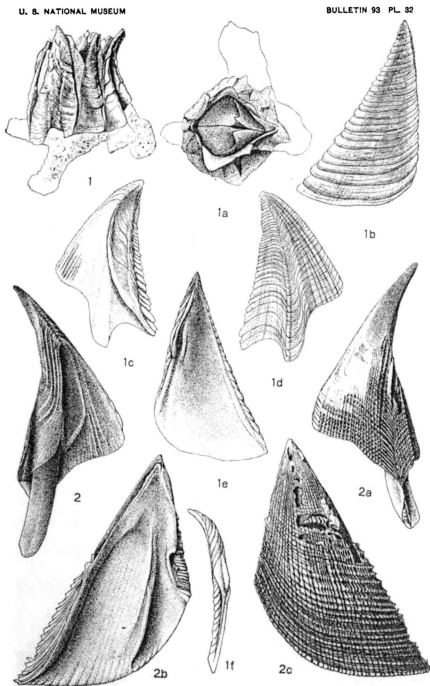

1-1F, BALANUS FLOS; 2-2C, B. AQUILA.

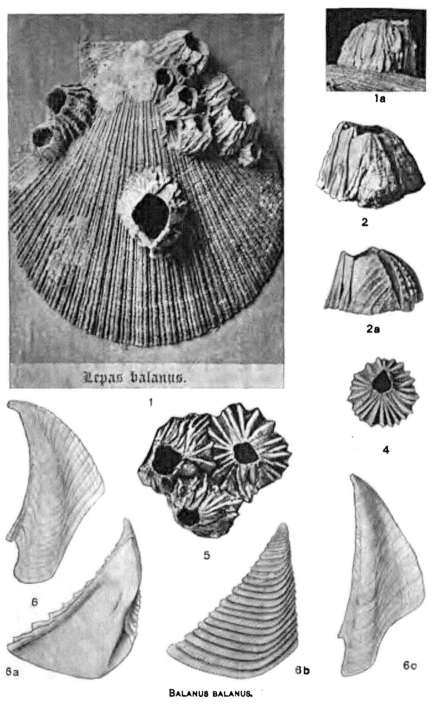

Lepas balanus.

1a

2

2a

4

1

5

6

6a

6b

6c

BALANUS BALANUS.

FOR EXPLANATION OF FIGURES SEE PAGE 346.

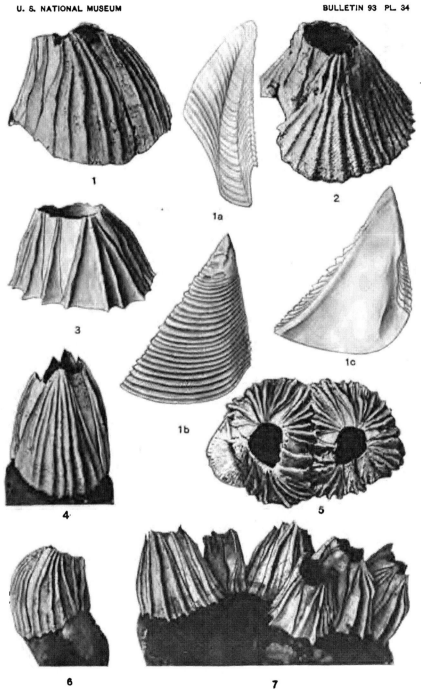

BALANUS BALANUS.

FOR EXPLANATION OF FIGURES SEE PAGE 346.

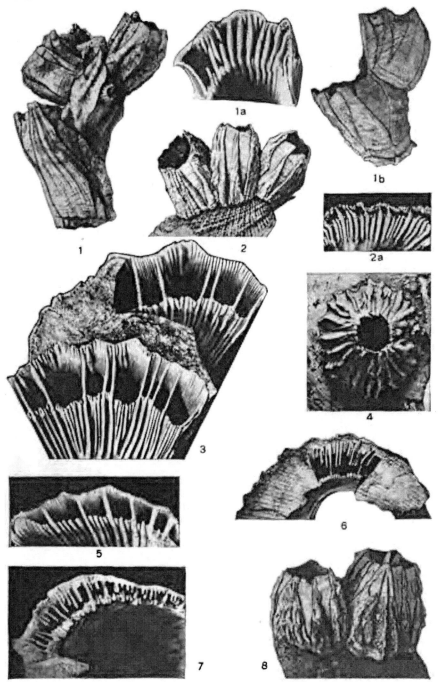

1a

1b

2a

1

2

3

4

5

6

7

8

BALANUS BALANUS.

FOR EXPLANATION OF FIGURES SEE PAGE 347.

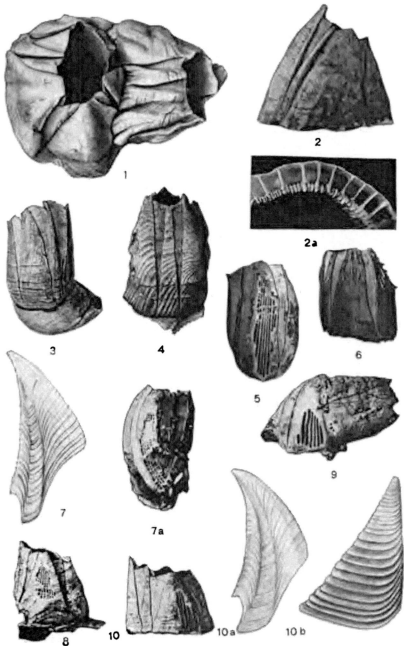

1-2A, BALANUS ROSTRATUS; 3-6, B. R. APERTUS; 7-8, B. R. HETEROPUS;
9-10B, BALANUS BALANUS PUGETENSIS.

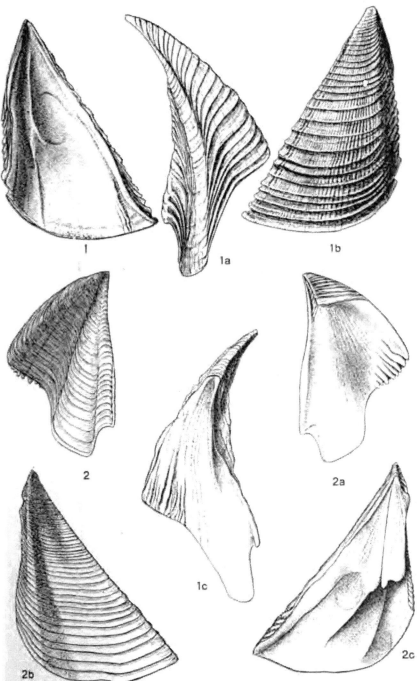

1-1C, BELANUS ROSTRATUS APERTUS; 2-2C, B. AMPHITRITE PERUVIANUS.

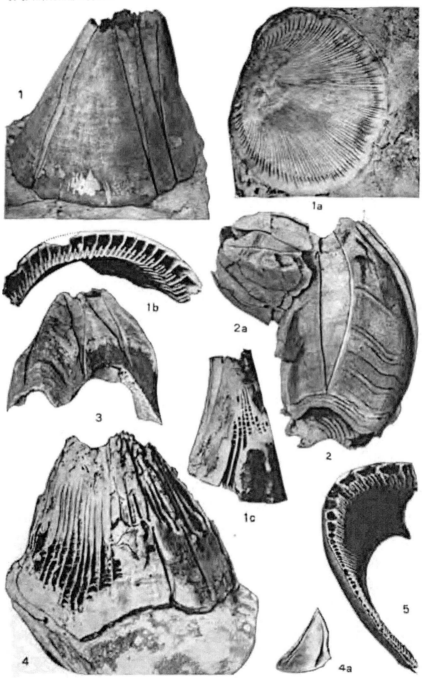

1-2, BALANUS ROSTRATUS DALLI; 2A, B. BALANUS; 3, B. ROSTRATUS SUTURALIS;
4-5. B. R. ALASKENSIS.

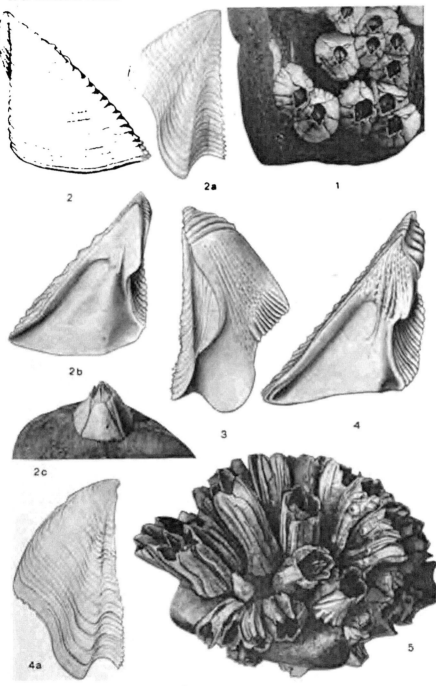

BALANUS CRENATUS.

FOR EXPLANATION OF FIGURES SEE PAGE 348.

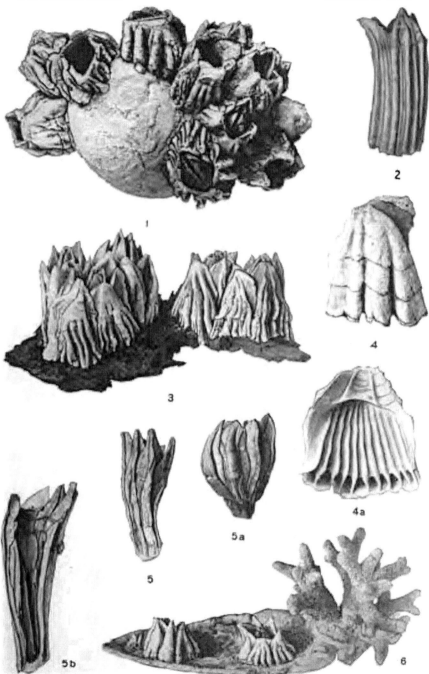

BALANUS CRENATUS.

FOR EXPLANATION OF FIGURES SEE PAGE 349.

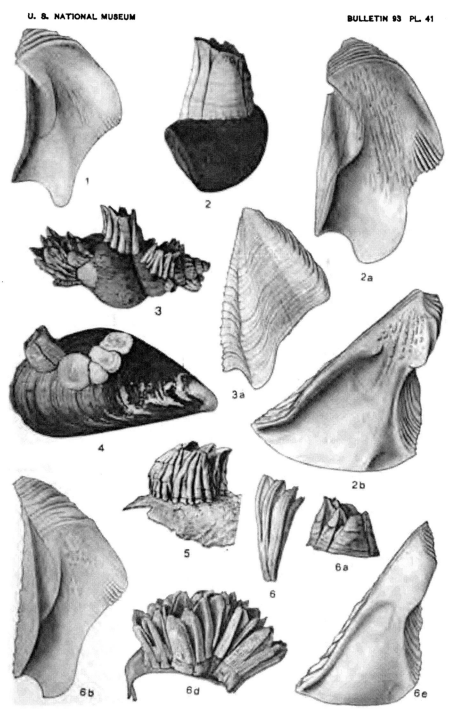

1, 4, BALANUS CRENATUS CURVISCUTUM; 2-6A, 5-6E, B. CRENATUS.

FOR EXPLANATION OF FIGURES SEE PAGE 349.

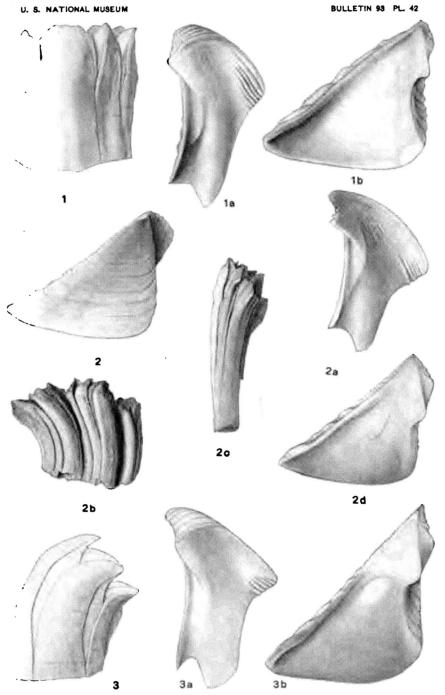

1-2D, BALANUS CRENATUS CURVISCUTUM; 3-3B, B. C. DELICATUS.

FOR EXPLANATION OF FIGURES SEE PAGE 349.

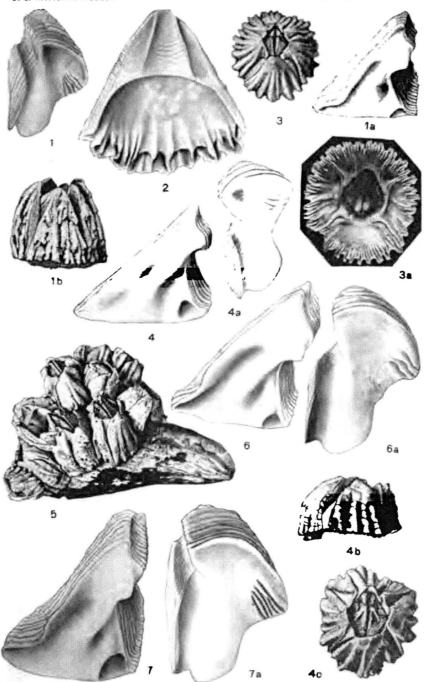

BALANUS GLANDULA.

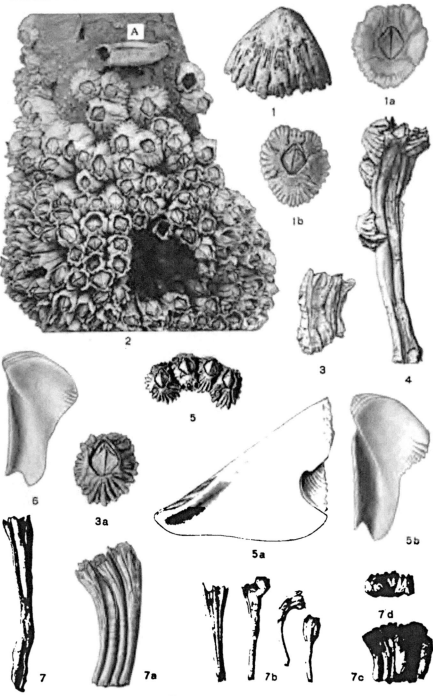

BALANUS BALANOIDES.

FOR EXPLANATION OF FIGURES SEE PAGE 350.

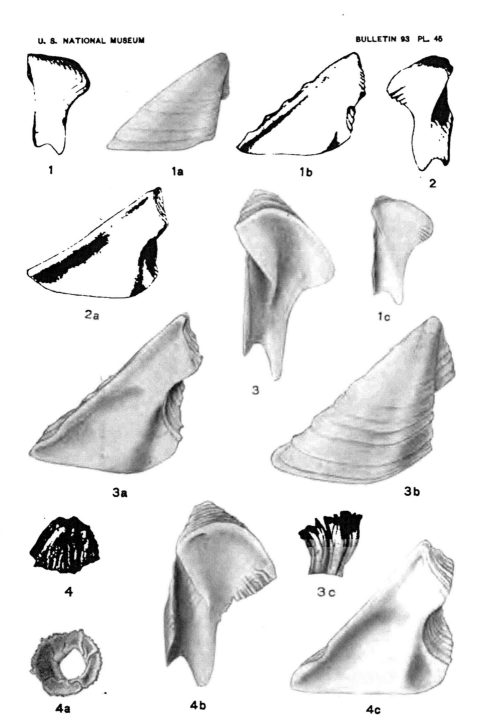

1-2A BALANUS BALANOIDES; 3-4C, B. B. CALCARATUS.

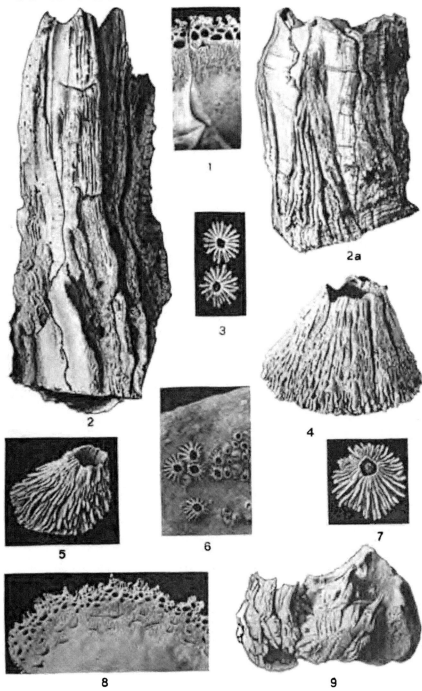

BALANUS CARIOSUS.

FOR EXPLANATION OF FIGURES SEE PAGE 351.

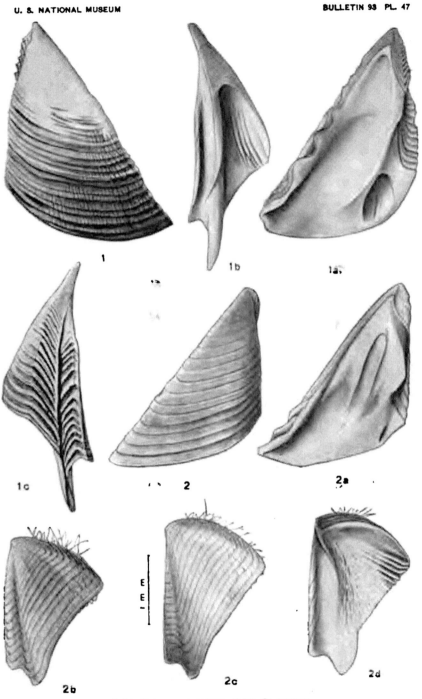

1   1b   1a,

1c   2   2a

2b   2c   2d

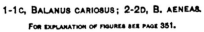

1-1c, BALANUS CARIOSUS; 2-2D, B. AENEAS.

FOR EXPLANATION OF FIGURES SEE PAGE 351.

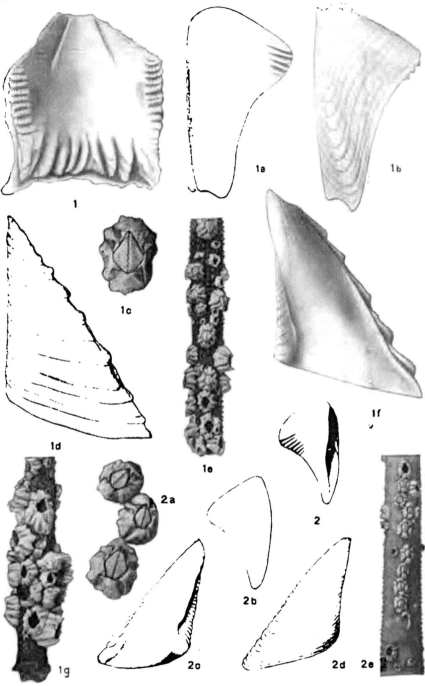

1-1G, BALANUS HAWAIENSIS; 2-2E, B. TANTILLUS.

FOR EXPLANATION OF FIGURES SEE PAGE 351.

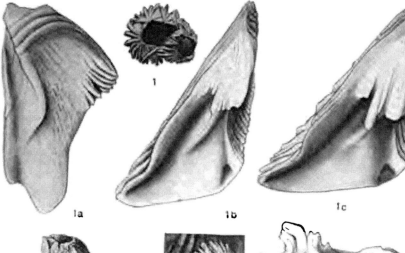

1

1a

1b

1c

2

1d

3

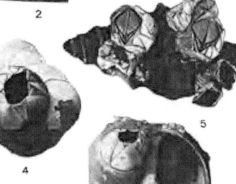

5

3a

4

6

7

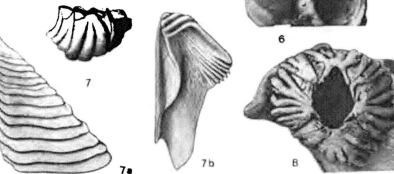

7a

7b

8

1-1D, 7-8, Balanus hesperius; 2-5, B. h. laevidomus; 6, B. h. nipponensis.

For explanation of figures see page 352.

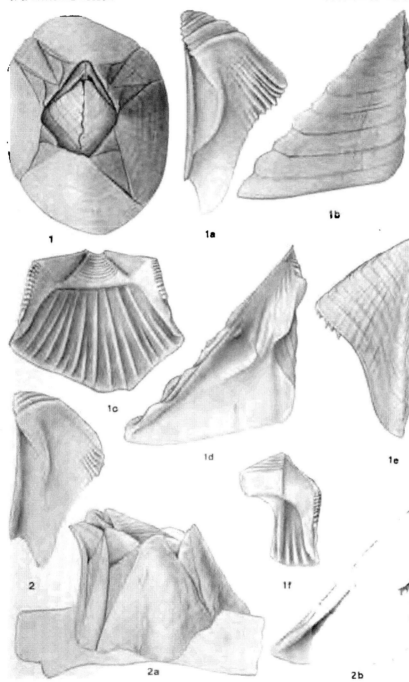

BALANUS HESPERIUS LAEVIDOMUS.

FOR EXPLANATION OF FIGURES SEE PAGE 352.

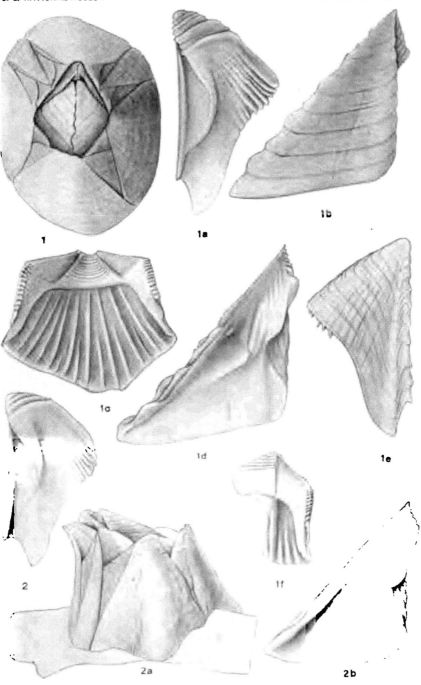

BALANUS HESPERIUS LAEVIDOMUS.

FOR EXPLANATION OF FIGURES SEE PAGE 352.

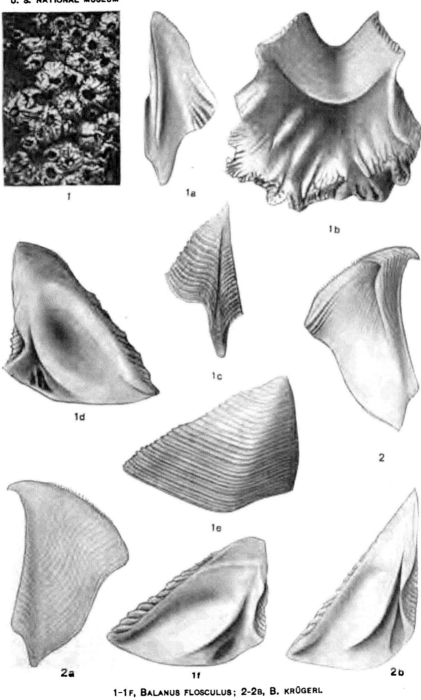

1 1a 1b 1c 1d 1e 1f 2a 2 2b

1-1F, BALANUS FLOSCULUS; 2-2B, B. KRÜGERI.

FOR EXPLANATION OF FIGURES SEE PAGE 352.

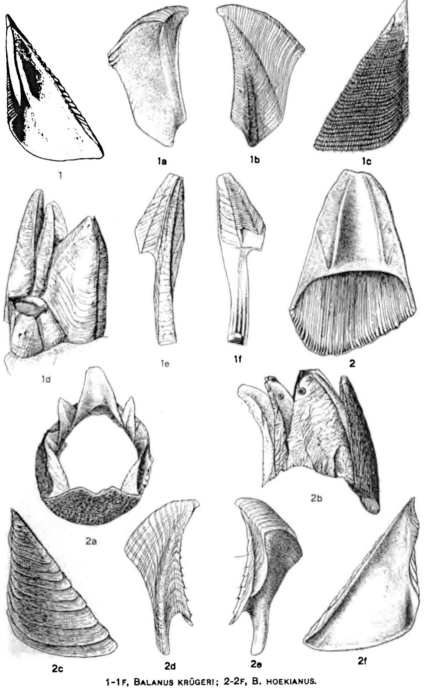

1-1F, BALANUS KRÜGERI; 2-2F, B. HOEKIANUS.

FOR EXPLANATION OF FIGURES SEE PAGE 352.

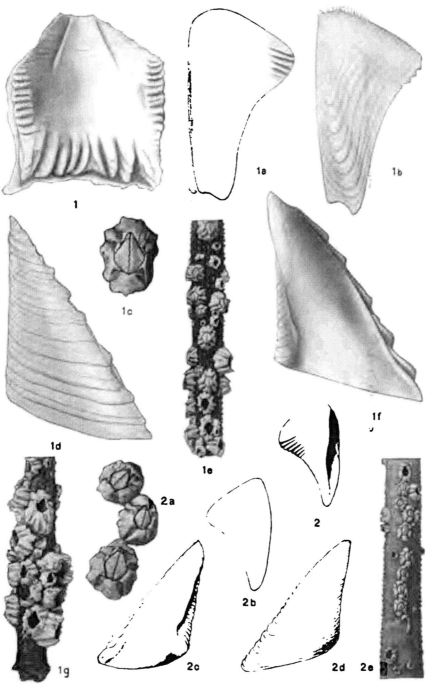

1-1G, BALANUS HAWAIENSIS; 2-2E, B. TANTILLUS.

FOR EXPLANATION OF FIGURES SEE PAGE 351.

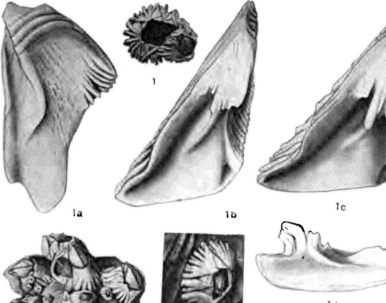

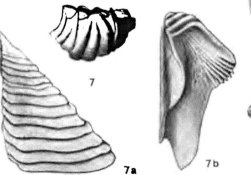

1-1D, 7-8, BALANUS HESPERIUS; 2-5, B. H. LAEVIDOMUS; 6, B. H. NIPPONENSIS.

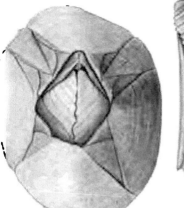
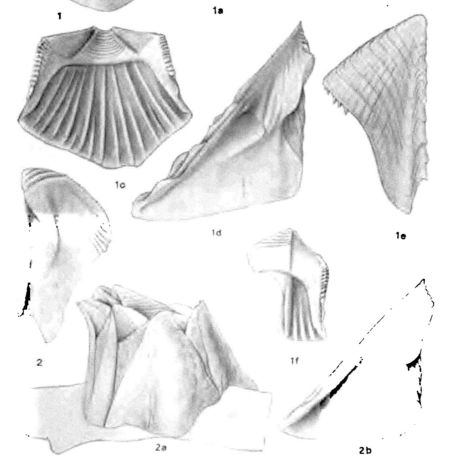

1

1a

1b

1c

1d

1e

1f

2

2a

2b

BALANUS HESPERIUS LAEVIDOMUS.

FOR EXPLANATION OF FIGURES SEE PAGE 352.

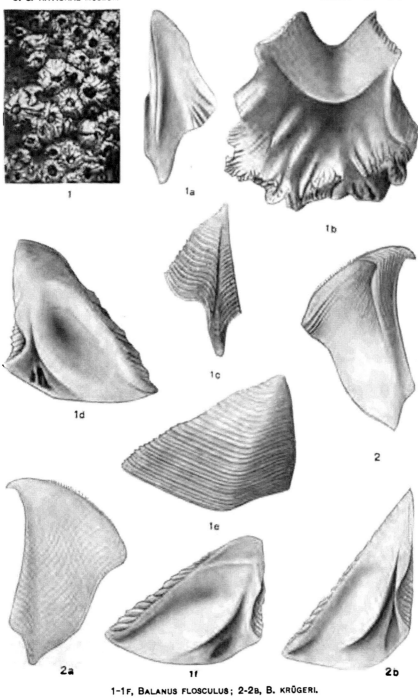

1-1F, BALANUS FLOSCULUS; 2-2B, B. KRÜGERI.

FOR EXPLANATION OF FIGURES SEE PAGE 352.

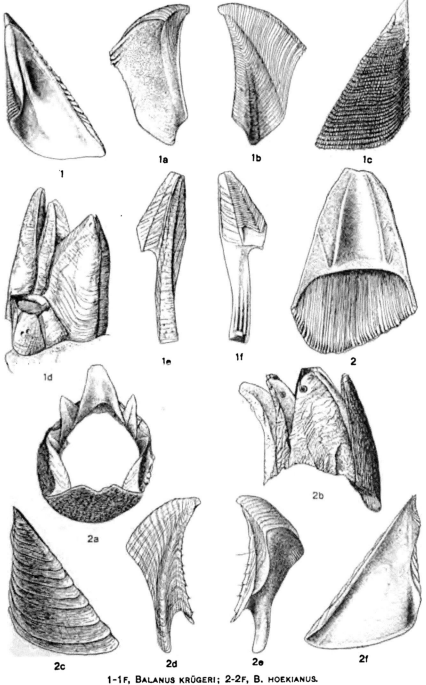

1a   1b   1c

1

1e   1f   2

1d

2b

2a

2c   2d   2e   2f

1-1F, BALANUS KRÜGERI; 2-2F, B. HOEKIANUS.

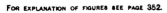

FOR EXPLANATION OF FIGURES SEE PAGE 352.

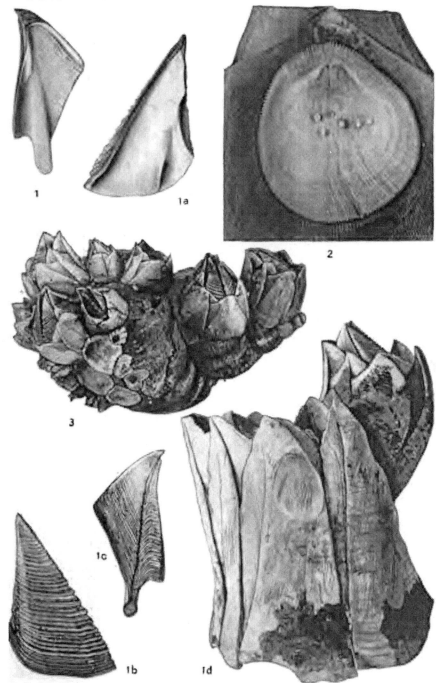

BALANUS HAMERI

FOR EXPLANATION OF FIGURES SEE PAGE 353.

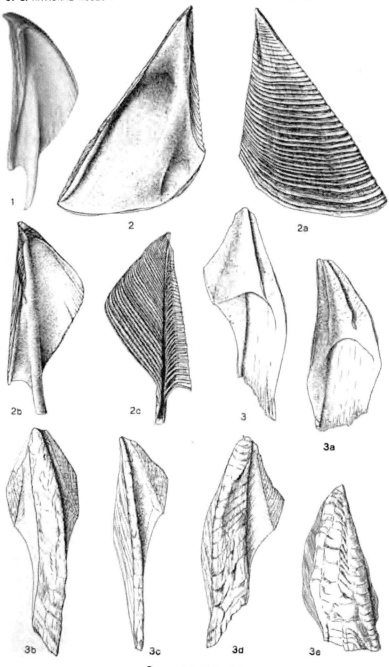

BALANUS EVERMANNI.

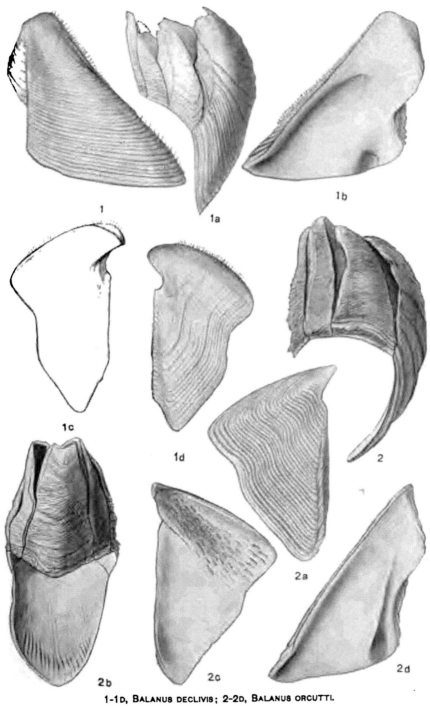

1

1a

1b

1c

1d

2

2a

2b

2c

2d

1-1D, BALANUS DECLIVIS; 2-2D, BALANUS ORCUTTI.

FOR EXPLANATION OF FIGURES SEE PAGE 353.

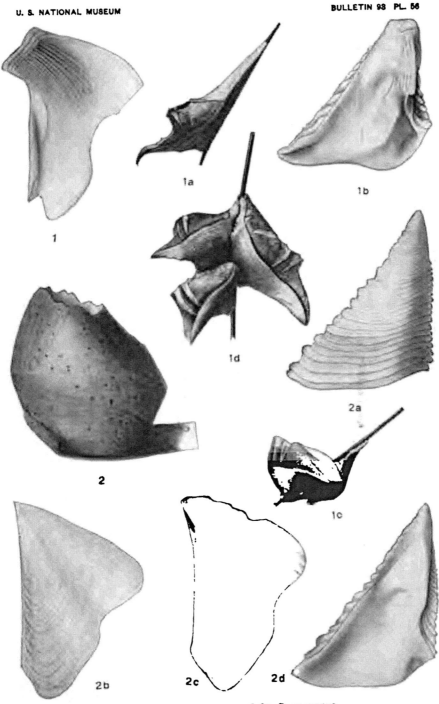

1-1D, BALANUS GALEATUS; 2-2D, B. SCANDENS.

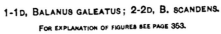

FOR EXPLANATION OF FIGURES SEE PAGE 353.

BULLETIN 93 PL. 57

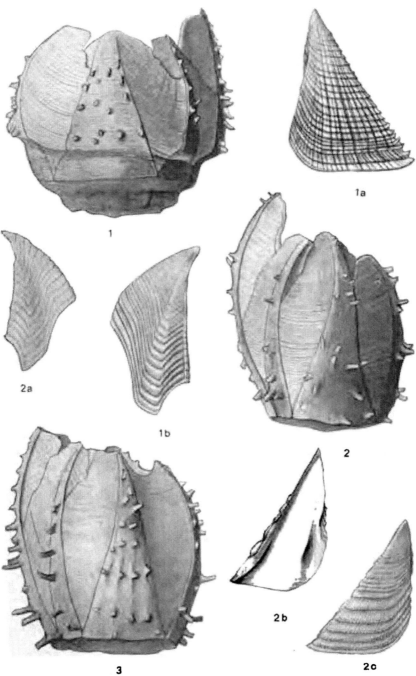

ACASTA CYATHUS.

FOR EXPLANATION OF FIGURES SEE PAGE 353.

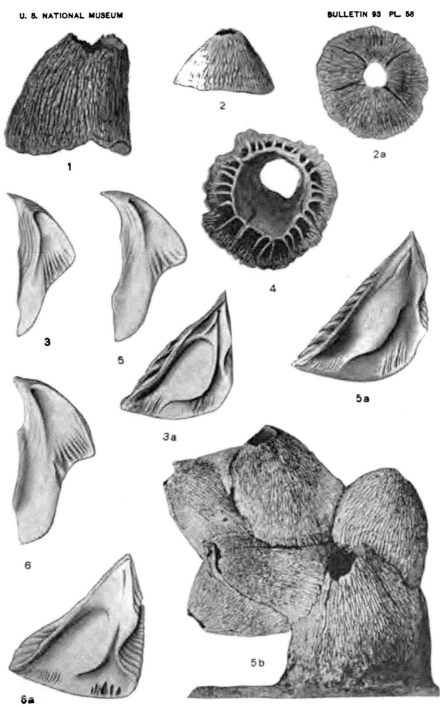

1-3A, TETRACLITA SQUAMOSA JAPONICA; 4, T. ROSEA; 5-6A, T. SQUAMOSA RUFOTINCTA.

FOR EXPLANATION OF FIGURES SEE PAGE 353.

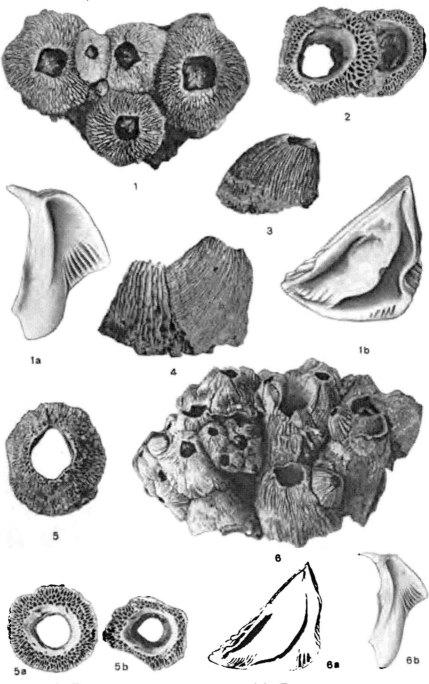

1-5B, TETRACLITA SQUAMOSA STALACTIFERA; 6-6B, T. S. STALACTIFERA FORM
FLORIDANA.

FOR EXPLANATION OF FIGURES SEE PAGE 354.

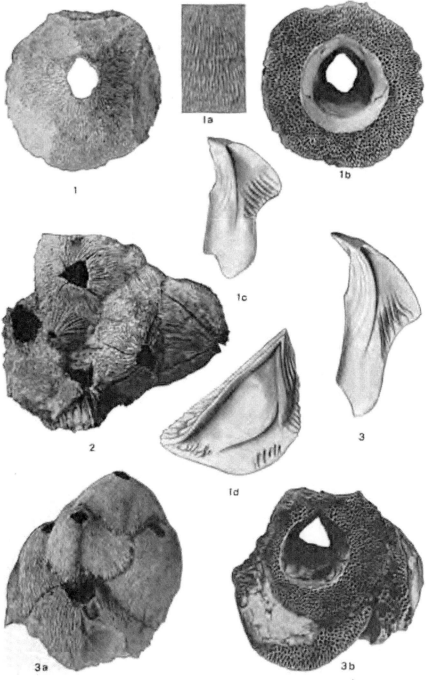

1-1D, TETRACLITA SQUAMOSA MILLEPOROSA; 2, T. SQUAMOSA FORM CONFINIS;
3-3B, T. S. PANAMENSIS.

For explanation of figures see page 354.

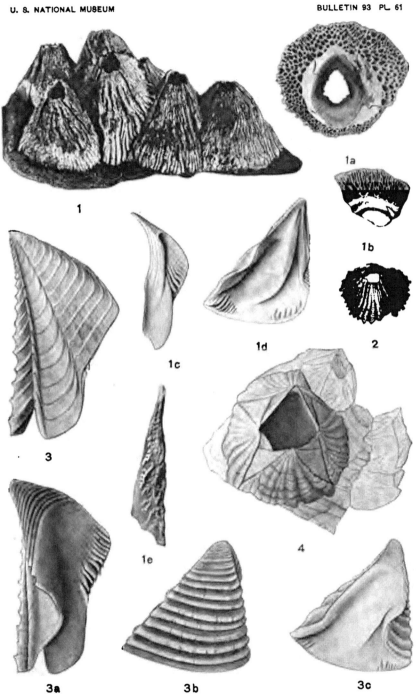

1-1E, TETRACLITA SQUAMOSA RUBESCENS; 2, T. S. RUBESCENS FORM ELEGANS;
3-4, T. RADIATA.

FOR EXPLANATION OF FIGURES SEE PAGE 354.

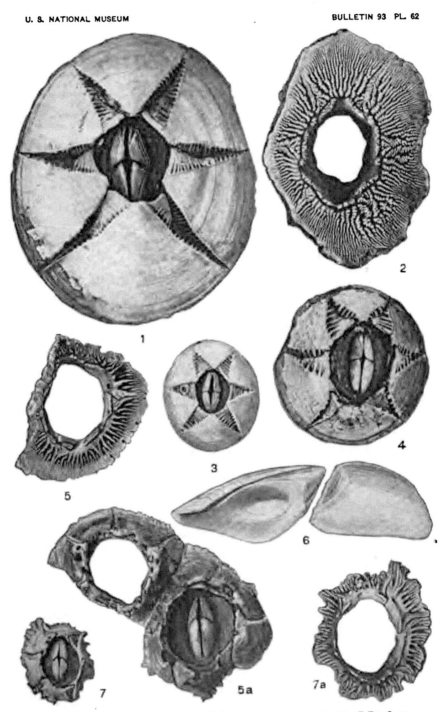

1-4, 6, CHELONIBIA TESTUDINARIA; 5-5A, C. MANATI CRENATIBASIS; 7-7A, C. M. LOBATIBASIS.

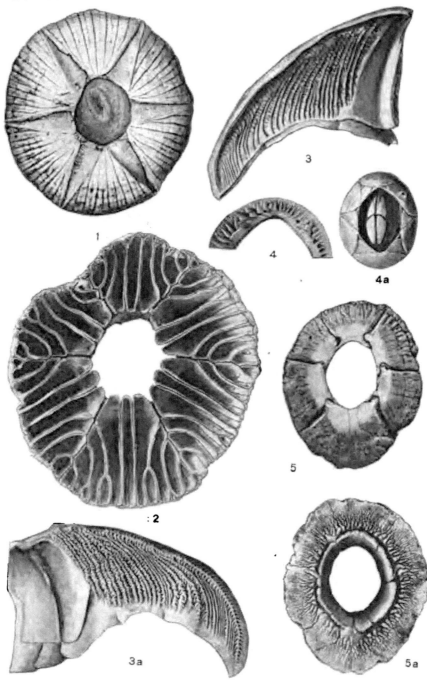

1-3A, CORONULA COMPLANATA; 4, 4A, CHELONIBIA PATULA; 5, 5A, CHELONIBIA
CARETTA.

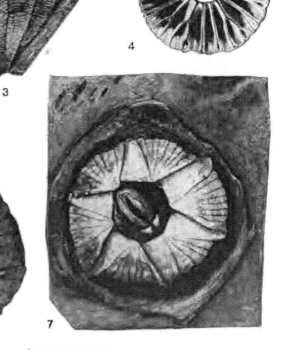

CORONULA REGINAE.

FOR EXPLANATION OF FIGURES SEE PAGE 355.

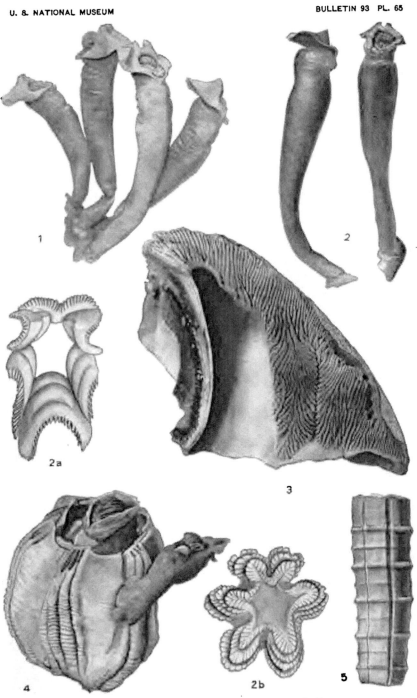

1-2B, XENOBALANUS GLOBICIPITIS; 3, 4, CORONULA DIADEMA; 5, TUBICINELLA MAJOR.

FOR EXPLANATION OF FIGURES SEE PAGE 355.

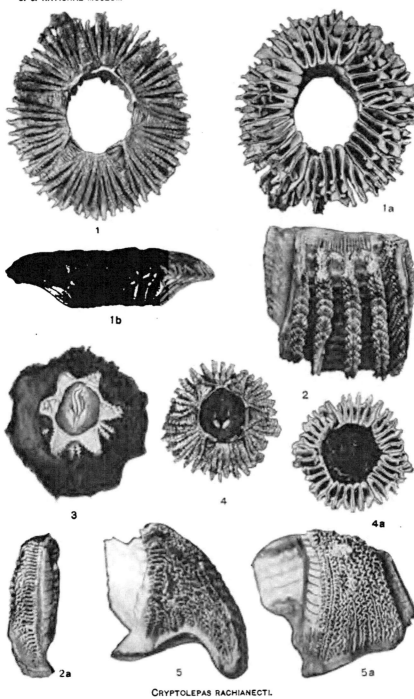

CRYPTOLEPAS RACHIANECTI.

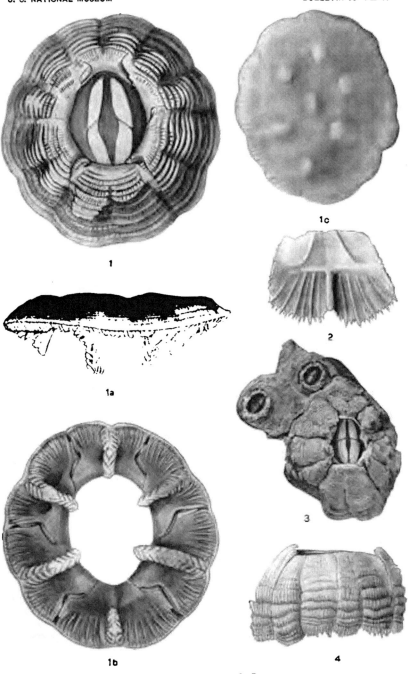

1-1c, 3, 4, PLATYLEPAS HEXASTYLOS; 2, P. H. ICTHTHYOPHILA.

For explanation of figures see page 356.

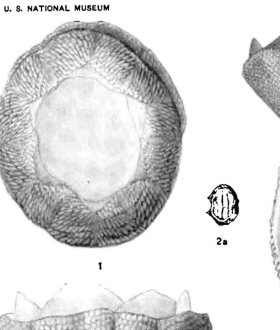

1

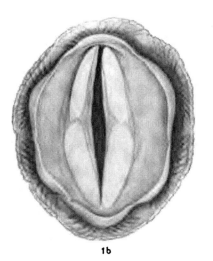

1a

2

2a

3

3a

1b

3b

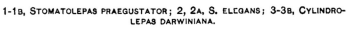

1-1B, STOMATOLEPAS PRAEGUSTATOR; 2, 2A, S. ELEGANS; 3-3B, CYLINDRO-
LEPAS DARWINIANA.

FOR EXPLANATION OF FIGURES SEE PAGE 356.

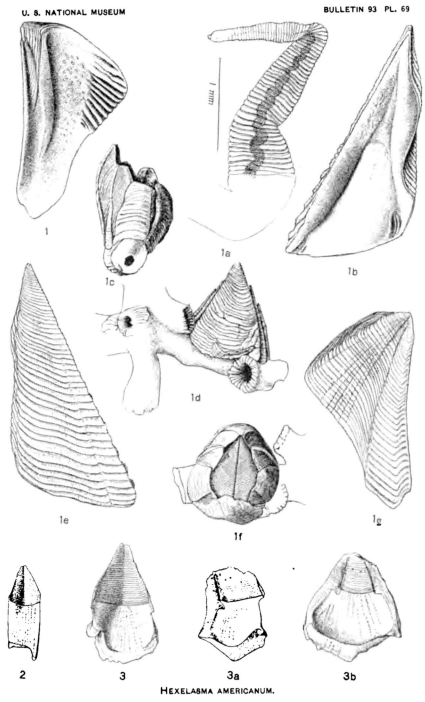

HEXELASMA AMERICANUM.

FOR EXPLANATION OF FIGURES SEE PAGE 356.

1a

1b

1c

1d

3

3a

2

3b

3c

4

CHTHAMALUS FRAGILIS.

FOR EXPLANATION OF FIGURES SEE PAGE 356.

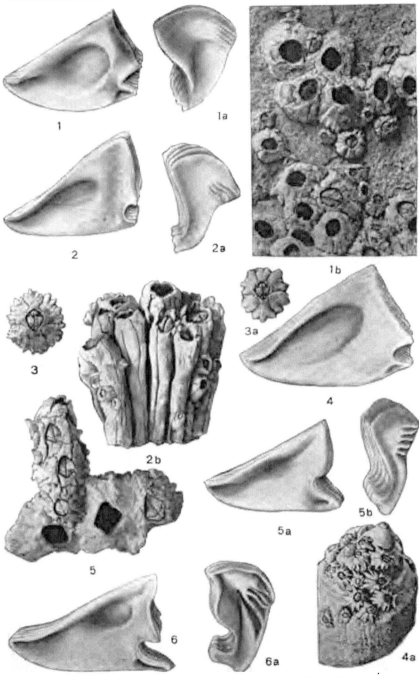

1-4A, CHTHAMALUS STELLATUS; 5-5B, C. S. ANGUSTITERGUM; 6, 6A, C. S. BISINUATUS.

FOR EXPLANATION OF FIGURES SEE PAGE 356.

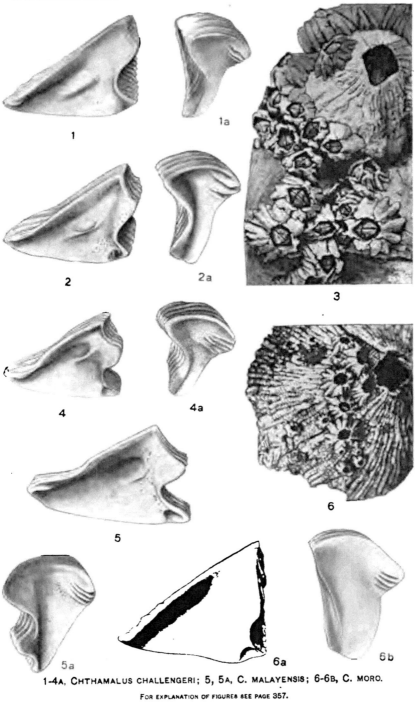

1-4A, CHTHAMALUS CHALLENGERI; 5, 5A, C. MALAYENSIS; 6-6B, C. MORO.

FOR EXPLANATION OF FIGURES SEE PAGE 357.

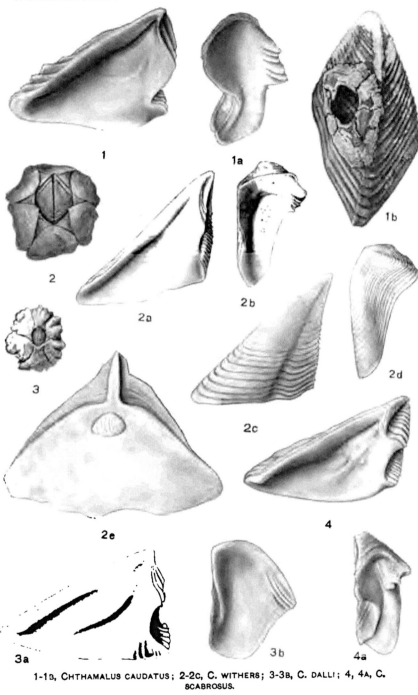

1-1B, CHTHAMALUS CAUDATUS; 2-2C, C. WITHERS; 3-3B, C. DALLI; 4, 4A, C. SCABROSUS.

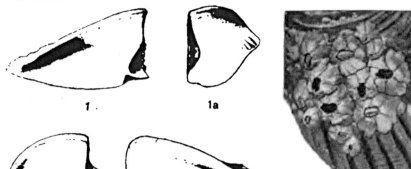

1 .

1a

1b

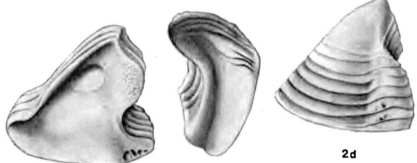

2

2b

2c

2a

2d

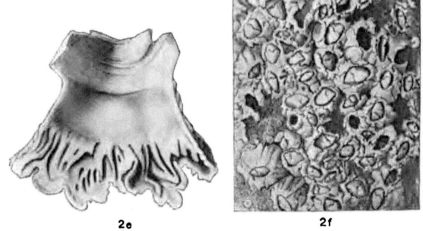

2e

2f

1-1B, CHTHAMALUS FISSUS; 2-2F, C. ANISOPOMA.

1

1a

1b

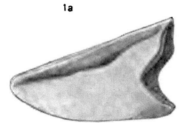

1c

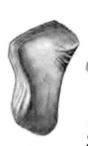

1d

2

2a

2b

2c

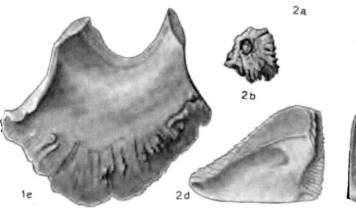

1e

2d

2e

1-1E, CHTHAMALUS IMPERATRIX; 2-2E, C. PANAMENSIS.

FOR EXPLANATION OF FIGURES SEE PAGE 357.

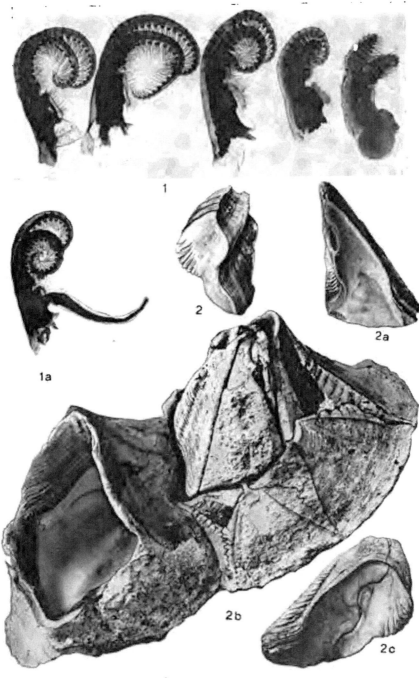

CHTHAMALUS HEMBELI.

FOR EXPLANATION OF FIGURES SEE PAGE 357.

INDEX.

CPSIA information can be obtained at www.ICGtesting.com
Printed in the USA
LVOW080839240712

291269LV00007B/66/P